ROUTLEDGE INTERNATIONAL HANDBOOK OF SUSTAINABLE DEVELOPMENT

This Handbook gives a comprehensive, international and cutting-edge overview of sustainable development. It integrates the key imperatives of sustainable development, namely institutional, environmental, social and economic, and calls for greater participation, social cohesion, justice and democracy as well as limited throughput of materials and energy. The nature of sustainable development and the book's theorisation of the concept underline the need for interdisciplinarity in the discourse as exemplified in each chapter of this volume.

The *Routledge International Handbook of Sustainable Development* employs a critical framework that problematises the concept of sustainable development and the struggle between discursivity and control that has characterised the debate. It provides original contributions from international experts coming from a variety of disciplines and regions, including the Global South.

Comprehensive in scope, it covers, among other areas:

- Sustainable architecture and design
- Biodiversity
- Sustainable business
- Climate change
- Conservation
- Sustainable consumption
- De-growth
- Disaster management
- Eco-system services
- Education
- Environmental justice
- Food and sustainable development
- Governance
- Gender
- Health
- Indicators for sustainable development
- Indigenous perspectives
- Urban transport

The *Handbook* offers researchers and students in the field of sustainable development invaluable insights into a contested concept and the alternative world-views that it has fostered.

Michael Redclift is Emeritus Professor of International Environmental Policy at King's College London, UK, where he has taught since 1999.

Delyse Springett formerly directed the Centre for Business and Sustainable Development at Massey University, New Zealand, and taught Master's courses on business and sustainability at Massey University and at the University of Hong Kong.

We urgently needed a guide to sustainable development – one of the most widely-used and least-understood concepts in existence. Now we have one. Led by two of the most respected authorities in the field, the team of experts assembled here covers all the expected dimensions – and a few more besides. 'Indispensable' is a word frequently found on book dust covers – here it means what it says.

Andrew Dobson, Keele University, UK

Sustainability refuses to be defined, or even stay put in the natural sciences. Rather, it has infected economic justice discourse, infused debates over how power works, wandered into our understanding of consumption and public health, and injected itself into governance dialog. Here is a handbook that documents the power of a rogue idea on how we think: across problems, locally and globally, present and future.

Richard B. Norgaard, University of California, Berkeley, USA

With the emergence in 2015 of new global Sustainable Development Goals, we reach a new stage in the development of the idea and promise of sustainable development. Over the past 30 years, the concept has come to be anchored in key debates about growth, environment and equity. This Handbook, bringing together an illustrious group of experts, looks at how sustainable development discourses have emerged and changed over that period, and looks forward to new debates now unfolding. It provides an unparalleled, state-of-the-art overview.

Frans Berkhout, King's College London, UK

ROUTLEDGE INTERNATIONAL HANDBOOK OF SUSTAINABLE DEVELOPMENT

Edited by Michael Redclift and Delyse Springett

Routledge
Taylor & Francis Group
LONDON AND NEW YORK
earthscan
from Routledge

First published 2015
by Routledge
2 Park Square, Milton Park, Abingdon, Oxon OX14 4RN

and by Routledge
711 Third Avenue, New York, NY 10017

Routledge is an imprint of the Taylor & Francis Group, an informa business

British Library Cataloguing-in-Publication Data
A catalogue record for this book is available from the British Library

Library of Congress Cataloging-in-Publication Data
Routledge international handbook of sustainable development / edited by Michael Redclift and Delyse Springett.
pages cm.—(Routledge international handbooks)
Includes bibliographical references and index.
1. Sustainable development. I. Redclift, M. R., editor of compilation. II. Springett, Delyse. III. Title: International handbook of sustainable development.
HC79.E5R675 2015
338.9'27—dc23 2014032740

ISBN: 978-0-415-83842-9 (hbk)
ISBN: 978-0-203-78530-0 (ebk)

Typeset in Bembo
by Keystroke, Station Road, Codsall, Wolverhampton

MIX
Paper from responsible sources
FSC® C013056

Printed and bound in Great Britain by
TJ International Ltd, Padstow, Cornwall

Professor Tony McMichael died before this book was published. We dedicate our book to his memory and the cause of enlightened research into sustainable development.

CONTENTS

FIGURES

TABLES

CONTRIBUTORS

William M. Adams is Moran Professor of Conservation and Development at the University of Cambridge, where he has been teaching about conservation and sustainable development in the Department of Geography since 1984. His books include *Future Nature* (Earthscan, 2003), *Against Extinction* (Earthscan, 2004) and *Green Development: Environment and Sustainability in a Developing World* (Routledge, 2009). He blogs at http://thinkinglikeahuman.wordpress.com/.

Gar Alperovitz is the Lionel R. Bauman Professor of Political Economy at the University of Maryland, and is the co-founder of the Democracy Collaborative. He is the author of numerous books, including most recently *What Then Must We Do? Straight Talk About the Next Revolution*; *America Beyond Capitalism*; and, with Lew Daly, *Unjust Deserts.* He is a founding board member of the New Economics Institute and of the Committee for the Political Economy of the Good Society (PEGS).

Keith Bothwell is an architect with over 30 years' experience and is Senior Lecturer at Kent School of Architecture, University of Kent, UK. He trained at the Bartlett School of Architecture UCL, in the 1970s. He has completed research for the Building Research Establishment on the pedagogy of sustainable design. His research interests focus on the obstacles to sustainable design, particularly within architectural practice.

Nicholas J. Clifford is Professor of Physical Geography at King's College London, and has over 20 years of research experience in fluvial and estuarine geomorphology. He has produced more than 150 scientific works and conference presentations, and a monograph, *Turbulence: Perspectives on Flow and Sediment Transport.* He is currently Managing Editor of the journal, *Progress in Physical Geography*, and serves on the editorial boards of *River Research and Applications* and *Catena*.

Robert William Collin joined the Centre for Public Policy at Willamette University in 2003 as its Senior Research Scholar, and also teaches as an adjunct Professor of Law at the Willamette University College of Law. He has served as a faculty member in the University of Oregon Environmental Studies program since 1993, and his books include, *The EPA: Cleaning Up America's Act* (2007), *Battleground: Environment* (2 volumes) (2008), and *The Encyclopedia of Sustainability* (3 volumes with Robin Morris Collin) (2010).

Robin Morris Collin is the Norma J. Paulus Professor of Law at Willamette University College of Law in Oregon. She is the first US law professor to teach sustainability courses in a US law school and was awarded the David Brower Lifetime Achievement Award and the National Environmental Justice Achievement Award from the Environmental Protection Agency for her work with the Oregon Environmental Justice Task Force.

Robert Costanza is Professor and Chair in Public Policy at the Crawford School of Public Policy, Australian National University. Prior to this, he was Distinguished University Professor of Sustainability, in the Institute for Sustainable Solutions at Portland State University (2010–2012), and Gund Professor of Ecological Economics and Founding Director of the Gund Institute for Ecological Economics at the University of Vermont (2002–2010). His transdisciplinary research integrates the study of humans and the rest of nature to address research, policy, and management issues at multiple time and space scales, from small watersheds to the global system. He is co-founder of the International Society for Ecological Economics and founding editor-in-chief of *Solutions* (www.thesolutionsjournal.org).

Herman E. Daly is currently Professor (Emeritus) at the University of Maryland. From 1988 to 1994, he was Senior Economist in the Environment Department of the World Bank. His interest in economic development, population, resources, and environment has resulted in over a hundred articles and numerous books. In 1996, he received Sweden's Honorary Right Livelihood Award and the Heineken Prize for Environmental Science awarded by the Royal Netherlands Academy of Arts and Sciences. In 2002, he was awarded the Medal of the Presidency of the Italian Republic and in 2014 he received the Blue Planet Award.

Joshua Farley is an ecological economist, Associate Professor in Community Development and Applied Economics, and Fellow at the Gund Institute for Ecological Economics at the University of Vermont. His broad research interests focus on the design of economic institutions capable of balancing what is biophysically possible with what is socially, psychologically, and ethically desirable.

Oscar A. Forero is an anthropologist, specialising in Development and Technology Studies. He has advised many Indigenous Peoples' organisations on the human rights approach to sustainable development and biodiversity conservation. He is a member of the IUCN Task Force on Cultural and Spiritual values of biodiversity. Oscar is currently a Senior Lecturer in International Development at University of East London and Consultant to the Centre for Development, Environment and Policy, SOAS, University of London.

Carol Franco supports projects on forest mapping and monitoring and fosters climate change policies in Latin America at the Woods Hole Research Centre. Her research has focused on environmental and socio-economic policies, food security, and climate change policies. She has worked as the Carbon Finance Officer of the United Nations Development Programme in the Dominican Republic, and prior to joining the Centre, she was a Research Assistant Professor at the Institute for Sustainable Solutions at Portland State University, Oregon.

Marco Grasso has a PhD from King's College London and is Associate Professor in Political Geography at the Università degli Studi di Milano-Bicocca, Italy. His research interests include the socio-economic study of climate change and international environmental policy and politics.

C. Michael Hall is a Professor in the Department of Management, Marketing & Entrepreneurship, University of Canterbury, New Zealand; Docent, Department of Geography, University of Oulu, Finland; and a Visiting Professor at Linneaus University, Kalmar, Sweden. Co-editor of *Current Issues in Tourism*, he has published widely on tourism, regional development, environmental history and change, and gastronomy.

Emma Hinton completed her PhD on third sector sustainable consumption advocacy in 2011. Since then, her post-doctoral research at King's College London and the University of Southampton has focused on understanding the influence of different kinds of policy intervention intended to encourage sustainable consumption on participants' everyday practices.

Ray Hudson is Professor of Geography and Deputy Vice Chancellor at Durham University. His research for the last 40 years has focused on the political economy of uneven spatial development, theorising capitalist development as involving temporally and spatially specific social processes of value creation and material transformation, and, as part of this, a concern with transitions to sustainability.

Tim Jackson is a leading international expert on sustainability. Since 2000, he has been Professor of Sustainable Development at the University of Surrey. In 2004, he was appointed as Economics Commissioner on the UK Sustainable Development Commission, where he led a five-year project called Redefining Prosperity. This ground-breaking work culminated in the publication of his controversial book, *Prosperity without Growth: Economics for a Finite Planet.*

Tommy Jensen is Professor in Business and Administration at the Stockholm Business School, Stockholm University, and holds a PhD from Umeå School of Business and Economics. His research interests are in the areas of organisation theory, sociology and moral philosophy with a focus on the intersection between 'private' and 'public' spheres and the social and environmental dilemmas that this intersection gives rise to.

Tony Johnston is the Head of the Department of Hospitality, Tourism and Leisure at the Athlone Institute of Technology, Ireland. He has previously lectured in Ecotourism (University of Derby), Development Geography (King's College London) and Tourism (University of the Highlands and Islands, Scotland). Tony's main research interests are in tourism and development geographies, particularly those concerning sustainability, conflict and poverty.

Martina Maria Keitsch is Associate Professor in Sustainable Design at the Department of Product Design, Norwegian University of Science and Technology. She has worked for over 15 years in the design field mainly with eco design, design theory, environmental ethics, user-driven innovation and aesthetics and has published several articles on these topics. She teaches Bachelor, Master's and PhD students.

Ida Kubiszewski is a Senior Lecturer at the Crawford School of Public Policy at Australian National University. Prior to this, she was an Assistant Research Professor and Fellow of the Institute for Sustainable Solutions at Portland State University, Oregon. She is a Fellow of the National Council for Science and the Environment and an Associate Research Fellow at the Veblen Institute for Economic Reforms.

Stewart Lockie is Professor of Sociology and Director of The Cairns Institute at James Cook University, Australia. He is an environmental sociologist with expertise in environmental and natural resource management policy, social impact assessment and the sociology of food and agriculture. His current research is primarily concerned with climate adaptation policy, food security and biodiversity conservation.

Timothy Luke is University Distinguished Professor, and Chair, Department of Political Science, Virginia Polytechnic Institute and State University in Blacksburg, Virginia. He also serves as Programme Chair for Government and International Affairs in the School of Public and International Affairs, and is the founding director of the Alliance for Social, Political, Ethical, and Social Theory (ASPECT). His research focuses on environmental politics, international affairs, and social theory.

Ashwina Mahanti is a PhD student at the School of Sustainability at Arizona State University. Prior to starting her PhD, she worked as a consultant for UNDP, India, and helped draft the State Climate Change Action Plan for the Andaman and Nicobar Islands. Her research interests include governance, globalisation, sustainable development and climate change adaptation.

David Manuel-Navarrete is Assistant Professor of Sustainability at Arizona State University. After working for the Sustainable Development Division of the United Nations Economic Commission for Latin America and the Caribbean, he returned to academia to teach sustainability and conduct research on climate change adaptation, socio-ecological systems, and sustainable tourism. He is lead author on over a dozen journal and book publications.

Anne Matan is a researcher and lecturer at Curtin University Sustainability Policy (CUSP) Institute at Curtin University in Perth, Western Australia. Her research interest is in creating sustainable, vibrant and people-focused urban places, focusing on active transport, particularly walking and cycling, pedestrian planning and urban design, and how people interact with the built environment. She is an honorary Sustainability Advisor for Bicycling Western Australia.

James McIntosh is a qualified Land Use Planner, Transport Planner and Registered Cadastral Surveyor, and is currently studying for a Doctor of Philosophy at the Curtin University Sustainability Policy (CUSP) Institute, developing a comprehensive assessment framework for valuing transport infrastructure projects. He has 16 years of international and Australian professional experience in multidisciplinary engineering and environmental consultancies in Australia.

Anthony J. McMichael, AO, environmental epidemiologist, was Professor Emeritus of Population Health at the Australian National University, Canberra, where he led the research programme on population health risks of climate change. He was an elected member of the US National Academies of Science, and advised on scientific assessments of health risks on the Intergovernmental Panel on Climate Change (IPCC) and the Millennium Ecosystem Assessment, and the World Health Organization.

Naho Mirumachi is Lecturer in Geography at the Department of Geography, King's College London. Trained in political science, international studies and human geography, her research interests are the politics of water resources management and the governance of trans-boundary river basins.

Arthur P. J. Mol is Professor in Environmental Policy at both Wageningen University, the Netherlands, and Tsinghua University, China. He is also Director of the Wageningen School of Social Sciences and joint editor of *Environmental Politics*. His main fields of interest and publications are globalisation, social theory and the environment, informational governance, ecological modernisation.

Mark Mulligan is Reader in Geography at King's College London and senior fellow of UNEP World Conservation Monitoring Centre. His research focus is the monitoring and spatial modelling of ecosystem processes as transformed by land use and climate change. He has published more than 50 peer-reviewed journal articles and supervised more than 30 PhDs in this area.

Raymond Murphy is Emeritus Professor at the University of Ottawa, Canada, and Past President of the Environment and Society Research Committee of the International Sociological Association. He is the author of various books, including *Social Closure* (Oxford University Press, 1988), *Rationality and Nature* (Westview, 1994), *Sociology and Nature* (Westview, 1997), and *Leadership in Disaster: Learning for a Future with Global Climate Change* (McGill-Queen's University Press, 2009).

Yamini Narayanan is an Australian Research Council Discovery Early Career Research Award (DECRA) Research Fellow at the Alfred Deakin Research Institute, Deakin University. Her specialisations are in the areas of urban development and planning (in South Asia), religion and development, and gender and development. Her book, *Religion, Heritage and the Sustainable City: Hinduism and Urbanisation in Jaipur* (Routledge) was published in 2015.

Peter Newman, AO, is the John Curtin Distinguished Professor of Sustainability at Curtin University and Director of the Curtin University Sustainability Policy (CUSP) Institute. He is on the Board of Infrastructure Australia and is a Lead Author for Transport on the IPCC. He is the author of over 263 publications including 15 books. In 2014, he was awarded an Order of Australia for his contributions to urban design and sustainable transport.

Hedda Ransan-Cooper is a post-doctoral researcher at the Australian National University. Her research interests include climate change adaptation, environmental migration and environmental sociology.

Michael Redclift is Emeritus Professor of International Environmental Policy in the Department of Geography at King's College London. His research interests include sustainable development, global environmental change, environmental security and the modern food system. In 1987, his ground-breaking book, *Sustainable Development: Exploring the Contradictions* was published by Routledge. In 2006, he was the first recipient of the 'Frederick Buttel Award', from the International Sociological Association (RC 24) for his 'outstanding contribution to environmental Sociology'.

Colin Sage is Senior Lecturer in Geography in the School of the Human Environment, University College Cork, Republic of Ireland. He is the author of *Environment and Food* (Routledge, 2012) and co-editor of *Food Transgressions: Making Sense of Contemporary Food Politics* (Ashgate, 2014). Besides work on food and sustainability, he is interested in exploring ways of making food a key element in civic engagement and effective public policy.

Juliet Schor is Professor of Sociology at Boston College. Previously, she taught at Harvard University for 17 years, in the Department of Economics and the Committee on Degrees in Women's Studies. Her research has focused on work, consumption, and sustainability. Her 'work and spend' cycle is an integrated approach to production and consumption. Most recently, her research emphasises political consumption, new patterns of time use, and alternative economic structures. As a member of a MacArthur Research Network, she is studying the emergence of collaborative consumption.

Annika Skoglund holds a PhD in Industrial Economics and Management (2011) and is currently Associate Senior Lecturer at Uppsala University and Visiting Fellow at the University of Essex Sustainability Institute, UK. She uses cross-disciplinary approaches with focus on social issues that evolve with knowledge production on climate change and sustainability. She has published in *Renewable Energy*, *Sustainable Development*, *Scandinavian Journal of Management* and *Children's Geographies*.

Joachim H. Spangenberg has a PhD in economics, but an academic background in natural sciences. He is an interdisciplinary researcher by education and dedication. He works professionally as a macro-economist for the Helmholtz Centre for Environment Research and the Sustainable Europe Research Institute (SERI), Germany, on sustainable development strategies, sustainability values and indicators, ecosystem services and their valuation, environmental conflicts, and on issues of sustainable consumption and economic growth.

Delyse Springett completed her PhD – a critical analysis of corporate conceptions of sustainable development – at Durham University. She has a strong interest in education for sustainable development that employs a critical pedagogy, and taught Master's courses on critical perspectives on business and sustainable development at Massey University, New Zealand, and at the University of Hong Kong. Now retired and working as an independent writer and researcher, she was formerly Director of The Centre for Business and Sustainable Development and Senior Research Officer in the College of Business at Massey University.

Peter Victor is an economist who has worked on environmental issues for over 40 years as an academic, consultant, and public servant. Victor was one of the founders of the emerging discipline of ecological economics and was the first President of the Canadian Society for Ecological Economics. He is a Professor in Environmental Studies at York University, Canada, and from 1996 to 2001 was Dean of the Faculty of Environmental Studies. This followed several years as Assistant Deputy Minister of the Environmental Sciences and Standards Division in the Ontario Ministry of the Environment.

Graham Woodgate trained as a forester before entering academia and, in addition to his post at University College London, he works as a forestry consultant and manages his own silvo-pastoral smallholding in southern England. He is co-editor of a series of volumes that map the development of environmental sociology from the nineteenth century to the present and is a member of the Editorial Board of *Agroecology and Sustainable Food Systems*.

ABBREVIATIONS

BRE	Building Research Establishment
BREEAM	Building Research Establishment Environmental Assessment System
BRS	Building Research Station
CBD	Convention on Biological Diversity
CEC	Commission on Education and Communication
CEPAL	Economic Commission for Latin America
CPUL	continuous productive urban landscapes
DESD	Decade of Education for Sustainable Development
DfE	Design for Environment
DHRIP	Declaration on the Rights of Indigenous Peoples
EBAs	Endemic Bird Areas
EPA	Environmental Protection Agency
ESD	education for sustainable development
FCPF	Forest Carbon Partnership Facility
FIP	Forest Investment Program
GAPESD	Global Action Programme for Education for Sustainable Development
GRULAC	African Group, The Asia-Pacific Group, The Eastern European Group, The Latin American and Caribbean Group
HF	human footprint
IBAs	Important Bird Areas
IE	industrial ecology
IPBES	International Panel on Biodiversity and Ecosystem Services
IWGIA	International Work Group on Indigenous Affairs
IWRM	Integrated Water Resources Management
LEED	Leadership in Energy and Environmental Design
MVHR	mechanical ventilation heat recovery system
OAS	Organisation of American States
PA	protected area
PAR	participatory action research
PRME	Principles for Responsible Management Education

REDD	Reducing Emissions from Deforestation and forest Degradation
SD	sustainable development
WEOG	The Western European and Others Group
WIPO	World Intellectual Property Organization

PART I

History and evolution of the concept of sustainable development

1

SUSTAINABLE DEVELOPMENT

History and evolution of the concept

Delyse Springett and Michael Redclift

When the Club of Rome[1] coined the term, 'The Global Problèmatique', for the environmental crisis of the early 1970s, it was intended to capture the connections and dynamic interactions between the various aspects of the problem – those linkages and knock-on effects that reverberate throughout the world (Reid 1995; Rockström et al. 2009). The institutional roots of the crisis, with its social, political and economic dimensions and the associated cultural, spiritual and intellectual implications, can be traced back to the emergence of the capitalist economy from the scientific and industrial revolutions in England (Merchant 1980; Capra 1983; Spretnak and Capra 1985; Carley and Christie 1992). Central to the changing world-view was the shift in attitudes towards nature wrought by the ideology of the Enlightenment, leading to nature's 'disenchantment' and the dissipating of its power over physical and spiritual aspects of human life (Merchant 1980; Eckersley 1992).[2] The new scientific paradigm at the core of the Enlightenment that transformed the human–nature relationship, combined with the capitalist model of production and consumption, produced a *degree* of change and *scale* of degradation not previously possible (Merchant 1980). Along with this, the Northern[3] process of domination, effected through colonization in pursuit of resources, markets and land – and later extended through the globalization of trade, technological expertise, the money market and communications (*The Ecologist* 1993) – eventually resulted in global impacts on nature and the lives of people. Two decades ago, Vitousek et al. (1986: 1861) stated: 'any clear dichotomy between pristine ecosystems and human-altered areas that may have existed in the past has vanished'. Today, the Earth is beyond the point where boundaries can be ascribed to environmental problems and the associated social impacts. However, the sharing of the impacts is not equitable, as the eco-justice movement underlines: the poor disproportionately shoulder the consequences of environmental degradation (Faber and O'Connor 1989; Dobson 1998; Agyeman et al. 2003; Martínez-Alier 2003). These social and environmental impacts and the struggle to deal with them led to the coining of the concept of 'sustainable development' and its appearance on the international agenda in the 1970s (Carley and Christie 1992).

There were early precedents for today's lack of ecological justice. In England, by the mid-nineteenth century, a far-reaching experiment in social engineering had been undertaken through state intervention. This had started with the appropriation of common land, which was presented as an ostensibly public and democratic process controlled by Parliament, while actually driven by big property owners (Gray 1998: 8). The transformation of England to an industrial society through the force of capitalist industrialization provided a microcosm of today's global money economy and prevailing paradigm of profit and domination.[4] It signalled how future trade that developed between the colonizers and the colonized would become skewed (Carley and Christie 1992), and how the lives of people in the South would be transformed by powerful and seemingly indomitable Northern interests. The new scientific and industrial revolutions of the twentieth century meant that Northern power would go on to impact on developing nations under the guise of 'development' and of 'aid'.[5] Adam Smith's concept of 'the invisible hand'[6] was reconstructed to endorse whatever operations the capitalist free market economy called for. The plans of the Allies crafted at Bretton Woods after the Second World War resulted in extended ways of exercising power over people and nature through the globalization of the economy, strengthened by the creation of Northern-dominated global structures such as the World Bank, the International Monetary Fund and the World Trade Organization (Lang and Hines 1993; Esty 1994; Brack 1998).[7, 8] These institutions, set up to run the world in a 'democratic' fashion, have proved to be deeply undemocratic (Monbiot 2003). They imposed liberal market structures onto the economic life of societies worldwide, creating what amounts in many ways to a single global, asymmetric 'free' market (Gray 1998: 2), which, to the poor and the powerless, has represented an 'invisible elbow' (Jacobs 1991: 127). From the early 1990s onwards this neoliberal ascendancy (the 'Washington Consensus') used fiscal incentives and sanctions at the international level to 'roll back' the state, in both developed and emerging economies, and to give free rein to the market through abolishing government subsidies to producers, combined with the overhaul of external tariffs ('structural adjustment'). These market reforms eventually paved the way for accelerated economic growth, notably in the BRIC countries (Brazil, Russia, India and China) at the expense of growing internal inequality and the plunder of natural resources.

The neo-Marxian contribution to the environmental debate that emerged in the late twentieth century helped to expose the effects of earlier domination, and tipped the discourse on 'sustainability' from a Northern-dominated focus on 'nature conservation', based on a scientific paradigm, to one which examined the inextricability of environmental and social responsibility, and exposed how power and knowledge are used to dominate the environment and people.[9] The root causes of the global problematic were deemed to be the capitalist means of production and consumption, the institutions set in place to support this, and the asymmetric power that those institutions represent. However, this analysis, with hindsight, was only partially accurate and seriously over-deterministic.

The global problematic today mirrors the intensified outcomes of the capitalist political economy and its historical colonization of much of the globe, encompassing both 'liberal democracies' and authoritarian capitalist economies, notably Russia. Moreover, in China, a hybrid economy developed in the period from 1990 that combined elements of state socialism with a highly dynamic market-based system. Massive increases in world trade, and especially the rise of China, have continued to benefit the developed world, not least from reducing living costs for its domestic populations,[10] while the broad secular trends of Northern capitalism have taken root in newly industrializing countries (NICs). Inequalities between rich and poor countries have forced the poor countries to adopt 'market-friendly' policies and to embrace a liberal market version of capitalism (Carley and Christie 1992). Developing countries have emulated Northern consumerist aspirations, with Southern elites enjoying new-found life-styles while basic levels of health, welfare and education for the majority fail to be attained (George 1976; 1988). The process of globalization, exercised through both 'old' and 'new' media and consumption patterns, has ensured the continuing hegemony of market-based values, notably through the dissemination of the Internet. This global reach of information technology and the new media might even be seen as a refinement of earlier processes such as the capture of the commons and the drive for imperialism (Newby 1980; *The Ecologist* 1993; Diani 2000; Van Aelst and Walgrave 2007; Van Laer 2010). However, today's 'imperialist' powers are likely to be transnational corporations, often richer and more powerful than individual governments (Korten 1995; Madeley 2007; Bonanno and Constance 2008), whose policies include at least token reference to 'corporate social responsibility'. They are also more elusive, and able to shift wealth and physical plant around the globe. The crisis provoked by economic and cultural globalization also has a physical parallel in the problem of anthropogenic climate change, which presents a challenge to international policy that is both enormously complex, and has created a new site for political contestation. Compliance with the requirements of climate change policy demands a serious reduction of the environmental impacts of industry, which in turn calls for fundamental changes in economic structures and processes which conventional economic analysis ignores, and which is denied and resisted at industry and institutional levels.

The essential character of production and consumption patterns is the basis of the most serious environmental problems (Jacobs 1996), as is the issue of values. Redclift (1996) points out that we have confused the 'standard of living' with the quality of life, making the consumer society that underpins the capitalist goals of business easier to manipulate (see also Marcuse 1964; Robertson 1990; Durning 1992), and destroying Marx's vision of the proletariat as agents of change. This legitimates corporate control over expectations and behaviour, where individual acquisition of the status symbols of the capitalist version of 'the good life' outpaces concern for 'the common good' (Daly and Cobb 1989). A corollary of this has been the emergence of social movements which, despite their epistemological and political differences, are linked by their concern for environmental, social and equity issues. These may represent a potential force for change which could provide a powerful alternative paradigm to that of the capitalist political economy (O'Connor, J. 1998; Doherty and Doyle, 2008).

The environmental backlash

The counter-attack against the power of globalization and market capitalism is observed in the outcry against their impact on the environment (if not against other institutional forms of hegemony). This was initiated with Rachel Carson's[11] exposé of the chemicals industry (1962), and is well documented, needing only a brief summary of key points here. The environmental discourses of the 1960s and 1970s were grounded in a perspective that was broader and more 'political' than the earlier 'conservation' discourse.[12] They exposed the outcomes of capitalist industry and economics and cast doubt on the dominant political conception that economic growth itself, left unfettered, would resolve environmental as well as social problems. The energy of that early movement, with its emphasis upon environmental and public virtues, may be reflected today in new social trends, such as the protests against genetically engineered food, globalization and the destruction of 'nature'. For its part, the 'environmental' movement itself has to a large extent become engulfed in the predominating *environmental management* paradigm and has relinquished some of the moral leadership it once represented (Sachs 1993). *A Blueprint for Survival* (*The Ecologist*, 1972) forecast the irreversible destruction of life-support systems and the breakdown of society. The establishment of the Club of Rome and the publication of *Limits to Growth* (Meadows et al. 1972)[13] re-launched a neo-Malthusian[14] discourse, expounding the problèmatique as arising essentially from exponential population growth and reinforcing Hardin's argument (1968) that people are incapable of putting 'collective' interests before 'individual' ones. As neo-Marxists joined the debate (for example, Redclift 1987), the *Limits to Growth* focus on 'scarcity' was exposed as ignoring the discourse of 'distribution'.[15] The contestation had already become a struggle as to who should define and construct the discourse, based on the nexus between power and knowledge. Detractors of the environmental backlash scoffed at both the 'doomsday scenarios' and the 'utopian' alternative that *A Blueprint for Survival* presented. Cornucopians[16] like Beresford (1971) and Maddox (1972) placed their faith in technical expertise – plentiful resources and energy, the ability of the 'green revolution' to feed starving populations, and technical solutions to problems of resource production. Business – caught on the back foot initially in the face of this backlash – soon gathered its considerable weight to undermine the environmental cause through various means of coercion, mostly based upon extending its control over public attitudes through a pervasive hegemony that colonized the life-world of the public through the media (Rowell 1996; Beder 1997; Mayhew 1997; Welford 1997).

A different kind of attack and a different hegemonic contestation arose from socially concerned groups who perceived the 'ecological crisis' as being employed to legitimate inattention to the problems of social injustice, of war and the impacts of capitalism, further disempowering the poor and weak. Clarke (1975: 62) pointed out at the time that the ecological crisis was not a diversion from social ills, but a *result* of them. However, the perception of a dichotomy emerging between 'environmental' and 'social' concerns and the suspicion that social justice was taking a back seat in favour of the Northern focus on environmental issues became a growing concern, especially in developing countries. It impacted on the international environmental discourse, particularly in the lead-up to the Stockholm Conference on the Human Environment (UNCHE 1972), and found its legitimation in the World Commission on Environment and Development (WCED) Report, *Our Common Future*, in 1987.[17]

Another potential form of hegemonic appropriation requires comment: the epistemological and ontological basis of the analysis of the global problematic has come chiefly from the North. Accounts of the growth of environmentalism have themselves mostly arisen from the industrialized world (Adams 1990); and Redclift (1984) warned against international comparisons based entirely on European or North American experience. These cautions from the North echoed those of writers from the South who claimed that Northern environmentalism was an extension of the pervasive Northern hegemony and its 'global' reach (Biswas and Biswas 1984; Shiva 1991; 1993; Beney 1993; Gudynas 1993). The 'framing' of the concept of 'sustainable development' reflected Northern constructions, and a particularly invasive form of Northern appropriation and domination that sometimes attempted to disguise the origins of the problematic while taking the higher moral ground. There is, for example, a continuing tendency to ascribe the causes of unsustainable development to other sources, such as the behaviour of the poor in the developing world (and see Martínez-Alier, 2003, on the environmentalism of the poor). We would seek to argue that what is required today, as in 1987, is a more inclusive problematization of the concept that takes into account world-views and cultures other than those of the North alone, and that takes a much broader-based, discursive approach.

The international contestation of sustainable development

The environmental movement of the 1960s was based largely upon a concept of nature that was scientifically constructed by the North (Hays 1959; Evernden 1992; Eder 1996a), chiefly rooted in the earlier American 'conservation' movement and perceived by O'Riordan (1981) as organized resource exploitation and regional economic planning. As the debate became affected by ideas and concepts from the field of development (Redclift 1987; Adams 1990; Goulet 1995a; 1995b), the dialectics of 'environment and development' produced a new discourse, though the North continued to identify the problems and solutions, chiefly from a 'conservation' perspective. The adoption of the term, 'sustainable development', brings with it epistemological and practical problems that have led to strong contestation; but it signifies a transformation being made in the environmental discourse. The contestation – even repudiation – of the term,[18] has not excluded its capture by some groups, to become a key concept in the rhetoric of 'green' business. Against negative perceptions, some authors always understood the concept as capable of emancipating more democratic and inclusive approaches to living with nature and each other (O'Connor, J. 1998); while others saw it as legitimating perspectives from the South (Redclift 1987; Jacobs 1991).

International fora on environment and sustainable development from the Stockholm Conference in 1972[19] to the UNCSD (Rio+20) in 2012, as well as key international Strategies and Reports, have tended to legitimate the North's power over and domination of the construct, while appearing to be seeking 'solutions'. A great deal of hope for the necessary discursivity in addressing sustainable development had been pinned on these fora. However, they were organized by the Northern-dominated United Nations and promoted largely North-driven agendas, even though they also formed sites of protest. The agendas have been as remarkable for their lacunae as their content; and the significance of the attendance or non-attendance at these fora of key political figures from the North, such as the President of the USA, and their powers of veto, signal where the power lies. Institutional hegemony at these fora has also been shown to be heavily dependent upon the support of corporate power. The fact that collusion between these dominant forces governs the outcomes of international debates on environment and sustainable development has been difficult to overlook. The voices of non-governmental organizations (NGOs) and the South have gradually been heard after much struggle, though without achieving equal power.

Such discord between North and South characterized the preparations for the Stockholm Conference (UNCHE, 1972), as it has all subsequent international fora and official rhetoric on environment and sustainable development. The South's struggle against a Northern-dominated vision of protecting the environment against industrialism and pollution (Adams 1990: 37) tipped the United Nations Conference on the Human Environment (UNCHE) agenda from a focus on 'environmental responsibility' to include the twin moral principle of 'social justice' (Redclift 1996: 13). The exposure of a one-sided discourse that bypassed the concerns of the poor majority, who sought their own right to developmental progress through industrialization, demonstrated the extent to which the North had taken for granted its economic 'superiority' and scientific 'expertise'. Its agenda rested upon a neo-Malthusian doctrine that was 'deeply unattractive to and mistrusted by' developing country representatives (Adams 1990: 37). The extent to which the views of developing countries actually influenced the discourse of UNCHE remains open to debate. Some new conceptual ground was broken (ibid.); but there was little focus on the dialectics of 'poverty and pollution'[20] – a foretaste of the lacunae of the United Nations Conference on Environment and Development (UNCED) debate 20 years later. At the same time, environmentalists contested the 'remedial focus' of limiting damage to the environment without checking development and the apparent determination '*to legalise the environment as an economic externality*' (Colby 1991: 201, original emphasis). Both analyses indicate that the struggle for economic power that was legitimated by the Conference would ensure that the losers would be the environment and the poor of the South. However, in a Foucauldian sense, the capacity of the developing world to exercise the power to influence the international agenda had been demonstrated. It could tilt the domination exercised over the environmental/sustainable development agenda, though the possibility that this would awaken renewed determination to maintain Northern power over the agenda was an outcome to anticipate in later fora.

The World Conservation Strategy (IUCN et al. 1980) did little to allay the South's fears that the North would continue to dominate the agenda. The stated overall aim of achieving sustainable development '*through the conservation of living resources*' (IUCN et al. 1980, IV, emphasis added) overlooked sensitive and controversial issues of international and political order, war and armaments, population and urbanization (Khosla 1987).[21] The World Conservation Strategy foreshadowed the World Commission on Environment and Development's (WCED) definition of sustainable development by focusing on the needs of future generations; but its Judaeo-Christian affirmation of domination over nature – and, by implication, humankind – was unpopular, as was the stance on 'scarcity' as opposed to 'redistribution' (Redclift 1992; Achterhuis 1993). The strategy was still environment-dominated with pervasive Malthusian overtones, 'repackaged for a new audience' (Adams 1990: 47; Reid 1995); and it failed to examine the social and political changes that would be necessary to meet its conservation goals (Redclift 1992). The essentially political nature of the development process was not grasped, the naïve assumption being that 'conservation', rather than being a social construct and essentially political (Redclift 1987; Eder 1996a), was above ideology. The Strategy failed to acknowledge that human societies construct their views of nature to reflect human problems and that the Northern construction of environment did not reflect the views of the South.

The power of Northern hegemony met some resistance from the World Commission on Environment and Development (WCED), which included a large number of Commissioners from the South. The Brundtland Report (1987) placed the discourse much more firmly in the economic and political context of international development. Efforts to limit the agenda to 'environmental' matters and a critique of conventional environmental management as practised in developed countries were resisted (Redclift 1987). The preliminary consultative process itself provided something of a model of democratic participation (ibid.), and the Report was altogether more 'political' and radical than the Stockholm Declaration (1972) or the World Conservation Strategy (1980). It took a stance that was more challenging of traditional power structures, acknowledging the inseparability of environmental and development issues and the link between poverty and environment – 'the pollution of poverty' that Indira Ghandi had brought to the attention of the Stockholm Conference (Adams 1990). It was motivated by the 'egalitarian' concept of sustainable development (Jacobs 1999) and the concern to find an equitable form of development (Reid 1995) closer to the understanding adhered to by the South (Jacobs 1999). Its dialectics, therefore, focus on the moral imperative of equitable sharing, intra- and inter-generationally, with more even distribution, foreshadowing profound effects for poor and rich. Nevertheless, the fact that the social and economic objectives for sustainable development were based on the premise that further growth was necessary encouraged scepticism among eco-centrists who did not equate the shift to sustainability with the growth paradigm, as well as ecological economists, who feared the surpassing of limits unless quantitative throughput growth could be stabilized and replaced by qualitative development (Daly 1990; 1992; Goodland et al. 1991; Goodland 1995). The Commission was castigated as having sold out to the power of big business. The Report emphasized producing more with less (a precept that business has readily absorbed for its profit motive, if not for reasons of sustainability), reduction of population levels and the introduction of a level of redistribution.[22] It catalyzed the ongoing debate about the nature and purpose of economic growth, strengthening the discourse about the 'political' role of growth as it dominates not only business but governmental policy-makers and consumers (Ayres 1998). Its radical force may also have reinforced the determined 'silences' that continue to characterize the debate on sustainable development, particularly in the business discourse.

Despite the criticisms, the Commission presented a political vision of sustainable development: it called for institutional restructuring of national politics, economics, bureaucracy, social systems of production and technologies, requiring a new system of international trade and finance.[23] It was, perhaps, the neo-Marxist movement, newly taking the environment into its consideration in the late 1980s, that best perceived the potential the Report brought for significantly new ways of doing things within a revised capitalist framework. The anticipated need for a five-to-tenfold increase in manufacturing output, the halt to the rising living standards of richer nations and the emphasis upon redistribution brought the Commission closer to a Marxian analysis of the environmental problematic, but possibly tolled the Report's death-knell. On account of its compromise with growth, it would be subject to both the force of the eco-centric critique, which dismissed it as a pawn of capitalist hegemony and to appropriation by business and dilution to fit the business-as-usual paradigm (Soussan 1992; Goodland et al. 1991). An epistemological perspective on its comparative failure to inspire change is that it offered a *consensus view* of sustainable development where none existed previously (Smith and Warr 1991: 267). This is still a problem of the discourse today, particularly in the light of limited dialectical discursivity and lack of inclusivity. The Report did, however, offer a challenge to traditional sources of power, of whatever hue, by lifting the debate from a focus on scarcity and counteracting 'the sectoral bias and compartmentalism' that had marked much of the work on the environment (Redclift 1992: 33).

The United Nations Conference on Environment and Development (UNCED 1992), the agenda of which arose largely from the Brundtland Report, demonstrated what may happen to any serious challenge to traditional forms of power. The Conference potentially represented a 'turning point' (Gore 1992; Frankel 1998) and the opportunity to address the worsening socio-economic disparities between North and South along with the environmental degradation associated with these. Opinions on the achievements of UNCED are divided between confidence in significant progress being made and the belief that the Conference was a failure, even a charade stage-managed by business.[24, 25] The UNCED process revealed that it served powerful interests. The critique of the process and the Alternative Treaties produced by an international consortium of NGOs reveal the key 'silences' and 'non-decision-making' that characterized the formal agenda. For example, Agenda 21 has clauses on 'enabling the poor to achieve sustainable livelihoods', but none on how the rich would do so; a section on women, but none on men. Only the Alternative Treaties speak of debt forgiveness and redistribution of wealth, or examine issues of militarism, transnational corporations (TNCs) and alternative economic models. Business, which had played a 'lukewarm' role at UNCHE, but had taken its place in the discourse after Brundtland, now assumed a central role at UNCED.[26] The discourse of the Conference took for granted that economic development was the *sine qua non* – where no growth meant more poverty and degradation to the environment, whereas continued economic growth would protect the environment and reduce both population and poverty.[27]

The UNCED process, which ideally would have provided a key site of contestation, proved to be another example of the exercise of power by the North to continue its own domination (Rich 1994) – even though the South had a bargaining chip this time in that its co-operation was needed for the major conventions. It became clear that the industrialized nations were ready to commit much less to the developing nations than had been hoped for. Important connections between institutional, social, environmental and economic policy failed to be made (Redclift 1996). Climate change, deforestation and biodiversity predominated over the 'issue that Rio forgot' – population – as well as the trade, poverty and debt crisis issues raised in the alternative proceedings. The implications of profligacy, rather than growth, and the neglect of poverty left an agenda still to be dealt with (ibid.). In 1992, it was clear that business had prepared itself very well to shape the sustainable development agenda and the outcomes of UNCED, and this embargo on real institutional change taking place continued at the World Summit on Sustainable

Development (WSSD) in 2002 and at Rio+20 in 2012. NGOs were also seen to have made a vast compromise by legitimizing a process they had been opposed to. Sustainable development is an essentially political project with the political power to bring about social change, possessing the agency to challenge the ideology of neo-liberal capitalism. It calls for emancipation, more equitable distribution of power and resources, shifts in human behaviour and the redefinition of the roles of public, private and political institutions. In short, the potential of sustainable development to be paradigm-changing, calling for structural change, would have been sufficiently radical to totally alienate business, providing corporations with an even stronger impetus to appropriate the sustainable development agenda (Springett 2013). Finger (1993) highlights the UNCED process as accelerating the move towards 'global management', using the environmental crisis as a *pretext* to hasten the establishment of a 'world technocracy', stemming generally from industrial development, which would manage resources and '*so-called* environmental risks' (ibid.: 36, emphasis added). The 'global crisis management' that this would lead to would use fear and threats to legitimize a militaristic and technocratic approach, leaving the world still with a '*profound absence of vision and leadership*' (ibid.: 47, emphasis added).

However, since UNCED, the balance of power has shifted. While the struggle at that and earlier fora can be seen as being between 'North' and 'South', the gap today is also between the poorest countries, with no resources to attract investment, the developed countries, and the new 'rapidly developing' economies. Notable among these are the BRICs,[28] which may symbolize a shift in global economic power away from the G8 towards the developing world. In the meantime, dominant discourses and the interests they reflect and defend guarantee that the EU and developed world countries, as well as rapidly developing countries such as China, will make adjustments to deal with the crises of debt in developed nations such as Greece, but fail to respond to similar needs of resource-poor developing countries in Africa and South America.

The process and outcomes of the WSSD (2002) were more widely disseminated through the development of the 'web': the commentaries of specific fora set up to discuss the WSSD agenda and process[29] meant that a considerable amount of dialogue from NGOs and others accompanied the 'formal' discourse. This revealed that corporate capital had not only continued to exercise enormous power since UNCED, but that governments appeared to have little control over corporate behaviour (Springett 2013). This focused especially on the lack of legal instruments and agencies capable of regulating TNCs. The fact that the UN Centre on Transnational Corporations and its Code of Conduct for TNCs had virtually disappeared close to the time of UNCED remained a cause for concern. New guidelines and frameworks were seen as lacking effective authority over corporate behaviour: for example, the OECD Guidelines for Multinational Enterprises (2000) contained the possibility of government intervention, but this was not widely recognized or acted upon (International Confederation of Free Trade Unions/ ICFTU 2002); and the UN Global Compact (2000), which prominent TNCs had signed up to, was viewed as the 'smuggling of a business agenda into the UN' (Bruno and Karliner 2002). The World Business Council for Sustainable Development (WBCSD) had assumed a prominent role since 1995 as an advocate of 'sustainable business', but this was doing little to alleviate the milieu of 'tremendous inequality' within which its corporate members operated (Bruno and Karliner 2002). During the decade since UNCED, corporations had lobbied to make a case for their 'sustainable' activities; but not to change an unjust and unsustainable global economic system that was the fundamental obstacle to solving the global environmental and social crisis (Hoedeman 2002).

A cause of extreme scepticism for many observers was the establishment of Type One (Statutory) and Type Two (Voluntary) partnerships between government, business and NGOs to tackle social and environmental problems in developing countries. This was perceived by some as NGOs selling out to business; and as paving the way for more corporate business opportunities. Government reliance on corporations to keep national economies afloat underlined their inability to put the required regulations in place without corporate retribution, so that government focus was perforce on the immediate rather than the future.[30] It was proposed that what was needed was a new 'Global Deal' – sustainable development legislation wherein corporations, civil society and governments could negotiate a binding international convention on the key issues. However, this did not emerge from the WSSD; and the idea of a rule-based International Institute for Sustainability was rejected by the USA.

It was to be anticipated that corporations and their front groups would play a similarly powerful role at the United Nations Conference on Sustainable Development (UNCSD) 2012 (Springett 2011; 2012a; 2012b; 2013). With its key overarching themes of a 'Green Economy' and an 'Institutional Framework for Sustainable Development', UNCSD caused some general concern. While the agenda appeared to promise a different approach to economic decision-making, the fear for many was that it was little more than a manoeuvre to replace sustainable development with 'ecological modernization' or 'greener business as usual': many perceived the 'green economy' as a pseudonym for the new OECD mantra of 'green growth' – a wolf in sheep's clothing. Jackson (2012) noted, post-Rio+20, that, rather than questioning the existing economic model, which is leading us to environmental and social disaster, Rio+20 betrayed the vision of a green economy through a staggering linguistic turnabout that equated 'green economy' with 'sustained economic growth'. People in developing countries were particularly suspicious of the new agenda, which was predominantly championed by the North: they perceived it as an attempt to re-write the sustainable development narrative, replacing it with one with a weaker emphasis on social concerns.

The big gamble at Rio+20, as at UNCED, was that governments would play safe under pressure from big business and avoid difficult decisions, while business organizations had again readied themselves for the conference (Guardian Sustainable Business 2011). For example, the draft International Chamber of Commerce (ICC) contribution (2011) for the Rio+20 Compilation document began with a dispute over the language of a 'green economy', preferring a reference to 'greener economies', which, it was claimed, better acknowledged the many challenges and opportunities present across sectors and value chains. While the ICC was not alone in considering that 'green economy' is a problematic concept, their own alternative might be accused of adding other levels of 'fuzziness'.

However, for the purpose of the upcoming UNCSD, the ICC acknowledged the term 'green economy' as a policy term and a unifying theme to articulate 'sustainable development' as the 'direction' towards which all economies need to strive while acknowledging existing tensions and current global economic turmoil. The general tone of the ICC's contribution, as is usual with the business groups, sounded 'reasonable'. Ten systems or conditions were advocated for a transition towards a 'green economy', including those for social, economic and environmental innovation with some mutually reinforcing cross-cutting elements and an emphasis on what would make markets more successful. Similarly, the key messages for improving the institutional framework for sustainable development focused strongly on the integral role of business and business interests.

In a sense, however, Rio+20 was doomed even before it began. Countries and the media were slow to engage with the agenda. Some of the malaise must be placed at the door of the UN, an institution set up in Cold War conditions more than 60 years ago, now proving unable to respond to contemporary challenges and casting doubt on its own suitability and effectiveness to further the agenda of sustainable development. People had not forgotten the 'débâcle' of UNCED (*The Ecologist*, 1992), nor the failure to agree a climate change settlement in Copenhagen in 2009 and Cancun in 2010. The apparently intractable geopolitical stand-offs in the negotiations pointed to a crisis within the international community. The lower profile but still significant failure of the nineteenth session of the UN Commission on Sustainable Development (May, 2011) to reach an agreement on a series of environmental and development issues provided further evidence of widening distrust and an unwillingness to co-operate on some of the most urgent global issues of our time.

New realities: the development of the 'emerging economies' and the progress of globalization

The hope that markets and technology would solve the environmental problems associated with accelerated economic growth and the enormous rise in global consumption were about to be challenged by a number of events at the beginning of the twenty-first century, which nation states came to prioritize over the institutional changes associated with public endorsement of sustainable development. Foremost among them was the 'financial crisis' that afflicted Europe and North America after 2007.

This major disruption in the economic development model was a crisis fed by the personal greed of many bankers and financial managers, and fuelled by the virtually unregulated production of credit – not because interest rates were low, but because in some countries the price attached to housing equity (the United States, the United Kingdom, Spain and Ireland) was unrealistically high. The financial crisis was fuelled by cheap credit, and in this sense the absence of sustainability made most consumers complicit with the model. The rise in 'sub-prime' lending and borrowing took place under systems of ineffective governance that emphasized everybody's right to property regardless of collateral and debt levels. Politically it was 'sold' as everybody's right to credit rather than their right to debt. The financial crisis revealed that it was completely unsustainable. There were several obvious corollaries:

1. The policy response paid lip service to the rapidly disappearing Green agenda, but did not support this rhetoric with effective interventions. (Compare the almost derisory role of new Green investment in attempts to address the financial crisis.)
2. There is now considerable evidence of the effects of the financial downturn on migration, as well as poverty, notably in China, which supported the United States' debt through buying in to its financial packages, and supported raised consumption in the West generally, by lowering the costs of manufactured goods there.
3. Another process that has gathered speed is that of transnational sourcing of food, minerals and other resources. The internationalization of capital movements and the need to secure resources have led to increased transnational acquisition of land and minerals, on the part of China and some of the Gulf States, principally in Africa. Rather than depend exclusively upon trade relations to meet their domestic resource deficiencies – trade contracts during an economic recession – the advantages of acquisition of land, water sources, food (via 'virtual water') became evident, especially for their geopolitical reach. Land displacement for crops like soya had already changed international food/land imbalances.

Natural resources and the modern food system

The modern food system developed to meet the needs of the industrialized countries, where technological changes and the growth of domestic markets served to initiate industrialized agriculture (Goodman and Redclift 1991). In the 1970s, the prevalent view was that food production could not keep pace with population growth – the first sense of 'natural limits' discussed at the beginning of this chapter. To some extent, the success of the much-vaunted 'Green Revolution' in basic grains was to discredit this rather simplistic view of limits. Throughout the 1970s and the 1980s impressive gains were made in the productivity of basic grains – especially rice, corn and wheat – aided by enhanced irrigation systems and chemical fertilizers and pesticides.

However, apart from growing inequality in many countries, between rural and urban sectors and within the rural sector itself, the Green Revolution gains could not be continued exponentially, and the costs of maintaining irrigation systems and dealing with the environmental 'externalities' from the Green Revolution grew in importance. Today about 12 per cent of global cereals are traded between states on the international market: about half the 300 million tons annually between the North and the South. The South is still a net importer of cereals: not Latin America but much of Asia and North Africa experience net deficits in cereals. In 2006, the United States exported 82 million metric tons of cereals, compared with 22 million metric tons from the European Union. Projections for the year 2020 suggest that the United States will trade about 119 million metric tons of cereals by this date (SCOPE 2009). The drivers of cereal imports in the South include population growth, changing diets (which substitute grain-fed animals for vegetable protein) and non-food land uses, particularly the development of biofuels. Additional factors which are likely to drive the import of cereals to developing countries include increasing energy and fertilizer prices and climate change effects in the tropics.

In addition, biofuel production has made the prospect of serious food shortages much worse than it might otherwise have been. The United States embarked on a very large-scale ethanol production programme under President George Bush, not primarily to address climate change but to provide an alternative source of energy to hydrocarbons. Biofuel production requires heavy use of nitrogen-based fertilizers and often diverts land away from food production or forest/grazing land. The increase in biofuels production thus reduces carbon sequestration from the atmosphere and serves to jeopardize climate change from a land use perspective, while making only small gains from substitution of hydrocarbons in energy systems. Biofuels are not 'carbon positive' in that nitrous oxide emissions increase with only modest benefits in reducing carbon emissions – the new effect on greenhouse gas emissions is negative.

The most serious effect of the growth in the biofuels market is that land and water uses are transformed in ways that increase food and water insecurity. The conversion of land from forests and grasslands to biofuels production is one of the key factors. However, biofuels also make enormous demands on scarce supplies of fresh water and contribute to air pollution by increasing vehicle emissions of nitrogen. Another important effect is the runoff from nitrates that contributes to water pollution, and has been a major factor in the water sources ending in the Gulf of Mexico. Finally, biofuels are very land-intensive: three and a half times as much energy can be produced from grassland as from biofuels conversion.

There are also several major new problems that have arisen as a result of the cereal dependency of the developing world, including the newly industrializing countries of Asia. First, land itself is being acquired by China, South Korea and some of the Gulf States. In addition to the crops that the South grows for trading with the North, notably soya, land is being bought by these countries to supply their own domestic markets. The poorest countries in the South are least able to avail themselves of this possibility, and as a result their own domestic food supply is in jeopardy.

Second, there is the continuing problem of trade barriers erected by the industrialized world against cheap food and fibre imports from the South. The protection afforded domestic agricultural producers in the North, especially the United States, the European Union and

Japan, continues to undermine food security in the South. At the same time the environmental services provided largely by tropical countries – such as forests, water courses and extensive grasslands – are not being paid for or supported by trading partners in the North. The global environment is being depleted without compensation being offered to most of those on the 'sharp end' of the process of depletion.

The financial crisis, sustainable development and consumption

The changes in the way that materials, food and energy are sourced globally have usually been discussed without much reference to sustainable development. The expansion of credit in much of the developed world, and the associated levels of personal and corporate debt that has affected most financial institutions since September 2008, led to an economic downturn and period of recession from which we have still not emerged in 2014. An understanding of the 'limits' imposed by shifts in demand needs to be complemented by an analysis of the rising levels of personal consumption and debt, not only in the developed world but in many middle-income and fast-growing developing economies.

The 'toxicity' of many financial institutions, which prompted national governments to bail out much of the banking sector, was triggered by excessive lending in a number of countries, including the United States, the United Kingdom, Spain and Ireland, and especially on house purchases. This brought about a loss of confidence in the ability of the lending institutions to recoup their assets, and national governments acted to guarantee the private banking sector against a feared 'run on the banks'. These developments occurred within a context of relatively high personal (and institutional) indebtedness since the 1980s.

At the same time, another shift had been occurring in consumer policy, this time prompted by the much wider acknowledgement of global climate change, especially after the Stern Report was published in 2007 (Stern 2007). The need to pursue 'low carbon' solutions to economic growth rapidly altered the policy discourses surrounding consumption, and it has become an article of faith for public policy that economic growth is only tolerable if it does not exacerbate existing concentrations of carbon in the atmosphere. At one level such an acknowledgement of the importance of 'sustainable development' is both positive and challenging. In 2008, the United Kingdom's Climate Change Bill was introduced, establishing a very ambitious target for carbon reductions of 80 per cent by 2050. This policy activity has been accompanied by sustained lobbying on the part of NGOs and others in the United Kingdom, including Rising Tide, the Campaign Against Climate Change, and the series of Climate Camps that have repeatedly mobilized the public in their thousands to call for urgent action on climate change and a new approach to economic organization. Nevertheless the impact of budget cuts in the UK and throughout many of the countries of southern Europe, has jeopardized pro-environment policy and targets.

The characterization of climate change as a 'market failure' immediately offered economists, businesses and governments a lifeline (Stern 2007). Rather than necessitating expensive and comprehensive restructuring in systems of provision, or even reduced volumes of production and consumption, Stern's neoclassical view that sustainability could be delivered through *increased* consumption of particular kinds of products, simultaneously feeding the economy, has come to typify the mainstream sustainable consumption discourse, while serving to turn sustainability thinking on its head. In addition, such developments in the economy and in public policy raise some awkward questions for our understanding of sustainable development and the policy discourses which have characterized the field. There is a very substantial literature (see, for example, Hobson, 2002; Seyfang 2005; Jackson 2005) that suggests there is still considerable confusion over the most effective way to achieve more sustainable consumption, and several of the assumptions about consumer behaviour – such as the role of an 'information deficit' about the environmental costs of products and services, and the targeting of personal responsibility for policy solutions as being sufficient to lead to voluntary behaviour change (Redclift and Hinton 2008). Remarkably, these assumptions are largely untested and circumstantial. While policy-makers and pundits alike tend to measure progress towards sustainable consumption in terms of the numbers of purchases of particular 'green' or 'ethical' commodities, where success is framed in terms of market share, an alternative discourse suggests that sustainable consumption involves frugality, thrift and a kind of voluntary austerity. If this is indeed the case, then a focus on economic growth – low carbon or otherwise – may still be unsustainable.

As the Stern Report suggests, climate change is now regarded as a 'given', markets are now considered more relevant to policy solutions than ever before, and the reduced dependency on hydrocarbons is widely regarded as the single most urgent policy challenge facing us. It is also widely assumed that evidence of a slow emergence from economic recession in the developed world will only serve to intensify this process, creating policy tensions and more opportunities for fiscal sacrifices.

This chapter began by arguing that the 'contradictions' of thinking about sustainability and development have merged into distinct policy discourses on the idea of 'natural limits', resource capacity and (un)sustainable consumption. These discourses can be usefully informed by recent work in the social sciences. A realist, science-driven policy agenda has been paralleled by a science-sceptical post-modern academic discourse. Neither position represents a threat to the other – since they inhabit quite different epistemological terrain, and address different audiences. In the process, however, we have seen an enlarged academic debate, and one that closely examines the way environmental language is deployed, while at the same time recognizing that public policy discourses themselves carry weight. The language of 'green consumerism' can reduce the politics of climate change to the size of a green consumer product. The policy debate has proceeded through assumptions about 'choice' and 'alternatives', that have been largely devoid of any critical, structural analysis, and frequently narrow the field of opportunity, by assuming that people act primarily as consumers, rather than citizens (Redclift and Hinton 2008). There is clearly room for more rigorous analysis of what is a very broad social terrain.

The discourse of sustainable development: problematizing the concept

This brief genealogy of sustainable development, the contestation for the concept at international level and the changing realities that the progress of globalization brings with it explain the power and hegemony exercised in the struggle for 'ownership' and definition of the concept. It discloses why the discourse has been narrowly controlled and why a dialectical, relational approach is needed to open up the still-evolving process (Harvey 1996). A more dialectical approach might produce, not a two-dimensional, undialectic 'map', but something more discursive, akin to multi-dimensional 'cognitive mapping' of the many discourses of sustainable development. The importance of maintaining discursivity is that it is the discourse that is 'creating' sustainable development (Foucault 1972); the process is a dynamic one, where the concept should not be allowed to become a naturalized, 'reified' thing (ibid.). It comes down to a struggle between discursivity and control, an inherently ideological process (Redclift 1996), which is witnessed at the international level. The international literature reflects the 'stakes in the ground' of specific groups:[31] economics, ecology, environmental management, environmental philosophy, the claims and contestations of academic disciplines, views from the South and political and corporate positions all reveal the political, ideological, epistemological, discipline-based and philosophical approaches that compete for legitimacy. Broadly speaking, these fall into three major camps: ecology-centred, market-based and neo-Marxist approaches. From a critical perspective, sustainable development is perceived, not only as a social construct, but a multi-constructed and strongly contested concept (Eder 1996b; Dobson 1996) that is political and radical (Jacobs 1991). The dismissive charge of 'vacuousness' that has been made needs to be explored to discover whether such 'vacuity' is used as an obfuscatory gag on the radical aspects of the concept – a way of excluding competing views in the struggle for ownership – or whether the concept is, indeed, vapid jargon.

'Sustainable development' or 'sustainability'?

The contestation for the definition of sustainable development[32] is made additionally problematic by the ways in which the terms, 'sustainable development' and 'sustainability', have been counter-posed (Dobson 1998). For purists, the terms are almost diametrically opposed, sustainable *development* represents a threat to sustainability on account of its 'dangerous liaison', particularly since the Brundtland Report, with economic growth. This liaison smacks of positivism and modernism, since the concept is seen as emanating from the very cultural and economic sources that gave rise to 'unsustainability'. Much of the concern focuses upon Northern domination and the assumption that (Northern) 'management' can solve the sustainable development dilemma. The increasing domination and 'eco-cracy' (Gudynas 1993) stem from the fact that, institutionally, we have bought into an all-engulfing management paradigm (Redclift 1996) that introduces new institutional structures for *environmental management*[33] that give scant attention to the actual processes through which the environment has been transformed and commodified. Against this is the body of opinion that believes that sustainable development encapsulates the understanding of the need for radical change to a different way of life – what has been characterized as a 'painfully difficult turn towards material simplicity and spiritual richness' (Worster 1993: 132). In this sense, it is a strongly normative goal imbued with values and implying that value judgements need to be made (Redclift 1996): a social goal for guiding behaviour at the individual, institutional, national and global levels. This shifts sustainable development out of the paradigm of management where business locates the concept (Springett 2006). It also confirms it as a political concept. It is not surprising, then, that discussions of sustainable development generally ignore the epistemological dimension of the construct, the assumption being that Northern knowledge and expertise have developed a 'universal epistemology', whereas, in reality, the ubiquity of Northern science succeeds in fragmenting the knowledge of the South (Redclift 1991), even though this knowledge may be increasingly important in terms of sustainable development.

Some argue that the ambiguous theoretical basis of sustainable development and the lack of consensus about its meaning make its implementation almost impossible: there are conceptual, political and ethical dilemmas in recasting 'development' activities as 'sustainable', and then declaring this a new paradigm for human interaction with the environment (Sneddon 2000). In its mainstream guise, sustainable development is in danger of privileging *global* environmental problems and global (i.e. 'powerful local', Shiva 1993) institutions which are largely the province of the North, and which choose to focus, for example, on the *problem* of poverty rather than the origins of poverty-*production*. This curtails the ability of the concept to act as an instrument for a 'transformative politics', whereas the concept of 'sustainability' is seen as not having been co-opted into the unilinear, mainstream hegemony to the same degree (Adams 1995; Sunderlin 1995; Sneddon 2000). It 'carries less political baggage' (Paehlke 1999), sparing us some of the problems associated with sustainable development. It is seen as having a 'multiplicity' of meanings, for example, leaving open the question of GNP (ibid.: 243), whereas sustainable development assumes that growth is possible and desirable. Both terms view the economy, the environment and society as inevitably bound up with each other, but sustainability does not assume that economic growth is essential, nor that economic growth will inevitably result in net environmental harm (ibid.).

However, like sustainable development, *sustainability* has a 'complex conceptual structure' (ibid.: 246), and is also deplored for its 'vague, ill-defined character' (Becker et al. 1999). It is also seen as introducing 'normative commitments to the development problematic', calling for justice for future generations and implying that the economic process should be 'subordinated to social and ecological constraints' (ibid.: 5). This strongly accords with the conception of sustainable development propounded by Redclift and others. Despite the calls for sustainability to be extricated from the sustainable development discourse – or to replace it – there is also evidence that a number of writers have in mind an all-embracing concept that eschews neo-classical economics, calls for better understanding and treatment of nature, demands social equity and eco-justice based on a less instrumental understanding of democracy, and that this overall conception of 'the good life' is sometimes referred to as 'sustainability', and sometimes as 'sustainable development'.

A question of definition: competing certainties versus discourse

Part of the 'problem' of sustainable development is the contestation for its definition: so intrinsically political is the concept that it elicits attempts by widely disparate vested interests to frame its meaning. The power of definition, and of determining the language that characterizes a concept, are seminal ways of staking and holding claims to domination (Beder 1996; Livesey 2001; Ralston Saul 2001); while dismissing that concept on account of its *lack* of clear definition also restricts any inherent potential for change from being liberated. The debate on sustainable development has ranged from a call for consensus on a definition that can lead to action (Carpenter 1994) to proposals that the term be abandoned on account of its 'vacuity' and 'malleability' (Lélé 1991; Sneddon 2000) and its lack of 'objective analysis' (Reboratti 1999). Redclift notes that it is 'about meeting human needs, *or* maintaining economic growth, *or* conserving natural capital, *or* all three' (1999: 37, emphasis added). The alleged vagueness and ill-defined character of the concept (Becker and Jahn 1999) have been attributed both to a lack of theoretical underpinning and to the ways in which the concept itself was constructed and framed (Sneddon 2000). Built upon the dual and opposing concepts of ecological sustainability and development/growth, the complexity of the construct promulgates not only different and conflicting theoretical perspectives, but also the ensuing 'semantic confusion' that arises from these (Sachs 1999). Its conceptual capacity and the normative and political dimensions of the concept only increase the ambiguity: it has come to be used *as though* it has 'universal and temporal validity' and general acceptance (Reboratti 1999: 209; see also Smith and Warr 1991), while, at the same time, its lack of objective analysis has led to its being dismissed as a cliché.

Some perceive the ideological repackaging of the discourse of development planning in the 1980s as a cynical attempt to construct a 'green cover' for business-as-usual and the ongoing exploitation of people and resources (Willers 1994; Adams 1995; Escobar 1995): a political cover for otherwise unacceptable corporate practices (Paehlke 1999) and an attempt at 'semantic reconciliation' of the irreconcilable ideologies of ecological transformation and economic growth. The lack of clear definition of sustainable development – its 'opaqueness' – is also seen as symptomatic of this underlying ideological struggle. However, it might also be argued that the failure to deliver a tight definition reflects the futility – even the danger – of trying to capture a complex construct in simplistic terms.[34] Perhaps the most serious aspect of the problematic for 'sustainable development' is that the ambiguous theoretical basis and lack of context-specificity and clarity (Sneddon 2000) disable *implementation* of a concept that does not have time on its side (Redclift 1987; Lélé 1991; Frazier 1997). The dismissal of the concept as a force for power has been widespread: its 'populism' is seen as resulting in confusion and ambiguity (Lélé 1991; Redclift 1991; Reboratti 1999), reducing it to a 'quasi-rhetorical term' and a 'must word' (Reboratti 1999). Lack of academic rigour in the initial formulation of the term has relegated it to the popular status of a 'catch-phrase' (Lélé 1991), with an accompanying 'fuzziness' surrounding its definition and interpretation. Indiscriminate use of the term disguises the fact that it is 'hard to pin down and convert into a useful methodological tool' (Reboratti 1999): even the 'relatively acceptable' WCED needs-based definition focusing on inter- and intra-generational equity is dismissed as 'wishful thinking rather than conceptual framework' (ibid.: 213). It has lost further credibility and meaning on account of the ease with which it has 'passed into the everyday language of politicians' (O'Brien 1991) with the consequent danger of losing all meaning, though it has not impacted substantially on the *platforms* of political parties (Reboratti, 1999). The other cause of scepticism is the ease with which the construct has been colonized by business and become part of its own rhetoric.

The debate reflects the contestation by those who aim to neutralize the potentially political role that lies at the heart of the concept. This prevents serious change from taking place (Lélé 1991) and disempowers its radical core of meaning. The general use of the concept indicates a poor understanding of the institutional causes of poverty and environmental degradation, confusion about the role of economic growth, lack of clarity about the concepts of sustainability and *participation*, with all of this constraining the democratic force of the concept (ibid.). It has also been argued that the vagueness surrounding the concept forms part of its 'appeal' (Redclift 1991): it can mean different things to ecologists, environmental planners, economists, business people and activists. Such 'vagueness' may be a politically expedient aspect of the concept, not only to play down its potential power, but also to emancipate that power (Lélé 1991): a more specific definition might represent a reactionary force, a means of control that restricts discourse (Ralston Saul 2001). In other words, the 'ambiguity'[35] of the concept may be its central virtue and strength, inviting discourse (Redclift, 1987; O'Riordan 1993; Wilbanks 1994).

Dryzek (2000) advocates, not a definition, but a discourse about sustainable development that is shaped by a shared set assumptions and capabilities and embedded in enabling language. Discourses are social and act as sources of order by co-ordinating the behaviour of individuals who subscribe to them.[36, 37] At the heart of the debate over sustainable development lies the question of power, and, specifically, the potential for political and structural change that is central to a radical interpretation of the concept (Springett 2005). Its political significance is underlined in part by the fact that it has been generated through the power of Northern institutions, as well as academic debate (Reboratti 1999). At the same time, the lack of specificity clouds its *normative* role as a social goal which can only be achieved through examination of our own behaviour (Redclift 1996), not 'fixed' by management and technology. For Redclift, it is a policy objective rather than a methodology – an overarching concept and 'unapologetically normative' (1996: 37), calling for a more 'human-focused' approach. The discourse is full of contradictions. Borrowing from the natural and social sciences, the concept is seen as a major constraint on human 'progress' – the price the conventional growth model must pay if the 'biospheric imperative' is ignored, calling for different technologies and more realistic assessment of environmental losses. Another contradiction concerns the implications of 'human progress' for nature, with people from different ideological persuasions calling for an examination of the 'ends' as well as the 'means' of development. Central to the problem are the unanswered questions about recovery of our control over consumption (ibid.). The Brundtland Report's focus on 'needs' still left unanswered questions about the needs of future generations, the changes in needs, the ways in which development contributes to or creates needs, and how needs are defined in different cultures. No answer has been found to the question of *what* is to be sustained (Redclift 1999: 60). Redclift defines the key question as being distributive, calling for a redefinition that would incorporate future population growth and the ensuing demands on the environment, as well as necessary changes in individual consumption patterns. The discourse rarely stops to examine those real needs (largely of the South and the poor of the North) that are consistently not being met (Durning 1992; Elkington 1995), and this brings the heart of the problem back to the materiality of the environmental experience without which culture itself cannot exist (Ingold 1992). Concepts of nature are always cultural statements (Beinart and Coates 1995; Redclift 1999), and the 'environment' is the creation of human activity, socially constructed like all discourses, and based upon ecological principles that are themselves constructs of a science that is part of human culture (Redclift 1999: 67).

One danger of the contestation over definition is that it will deflect attention from these unanswered questions that signify the need for an essentially political project to bring about changes in human behaviour (1997). Competition over definition helps to obscure the more basic need to redefine the roles and functions of public and private institutions that support unsustainable behaviour – not only business, but political and administrative institutions. It is a political act to contest the definition of sustainable development, and the endless contestation may cover up embarrassing questions such as government unwillingness to promote, for example, major fiscal or financial reforms; or to significantly decentralize power; or to recognize that scientific knowledge as a basis for 'rational' decision-making has limitations. In a sense, the debate about definition can be seen as a displacement activity or a deliberate barrier to the recognition of the sustainable development imperative. Contemporary market economies have ideological mechanisms for silencing opposition (O'Connor, J. 1994), one being the act of 'semiotic conquest' of language and agenda. Endless contestation deflects the radical core of sustainable development into a confusing, de-energizing struggle for 'meaning' rather than action. In terms of business, the capitalist appropriation of nature and communities is seen by O'Connor as attempting to find its own legitimation through the 'sinister double play' of the rhetoric of 'greened growth' as opposed to a focus on sustainable development. Radical constructions of sustainable development view it as a potentially energizing force in its own right (Redclift 1987; Dovers 1989; O'Connor, M. 1994; O'Riordan and Voisey 1997), with the potential to create important social change, but calling for a myriad of institutional changes that are not necessarily promoted by the sustainable development agenda. This radical view suggests that many strategies will be employed to obscure or dilute that power, not least by capitalist business itself.

For social change to take place, there needs to be, not a 'definition', but some consensus about the *core meaning* of the term and the moral imperative it offers for 'the good life'. This is not easy when the concept is viewed as propping up the fundamental processes of capitalist exploitation (Jacobs 1999: 22). The demand for a cut-and-dried – and, therefore, almost inevitably 'technological' – definition raises the spectre of 'reason' metamorphosing into 'technology' (Horkheimer 1947), already seen in the domination and instrumentalization of nature. A dialectical approach to sustainable development, not pinned to a specific definition, would be more likely to question the instrumentalist epistemic shift of science in the 1920s, the rapid growth of big bureaucracies in public administration, humanity's colonization of nature through technology, and the capitalist management of the administrative apparatus of the state that worked together to create the need for the construct. Such dialectical discourse would be more likely to unearth the origins of the term, and the archaeology of the institutional infrastructure that supports these systems. Shifting from 'definition' to 'discourse' might elevate the power of sustainable development as a 'site of political contest', the source of a new political world-view that contests the status quo (Jacobs 1999). It would suggest that sustainable development may become part of the deliberative turn to a more discursive theory of democracy (Dryzek 2000), whereby, through a process of dialectical discourse, sustainable development could contribute to a new, more inclusive theory of 'the good life'. Inherent in such a theory would be considerations of environment, equity and ethical issues – factors it is difficult to 'value'.

The areas of core meaning that characterize the belief in the political power of sustainable development, as identified by Jacobs (1991), are:

- the entrenchment of environmental considerations in economic policy-making;
- a commitment to equity;
- an appreciation that 'development' is wider than growth.

Based on this, any interpretation implies change for economic policy and exposes the additional conflict that sustainable development is the beginning, not the end, of the debate: it provides a 'common currency', bringing together conflicting vocabularies to a common, though contested, one (Jacobs 1999). The focus on social equity, global justice and human rights presents a constructivist interpretation based on human relations, culture and politics (Lash et al. 1996). This moves away from the major response since Brundtland, focused on 'managing' the Earth through technological expertise, and the framing of the concept by powerful groups of the North (Becker 1999). Nevertheless, much of the debate has continued to focus on 'definition' rather than imperatives; and the business incursion into the debate has increased the focus on both definition and 'management'.

A 'beggar at the feast?' Peak oil, and de-growth theory

As we have seen, much of the recent debate about 'sustainable development' has focused on the 'capture' or normalization of the term, especially by business and government. However, parallel with this process is another – which casts the discussion rather differently and refers back, albeit sometimes obliquely, to the concept's origins in 'steady state economics' and the ideas of 'sufficiency' (Daly 1977). This is the discussion and practices around 'peak oil' and, more particularly, the 'de-growth theory' and related social movements.

The debate around 'peak oil', which gained renewed momentum in the first decade of the twenty-first century, has parallels in the discussion of the 'limits to growth' in a previous epoch. Adherents of the 'peak oil' thesis argue that production capacity in the hydrocarbon industries will remain the principal brake on supply, and that the decrease in production, to which this will lead, constitutes a bottleneck in the economy (Sorrell et al. 2010; Chapman 2014; Madureira 2014).

The revival of concern with the resource side of the resource/consumption equation is attributable to the fact that, since 1980, global oil discoveries have lagged behind annual production: global production has fallen since 2006 and population and oil consumption have continued to grow faster than oil production. International oil companies are now prospecting in remote fields or utilizing other forms of hydrocarbons, notably shale gas. In the view of 'peak oil' adherents the decrease in oil production will seriously undermine modern technological society, unless alternatives are found to the host of products with a basis in hydrocarbons, including fertilizers, detergents, solvents, adhesives and most plastics. The publication of the Hirsch Reports in 2005 and 2007, by the United States Department of Energy, suggested that to avoid the unprecedented risk of oil price volatility, viable policies to mitigate the crisis needed to be put in place at least 'a decade in advance of peaking'. Needless to say, at the time of writing, such mitigation policies have not been implemented globally.

At the same time another debate has ensued with closer links to the 'anti-globalization' movement, and with roots in the more radical iterations of sustainable development, prior to the mainstreaming of the concept and its incorporation in government and business lexicons. We refer to the literature and social movements associated with 'de-growth', which have proved particularly important in France and North America. The 'de-growth' movement (or *decroissance* in French) is not simply a movement and intellectual position that supports negative growth, as the term implies in English. Rather, it represents a paradigm shift of some complexity, which parts company with the dominant model and culture of industrial society, based on the accumulation of goods through enhanced personal and social consumption. In this sense the 'de-growth' position is the complement to 'peak oil', arguing that radical shifts in demand are called for, in part to manage the expected fall in output of hydrocarbon-based consumer goods. Drawing on a key facet of sustainable development, the 'de-growth' position advocates reduced consumption, though this is presented by different advocates in markedly different ways. As Barry (2012) has suggested, the ideology of growth is structurally coupled with capitalist political economy, and is increasingly identified as a major underlying cause of climate change and natural resource depletion. Manuel-Navarrete (2012: 153), like Barry and most of the 'de-growth' theorists, argues for a 'post-capitalist political economy' that questions the very essence of economic growth as the driving force in the economy. The 'de-growth' theorists have, then, reopened a Pandora's box of global capitalism's ills, including, *inter alia*: how to delink wages from personal incomes to facilitate non-material co-operation, especially over leisure time; alternative types of currency and exchange free from commercial banking; new forms of democratic power-sharing and the reversal of inequitable income and wealth distribution (Binswanger 2001; Fournier 2008). Increasingly 'de-growth' adherents, like others advocating a 'well-being' approach to society, while still favouring the downscaling of production and consumption, do not seek individual 'martyrdom' and personal asceticism but an increase in the rewards of labour and recreational time from sharing work, consuming less and devoting more time to art, music, family and community. At the level of local communities, these objectives have been incorporated in the 'Transition Towns' movement in the United Kingdom, which places local accountability at the forefront of the 'transition' away from dependence on hydrocarbons and the practice of sustainable transport, agriculture and housing (North and Scott Cato 2012).

The scale and ambition of this alternative Green agenda reflect the intellectual contribution of a host of radical thinkers and practitioners from the past, including Thoreau, Ruskin, William Morris and Tolstoy. It also reflects the influence of a more recent generation, without whom the idea of 'sustainable development' would have been impossible: Nicholas Georgescu-Roegen, Jean Baudrillard, Andre Gorz, Ivan Illich and Edward Goldsmith among others.

Sustainable development: an oxymoron?

Polanyi (1967) stressed that economic rationalism, in the strict sense, does not answer questions of motivations and valuations of a moral and practical order. Yet the compromise constructed between sustainable development and economic growth suggests that equity, conservation and economic growth, while uncomfortable companions, are not incompatible (Jacobs 1991). Opponents view this as 'a fatal co-option' into technocentric management designed not to disturb the power processes of the growth economy and capitalist exploitation (Reboratti 1999: 22). Sustainable development has become part of the historical process linked to economics and political structures, transformed both existentially and by economic growth, but inextricably linked with the expansion and contraction of the world economic system (Redclift 1987). However, it calls for a competing paradigm that breaks with the linear model of growth and accumulation. This would be more inclusive, with economic forces seen as related to the behaviour of social classes and the role of the state in accumulation.The social and environmental impacts of capitalist development would not be regarded as beyond the aegis of market economics: they would no longer be permitted as 'externalities borne chiefly by those without power, and which now need to be internalized within the economic model' (Redclift 1987: 13). By strengthening the emphasis upon human need, the Brundtland Report itself provided an opportunity for a radical shift away from an economics epistemologically predisposed to a modernist, reductionist view of resources and exchange value (Norgaard 1985). Nevertheless, it is a 'dangerous liaison' (Sachs 1991; 1999): an attempt to reconcile the irreconcilable (Benton 1999). It can be read as appropriation of the agenda of environmental responsibility and social justice by economists, still reliant upon economic instruments for environmental protection; and no more than a vehicle for 'free market environmentalism' dominated by neo-classical concepts for allocating resources (Beder 1996: 89). International agencies such as the OECD and fora such as UNCED have favoured such ideologically-based market solutions; but others see it as resulting in economic valuation that is another kind of 'semiotic conquest' (O'Connor, J. 1994), converting ecological entity to 'natural capital' and placing it on a par with other forms of capital.[38]

It seems improbable that any agreement about sustainable development that adheres to the core themes identified in this chapter can be based on current global, cultural and political tradition (Reboratti 1999). Rather, it needs a new social covenant and a new set of 'rules', including economic rules and ways of thinking about growth. For example, instead of following the neo-liberal theory of the free play of markets as the system of economic regulation, economic activity would be re-located within society (Gowdy 1999). An emancipatory shift of this kind might mean learning from the complex social systems that have been sustained for long periods of time by people in developing nations, requiring a powerfully different conception of the role of economics in creating the 'good life'.

Conclusion and structure of the Handbook

The dominant and contested discourses on sustainable development overviewed in this introductory chapter indicate that a more discursive theorization of the concept is emerging that challenges the control and hegemony that have been exercised over the discourse. In some cases, these discourses question reified institutions and the domination of the globalized economy, subjecting them to deconstruction of their origins and purposes, and their agendas in appropriating sustainable development. In other cases they put in place the need and the space for emancipatory shifts to what history has set in place, but which is 'not allowed to settle' (Foucault 1972).They represent an antithesis, and provide a 'thinkable opposition' to the modern meta-theory of economic rationality promoted through capitalist development by one that is based upon environmental justice, equity and ecological rationality (O'Connor, J. 1998; Dobson 2003; Barry 2013). A narrative of 'the good life' emerges that is characterized by democratic participation (Jacobs 1991) and deliberative democracy (O'Mahoney and Skillington 1996; Dryzek 2000) as well as a heightened concern with 'well-being' (Dasgupta 2001; Sachs and Reid 2006) and conceptions of what constitutes 'happiness' (Layard 2005). Such a vision is based on constructing sustainable development as problematic: not a discourse of environment and conservation and growing 'eco-cracy', but one of social crisis and human agency. The themes are echoed by voices from the South which also locate the roots of the crisis in global and Northern institutions which need democratizing (Shiva 1993).

The agendas of social and political institutions, and the institutionalization of the sustainable development agenda itself, need to be questioned (Redclift 1992; Sachs 1993; Martínez-Alier 1999). Indeed, one conclusion that can be drawn from the contestation for sustainable development is that power in itself does not provide vision or leadership. In a Foucauldian sense, that very exercise of power may give impetus to such leadership and vision being emancipated *from below*. Foucault (1980) maintained that power, while hierarchized, is not simply a top-down phenomenon, but also comes from below. The global and hierarchical structures in a society operate through local and low-level 'capillaries' of power relationships, raising the question of who holds 'power' over the concept of sustainable development and how sustainable development is constructed. The voices heard from NGO and grassroots groups at UNCED and Rio+20 as well as recent popular movements indicate that people are ready to exercise that power. Other 'spaces of hope' are opening up that may foster horizontal conjunctions of individuals to be included in the discourse, delivering greater social cohesion. We are witnessing new expressions of people power that may define ways of further democratizing the discourse, though not without bitter struggle.

The role of technology in empowering people to communicate and make their voices audible is changing the balance of power and providing new 'capillaries' for communication: the 'Arab Spring' signified a radical call for new institutions, while the 'Occupy' movement challenged the status quo and fired the imagination of many – 'convulsions' (Žižek 2012) that may be seen as contradictory, often perverse, sometimes reactionary, but which signal the possibility of an emancipatory future leading to social transformation. Such movements may drive more discursive or consensual decision-making. Hinton's research (2011), focusing on sustainable consumption, examines the ways in which advocacy may be delivered by a range of cultural political actors including third sector organizations (TSOs). She argues that these groups occupy a privileged and interesting position within the advocacy landscape as trusted and apparently impartial experts, primarily motivated by altruistic concerns and causes. This indicates the possibility of a different administrative coalition assuming a focal role in the sustainable development discourse – one that is more inclusive and horizontal, that advocates for democratic participation, more in keeping with a radical construction of sustainable development. If the discourse were driven by deliberative principles, by collective deliberation, a more equal opportunity to contribute to the ethical project of sustainable development might result in a stronger movement towards 'the sustainable good life' and 'our common future'. This opposing discourse of emancipation pre-supposes radical forms of political democracy (O'Connor, J. 1994: vii). To construct an 'ecological' society, we need liberal democratic forms of institutions and policies. It suggests a very different agenda from the one promulgated by corporations and the institutions that support them, and from the theorization of business and 'greening' that largely constructs their case.

This account of the history of the concept of sustainable development signally shaped the structure and content of the Handbook. It demonstrates that sustainable development is a contested concept, constructed, even appropriated, to meet a diversity of agendas. Because of this, the Handbook eschews the 'triple bottom line' agenda, promoted largely by business ('the business case'), but now current in the academic literature, which focuses on social, environmental and economic issues. The Handbook addresses the multiple dimensions of sustainable development and its contradictions. It is structured around four key imperatives of sustainability, based on the 'Prism of Sustainability' (Spangenberg 2002) as they apply to sustainable development: the institutional, environmental, social and economic imperatives, as well as consideration of the future challenges that sustainable development holds for us. The four imperatives are closely interconnected, highlighting participation, burden sharing, justice, democracy, social cohesion, care, access, limited environmental throughput, eco-efficiency and a sustainable economy that advantages all at reduced environmental cost.

While it is not feasible to cover all possible perspectives within the limitations of the Handbook, this structure has enabled us to address major aspects of the discourse. For example, in Part II, addressing the institutional dimensions of sustainable development, Ray Hudson, in Chapter 2, notes that the extensive literature on relationships between the economy and environmental and socio-political sustainability generally overlooks both the prevalence of the illegal as a significant proportion of activity in the global capitalist economy and its significance for the legal economy. What does recognition of the significance of the illegal mean for the conceptualization of the economy, for the sustainability of the economy of contemporary capitalism and for environmental and socio-political sustainability? In Chapter 3, Michael Hall discusses the importance of island studies as a means of understanding broader issues of sustainable development writ small. He provides an analysis of small island developing states (SIDs) and notes the potential contribution of island studies to theories of sustainability and framing problems of sustainable development. He discusses the notion of islands of sustainability (IOS) and the consideration of islands from industrial ecology perspectives, and utilizes island biogeographical theory to provide insights not only into problems of maintaining island biodiversity, but also as a means of understanding issues faced by human ecological systems. In Chapter 4, Annika Skoglund and Tommy Jensen employ a post-Foucauldian approach to trace how the IPCC has refined its work around 'uncertainty' since the 1990s and promoted the professionalization of sustainable development as a solution. They reveal that talk about uncertainty justifies further knowledge production, moulds a scientific-consensual collective author subject, prepares for surprises and complexities and enforces reflection on and confession of the difficulty of policy-making where complexity prevails. These effects of uncertainty contribute to a forceful ethical programme for change in the neo-liberal sustainable development-resilience nexus. In Chapter 5, Tony McMichael points out that human health has much greater significance in the conceptualization of sustainability than being a mere consequence of environmental and social living conditions and personal choices. Trends in the profile of biological health and survival within a human population, measured over intergenerational time, provide a critical index of whether the combination of population size, social-cultural profile, prevailing technologies and economic intensity is environmentally sustainable. Environmental deterioration and social inequity undermine the prospects for health; indeed, the basic foundations of human health and survival (as for other species) reside in the natural world: food, water, energy, constraints on infectious agents, and physical buffering against natural disasters.

Delyse Springett notes in Chapter 6 that commentaries and policies on the transition to sustainable development have frequently emphasized the central role that education must play in that paradigm shift. She argues that, in order for education for sustainable development (ESD) to assume the transformational role often ascribed to it, and in view of the urgency of the sustainability agenda and the radical re-think of societal priorities it demands, the challenge is to develop a critical theorization of ESD and a critical pedagogy for its delivery. Key stages in the history of education for sustainable development, including initiatives by multilateral organizations such as the United Nations, are overviewed to seek out similar calls for a critical pedagogy, and the institutional impediments that have made this a problematic area of the curriculum at all levels are considered. Major challenges include the education both of those who are to deliver ESD and of the decision-makers who manage key areas of our lives. Finally, she asks if ESD is addressing the real issues of sustainable development and how it might develop the transformational power to make a difference.

In Part III, focusing on the environmental dimensions of sustainable development, Stewart Lockie and Hedda Ransan-Cooper point out in Chapter 7 that biological diversity contributes to numerous ecosystem processes that support ecological, economic and social well-being. Reflecting this, the 1992 Convention on Biological Diversity explicitly incorporates the concept of sustainable development by aiming to ensure conservation of biodiversity, sustainable use of its components and fair and equitable sharing of the benefits that arise from utilization of genetic resources. Evidence to date, however, suggests that action to preserve and enhance biodiversity is either insufficient or ineffective. The chapter examines thus two relatively novel and globally-oriented initiatives with major implications for biodiversity governance: Reducing Emissions from Deforestation and Forest Degradation and the International Panel on Biodiversity and Ecosystem Services. In particular, the chapter examines how these initiatives deal with the demands sustainability makes on learning, deliberation and accountability.

In Chapter 8, Naho Mirumachi writes about issues relating to water for sustainable development and the sustainable development of water. She points out that political recognition of the importance of water for sustainable development has resulted in the establishment of many policy initiatives, concepts and water management frameworks to facilitate the sustainable management of water resources. Nevertheless, challenges remain and critical analyses of the socio-economic conditions of water use and management are still needed.

In Chapter 9, Keith Bothwell, turning to sustainable architecture, uses examples of recent practice to describe the characteristics of sustainable buildings. From its roots in the counter-culture movement of the late 1960s and in buildings constructed before the Industrial Revolution, sustainable architecture has grown to become mainstream, with sustainability now entrenched in building codes. However, environmental assessment methodologies used to calibrate sustainability indicators against a common scale are not altogether successful. Bothwell probes the possible future direction of sustainable architecture, acknowledging that buildings standing today will still be there in 50 years' time and that their adaptation must form part of the overall picture. Focusing on sustainable design more generally, Martina Maria Keitsch reminds us in Chapter 10 that the *Rio Declaration* of 2005 states that designers can contribute to improved sustainability: this means creating products and services in line with the climate, the region and cultural conditions. To establish harmonious interactions with users, products should be well designed, easy to use and beautiful. Key ideas and practices in sustainable industrial design are presented with the help of examples. The sustainable design curriculum is explored along with discussion of how sustainable design strategies contribute to societal development.

The principles of sustainable development and ecosystem services (management) are tightly linked. In Chapter 11, Mark Mulligan and Nicholas Clifford clarify some aspects of the ecosystem services concept, highlighting, by use of examples, some operational principles and consequences for sustainable development of working with this concept. They describe the management of ecosystem services: whether it is possible; what the information requirements are and some key interventions that can be applied. They discuss whether ecosystem services management is necessary for sustainable development with a particular focus on water provision services. Finally, they consider whether ecosystem services management alone is sufficient for sustainable development or whether it represents one of many necessary tools. They argue that the ecosystem services concept provides a planning framework (a means of governance) but that its use as a tool for sustainable development is largely focused on the management (organization of) the interactions between societies and environment.

In Chapter 12, William Adams considers the close and paradoxical relations between conservation and economic growth through the long twentieth century, and analyses the long-standing dependence of conservation on market-based strategies with built-in high throughputs of energy and materials. He explores the possibility of conservation strategies that embrace de-growth, and considers the transitions in scale, definitions of nature, priorities, forms of organization and democratic control that such a model would demand.

In Part IV, focusing on the social dimensions of sustainable development, Robin Morris Collin and Robert W. Collin emphasize in Chapter 13 that sustainability and environmental justice are both tied to the distribution of environmental benefits and burdens. Processes for sustainable development expose disproportionate environmental and economic burdens. They point out that environmental injustices damage the economy, the environment, and the community and that sustainable development ignores any of these impacts at the peril of compounding mounting damage. In Chapter 14, Oscar Forero reviews the contribution of indigenous peoples to the transformation of the sustainable development concept and its practices. Indigenous peoples have fought hard to make it obligatory under national and international laws that biodiversity conservation and sustainable development projects in their territories should only be attempted when these initiatives unequivocally endorse the complete implementation of their human rights as individuals and as peoples. By discussing how indigenous peoples have dealt with the challenges posed by the sustainable development paradigm, Forero also contributes to the ongoing discussion that links management of sustainable development to implementation of human rights.

Emma Hinton, in Chapter 15, discusses some of the ways in which the politics of sustainable consumption can be understood. She outlines key milestones in international governance, discusses a range of types of sustainable consumption – including green and ethical consumerism, voluntary simplicity and anti-consumption – and considers the roles, responsibilities and agency of citizen-consumers. She critically examines the extent to which contemporary sustainable consumption politics may be considered to be an adequate response to consumption issues by working with distinctions between 'weak' and 'strong' forms of sustainable consumption and considering the extent to which they may take on a 'post-political' character. In Chapter 16, Tony Johnston reviews the key literature on sustainable tourism development, particularly reflecting on new agendas in sustainable tourism development and the relationship between academy and practitioner research. A broad perspective on sustainable development is adopted throughout the chapter, incorporating economic discourse alongside institutional and socio-cultural perspectives. He provides a brief chronology of sustainable tourism development, from its primarily economic-oriented foundations to its current broader socio-environmental perspective. Later discussion in the chapter is focused on the sociology of academic and practitioner research in tourism.

In Chapter 17, Colin Sage explores a number of issues connecting food and sustainable development. He highlights some of the ways the dominant twentieth-century paradigm, productivism, exerts particular pressure upon resources and squeezes the entitlements of the poor. An alternative approach informed by sustainability not only works with nature but supports the claims of farmers and citizens to recover their rights to feed themselves. Nevertheless, meat remains a difficult issue to resolve, given its enormous environmental impact, yet with universal expectations around consumption.

In Part V, examining the economic dimensions of sustainable development, Robert Costanza et al. in Chapter 18 sketch a vision of what an 'ecological economy' might look like and how we could get there. They suggest that this option can provide full employment and a high quality of life for everyone into the indefinite future while staying within the safe environmental operating space for humanity on Earth. To get there, we need to stabilize population; more equitably share resources, income, and work; invest in the natural and social capital commons; reform the financial system to better reflect real assets and liabilities; create better measures of progress; reform tax systems to tax 'bads' rather than goods; promote technological innovations that support well-being rather than growth; establish 'strong democracy', and create a culture of well-being rather than consumption. The substantial challenge is making the transition to this better and more sustainable world in a peaceful and positive way. There is no way to predict the exact path this transition might take, but the authors hope that painting this picture of a possible end-point and some milestones along the way will help make this choice and this journey a more viable option.

Michael Redclift and Emma Hinton take a 'long view' in Chapter 19 of the attempts to grapple with the challenges of economic austerity during the economic recession that has characterized several major economies since 2008, by briefly examining the wartime austerity policies in the United Kingdom, which lasted from 1940 until the mid-1950s. The policies during this earlier period were not in themselves a response to the demand for sustainable development but, it is argued, provide a useful comparison with today's attempts to develop sustainable development policy at a time of indebtedness and economic retrenchment. The chapter concludes that the period of austerity in the 1940s and the 1950s was not an historical parallel with today but can be understood as a preceding historical phase, in which enhanced personal and family security eventually prompted a large measure of personal and collective indebtedness.

Joachim H. Spangenberg points out in Chapter 20 that sustainable development indicators are tools for monitoring progress, specifically chosen according to targets and user groups. Consequently, the holding of different world-views leads to setting different kinds of targets, and to using different indicators. The two main schools represent the modificationists, who opt for minor changes of the current model, and the transformationists, who consider that a deep structural change is necessary. While the former often use monetary indicators, the latter hold physical measurement to be indispensable. The chapter presents the world-views and the resulting choices of indicators, indices and indicator systems of both camps, and the indicator quality criteria applicable for both. Tim Luke's Chapter 21 revisits the growth of corporate social responsibility programmes as they have developed in response to cultural, political, and social pressures to reform various business practices to implement workable policies and practices in pursuit of environmental sustainability. He notes that, while some more far-sighted entrepreneurs in the USA took the initiative on their own accord, many firms responded only when pushed toward such changes by new social movements seeking greater ecological responsibility, government environmental regulations to encourage corporate social responsibility, and more aggressive commercial competitors that appeared more caring, innovative or responsible than companies that held back from making such changes in their business operations. His analysis reviews the gradual shift by many companies to at least appear as if they are equally worried about people, the planet, and profit, but he concludes that these campaigns, by and large, are sophisticated efforts at greenwashing, marketing changes or community co-optation. Peter Newman, Anne Matan and James McIntosh argue in Chapter 22 that the challenge for urban transport and sustainable development is to radically reduce resource consumption and the ecological footprint while improving the liveability of cities. While this seems rather daunting, the data from most developed cities suggest that the transition has begun. The peaking of car use, the rapid growth in public transport, bicycling and walking, the regeneration of central areas, all suggest a major transformation to reduce car dependence is underway. The growth of Walking City and the Transit City fabric will be the transformative force that can maintain the momentum of this process.

In an important case study that has implications for sustainable development in all of its manifestations, Arthur Mol points out in Chapter 23 that one of the key global battlefields for environmental sustainability is located in China. We felt it was important to include a chapter devoted to one country, China, for specific reasons. China is today a global leader in greenhouse gas emissions, active globally in natural resources consumption, with per capita greenhouse gas emissions already equal to the EU, and an ongoing high level of economic growth. Representing almost one quarter of the world's population, China's environmental policies deserve particularly close attention. The prospect of more sustainable development in China carries unique implications for the rest of the world. Mol formulates and assesses four discourses that can be extracted from the current literature on how China can/should/does address its sustainability challenges: (1) environmentally unequal exchange; (2) environmental authoritarianism; (3) (reflexive) ecological modernization; and (4) (local) environmental democracy. He points out that none of these discourses has yet a hegemonic position, and ideas from all four discourses are currently to some extent materialized in policies and practices.

Part VI turns to the future challenges that sustainable development still holds for us. Graham Woodgate focuses on agroecology in Chapter 24 as post-development discourse and practice. While detractors criticize post-development discourse for not offering viable alternatives, post-development processes since the 1980s have been building from the bottom up, one of the clearest examples of post-development in action being in agroecology which brings together agricultural practice, transformative agroecological science and agrarian social movements, set in motion through the politics of food sovereignty. As such, agroecology represents a clear and potent challenge to the corporate food regime and its neo-liberal discourse of 'sustainable development' and 'food security'. In Chapter 25, Marco Grasso comments on the social dimension of sustainable development in major carbon-emitting countries. After pointing out why climate policy should be guided by sustainable development, he investigates the social dimension of sustainability through specific assessment of the equity and political feasibility of the major emitters' climate policy. To conclude, he briefly describes some shared features of, and issues emerging from, the top emitters' climate policy as evidenced by analysis. Raymond Murphy argues in Chapter 26 that learning how past disasters have been incubated is crucial to avoid the incubation of *un*sustainability. This involves learning to avoid the failure of foresight, the atrophy of vigilance, indifference to danger signs, error-inducing systems, the normalization of deviance, tightly coupled systems that magnify normal human errors, fantasy risk analyses, laxity of regulations and enforcement, the capture of regulatory institutions by industries being regulated, limited liability laws incentivizing recklessness, and the uselessness of potential market losses in preventing calamities. He argues that sustainable development is fostered only if societies accept the chronic burden of vigilance and the up-front costs necessary to maintain the services nature provides.

Yamini Narayanan, in Chapter 27, applies a religion and human rights perspective to the discussions on women and their participation in sustainable development, and demonstrates that it is a crucial way of understanding the particular ways in which these connections actively restrict – or, alternatively, provide the opportunity to enable – women's active leadership and role in sustainable development. Specifically, she shows that religion impacts on four major fundamental rights of women, which in turn compromise their right to overall sustainable development: (1) the right to environment; (2) the right to safety and security; (3) the right to health and education; and (4) the right to mobility.

Finally, in Chapter 28, Ashwina Mahanti and David Manuel-Navarrete point out that governance and sustainability are inextricably linked. They discuss how different disciplinary approaches have framed the relationship between sustainability and governance and identify and discuss two dominant perspectives: the socio-political and the socio-ecological. They argue that these two perspectives have structured debates on the alternative ways in which sustainable development and sustainability transitions can be promoted through 'governance'. Each perspective has provided a particular conceptualization of governance by placing different emphases on power, scale, systems dynamics, uncertainty, participation and solutions. However, the recent emergence of sustainability science has presented the need to transcend these two dominant perspectives and re-think governance along a solution-oriented approach that promotes structural transformations, both socio-politically and socio-ecologically.

The aim of the Handbook has been to show the continuity, if not coherence, of the concept of sustainable development over the last half-century and the contributions outlined above illuminate the evolving discourse. While grounded in theory, the chapters explicitly link theory to practices, redefine existing areas of research and highlight emerging areas within international scholarship and public policy. The Handbook is international in scope and interdisciplinary in outlook, suitable for audiences in the public and science policy areas, as well as academic social science departments. It will appeal to different audiences from academia, including students in the many academic courses now offered internationally, as well as to more general audiences who are keen to acquire a sound understanding of sustainable development as a basis for their own activities. It presents the implications of thinking about sustainable development for civil society, the international community, business and activist groups. It suggests that though the meaning and practice of 'sustainable development' have a disputed history, the idea has also served as an inspiration, for theorists and practitioners alike. It is far too early to write its obituary.

Notes

1 The Club of Rome comprised industrialists, educators, scientists and others who saw that the interdependence of the world's economic, social, financial and cultural systems had resulted in the Earth becoming 'a stressed system', and feared the exhaustion of many key resources.

2 The scene was set for modernism and unsustainable development through the destruction of the organic world-view of nature and of her role as 'nurturing mother', effected through the new science of Newton, Hobbes, Descartes, Bacon and Locke. The shift was made from the world perceived as 'organic, living, spiritual universe' to 'the world as machine' (Merchant 1980).

3 The terms, 'the North', signifying the 'developed' countries, and 'the South' for the 'developing' countries (and bearing in mind that these terms emanated from 'the North'), are used as convenient labels in this history of sustainable development until the post-UNCED shift in global economic power.

4 The changes in England did not take place without contemporary comment and action (see, for example, Engels, 1884, *The Conditions of the Working Class in England*), and social and political upsurge characterized the reaction of people denied their traditional ways of life then, just as globalization gives rise to a force of protest today. In a country rapidly increasing its colonial empire, 'Luddites', as well as 'surplus' population that it was sometimes difficult to feed, could be disposed of through a combination of transportation and settlement to colonies (Thompson 1963).

5 Northern domination of the developing world has resulted in the poor subsidising the rich through both debt repayment and parting with resources (Ekins 1992: 20). For example, Sub-Saharan Africa paid twice the sum of its total debt in the form of interest between 1980 and 1996, yet still owed three times more in 1996 than it did in 1980 (Monbiot 2003). McNeill (1989) points out that, while the world's population tripled during the twentieth century, and industrial production increased 50 times, with 80 per cent of that increase taking place since the 1950s, intensified agricultural production has kept pace with population growth, but has also brought desertification, soil erosion and salination.

6 Adam Smith's *The Wealth of Nations* (1776) advocated local accountability, moral reasoning and a limit to the large size of business, but his theories are now used to vindicate the actions of modern capitalism (Korten 1995).
7 Decisions made by the Allies at Bretton Woods in 1944 defined important aspects of the debate about political and environmental justice (Rich 1994) by setting in place the structures for increased control by the North – the 'bailiffs' of the world economy – putting the burden of maintaining the balance of international trade on the poorest debtor nations (Monbiot 2003).
8 The World Trade Organization (WTO) enforces free trade on weaker nations according to rules with which the richer nations do not comply. 'Structural adjustment' entails removing barriers to trade and capital flows, liberalizing banking systems, reducing government spending on everything except debt repayments, and privatizing assets to foreign investors (Redclift 1987; Lang and Hines 1993; Rich 1994; Monbiot 2003). In the meantime, rich nations maintain their own protection through tariffs, import restraints and subsidies that keep out imports from poorer nations.
9 See, for example, Commoner (1971); Bahro (1984); Adams (1990); Jacobs (1991); Smith and Warr (1991); Carley and Christie (1992); O'Connor (1994; 1998); Harvey (1996); Redclift (1987); Kovel (2002); and Panayotakis (2011).
10 The UN Annual Human Development Report (2003) charted increasing poverty in the 1990s for more than a quarter of the world's countries owing to the combination of famine, HIV/Aids, conflict and failed economic policies (*The Guardian*, 9 July 2003: 1–2).
11 The way in which industry responded to Carson's exposé was one of the first instances of industry 'lash-back' on the environmental critique (see Graham 1980).
12 See, for example, Marcuse (1964); Boulding (1966); Brower and Erlich (1968); Commoner (1971); *The Ecologist* (1972); Ward and Dubos (1972); Meadows et al. (1972); Schumacher (1973), Ward (1979); among others.
13 Updated in 1988, *Beyond the Limits: Confronting Global Collapse, Envisioning a Sustainable Future*, and in 2004, *The Limits to Growth: The Thirty Year Update*.
14 So called after Thomas Malthus, whose *Essay on the Principles of Population* (1798) propounded the theory that the Earth would run out of resources as population and consumption increased.
15 The 'constructed' nature of 'scarcity' had been critiqued earlier by Bookchin (1971) and Marcuse (1972). See also Achterhuis (1993).
16 This 'scepticism' is kept alive today through the alternative discourses on the environment of writers such as Beckerman (1994; 1996, 1999); Lomborg (2001) and numerous climate change deniers.
17 The WCED was the third commission set up by the UN in the 1980s, the others being the Independent Commission on International Development Issues (ICIDI), which produced the Brandt Reports, *North-South: A Programme for Survival* (1980) and *Common Crisis* (1983); and the Independent Commission on Disarmament and Security Issues (ICDSI), which produced the Palme Report, *Common Security: A Blueprint for Survival* (1983).
18 It is perceived as an 'oxymoron' (*The Ecologist* 1992; Rich 1994); a 'dangerous liaison' (Sachs 1993) or a 'new jargon phrase in the development business' (Conroy and Litvinoff 1988).
19 The UN Conference on the Human Environment (Stockholm, 1972).
20 Several of the Principles and Recommendations produced in the major UNCHE outcome, the 'Declaration on the Human Environment', have been perceived not only as Northern-dominated, but 'mildly eco-fascist' (Adams 1990: 39).
21 The Strategy's stated goal of the 'integration of conservation and development' based on 'a more focused approach to *management* of living resources and ... *policy guidance*' (IUCN et al. 1980: vi, emphasis added) underlined the potential for ideological dissent and the emerging struggle for 'ownership' of the construct of sustainable development. It framed the goals in a Northern, scientific construction of the problem and a reductionist, managerial 'solution' by experts.
22 How such a massive transition from input growth to 'qualitative development' was to be made was not explained, possibly for the politically expedient motive of gaining a wider audience (Goodland et al. 1991; Soussan 1992). The dilemma for the Commission was how to take a strong stand on fundamental concerns while gaining political acceptance and support (Lélé 1991).
23 It was possibly this challenge to the major hegemonic forces of the capitalist economy that led to the Report's being strongly criticized and largely ignored.
24 *The Ecologist* (1992: 1) underlined the control and self-promotion that the Conference endorsed:

> The World Bank emerged in control of an expanded Global Environmental Facility, a prize it had worked for two years to achieve. The US got the biodiversity convention it sought simply by not signing the convention on offer. The corporate sector, which throughout the UNCED process enjoyed special access to the secretariat, was confirmed as the key actor in the 'battle to save the planet'. Free-market environmentalism – the philosophy that transnational corporations brought to Rio through the Business Council for Sustainable Development – has become the order of the day, uniting Southern and Northern leaders alike.

25 See Holmberg et al. (1991); Luke (1997).
26 The privileged position afforded to business at UNCED is discussed in Chapter 5.
27 The increased level of growth based upon economic indicators since the early 1950s has been accompanied by the widened gap between rich and poor and the acceleration of environmental destruction (*The Ecologist* 1993; Monbiot 2003).
28 The countries, Brazil, Russia, India and China.
29 For example, summit@oneworld.net; www.EarthSummit2002.org
30 See www. Earthsummit2002.org/es/life/default/htm
31 See Tisdell (1988).
32 See, for example, Pezzey (1989); Munro (1995).
33 Environmentalists themselves bought into the prevalent management paradigm, calling for *better management strategies*, where once they had called for *new public virtues* such as democracy, local self-reliance and cultural diversity, all championed within a 'spirit of contention' (Sachs 1993: xv).
34 Similar difficulties are associated with other fundamentally political 'meta-constructs' such as 'freedom' and 'justice' when it comes to precise, contextual definition; yet there is a broad core of understanding of what they signify.
35 Jacobs (1999) identifies the irony of this 'ambiguity' that may have enabled the development of a radical discourse of sustainable development to emerge *under the noses* of the very structures that the concept opposes and that have, in turn, attempted to appropriate and neutralize sustainable development.
36 However, Dryzek (2000) does not see sustainable development as necessarily forming a part of the deliberative turn to a more discursive democracy on account of its *accommodation* to the capitalist economic system, though he does acknowledge that there is a radicalization of the discourse developing that might make it part of the discursive turn, and concedes that the concept seems 'reasonably conducive to democracy' as it emphasizes the role of a transnational civil society (ibid.: 123).
37 As noted in the previous note, Dryzek is more inclined to see sustainable development as being 'accommodated' to the capitalist economic system.
38 Harvey (1996: 156) points out that economic valuation represents a double-edged sword for its critics: they must beware of either eschewing the monetary evaluation of nature and thus remaining 'irrelevant' to the political debate; or risk reducing complex ecological processes to 'the crude language of money'.

References

Achterhuis, H. (1993) Scarcity and sustainability. In W. Sachs (ed.) *Global Ecology*. London: Zed Books, pp. 104–116.

Adams, W. M. (1990) *Green Development: Environment and Sustainability in the Third World*. London: Routledge.

Adams, W. M. (1995) Green development theory? Environmentalism and sustainable development. In J. Crush (ed.) *Power of Development*. London: Routledge, pp. 87–99.

Agyeman, J., Bullard, R. D. and Evans, B. (2003) *Just Sustainabilities: Development in an Unequal World*. Cambridge, MA: MIT Press.

Ayres, R. U. (1998) *Turning Point: The End of the Growth Paradigm*. London: Earthscan.

Bahro, R. (1984) *From Red to Green*. London:Verso/NLB.

Barry, J. (2012) Climate change, 'the cancer stage of capitalism' and the return of limits to growth: towards a political economy of sustainability. In M. Pelling, D. Manuel-Navarrete and M. Redclift (eds) *Climate Change and the Crisis of Capitalism*. London: Routledge, pp. 129–143.

Barry, J. (2013) *The Politics of Actually Existing Unsustainability*. Oxford: Oxford University Press.

Becker, E. (1999) Fostering transdisciplinary research into sustainability in an age of globalization: a short political epilogue. In E. Becker and T. Jahn (eds) *Sustainability and the Social Sciences: A Cross-Disciplinary*

Approach to Integrating Environmental Considerations into Theoretical Reorientation. London: Zed Books, pp. 284–289.

Becker, E and Jahn, T (eds) (1999) *Sustainability and the Social Sciences. A Cross-Disciplinary Approach to Integrating Environmental Considerations into Theoretical Reorientation*. London. Zed Books.

Becker, E., Jahn, T. and Stiess, I. (1999) Exploring uncommon ground: sustainability and the social sciences. In E. Becker, and T. Jahn (eds) *Sustainability and the Social Sciences: A Cross-Disciplinary Approach to Integrating Environmental Considerations into Theoretical Reorientation*. London: Zed Books, pp. 1–22.

Beckerman, W. (1994) Sustainable development: is it a useful concept? *Environmental Values*, 3: 191–209.

Beckerman, W. (1996) *Through Green-Coloured Glasses: Environmentalism Reconsidered*. Washington, DC: Cato Institute.

Beckerman, W. (1999) Sustainable development and our obligations to future generations. In A. Dobson (ed.) *Fairness and Futurity: Essays on Environmental Sustainability and Social Justice*. Oxford: Oxford University Press, pp. 71–92.

Beder, S. (1996) *The Nature of Sustainable Development*, 2nd edn. Melbourne: Scribe Publications.

Beder, S. (1997) *Global Spin: The Corporate Assault on Environmentalism*. Melbourne: Scribe Publications.

Beinart, W. and Coates, P. (1995) *Environment and History*. London: Routledge.

Beney, G. (1993) Gaia: the globalitarian temptation. In W. Sachs (ed.) *Global Ecology*. London: Zed Books, pp. 179–188.

Benton, T. (1999) Sustainable development and accumulation of capital: reconciling the irreconcilable? In A. Dobson (ed.) *Fairness and Futurity: Essays on Environmental Sustainability and Social Justice*. Oxford: Oxford University Press, pp. 199–229.

Beresford, M. (1971) Doomsayers and eco-nuts: a critique of the ecology movement. *Politics*, 12: 98–106.

Binswanger, M. (2001) Technological progress and sustainable development: what about the rebound effect? *Ecological Economics*, 36: 119–132.

Biswas, M. R. and Biswas, A. K. (1984) Complementarity between environment and development processes. *Environmental Conservation*, 11: 35–44.

Bonanno, A. and Constance, D. H. (2008) *Stories of Globalization: Transnational Corporations, Resistance, and the State*. Philadelphia, PA: Penn State University Press.

Bookchin, M. (1971) *Post-Scarcity Anarchism*. Berkeley, CA: Ramparts.

Boulding, K. E. (1966) The Economics of the Coming Spaceship Earth. In H. Jarrett (ed.) *Environmental Quality in a Growing Economy*. Baltimore, MD: Johns Hopkins University Press, pp. 3–14.

Brack, D. (ed.) (1998) *Trade and Environment: Conflict or Compatibility?* London: RIIA and Earthscan.

Brower, D. and Erlich, P. H. (1968) *The Population Bomb*. New York: Ballantine Books.

Bruno, K. and Karliner, J. (2002) The UN's global compact accountability and the Johannesburg Earth Summit. *Development*, 45(3): 33–38.

Capra, F. (1983) *The Turning Point: Science, Society and the Rising Culture*. London: Wildwood House.

Carley, M. and Christie, I. (1992) *Managing Sustainable Development*. London: Earthscan.

Carpenter, R. (1994) Can sustainability be measured? *Ecology International Bulletin*, 21: 7–36.

Carson, R. (1962) *Silent Spring*. New York: Fawcett Crest.

Chapman, I. (2014) The end of peak oil? *Energy Policy*, 64: 93–101.

Clarke, R. (ed.) (1975) *Notes for the Future: An Alternative History of the Last Decade*. London: Thames and Hudson.

Colby, M. E. (1991) Environmental management in development: the evolution of paradigms. *Ecological Economics*, 3: 193–213.

Commoner, B. (1971) *The Closing Circle: Nature, Man and Technology*. New York: Knopf.

Conroy, C. and Litvinoff, M. (eds) (1988) *The Greening of Aid: Sustainable Livelihoods in Practice*. London: Earthscan.

Daly, H. E. (1977) *Steady-State Economics: The Economics of Biophysical Equilibrium and Moral Growth*. San Francisco: W.H. Freeman, revised edition (1992) London: Earthscan.

Daly, H. E. (1990) Sustainable growth: an impossibility theorem. *Development*, 3/4: 45–46.

Daly, H. E. (1992) *Steady-State Economics*. London: Earthscan.

Daly, H. E. and Cobb, J. B. Jr. (1989) *For the Common Good: Redirecting the Economy Towards Community, The Environment and a Sustainable Future*. London: Green Print.

Dasgupta, P. (2001) *Human Well-Being and the Natural Environment*. Oxford: Oxford University Press.

Diani, M. (2000) Social movement networks, virtual and real. *Information, Communication and Society*, 3(3): 386–401.

Dobson, A. (1996) Environment sustainabilities: an analysis and a typology. *Environmental Politics*, 5(3): 401–428.

Dobson, A. (1998) *Dimensions of Social Justice: Conceptions of Environmental Sustainability.* Oxford: Oxford University Press.

Dobson, A. (ed.) (1999) *Fairness and Futurity: Essays on Environmental Sustainability and Social Justice.* Oxford: Oxford University Press.

Dobson, A. (2003) *Citizenship and the Environment.* Oxford: Oxford University Press.

Doherty, B. and Doyle, T. J. (eds) (2008) *Beyond Borders: Environmental Movements and Transnational Politics.* London: Routledge.

Dovers, S. (1989) Sustainability: definitions, clarifications and contexts. *Development*, 2/3: 33–36.

Dryzek, J. (2000) *Deliberative Democracy and Beyond: Liberals, Critics and Contestations.* Oxford: Oxford University Press.

Durning, A. T. (1992) *How Much Is Enough? The Consumer Society and the Future of the Earth.* New York: Norton.

Eckersley, R. (1992) *Environmentalism and Political Theory: Toward an Ecocentric Approach.* London: UCL Press.

Eder, K. (1996a) *The Social Construction of Nature: A Sociology of Ecological Enlightenment.* London: Sage.

Eder, K. (1996b) The institutionalisation of environmentalism: ecological discourse and the second transformation of the public sphere. In S. Lash, B. Szerszynski, and B. Wynne (eds) *Risk, Environment and Modernity: Towards a New Ecology.* London: Sage, pp. 203–221.

Ekins, P. (1992) Sustainability first. In P. Ekins and M. Max-Neef (eds) *Real-life Economics: Understanding Wealth Creation.* London: Routledge, pp.: 212–222.

Elkington, J. (1995) *Who Needs It? Market Implications of Sustainable Life-Styles.* London: SustainAbility Ltd. and ERP.

Engels, F. (1884) *The Condition of the Working Class in England*, 2nd edn., trans. and edited 1971 by W. O. Henderson and W. H. Chaloner. Oxford: Blackwell.

Escobar, A. (1995) Imagining a post-development era. In J. Crush (ed.) *Power of Development.* London: Routledge, pp. 211–227.

Esty, D. C. (1994) *Greening the GATT: Trade, Environment, and the Future.* Washington: IIE.

Evernden, N. (1992) *The Social Creation of Nature.* Baltimore, MD: John Hopkins University Press.

Faber, D. and O'Connor, J. (1989) The struggle for nature: environmental crisis and the crisis of environmentalism in the United States. *Capitalism, Nature, Socialism*, 2: 12–39.

Finger, M. (1993) Politics of the UNCED process. In W. Sachs (ed.) *Global Ecology: A New Arena of Political Conflict.* London: Zed Books, pp. 36–48.

Foucault, M. (1972) *The Archaeology of Knowledge.* London: Tavistock.

Foucault, M. (1980) *Power/Knowledge.* New York: Pantheon.

Fournier, V. (2008) Escaping from the economy: politics of degrowth. *International Journal of Sociology and Social Policy*, 28(11/12): 528–545.

Frankel, C. (1998) *In Earth's Company: Business, Environment and the Challenge of Sustainability.* Gabriola Island, BC, Canada: New Society Publishers.

Frazier, J. (1997) Sustainable development: modern elixir or sack dress?' *Environmental Conservation*, 24: 182–193.

George, S. (1976) *How the Other Half Dies: The Real Reason for World Hunger.* London: Penguin.

George, S. (1988) *A Fate Worse Than Debt: A Radical Analysis of the Third World Debt Crisis.* London: Penguin.

Goodland, R. (1995) The concept of environmental sustainability. *Annual Review of Ecological Systems*, 26: 1–24.

Goodland, R., Daly, H., El Sarafy, S. and von Droste, B. (1991) *Environmentally Sustainable Economic Development: Building on Brundtland.* Paris: UNESCO.

Goodman, D. and Redclift, M. (1991) *Environment and Development in Latin America.* Manchester: Manchester University Press.

Gore, A. (1992) *Earth in the Balance: Forging a New Common Purpose.* London: Earthscan.

Goulet, D. (1995a) *Development Ethics: A Guide to Theory and Practice.* London: Zed Books.

Goulet, D. (1995b) Authentic development: is it sustainable? In T.C. Trzyna (ed.) *A Sustainable World.* London: IUCN/Earthscan, pp. 44–59.

Gowdy, J. (1999) Economic concepts of sustainability: relocating economic action within society and the environment. In E. Becker and T. Jahn (eds) *Sustainability and the Social Sciences: A Cross-Disciplinary*

Approach to Integrating Environmental Considerations into Theoretical Reorientations. London: Zed Books, pp.162–181.

Graham, F. (1980) The witch-hunt of Rachel Carson. *The Ecologist*, 10(3): 75–77.

Gray, J. (1998) *False Dawn: The Delusions of Global Capitalism*. London: Granta Books.

Guardian Sustainable Business, 28 October (2011) Why the message from Rio+20 matters more than ever. Available at: www.guardian.co.uk/.../rio-2012-climate-change-paulhohnen (accessed 20 June 2012).

Gudynas, E. (1993) The fallacy of eco-messianism: observations from Latin America. In W. Sachs (ed.) *Global Ecology: A New Arena of Political Conflict*. London: Zed Books, pp. 170–178.

Hardin, G. (1968) The tragedy of the Commons. *Science*, 162: 1243–4128; reprinted in *Environmental Ethics*, ed K.S. Shrader-Frechette. Pacific Grove, CA: Boxwood, pp. 242–252.

Harvey, D. (1996) *Justice, Nature and the Geography of Difference*. Cambridge, MA: Blackwell.

Hays, S. (1959) *Conservation and the Gospel of Efficiency – The Progressive Conservation Movement 1890–1920*, 1979 edn. New York: Atheneum.

Hinton, E. D. (2011) Virtual spaces of sustainable development: governmentality and third sector advocacy in the UK. PhD thesis. King's College London.

Hirsch, R. L., Bezdek, R. and Wendling, R. (February 2005). *Peaking of World Oil Production: Impacts, Mitigation, and Risk Management*. Science Applications International Corporation/US Department of Energy, National Energy Technology Laboratory.

Hirsch, R. L. (2007) *Peaking of World Oil Production: Recent Forecasts*. Science Applications International Corporation/US Department of Energy, National Energy Technology Laboratory. February.

Hobson, K. (2002) Competing discourses of sustainable consumption: does the 'rationalisation of lifestyles' make sense? *Environmental Politics*, 11(2): 95–120.

Hoedeman, O. (2002) Rio+10 and the greenwash of corporate globalization. *Development*, 45(3): 39–42.

Holmberg, J., Bass, S. and Timberlake, L. (1991) *Defending the Future: A Guide to Sustainable Development*. London: Earthscan.

Horkheimer, M. (1947) *Eclipse of Reason*. New York: Oxford University Press.

Ingold, T. (1992) Globes and spheres: the topology of environmentalism. In K. Milton (ed.) *Environmentalism: The View from Anthropology*. London Routledge, pp. 31–42.

International Confederation of Free Trade Unions (ICFTU)(2002) *Making Sustainability Work*. Brussels: Trade Union World Briefing.

International Chamber of Commerce (ICC) (2011) *Draft ICC Contribution for the UNCSD Compilation Document, 2012*. Document 213/89.

IUCN, WWF and UNEP (1980) *World Conservation Strategy*. International Union for the Conservation of Nature. Gland, Switzerland.

Jackson, T. (2005) Live better by consuming less? Is there a 'double dividend' in sustainable consumption? *Journal of Industrial Ecology*, 9(1 –2): 19–36.

Jackson, T. (2012) How fear led world leaders to betray green economy. *Guardian Sustainable Business*, 25 June 2012. Available at: www.guardian.co.uk/sustainable.../rio-20-tim jackson-leaders-green-economy (accessed 30 November 2012).

Jacobs, M. (1991) *The Green Economy: Environment, Sustainable Development and the Politics of the Future*. London: Pluto Press.

Jacobs, M. (1996) *The Politics of the Real World: Meeting the New Century*. London: Earthscan.

Jacobs, M. (1999) Sustainable development as a contested concept. In A. Dobson (ed.) *Fairness and Futurity: Essays on Environmental Sustainability and Social Justice*. Oxford: Oxford University Press, pp. 21–45.

Khosla, A. (1987) Alternative strategies in achieving sustainable development. In P. M. Jacobs and D. Munro (eds) *Conservation with Equity: Strategies for Sustainable Development*. Cambridge: IUCN, pp. 191–208.

Korten, D. (1995) *When Corporations Rule the World*. London: Earthscan.

Kovel, J. (2002) *The Enemy of Nature: The End of Capitalism or the End of the World?* London: Zed Books.

Lang, T. and Hines, C. (1993) *The New Protectionism: Protecting the Future against Free Trade*. London: Earthscan.

Lash, S., Szerszynski, B. and Wynne, B. (1996) *Risk, Environment and Modernity: Towards a New Ecology*. London: Sage.

Layard, R. (2005) *Happiness: Lessons from a New Science.* London: Allen Lane.
Lélé, S. M. (1991) Sustainable development: a critical review. *World Development*, 19(6): 607–621.
Livesey, S. (2001) Eco-identity as discursive struggle: Royal Dutch/Shell, Brent Spar and Nigeria. *The Journal of Business Communication*, 8(1): 58–91.
Lomborg, B. (2001) *The Skeptical Environmentalist.* Cambridge: Cambridge University Press.
Luke, T. W. (1997) Sold down the river: the Rio Summit and the New World Order in the United States. *Environmental Justice Conference: Global Ethics for the 21st Century.* Melbourne University, October 1997. (No proceedings).
McNeill, J. (1989) Strategies for sustainable economic development. *Scientific American*, 261: 105–113.
Maddox, J. (1972) *The Doomsday Syndrome.* Harmondsworth: Penguin.
Madeley, J. (2007) *The Enemy of Nature: The End of Capitalism or the End of the World?* 2nd edn. London: Zed Books.
Madureira, N. L. (2014) *Key Concepts in Energy.* London: Springer International Publishing.
Malthus, T. (1798) *Essay on the Principles of Population*, Edition 1973. London: Dent.
Manuel-Navarrete, D. (2012) The ideology of growth: tourism and alienation in Akumal, Mexico. In D. Pelling, M. Manuel-Navarrete and M. Redclift (eds) *Climate Change and the Crisis of Capitalism.* London: Routledge, pp. 143–156.
Marcuse, H. (1964) *One-Dimensional Man: Studies in the Ideology of Advanced Industrial Society.* London: Routledge and Kegan Paul. Reprinted Abacus, London, 1972.
Marcuse, H. (1972) *Counterrevolution and Revolt.* London: Allen Lane.
Martínez-Alier, J. (1999) The socio-ecological embeddedness of economic activity: the emergence of a transdisciplinary field. In J. Becker and T. Jahn (eds). *Sustainability and the Social Sciences: A Cross-Disciplinary Approach to Integrating Environmental Considerations into Theoretical Reorientation.* London: Zed Books, pp. 112–140.
Martínez-Alier, J. (2003) *The Environmentalism of the Poor: A Study of Ecological Conflicts and Valuation.* Cheltenham: Edward Elgar Publishing.
Mayhew, N. (1997) Fading to grey: the use and abuse of corporate executives' 'Representational power'. In R. J. Welford (ed.) *Hijacking Environmentalism: Corporate Responses to Sustainable Development.* London: Earthscan, pp. 63–95.
Meadows, D. H., Meadows, D. L., Randers, J. and William, W. III. (1972) *The Limits to Growth: A Report for the Club of Rome's Project on the Predicament of Mankind.* New York: Universe.
Meadows, D. H., Meadows, D. L. and Randers, J. (1988) *Beyond the Limits: Confronting Global Collapse, Envisioning a Sustainable Future.* Vermont: Chelsea Green Publishing.
Meadows, D. H. and Randers, J. (2004) *Limits to Growth: The Thirty Year Update.* Vermont: Chelsea Green Publishing.
Merchant, C. (1980) *The Death of Nature: Women, Ecology and the Scientific Revolution.* London: Wildwood House.
Monbiot, G. (2003) *The Age of Consent.* London: Flamingo.
Munro, D. A. (1995) Sustainability: rhetoric or reality? In T. C. Trzyna (ed.) *A Sustainable World: Defining and Measuring Sustainable Development.* London: Earthscan, pp. 27–35.
Newby, H. (1980) *Green and Pleasant Land? Social Change in Rural England.* Harmondsworth: Penguin.
Norgaard, R. (1985) Environmental economics: an evolutionary critique and a plea for pluralism. *Journal of Environmental Economics and Management*, 12: 382–394.
North, P. and Scott Cato, M. (2012) A suitable climate for political action? A sympathetic review of the politics of transition. In M. Pelling, D. Manuel-Navarrete and M. Redclift (eds) *Climate Change and the Crisis of Capitalism.* London: Routledge.
O'Brien, P. (1991) Debt and sustainable development in Latin America. In D. Goodman and M. Redclift (eds) *Environment and Development in Latin America.* Manchester: Manchester University Press, pp. 24–47.
O'Connor, J. (1994) Is capitalism sustainable? In M. O'Connor (ed.) *Is Capitalism Sustainable? Political Economy and the Politics of Ecology.* New York: Guilford, pp. 152–175.
O'Connor, J. (1998) *Natural Causes: Essays on Ecological Marxism.* New York: Guildford.
O'Connor, M. (1994) Introduction: liberate, accumulate – and bust? In M. O'Connor (ed.) *Is Capitalism Sustainable? Political Economy and the Politics of Ecology.* New York: Guilford, pp. 1–21.
O'Mahoney, P. and Skillington, T. (1996) 'Sustainable Development' as an organising principle for discursive democracy? *Sustainable Development*, 4(1): 42–52.
O'Riordan, T. (1981) *Environmentalism*, 2nd edn. London: Pion.

O'Riordan, T. (1993) The politics of sustainability. In R. K. Turner (ed.) *Sustainable Environmental Management: Principles and Practice*. London: Belhaven and ESRC, pp. 37–69.

O'Riordan, T. and Voisey, H. (1997) The political economy of sustainable development. *Environmental Politics*, 6: 1–23.

OECD (2000) *Guidelines for Multinational Enterprises*. Paris: OECD.

Paehlke, R. (1999) Towards defining, measuring and achieving sustainability: tools and strategies for environmental evaluation. In J. Becker and T. Jahn (eds) *Sustainability and the Social Sciences. A Cross-Disciplinary Approach to Integrating Environmental Considerations into Theoretical Reorientation*. London: Zed Books, pp. 243–264.

Panayotakis, C. (2011) *Remaking Scarcity: From Capitalist Inefficiency to Economic Democracy*. London: Pluto Press.

Pelling, M., Manuel-Navarrete, D. and Redclift, M. (eds) (2012) *Climate Change and the Crisis of Capitalism*. London: Routledge.

Pezzey, J. (1989) Definitions of sustainability. Paper developed as Visiting Harkness Fellow, Environment and Behavior Programme, University of Colorado: Institute of Behavioral Sciences.

Polanyi, K. (1967) *The Great Transformation*. Boston: Beacon.

Ralston Saul, J. (2001) *On Equilibrium*. Toronto: Penguin.

Reboratti, C. E. (1999) Territory, scale and sustainable development. In J. Becker and T. Jahn (eds) *Sustainability and the Social Sciences. A Cross-Disciplinary Approach to Integrating Environmental Considerations into Theoretical Reorientation*. London: Zed Books, pp. 207–222.

Redclift, M. (1984) *Development and the Environmental Crisis: Red or Green Alternatives*? London: Methuen.

Redclift, M. (1987) *Sustainable Development: Exploring the Contradictions*. London: Routledge.

Redclift, M. (1991) The multiple dimensions of sustainable development. *Geography*, 36–42.

Redclift, M. (1992) Sustainable development and global environmental change: implications of a changing agenda. *Global Environmental Change*, March 1992: 32–42.

Redclift, M. (1996) *Wasted: Counting the Costs of Global Consumption*. London: Earthscan.

Redclift, M. (1999) Sustainability and sociology: northern preoccupations. In E. T. Becker and T. Jahn (eds) *Sustainability and the Social Sciences. A Cross-Disciplinary Approach to Integrating Environmental Considerations into Theoretical Reorientation*. London: Zed Books, pp. 59–73.

Redclift, M. R. and Hinton, E. D. (2008) *Living Sustainably: Approaches for the Developed and Developing World*. London: Progressive Governance.

Reid, D. (1995) *Sustainable Development: An Introductory Guide*. London: Earthscan.

Rich, B. (1994) *Mortgaging the Earth: The World Bank, Environmental Impoverishment and the Crisis of Development*. London: Earthscan.

Robertson, J. (1990) *Future Wealth: A New Economics for the 21st Century*. New York: The Bootstrap Press.

Rockström, J. et al. (2009) A safe operating space for humanity. *Nature*, 461: 472–475.

Rowell, A. (1996) *Green Backlash: Global Subversion of the Environmental Movement*. London: Routledge.

Sachs, I. (1999) Social sustainability and whole development: exploring the dimensions of sustainable development. In J. Becker and T. Jahn (eds) *Sustainability and the Social Sciences. A Cross-Disciplinary Approach to Integrating Environmental Considerations into Theoretical Reorientation*. London: Zed Books, pp. 25–36.

Sachs, W. (1991) Environment and development: the story of a dangerous liaison. *The Ecologist*, 21(6) November/December: 252–257.

Sachs, W. (ed.) (1993) *Global Ecology: A New Arena of Political Conflict*. London: Zed Books.

Sachs, J. D. and Reid, W. (2006) *Investments toward Sustainable Development*. New York: Columbia University: Earth Institute.

Schumacher, E. F. (1973) *Small is Beautiful: Economics as if People Really Mattered*. London: Abacus.

SCOPE (2009) Finance, food and energy crises: the consequence for the environment and land use change. Paper presented at conference at Imperial College London, June 12 2009.

Seyfang, G. (2005) Shopping for sustainability: can sustainable consumption promote ecological citizenship?' *Environmental Politics*, 14(2): 290–306.

Shiva, V. (1991) *The Violence of the Green Revolution: Third World Agriculture, Ecology and Politics*. London: Zed Books.

Shiva, V. (1993) The greening of the global reach. In W. Sachs (ed.) *Global Ecology: A New Arena of Political Conflict*. London: Zed Books, pp. 149–156.

Smith, P. M. and Warr, K. (1991) *Global Environmental Issues*. London: Hodder and Stoughton.

Sneddon, C. S. (2000) 'Sustainability' in ecological economics, ecology and livelihoods: a review. *Progress in Human Geography*, 24(4): 521–549.

Sorrell, S., Miller, R., Bentley, R. and Speirs, J. (2010) Oil futures: a comparison of global supply forecasts. *Energy Policy* 38: 4990–5003.

Soussan, J. G. (1992) Sustainable development. In A. M. Mannion and S. R. Bowlby (eds) *Environmental Issues in the 1990s*. Chichester: John Wiley and Sons, pp. 131–146.

Spangenberg, J. H. (2002) Environmental space and the prism of sustainability: frameworks for indicators measuring sustainable development. *Ecological Indicators*, 2(3): 295–309.

Spretnak, C. and Capra, F. (1985) *Green Politics: The Global Promise*. London: Paladin.

Springett, D. V. (2005) Structural limits to sustainable development: managers and progressive agency. *International Journal of Innovation and Sustainable Development*, 1(1–2): 127–148.

Springett, D. V. (2006) Managing the narrative of sustainable development: 'Discipline' of an 'inefficient' concept. *International Journal of Green Economics*, 1(1–2): 50–67.

Springett, D. V. (2011) Waiting for Rio. *ISDRS Newsletter*, 3, 2011: 14–16.

Springett, D. V. (2012a) Rio+20: More than hot air? *ISDRS Newsletter*, 2, 2012: 4–5.

Springett, D. V. (2012b) How corporations hijacked the sustainable development agenda. *Global Responsibility*, 64, June 2012: 7–9.

Springett, D. V. (2013) Critical perspectives on sustainable development. *Sustainable Development*, 21(3): 73–83.

Stern, N. (2007) *The Economics of Climate Change: The Stern Review*. New York: Cambridge University Press.

Sunderlin, W. D. (1995) Managerialism and the conceptual limits of sustainable development. *Society and Natural Resources*, 8: 481–492.

The Ecologist (1972) *A Blueprint for Survival*. Harmondsworth: Penguin.

The Ecologist (1992) The Earth Summit Débâcle. 22(4): 122.

The Ecologist (1993) *Whose Common Future?* London: Earthscan.

The Independent Commission on International Development Issues (ICIDI) (1980) *North-South, a Programme for Survival* (The Brandt Report).

The Independent Commission on International Development Issues (ICIDI) (1983) *Common Crisis: North-South Co-operation for World Recovery* (The Brandt Report).

The Independent Commission on Disarmament and Security Issues (ICDSI) (1983) *Common Security: A Blueprint for Survival* (The Palme Report).

Thompson, E. P. (1963) *The Making of the English Working Class*. London: Gollancz.

Tisdell, C. (1988) Sustainable development: different perspectives of ecologists and economists, and relevance to LDCs. *World Development*, 16(3): 373–384.

UNCED (United Nations Conference on Environment and Development) (1992) *Agenda 21: Programme of Action for Sustainable Development*. New York: United Nations Publications.

UNCHE (United Nations Conference on the Human Environment) (1972) *The Stockholm Declaration*. New York: UN.

UNCSD (United Nations Conference on Sustainable Development) (2012) *Report*. New York: United Nations.

United Nations Human Development Report (2003) *Millennium Development*. Oxford: Oxford University Press.

United Nations World Summit on Sustainable Development (WSSD) (2002) *The Johannesburg Declaration on Sustainable Development*. New York: United Nations.

Van Aelst, P. and Walgrave, S. (2007) New media, new movements? The role of the Internet in shaping the anti-globalisation movements. *Information, Communication and Society*, 5(4): 465–493.

Van Laer, J. (2010) Internet and social movement: action repertoires. *Information, Communication and Society*, 13(8): 1146–1171.

Vitousek, P. M., Erlich, P. R., Erlich, A. H. and Matson, P. A. (1986) Human appropriation of the products of photosynthesis. *Bioscience*, 34: 368–373.

Ward, B. (1979) *Progress for a Small Planet*. Harmondsworth: Penguin.

Ward, B. and Dubos, R. (1972) *Only One Earth*. New York: Norton.

Welford, R. J. (ed.) (1997) *Hijacking Environmentalism: Corporate Responses to Sustainable Development*. London: Earthscan.

Wilbanks, T. J. (1994) 'Sustainable development' in geographic perspective. *Annals of the Association of American Geographers*, 84(4): 541–556.

Willers, B. (1994) A new world deception. *Conservation Biology*, 8: 1146–1148.

World Commission on Environment and Development (WCED) (1987) *Our Common Future: The Report of the World Commission on Environment and Development*. Oxford: Oxford University Press.

Worster, D. (1993) The shaky ground of sustainability. In W. Sachs (ed.) *Global Ecology: A New Arena of Political Conflict*. London: Zed Books, pp. 36–48.

Žižek, S. (2012) *The Year of Dreaming Dangerously*. London: Verso.

PART II

Institutional dimensions of sustainable development

2

DOES ILLEGALITY ENABLE OR UNDERMINE THE SUSTAINABILITY OF THE GLOBALISING ECONOMY?

Ray Hudson

Introduction

There is an extensive and well-known literature that examines relationships between the economic, environmental, political and social dimensions of sustainability and the potential synergies, conflicts and trade-offs among them. Understanding them poses both theoretical and practical challenges. There undoubtedly are hard choices to be made as to priorities and differing views as to the compatibility of objectives relating to these four dimensions. In particular, there is continuing disagreement as the extent to which and ways in which an economy driven by the imperatives of capital can be made compatible with the pursuit of environmental and social sustainability.

Capitalist economies involve transformations of elements of the natural world via social processes of commodity production, organised and regulated in particular ways in specific times and places (Boyer 1990; Jessop 1990). The legal arrangements that govern relations between economy, society and the natural world have implications both for the sustainability of the economy and for environmental, political and social sustainability. Crucially, legal economic activities can and do unavoidably have adverse sustainability outcomes as a part of 'business as usual' in the capitalist economy.

By and large, however, discussion of these issues in the literature is limited to a conceptualisation of the economy that is composed of formally regulated and legally sanctioned activities. What is generally unrecognised is the prevalence of the illegal and its centrality to the legal economy, as a significant proportion of activity in the global capitalist economy is in one way or another illegal. Failure to acknowledge this results, therefore, at best, in a partial conceptualisation of the economy and of the links between the economy and other dimensions of sustainability. Recognition of the significance of the illegal raises important questions as to its relationship to the legal and the implications of the prominence of the illegal for sustainability: what does this mean for environmental, political and social sustainability and also, crucially, for the sustainability of the economy of contemporary capitalism? Does this help sustain the economy while further eroding the non-economic aspects of sustainability, since whatever the impacts within the legal regulatory framework, these are more damaging when the legal limits are transgressed?

How big is the illegal economy and why does that matter for sustainability?

Defining illegal economic activities is seemingly straightforward: '[t]hose productive activities that generate goods and services forbidden by law or that are unlawful when carried out by unauthorised producers' (OECD 2002: 13). The legal and illegal are therefore relationally defined. The boundary between them varies among different territorial jurisdictions at different spatial scales, most commonly the scale of the national state, and over time. What is illegal in one time and place may be legal in another; and vice versa. Bearing this definitional qualification in mind, it is estimated that the illegal economy accounts for perhaps 20 per cent of global GDP and considerably more in particular territories and jurisdictions (for example, 40–50 per cent or more in (so-called) transitional and developing economies: Glenny 2008, 2011). However, illegal activities are by no means confined to these peripheral parts of the world economy. They are also present in a range of spaces in the core capitalist economies of the developed world – ranging from pivotal financial districts in major metropolitan city-regions to diverse deindustrialised and marginalised places.

The extent of illegality suggests that understandings of the capital accumulation process and the sustainability of the economy and its wider social and ecological impacts that rely solely upon published statistics relating to the formal legal economy are, at best, partial. There is an obvious difficulty in estimating the magnitude and effects of illegal activity and its articulations with the legal precisely because it is beyond the gaze of national states and other regulatory bodies that generate the data that describe the legal economy (although that is not to say without their connivance on occasion). However, as Castells (2010: 173) emphasises, difficulties in obtaining precise empirical data on the extent of illegality should not stand in the way of seeking to understand its function and practices and the relations between the legal and illegal – to which I would add the relations between the economy and various dimensions of sustainability.

While always present within capitalist economies, the illegal has become an integral part of the contemporary phase of capitalist development, given greater prominence because of the tendency to neo-liberalism, giving greater freedom to lightly regulated markets which create spaces in which the illegal can flourish more easily. While acknowledging the definitional difficulties, illegal activities clearly typically form a substantial enough part of total economic activity for them to be considered as an integral part of the normal workings of the capitalist economy rather than a marginal anomaly (Brown and Cloke 2007; Murphy 2011). Illegal practices are present in routine production in factories and workplaces, in the widespread theft of intellectual property (IP) and the growth of counterfeit 'knock offs' and forgeries, in a variety of exchange and trading activities (flows of people, arms, cigarettes, and drugs, for example) and crucially in flows of money and money laundering activities in centres of global finance that convert massive sums of money generated in illegal activities into legitimate money capital in the formal mainstream economy. These issues are explored below.

The spatial and temporal variation in the significance of the illegal and in its coupling with legal suggests that while each depends upon the other, the relationship between them is asymmetrical and contingent as well as symbiotic. Though related, they are regulated and governed in different ways in the same time and space. In addition, like legal activities, illegal activities are governed and regulated differently in different spaces and times, although a combination of trust, often within the social relations of family or clan, and the threat of extreme violence is typically important in their regulation (Gambetta 2011). Consequently, how, when and where legal and illegal activities intersect and relate to one another in the circuits of capital and spaces of capitalist economic activity is critical (Nordstrom 2007; Castells 2010) both for the economy and socio-ecological sustainability more generally. Since the significance of the illegal to economic sustainability varies spatially and temporally, so too does its effects upon environmental, political and social sustainability. Activities that are legal in some jurisdictions may have more damaging effects on environmental and social sustainability than the same activities that are illegal in others. Consider, for example, the effects of the expansion of coal-fired power stations and heavy industry in contemporary China – legal, but environmentally very damaging.

The ways in which the economy is regulated and the line between the illegal and legal is defined is particularly important as there is a tension, inherent in the primacy of the profit motive in capitalism, between the need for competing companies to operate according to the 'rules of the game', and the pressure to bend those rules (Murphy 2011: 135). While some companies have a competitive interest in enforcing strong regulation, for others, the route to economic survival necessarily involves circumventing regulatory restrictions and acting illegally. A similar point can to an extent be made about national states in their competition for economic activity and investment. The primacy of competition and the profit motive results in a tendency to blur, if not outright transgress, the legal/illegal boundary and for such blurring to be structurally embedded in the day-to-day operations and practices of capitalist economies. Where the line between legal and illegal is drawn and how, where and to what extent such blurring of that line occurs, however, vary temporally and spatially. This demarcation and its transgression and the links between the legal and illegal are critical to the dynamic trajectory, spatiality and sustainability of accumulation globally and have implications for other dimensions of sustainability.

In short, the illegal is rife and permeates the space-economy of contemporary capitalism in diverse and complex ways. It cuts across and problematises binaries such as core/periphery, developed/underdeveloped and North/South. Its presence may indicate that the limits imposed by laws and regulatory processes to manage the adverse effects of economic activities on environmental and social sustainability within 'acceptable' limits are chronically transgressed. Recognising this and also that those legal activities may compromise sustainability, a number of questions are explored in this chapter: to what extent do illegal activities further undermine the sustainability of the contemporary legal global economy? On the other hand, conversely and perhaps seemingly counter-intuitively, to what extent are illegal activities integral to the sustainability of that economy? How far does illegality in the economy contribute to further erosion of the environmental (via illegal production and dumping of polluting wastes, for example), political (via challenging the legitimacy of national states, for example) and social (as a result of the effects of illegal labour migration, employment of child labour and the growing scale of the consumption of illegal drugs, for example) dimensions of sustainability?

Illegality and the erosion of environmental sustainability

The transformation of elements of the natural world forms the starting point for creating socially useful and valued commodities under capitalist relations of production. An important strand of this initial stage in the production process involves winning minerals from the earth. With the expansion and growing globalisation of the economy, there have been increasing pressures to extend the search for valuable minerals and other natural materials on a global scale. Much of this activity is regulated within the formal economy. With the growth of the Chinese economy, for example, large parts of Australia have become a regulated source of such materials. Many critical minerals are found in other parts of the world conventionally regarded as underdeveloped, however, such as Africa and parts of Asia and South America. In these locations political elites often continue to look favourably on investment in mining by multinational corporations (MNCs) as, allegedly, a post-colonial route to development. While much of this mining activity is legal and regulated as such, regulation is often light so that there are deleterious environmental impacts. In addition, however, there are also numerous instances of illegal mining of minerals such as copper, palladium, platinum and tin, with scant if any regard for the effects of such activity on environmental sustainability, with widespread dumping of untreated toxic waste materials and pollutants into the environment adjacent to the mining areas. Illegal mining activities can therefore further exacerbate and undermine ecological sustainability with deleterious effects upon both environmental and human health and well-being (Action Against Impunity for Human Rights 2011; Erman 2007; Nordbrand and Bolme 2007; Pöyhönen and Simola 2007).

Such minerals then enter complex patterns of international trade and the supply chains and manufacturing processes of major multinationals. Illegality in the manufacturing process can further impact adversely on environmental sustainability. Because manufacturing necessarily involves the chemical and physical transformation of materials (natural and synthetic), processes of transformation that often involve noxious by-products, it can have adverse environmental impacts. As a result, modes of regulation incorporate legal frameworks to limit their extent. However, as biophysical processes cannot necessarily be contained to produce only their intended effects, they can also produce unintended and unwanted adverse impacts beyond regulatory limits and erode environmental sustainability as a result. In addition, however, in many parts of the world competitive pressures lead companies intentionally to ignore legal limits and to produce illegally, deliberately producing adverse and illegal environmental impacts, further eroding environmental sustainability. For example, companies may knowingly deploy illegal production processes that lead to environmental pollution via illegal emissions into the atmosphere or the illegal dumping of toxic wastes (Hudson 2010).

Globalisation, illegality and the erosion of social sustainability

Capitalist production is predicated upon sharp class differences in the conditions under which people live and work. Typically, laws are enacted and social norms established within modes of regulation designed to keep the resultant tensions within tolerable limits and enable societies to be sustainably reproduced. While such limits vary temporally and spatially, they establish a benchmark in a particular jurisdiction as to an 'acceptable' degree of economic inequality that is seen as compatible with social sustainability. Capital, however, is of necessity engaged in a ceaseless competition for profits, pushing at the boundaries of what is acceptable as companies seek to cut costs and maximise profits.

Since the initial discovery of the New International Division of Labour (Fröbel et al. 1980), there has been keen interest in new forms of corporate organisation and, as part of this, of capital producing and using spatial difference in pursuit of profit (Hudson 2001). This enhanced interest in spatial differences has reflected the growing emphasis on the activities of MNCs and their transition to becoming brand managers while seeking to out-source various functions to the cheapest feasible location (Hudson 2005: 63–75), enabling their corporate owners to reap surplus profits. Companies have out-sourced and increasingly off-shored routine production of components and assembly work and some aspects of back office work and routine R&D, forming globally distributed production systems with complex links and flows of materials and value between diverse spaces in different parts of the world (Hudson 2008). As production systems have penetrated into still more marginal and peripheral spaces in the globalising economy, and pressures to cut costs further have intensified, so too has the potential for the illegal to flourish.

Increasingly much routine work is re-located not simply to spaces in which labour and other production costs are lower but to spaces in which they can be further lowered by the widespread use of illegal working practices. In many places illegality lies at the heart of mining and production processes, involving unauthorised workers and/or workers working under conditions that otherwise violate labour laws. There is, for example, compelling evidence of this in mining in Africa and in manufacturing in China, Indonesia, India, Burma and other parts of Southeast Asia as well as central and eastern Europe, across a wide range of industries including clothing and textiles and consumer electronics (mobile phones, PCs and their various components and offshoots such as tablets) in the new 'workshops of the world' of twenty-first century capitalism. In their journey through global networks many commodities may therefore routinely pass through both legally and illegally regulated spaces and involve both legal and illegal workers. However, the centrality of illegal labour and working practices in the emergence and economic sustainability of global production systems and their implications for other dimensions of sustainability have not been properly considered.

The erosion of social sustainability I: illegality, migration and labour markets

While illegal labour can be provided by members of an indigenous population, for example, via child labour or indentured labour (for example, see Coninck et al. 2011) and there is widespread evidence of this, the supply of illegal labour is also linked to flows of migrant workers and this has increased in significance as processes of globalisation have widened and deepened. Illegal migrant labour may be deployed as labour-power in activities that are legal, although those who perform such work are not authorised to do so. This has profound implications for both capital and labour. For the companies involved, it enables production costs to be driven down further and competitiveness to be increased. In this way, it enhances their sustainability as capital. For those who provide labour-power, it has serious implications for the precariousness of their position in the labour market, level of wages, and working and living conditions as labour market inequality and social inequality more generally widen as a result. In this way it threatens social sustainability.

Since labour always has to be produced as a fictive commodity in order that commodified labour-power can come into existence (Polanyi 1944; Elson 1979), the price that capital pays to secure labour-power reflects the conditions under which labour is reproduced, and the distribution of the costs of that reproduction (as between family, community, and state) over time and space. Consequently, migrant labour can depress the price of labour-power in three ways. First, within legal systems of intra-national (notably China in recent years) and international (for example, from the Mediterranean region to northern Europe) migrant labour flows, because the costs of reproduction of such labour have been displaced elsewhere in time/space. Second, and in addition, because illegal migrant labour by definition lacks citizenship and legal rights, it is particularly vulnerable to further hyper-exploitation, leading to a further lowering of wages. Furthermore, third, illegal migrants can expand labour reserves, further pushing down wages and the value of labour-power and enhancing rates of exploitation, profit and accumulation more generally. In some cases workers who were initially legal migrants lose their jobs and so become illegal migrants as their work permits expire. Often, in these circumstances, they are unable to return to their country of origin because of indebtedness incurred through the payment of fees to agents in order to become migrants in the first place. As a result, they become vulnerable to recruitment as illegal labour with a very precarious existence. In other cases, employment agencies deliberately arrange for contract workers to become illegal immigrants in order that they can be employed on inferior conditions and lower wages (SOMO 2009). National states may on occasion turn a blind eye to such practices and illegal migration in order to intensify labour market competition as one strand of broader neo-liberal strategies (Evans et al. 2006: 61).

Thus, while the increase in illegal migrant workers and work may benefit capital and enhance corporate sustainability, it does so at the risk of a considerable threat to social sustainability. Illegal labour migration can deepen labour market segmentation, often on the basis of ethnicity, and exacerbate inequality in labour markets and in incomes, with corrosive effects on social relations beyond the labour market that further endanger social sustainability.

The erosion of social sustainability II: Illegal working practices in the circuit of productive capital

Formally regulated labour markets define the terms and conditions on which labour is legally hired and labour-power purchased. There are, however, significant spatial differences in labour market regulation both over time and between and within national territories: working practices that are legal in some may be illegal in others, for example. Acknowledging this, it is also the case that labour-power that is legally purchased on the labour market from workers whose status is legal can be illegally employed because of the structural weakness of labour and/or the inability or unwillingness of state officials to enforce even weak regulation in particular locations. For example, companies may withhold wages and force workers to work beyond the legal limit for overtime, violating both national legislation and international agreements such as the ILO's Hours of Work Convention and exacerbating labour market inequality as a result. In addition, workers may be forced to work in conditions that contravene labour and health and safety legislation. Often they have little choice but to work excessive and illegal overtime because their legal basic wage is below the level of a 'living wage' or because they are forced to work 'voluntary' unpaid overtime on pain of the threat of dismissal or other sanctions if they refuse to do so (Nordbrand and de Haan 2009). Consequently, the boundaries between legal and illegal in production are frequently fuzzy and unclear. Furthermore, illegally produced goods may be packed and distributed by legal businesses (or vice versa), further blurring the boundary between legal and illegal.

Illegal employment practices in production, such as those described above, are often facilitated by the legally-sanctioned absence of trades unions (for example in 'no union no strike' Export Production Zones) or the presence of unions that are effectively under state control and/or the influence of employers. Such practices are widespread over much of Southeast Asia and in central and eastern Europe, both in sectors such as consumer electronics and IT that are commonly represented as involving 'high tech' methods of production (Mackay 2004; Chan et al. 2008; Pöyhönen and Wan 2011) as well as industries commonly seen as deploying 'traditional' production methods, such as brick making or clothing production (Oonk et al. 2012). Commodities produced under these circumstances via illegal labour (whether directly or indirectly, knowingly or unknowingly) can then undercut those that are legitimately produced, reducing the market share and profits of producers operating legally and conforming to the requirements of labour legislation. Employing illegal labour thereby contributes to uneven development among companies and spaces of production. While beneficial to some, it threatens social and systemic sustainability.

Under pressure from NGOS and consumers in countries that are the predominant markets for products produced in this way, major MNCs have often put in place Corporate Social Responsibility policies that prescribe working conditions and practices, but these rarely extend beyond first-tier suppliers. Moreover, these policies are routinely breached because they conflict with competitive pressures to cut costs, leading to managers deliberately falsifying employment records to disguise illegal overtime and to underpayment of wages (Sum and Ngai 2005). As a result, because economic imperatives trump concerns with social justice and sustainability, economic inequality is exacerbated and societal sustainability undermined.

At the same time, however, the switch of much routine production away from 'traditional' industrial cities and regions in core countries has created spaces in which other forms of illegality have emerged, in part as people there seek to ensure some sort of social sustainability by constructing survival strategies in spaces that have become marginal to, or expelled from, mainstream circuits of capital. Such spaces form fertile ground in which a range of illegal trading activities – such as those focused on drugs – as well as illicit and/or illegal production activities, often involving illegal migrant workers, have taken root and expanded (Evans et al. 2006). As a result, these spaces in core countries have come to resemble those thought typical of the booming cities of Africa, Asia and Central and South America (Portes et al. 1989), with ambivalent effects on sustainability. Activities intended to sustain some sort of societal cohesion may result in the erosion of environmental sustainability because of the illegal dumping of wastes and pollutants (Saviano 2008).

Illegality, the 'blind eyes' of the state and political sustainability

The proliferation of illegal activities in many parts of the world, especially those on the margins, often involves the entanglement of elements of the legal state and its officials in illegal activities either directly or indirectly, sanctioning them by turning a 'blind eye' (in return for a financial consideration) to their existence (Hill 2005; Pöyhönen and Simola 2007; Glenny 2008; Saviano 2008; Castells 2010). Alternatively, state officials may ignore illegal practices because of a desire to encourage economic growth in their area (CIVIDEP 2009; Kynge 2009). This selective blindness extends from the start to the finish of the production system, as I have already indicated in comments about mining and manufacturing in various parts of the world.

The tremendous growth in containerised sea transport on a global scale also had a major effect in facilitating the expansion of the global trade in illegal products and substances. Containerisation has complicated the process of identifying illegally produced goods and illegal substances as these can be mixed in with legally produced goods. An estimated 420 million containers are shipped around the world every year, virtually uninspected (United Nations 2008). The volume of containers moving through the major ports that form the key nodal points in global transport networks, allied to the low priority attached to checking them, make it impossible for customs officials to inspect more than a tiny sample of containers moving through them (Sterling 1994; Nordstrom 2007; Clerix 2011). Maximising the flow of containers and ensuring the continuous uninterrupted circulation of capital is seen as a much more pressing imperative than concerns over illegal materials that containers might contain. As a result, drugs, principally cocaine from South America (Colombia, Ecuador, Panama, Peru), continue to be smuggled through European ports in significant amounts, concealed in containers among legitimate cargo, such as fake fruit (bananas and pineapples) or timber. Sold on the streets of Europe, they boost the profits of drug cartels and create social problems that threaten the sustainability of European societies. In other parts of the world there is a long history of smuggling across national land borders and this continues, as the Mexican-US border zone and places such as Ciudad del Este on the 'Triple Frontier' of the Paraguayan–Brazilian–Argentinian border clearly reveal (Naím 2007; Neuwirth 2012). This helps sustain local communities economically but at considerable risks to social sustainability.

It is axiomatic that unless commodities can be sold, the surplus-value embodied in them remains unrealised. Consequently, in addition to the wide range of legally sanctioned spaces and associated practices of sale for commodities (Hudson 2005: 145-166), there are also specific spaces in marginalised locations as well as iconic and well-known street markets in global cities such as Beijing, London, Los Angeles, New York and Paris in which illegally produced commodities are sold (Chaudhry and Zimmerman 2010: 42–43). Such markets, which state regulators regard with 'blind eyes' and effectively ignore, legitimate the illegal activities involved in the prior production of the commodities on sale there. In so doing, they enable producers to realise surplus-value and consumers to acquire the symbolic value and prestige of premium brands at a fraction of the price of the genuine article, undercutting the latter in the market while to all intents and purposes appearing to be genuine. One consequence of systematically turning a blind eye to illegal activities, however, is a loss – often considerable – to the state of revenue that could be used for progressive developmental purposes and indeed to promote more sustainable forms of economic activity and practice. Another is to threaten the legitimacy of the state as its officials condone and/or participate in these activities. From another – and potentially more progressive – perspective, however, insofar as the reproduction of uneven development creates spaces in which challenges emerge to the existing capitalist order, it potentially threatens its sustainability. Whether and how such potential will be realised is of course a different matter.

Challenging illegality in globalising circuits of productive capital?

In conclusion, from the perspective of capital the reason for the expansion and widespread presence of illegal working practices is crystal clear: the imperative to make a higher mass and/or rate of profit than one's competitors. This is a very visible manifestation of the competitive pressures that are genetically encoded into capitalist relations of production and drive the accumulation process. In this sense, illegality is critical to the success of competing companies and to the short-term sustainability of contemporary capitalist arrangements. However, as Polanyi (1944) noted, disembedding the economy through deepening capitalist social relations and market disciplines, challenging existing cultural norms and accepted forms of social behaviour, characteristically triggers a response that contests the direction of change. Consequently, economic growth is characterised by a 'double movement', a tension between social forces pushing for increased marketisation and the deepening and extension of capitalist social relations and those opposing these processes. There is growing resistance to the flouting of environmental legislation and the consequent erosion of environmental sustainability and to working practices that are seen as immoral as well as illegal and so a growing threat to the longer-term political and social sustainability of forms of production that are dependent on the hyper-exploitation of labour. This is not simply a tension to be resolved via trade-offs between different dimensions of sustainability but an existential condition of capitalist social relations. While illegal economic activity clearly further undermines aspects of environmental and social sustainability, however, at the same time it is critical to the sustainability of the mainstream legal economy and this is explored further in the next section.

Illegal flows of money, spaces of sanitisation and disguise: the heightened significance of the illegal in sustaining globalising capitalism

The contemporary economy is characterised by enhanced flows of money, legal and illegal, and the extensive laundering of money from the illegal economy back into the mainstream legal economy as 'clean' money capital. The neoliberalisation of capital markets led to an eightfold expansion of cross-border financial flows between 1990 and 2006 (McKinsey Global Institute 2008), of which around 20 per cent are illegal. An estimated USA$1.6 trillion annually flows illegally into offshore accounts (Baker 2006). Proceeds from illegal activities account for around 35 per cent of such cross-border flows originating from developing and transitional economies. In contrast, the remaining 65 per cent originate from the proceeds of illegal commercial activity - mispricing, abusive transfer pricing, and fake and fraudulent transactions - indicative of the pervasive character of illegality *within* the mainstream 'legal' economy.

Money laundering is of particular significance in the context of the systemic sustainability of contemporary economic arrangements and illegal flows of money follow complex and, by design, opaque pathways. At least two-thirds of the money earned in the illegal economy is immediately spent in the legal economy (Schneider and Enster 2000). National states and regulatory organisations are deeply implicated in facilitating such flows from the illegal to legal economy. While the precise magnitude may be a matter for debate, the existence and significance of these flows are not. Some of this money is used to support livelihoods and enables increased commodity consumption. A much greater proportion becomes money capital, invested in diverse legitimate activities and spaces in mainstream markets. This both enhances the competitive position of those who own it and contributes systemically to the expanded reproduction of capital and to the sectoral and spatial distribution of growth. As Castells (2010: 183) points out, '[t]he whole criminal system only makes sense if the profits generated can be used and reinvested in the legal economy'.

Where do illegally acquired profits become 'clean' money? This is a critical question. This cleansing principally occurs in a particular type of space – offshore tax havens (OTHs), though by no means exclusively so there. For example, in 1997 the 55 banks in the Paraguayan city of Ciudad del Este, located where its border meets those of Argentina and Brazil, laundered an estimated $45 billion generated mainly from cocaine revenues from the Andean countries (Naím 2007: 142–143). OTHs are legal jurisdictions created through collusion between national states and major capitalist interests, 'secrecy spaces' (Christensen and Hampton 1999) that provide an interface between legal and illegal economies. OTHs were originally established as spaces in which legal (though ethically and morally dubious) tax avoidance activities were permissible. Subsequently they have become the sites of many financial transactions in the global economy: over 50 per cent of international bank lending, approximately 33 per cent of foreign direct investment and 50 per cent of global trade are routed on paper via tax havens which account for only 3 per cent of world GDP (Christensen 2011: 178). The expansion of OTHs has been enabled by developments in ICTs and closely linked to the neo-liberalisation of global capital markets (Sikka 2003). Powerful national states and international institutions that they dominate, notably the World Bank and IMF, and the interests represented and prioritised through them, have therefore been instrumental in constructing both the more publicly visible institutional forms and the invisible architecture of globalisation. As a result, 'legal institutions granted special status and privilege by society have been subverted to purposes for which they were never intended' (Christensen 2011, 183).

The secretive legal instruments used for legal tax avoidance have become abused for illegal tax evasion linked to a wide range of criminal activities. OTHs encourage and enable large-scale corruption by providing an operational base for legal and financial professionals and their clients to exploit the limits to legislation and gaps within and between national systems of tax regulation. The bulk of money laundering operates via investments in securities and transfers of funds in global financial markets. Elaborate schemes are devised to 'weave dirty money' (Christensen 2011: 183) into commercial transactions and disguise the proceeds of crime and tax evasion. Hidden behind a cloak of legal regulations, the legislative gaps are significant – while capital flows have become globally hypermobile, regulatory systems remain largely based on national territories, allowing 'dirty' money to be laundered via complex multi-jurisdictional ladders operating through the global banking system in which OTHs are key locations, permissive spaces that allow – indeed encourage – transactions and flows that elsewhere would be deemed illegal and so enable profits generated in illegal economies elsewhere to be sanitised and recycled into the circuits of the legal. In this way they facilitate the exploitation of the uneven development of and asymmetries among regulatory spaces.

Most OTHs are closely linked to major OECD economies, with about half linked to the UK, as Overseas Territories, Crown Dependencies or members of the Commonwealth. Moreover, many OTHs are not literally 'offshore' as the term is strictly a political statement about the relationship between the state and parts of its related territories (Palan 1999). Indeed, such spaces have been created at the heart of the globalising economy in cities such as London and New York, with differential regulatory regimes that share one characteristic in common: they differentiate regulatory standards as between domestic resident capital and non-resident international capital (Unger and Rawlings 2008). As the spate of press reports in 2012 emphasised, major banks such as Barclays, HSBC and Standard Charter may well have been routinely involved in money laundering through their bases in London, New York and so on.

Advanced capitalist states (such as Switzerland, the UK and the USA) frequently collude in preventing the development of effective international regulation to tackle illegal financial flows and police financial flows into and out of the OTHs, precisely because they play a pivotal role in the global accumulation process. National states and multilateral agencies have largely downplayed concerns about 'dirty money' and money laundering, except, revealingly and significantly, in relation to drugs and terrorism, which account for only a small proportion of illegal cross-border flows. This discursive selectivity reflects a tacit recognition of the intimate relationships between legal and illegal activities in the routine constitution of capitalist economies and of the pivotal role of OTHs as the spaces in which the financial flows between them takes place. As Castells (2010: 172) puts it:

> At the heart of the system is money laundering by the hundreds of billions (maybe trillions) of dollars. Complex financial schemes and international trade networks link up the criminal economy to the formal economy, thus deeply penetrating financial markets and constituting a critical, volatile element in a fragile global economy.

Castells thus emphasises the way in which the contemporary capitalist economy encourages and facilitates the systematic and large-scale laundering of 'dirty money'. In stark contrast, such limited attention as is given to seeking to halt such flows is focused upon 'bribery of public officials and looting by despots and their cronies . . . the prevailing corruption discourse remains largely focused on pointing fingers at petty officials and ruling kleptomaniacs' (Christensen 2011: 181–184).

In summary, since the criminal economy is a capitalist economy, the economic rationale for illegal activities depends upon the money that they realise becoming money capital invested in legitimate legal activities in the formal economy – and this crucially depends upon successful money laundering operations. At the same time, however, the economic sustainability of the mainstream depends both upon the widespread deployment of illegal activities and upon continuous and substantial inflows of money from the illegal to the legal economy. Legal and illegal economies thus co-exist in a symbiotic relationship. OTHs have enabled the dramatic expansion of global financial flows and as a result have become major sites of activity in global financial markets. They have become closely entangled with servicing illegal economic activities, precisely because of the lack of transparency that surrounds transactions carried out in and through them, either because of banking secrecy laws or through *de facto* judicial arrangements and banking practices. Precisely because they are dealing in financial activities on the fringes, or beyond the boundaries, of formal legal regulation, economic agents involved in OTHs have necessarily developed a high degree of trust to enable these places to function successfully as socially constructed key nodes in global financial networks (Hudson 1998). Facilitated by lightly and loosely regulated institutions that permitted the opaque practices that spawned innovative financial products such as complex derivatives that lay at the heart of both money laundering networks and the global financial crisis that exploded in 2008 (Kaletsky 2010; Patterson 2010), OTHs have been central to the emergence of neoliberal globalisation.

This has systemic implications. Since criminal capital is involved in high-risk activities in markets in which the speed, volatility and volume of electronic market transactions has increased greatly, it follows, and amplifies, speculative turbulence in financial markets. Thus, it has become an important source of destabilisation of international financial and capital markets, not least in contributing to the global financial crisis that began in 2008. The systemic threats that this poses to capitalist development and particular class interests are self-evident. Thus the explosive growth of illegal monetary operations and money laundering is both central to the sustainability of neoliberal capitalism and at the same time poses risks to its future sustainability. This highlights the tensions generated by the growth of illegality as both enabling but also posing a severe threat to the sustainability of the contemporary form of capitalism.

Conclusion

The symbiotic relationships between illegal and legal activities in ensuring the sustainability of the contemporary form of global capitalism are both deeply embedded and deeply contradictory. These relationships, while systemically structural, are also contingent and the significance of the illegal varies in the extent to which it emerges and becomes dominant in specific times and spaces. From one point of view, the competitive success and economic sustainability of particular companies and states are clearly crucially dependent upon their involvement in illegal production and/or trading activities. In particular, illegal practices in the financial sector are often linked to and enable and facilitate money laundering activities through which illegally acquired money becomes cleansed, transformed and deployed as legitimate money capital in the legal economy. On the other hand, illegal activities within production systems may threaten the environmental, social and political sustainability of the spaces in which they occur.

There is, however, another twist to the tale. The major global financial crisis that erupted in 2008 dramatically revealed that unfettered markets – which permitted if not encouraged the growth of illegal practices – in fact eroded the systemic sustainability of the globalising capitalist economy and threatened to provoke an unparalleled depression that was only averted as a result of unprecedented and very class-specific and territorially specific national state action and intervention. This included printing money on a massive scale and the *de facto* nationalisation of banks and other major financial institutions by national governments, along with action by supra-national organisations that, at one level at least, espoused a neo-liberal rhetoric, championing the virtues of minimal regulation and unfettered markets as economic steering mechanisms.

Crucially, however, such state interventions can only displace rather than abolish economic crisis tendencies. This displacement is reflected in the deepening social inequalities and political instability visible in many parts of the world, not least in the European Union and other parts of Europe in recent years, developments that are exacerbated by the expansion of illegal economic activities. As a result, risks to political and social sustainability intensify. At the same time, a global ecological crisis is immanent, largely a result of activities that are legal but again exacerbated by the growth of illegal activities, registered most visibly in the effects of human activity on the global climate and global warming but in a plethora of other ways at more local scales. The prospect of the coupling of economic, ecological and socio-political crises raises serious questions as to the future sustainability of capitalism as we have come to know it. What sustainable forms of capitalism or, more radically, non-capitalist alternatives – ecologically, socially and politically as well as economically – might be possible in future, and what would they look like? These remain open questions to which, worryingly, there seem to be few persuasive answers.

References

Action Against Impunity for Human Rights (2011) *Unheard Voices: Mining Activities in the Katanga Province and the Impact on Local Communities*. Amsterdam: ACIDH and SOMO – Centre for Research on Multinational Corporations: 49.

Baker, R. (2006) *Capitalism's Achilles Heel*. Hoboken, NJ: Wiley.

Boyer, R. (1990) *The Regulation School: A Critical Introduction*. New York: Columbia University Press.

Brown, E. and Cloke, J. (2007) Shadow Europe: alternative European financial geographies. *Growth and Change*, 38: 304–327.

Castells, M. (2010) *End of Millennium*, 2nd edn. Oxford: Blackwell.

Chan, J., de Haan, E., Nordbrand, S. and Torstensson, A. (2008) *Silence to Deliver: Mobile Phone Manufacturing in China and the Philippines*. Amsterdam: SOMO and Swedwatch.

Chaudhry, P. and Zimmerman, A. (2010) *The Economics of Counterfeit Trade: Governments, Consumers, Pirates and Intellectual Property Rights*. Berlin: Springer.

Christensen, J. (2011) The looting continues: tax havens and corruption. *Critical Perspectives on International Business*, 7: 177–196.

Christensen, J. and Hampton, M. (1999) A legislature for hire: the capture of the state in Jersey's Offshore Finance Centre. In M. Hampton and J. Abbott (eds) *Offshore Finance Centres and Tax Havens: The Rise of Global Capital*. Basingstoke: Macmillan, pp. 166–191.

CIVIDEP (2009) *Corporate Geography, Labour Conditions and Environmental Standards in the Mobile Phone Manufacturing Industry in India*. Amsterdam: SOMO – Centre for Research on Multinational Corporations: 30.

Clerix, K. (2011) The Port of Antwerp is a honey jar for organized crime, trans. B. Cosyns. Available at http://mo.be/en/article/port-antwerp-honey-jar-organized-crime (accessed 17 October 2013).

Coninck, N., Theuws, M. and Overeem, P. (2011) *Captured by Cotton: Exploited Dalit Girls Produce Garments in India for US and European Markets*. Amsterdam and Utrecht: SOMO and ICN.

Elson, D. (1979) The value theory of labour. In D. Elson (ed.) Value: *The Representation of Labour in Capitalism*. London: CSE Books.

Erman, E. (2007) *Rethinking Legal and Illegal Economy: A Case Study of Tin Mining in Gangka Island*. Available at http://globetrotter.berkeley.edu/GreenGovernance/papers/Erman2007.pdf (accessed 14 January 2012).

Evans, M., Syrett, S. and Williams, C. (2006) *Informal Economic Activities and Deprived Neighbourhoods*. London: Department of Communities and Local Government.

Fröbel, F., Heinrichs, J. and Kreye, O. (1980) *The New International Division of Labour*. Cambridge: Cambridge University Press.

Gambetta, D. (2011) *Codes of the Underworld: How Criminals Communicate*. Princteon, NJ: Princeton University Press.

Glenny, M. (2008) *McMafia: A Journey through the Global Criminal Underworld*. Toronto: House of Anasi Press.

Glenny, M. (2011) *Dark Market: Cyberthieves, Cybercops and You*. London: The Bodley Head.

Hill, P. (2005) The changing face of the Yakuza. In M. Galeotti (ed.), *Global Crime Today: The Changing Face of Organised Crime*. London: Routledge, pp. 97–116.

Hudson, A. C. (1998) Placing trust, trusting places: on the social construction of offshore financial centres. *Political Geography*, 17: 915–937.

Hudson, R. (2001) *Producing Places*. New York: Guilford Press.

Hudson, R. (2005) *Economic Geographies: Circuits, Flows and Spaces*. London: Sage.

Hudson, R. (2008) Cultural political economy meets global production networks: a productive meeting? *Journal of Economic Geography*, 78: 421–440.

Hudson, R. (2010) Multiplicant els riscs per a la salut I el benestar: els costos inadmissibles de la globalització/Multiplying risks to Health and Wellbeing: the unacknowledged costs of globalisation. *Treballs de la Societat Catalana de Geografia*, 70: 101–127.

Jessop, B. (1990) *State Theory: Putting Capitalist States in Their Place*. Cambridge: Cambridge University Press.

Kaletsky, A. (2010) *Capitalism 4.0: The Birth of a New Economy*. London: Bloomsbury.

Kynge, J. (2009) *China Shakes the World: The Rise of a Hungry Nation*. London: Phoenix.

Mackay, S. (2004) Zones of regulation: restructuring labor control in privatized export zones. *Politics and Society*, 32: 171–202.

McKinsey Global Institute (2008) *Mapping Global Capital Markets: Fourth Annual Report*. San Francisco: McKinsey Global Institute.

Murphy, J. (2011) Capitalism and transparency. *Critical Perspectives on International Business*, 7: 125–141.

Naím, M. (2007) *Illicit: How Smugglers, Traffickers and Copycats are Hijacking the Global Economy*. London: Arrow Books.

Neuwirth, R. (2012) *Stealth of Nations*. New York: Anchor Books.

Nordbrand, S. and Bolme, P. (2007) *Powering the Mobile World: Cobalt Production for Batteries in the DR Congo and Zambia*. Swedwatch: 83.

Nordbrand, S. and de Haan, E. (2009) *Mobile Phone Production in China: A Follow up Report on Two Suppliers in Guangdong*. Amsterdam: SOMO and Swedwatch: 27.

Nordstrom, C. (2007) *Global Outlaws: Crime, Money, and Power in the Contemporary World*. Berkeley, CA: University of California Press.

OECD (2002) *Measuring the Non-Observed Economy: A Handbook*. Paris: OECD.

Oonk, G., Overem, P., Peepercamp, M. and Theuws, M. (2012) *Maid in India: Young Dalit Women Continue to Suffer Exploitative Conditions in India's Garment Industry*. Amsterdam: SOMO and ICN:.

Palan, R. (1999) Offshore and the structural enablement of sovereignty. In M. Hampton and J. Abbott (eds) *Offshore Finance Centres and Tax Havens: The Rise of Global Capital*. Basingstoke: Macmillan, pp. 18–42.

Patterson, S. (2010) *The Quants: How a Small Band of Maths Wizards Took Over Wall Street and Nearly Destroyed It*. London: Random House.

Polanyi, K. (1944) *The Great Transformation*. Boston: Beacon Press.

Portes, R., Castells, M. and Benton, L. A. (eds) (1989) *The Informal Economy: Studies in Advanced and Less Developed Countries*. Baltimore, MD: Johns Hopkins University Press.

Pöyhönen, P. and Simola, E. (2007) *Connecting Components, Dividing Communities: Tin Production for Consumer Electronics in the DR Congo and Indonesia*. Amsterdam: FinnWatch and SOMO.

Pöyhönen, P. and Wan, D. (2011) *Game Console and Music Player Production in China*. Finnwatch, SACOM and SOMO: 39. Available at www.makeITfair.org (accessed 11 January 2012).

Saviano, R. (2008) *Gomorrah: Italy's Other Mafia*. London: Pan.

Schneider, F. and Enster, D. H. (2000) Shadow economies: size, causes and consequences. *Journal of Economic Literature*, 37: 77–78.

Sikka, P. (2003) The role of offshore financial centres in globalization. *Accounting Forum*, 27: 365–399.

SOMO (2009) *On the Move: The Electronics Industry in Central and Eastern Europe*. Available at: www.makeITfair.org (accessed 10 January 2012).

Sterling, C. (1994) *Thieves World: The Threat of the New Global Network of Organised Crime*. New York: Simon and Schuster.

Sum, N-L. and Ngai, P. (2005) Globalization and paradoxes of ethical transnational production: code of conduct in a Chinese workplace. *Competition and Change*, 9: 181–200.

Unger, B. and Rawlings, G. (2008) Competing for criminal money. *Global Business and Economics Review*, 10: 331–352.

United Nations (2008) Ten stories the world should hear more about. Crime in a box: Ports crack down on trafficking of arms, drugs and human beings. Available at: http://www.un.org/en/events/tenstories/08/printable/crime.shtml (accessed 17 October 2013).

3

GLOBAL CHANGE, ISLANDS AND SUSTAINABLE DEVELOPMENT

Islands of sustainability or analogues of the challenge of sustainable development?

C. Michael Hall

Introduction

Islands, and especially tropical islands, have a prominent place in the Western cultural imagination. Yet their image has undergone substantial change over time shifting from a focus on mercantile resource exploitation, to a more Romantic portrayal in the nineteenth century. In the modern era Romantic themes have often been essential to the tourism imaginary of islands for the markets of the developed world (Hall and Page 1996). More recently islands have become one of the focal points of contemporary environmental and, hence, economic and political change (Moore 2010). Images and stories of islands disappearing beneath the waves have become major symbols of global change (Hall 2010a). But more than that, they have also become both actual and symbolic representations of the central challenge of sustainable development to reconcile human demands with the limits of natural resources.

Islands are significant to help an understanding of the problem of transitioning to sustainable development because their finite space represents an analogue with that of the Earth with respect to issues of managing resource use and waste within a relatively bounded system. An important line of thinking in sustainable development is the significance of islands of sustainability (IOS) (Wallner et al. 1996; Bebbington 1997; Deschenes and Chertow 2004; Péti 2012) whereby global sustainability will be achieved when regions live according to their carrying capacity, i.e. the ability to live and develop without running down natural capital. According to Wallner et al. (1996: 1764) this means that:

> In order to reach regional sustainability the area balance—taking into account the appropriated area from other regions (imports), the area actually occupied for a region's own purposes, and the area made available for other regions (exports)—should not be negative in such a way that the appropriated area exceeds the others.

IOS are also regarded as important 'innovative disturbances' (Wallner and Narodoslawsky 1996) that are able to jeopardise the structural stability of unsustainable systems whether they be at a macro-regional, national or global scale, and may provide opportunities to introduce elements of sustainable development into the wider system. Such potential shifts as a result of IOS, Wallner et al. (1996) argue, would therefore contribute to the transition toward wider sustainable development as a result of the accompanying paradigm change from a mechanistic to a holistic (synergetic, network) or integrated paradigm.

Although the desired outcome of the IOS appears optimistic, the bounded systems of the IOS approach are a potentially useful analogue to examine issues of island transition. However, real islands as well as IOS are never completely bounded (Kerr 2005). Physical flows of matter and energy extend over products, processes, and firms, and local, regional or national boundaries and borders, as well as flows of capital and people. The latter are especially important for Small Island Developing States (SIDS), given the critical role of migrant flows and remittances (UN DESA 2010). Moreover, different islands and SIDS can have substantially different political jurisdictions and governance capacities and socio-cultural structures. Nevertheless, issues of scale and relative isolation remain key characteristics of islands. The relatively 'simpler ecologies' of islands are also matched by their economies which tend to have a narrow base. Islands are systems that are closed and bounded in many respects and thus provide a manageable unit of research and a 'living laboratory' on the realities of sustainable development including with respect to scales of application and analysis (Hall 2010a; Pungetti 2012). Of course, these same properties 'present island populations with the challenges of limited resource availability, tenuous resource security and limited natural carrying capacity' (Deschenes and Chertow 2004: 202). Many island microstates are also among the most at risk jurisdictions from environmental change such as sea level rise, ocean acidification and biodiversity loss, as well as being some of the least developed countries in the world (United Nations Department of Economic and Social Affairs [UN DESA] 2010). As Deschenes and Chertow (2004: 202) suggest, 'While every human population faces these challenges, the need to find solutions for sustainable development is much more immediate for island systems.'

This chapter therefore examines the main challenges facing SIDS with respect to sustainable development including climate change, a narrow resource and economic base, population change, natural disasters and biodiversity loss. At a more conceptual level, and using notions of island biogeography in particular, the chapter then examines the extent to which SIDS may serve as islands of sustainability and the insights that can be gained from island studies of the prospects of sustainable development.

Small Island Developing States (SIDS)

Although typically portrayed in tourism promotion as idyllic destinations with waves lapping palm-tree-ringed sandy beaches, the reality of SIDS is far more complex. The challenges of SIDS within the context of sustainable development was first formally recognised by the international community at the 1992 United Nations Conference on Environment and Development (UNCED) held in Rio de Janeiro. Chapter 17, paragraph 124 of Agenda 21 states:

> [SIDS] and islands supporting small communities are a special case both for environment and development. They are ecologically fragile and vulnerable. Their small size, limited resources, geographic dispersion and isolation from markets, place them at a disadvantage economically and prevent economies of scale.
>
> *(UN DESA 2010: iii)*

However, there is no agreed definition of SIDS, even within the United Nations Community. UNCTAD (2012) recognises 29 SIDS, of which eight are included in the group of 48 Least

Developed Countries (LDCs), while the Department of Economic and Social Affairs, Division for Sustainable Development, identifies 39, two of which also qualify as LDCs (Table 3.1). The UN Office of the High Representative for the Least Developed Countries, Landlocked Developing Countries and Small Island Developing States (UN-OHRLLS) recognised 57 SIDS as of the start of 2014, 38 of which are UN members, with the remaining 19 states being either non-UN members or associate members of regional commissions.

Population growth and urbanisation

A common element with SIDS is the extent to which they have highly vulnerable economic, social and natural environmental systems as a result of their small size, narrow resource base and insularity (Kerr 2005). Many SIDS also exhibit relative remoteness from major markets, vulnerability to external shocks, and substantial exposure to global change. Such vulnerabilities are exacerbated by population increase and growing urbanisation. The percentage of the population living in urban areas across all SIDS increased 11 per cent, from 49.5 per cent in 1990 to 55 per cent in 2008 (UN DESA 2010), with urbanisation showing no signs of decrease. Because of their limited size the combination of population growth and urbanisation also leads to greater population density in urban areas. For example, Ebye Atoll, the capital of the Marshall Islands, is an island that is now 100 per cent urban and has the highest population density in the Pacific (Wilkinson 2011), at over 40,000/km^2 (Chui and Terry 2013).

A classic example of SIDS urbanisation is Funafuti, the capital island of Tuvalu, with an area of approximately 2.79 km^2. In 1973, Funafuti had 14.8 per cent of the total population and a population density of just less than 900/km^2. By 2002, it had grown to approximately 47 per cent of the total population with a population density of just over 1,600/km^2 (Wilkinson 2011). In the Indian Ocean, the capital of the Maldives, Malé, is home to nearly a third of the country's population and has a density of over 17,000/km^2 (UN DESA 2010).

Urban centres are therefore significant sites of environmental change (Connell 2011). Although high urban population densities may be interpreted on the one hand to have relieved pressure on natural habitats and biodiversity in rural areas, the impact on coastal ecosystems is intensifying in areas of urban growth, while also placing urban populations at increasing risk of disease, coastal erosion, and flooding (Donnelly and Jiwanji 2010; Wilkinson 2011; Chui and Terry 2013). For example, Betio, the capital of Kiribati, on the atoll island of Tarawa, has a population of 12,509 people on 1.45 km^2. Approximately 40 per cent of households are connected to the sewerage system which pumps raw sewerage directly into the sea. Those not connected use either pit latrines, small septic tanks or the beach (Butcher-Gollach et al. 2007).

Environmental change

Many low-lying small island countries are extremely vulnerable to sea level rise. The Intergovernmental Panel on Climate Change (IPCC) forecast that global sea levels will rise on average between 24 and 30 cm by 2046–2065 and between 40 and 63 cm by 2081–2100 (IPCC 2013). A large proportion of the population of many SIDS live in a low elevation coastal zone (LECZ), or the contiguous area along the coast that is less than 10 metres above sea level. Nineteen SIDS have population shares greater than 39 per cent in the LECZ with the Maldives, Bahamas, Bahrain and Suriname among those most at risk (UN DESA 2010). The situation for SIDS is further complicated by a high coastline-to-land-area ratio. This means that many settlements and critical infrastructure are increasingly vulnerable to erosion, storms and tidal surges,

Table 3.1 Characteristics of SIDS

SIDS (UN 2010)	*SIDS (UNCTAD 2012)*	*UN-OHRLLS (2014)* [1]	*LDC* [2]	*High environmental vulnerability* [3]	*CO^2 per capita (tonnes) (2008)* [4]	*CO^2 per capita (average annual growth) (1970–2008)* [5]	*Endangered species (% of all animal species) (2011)* [6]	*Fresh water withdrawals (% of total renewable water resources) (2003–12)* [7]	*No. of deaths due to natural disasters (annual average per million people) (2005–11)* [8]	*Human Development Index (HDI) (rank) (2012)* [9]
American Samoa		N		NA	10.35 [1]	NA	NA	NA	NA	NA
Anguilla		N		NA	NA	NA	NA	NA	NA	NA
Antigua and Barbuda	X	UN		X	5.1	-0.8	8.3	3.3	0	0.760 (67)
Aruba		N		NA	21.7[1]	NA	NA	NA	NA	NA
Bahamas	X	UN		NA	6.5	-2.2	10.0	NA	3	0.794 (49)
Bahrain		UN		X	21.4	1.5	7.2	219.8	NA	0.796 (48)
Barbados	X	UN		X	5.0	2.7	8.7	76.1	0	0.825 (38)
Belize		UN			1.3	0.7	6.4	0.8	13	0.702 (96)
Bermuda		N		NA	NA	NA	NA	NA	NA	NA
British Virgin Islands		N		NA	NA	NA	NA	NA	NA	NA
Cape Verde	X	UN		X	0.6	4.2	12.5	6.8	0	0.586 (132)
Cayman Islands		N		NA	NA	NA	NA	NA	NA	NA
Comm. of Northern Marianas		N		NA	NA	NA	NA	NA	NA	NA
Comoros	X	UN	X	X	1.0	NA	11.7	0.8	0	0.429 (169)
Cook Islands		N		NA	12.7[1]	NA	NA	NA	NA	NA
Cuba		UN		X	2.8	0.7	18.1	19.8	0	0.780 (59)
Curacao		N			NA	NA	NA	NA	NA	NA
Dominica	X	UN		NA	1.9	4.4	8.6	NA	15	0.745 (72)

Dominican Republic		UN		X	2.2	3.1	16.1	16.6	9	0.702 (96)
Federated States of Micronesia	X	UN		NA	0.6	NA	13.7	NA	45	0.645 (117)
Fiji	X	UN		X	1.5	1.0	13.1	0.3	8	0.702 (96)
French Polynesia				NA	NA	NA	NA	NA	NA	NA
Grenada	X	UN		X	2.4	4.4	10.5	NA	38	0.770 (63)
Guadeloupe		N		NA	NA	NA	NA	NA	NA	NA
Guam		N		NA	NA	NA	NA	NA	NA	NA
Guinea-Bissau		UN	X		0.2	1.4	5.7	0.6	1	0.364 (176)
Guyana		UN			2.0	-0.2	3.8	0.7	4	0.636 (118)
Haiti		UN	X	X	0.3	3.0	19.4	8.6	65	0.456 (161)
Jamaica	X	UN		X	4.5	1.4	15.2	6.2	3	0.730 (85)
Kiribati	X	UN	X	X	0.3	-1.0	12.4	NA	0	0.629 (121)
Maldives	X	UN		X	3.0	NA	9.1	15.7	0	0.688 (104)
Marshall Islands	X	UN		X	1.9	NA	11.0	NA	NA	NA
Martinique		N		NA	NA	NA	NA	NA	NA	NA
Mauritius	X	UN		X	3.1	4.4	15.2	26.4	1	0.737 (80)
Montserrat		N		NA	NA	NA	NA	NA	NA	NA
Nauru	X	UN		X	3.9	NA	12.1	NA	NA	NA
New Caledonia		N		NA	NA	NA	NA	NA	NA	NA
Niue		N		NA	NA	NA	NA	NA	NA	NA
Palau	X	UN		X	10.5	-0.3	11.4	NA	NA	0.791 (52)
Papua New Guinea	X	UN		X	0.3	0.3	11.4	0.0	4	0.466 (156)
Puerto Rico		N		NA	NA	NA	NA	NA	NA	NA
Samoa	X	UN	X	X	0.9	3.9	10.8	NA	5	0.702 (96)
São Tome and Principe	X	UN	X		0.8	3.7	14.9	0.3	NA	0.525 (144)
Seychelles	X	UN		X	7.8	7.3	16.1	NA	0	0.806 (46)
Singapore		UN		NA	6.7	-0.7	13.7	31.7	NA	0.895 (18)

(Continued)

Table 3.1 (Continued)

SIDS (UN 2010)	*SIDS (UNCTAD 2012)*	*UN-OHRLLS (2014)* [1]	*LDC* [2]	*High environmental vulnerability* [3]	*CO^2 per capita (tonnes) (2008)* [4]	*CO^2 per capita (average annual growth) (1970–2008)* [5]	*Endangered species (% of all animal species) (2011)* [6]	*Fresh water withdrawals (% of total renewable water resources) (2003–12)* [7]	*No. of deaths due to natural disasters (annual average per million people) (2005–11)* [8]	*Human Development Index (HDI) (rank) (2012)* [9]
Solomon Islands	X		X	X	0.4	1.1	14.8	NA	4	0.530 (143)
St. Kitts and Nevis	X	UN		X	4.9	NA	8.6	NA	NA	0.745 (72)
St. Lucia	X	UN		NA	2.3	3.4	9.4	NA	6	0.725 (88)
St. Vincent and the Grenadines	X	UN		X	1.8	4.7	9.0	NA	0	0.733 (83)
Suriname		UN			4.7	0.2	3.5	0.5	2	0.684 (105)
Timor-Leste	X	UN	X	NA	0.2	NA	5.2	NA	1	0.806 (134)
Tonga	X	UN		X	1.7	4.6	8.5	NA	0	0.702 (95)
Trinidad and Tobago	X	UN		X	37.4	3.7	6.8	6.0	0	0.760 (67)
Turks and Caicos Islands		N		NA	NA	NA	NA	NA	NA	NA
Tuvalu	X	UN	X	X	NA	NA	13.0	NA	NA	NA
US Virgin Islands				NA	NA	NA	NA	NA	NA	NA
Vanuatu	X	UN	X	X	0.4	-0.4	12.0	NA	0	0.626 (124)
LDCs[10]					0.2	-0.5	7.6	2.8	20	0.449
SIDS[10]					2.7	1.4	14.9	NA	16	0.648
World[10]					4.5	0.4	11.7	7.3	6	0.694

Notes:

1 The United Nations Office of the High Representative for the Least Developed Countries, Landlocked Developing Countries and the Small Island Developing States (UN-OHRLLS) (2014) Country profiles Profils des pay. Online. Available HTTP: http://unohrlls.org/about-sids/country-profiles/ (accessed 5 January 2014).

2 Least Developed Country category according to UNCTAD (2012).

3 Above average environmental vulnerability on UNEP environmental vulnerability index compared with average for all LDCs (UN DESA 2010). The Environmental Vulnerability Index is based on 50 indicators covering natural/anthropogenic risks, resilience and ecosystem integrity, and covers issues related to climate change, biodiversity, water, agriculture and fisheries, human health, desertification, and exposure to natural disasters (UN DESA 2010).

4 Anthropogenic carbon dioxide emissions stemming from the burning of fossil fuels, gas flaring and the production of cement, including carbon dioxide emitted by forest biomass through depletion of forest areas; divided by midyear population (UNDP 2013). Figure does not include non-CO_2 greenhouse gas emissions. World Bank (2012) in UNDP (2013).

5 UNDP (2013) calculations based on data from the World Bank.

6 Percentage of animal species classified as critically endangered, endangered or vulnerable by the International Union for the Conservation of Nature (IUCN) (2012) in UNDP (2013).

7 Total freshwater withdrawn in a given year, expressed as a percentage of total renewable water resources. FAO (2011) in UNDP (2013).

8 Number of people confirmed as dead and missing and presumed dead as a result of a natural disaster. Natural disasters are classified as climatological, hydrological and meteorological disasters, which include drought, extreme temperature, flood, mass movement, wet storm and wildfire. UNDP (2013) using United Nations Department of Economic and Social Affairs and Centre for Research on the Epidemiology of Disasters data.

9 The Human Development Index (HDI) is a composite index measuring average achievement in three basic dimensions of human development—a long and healthy life, knowledge and a decent standard of living (UNDP 2013).

10 Figures from UNDP (2013)

saline intrusion, and the intersection of groundwater with the surface, all of which can lead to inundation of low-lying areas (Nunn 2013).

Rapid urbanisation and environmental degradation can also lead to the loss of coastal forests, mangroves, and coral reefs that act to cushion the impacts of storm events. However, the implications of climate change are not isolated to sea level rise and problems for SIDS are magnified by forecast increases in the intensity of weather events (Mimura et al. 2007; IPCC 2013), as well as, in some cases, damage to surrounding coral reefs that serve to reduce wave impact and tidal surges as a result of coral bleaching events and ocean acidification (Forbes et al. 2013). According to the Alliance of Small Island States' (AOSIS) Declaration on Climate Change, 'climate change poses the most serious threat to our survival and viability, and . . . undermines our efforts to achieve sustainable development goals and threatens our very existence' (AOSIS 2009: 1). As is the case with many developing countries the majority of SIDS are low contributors to greenhouse gas emissions on a per capita basis (Table 3.1), yet bear the brunt of many of the effects of climate change.

Climate change has exacerbated weather-related natural disasters, and cyclones, floods, and droughts have increased in frequency and intensity since the 1960s (Scott et al. 2012). The capacity of SIDS to adapt to climate change is affected by their overall level and rate of economic development, and possibly distribution of wealth, as well as their propensity to be affected by sea level rise and significant climate variability in the form of severe weather events. The IPCC (2014) notes that barriers to adaptation strategies in island settings include 'inadequate access to financial, technological and human resources, issues related to cultural and social acceptability of measures, constraints imposed by the existing political and legal framework', and significantly given the focus of the present volume, an 'emphasis on island development as opposed to sustainability' (ibid.: 27). Nevertheless, despite the media profile often given to climate change and SIDS, there is still substantial lack of understanding and awareness on many islands with respect to climate change (Nunn 2009). This may be further complicated by the failure of adaptation and vulnerability communication and planning strategies to address the role of traditional belief systems of island inhabitants (Mortreux and Barnett 2009). Even where problems are recognised, continuing community preferences for 'hard' adaptation measures such as seawalls instead of 'soft' measures such as beach nourishment (IPCC 2014) also suggest a failure to adequately communicate climate change adaptation measures and their long-term effectiveness and implications (Hall 2014).

Because of their small size and disproportionate share of population living in hazard prone coastal areas SIDS are particularly vulnerable to natural disasters. Samoa, Saint Lucia, Grenada, Vanuatu, Tonga and Maldives are among the top 12 countries with the highest economic losses on capital stock in relative terms due to natural disasters from 1970 to 2006 (Baritto 2009). In the case of Samoa, due to the relatively small size of its economy, the damage caused by a tropical storm and a forest fire in 1983 as well as three tropical storms in a row from 1989 to 1990, may have led to the destruction of its capital stock equivalent to a reverse of more than 35 years (ibid.). It is also important to recognise that hydro-meteorological disasters are significant not only because of their direct effects on infrastructure and economic and population well-being but also because they can affect investor and tourist perceptions (Scott et al. 2012). The latter is especially important because of the disproportionate economic importance of tourism in SIDS compared to other countries (Gössling et al. 2009).

The combination of population increase, urbanisation and environmental change is also placing pressure on SIDS' water supplies with the amount of available renewable freshwater in decline in the majority of island states in the Caribbean and the Pacific (World Bank 2012). Sea level rise, surges and flooding can lead to saltwater intrusion into freshwater aquifers

(Chui and Terry 2013), with the water supply also being affected by the groundwater contamination and over-extraction associated with urbanisation, population growth, and industrial demands. Some countries comprised of groups of low-lying small islands, such as Barbados, Kiribati, and Tuvalu, have chronically limited freshwater resources, low annual rainfall, and shallow water tables (UN DESA 2010), which have necessitated shipping of water to some islands at times of drought as well as the purchase of desalinisation plants.

Because of the nature of islands, coastal and marine resources invariably tend to be economically as well as ecologically important. Yet they are also among the resources most susceptible to global change. SIDS' fish stocks are coming under increasing pressure (Allison et al. 2009), with potentially substantial implications for economic and environmental well-being (Ghina 2003; Kerr 2005). For example, in the Pacific, tuna fisheries make up more than 10 per cent of GDP and over 50 per cent of exports in some SIDS, and subsistence fishing supplies between 50 and 90 per cent of the animal protein diet for people in rural areas and remote islands (UN DESA 2010).

The decline of fish stocks mirrors a broader problem of indigenous species loss in island states. Islands are often important centres of biodiversity as their relative isolation contributes to high degrees of endemism as a result of speciation and the presence of flora and fauna that otherwise may have become extinct elsewhere. The relative isolation of many islands that are now part of SIDS that may have protected them from human activities or the introduction of predators for thousands of years unfortunately was lost in many cases first due to colonial mercantile expansion. Features of contemporary globalisation including the growth of international trade and tourism combined with faster modes of transport and liberalised economies only further encouraged the biotic movement that, together with urbanisation, land-use change and population growth, have provided the basis for the enormous loss of indigenous biodiversity in many islands.

Information on changes over time in the number of threatened species is only available for a limited number of categories of animals (birds, mammals, and amphibians) and plants for most small island countries. Taking these limitations into account, however, it is still apparent that the number of threatened species continues to increase (Hall 2010b). In the Caribbean, the number of threatened animal species as a proportion of all animal species in a given country ranges from a low of 6.6 per cent in Trinidad and Tobago to a high of 18.1 per cent in Bermuda. The proportion of threatened animal species is generally much higher in the Pacific Islands, and ranges from a low of 14.8 per cent in Tonga to 22.4 per cent in French Polynesia (ibid.).

Studies of species-to-area relationships suggest that between 30 per cent and 50 per cent of a given community or ecosystem type needs to be conserved in order to maintain between 80 per cent and 90 per cent of species (Groves 2003). Yet only two Caribbean island states (the Cayman Islands, and Trinidad and Tobago) and one in the Pacific, Karibati, have designated more than 30 per cent of their landmass as nature protection (Hall 2010b). These figures only refer to the overall area being conserved and not the proportion of specific ecosystems that are set aside. Island ecosystems that are suitable for conversion to agriculture are the most under-represented areas in conservation strategies. Furthermore, despite the economic and environmental importance of marine resources – especially fish stocks – the proportion of marine area in the Caribbean and Oceania that is protected is much lower than that for terrestrial areas. In the Caribbean, Jamaica has the highest proportion of marine area set aside (3.56 per cent), while in the Pacific, Palau has protected 8.74 per cent of its marine territory (Hall 2010b).

This overview of SIDS highlights why their vulnerability and resilience are of significance to understanding broader issues of sustainable development and the capacity for social and economic development without running down natural capital. Kerr (2005) suggests that models of sustainable development grounded in constant stock approaches, i.e. if one generation bequeaths to the next a stock of resources equivalent to that which it has inherited, and the development of sustainable decision-making practices, may have something to offer islands in terms of the management of resources. However, islands have 'very limited control over exogenous threats or the economic drivers of development' (Kerr 2005: 519). While Kerr's observation may be supported by the contemporary situation of many SIDS, it raises broader questions about the extent to which islands of sustainability can ever be established within a sea of global change. Given the exigency of global environmental change and a globalised economy that emphasises the permeability of borders, at least for trade, capital, the highly skilled and wealthy, are the problems of sustainable development for islands and SIDS to be regarded as a special case or do they represent the problems of sustainable development writ small?

Islands and sustainable development: an island biogeographical approach

Islands have played a key role in the development of ecological thinking, perhaps most famously with respect to the development of evolutionary thought but also with respect to the theory of island biogeography (Quammen 1996). The concept of island biogeography examines the relationships between species and a given area (MacArthur and Wilson 1963, 1967) and is therefore especially significant for conservation science. The conventional expression of the species–area relationship is $S = CA^z$ where *S* and *A* are species count and area, respectively, and *C* and *z* are fitted species specific constants. However, significantly for the wider applicability of the species–area relationship, an 'island' can be regarded as any area of suitable habitat that is surrounded by unsuitable habitat. This therefore includes not only terrestrial islands but can also be any appropriate bounded space.

The number of species that are found on an island depends on several factors, including its area and topography, habitat diversity, shape, spatial and temporal isolation, climate, previous connection to landmasses, accessibility to its source of colonists (i.e. not just distance to nearest source region but location relative to ocean and wind currents), and the equilibrium rate of colonisation by new species and the rate of extinction of existing species (Cox et al. 1973). The equilibrium model of the biota of a single island proposes that the equilibrial species number is reached at the intersection between the curve of the rate of new species immigration, not already on the island, and the curve of extinction of species on the island (Figure 3.1). The model therefore suggests that although fluctuations will occur over time there is a finite limit on the species biodiversity of a given area. This is highly significant in biodiversity conservation terms as, because every species runs the risk of extinction, 'the more that have arrived, the more species there are at risk. In addition, as more species arrive, the average population size of each will diminish as competition increases' (Cox et al. 1973: 98).

MacArthur and Wilson favoured logarithmic transformations of both axes thereby enabling the constants c and z to be determined by least squares (linear) regression (Whittaker and Fernández-Palacios 2007). MacArthur and Wilson (1967) found that in most cases z falls between 0.20 and 0.35 for islands. The model is highly significant in that, even though it has substantial heuristic value without it, the contribution of the theory to biogeography and environmental conservation provides a high degree of rigour with respect to dynamic modeling of ecological population processes.

Island biogeography has been extensively applied to studies of the suitability of habitats and ecosystems for conservation purposes (Whittaker and Fernández-Palacios 2007; Ford 2011; Hanski 2011; Van Teeffelen et al. 2012; Heinken and Weber 2013). However, while there is recognition of its relationship to the human appropriation of net primary production/natural

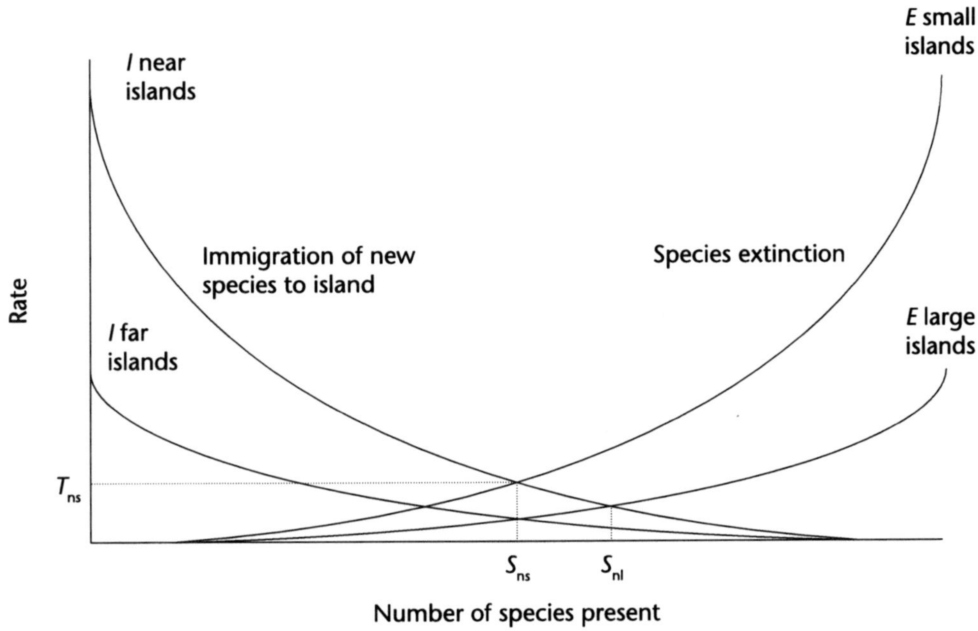

Figure 3.1 Equilibrium model of the single island biota. The equilibrial species number is reached at the intersection between the curves of the rate of immigration of new species, not already on the island, and the curve of extinction of species on the island. Immigration rates are postulated to vary as a function of distance, and extinction rate as a function of island area (increased competition for finite natural resources). The model predicts different values for *S* (number of species), which can be read off the ordinate and for turnover rate (*T*) (the number of species that become extinct and are replaced by immigrants and speciation over unit time). Each combination of island area and isolation should produce a different and unique combination of *S* and *T*. For reasons of uncluttered illustration only limited values are shown. The equilibrium point at which *I* equals *E* is never completely constant as it will shift over time in relation to a range in external and internal factors however the key point is that there is a 'capacity' to how many species can successfully inhabit a finite area over time (Whittaker and Fernández-Palacios 2007; Hall 2010b).

capital as an environmental indicator of sustainable development (Haberl 1997, 2006) and ecological footprinting (Haberl et al. 2004; Galli et al. 2012), some of the practical and theoretical implications of theories of island biogeography for economic dimensions of sustainable development have perhaps not been fully explored despite islands being sites of theoretical novelty (Baldacchino 2007). This is even more surprising given the awareness of issues of resilience and vulnerability for island species and ecosystems that arise from island biogeographical research (Marzluff 2005; Levin and Lubchenco 2008).

Islands provide an opportunity to provide a boundary to study competition between human consumption and wildlife for natural capital (Figure 3.2) (Czech 2004). With such competition, of course, being one of the major reasons why many island ecosystems have suffered such a high degree of loss of endemic biodiversity as a result of habitat loss and land use change. Figure 3.3 illustrates the interconnectedness of human economic systems and natural systems in more detail, with the central box showing the interrelationships between human and ecological systems in an island as well as inputs and outputs in terms of energy and waste as well as the

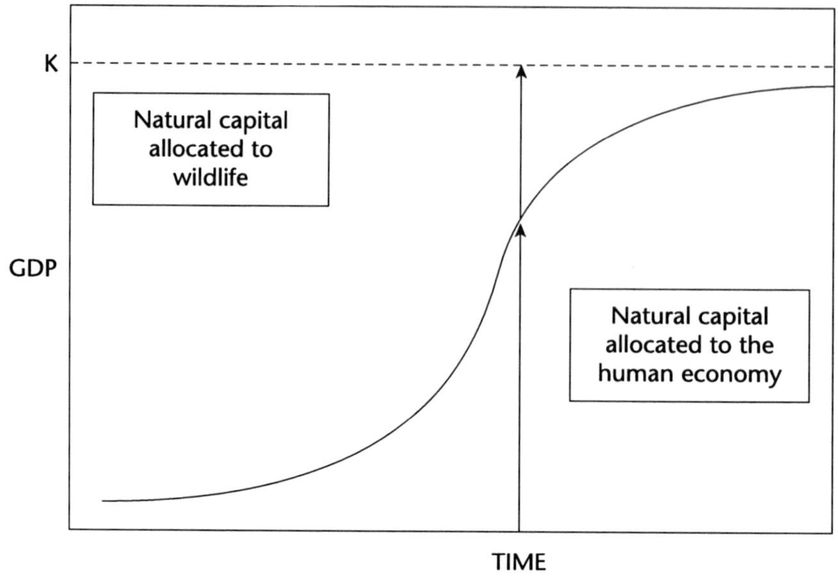

Figure 3.2 Competition for natural capital between people and wildlife

circulation of capital, people and species. Following industrial ecological thinking (Korhonen 2005), the human or industrial system is reflected as an analogue of the natural system. However, given the finite nature of natural capital, the human system will often grow at the expense of the natural capital stocks available in the natural system at a rate faster than it can be renewed – what is otherwise described as unsustainable development. Such 'drawdowns' of natural capital as a result of human disturbance and extraction can lead to substantial perturbations of natural systems leading to species extinctions. This process is especially pronounced on islands.

Nevertheless, islands are inherently dynamic (Lomolino 2000a; 2000b). A more accurate assessment is therefore provided in Figure 3.4 which presents a tripartite model of island biogeography with respect to the three fundamental biogeographic processes of immigration, extinction and evolution as a function of island characteristics of area and isolation. Under Lomolino's (2000a) approach immigration rates should increase with proximity to a source region and the ability of species to travel or transported across immigration barriers and filters. Extinction rates should decrease as island area increases, or increase with growing resource requirements of the focal species. Finally, speciation should be most important where extinction and immigration are lowest and therefore it increases in relation to increase in island area and isolation and decreases with respect to resource requirements and the capacity of species to move or disperse within their environments (Lomolino 2000a). The model, especially when considered in conjunction with figure 3.3, also suggests the importance of both the independent and interacting affects of anthropogenic stressors on natural capital, e.g. climate change, habitat loss, over-exploitation and the introduction of exotic species (Mora and Zapata 2013). However, just as significantly, the interrelationships between island characteristics and biogeographical processes provide for the relative resilience of islands to disturbance, whether from storms or drought, or from direct anthropogenic pressures (Hall 2010b; Jackson and Sax 2010; Yackulic et al. 2011).

Island biogeography clearly provides a means to help explain and analyse island conservation issues. However, the application of the island biogeography approach to sustainable development of islands also provides a clear analogue to the human and economic ecology of islands as well.

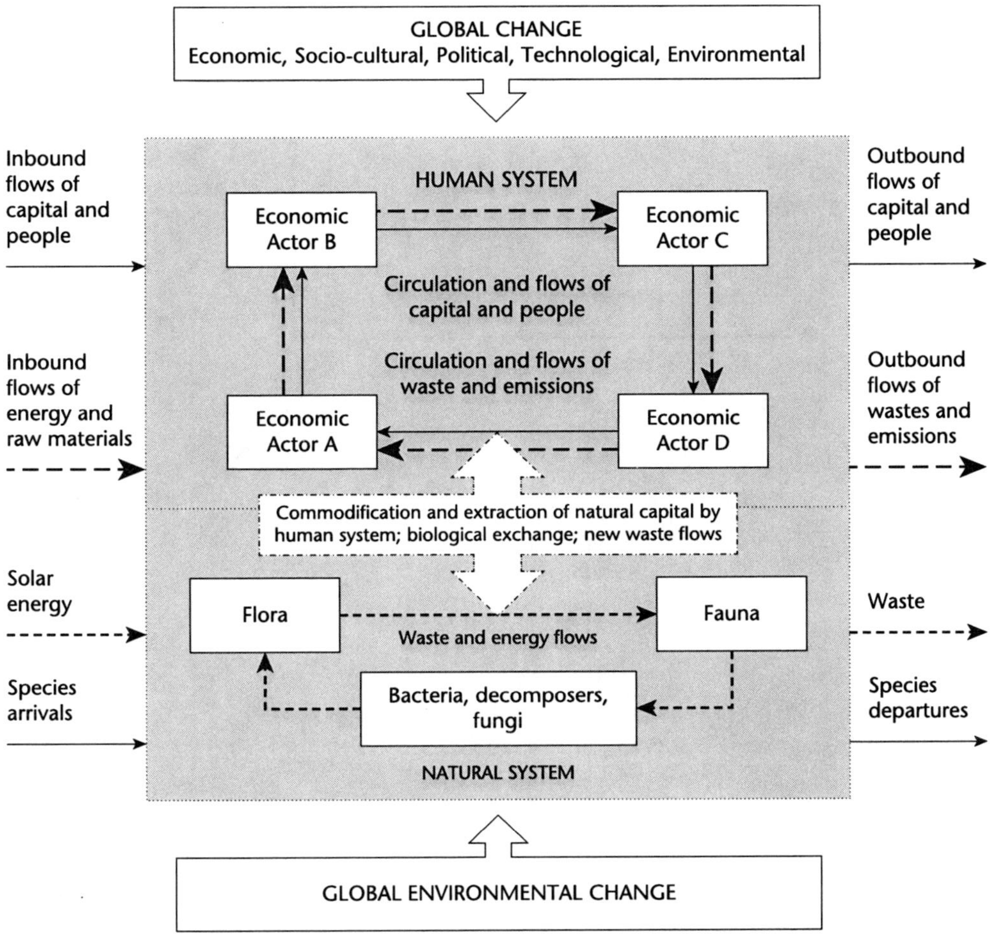

Figure 3.3 Interaction of human and ecological systems

Figure 3.5 presents a model of the application of island biogeographical theory to the understanding of adaptation, resilience, and vulnerability of island economies. From this approach, the equilibrial or steady state number of businesses is reached at the intersection of the rate of immigration of new firms and capital, and the emigration or closure (extinction) of businesses on the island, along with the capacity of businesses to innovate and adapt (which is analogous to species evolution over time and the occupation of new ecological niches). Immigration rates are postulated to vary as a function of distance (which may be economic, cultural or perceptual rather than Euclidean), and closure rate as a function of island area and resources that determine the competition for finite natural and human capital. Although heuristic, the model can potentially predict different values for S (e.g. number of firms and/or capital) (in substituting values for Figure 3.1), and for turnover rate (T) (the number of firms that close and are replaced by immigrants and innovation over unit time). Each combination of island area and isolation should produce a different and unique combination of S and T. The equilibrium point at which I equals E is, of course, never completely constant as it will shift over time in relation to a range in external and internal factors however the key point is that there is a 'capacity' to how many businesses – or people, including visitors – can successfully inhabit a finite area over time without there being loss of natural capital

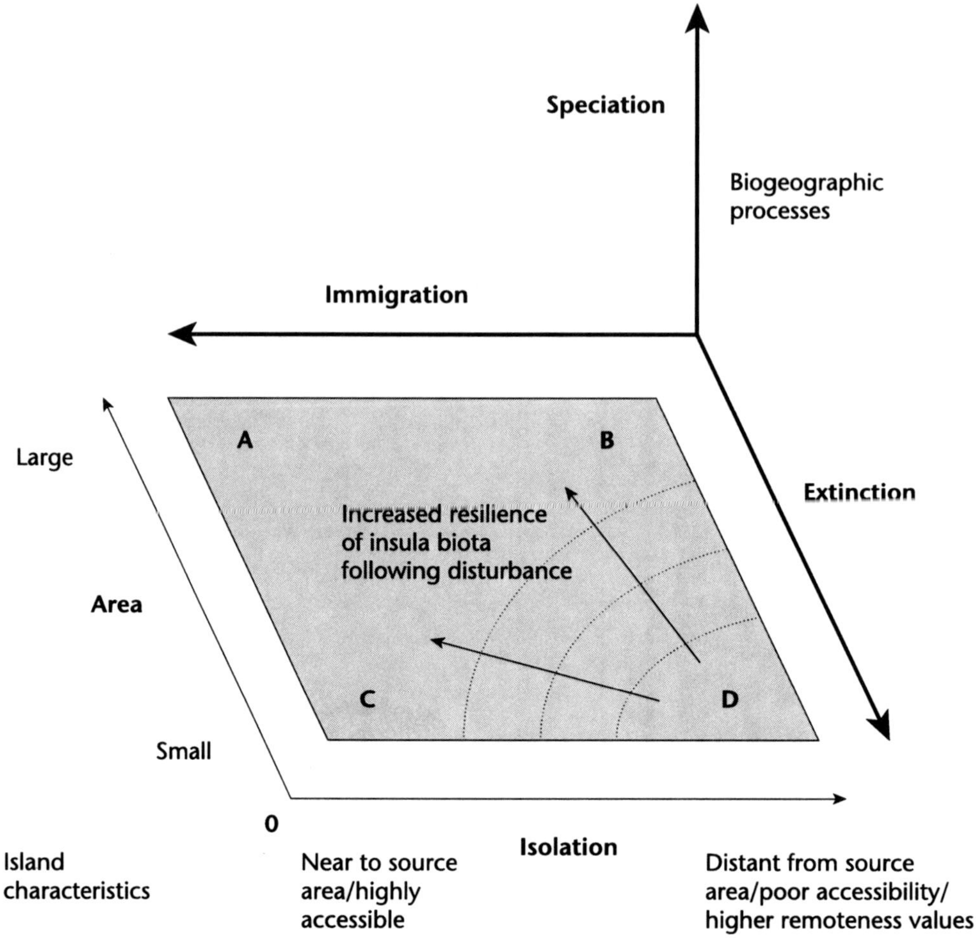

Community characteristics of labelled regions are as follows:
A: Moderate to high species richness, low endemicity and low turnover
B: Moderate to high species richness, high endemicity and low turnover
C: Moderate to low species richness, low endemicity and high turnover
D: Low species richness, low endemicity and high turnover – a depauperate island.
Species richness is the number of different species represented in a set or collection of individuals it does not take into account the abundances of the species or their relative abundance distributions.
Endemism is the ecological state of being unique to a defined geographic location. Species that are indigenous to an island are not endemic if they are also found elsewhere.

Figure 3.4 Relationships between biogeographical processes and island characteristics

Source: Adapted from Lomolino (2000a; 2000b); Hall (2010b; 2012).

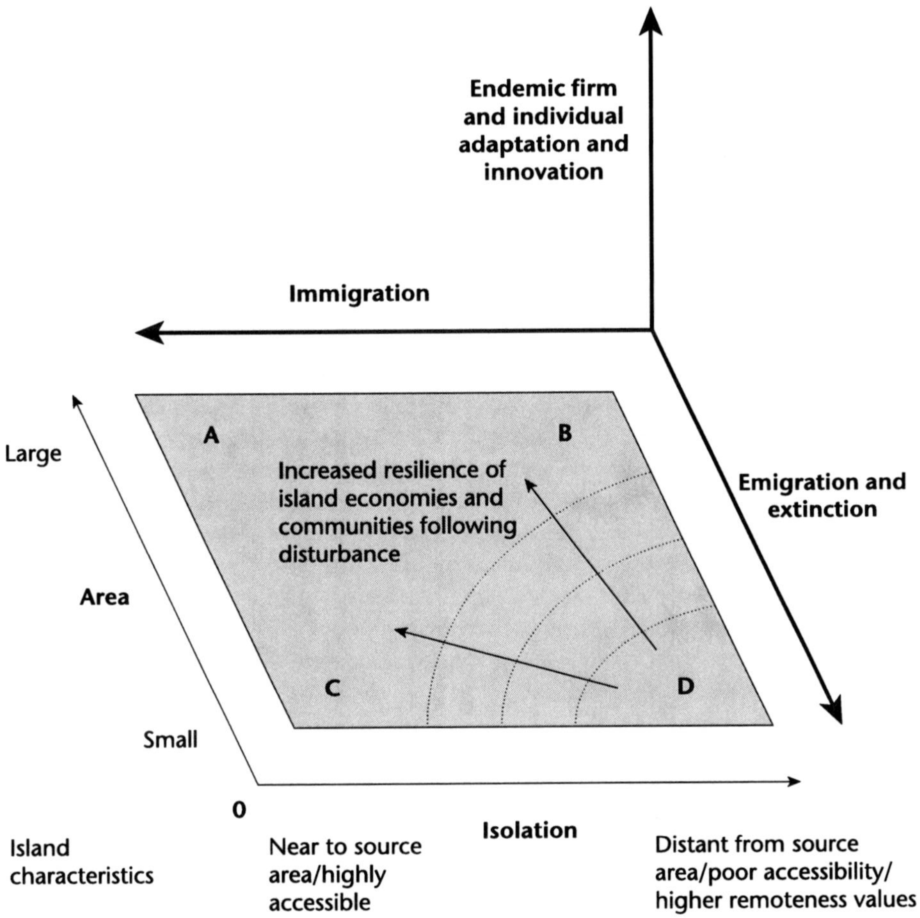

Community characteristics of labelled regions are as follows:
A: Moderate to high economic richness, low endemicity and low turnover (e.g. Singapore);
B: Moderate to high economic richness, high endemicity and low turnover (e.g. Cuba);
C: Moderate to low economic richness, low endemicity and high turnover (e.g. Bahamas);
D: Low economic richness, low endemicity and high turnover – a depauperate island economy (e.g. Nauru).
Economic richness is the number and variety of different businesses.
Endemicity is the number of businesses unique to the island/location. It does not include international chains.
Immigration refers to the inflow of firms, people and/or funds.
Extinction refers to firms ceasing to operate.

Figure 3.5 Island biogeographical perspectives on island adaptation, resilience, vulnerabilty and sustainability

Source: After Hall (2010b, 2012).

(Hall 2010b) and without there being substantial importing of external resources, e.g. energy, food, water and/or economic capital, to maintain a given population base.

Anthropogenic impacts on islands provide clear illustrations of the environmental pressures on island resources, which can only be satisfied by importing resources from elsewhere unless such resources are either going to be depleted and/or limits are placed on the number of resource users. This is evidenced, for example, in the import of food and water to many island tourism destinations to supplement what cannot be provided locally in order to meet a given level of real population demand (real population is the permanent population plus the temporary tourist population at any given time) (Hall 2010b; Gössling et al. 2012). In such situations if land resources are available, it may be possible to develop higher degrees of economic endemism so as to reduce external resource inputs. However, in many SIDS this will not be possible given their extremely limited area.

Using an island biogeographic approach to examine issues of sustainable island development and hence the notion of islands of sustainability clearly raises substantial questions as to whether this is possible or not. It may be the case that islands that are located close to mainland areas in the developed regions of the world with ample resources and relatively low population levels may have the potential to develop dense self-sustaining network economies within existing resource and human capacities, but for many SIDS it is a highly doubtful prospect. As with many of the animal species on islands, many businesses occupy a specialised niche in order to survive. The limited resource base of most islands means that if a relative advantage exists, it only does so in a small number of sectors, usually fisheries, tourism, financial services, and traded agricultural products (Kerr 2005). However, such specialisation not only leads to lack of diversity in the business base but also makes the economy extremely vulnerable to external economic and environmental change and even more dependent on remittances and aid payments (Pelling and Uitto 2001; McGillivray et al. 2010).

Conclusion: islands – an analogue of what?

Much of the focus of the sustainable development of islands has been on climate change with respect to the threats of sea level rise and increased high magnitude weather events. Undoubtedly, such threats are extremely important. But as this chapter has suggested, the threats to SIDS are much wider and lie in the synergistic nature of global change factors as well as the inherent characteristics of islands themselves. Yet, SIDS remain committed to a growth economy instead of one focused on development.

There is very little to suggest in the data on SIDS that they illustrate the possibility of becoming islands of sustainability, defined in terms of 'a constant flow of throughput at a sustainable (low) level, with population and capital stock free to adjust to whatever size can be maintained by the constant throughput beginning with depletion and ending with pollution' (Daly 2008: 3). Population pressures are often being reduced by emigration that also provides a means to return economic capital to the SID via remittances. Some economists have argued that this is a logical approach to maintaining material welfare in island states (Bertram 1993). However, remittances and aid are dependent on economic growth in metropolitan areas and sympathetic policy settings with respect to migration and aid. The degree of specialisation in island economies is highly vulnerable to competition as well as changes in demand and accessibility. Undoubtedly, many SIDS are also seeking to innovate through community-based projects as well as via new business initiatives often as part of aid programmes but the long-term economic prospects remain bleak especially as many individuals continue to be attracted by employment elsewhere.

The combination of social and economic factors means that the capacity of the majority of SIDS to undertake effective environmental and climate change adaptation measures are constrained by a short-term policy focus and limited budgets. Such a situation affects the urgent need of many SIDS to mainstream or integrate climate change adaptation and sustainable planning strategies into development plans and policies (IPCC 2014; Swart and Raes 2007), a situation that is only exacerbated by the often failure to effectively communicate climate change information to island peoples with traditional belief and decision-making systems (Nunn et al. 2014).

It can be argued of course that even within SIDS there may be small-scale islands of sustainability that seek to create the transitions required for sustainable development. Perhaps. But the fact that they are slow in coming and the enormous difficulties facing SIDS provides a mirror to the problem of sustainable development writ large. For many islands, carrying capacity is being maintained artificially high by inflows of capital, often via aid and remittances, often to fund food, energy and even water supplies that cannot be provided locally and/or by people emigration. Endemic innovation is important in using indigenous resources more efficiently, but is not by itself sufficient to maintain levels of natural capital. Such a situation is a good metaphor for sustainability, but at a global scale. The lesson of island biogeography is that, given with current technologies the potential to emigrate to a long-term survivable environment elsewhere in the solar system being slim, we instead face the prospect of extinction for many species, and ongoing anthropogenic transformation of natural capital.

References

Allison, E. H., Perry, A. L., Badjeck, M. C., Adger, W. N., Brown, K., Conway, D., Halls, A. S., Pilling, G. M., Reynolds, R. D., Andrew, N. L. and Dulvy, N. K. (2009) Vulnerability of national economies to the impacts of climate change on fisheries. *Fish and Fisheries*, 10: 173–96.

AOSIS (Alliance of Small Island States) (2009) *Declaration on Climate Change 2009*. Available at: www.aosis.info/documents/AOSISSummitDeclarationSept21FINAL.pdf

Baldacchino, G. (2007) Islands as novelty sites. *Geographical Review*, 97(2): 165–74.

Baritto, F. (2009) *Disasters, Vulnerability and Resilience from a Macro-economic Perspective. Lessons from the Empirical Evidence*. Background paper for the 2009 ISDR Global Assessment Report on Disaster Risk Reduction. New York: UN-ISDR.

Bebbington, A. (1997) Social capital and rural intensification: local organizations and islands of sustainability in the rural Andes. *Geographical Journal*, 163: 189–97.

Bertram, I. G. (1993) Sustainability and material welfare in small South Pacific Island economies, 1900–1990. *World Development*, 21: 247–58.

Butcher-Gollach, C., Banes, C., Jones, P., Liousse, C. and Onorio, K. (2007) *Kiribati Urban Renewal Program Scoping Study (KURPSS):* Volume I *Background Study*. The Ministry of Internal and Social Affairs, Government of Kiribati; New Zealand Agency for International Development; and Australian Agency for International Development.

Chui, T. F. M. and Terry, J. P. (2013) Influence of sea-level rise on freshwater lenses of different atoll island sizes and lens resilience to storm-induced salinization. *Journal of Hydrology*, 502: 18–26.

Connell, J. (2011) Elephants in the Pacific? Pacific urbanisation and its discontents. *Asia Pacific Viewpoint*, 52(2): 121–135.

Cox, C. B., Healey, I. and Moore, P. (1973) *Biogeography: An Ecological and Evolutionary Approach*. Oxford: Blackwell.

Czech, B. (2004) A chronological frame of reference for ecological integrity and natural conditions. *Natural Resources Journal*, 44: 1113–1116.

Daly, H. E. (2008) *A Steady-State Economy*. London: Sustainable Development Commission.

Deschenes, P. J. and Chertow, M. (2004) An island approach to industrial ecology: towards sustainability in the island context. *Journal of Environmental Planning and Management*, 47: 201–217.

Donnelly, J. and Jiwanji, A., (2010) *Urbanization and Children in the Pacific*, Suva: UNICEF Pacific.

FAO (Food and Agriculture Organization) (2011) AQUASTAT database. Available at: www.fao.org/nr/water/aquastat/data

Forbes, D. L., James, T. S., Sutherland, M. and Nicholls, S. E. (2013) Physical basis of coastal adaptation on tropical small islands. *Sustainability Science*, 8: 327–344.

Ford, H. A. (2011) Twinkling lights or turning down the dimmer switch? Are there two patterns of extinction debt in fragmented landscapes?. *Pacific Conservation Biology*, 17(4): 303–309.

Galli, A., Wiedmann, T., Ercin, E., Knoblauch, D., Ewing, B. and Giljum, S. (2012) Integrating ecological, carbon and water footprint into a 'footprint family' of indicators: definition and role in tracking human pressure on the planet. *Ecological Indicators*, 16: 100–112.

Ghina, F. (2003) Sustainable development in small island developing states. *Environment, Development and Sustainability*, 5(1–2): 139–165.

Gössling, S., Hall, C. M. and Scott, D. (2009) The challenges of tourism as a development strategy in an era of global climate change. In E. Palosou (ed.) *Rethinking Development in a Carbon-Constrained World: Development Cooperation and Climate Change*. Helsinki: Ministry of Foreign Affairs.

Gössling, S., Peeters, P., Hall, C.M., Ceron, J-P., Dubois, G., Lehmann, L. and Scott, D. (2012) Tourism and water use: supply, demand, and security: an international review. *Tourism Management*, 33: 1–15.

Groves, C. (2003) *Drafting a Conservation Blueprint: A Practitioner's Guide to Planning for biodiversity*. Washington, DC: Island Press.

Haberl, H. (1997) Human appropriation of net primary production as an environmental indicator: implications for sustainable development. *Ambio*, 26(3): 143–146.

Haberl, H. (2006) The global socioeconomic energetic metabolism as a sustainability problem. *Energy*, 31: 87–99.

Haberl, H., Wackernagel, M., Krausmann, F., Erb, K. H. and Monfreda, C. (2004) Ecological footprints and human appropriation of net primary production: a comparison. *Land Use Policy*, 21: 279–288.

Hall, C. M. (2010a) Island destinations: a natural laboratory for tourism. *Asia Pacific Journal of Tourism Research*, 15: 245–249.

Hall, C. M. (2010b) An island biogeographical approach to island tourism and biodiversity: an exploratory study of the Caribbean and Pacific Islands. *Asia Pacific Journal of Tourism Research*, 15: 383–399.

Hall, C. M. (2012) Island, islandness, vulnerability and resilience. *Tourism Recreation Research*, 37(2): 177–181.

Hall, C. M. (2014) *Tourism and Social Marketing*. London: Routledge.

Hall, C. M. and Page, S. J. (eds) (1996) *Tourism in the Pacific*. London: Thomson Press.

Hanski, I. (2011) Habitat loss, the dynamics of biodiversity, and a perspective on conservation. *AMBIO: A Journal of the Human Environment*, 40: 248–255.

Heinken, T. and Weber, E. (2013) Consequences of habitat fragmentation for plant species: do we know enough?. *Perspectives in Plant Ecology, Evolution and Systematics*, *15*(4): 205–216.

IPCC (Intergovernmental Panel on Climate Change) (2013) Summary for policymakers. In T. F. Stocker, D. Qin, G.-K. Plattner, M. Tignor, S. K. Allen, J. Boschung, A. Nauels, Y. Xia, V. Bex and P. M. Midgley (eds) *Climate Change 2013: The Physical Science Basis*. Cambridge: Cambridge University Press.

IPCC (Intergovernmental Panel on Climate Change) (2014) Small islands. In T. F. Stocker, D. Qin, G.-K. Plattner, M. Tignor, S. K. Allen, J. Boschung, A. Nauels, Y. Xia, V. Bex and P. M. Midgley (eds) *Climate Change 2014: Impacts, Adaptation, and Vulnerability*. Final Draft Working Group II, Fifth Assessment Report. Cambridge: Cambridge University Press.

Jackson, S. T. and Sax, D. F. (2010) Balancing biodiversity in a changing environment: extinction debt, immigration credit and species turnover. *Trends in Ecology & Evolution*, 25(3): 153–160.

Kerr, S. A. (2005) What is small island sustainable development about? *Ocean and Coastal Management*, 48: 503–524.

Korhonen, J. (2005) Industrial ecology for sustainable development: Six controversies in theory building. *Environmental Values*, 14: 83–122.

Levin, S. A. and Lubchenco, J. (2008) Resilience, robustness, and marine ecosystem-based management. *Bioscience*, 58(1): 27–32.

Lomolino, M. V. (2000a) A call for a new paradigm of island biogeography. *Global Ecology and Biogeography*, 9: 1–6.

Lomolino, M. V. (2000b) A species-based theory of insular zoogeography. *Global Ecology and Biogeography*, 9: 39–58.

Macarthur, R. H. and Wilson, E. O. (1963) An equilibrium theory of insular zoogeography. *Evolution*, 17: 373–387.

Macarthur, R. H. and Wilson, E.O. (1967) *The Theory of Island Biogeography*. Princeton, NJ: Princeton University Press.

McGillivray, M., Naude, W. and Santos-Paulino, A. U. (2010) Vulnerability, trade, financial flows and state failure in small island developing states. *The Journal of Development Studies*, 46: 815–827.

Marzluff, J. M. (2005) Island biogeography for an urbanizing world: how extinction and colonization may determine biological diversity in human-dominated landscapes. *Urban Ecosystems*, 8: 157–177.

Mimura, N., Nurse, L., McLean, R., Agard, J., Briguglio, L., Lefale, P., Payet, R. and Sem G. (2007) Small islands. In M. Parry, O. Canziani, J. Palutikof, P. van der Linden and C. Hanson (eds) *Climate Change 2007: Impacts, Adaptation and Vulnerability*. Cambridge: Cambridge University Press.

Moore, A. (2010) Climate changing small islands: considering social science and the production of island vulnerability and opportunity. *Environment and Society: Advances in Research*, 1(1): 116–131.

Mora, C. and Zapata, F. A. (2013) Anthropogenic footprints on biodiversity. In K. Rohde (ed.) *The Balance of Nature and Human Impact*. Cambridge: Cambridge University Press.

Mortreux, C. and Barnett, J. (2009) Climate change, migration and adaptation in Funafuti, Tuvalu. *Global Environmental Change*, 19: 105–112.

Nunn, P. D. (2009) Responding to the challenges of climate change in the Pacific Islands: management and technological imperatives. *Climate Research*, 40: 211–231.

Nunn, P. D. (2013) The end of the Pacific? Effects of sea level rise on Pacific Island livelihoods. *Singapore Journal of Tropical Geography*, 34: 143–171.

Nunn, P. D., Aalbersberg, W., Lata, S. and Gwilliam, M. (2014) Beyond the core: community governance for climate change adaptation in peripheral parts of Pacific Island Countries. *Regional Environmental Change*, 14: 221–235.

Pelling, M. and Uitto, J. I. (2001) Small island developing states: natural disaster vulnerability and global change. *Global Environmental Change Part B: Environmental Hazards*, 3(2): 49–62.

Péti, M. (2012) A territorial understanding of sustainability in public development. *Environmental Impact Assessment Review*, 32(1): 61–73.

Pungetti, G. (2012) Islands, culture, landscape and seascape. *Journal of Marine and Island Cultures*, 1(2): 51–4.

Quammen, D. (1996) *The Song of the Dodo: Island Biogeography in an Age of Extinction*. New York: Touchstone.

Scott, D., Gössling, S. and Hall, C. M. (2012) *Tourism and Climate Change: Impacts, Adaptation and Mitigation*. London: Routledge.

Swart, R. and Raes, F. (2007) Making integration of adaptation and mitigation work: mainstreaming into sustainable development policies. *Climate Policy*, 7: 288–303.

UNCTAD (United Nations Conference on Trade and Development) (2012) *UNCTAD Handbook of Statistics 2012*. New York and Geneva: UNCTAD.

UN DESA (United Nations Department of Economic and Social Affairs) (2010) *Trends in sustainable development: Small Island Developing States*. New York: UN DESA.

United Nations Development Programme (UNDP) (2013) *Human Development Report 2013. The Rise of the South: Human Progress in a Diverse World*. New York: UNDP.

Van Teeffelen, A. J., Vos, C. C. and Opdam, P. (2012) Species in a dynamic world: consequences of habitat network dynamics on conservation planning. *Biological Conservation*, 153: 239–253.

Wallner, H. P. and Narodoslawsky, M. (1996) Evolution of regional socio-economic systems toward 'islands of sustainability'. *Journal of Environmental Systems*, 24: 221–240.

Wallner, H. P., Narodoslawsky, M. and Moser, F. (1996) Islands of sustainability: a bottom-up approach towards sustainable development. *Environment and Planning A*, 28: 1763–1778.

Whittaker, R. J. and Fernández-Palacios, J. M. (2007) *Island Biogeography: Ecology, Evolution, and Conservation*, 2nd edn. Oxford: Oxford University Press.

Wilkinson, A. (2011) Urban challenges in the Pacific. Paper presented at Fifth Asia-Pacific Urban Forum. Cities of Opportunity: Partnerships for an Inclusive and Sustainable Urban Future, Bangkok: ESCAP.

World Bank (2012) *World Development Indicators 2012*. Washington, DC: World Bank.

Yackulic, C. B., Sanderson, E. W. and Uriarte, M. (2011) Anthropogenic and environmental drivers of modern range loss in large mammals. *Proceedings of the National Academy of Sciences*, 108(10): 4024–4029.

4

'UNCERTAINTY' IN THE PROFESSIONALISATION OF SUSTAINABLE DEVELOPMENT

The case of the Intergovernmental Panel on Climate Change (IPCC)

Annika Skoglund and Tommy Jensen

Introduction

The belief in making the world a 'sustainable' one is widespread, and sustainable development has been presented as a solution to various environmental, social and economic crises. In particular, we have heard calls for a change in 'development paths' to mitigate climate change (IPCC WG III 2007: 21). With a dissemination of knowledge about the climate, and how it is linked to ecological systems, sustainable development has increasingly tuned into complexity, vulnerability and resilience (Reid 2013). Furthermore, vulnerability is underpinned by 'uncertainty', which is not only visible in descriptions of catastrophic processes in general, but especially in the case of the IPCC (e.g. see Evans and Reid 2013). However, 'uncertainty' can be construed in different ways and accomplish different things. We therefore aim to get closer to how the IPCC has refined its work practices around 'uncertainty' since the 1990s and promoted the professionalisation of sustainable development as a solution to climate change.

This professionalisation of sustainable development can be analysed with the aid of several fruitful approaches. In this chapter, the focus is on the growing field of climate governmentality studies (e.g. see Oels 2005, 2013; Lövbrand et al. 2009; Methmann 2013; Paterson and Stripple 2010; 2012; Stripple and Bulkeley 2013b). Climate governmentality studies are useful, because they offer an alternative to the more established global climate governance studies (Lövbrand and Stripple 2013: 34). In comparison to the traditional governance approach, the governmentality framework focuses on how the climate is made governable and the correlating qualities of individuals and collectives that this rationality of government presupposes. In contrast to a research interest in solutions to how we can live in accordance with sustainable development in a world threatened by climate change, climate governmentality is useful for gaining insights into how 'sustainable' solutions are offered. How we are helped and guided to live with climate risk and biospheric life is thus investigated. This type of analysis traces how knowledge about climate change shapes us and creates new ontologies of ourselves (cf. Rose 2007: 105).

In climate governmentality studies the emphasis is on how the human is affected by human constructions of climate change and its solutions. Within the governmentality framework, sustainable development can be analysed as a so-called 'ethical programme for change', by which certain self-technologies are offered to the human to create a specific outcome (cf. Dean 2007: 63; 2010: 27). Despite this, the outcome should never be viewed as guaranteed, but analysed as an idea that seeks to help more or less willing individuals to become better able to regulate themselves.

This anti-essentialist perspective aims to unravel how realities are produced and co-constructed by an abundance of actors. This is done by analysing single statements, policy documents, business commercials and social movement protests, to mention only a few examples of proposals to make the world a more 'sustainable' one. In comparison to those who focus on a presumed weakened state and hegemonic companies, the governmentality framework treats power as relational and exercised. Hence, the state is not envisioned as a universal or an 'autonomous source of power', it has no heart or essence, but is made up of 'multiple governmentalities' (Foucault [1978–79] 2010: 77). This analytical focus on productive forms of power highlights power as exercised through the formation and extension of possible subjectivities/identities and ways of living. How 'conducting the conduct of others' (Foucault [1982–83] 2011:4), i.e. aid to self-management, unfolds via knowledge production about climate change and its solutions, is the analytical target. This means that constructions of climate change and sustainable development can be investigated in relation to a potential reformation of indirect rule, supported by an enabling state. This is also called government at a distance, or 'advanced liberal government' (Rose 1996: 139–142). Non-state actors may thus take it upon themselves to form an 'apparatus', with the aim of managing the population and optimising vitality or '"make" live and "let" die' (Foucault [1976–1997] 2004: 241). In addition, the formation of this apparatus leads to the formation of new professions that assay 'life' or ways of living, often coupled to specific knowledge production. According to this perspective, professionalisation can also be spread through a dissemination of knowledge, expertise and responsibility to those who are not normally perceived as 'professionals', such as housewives, unemployed activists or even children. However, such a professionalisation of sustainable development, enforced by concerns for climate change, is empirically hard to grasp. We will therefore illustrate how climate governmentality can be used analytically to trace a refinement of work practices around climate change and sustainable development in a limited set of IPCC texts.

We start by introducing the existing literature in climate governmentality studies, after which we turn to the empirical case – the IPCC. Here we use the Panel's socio-economic summaries to policy-makers from 1990–2007 as a backdrop in order to focus on: (1) how uncertainty is constructed; and (2) what the effects are. In other words, we aim to get closer to how the IPCC talks about uncertainty, and how this can be conceived as a refinement of its work practices, explored as a potential professionalisation of sustainable development. The analysis also contributes to climate governmentality studies by analysing 'uncertainty' as fundamental for the proposed change of 'development paths' that also requires a transformation from high to low carbon subjectivities. The professionalisation of sustainable development is thus closely connected to invitations to live (or die) in a world threatened by climate change.

Climate governmentality studies

Michel Foucault introduces and develops governmentality, or 'the problem of government', in various ways in his lectures, essays, interviews and books. By raising the question of how we first came to think about 'how to govern' in a frugal way, he not only traces the effects of liberal philosophy and its link to population management, Biopolitics (Foucault [1976] 2002a: 50), but also Stoicism's re-activation of how to govern the self, Catholic and Pastoral doctrine's government of souls and conduct, pedagogy's government of children, and the government of the State by the Prince (Foucault [1977–78] 2007: 88). Hence, Western forms of rule have developed through complexes of knowledge and formation of subjectivities. Foucault also mentions how changes in the climate were linked to dietary rules and sexual activity in ancient Greece (Foucault [1976] 2002b: 54). Furthermore, Foucault stresses the importance of situating any analysis of 'the government of the self and the government of others' in relation to time and place (Foucault [1982–83] 2011: 8–9).

Initially, Foucault's genealogies were picked up in relation to environmental problems in general (e.g. see 'Environmentality' in Agrawal 2005; Darier 1999; and 'green governmentality' in Rutherford 2007). Recent post-Foucauldian studies have also been conducted on the re-configuration of Biopolitics with climate change and sustainable development (e.g. see Brand 2007; Duffield 2007; Grove 2010; Reid 2012). These studies include how 'the self' is governed in relation to 'something else', such as representations of the vulnerable other, 'life' redefined, or children (e.g. see Skoglund and Börjesson 2013).

Stripple and Bulkeley (2013: Introduction) suggest that governmentality should enter new empirical arenas and ask new questions by looking into politics as an immanent process that evolves through social relations. This 'provides an analytical toolbox that can advance new perspectives on the climate as a political space, and enables us to grasp and highlight the existence of changing discursive productions of a warming world and their effects in mitigating or adapting to that world' (ibid.: 10). Hence, it is a perspective that is concerned with how we are invited to govern ourselves and others in relation to climate change (Bulkeley and Stripple 2013). The empirical arenas are thus extended from state politics to sites such as the production of star species (e.g. polar bears, see Yusoff 2010), forests, migration, the household and children.

How the local environment needs to be represented and defined in order to be governed has been elaborated on by Rutland and Aylett (2008). They focus on how climate change became a political priority in Portland, and how the local state sought to enlist the self-governing capacities of its residents. How political programmes become shared ideas within the population through knowledge is thus analysed for a specific case. According to the authors, knowledge is important for opening up for action and for helping subjects to regulate themselves in a more environmentally-friendly direction.

In comparison, Oels (2005:185) suggests that it is climate change, and not a specific formation of subjectivity, that is rendered governable by biopower. This form of biopower 'justified global management of spaceship Earth in the name of the survival of life on Earth'. According to her analysis, this biopolitical focus changed in the mid-1990s and climate change became increasingly governed by technologies for self-management, i.e. advanced liberal government. Solutions to climate change predominantly followed economic logic, market-based solutions and a language of cost-effectiveness.

It has also been illustrated that organisations try to localise the problem of climate change and position it closer to the everyday life of the citizen, for example by discussing individual energy use (Slocum 2004). It is assumed that localising the issue in this way inspires people to act, and that it is possible to deploy political strategies that make the relationship between the local and global visible (ibid.). Energy use and dollars saved thus become speakable issues, Slocum continues, and concludes that situated knowledge and the constitution of commonness could be used in campaigns designed to spur citizen concern.

Paterson and Stripple (2010) use governmentality to elaborate on the effects of practices linked to carbon offsetting. They exemplify various calculative and comparative techniques and ways of visualising the confessing, connective and even narcissistic self for the limitation of carbon emissions. Hence, they delve into how subjects are formed around climate change in order to understand how the responsibilisation of the individual is linked to global climate governance. They conclude that the individual is encouraged to problematise his/her climate related activities in a plurality of ways, so as to optimise self-regulation with the help of peer pressure. Carbon governmentality individualises by producing individuals who problematise themselves and totalises by targeting the overall effects of emitting individuals. In a follow-up study tracing how the commodification of carbon has become morally correct, Paterson and Stripple (2012) focus on biopolitical techniques (data assessments and planning) in relation to the self-regulation that is facilitated.

In comparison, Methmann (2013) situates his climate governmentality study in relation to an academic discussion by using global climate politics as a paradigmatic case for illustrating how global governmentality operates. He argues that the Clean Development Mechanism depoliticises climate politics and disseminates advanced liberal government. Lövbrand et al. (2009) have a more historic approach, and examine the assumptions and political implications of the Earth System metaphor. They derive how the assumptions of 'environmental change research' that interconnect ecological and human systems produce a new population – humankind – as a geological force.

Another issue that is raised in discussions about climate change is security and how security claims unfold; who is suggested to deliver it?; with what means?; and for whom (Stripple 2012)? Studied as assembled through performative practices, security is a discourse that constantly changes the subject of insecurity, where climate change assessments pattern vulnerability, with significant implications for how politics is organised in the name of security. The liberal problematic of security keeps re-addressing the risk, uncertainty and insecurity that follows from unleashed freedom (see also Lentzos and Rose 2009). Politics is no longer mainly recognised as a modern innovation of national security, i.e. security of states in relation to other states, but as a dissemination of liberal rationality through strategies and tactics that aim to shape a subject who is prone to reproduce the resilience of the liberal rationality itself (Reid 2011). We have been confronted with a potential replacement of the 'development-security nexus' by the more disaster-accepting 'sustainable development-resilience nexus'. According to Reid (2013), we are now increasingly made governable with the aid of a neoliberal biopolitical rationality that comes with a shift from development to sustainable development and a shift from security to resilience.

Oels (2013) further presents how a re-configured biopolitics has affected a 'securitisation' of climate change. She contends that risk management is now operationalised through contingence, by which even higher temperatures than the 2°C are accounted for and addressed. Reid (2012) alternatively shows how this reconfiguration of biopolitics now takes biospheric life into consideration, which results in a transformation of the former liberal security problematic into a neoliberal resilience ultimatum. He scrutinises how ecological reasoning is formative of neoliberalism and sustainable development (ibid.: 70), and how it is increasingly through resilience as a 'capacity of life itself', and not a state, that neoliberalism expands globally to foster adaptive self-reliant subjects. Some are invited to abandon security, buffer change, absorb threats and adapt, i.e. bear the risks upon themselves to become self-reliant (Reid 2012: 71–74; see also Duffield 2007), although this is specifically demanded of the poor since they are targeted by UNEP as 'ecologically ignorant' due to their lack of sufficient markets, property rights and flexible institutions (Reid 2012: 74). Not only does sustainable development prescribe peoples to live within markets, it also enforces them to become resilient, by which their political capacities are degraded (ibid.: 77).

The strand of literature that explores the broader biopolitical effects linked to climate change illustrates that the ontology that underpins resilience is vulnerability (Evans and Reid 2013). Vulnerability has become fundamental for management of catastrophic processes in general, and especially in the case of climate change. This can be observed in the 2012 Special Report of the IPCC. Evans and Reid outline how the IPCC preconditions vulnerability for the resilient subject. Specifically, they show how the uncertain is brought together with the certain to form 'subject-centred events' (ibid.: 84). Hence, by relying on the uncertainty of catastrophic events, which cannot be known in advance, the IPCC assumes that the subject can deal with these occurrences, which 'foster behavioural claims to empirical truth' (ibid.). In extension, the authors describe how disaster management underpins most of the social scientific work on climate change, by which the vulnerable subject is constituted as the lead actor in, and storyteller of, catastrophic futures.

The 'concept of resilience openly promotes insecurity' to which the vulnerable subject is attuned (Evans and Reid 2014: 72). That is, the enterprising self is invited to accept insecurities and use these as opportunities of flourishing. Thus, contemporary forms of resilience-making still foster a subject who voluntarily relinquishes the state as a means of security and supports the advanced liberal rule that it is offered to contribute to in remoulded ways. However, how insecurity and the making of the vulnerable in efforts of sustainable development are linked to various constructions of 'uncertainty' in relation to climate change has not been thoroughly investigated. Our intention is to address this in our analysis of the IPCC socio-economic reports.

The IPCC: a centre for the re-presentation of knowledge

The IPCC has become one of the more influential providers of knowledge about climate change and its solutions (Hoffman 2011) and is considered as 'the largest and most rigorously peer-reviewed scientific collaboration in history' (Gelbspan 2005: 187), synthesising 'the best existing research on climate change' (Aylett 2010: 104). Due to this, the IPCC is proposed to be 'the engine of our scientific knowledge on climate change' (Peake 2005: 495). However, the work practices of the Panel have also been criticised for allowing political processes to pollute scientific fact production. Such criticism is not surprising if we look at Figure 4.1 illustrating the IPCC's review process, in which governments and appointed experts act as reviewers/contributors (see also IPCC 2013a).

However, whether the IPCC openly discusses how it might deal with various forms of uncertainties in this review process and the mismatch between different contributors to their knowledge-generating process have not been acknowledged. The IPCC has even found it necessary to create a framework for how it should communicate uncertainty in a standardised way. An external body has also reviewed this framework and constructively suggested changes (InterAcademy Council 2010: xiv–xv). In its own reports, the IPCC acknowledges the lack of information and the need for transparency (IPCC WG II/WG III 2012). For example, sustainable development is coupled to uncertainty about the possible mitigation and adaptation options and the impossibility of predefining future development paths. In particular, the IPCC problematises assumptions about population growth and consumption.

We now turn to the IPCC socio-economic summaries for policy-makers between 1990 and 2007 to illustrate how uncertainty is described and what its effects are. We have used the search function to find all the paragraphs that include the words 'uncertain/ty/ties'. This search is summarised by a detailed re-presentation of the relevant paragraphs, in which repetitive paragraphs are excluded.

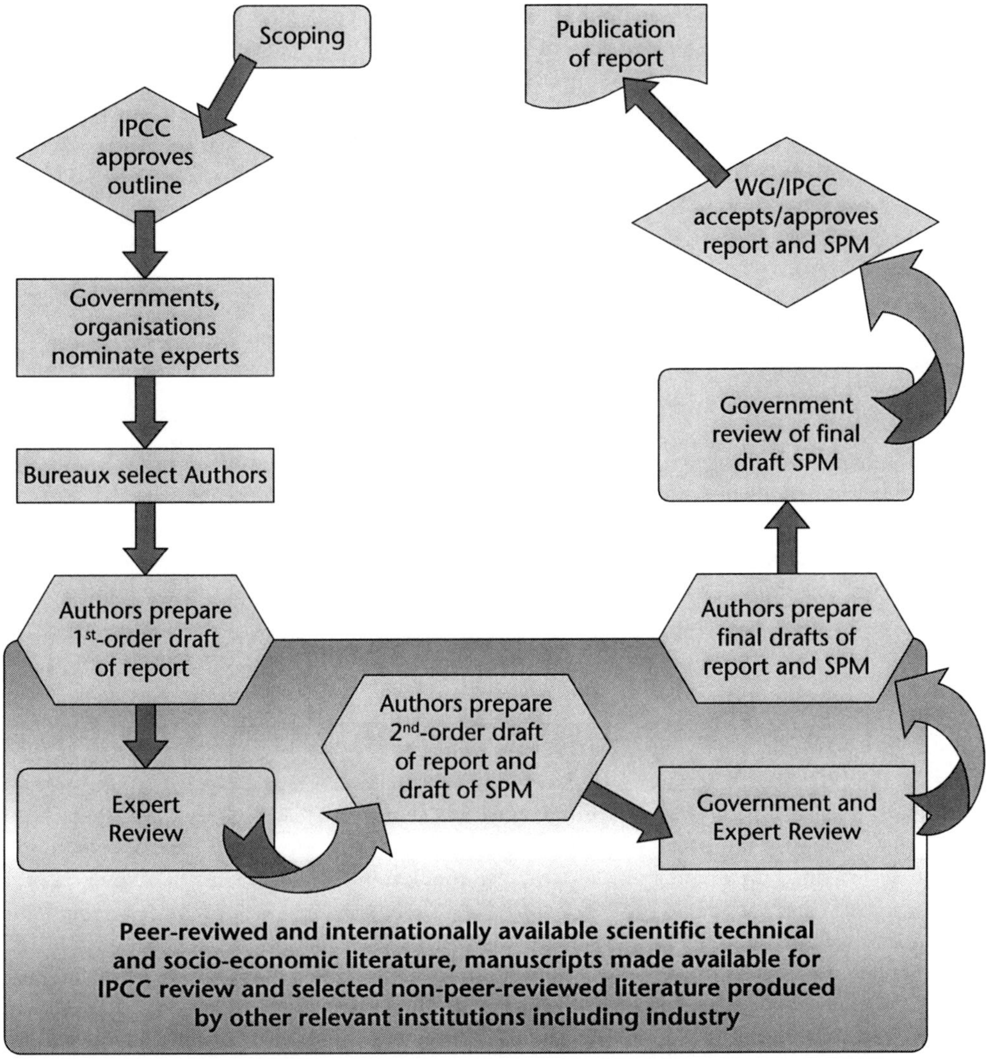

Figure 4.1 Summary description of the IPCC writing and review process

Source: IPCC (2013b).

IPCC 1990 WG II and WG III

In 1990, the IPCC Working Group II states that '[c]omprehensive estimates of the physical and biological effects of climate change at the regional level are difficult' (IPCC WG II 1990: 1). There is not enough '[c]onfidence in regional estimates', and there is 'considerable disagreement between various general circulation model and palaeoanalog results' (ibid.). Furthermore, the report openly discusses that there are 'several scientific uncertainties regarding the relationship between climate change and biological effects and between these effects and socioeconomic consequences' (ibid.). Apart for constructing uncertainty about scientific facts, and how these are linked to socio-economics, the IPCC states that 'surprises cannot be ruled out' (IPCC WG II 1990: 2), especially as the rate of change is at this point unknown. However, uncertainties are not seen as obstacles to drawing conclusions: 'Despite these uncertainties, Working Group II has been able to reach some major conclusions' (ibid.).

In 1990, the IPCC Working Group III illustrates that there are uncertainties in the emission scenarios. The mean temperature rise is given 'an uncertainty range of 0.2°C to 0.5°C per decade', and in the same scenario there is 'an uncertainty range of 3–10 cm per decade' for the rise in sea levels (IPCC WG III 1990: xxv). These uncertainties are due to a limited 'ability to estimate future rates of population and economic growth, etc.' (ibid.). The report also proposes that 'some uncertainty in the projections of greenhouse gas emissions, individual behavior, technological innovation, and other factors ... are crucial for determining emission rates over the course of the next century' (ibid.: xxx).

Moving on to the 'response strategies', these are suggested to present 'formidable difficulties for policymakers' (IPCC WG III 1990: xxxiv). The available information 'to make sound policy analyses is inadequate' (ibid.), due to:

> (a) remaining scientific uncertainties regarding the magnitude, timing, rate, and regional consequences of potential climate change; (b) uncertainty with respect to how effective specific response options or groups of options would be in actually averting potential climate change; and (c) uncertainty with respect to the costs, effects on economic growth, and other economic and social implications of specific response options or groups of options.
>
> *(IPCC WG III 1990: xxxiv)*

IPCC 1995 WG II and WG III

In 1995, the IPCC Working Group II discusses how patterns of climate change are interwoven with climate variability, which also brings more uncertainty (IPCC WG II 1995: Preface). A 'confidence' category is introduced, where 'Low Confidence ... is reserved for cases when lead authors were highly uncertain about a particular conclusion' (ibid.: x). The IPCC further outlines how such uncertainty can arise by pointing to 'a reflection of a lack of consensus' and 'the existence of seriously competing hypotheses' (ibid.: x).

Complementary to this problematisation of consensus seeking and discussion of uncertainty in IPCC's own practices, the authors speak directly to the reader: 'Readers of the assessment need to keep in mind' that the confidence levels provide 'a rough sense of the collective judgment by the authors of the degree of certainty or uncertainty' and that 'they are an imperfect tool' (IPCC WG II 1995: x). Hence, the IPCC seeks to make the reader aware of the problems associated with the 'subjective process' of assigning 'confidence levels' to scientific results: 'different individuals will assign different levels of confidence to the same findings and the same base of evidence because they demand different standards of proof' (ibid.: x). A sound relation between the authors and the reader is therefore suggested, without further explanation of what that would entail. Nevertheless, the IPCC adds that there are dangers with 'multiple sources of uncertainty, some of which are difficult to identify with precision, leading different individuals to make different judgments' (ibid.: x).

When it comes to solutions to this uncertainty, the IPCC proposes that '[u]ncertainty does not mean that a nation or the world community cannot position itself better to cope with the broad range of possible climate changes or protect against potentially costly future outcomes' (IPCC WG II 1995: 4). All in all, 'precautionary measures' and mitigation of emissions, as well as 'enhancing the resilience of vulnerable systems by means of adaptation', are recommended (ibid.: 4).

In 1995, Working Group III focuses on the socio-economic aspects of climate change and discusses 'decision making under uncertainty' (IPCC WG III 1995: Foreword); an area which together with 'risk aversion, technology development and diffusion processes, and distributional considerations are ... relatively poorly developed in international environmental economics, and especially in the climate change literature' (ibid.: 7). Specifically, it is the 'traditional cost-benefit analysis' that is problematised regarding uncertainty, since the problem of climate change is 'global, regional, and intergenerational' (ibid.: 9). Estimates are therefore seen to 'vary widely' together with low 'confidence in monetary estimates' (ibid.: 9). 'These uncertainties and the resolution of uncertainty over time may be decisive for the choice of strategies to combat climate change. The objective of decision analysis is to deal with such problems' (ibid.: 9).

In addition, other unknown non-market consequences are introduced as 'a source of major uncertainty in assessing the implications of global climate change for human welfare' (IPCC WG III 1995:10). Here, the IPCC informs the reader how monetary valuation has been negotiated within the Panel:

> Some regard monetary valuation of such impacts as essential to sound decision making, but others reject monetary valuation of some impacts, such as risk of human mortality, on ethical grounds. Additionally, there is a danger that entire unique cultures may be obliterated. This is not something that can be considered in monetary terms, but becomes a question of loss of human diversity, for which we have no indicators to measure economic value.
>
> *(IPCC WG III 1995: 10)*

Damages are furthermore coupled to highly uncertain estimates and 'given the widely differing assumptions and methodologies in the studies' (IPCC WG III 1995: 10). Models are even said to 'remain simplistic and are limited representations of the actual climate processes and are based on earlier IPCC scientific reports' (ibid.: 11). In addition to the 'limited knowledge of impacts, uncertain future technological and socio-economic developments', catastrophes and surprises are introduced as adding to the overall uncertainty (ibid.). The IPCC concludes that '[b]ecause of the lack of appropriate scientific knowledge, there would remain a high degree of uncertainty about the results of limiting emissions at specific levels' (ibid.: 15).

IPCC 2001 WG II and III

In 2001, the IPCC Working Group II 'describes the current state of understanding of the impacts, adaptation, and vulnerability to climate change and their uncertainties' (IPCC WG II 2001: 3). Now, vulnerability is emphasised and climate extremes are discussed as leading to 'damage, hardship, and death' (ibid.: 3). These extremes are recognised as difficult to estimate, and the IPCC therefore warns the reader of the uncertainties of estimations, concluding that 'it can be expected that the severity of their impacts will also increase in concert with global warming' (ibid.: 6). Furthermore, economic models are recognised as insufficient, since they do 'not clearly distinguish the climate change signal from other sources of change' (ibid.: 6).

Uncertainty is also illustrated as existing in relation to how vulnerable populations will be affected. 'Further research' is requested to limit this uncertainty (IPCC WG II 2001: 11) and 'to strengthen future assessments and to reduce uncertainties in order to assure that sufficient information is available for policy-making about responses to possible consequences of climate change, including research in and by developing countries' (ibid.: 17).

The IPCC continues to emphasise the uncertainties of scenarios and methods, now linked to 'uncertainties regarding the sensitivities and adaptability of natural and social systems' (ibid.: 17). These uncertainties are suggested to be of such a character that the 'assessment of regional vulnerabilities' necessarily has to be 'qualitative' (ibid,: 17).

In 2001, the IPCC Working Group III elaborates on how the response to climate change is 'characterised by decision-making under uncertainty and risk, including the possibility of non-linear and/or irreversible changes (IPCC WG III 2001: 3). Scenarios are again constructed as being uncertain, since they 'do not provide information on equity implications and how such changes may be achieved or who may bear any costs incurred' (ibid.: 3). Moreover, 'significant differences and uncertainties surround specific quantitative estimates of the costs and benefits of mitigation options' (ibid.: 9).

The discussion about uncertainties now turns to non-Annex I countries, which may be 'adversely affected by reductions in demand for their exports to OECD nations and by the price increase of those carbon intensive and other products they continue to import' (IPCC WG III 2001: 11). However, these are said to 'benefit from the reduction in fuel prices, increased exports of carbon-intensive products and the transfer of environmentally sound technologies and know-how' (ibid.: 1). Even so, there are 'complexities', the IPCC states, since 'the breakdown of winners and losers remains uncertain' (ibid.). In addition, it proposes that '[c]limate change decision-making is essentially a sequential process under general uncertainty' that requires 'a prudent risk management strategy' (ibid.: 12). Again, further research is called for 'to strengthen future assessments and to reduce uncertainties as far as possible in order that sufficient information is available for policy making about responses to climate change, including research in developing countries' (ibid.: 13).

IPCC 2007 WG II and WG III

In 2007, the IPCC Working Group II introduces a strategy for the communication of uncertainty. In 'Endbox 2', the IPCC states that there are 'a set of terms that describe uncertainties in current knowledge' (IPCC WG II 2007: 21). In 'Endbox 1: Uncertainty representation', the IPCC proposes that '[u]ncertainty is an inherent feature of any assessment. The fourth assessment report clarifies the uncertainties associated with essential statements' (ibid.: 23). The report continues by problematising the '[f]undamental differences between the underlying disciplinary sciences of the three Working Group reports' (ibid.: 23). These differences, it is consequently argued, 'make a common approach impractical' (ibid.: 23).

> The 'likelihood' approach applied in 'Climate change 2007, the physical science basis' and the 'confidence' and 'likelihood' approaches used in 'Climate change 2007, impacts, adaptation, and vulnerability' were judged to be inadequate to deal with the specific uncertainties involved in this mitigation report, as here human choices are considered.
>
> *(IPCC WG II 2007: 23)*

In 2007, the IPCC Working Group III addresses uncertainties concerning 'carbon leakage' and 'long-term costs' (IPCC WG III 2007: 12). The report repeats the lack of full knowledge, especially for mitigation possibilities in developing countries. Additional research is called for in order to address those gaps and 'further reduce uncertainties and thus facilitate decision-making related to mitigation of climate change' (ibid.: 22).

Analysis

The IPCC reports exemplify how policy discourse on climate change transforms (cf. Oels 2013). What has been implemented in the case of the IPCC is the widespread and loose boundaries of the organisation as such, its ways of collecting and evaluating information, its inclusion and reviewing of opinions, its production and dissemination of knowledge, and its re-presentation of negotiations and agreements. Hereby, we are given continuously remoulded versions of reality, where several things are accomplished when uncertainty is introduced to the scene for possible articulation. We have chosen to highlight four main accomplishments that occur via the IPCC's constructions of 'uncertainty': (1) requests for more knowledge; (2) merging science and consensus; (3) preparations for surprise and complexity; and (4) opening up for reflection and confession. We also aim to explore how these accomplishments relate to a professionalisation of sustainable development and its correlating forms of subjectivity.

Requests for more knowledge

By uncovering and re-presenting uncertainties, the IPCC opens up for extended negotiations and discussions about what can be said and done. Uncertainty, thus, accomplishes something more than a scientific discussion about the probability of results. It accomplishes a need for the growth of expertise and fields of visibility. This was observable in 1990, when the IPCC complained about the lack of information to make sound policies and the lack of knowledge about individual behaviours (IPCC WG III 1990: xxxiv and xxx).

The problem of how to govern in a frugal way, and preferably through self-regulation in order to avoid resistance, was initially solved by a growing apparatus for acquiring knowledge about those who were to be governed (Foucault [1977–78] 2007). With assessments of climate change information is sought about how the climate is coupled to the human in various regions. This includes a wish for the extended intake of information about possible future development paths via the co-production of knowledge. Consequently, uncertainty justifies a prolongation of interest in climate change and its solution, sustainable development. Requests for more knowledge are dispersed and broadened with the aid of claims of uncertainty.

For anthropogenic climate change, this opens up for more detailed assessments and the inclusion of developing countries, as exemplified in 2001 and 2007 (e.g. see IPCC WG II 2001: 17; IPCC WG III 2001: 13; 2007: 22). Not only do we see a will to link the global with the local (Slocum 2004), but also an opening up of new fields of visibility and more knowledge production about those who are to be governed. This is specifically noticeable for people living in the developing countries, who are now increasingly confronted with sustainable development as a way of addressing climate change. A professionalisation of sustainable development thus goes hand in hand with the wish to transform the underdeveloped into sustainably developed.

Furthermore, the emphasis on the lack of certainty between scientific assessments and socio-economic consequences legitimises invitations to cross-disciplinary collaboration. Requests for more knowledge not only target a geographical expansion, but also an intellectual one. Tellingly, we have recently seen new efforts of 'Environmental Humanities' that specifically address climate change (cf. KTH 2013) and sustainability (ISSC 2013). Hence, uncertainty also seems to enlarge the intellectual space for climate change and its sought solution, sustainable development.

Merging science and consensus

The policy reports draw on scientific assessments of climate change as a physical phenomenon. This implies that there is a requirement to follow a somewhat objective knowledge production; one that grounds truth in an external world that is free from bias and desire. This objectivity ideal, free from individual standpoints, is well known in the scientific community, but has been criticised from the point of view of the social sciences. Knowledge production is from this perspective conceived as a social phenomenon. These differences between the disciplines is also problematised by the IPCC itself (e.g. see IPCC WG II 2007: 23). However, in the case of the IPCC, a tension between the ideal of objectivity and the practice of consensus arises. In a discussion of uncertainties, the Panel seeks to balance its objective knowledge claims and its outspoken subjective processes of collective agreements (e.g. see IPCC WG II 1995: x; IPCC WG II 2007: 23).

We assume that the negotiation of the version of reality presented by the IPCC has been ongoing throughout the extensive review process, as depicted in Figure 4.1. The negotiation of what climate change can be said to be is also directly visible in the reports, specifically through the open discussion of uncertainty and the various confidence levels presented as linked to agreements between experts. Negotiations are thus driven by an open acknowledgement of the uncertainty of scientific results, uncertainty about the impacts of climate change, and uncertainty about the effects of solutions to these impacts. Here, the discussion about uncertainty functions as a disclaimer for presentations of objective knowledge and, in general, the reports seek to establish the results of the IPCC as a scientific accomplishment.

The negotiations on uncertainties in the reports create a specific subject position, in that they openly outline that the limits of scientific knowledge and the limits of qualitative conclusions create a more credible scientifically-based authority. When the IPCC talks about its own fact construction as subjective, the organisation is transformed into a more transparent author subject. In addition, the reports openly mould a systematic approach to reaching consensus about uncertainties. The collective author subject seeks transparency and consensus at the same time as it subscribes to the mission of making conclusions reproducible by an external party. Hence, a new form of objectivity by consensus is pursued through the outspoken problem of individual standpoints and disagreements between the members – that have now been systematically processed into, for example, 'confidence levels'. The IPCC reports also invest in confidence by describing its wish to fine-tune the scientific ways in which the calculations are made and the consequences drawn. The objective knowledge claims are thus repeated in links to systematic scientific methods and procedures. The full circle is thus drawn, from objective truth claims to subjectivity handled by consensus and back to a wish to refine scientific methods that can advance science itself and the specific knowledge of climate change. It is also recognised that the scientific methods with which to investigate the changing climate are changing too – and a final truth is not proposed to be possible to reach. This is related to sustainable development in one crucial way – the possibility of outlining more correct assumptions about possible future development paths (e.g. as in IPCC WG III 2007).

Prepare for surprise and complexity

The form that uncertainty takes also shifts over the years. From being related to the basic assumptions and calculations, uncertainties are increasingly positioned as belonging to the future. According to the IPCC, uncertainty is in many ways constructed as inherent in the future. This includes 'surprises' (IPCC WG II 1990: 2), 'hardship and death' (e.g. see IPCC WG II 2001: 3), as well as possibilities of irreversibility (IPCC WG III 2001: 3). In short, the IPCC consequently narrates certainty about future uncertainties that are grave and disastrous for us.

Uncertainty is in this form rather about the future itself than the human practices of objective knowledge production. One of the present effects of positioning uncertainty in the future is that it brings an unassailable form of uncertainty. In the socio-economic summaries, this does not open up for more scientific work on the causal relation between human behaviour and climate change disasters. Rather, the IPCC paves the way for more social scientific work and precautionary measures. As others have shown, assumptions about vulnerability and human conduct are instead directly targeted (Evans and Reid 2013). The unassailable uncertain future opens up for preparations in the form of adaptation and resilience (e.g. see IPCC WG II 1995: 4). As in its broader reforms of sustainable development, the IPCC's discussion of unforeseeable and present complexities prioritises adaptation and resilience (Reid 2012).

Whereas the previous analytical theme partly treated uncertainty as something that could be worked on scientifically, the uncertain future is directly embraced by sustainable development. Sustainable development is a solution that seeks to include thoughts about the future life and its generations. This form of uncertainty with the future thus supports sustainable development as a political agenda that simply accepts the future as non-determinable. Nevertheless, the IPCC's inclusion of science as a way of moulding as exact sustainable paths as possible, merged with sustainable development as a more general political idea of embracing the future as uncertain, creates a prosperous link between the 'objective' scientific sphere and governing. This is also how a professionalisation of sustainable development is extended into a broader 'ethical programme for change' (Dean 2007: 63).

Reflection and confession

Throughout the reports, the uncertainties are highlighted as giving rise to difficult policy decisions. Complexities are increasingly referred to, and economic aspects intertwined in a polarisation between winners and losers (IPCC WG III 2001: 11). Hence, much is openly discussed as being at stake when providing guidance for policy-makers and others. The systematics for consensus is extended into a confessional practice, as the IPCC problematises how it has reasoned in its representations of uncertainty. As the years go by, it also provides more detailed accounts of how to correctly communicate uncertainty (IPCC WG II 2007: 21–23). It explicitly attempts to make its communication strategy on uncertainty as transparent as possible. This can be seen as a way of meeting both political and scientific criticism.

In effect, the Panel constitutes itself as developing greater self-reflection on what is involved in the knowledge process it is contributing to, from the production of objective knowledge to the communication of general uncertainties. Uncertainty, thus, opens up for moulding a scientifically and politically proper way in which to communicate. Constructions of uncertainty function as a technology for shaping and guiding the author 'self' in relation to others. In a direct way, the individual contributors are also addressed by how they are told to talk about and communicate uncertainty. Hence, the Panel seeks to outspokenly direct the conduct of the members. It also seeks to constitute a more trustworthy bond to those policy-makers who are to make decisions under uncertainty. They too are to reflect upon the difficulties ahead. Prudent risk management is not only openly asked for (IPCC WG III 2001: 12), but presented as a necessary confession to make to the reader.

In comparison to broader efforts to create a 'sustainable' world, this resembles how those who promote sustainable development have called for more self-reflection from the 'Western' camp (see Skoglund and Jensen 2013). Uttering uncertainty as a self-technology for confession among academics, policy-makers and politicians seek to establish an ethical approach to the delivery of solutions to climate change. Adhering to decision-making under uncertainty spurs quests for reflection about policy-making as an insecure practice. Responsibility can thus be dispersed, whereby sustainable development is spread to groups formerly not known or recognised as 'professional' enough to deal with it.

Conclusion

Informed by post-Foucauldian perspectives, this chapter has presented an analysis of how the IPCC constructs uncertainty in its knowledge production on climate change and its solution, sustainable development. By deploying an anti-essentialistic perspective, we have offered an analysis of what a text accomplishes, instead of an analysis of the motives of the individual participants of the Panel. This approach emphasises how realities are produced, versions of the world are re-constructed and possible ways of speaking about oneself (or the IPCC) are established. This means that we have highlighted uncertainty as something ingrained in the policy discourse of the IPCC as a centre of re-presentation (cf. Rose 1999: 211), and not as being only in the hands of climate sceptics who wish to discredit the IPCC and its proposals for sustainable development.

This form of analysis affords insights into how uncertainty is continuously re-constructed by the IPCC and mobilises its efforts to refine its work practices. Uncertainty justifies further knowledge production, moulds a scientific-consensual author position, prepares for surprise and complexities, and enforces reflection on and confession about how difficult policy-making can be when complexity prevails. Consequently, through the governmentality literature, we have analysed uncertainty as opening up for new problem spaces, fields of visibility and a dissemination of expertise on both climate change and sustainable development. In addition, we have attempted to pin down how 'conducting the conduct of others' (Foucault [1982–83] 2011: 4) unfolds with uncertainty. Using the traditional take on governmentality, we could have emphasised a responsibilisation of the individual in terms of how uncertainty opens up for reflection about how individual's contribute to climate change and its uncertain impacts. However, we have instead chosen to emphasise how uncertainty opens up for various interrogative practices in a more general vulnerabilisation, with a request for more knowledge about those who are not yet sustainably developed, i.e. those who are not yet practising the correct form of adaptation and resilience.

We have complemented the established climate governmentality studies by exploring the varied descriptions of uncertainty in the reports, and how these variations contribute to the broader agenda of the sustainable development–resilience nexus. Concrete articulations of uncertainty not only reproduce the vulnerable subject of neoliberalism, but also open up for investigations of how a 'sustainable' world could be shaped in a frugal way by a collective scientific-consensus author subject who confesses and reflects on its complicated profession and possible refinement. Climate governmentality studies can thus teach us how statements about uncertainty are fundamental to contemporary ethical programmes for change that seek to manage populations and assess, protect and vitalise biospheric life processes.

References

Agrawal, A. (2005) *Environmentality: Technologies of Government and the Making of Subjects*. Durham, NC: Duke University Press.

Aylett, A. (2010) Participatory planning, justice, and climate change in Durban, South Africa. *Environment and Planning A*, 42(1): 99–115.

Brand, P. (2007) Green subjection: the politics of neoliberal urban environmental management. *International Journal of Urban and Regional Research*, 31(3): 616–632.

Bulkeley, H. and Stripple, J. (2013) Conclusion: towards a critical social science of climate change? In J. Stripple and H. Bulkeley (eds) *Governing the Climate, New Approaches to Rationality, Power and Politics*. New York: Cambridge University Press.

Darier, É. (ed.) (1999) *Discourses of the Environment*. Oxford: Blackwell Publishers.

Dean, M. (2007) *Governing Societies, Political Perspectives on Domestic and International Rule*. New York: Open University Press.

Dean, M. (2010) *Governmentality, Power and Rule in Modern Society*, 2nd edn. London: Sage.

Duffield, M. (2007) *Development, Security and Unending War, Governing the World of Peoples*. Cambridge: Polity Press.

Evans, B. and Reid, J. (2013) Dangerously exposed: the life and death of the resilient subject. *Resilience: International Policies, Practices and Discourses*, 1(2): 83–98.

Evans, B. and Reid, J. (2014) *Resilient Life, The Art of Living Dangerously*. Cambridge: Polity.

Foucault, M. ([1976–1997] 2004) *Society Must Be Defended*, trans. D. Macey. London: Penguin.

Foucault, M. ([1976] 2002a) *Sexualitetens historia – del 1 – Viljan att veta*. Södertälje: Axlins tryckeri.

Foucault, M. ([1976] 2002b) *Sexualitetens historia del 2 – Njutningarnas bruk*. Göteborg: Daedalos.

Foucault, M. ([1977–78] 2007) *Security, Territory, Population*, trans. G. Burchell. New York: Palgrave Macmillan.

Foucault, M. ([1978–79] 2010) *The Birth of Biopolitics*, trans. G. Burchell (Paperback ed.). Hampshire: Palgrave Macmillan.

Foucault, M. ([1982–83] 2011) *The Government of Self and Others, Lectures at the Collège de France, 1982–1983*, trans. G. Burchell. Hampshire: Palgrave Macmillan.

Gelbspan, R. (2005) Global warming and political power. *Organization and Environment*, 18(2): 186–192.

Grove, J. K. (2010) Insuring 'Our Common Future?' Dangerous climate change and the biopolitics of environmental security. *Geopolitics*, 15(3): 536–563.

Hoffman, J. A. (2011) Talking past each other? Cultural framing of skeptical and convinced logics in the climate change debate. *Organization and Environment*, 24(1): 3–33.

InterAcademy Council (2010) *Climate Change Assessments: Review of the Processes and Procedures of the IPCC*.

IPCC (2007) *Summary for Policymakers*. In *Climate change 2007: Impacts, Adaptation and Vulnerability. Contribution of Working Group II to the Fourth Assessment Report of the Intergovernmental Panel on Climate Change*, M. L. Parry, O. F. Canziani, J. P. Palutikof, P. J. van der Linden and C. E. Hanson, (eds). Cambridge: Cambridge University Press, 7–22.

IPCC (2013a) *IPCC Factsheet: How Does the IPCC Review Process Work?* Geneva: IPCC.

IPCC (2013b) Summary description of the IPCC writing and review process. Available at: www.ipcc.ch/organization/organization_procedures.shtml - .UpZBVyhno5A (accessed 27 November 2013).

IPCC WG II (1990) *Impacts Assessment, Summary for Policymakers, Working Group II*. Geneva; IPCC.

IPCC WG II (1995) *Impacts, Adaptations, and Mitigation – Contribution of Working Group II to the Second Assessment Report of the Intergovernmental Panel on Climate Change, Summary for Policymakers*. Cambridge: Cambridge University Press.

IPCC WG II (2001) *Impacts, Adaptation and Vulnerability, Working Group II, Summary for Policymakers*. Cambridge: IPCC.

IPCC WG II/WG III (2012) *IPCC Expert Meeting on Economic Analysis, Costing Methods, and Ethics. Meeting Report*. Lima.

IPCC WG III (1990) *Response Strategies, Summary for Policymakers, Working Group III*. Geneva: IPCC.

IPCC WG III (1995) *The IPCC Economic and Social Dimensions of Climate Change, Working Group III, Summary for Policymakers*. Cambridge: Cambridge University Press.

IPCC WG III (2001) *Mitigation, Working Group III, Summary for Policymakers*. Geneva: IPCC.

IPCC WG III (2007) *Summary for Policymakers*. In *Climate Change 2007: Mitigation. Contribution of Working Group to the Fourth Assessment Report of the Intergovernmental Panel on Climate Change*. B. Metz, O. R. Davidson, P. R. Bosch, R. Dave, L. A. Meyer (eds). Cambridge, UK.: Cambridge University Press and New York, USA.

ISSC (2013) *World Social Science Report 2013: Changing Global Environments*.

KTH, E. H. L. (2013) KTH Environmental Humanities Laboratory (EHL) is a new initiative at the Division of History of Science, Technology and Environment. Available at: https://http://www.kth.se/en/abe/om-skolan/organisation/inst/philhist/2.3231/ehl/ (accessed 9 December 2013).

Lentzos, F. and Rose, N. (2009) Governing insecurity: contingency planning, protection, resilience. *Economy and Society*, 38(2): 230–254.

Lövbrand, E. and Stripple, J. (2013) Part I: Governmentality, critical theory and climate change, bringing governmentality to the study of global climate governance. In J. Stripple and H. Bulkeley (eds) *Governing the Climate: New Approaches to Rationality, Power and Politics*. New York: Cambridge University Press.

Lövbrand, E. Stripple, J. and Wiman, B. (2009) Earth system governmentality: reflections on science in the Anthroposcene. *Global Environmental Change*, 19(1): 7–13.

Methmann, C. P. (2013) The sky is the limit: global warming as global governmentality. *European Journal of International Relations*, 19(1): 69–91.

Oels, A. (2005) Rendering climate change governable: from biopower to advanced liberal government? *Journal of Environmental Policy and Planning*, 7(3): 185–207.

Oels, A. (2013) Rendering climate change governable by risk: from probability to contingency. *Geoforum*, 45, 17–29.

Paterson, M. and Stripple, J. (2010) My Space: governing individuals' carbon emissions. *Environment and Planning D: Society and Space*, 28(2): 341–362.

Paterson, M. and Stripple, J. (2012) Virtuous carbon. *Environmental Politics*, 21(4): 563–582.

Peake, S. (2005) Epistemologies of climate change. *Organization and Environment*, 18(4): 495–499.

Reid, J. (2011) The vulnerable subject of liberal war. *South Atlantic Quarterly*, 110(3): 770–779.

Reid, J. (2012) The disastrous and politically debased subject of resilience. *Development Dialogue: The End of the Security-Development Nexus? The Rise of Global Disaster Management*, 58: 67–80.

Reid, J. (2013) Interrogating the neoliberal biopolitics of the sustainable development-resilience nexus. *International Political Sociology*, 7(4): 353–367.

Rose, N. (1996) Governing 'Advanced' liberal democracies. In A. Barry, T. Osborne and N. Rose (eds) *Foucault and Political Reason*. London: UCL Press Limited.

Rose, N. (1999) *Powers of Freedom: Reframing Political Thought*. Cambridge: Cambridge University Press.

Rose, N. (2007) *The Politics of Life Itself. Biomedicine, Power and Subjectivity in the Twenty-First Century*. Princeton, NJ: Princeton University Press.

Rutherford, S. (2007) Green governmentality: insights and opportunities in the study of nature's rule. *Progress in Human Geography*, 31(3): 291–307.

Rutland, T. and Aylett, A. (2008) The work of policy: actor networks, governmentality, and local action on climate change in Portland, Oregon. *Environment and Planning D: Society and Space*, 26(4): 627–646.

Skoglund, A. and Börjesson, M. (2013) Mobilizing 'juvenocratic spaces' by the biopoliticization of children through sustainability. *Children's Geographies*. doi. org/10.1080/14733285.2013.824739.

Skoglund, A. and Jensen, T. (2013) The professionalization of ethics in the Intergovernmental Panel on Climate Change (IPCC). *Sustainable Development Journal*, 21(2): 122–130.

Slocum, R. (2004) Polar bears and energy-efficient lightbulbs: strategies to bring climate change home. *Environment and Planning D: Society and Space*, 22.

Stripple, J. (2012) The subject of security in a warming world. *Brown Journal of World Affairs*, 18(2): 181–194.

Stripple, J. and Bulkeley, H. (eds) (2013) *Governing the Climate, New Approaches to Rrationality, Power and Politics*. New York: Cambridge University Press.

Stripple, J. and Bulkeley, H. (2013) Introduction: on governmentality and climate change. In J. Stripple and H. Bulkeley (eds) *Governing the Climate, New Approaches to Rationality, Power and Politics*. New York: Cambridge University Press.

Yusoff, K. (2010) Biopolitical economies and the political aesthetics of climate change. *Theory, Culture and Society*, 27(2–3): 73–99.

5

POPULATION HEALTH

A fundamental marker of sustainable development

Anthony J. McMichael

Introduction

The profile of human population health has greater significance in relation to sustainability than that of a mere 'collateral' consequence, an epiphenomenon, of daily living conditions and its available personal choices. Rather, trends in the biological health, disease and death rates in a population, measured over decadal or inter-generational time, provide a critical outcome-marker of whether the aggregated demand pressure due to population size, social-cultural practices, prevailing energy generation and other technologies, economic intensity and consequent environmental disruption is sustainable.

Environmental damage and depletion and social inequity all erode the prospects for health. Indeed, the basic foundation of population health and survival resides in the natural world: access to food, water and energy, constraints on infectious agents, and physical buffering against natural disasters. Human health, monitored and understood *ecologically* at this population or 'herd' level, provides an integrated outcome measure of the extent to which human societies are managing to live within the sustainable limits of the environment at regional and, ultimately, global levels.

In a disrupted, depleted and less productive environment, nature's life-supporting processes will falter and fail, later if not sooner – and cause the health of human populations and countless other species to decline over time (McMichael 1993). If the escalating human demands on the natural environment create a degraded world that diminishes the average levels of health, physical functioning and longevity in humans populations, future historians will deduce that today's generations did not understand that the eco-physical systems of the natural world are the true foundation of biological health. They will wonder: 'What was the point of all that expansive ideologically-enshrined wealth creation, environmental commandeering and relentless technological advance?'

Some will argue that, from society's perspective, after ten millennia of predominantly agrarian living with its privations, poverty, crises and shorter life-spans, the point of contemporary economic expansion and material consumption has been to achieve physical security, food sufficiency, comfortable living, better health care, diversity of opportunity and, in the poorer countries, a chance yet to achieve living standards comparable to today's developed world. That is at the core of the orthodox account of 'progress'.

However, many other commentators focus on the historical, political and cultural drivers of the evolution of today's prevailing model of societal development, including the kick-starting stimulus of industrialization, the rise of market capitalism, the emergence of consumerism, the escalation of wealth differentials within and between populations, the deep-rooted belief in continuing economic growth, and whether feedback influences from the environmental and social consequences of this intensified economic activity are now occurring. Those commentaries thus highlight humanity's increasingly excessive demands on the wider environment, and how they relate to increases in population size, fossil energy use, economic and corporate globalization, the spread and growth of a middle-class consumer culture, and escalating rates of resource extraction and waste generation. This recent 'great acceleration' in humankind's environmental impacts accounts for the mounting evidence that the global population is now operating beyond the sustainable limits of the Earth system (Hibbard et al. 2007; Rockström et al. 2009).

The global ecological footprint of humankind is now an estimated 1.5 times the size of Earth's biocapacity – its capacity to supply, replenish, recycle, restore and absorb (Wackernagel et al. 2002; Ewing et al. 2010). The cross-over into global ecological debt occurred around 1980 (see also Figure 5.3) and the gap between demand and supply has widened steadily since then. The 'ecological footprint' estimates the total amount of Earth's productive surface needed to supply a particular population with materials (food, water, fibres, timber, etc.) and to absorb its effluent, although it does not include depletion of some non-renewable forms of natural capital (McMichael and Butler 2011). This composite index, along with other systemic large-scale environmental indicators, makes clear that the world community is on an environmentally unsustainable path; one that will increasingly erode the foundations of health, vitality and longevity of human populations.

As we shall see later in this chapter, various of the contemporary disruptions in Earth's environmental systems such as human-induced climate change, aquifer depletion, soil degradation and biodiversity losses – all historically unprecedented in scale and rate – are already impairing health in many regions. These adverse health impacts occur unevenly around the world because of differences in the local manifestations of environment-ecological disruption, in local topography, and in levels of wealth, infrastructural robustness, governance, expertise and the pre-existing profile of health and disability. Early impacts of recent climate change have impinged predominantly on poor and vulnerable populations. However, the recent experience of super-hurricanes in the USA, floods in Europe, and extreme heatwaves and bushfires in Australia underscore the fact that the power and reach of disrupted nature are no respecter of persons, rich or poor, urban or rural.

Socio-economic development, viewed as gains in food and water security, physical security, settled living and basic physical comforts, may, if maintained in a dynamic near-steady state and with modest population growth, may be environmentally sustainable – but, paradoxically, still detrimental to population health. History offers several examples, mostly from earlier and technologically simpler societies where technological and demographic change was slow. The early agrarians of the Fertile Crescent 10–11 millennia ago were typically under-nourished, deprived of a range of micronutrients in their new and more limited diet. Their attained adult height was around 12 centimetres less than their immediate regional hunter-gatherer forebears, and their skeletal remains attest to delayed growth of long bones, weakened bony architecture, dental deformities and other signs of nutritional deprivation (Diamond 1987; Shermer 2001).

Conversely, assessed within an immediate time-frame, social-economic development can be good for health but environmentally and socially unsustainable. The so-called 'environmental paradox' refers to evidence that wide-ranging degradation and disruption of the natural environment do not endanger human health (Raudsepp-Hearne et al. 2010). The key evidence invoked is that health and longevity have improved *despite* the environmental pollution, damage and disruption over the past few decades. But this logic misses the key point that exceeding environmental limits and the natural world's fundamental life-support capacity has longer-term consequences for population health. Human-induced climate change illustrates that issue. Significant human alterations to the composition of the world's atmosphere and climate system began to escalate during the twentieth century, and particularly since the mid-1970s, but only now are we beginning to see various adverse human health consequences at least partly attributable to that change in the world's climate – namely, the widely evident increases in heat-related deaths, spread of various infectious diseases, influences on some regional food yields, displacement of vulnerable coastal and island populations, and, of course, the mounting toll from a generalized upturn in the frequency and severity of extreme weather events, an integral component of a warming climate (Coumou et al. 2013).

In 1990, Maurice King, a pioneer of surgery and maternal and child health in Eastern Africa, published a paper entitled, 'Health is a Sustainable State' (King 1990). His argument was that, while plaudits abounded for various new medical interventions to prevent serious illness and death in infants and children in poor countries blighted by persistent poverty, overcrowding and poor hygiene, there was no serious attempt to constrain population growth. That growth would now be further boosted by child survival. As child health improved, he argued, the seeds of a future demographic crisis were being sown in which human numbers would exceed the local environment's carrying capacity, particularly food production and water supplies. Hence his conclusion that, in basic health and survival terms, this was not a sustainable strategy.

King's argument, in essence, is that short-term gains in population health can be achieved without taking care to ensure a sustainable future configuration of population size and environmental vitality able to sustain good population health.

Figure 5.1 captures King's concept of 'demographic entrapment' within a larger historical frame. In the past two centuries much of the gain in world population size has resulted from the direct or indirect benefits of health-related interventions and technologies. During this time there has been no substantive coordinated international effort to constrain population growth. Powerful forces and beliefs, sometimes allied with defiant national pride, have precluded such policy. And so, while the imperative of achieving a sustainable way of living within environmental limits assumes increasing urgency, we remain on track for a likely global population of around 9.6 billion people by 2050 (UN Department of Economic and Social Affairs 2013). The *sustainability* dimension of the environment's capacity to continue providing essential supports for ongoing good health in populations now looms increasingly large and problematically in the equation.

This chapter begins with a review of how environmental biophysical and ecological systems and processes bear on the health of human communities and populations. The dual role of population health will be explored as a marker (albeit with built-in delay) of environmental trends, and as a resource for social and economic development and the achievement of a sustainable way of living. Population health should be understood and incorporated as a central consideration in the ongoing sustainability discourse and not viewed as mere collateral gain or loss. From an anthropocentric perspective population health is the ultimate criterion of whether humankind in the evolving post-industrial era has attained globally an environmentally sustainable way of living (McMichael 2009). The case for integrating consideration of human population health within multi-sectoral 'sustainability' policies and their evaluation will therefore be assessed. Historical examples will be included where they enrich the text and argument.

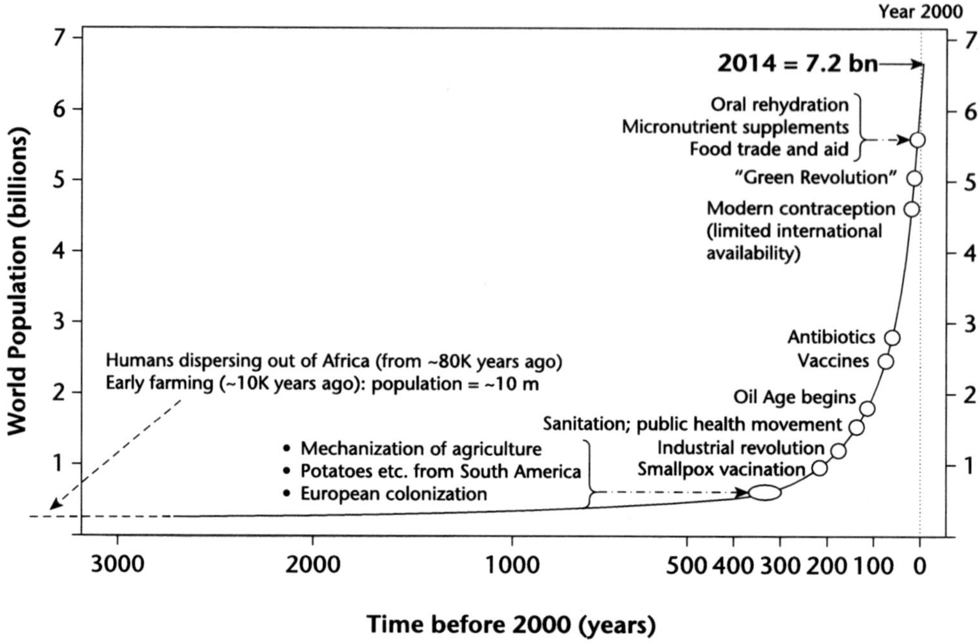

Figure 5.1 Growth in world population over past 2000 years. Much of the recent surge in numbers since around 1800 CE has resulted from the direct or indirect benefits of health-related interventions and technologies. The resultant increase in population pressure on the natural environment is now a major factor in the disruption of Earth's life-supporting systems.

Before exploring this topic in detail, however, the key words *health* and *population health* must be defined. Their scope, conceptualization and scale are widely misunderstood.

Health *and* population health *defined*

The concept of 'health' assumes different scope, form and meaning in different cultures. The word is often applied to collectivities, aggregations, of living organisms: farmers refer to the health of their herd, vignerons delight in a disease-free vineyard, and ecologists assess the health of ecosystems such as coral reefs and wetlands. The equivalent, for the human species, is the health of a community or a population. That is, population health is not about the occurrence of individual cases of illness and disease and the health care system's response to them; it is about understanding and responding to changes in rates of illness and disease and their distribution within the population. This is an *ecological* perspective.

Within the sustainability discourse, the population health perspective is the key health-related concept: environmental sustainability would enable the health of the whole population to be maintained at a positive level and in a well-shared fashion. But that conditional word 'enable' is a reminder that, in a future environmentally and socially sustainable world, other unrelated factors may encroach on the population's health, such as a tsunami, the evolution of a new and virulent infectious agent, or conflict based on religious or ethnic hatred.

Unhelpfully, and particularly in modern Western cultures, the prevailing mental model of health and its determinants is narrow and individual-focused. This is hardly surprising, since personal health is a central concern and an influence on daily living options. But this

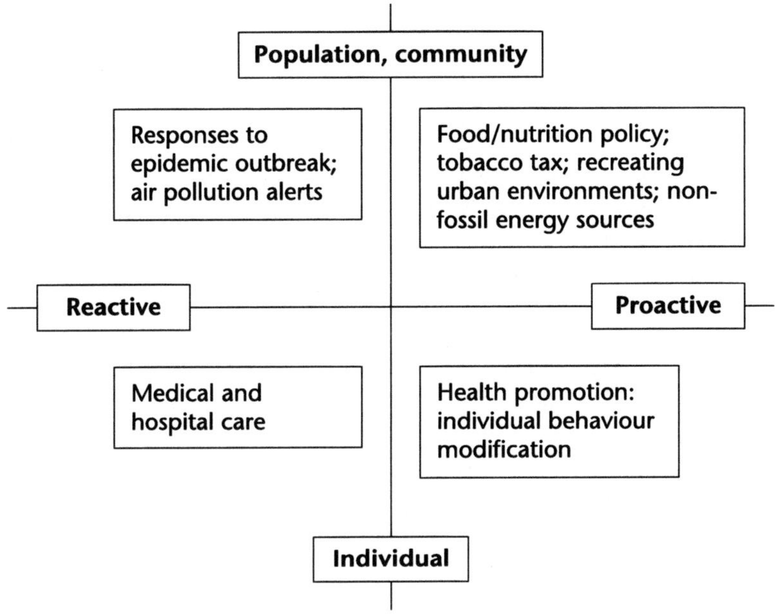

Figure 5.2 Dimensions of 'health', in relation to two orthogonal criteria, temporal and scalar. Much of the focus of developed society is in the individual-oriented repair-and-restore quadrant at bottom left. The need for policy integration and forward-planning within a *human ecology* frame is the focus of the top-right quadrant.

individualist view also reflects the powerful recent influence of neoliberalism and its assumption that individuals are free agents, responsible for their own actions and consumer choices; they are thus the arbiters of their own health. That individualist framing of the causes, prevention and treatment of illness and disease is shown in the lower half of Figure 5.2.

A detrimental consequence of this restricted and belittling view of 'health' is a reduced awareness within the community that the population's way of living, its economic system, and the conditions of the ambient environment exert powerful influence on the overall pattern and rates of disease. All boats rise or fall together (though often unevenly) as tides flow or ebb. That awareness requires understanding the significance of *population-level* relationships between the prevailing environmental circumstances (animate and inanimate), local culture, and how the interplay between those domains influences patterns of behaviour, consumption and social interactions within the population.

Current concerns over human-driven climate change provide an example. Climatic conditions and variable weather patterns belong to the category of environmental conditions (exposures) that impinge on whole communities, whole populations. If, for example, adverse climatic conditions impair food harvest in a local subsistence-based population, then a generalized food shortage is likely to occur, and many will suffer – especially those with little money or power. If warmer and wetter conditions foster mosquito proliferation, then the regional risks of malaria and dengue may increase, as might the geographic range of their transmission.

In reality, of course, patterns of health and disease are influenced by combinations of factors operating at different scales of space and time, ranging from conditions affecting the whole population to those impinging directly on the individual and his/her psychological, metabolic, molecular and genetic characteristics. To understand the pervasive and long-term risks from climate change and other unsustainable systemic environmental changes requires that we shift our primary focus from the individual and family level to the population level.

Influences of the environment's biophysical and ecological systems on health

During the third quarter of the twentieth century the predominant concern over environmental health hazards focused on exposures to specific, usually localized, toxic chemicals, ionizing radiation, and infectious microbes in food and water. Often these were controllable via effective local intervention. However, in *Silent Spring*, Rachel Carson had drawn attention in the early 1960s to a more insidious environmental risk to biological organisms and their health, including humans feeding high in the food chain (Carson 1962). Her stimulus was evidence that DDT and other persistent chlorinated organic pesticides and industrial chemicals were entering ecosystems and undergoing bioaccumulation up the food chain. This was an early forewarning of the greater modern risks to vitality, health and survival posed by systemic disruptions to the Earth system.

Many of the environmental conditions and exposures resulting from these systemic disruptions will tend to exacerbate pre-existing states of poor health. For example, flooding will amplify diarrhoeal diseases, heatwaves will cause heart attacks in those with underlying disease, and crop failures will cause death in already chronically under-nourished children. And so it is relevant to review briefly the current global health profile.

Recent results from the comprehensive Global Burden of Disease 2010 project provide a stock-take of the current health profile of the world and its major regions. The data show that as nations undergo economic development, as globalized influences on production, marketing and consumption increase, and as infectious diseases are increasingly constrained by gains in hygiene, surveillance, vaccination, treatment and (at least for the moment) antimicrobials, the global disease burden is shifting from communicable to non-communicable diseases (Murray et al. 2013). This health transition is also shown in Figure 5.3. These rising non-communicable (or 'chronic') diseases include heart and blood vessel diseases, respiratory diseases (including lung cancer from the international spread of cigarette marketing), type 2 diabetes and mental health disorders. Meanwhile, gains in life expectancy have been widespread, although as premature death rates decline there has been an ongoing increase in the number of years lived with disabling conditions. In Sub-Saharan Africa, however, many communicable, maternal, neonatal, and nutritional disorders remain the dominant causes of disease burden.

Of the many risk factors for disease assessed by this project, the leading global cause of health deficit in 2010 was high blood pressure (7 per cent of the global disease burden), followed closely by tobacco and alcohol. Of the seven specific *environmental* hazards assessed, the largest adverse impacts on health were from indoor household air pollution (4.5 per cent of the burden), ambient environmental particulate air pollution (3.1 per cent), followed by unimproved sanitation and exposure to environmental lead (Lim et al. 2012). Those seven itemized hazards, however, represent a very narrow and incomplete approach to encapsulating, understanding and estimating environmental influences on human health.

Indeed, that disaggregated and selective methodology also helps explain the marginalization of these great emerging threats to population health in the formulation of the UN's Millennium Development Goals for 2001–2015. These goals sought to reduce disparities in poverty, hunger, malnutrition, maternal mortality, diarrhoeal diseases, malaria, HIV/AIDS, tuberculosis, and unsafe drinking water. Yet the many pervasive environmental impacts and health consequences of climate change will almost certainly impede achieving such goals and will increase health disparities. Similarly, the seminal 'Brundtland Report' of the World Commission on Environment

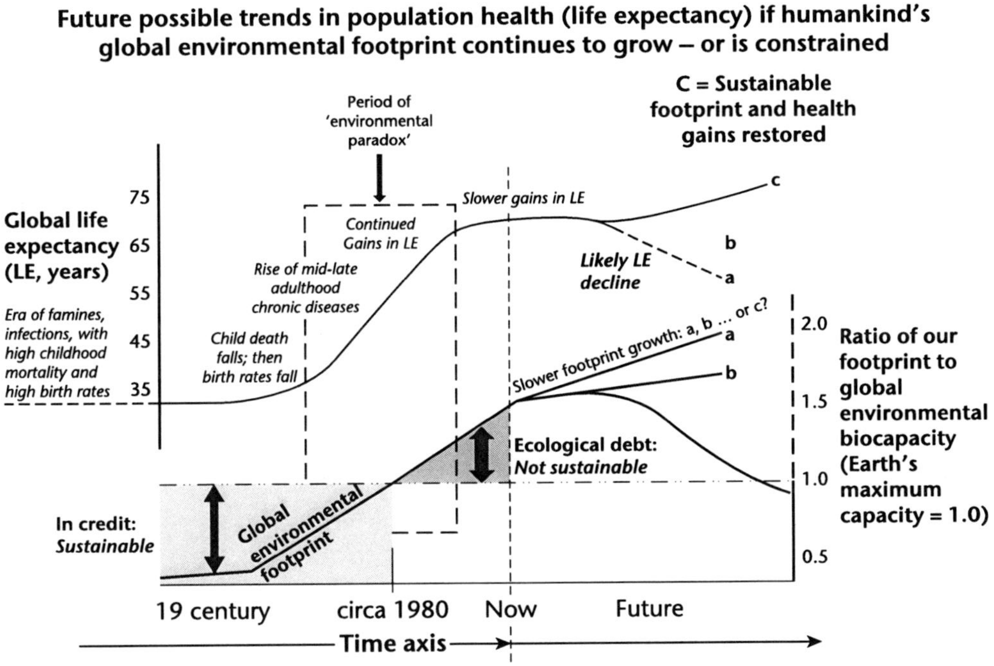

Figure 5.3 Schematic diagram of future possible trends in population health (life expectancy) if humankind's global environmental footprint continues to grow – or is constrained.
Pathway c leads to the sustainable ideal. (The dashed empty rectangle indicates where the misleading idea of the 'environmental paradox' arises.) The collective challenge to the world's human societies is to agree on and then implement an action plan that would redirect our future onto the paths marked 'c' – a rapid shrinking of the footprint and resumption of the gains in good and equitably shared health.

Source: Adapted/extended from: McMichael and Butler (2011).

and Development (World Commission on Environment and Development 1987) also provided an incomplete blueprint for governments, with little explicit attention to the human face of the problems being addressed. The Commission's preoccupation was with the politically sensitive issue of seeking strategies to balance the needs of current economic development with the long-term protection of the natural environment's many assets and 'services'. The text had little to say about the role, levels and significance of human well-being and health within this frame.

Meanwhile, the age-old scourges of population health persist in many countries. People in many low-income countries, and especially those in congested slum-dwelling populations, will be at particular risk from environmental and climatic disruptions. Bangladesh is particularly vulnerable to climate change because of widespread poverty and food insecurity, high rates of tropical infectious diseases, a very large coastal population exposed to cyclones and storm surges, and threats to river water flows from the melting of most of the Himalayan glaciers and the likely future upstream damming of rivers by water-short China and India.

Systemic environmental disruptions and human health

During any one of its geologically stable eras, Earth functions as an integrated biophysical system that moderates the climate, ocean chemistry, the circulation of major elements such as nitrogen and phosphorus, water evaporation and circulation, the generation of fertile soils and other life-supporting processes. In human-utility terms, ecosystems provide many essential 'goods and services', including foods, the recycling of nutrients and the cleansing of surface water. Biological diversity underpins many of those ecological processes. Many of the existing solutions in nature, such as the penicillin secreted defensively by moulds, can be applied to the advance of medicine and agriculture – and, perhaps, to helping resolve the macroscopic environmental challenges that we now face.

Today's human-induced disruptions to large-scale, often global, environmental systems are the consequence of the unprecedented aggregate human pressures on the natural world. Those disruptions comprise a syndrome, of which climate change is the best-known. That syndrome signals that the human species has now substantially transgressed the limits of Earth's biocapacity and is operating in an unsustainable and increasingly dangerous mode (Rockstrom et al. 2009). Two of the most seriously disrupted aspects of the Earth system are biodiversity losses and human-induced climate change.

Biodiversity and human health

The 'Great Dying' extinction 250 million years ago at the junction of the Permian and Triassic periods extinguished an estimated 90–95 per cent of (mostly marine) species. A major triggering cause is likely to have been a massive lava flow and carbon dioxide emissions in the Siberian region that heated the planet by an estimated 6°C. Whereas this overall process took around 80,000 years, the rate of biodiversity loss in today's world appears to be much faster, and is many hundred times more rapid than the natural background extinction rate. Many species and regional populations have already been lost because of modern human pressures. Around one-seventh of the world's remaining mammal species and one-tenth of bird species are currently classified as threatened with extinction.

The ramifications for human health and survival are many and potentially great (Chivian and Bernstein 2009) – though much more difficult to specify and estimate than are the health consequences of changes to the composition of the stratosphere and troposphere. Biodiversity supports and nurtures human health via six main paths:

- Much of the world's food yield depends on pollinators: bees, other insects, birds, bats and small mammals. Mostly beyond the urbanized field of vision, some of these pollinator species are in decline for reasons not yet well understood.
- Many species of plants and animals are sources of useful, even precious, chemical substances: medicinal compounds, agricultural chemicals, laboratory adjuvants for molecular biological research, and others. Around half of all new drugs approved by the US Food and Drug Administration in the past 2–3 decades have come from nature. Taxol, a mainstay chemotherapy drug that kills cancer cells, comes from the bark of the Pacific Yew tree – once considered commercially useless 'trash' by loggers. Sharks, now seriously over-fished, have powerful infection- and cancer-fighting molecules such as squalamine.
- There are, for the moment, still countless as yet undiscovered substances 'out there' in nature.
- Many species and ecosystems are important in the cleansing of water and air. For example, the filter-feeding oysters in Chesapeake Bay, eastern USA, have long kept the bay's water relatively free of toxins – but their numbers have declined severely since the 1950s (*The Economist*, Editorial, 2008).

- Other species naturally constrain infectious disease agents and (where applicable) their vector organisms. Birds and frogs eat mosquitoes, and fish eat mosquito larvae.
- Access to wilderness and contact with a diversity of plants and animals provides fascination, exhilaration and peace of mind. The aesthetic and spiritual dimensions of the natural world are of great importance to individuals and to most cultures. The Australian Aboriginals have a 'dreamtime' account of Creation, describing the origins of humans alongside their totemic ancestral animals, and the resultant connectivity of each tribal group to the descendants of a specific ancestral animal species.

On the long view, protecting biodiversity is not just a prerequisite to sustaining population health around the world but is also very cost-effective. The economic benefits from saving bio-ecological functions such as pollination, medicinal substances, fertile soils, clean air and water are 10–100 times greater than the cost of saving the habitats and species that provide these supportive functions. But, despite solemn international agreement, few governments have taken definitive policy-based action to protect their country's fauna and flora.

Climate change, health impacts and sustainability

As with biodiversity losses and health, climate change is a complex and dynamic process with many manifestations. It therefore impinges on human biology, health and survival via diverse pathways, direct and indirect, immediate and deferred (McMichael 2013a). In many situations a change in climatic conditions acts as a risk multiplier, exacerbating a population's pre-existing health problems.

Despite the difficulties in attributing causal influence to a complex climate system that often acts via indirect paths, a persuasive body of evidence is emerging from various populations that recent changes in climate have affected some health outcomes (Smith et al. 2014). These include uptrends in numbers of deaths from heatwaves in various countries, warming-associated geographic shifts in some infectious diseases (or, where applicable, their vector organisms), and an increasingly apparent and widespread increase in weather-related disasters and their toll of deaths, injuries, consequent infections (especially diarrhoeal disease, cholera and respiratory infections), food shortages, and post-traumatic stress disorders. Historically, climate-related food shortages have been the most frequent scourge of population health, and they in turn have often predisposed to infectious disease outbreaks – as too have climatic conditions (McMichael 2012).

Humans, unlike other species, can harness their culture to buffer themselves against many types of external risks, using technologies, infrastructure and good governance. The initial generation of 'adaptive' strategies may entail changes to the built environment, water engineering, trade arrangements, food aid, crop substitution, and public education and alert programs. Wealthier, well-governed and less geographically vulnerable societies may thus notice little adversity from early climate change. This, unfortunately, encourages the delusion that incremental adaptation will suffice to muddle through this presumed merely inconvenient climatic hiccup. This, an easy cop-out strategy for national governments, is *not* part of meaningful sustainability; indeed, by deferring primary abatement action it makes the future attainment of genuine sustainable living even more difficult. It also compounds the ethical dilemma in a world where climate-vulnerable populations are suffering already while lacking the experience, resources and information-and-policy base with which to make optimal adaptation choices.

Besides, for how long could a sequence of incremental adaptive strategies suffice to hold the adverse impacts of climate change at bay? According to climate change science the world population is now quite likely to encounter an increase in average global surface temperature of around 4°C by the century's end (Stocker et al. 2013; Sherwood and Bony 2014). An average global temperature that high has not prevailed on Earth for at least the last 30 million years. It would change the face of the natural world, cause massive social disorder and displacement, and would very probably undermine social and political institutions. The consequences for human health would be dire, though difficult to foresee with clarity, since social, economic and political disruptions would also multiply (McMichael 2013b).

Climate, food yields, and sustainable agriculture

While much public and policy attention has been paid to how climate change might affect food export earnings, the balance of trade, and rural livelihoods, the ultimate manifestation of reduced food yields is impaired health – hunger, under-nutrition, child stunting, susceptibility to infection, impaired adult health, and premature death. Further, in a world of great disparities in wealth, climate-related falls in crop yields and surging food prices can have potentially disastrous effects on the poor. The 2011 world price spike, implicated in the uprisings in Egypt that propelled the Arab Spring, reflected in part the disastrous impact of mid-2010 heat and fires to the Russian wheat crop; Egypt has been the main importer of Russian wheat (Werz and Hoffman 2013).

Yields of crops and livestock are generally sensitive to climatic conditions, and can be impaired by quite small changes in temperatures during the growing season (Lobell and Field 2007). Between 1980 and 2008, potential gains in crop yields from technological and other advances appear to have been largely offset by rising temperatures in many cropping regions (Lobell et al. 2011). Yields of wheat, rice and corn from one-third of the main cropping regions in eastern Asia, Europe and North America appear to have peaked in recent times (Grassini et al. 2013). India's rice yields peaked a decade ago, and South Asia's 'green revolution' has tailed off. Downturns in yield are anticipated to spread to parts of Sub-Saharan Africa, southern Europe, the US Midwest, and southern Australia.

The consistent finding from modelling studies is that currently-projected climate change would have a net negative impact on future global yields. Viewed at regional level that finding is ethically and politically troubling. While some temperate mid-high latitude regions may benefit, many countries in the tropics and subtropics such as much of South Asia and the savannah zone of West Africa, where both warming and reduced rainfall are likely to occur, are likely to experience declining yields – so too are parts of southern Europe, southern US and southern Australia (IPCC 2014).

The adverse impacts of local food shortages on human nutrition and health, especially in young children, are potentially serious, affecting growth, stunting, immune function and survival (Lloyd et al. 2011). Nutritional deficits also have life-long consequences for non-communicable diseases in adulthood and overall bodily functioning. Climate change, of course, is not a lone actor. Trends in food yields this century are already a pivotal concern, as population numbers and environmental stressors press increasingly upon the agricultural and marine food-producing base – a base that will have to produce twice as much food as today to feed, sufficiently and equitably, a population that is about 30 per cent larger than today's and with more demanding food preferences.

Again, climate change will not act alone. Consider three other critical factors: First, soil: around one-third of the world's cropland is losing top soil faster than new soil can form naturally. This is one major cause of the decline in agricultural yields, despite heightened compensatory inputs, and now evident in a range of countries including Japan, South Korea, and a number of

European countries (Davidson and Andrews 2013). Immense dust bowls are forming, in the region of northwest China, western Mongolia and adjoining central Asia, and in central Africa. In northern China thousands of rural villages have been abandoned, their grasslands destroyed by overgrazing and farm-lands inundated by migrating sand dunes.

Second, meat production: Humans come from a long line of meat-eaters, extending back more than two million years. Our anatomy has evolved accordingly. What was once a scavenged luxury, and later a hunted commodity that enabled occasional feasts, has now become the centre-piece of modern middle-class dining. Red meat consumption is escalating in many developing countries, especially China, South Korea, Taiwan and Brazil as three billion people move up the food chain, eating more grain-fed livestock and poultry products.

Domesticated livestock, reared at industrial scale, cause damage to soils, use vast volumes of water, contaminate surface waters with nitrogenous wastes, and displace native species. Globally, over half of all harvested bioactive nitrogen and phosphorus compounds is now consumed as feedstock (grains, corn, tubers) by livestock rather than directly by people. Further, livestock account for over half of agriculture's substantial climate footprint, particularly the digastric ruminant animals – cattle, sheep, goats, camels – that each belch up hundreds of litres of the potent greenhouse gas methane daily. Hence a reduction in average per-person red meat consumption in high- and middle-income populations would be good for the local environment, the global climate, the cardiovascular health of diners (Koeth et al. 2013), and the welfare of animals (McMichael et al. 2007).

Third, gender participation: Sustainable agricultural practice would also assign greater responsibility and opportunity to women in food production, especially in lower-income countries where the future may lie with well-managed small-hold farming. The Food and Agricultural Organization (FAO) estimates that according women the same status as men in agriculture would boost total agricultural output in developing countries by up to 4 per cent, a critical gain in under-nourished food insecure populations. Further, those food and income resources that are controlled by women are more likely to be applied to educating and feeding children (Walsh 1998). An ongoing five-year project collaborative project between aid agencies and the Tanzanian and Zambian governments is promoting women's roles in both poultry management and crop growth, thus reducing both poverty and food insecurity. Household poultry has a special significance for nutrition security since most families own poultry and chickens are often the only livestock looked after by women.

Migration and displacement

By around 2050, an estimated 200 million to one billion people may be displaced internally or across borders due to human-driven climate change and other population and environmental pressures (Kolmannskog 2009; Asian Development Bank 2012). Many other as yet unpredictable biophysical and social-cultural changes will also influence future displacement and migration. In the case of climate change, regional changes in precipitation and associated droughts and flooding, more frequent natural meteorological disasters like tropical cyclones and extreme forest fires, local crop failures, and severe water scarcity are all likely to cause people to abandon their homes. Coastal vulnerability puts many people at risk of displacement, particularly since over one-third of the human population now live within 100 kilometres of the coasts, many of them on low-lying coastal fringes and small islands. The combination of sea level rise, increasingly intense storms, and destruction of coastal barriers (mangroves, wetlands, vegetated dunes, and coral reefs) will increasingly threaten these exposed populations.

Displaced persons very often suffer adverse health outcomes (McMichael et al. 2012). Non-immune people migrating into an area in which a particular infectious disease, not previously encountered, is endemic are more susceptible to infection. Poor housing, sanitation, and access to safe drinking water combined with poor nutrition lead to disease epidemics, particularly diarrheal disease, measles, and acute respiratory infections. Displaced people also suffer from high rates of violence, sexual abuse, and – particularly in resettled refugee children and adolescents – mental health disorders (McCloskey and Southwick 1996).

Population health as a sustainability marker – and a resource

The rise of city living provides a good illustration of how changes in *rates* and the *distribution* of health disorders reflect shifts in human ecology and, in many cases, their unsustainable nature. Indices of population health can thus become critical 'sustainability markers'.

Patterns of modern urban living have radically altered human ecology, in the cities and in dependent relationships with the environmental hinterland (Seitzinger et al. 2012). Much of the rising tide of non-communicable diseases, particularly in urban populations, and spanning the income spectrum reflects the mismatch, the 'evodeviation', between evolutionarily-based human biological and psychological needs and environmental and social living conditions and associated cultural behaviours (Boyden 1987). Those conditions are determined substantially by historical momentum, mono-sectoral policy decisions, narrow economic priorities and the form of physical infrastructure, mostly blind to implications for human well-being and health. The epidemics of obesity and (consequent) type II diabetes, the globalization of antimicrobial resistance, and the pervasive spread of the car-and-roads culture and its associated trauma, air pollution and sedentary living all illustrate how technologically-driven and culturally-mediated changes in human ecology can affect health and well-being in globally inter-connected cities.

These historically novel, community-wide, blights on human health are largely intractable to conventional public health approaches. Despite recent health gains associated with urbanization and increased incomes, trends in various 'urban health penalties' are rising as middle-class consumerism flourishes, dietary preferences change, physical activity decreases, and community ethos dissolves. Health inequities and vulnerabilities persist between rich and poor, highlighted dramatically by the much higher death rates among the poor and socially disadvantaged and in Chicago during the extreme heatwave of 1995 (Semenza et al. 1996) and in New Orleans during Hurricane Katrina (Brunkard et al. 2008).

Viewed more generally, the level of human population health and life expectancy provide a fundamental measure, over intergenerational time, of whether a society has achieved an environmentally sustainable way of living. This relationship can be visualized in relation to the increase in a society's 'environmental footprint'; indeed, assessed approximately, this can be portrayed at global scale, as in Figure 5.3. Note that, after the initial flush of successful health gains associated with increasing exploitation of the environment, energy usage and material consumption (in the period of 'environmental paradox'), health gains slow, flatten and may then be eroded as environmental degradation and disruption becomes more widespread and severe. Human-driven climate change is a likely agent of such reversal.

If the underlying dependence of long-term population health on natural or sustainably managed environmental support systems were better understood by public and policy-maker, more effective restorative action would surely be taken – despite the impediments of human nature, vested interest and political inertia. To achieve this understanding, there is need to integrate learning, first, about the human species' place in nature and about its evolutionary origins in relation to climate, physical environment, food sources and infectious disease contacts into school education, and, second, about how our biology, psychology and health reflect closely the conditions of the environment in which we live.

The case for improving human health can also be framed, indeed reinforced, by the rationale that population health is a resource for enhancing vitality, creativity and engagement in the tasks of working for a sustainable future. Economists have consistently made this argument in relation to fortifying the process of economic and social development. Now it must be remade in relation to the pursuit of an environmentally sustainable future.

Ethical considerations

The reasons for stabilizing and, where necessary, repairing aspects of Earth's operating system and the integrity and vitality of the natural environment to a sustainable state are several (Gardiner 2011). Inevitably, self-interest is part of the mix. Environmental justice, too, is a central consideration able to invoke both ethical and political motivations (Butler and McMichael 2013). Consider, again, the prominent example of climate change. This poses threats to human well-being and health on two distinct time scales: first, the ongoing long-term changes in *average* climatic conditions due to human actions and, second, the consequent increase in climate *variability* and in extreme weather events. These entail very different time-frames and evoke different patterns of emotional, ethical and political response.

The former long-term category points to the obligation of the present generation, the majority of whom are the beneficiaries of an excessively large environmental footprint, to accept the up-front costs of slowing or arresting climate change and its environmental-change bed-fellows in order to lessen potentially catastrophic impacts on future generations of a system undone by unsustainable collective behaviours. That ethical concern is about basic intergenerational fairness, and should not become entangled with considerations of the economic efficiency of taking mitigation action at different future times and the attendant, presumptuous, choice of discount rates.

The second category, however, refers to the more immediate impacts of environmental disasters and weather extremes on existing populations and communities. Hence, decisions about how to respond relate primarily to the interests of present and immediate future generations. The ethical horizon in that case is much shorter.

Conclusion

Sustainability, as a word, is at risk of losing focus in a mist of promiscuous over-use and uncritical understanding of the concept. In the now high-priority recharting of a course to the future, understanding that the attainment of environmental and social sustainability has enormous consequences for human well-being, happiness, health and survival is essential. Historically the first-order task of societies, in principle, has been to harness within-population resources to feed, house and clothe people, to provide physical security, to generate wealth and to maintain social stability. For nearly all of human history that has been achieved, by variable means, without disrupting major components of the Earth system. Local soils and water supplies were often impaired, but ecological footprints did not threaten whole systems. Today, however, our collective footprint *does* threaten global and major regional environmental systems, and, in consequence, social stability and equity. That is not sustainable.

Assigning blame to particular societies or cultures for damage to Earth's natural systems is counter-productive. Time is lost, hostilities and resentments are exacerbated. One reading of the historical evidence reveals a *universal* human culpability for the now precarious conditions of the planet's fabric of life-support systems; a culpability that transcends culture, race, religion, nationality, ethnicity and gender (Crist 2012). On that reading the problem arises from the essentially universal *theology* of assumed continuing economic growth in a finite world and the accompanying assumption that solutions will, as ever, arise from human ingenuity.

In *The Price of Inequality* (2012), Joseph Stiglitz, erstwhile Chief Economist at the World Bank, argues that by paying attention to the common welfare, to everyone else's self-interest, we create the precondition for our own ultimate well-being. If we extend that proposition beyond the relations between humankind's rich and poor, advantaged and disadvantaged, present and future generations, to include the world's plant, animal and insect populations this would enhance the sustainability of all in the natural world that human populations depend on for their well-being, health and survival.

References

Asian Development Bank (2012) *Addressing Climate Change and Migration in Asia and the Pacific*. ADB, ISBN: 978-92-9092-610-8 (print) 978-92-9092-611-5 (web).

Boyden, S. (1987) *Western Civilization in Biological Perspective: Patterns in Biohistory*. Oxford: Oxford University Press, pp. 39–41.

Brunkard, J., Namulanda, G. and Ratard, R. (2008) Hurricane Katrina deaths, Louisiana, (2005) *Disaster Medicine and Preparedness* August 28, 2008: 1–9. Available at: http://new.dhh.louisiana.gov/assets/docs/katrina/deceasedreports/KatrinaDeaths_082008.pdf

Butler, C. D. and McMichael, A. J. (2013) Environmental health. In V. Sidel and B. Levy (eds) *Social Injustice and Public Health*. Oxford: Oxford University Press, pp. 318–338.

Carson, R. (1962) *Silent Spring*. Boston: Houghton Mifflin.

Chivian, E. and Bernstein, A. (eds) (2009) *Sustaining Life: How Human Health Depends on Biodiversity*. New York: Oxford University Press.

Coumou, D., Robinson, A. and Rahmstorf, S. (2013) Global increase in record-breaking monthly-mean temperatures. *Climatic Change* 118 (3–4): 771–782. DOI, 10.1007/s10584-012-0668-1.

Crist, E (2012) Abundant Earth and the population question. In P. Cafaro and E. Crist (eds) *Life on the Brink*. Atlanta, GA: University of Georgia Press.

Davidson, D. and Andrews, J. (2013) Not all about consumption. *Science* 339: 1286–87.

Diamond, J. (1987) The worst mistake in the history of the human race. *Discover Magazine*, May: 64–66.

The Economist (2008) Editorial, Oysters, Gem of the ocean. December 8, 2008, 13.

Ewing, B., Moore, D., Goldfinger, S. et al. (2010) *The Ecological Footprint Atlas 2010*. Oakland, CA: Global Footprint Network.

Gardiner, S. (2011) *A Perfect Moral Storm: The Ethical Tragedy of Climate Change*. Oxford: Oxford University Press.

Grassini, P., Eskridge, K. and Cassman, K. (2013) Distinguishing between yield advances and yield plateaus in historical crop production trends. *Nature Communications* 4, DOI: doi:10.1038/ncomms3918.

Hibbard, K. A., Crutzen, P., Lambin, E. et al. (2007) The great acceleration. In R. Costanza, J. Graumlich and W. Steffen (eds) *Sustainability or Collapse? An Integrated History and Future of People on Earth*. Dahlem Workshop Report 96, Cambridge, MA: MIT Press, pp. 417–446.

IPCC (Intergovernmental Panel on Climate Change) 2014 *Fifth Assessment Report (AR5)*.

King, M. H. (1990) Health is a sustainable state. *Lancet* 336: 664–667.

Koeth, R. A., Wang, Z., Levison, B. et al. (2013) Intestinal microbiota metabolism of l-camitine, a nutrient in red meat, promotes atherosclerosis. *Nature Medicine*, DOI, 10.1038/nm.3145.

Kolmannskog, V. (2009) Climate change, disaster, displacement and migration: initial evidence from Africa. Research Paper No. 180, United Nations High Commissioner for Refugees, Geneva.

Lim S., Vos, T., Flaxman, A. et al. (2012) A comparative risk assessment of burden of disease and injury attributable to 67 risk factors and risk factor clusters in 21 regions, 1990–2010, a systematic analysis for the Global Burden of Disease Study 2010. *Lancet*, 380: 2224–2260.

Lloyd S. J., Kovats, R. S. and Chalabi, Z. (2011) Climate change, crop yields and malnutrition: development of a model to quantify the impact of climate scenarios on child malnutrition. *Environmental Health Perspectives*, 119: 1817–1823.

Lobell, D. B. and Field CB (2007) Global scale climate-crop yield relationships and the impacts of recent warming. *Environment Research Letters*, 2 014002.

Lobell, D. B., Schlenker, W., Costa-Roberts, J. et al. (2011) Climate trends and global crop production since 1980. *Science*, 333 (6042): 616–620.

McCloskey, L. A. and Southwick, K. (1996) Psychosocial problems in refugee children exposed to war. *Pediatrics*, 97: 394–97.

McMichael, A. J. (1993) *Planetary Overload. Global Environmental Change and the Health of the Human Species*. Cambridge: Cambridge University Press.

McMichael, A. J. (2009) Human population health, sentinel criterion of environmental sustainability. *Current Opinions in Environmental Sustainability*, 1: 101–106.

McMichael A. J. (2012) Insights from past millennia into climatic impacts on human health and survival. *Proceedings of National Academy of Sciences USA*, 109: 4730–4737.

McMichael, A. J. (2013a) Globalization, climate change and health. *New England Journal of Medicine*, 368: 1335–1343.

McMichael, A. J. (2013b) Health impacts in Australia in a four degree world. In P. L. Christoff (ed.) *Four Degrees of Global Warming, Australia in a Hot World*. London: Routledge/Earthscan, pp. 155–171.

McMichael C. E., Barnett, J. and McMichael, A. J. (2012) An ill wind? Climate change, migration and health. *Environmental Health Perspectives* 120(5): 646–54.

McMichael, A. J., and Butler, C. D. (2011) Promoting global population health while constraining the environmental footprint. *Annual Review of Public Health* 32: 179–197.

McMichael, A. J., Powles, J. W., Butler, C. D. and Uauy, R. (2007) Food, livestock production, energy, climate change and health. *Lancet*, 370:1253–1263.

Murray C. J. L., Vos, T., Lozano, R. et al. (2013) Disability-adjusted life years (DALYs) for 291 diseases and injuries in 21 regions, 1990–2010, a systematic analysis for the Global Burden of Disease Study 2010. *Lancet* 380 (9859): 2197–2223.

Raudsepp-Hearne C., Peterson, G. D., Tengö, M. et al. (2010) Untangling the environmentalist's paradox. Why is human well-being increasing as ecosystem services degrade? *Bioscience*, 60(8): 576–589.

Rockström J., W. Steffen, W., Noone, K. et al. (2009) A safe operating space for humanity. *Nature*, 461: 472–475.

Seitzinger C., Svedin, U., Crumley, C. et al. (2012) Planetary stewardship in an urbanising world: beyond city limits. *Ambio* November 2012. DOI: 10.1007/s13280-012-0353-7.

Semenza, J. C., Rubin C. H., Falter, K. et al. (1996) Heat-related deaths during the July 1995 heat wave in Chicago. *New England Journal of Medicine*, 335(2): 84–90.

Shermer, M. (2001) *The Borderlands of Science*. Oxford: Oxford University Press.

Sherwood, S. C. and Bony, S. (2014) Spread in model climate sensitivity traced to atmospheric convective mixing. *Nature*, 505: 37–42.

Smith, K. R., Woodward, A., Campbell-Lendrum, D. et al. (2014) Chapter 11. Human health: impacts, adaptation and co-benefits. In C. B. Field, V. Barros, D. Dokken, et al. (eds.) *Climate Change 2014: Impacts, Adaptation, and Vulnerability*. Volume I: *Global and Sectoral Aspects. Contribution of Working Group II to the Fifth Assessment Report of the Intergovernmental Panel on Climate Change*. Cambridge: Cambridge University Press.

Stiglitz, J. (2012) *The Price of Inequality: The Avoidable Causes and Invisible Costs of Inequality*. London: Norton.

Stocker, T. F., Qin, Q., Plattner, G. K. et al. (eds) (2013) *Climate Change 2013: The Physical Science Basis. Contribution of Working Group I to the Fifth Assessment Report of the Intergovernmental Panel on Climate Change*. Cambridge: Cambridge University Press.

UN Department of Economic and Social Affairs, Population Division (2013) *World Population Prospects. The 2012 Revision, Key Findings and Advance Tables. Working Paper Number ESA/P/WP.227*. New York, USA: United Nations. Available at: www.unfpa.org/webdav/site/global/shared/documents/news/2013/KEYper cent20FINDINGSper cent20WPP2012_FINAL-2.pdf

Wackernagel M., Schulz, N., Deumling, D. et al. (2002) Tracking the ecological overshoot of the human economy. *Proceedings of National Academy of Sciences USA*, 99: 9266–9271.

Walsh, M. (1998) *Women in Food Aid Interventions, Impacts and Issues, FAO's Program on 'Time for a Change, Food Aid and Development.'* Rome: Food and Agricultural Organization, 23–24 October, 1998. Available at: http,//one.wfp.org/policies/introduction/background/faad/FAAD_English/faaq1_532e98.html.

Werz, M. and Hoffman, M. (2013) Climate Change, Migration, and Conflict. In E.C. Werrell and F. Femia (eds) *The Arab Spring and Climate Change. A Climate and Security Correlations Series.* Washington DC: Center for American Progress.

World Commission on Environment and Development (1987) *Our Common Future.* Oxford: Oxford University Press.

6

EDUCATION FOR SUSTAINABLE DEVELOPMENT

Challenges of a critical pedagogy

Delyse Springett

Introduction

This chapter argues that education for sustainable development (ESD), to be effective and to assume the transformational role often ascribed to it, requires both a critical theorization and a critical pedagogy that empower learners to envision 'a moral economy of social justice, citizenship and sustainability, based in social democracy' (Huckle 1996:15; 2012). The urgency of the sustainability agenda requires a radical re-think of societal priorities, and commentaries and policies on the transition to sustainable development have frequently emphasized the central role that education must play in that paradigm shift.[1] Key stages in the history of education for sustainable development are overviewed here to seek out similar calls for a critical pedagogy, and to highlight some of the institutional impediments that have made this a problematic area of the curriculum at all levels. A significant recent initiative at institutional level is the United Nations Decade of Education for Sustainable Development (DESD 2005–2014). By the time the chapter is published, the first stage of the DESD will be at its close, to be followed by the Global Action Programme on Education for Sustainable Development (GAPESD). This provides a timely juncture for assessing the progress made in a crucial area of education and whether we are yet on the path to developing a transformational role for education that may make a difference.

From environmental education to education for sustainable development

The formalization of the concept of sustainable development that the World Commission on Environment and Development established in *Our Common Future* (WCED 1987) not only marked a watershed for the robust environmental discourse that had flourished since the 'environmental crisis' of the 1960s but deeply influenced the re-theorization of environmental education (EE) while introducing further contestation to that discourse. The foundations of environmental education may be traced back to Rousseau's theories of education and his belief in the importance of the role of the environment in our lives, as propounded in *Emile: or, On Education* (trans. 1979). The Treatise considers how the basic human goodness that Rousseau believed in – *the natural man* (*sic*) – could be safeguarded from a corrupt society. In the late nineteenth century and the twentieth century, his educational theories and the normative questions they raised fed into the focus on Nature Study, Conservation Education and Outdoor

Education, from which emerged the environmental education movement that burgeoned in the 1960s and 1970s. A popular, vernacular, quasi-communal style of community schooling in ecology, green lifestyles and intentional frugality had also emerged in the 1950s and 1960s, linked to civil rights movements and the search for alternative life-styles, and culminating in such initiatives as Earth Day and the establishment of the Club of Rome.[2] These movements and the concerns they raised, along with publications such as Carson's *Silent Spring* (1962) and Ward's *Spaceship Earth* (1966), helped to jump-start the environmental education movement. By 1969, a definition of environmental education was provided in the first issue of *The Journal of Environmental Education*: 'Environmental education is aimed at producing a citizenry that is knowledgeable concerning the biophysical environment and its associated problems, aware of how to solve these problems, and motivated to work toward their solution' (Stapp 1969).

Environmental education now received support from intergovernmental organizations, though not necessarily from the institutions that govern the delivery of formal education at all levels. The IUCN issued the first internationally accepted definition of environmental education:

> the process of recognizing values and clarifying concepts in order to develop skills and attitudes necessary to understand and appreciate the interrelatedness among man (*sic*), his culture and his biophysical surroundings. EE also entails practice in decision-making and self-formulation of a code of behaviour about issues concerning environmental quality.
>
> *(IUCN 1971)*

In 1972, the United Nations Conference on the Human Environment (UNCHE) produced the Stockholm Declaration 'to inspire and guide the peoples of the world in the preservation and enhancement of the human environment', and established the International Environmental Education Programme coordinated by UNESCO and UNEP. The UNESCO-UNEP conference held in Belgrade in 1974 delivered the *Belgrade Charter* (UNESCO-UNEP 1975), based on the Stockholm Declaration, and set up international and regional meetings on environmental education that culminated in the International Intergovernmental Conference on Environmental Education, held in Tbilisi in 1977. The *Tbilisi Declaration* provided goals, aims, objectives and guiding principles that already signalled the need for a transformative education. The focus was on education that would:

- foster clear awareness of, and concern about, economic, social and political interdependence in urban and rural areas;
- provide every person with opportunities to acquire the knowledge, values, attitudes, commitment and skills needed to protect and improve the environment; and,
- create new patterns of behaviour of individuals, groups and society as a whole toward the environment (UNESCO-UNEP 1978: 3).

Three major perspectives on environmental education emerged (Lucas 1979):

- education *in* the environment (experiential education);
- education *about* the environment (providing information); and,
- education *for* the environment (critical and political education examining the origins of the environmental problematic and preparing learners for an active role as agents of change).

Clearly, the ideal goal would be for all three approaches to complement each other and be employed as parts of an overall educational strategy. However, it is 'education *for* the environment' that, ontologically and epistemologically, prepares the way for the transition to be made from 'environmental education' (and, frequently, a focus on science education as the basis for EE, since the 'problems' were often framed as scientific problems) to 'education *for* sustainable development' and the critical theorization promoted in this chapter. It highlights the fundamental change in the nature of education that ESD calls for and signals the changes to policy, curricula, pedagogy and institutional structures that are needed – a re-imagining of education (Corcoran 2009; Wals and Corcoran 2012) and a transformation that has proved both elusive and difficult over the years. Potentially, education *for* the environment/sustainable development is more openly ideological in its aims and approach and capable of exploring ideological perspectives in the discourse.

After *Our Common Future* (WCED 1987), many educators and authors adopted the rhetoric of 'Education for *Sustainable Development*' (ESD). However, just as the broader discourse contests the concept of 'sustainable development', with some favouring the different concept of 'sustainability', the educational discourse is challenged by those who would nominate 'Education for Sustainability' (EfS) or 'Sustainability Education' (SE) or 'Learning for Sustainability' (LfS) over 'Education for Sustainable Development'. More will be said about this later in the chapter. Some researchers still prefer to talk about 'environmental education', while confronting the challenges of sustainable development and sustainability, as notably demonstrated by the recent *International Handbook of Research on Environmental Education* (Stevenson et al. 2013).

A major outcome of the United Nations Conference on Environment and Development (UNCED 1992), which was based on the WCED outcomes, was Agenda 21, a blueprint for the future. Chapter 36 focuses on the role of education as a means of implementing the goals of Agenda 21, emphasizing that:

> Education is critical for promoting sustainable development and improving the capacity of the people to address environment and development issues . . . It is critical for achieving environmental and ethical awareness, values and attitudes, skills and behaviour consistent with sustainable development and for effective public participation in decision-making.
>
> *(UNCED 1992, Chapter 36: 2)*

However, it was the NGO 'Alternative Treaty on Environmental Education for Sustainable Societies and Global Responsibility' (1992), presented at the Global Forum, the alternative Earth Summit, that provided a more critical and transformational set of principles. It promoted a strong and open values position to the debate, calling for profound institutional change that would challenge the dominant social paradigm. It called for inclusive and participatory education at all levels, delivered through programmes that are holistic and systemic in approach, that take an interdisciplinary or multi-disciplinary stance, and are critical in their theorization. Its comprehensive goals come close to Huckle's (2012) ideal of 'concrete utopianism' in education and include:[3]

- Environmental education, whether formal, non-formal or informal, should be grounded in *critical and innovative thinking* in any place or time, *promoting the transformation and construction of society*.
- Environmental education is both individual and collective. It aims to develop *local and global citizenship with respect for self-determination and the sovereignty of nations*.

- Environmental education is not neutral but *is values based*. It is *an act for social transformation*.
- Environmental education must stimulate *solidarity, equality, and respect for human rights involving democratic strategies and an open climate of cultural interchange*.
- Environmental education should treat critical global issues, *their causes and interrelationships* in a systemic approach and within their social and historical contexts. Fundamental issues in relation to development and the environment, such as population, health, peace, human rights, democracy, hunger, degradation of flora and fauna, should be perceived in this manner. (Emphasis added).

Since UNCED, much energy has gone into promoting, practising and critiquing education for sustainable development, with continuing involvement from UNESCO, UNEP and the IUCN's Commission on Education and Communication (CEC). Yet relatively little has occurred that could convince us that the principles of the Alternative Treaty on Environmental Education and the transformative curriculum it promotes have been taken to heart.

The United Nations Decade of Education for Sustainable Development

Over the last ten years, some leadership has again been provided by the United Nations with the Decade of Education for Sustainable Development. The UN acknowledged that nurturing education for sustainable development in a neoliberal climate presented a challenge that required institutional change. Consequently, governments were to be encouraged to consider measures to implement the goals of the DESD in their education systems and strategies and even in their national plans. The aim was to integrate values, activities and principles that were inherently linked to sustainable development into all forms of education and learning, helping to bring about changes in attitudes, behaviours and values to ensure a more sustainable future in social, environmental and economic terms. Notably, emphasis is placed here, as so often, on *individual responsibility* and changes in *individual values and behaviour* rather than on structural change at institutional level. This is a not uncommon feature of the broader discourse on sustainable development, where it seems easier to focus on changing the individual (who clearly does have a key role to play in bringing about change) rather than on the need for institutional change. The transformation of individual values and behaviour is emphasized rather than the ability of that individual to understand issues around power or to achieve the empowerment and progressive agency to confront these: to *become* a *transformer*. Furthermore, the DESD goals are based upon the UNDP's 'three pillars of sustainable development', a phrase that precisely echoes the 'three pillars of sustainable development' or 'triple bottom line' that have been central to the rhetoric of business groups such as the World Business Council for Sustainable Development from the time of UNCED, and a signal, possibly, that business rhetoric is proving pervasive in the educational as well as other areas of the sustainable development discourse (Beder 1997; Beder et al. 2009; Springett 2009; 2013). Yet, by 2005, when the DESD was launched, one conception of sustainability (and, it is argued here, sustainable development) that was already current was the 'Prism of Sustainability' (Spangenberg 1995) embracing *four*, not three, imperatives: the environmental, economic, social, and, importantly, the *institutional* imperative. While UN statements about the DESD do underline that 'the concept of sustainable development touches upon all aspects of the social and institutional fabric' (UNEP 2007: 1), it appears that the terms of the DESD, while acknowledging the need for institutional *involvement*, had not pinpointed the 'institutional imperative' as such – the need for fundamental change at all levels of governance, and something that the 'three pillars' or 'triple bottom line' fail (deliberately?) to capture. Tellingly, when Huckle (2012) conducted an analysis of four major publications linked to the UNDESD for key words and phrases that would indicate that the authors had an understanding of issues that are central to a critical pedagogy for ESD – 'political economy', 'politics', 'capitalism', 'socialism' and 'critical pedagogy' – he discovered that 'politics' featured only in two of these and that 'political economy', 'capitalism', 'socialism' and 'critical pedagogy' appeared in none of them. Even when 'a critical perspective' is advocated as key to ESD, it does not mean that such structural and political issues are addressed.

Nevertheless, the basic vision of the DESD reflected some of the principles that the Alternative Treaty (1992) had outlined. The goal was that education, in formal, non-formal and informal settings, should provide an effective vector to bring about the changes in values, attitudes and lifestyles to ensure a sustainable future and the evolution of just societies. This indicated a role for national governments in re-thinking and re-orienting education and skills training to make the learning process locally relevant to real-life applications while engendering a broad concern for sustainability and sustainable development. The objectives to achieve these results aimed:

- to facilitate networking, linkages, exchange and interaction among stakeholders in ESD;
- to foster an increased quality of teaching and learning in education for sustainable development;
- to help countries make progress towards and attain the Millennium Development Goals through ESD efforts; and,
- to provide countries with new opportunities to incorporate ESD into education reform efforts (UNESCO 2004).

Education for sustainable development was to be interdisciplinary and holistic and embedded across the curriculum; explicitly driven by values and with these values openly examined, debated and applied; it was to be built around critical thinking and problem-solving, helping to build confidence in facing the dilemmas and challenges of sustainable development; it would be multi-method and participatory, applying different pedagogies and fostering cooperative learning and decision-making between teachers and learners, while being locally relevant and grounded in local languages and culture (UNESCO 2004: 6; UNESCO 2007; 2009a).

The transformational role of education for sustainable development

From the start, early pioneers of education for the environment had taken into account the ontological and epistemological challenges implicit in the development and delivery of EE if it was to foster real change, as well as the pedagogical approaches most likely to empower learners. It was clear that EE challenged the dominant social paradigm and called for social transformation and the transformation of education – which largely explains why it has proved so difficult to find a permanent niche for EE in the standard curricula of schools and institutions of higher education. While programmes that promote education *in* and *about* the environment have been more easily accommodated into the standard curriculum, education *for* the environment has found it harder to achieve a footing: the critical perspective it calls for is overtly political, encouraging learners to understand and critique the way the world works. At its most powerful, education *for* the environment – and, consequently, education *for* sustainable development – calls for the transformation of society and of educational systems that have become increasingly managerial and commercial in their goals and approaches. Such transformative goals may be dismissed as 'utopianism', but Huckle (2012: 43) perceives the goal as 'concrete utopianism' requiring greater 'realism' in education about the realities of how the world works.

Such a transformational role represents a serious challenge to the overall educational systems of countries. The exposure of ideology that education for sustainability may provide constitutes what Maher (1985) terms 'dangerous knowledge' that makes it difficult to fit comfortably in the formal curriculum. The formal education curriculum plays a key role in sustaining and reinforcing social hegemony, leading to the acceptance and reproduction of the ideology of the dominant social paradigm (see Apple 1979). It does this through the overt and the hidden curricula, perpetuating utilitarian attitudes toward nature while maintaining the class and societal division that serves the values and ideology of dominant social groups (see, for example, Trainer 1990; Orr 1992; 1994; Fien 1993; O'Connor 1998). Trainer (1990) described the curricula of schools and colleges, in their overt and hidden manifestations, as reproducing the socially and ecologically unsustainable values and practices of the industrial affluent society – promoting the desirability of economic growth and a competitive economy, the importance of individualism and competitive advantage, and market determination of economic and social priorities. O'Connor (1998: 149) similarly notes that the education system 'performs most activities that are necessary for the production of labour power'. Consequently, the emancipatory and change-agent roles of education for sustainable development are problematic for the 'reproductive' function education has assumed, alerting learners to the potentially hegemonic role of education and developing the skills to interrogate existing knowledge (Sultana 1989).

An important aspect of the perceived 'problem' is that a critical pedagogy is openly ideological, which is not to say that the intention is to co-opt learners to a particular perspective, although detractors might claim this. The goals of a critical pedagogy are emancipatory, intended to foster a habit of critical inquiry that *prevents* such capture. The goal is to involve learners in thinking through both personal and broader societal issues and to 'hold a mirror to the world and show it as it is and as it has produced and shaped its own nature' (O'Connor 1998: 52) – again, what Huckle (2012) refers to as 'realism' in education. This requires that we listen to voices that are seldom empowered and hear perspectives on sustainability and sustainable development that do not solely reflect the views of 'management' at whatever level (Springett 2006a; 2006b). Such education is openly 'political' in intent: it does not claim the supposed 'neutrality' of the orthodox curriculum that helps to reinforce societal hegemony in covert and purportedly neutral and unbiased ways (Apple 1979; Fien 1993; Huckle 1996; O'Connor 1998; Springett 2009), nor perpetuate a 'sanitized' picture of the world (Willmott 1994).

Contesting the concept of sustainable development

There remains the division that has arisen between those who would advocate 'education for sustainable development' and those who prefer to speak of 'education for sustainability'. Chapter 1 (p. 15f) has overviewed the 'contradictions' that surround the concept of sustainable development. However, this contestation and the epistemological contradictions it raises may also provide a learning advantage. A key requirement of any course on sustainability/sustainable development in whatever discipline will be to problematize the concepts of 'sustainable development' and 'sustainability', to unpick the contested ways in which they are framed and the reasons for this and to expose hegemony. It is an essential part of a critical approach to the discourse on sustainable development and sustainability and an example of how a critical theorization shapes content. It is a different route from courses that alert learners to 'issues' and 'solutions' without a grounding in the genealogy and politics of those 'symptoms' of the ecological and social problematic. The sustainability/sustainable development discourse itself provides a powerful way of understanding the role asymmetric power relations play in determining which constructions become legitimated, and the fundamental relevance of the discourse to students' own lives encourages their engagement in the debate.

Institutional impediments to education for sustainable development

In terms of what has happened to education at the institutional level over the last decades, Beder et al. (2009) maintain that many of the difficulties that have been encountered in transforming education arise from changes in its provision and delivery at all levels and from the increasing influence that neoliberal politics and the corporate world have on the nature of education. These changes start at schools level. It is not difficult to find 'environmental' components of the curriculum in schools – as noted, nature study and outdoor education have long featured on the curriculum, and the 1990s saw the rising popularity of 'whole-school' approaches through such programmes as 'eco-schools'. Against this, Beder et al. reveal the ways and means by which corporates have attempted to capture childhood, creating 'hyper-consumers' of their products and services and, in the longer term, submissive employees and passive citizens, more engaged with 'what they have' than 'who they are'. The formal education system itself has played a part in the transformation of *what education is for* since government funding, or the lack of it, renders schools vulnerable to the pressure of business selling its products to children via schools through sponsorships, competitions, communication technologies and classroom materials that help to grow brand loyalty. More broadly, the focus on 'consumer choice' has seen increases in the privatization of education and the provision of charter schools – often with corporate funding and involvement. Teachers feel besieged by the demands of time-consuming new testing regimes, lack of control over what is taught, additional 'welfare' responsibilities for their students and uncertainty about their own futures where tenure is threatened and unionization is discouraged. It takes little imagination to grasp that education for sustainable development is likely to struggle under these conditions. Corporate-sponsored classroom materials provide a distorted view of environmental, health and social issues (Beder et al. 2009; Huckle 2013). Schools have been driven to shift the goals of education from 'quality' to 'efficiency', imperilling the goals of education for sustainable development. As Beder et al. underline, business coalitions are powerful, capable of influencing government policy to transform schools into competing business enterprises and of engineering a narrowing of the curriculum to focus on numeracy and literacy, computer skills and a business-friendly view of history and society.

Despair about the changes taking place in the education system reaches beyond the schools. Concern about ideological premises that increasingly dominate the tertiary system of education has been vociferously expressed. The tertiary education sector, as 'conscience and critic' of society, might have been expected to take the leadership role in the discourse about sustainability and sustainable development and to embrace it as a moral responsibility: it is here that our teachers and leaders are prepared for their future roles. However, the increasingly reductionist turn the agenda of Higher Education has taken in recent years is characterized by competition and market-driven values that mimic the corporate ethos (Collini 2003; Parks 2013) rather than a collaborative culture, resulting in the commercialization and commodification of Higher Education. Slaughter and Rhoades (2004), reviewing changes in American universities, have identified this as 'academic capitalism'; while Anderson (2014: 39) notes that, in the UK, 'universities risk reduction to so many sales outlets for customers in need of livery for the market'. The UK report of the Higher Education Funding Council for England (HEFCE 2008), and the 'Browne Report' on Higher Education and Student Finance (2010), underlined the increasing bureaucratic control of higher education seen as a 'market' in which consumer demand (not least the requirements of business) will be sovereign (Collini 2010; McKibbin 2010). These are not trends that are likely to encourage either a critical perspective or a focus on sustainability. Schools and Higher Education institutions are in danger of becoming 'edu-businesses'.

There have been glimmers of hope. As early as 1990, initiatives were instigated to form international alliances of universities with other groups to promote commitment to a sustainability ethic. In the USA, *The Forum for University Leaders for a Sustainable Future* (ULSF 1990) underlined the key role of the university in promoting the transition to sustainable development. *The Talloires Declaration* in 1994 called for changes to curricula, teaching and learning and encouraged signatories to commit to programmes for environmentally responsible citizenship, teaching environmental literacy and developing interdisciplinary approaches to curricula, research initiatives, operations and outreach activities. This inspired the Conference of EuropeanRectors of European Universities that resulted in the COPERNICUS programme and *The University Charter for Sustainable Development* (CRE-COPERNICUS 1994) that also emphasized the importance of embedding sustainable development in the curricula, teaching and learning at university level. COPERNICUS-CAMPUS, the European University network for sustainable development, was tasked with developing Guidelines for the incorporation of sustainable development into the European Higher Education Area. This was followed in 2009 by UNESCO's *Bonn Declaration* (UNESCO 2009b) to strengthen knowledge about ESD through the teaching, research and community engagement of universities. Preparing for the DESD, UNESCO also envisioned Higher Education as having a key role to play in the transition to sustainability. Nevertheless, universities may be viewed as having largely ceded leadership in the sustainable development discourse to powerful business organizations. The corporate world has not suffered from the inertia that can characterize the university; rather, it has sought to shape, if not appropriate, the narrative of sustainable development, at least since UNCED (Springett 2013).

Kearins and Springett (2001), Springett and Kearins (2005) and Jones et al. (2009) summarize some of the principal inhibitors that have prevented universities and other establishments of higher education from taking the lead. These include staff concern for academic freedom and not wanting sustainable development 'imposed' on them; discomfort with interdisciplinary teaching; their own lack of knowledge in the field of sustainability; and concern that the ethos of the institution does not favour successful integration of sustainability across the teaching, learning and research programmes of the university. The last point is, possibly, the key inhibitor on account of the ideological conflict between the goals of education for sustainable development and institutions that have become increasingly commercialized and market-oriented. There has been a reaction against Higher Education's abdication of responsibility, its lack of action in the face of increasing environmental, social and economic dilemmas and its failure to grasp the institutional imperative of sustainable development (Corcoran and Wals, 2004; Springett 2009). Teaching and research programmes have emerged that focus on multiple aspects of sustainable development, along with a re-thinking of how the institution is managed. In addition to the traditional academic league tables, we now find universities, like companies, competing for places on 'Green League' tables in order to demonstrate their commitments to sustainability. While this entails greater attention to management functions – 'green housekeeping' that covers indisputably essential initiatives – it falls well short of sustainable development. Some universities take this further and make the claim to be 'sustainable universities' in terms of curricula, research programmes and corporate management. However, the critique of the eroding role of the university suggests that a more fundamental transformation is required. The very purpose of the institution needs to be revisited if its role in the shift to sustainability is to be one of leadership. Jones (2012) argues for a new metaphor of a 'restorative' or 'biophilic' university (p164), calling for a systemic, transitional change to 'sustaining universities' as facilitators of the shift to sustainability, rather than 'sustainable' universities competing for prowess on green league tables.

At NGO level, there has been a fierce struggle to ensure that Higher Education plays its part in the shift to sustainability. At the UN Conference on Sustainable Development – Rio+20 – (UNCSD 2012) the alternative Peoples' Sustainability Treaties again provided an example of deliberative democracy in action. They evolved through a consultative process with hundreds of civil society organizations that converged at Rio+20 to launch their Manifesto on the final day of the summit, declaring that another world is possible after Rio+20 and pledging their commitment to a transition toward increasingly sustainable futures on earth. The *Peoples' Sustainability Treaty on Higher Education Towards Sustainable Development* (2012) again emphasizes the need to transform higher education if it is to foster the principles of sustainable development.

The discussion brings into question the matter of who is to lead the turn to sustainable development in the future. A key goal of the DESD has been to 'foster an increased quality of teaching and learning in education for sustainable development', pinpointing the fact that many of our teachers and academics have had little education for sustainable development themselves in their formal education and training and have had to become pioneers in the area – to take in hand their own professional self-development for teaching environmental education or education for sustainable development. They have generally been taught and trained within tight disciplinary traditions. Sustainability, however, is a cross-disciplinary concept (Becker et al. 1997; Becker 1999), and education for sustainable development embraces 'aesthetic, cultural, ecological, economic, environmental, ethical, philosophical, political, scientific, social, spiritual and technological' dimensions, calling for 'permeability' between disciplinary boundaries (Selby 2006: 7). UNESCO (2004) also characterized education for sustainable development education for sustainable development as being interdisciplinary, cross-curricular and holistic, values-driven and built around critical thinking and problem solving. However, this ideal approach to education for sustainable development – or any area of education – is professionally and practically demanding where few educators have been taught or trained in such a range of theoretical, pedagogical or methodological approaches.

Challenges of a critical pedagogy

A further challenge for teachers arises from the advocacy for a critical theorization of the sustainable development curriculum, posing the question of how educators are to gain preparation for teaching critical perspectives if that perspective is generally lacking from their own professional development. There are political difficulties and possible career consequences for educators who promote a critical agenda or who focus on education for sustainable development or both (Springett and Kearins 2001). Academics are constrained to seek publication in top tier journals in order to strengthen their academic assessments and to compete for promotion and research funding, so that forays outside traditional disciplinary boundaries represent risk. It is not surprising that, in the business studies curriculum, for example, where the ideological struggle between the legitimacy of the traditional curriculum and the challenges that sustainable development poses are most obvious, there has tended to be a focus on the rhetoric of eco-modernism and incremental change and the 'gains' these bring to business. The focus has not infrequently been on the 'management' of the agenda of sustainable development (Luke 1999; Springett 2006b) rather than a radical perspective on the need for fundamental systemic change to modes of production and consumption.

Educating the decision-makers

Another important issue is the level of education for sustainable development that has been available to the leaders who make key decisions on our behalf and the managers who provide leadership at corporate level: to what extent is sustainable development embedded in the learning of those responsible for governance at all levels? Martin and Jucker (2005) question the education of future generations of professionals and note the prevalence of leaders who lack the qualities that would promote sustainable development. Huckle (1996) maintains that education for sustainable development focuses on the ethics and politics of sustainability and *un*sustain-ability to engage in 'shared reflection and action on forms of political economy that would enable us to live sustainably with one another and the rest of nature' (ibid.: xiv). Clearly, the capacity for such reflection and action on the part of political and business leaders urgently needs to be nurtured through the manner in which they are educated. Unsurprisingly, then, one part of the curriculum of higher education that has received considerable critical comment is the business studies curriculum where many of our future decision-makers receive their education. As noted, this is an area of the curriculum where the ideological struggle between the goals of sustainable development and the rationality of the capitalist paradigm of production and consumption collide (Springett 2005; 2009). The United Nations Principles for Responsible Management Education (PRME) (2007) – ostensibly designed to promote sustainable development in business schools – promulgates six 'Principles': Purpose; Values; Method; Research; Partnership and Dialogue. However, the rhetoric fails to suggest that the ideology of business education or of business *per se* needs to change if the goals of sustainable development are to be met.

There is some evidence that business managers themselves regret the lack of education for sustainable development in their own initial education and training (Springett 2006c). Moreover, education for sustainable development does not cease at the end of formal education (and not all managers and leaders receive tertiary education). Education for sustainable development needs to be available for managers already in the workplace and at all levels of seniority. This provides an important opportunity; and, in fact, one aspect of education for sustainability that has gone from strength to strength over the past two decades has been the focus on 'executive education' for sustainable development, mostly of leaders already functioning in the corporate world, and largely delivered as post-formal educational programmes (see, for example, Roome 2005; Wheeler et al. 2005). Luke, in this volume (Chapter 21), draws attention to the Master of Science Program in Sustainability Management offered to graduate students at Columbia University.

Is ESD addressing the real questions of sustainable development?

The potential scope of a curriculum for education for sustainable development is demonstrated by the breadth of topics covered in this Handbook – and represents one of its daunting aspects. Jones et al. (2009) reveal the interdisciplinary potential and benefits of infusing sustainability concepts, issues and case studies into all areas of learning and teaching, as well as the student motivation, teacher satisfaction and opportunities for innovative and active learning that this provides. So the fact that education for sustainable development may not have had the level of institutional support that its crucial role merits does not mean that nothing has happened in the area, but it does mean that the task of providing education for sustainable development for all peoples of all ages has been harder. It may also have resulted, in some cases, in a more strenuous effort to ground SD in curricula at all levels, and has certainly fuelled a good deal of cross-curriculum research (see Stevenson et al. 2013).

However, this leads to the crucial question that remains: are the curricula and programmes currently operating addressing the real and substantial questions of sustainable development? Are they 'realistic' (Huckle 2012)? We might start by considering accounts of the qualities that characterize the 'sustainability literate citizen' - the person educated to understand the causes and problems of unsustainable development and to develop the personal agency to challenge the status quo. This seems essential considering the emphasis placed on personal responsibility, values and behaviour change in the shift to sustainable development; and crucial in view of the changes in subjectivity the shift to sustainability will both rely upon and engender in the learner. A UNEP-UK document (Sterling and EDET 1992) was one of the first to take up this challenge and focuses on eight qualities that we might strive to nurture in all learners:

- a sense of responsibility to the environment, to other people and to the future of both;
- the will, knowledge and skills to translate this responsibility into action in both personal and public life;
- the ability to respond positively to change and uncertainty;
- a capacity to see the links between individual and group actions, external events, and other factors;
- an interdisciplinary and holistic outlook;
- a healthy scepticism alongside the ability and freedom to be creative;
- a balance of rationality with feeling and intellect with intuition; and
- a sense of self-worth combined with a respect for other individuals and cultures (Sterling 1996: 35).

A critical pedagogy would see 'a healthy scepticism' strengthened to the development of a critical capacity and the agency to identify structural irrationalities and to seek change at institutional level. Huckle (1996), for one, prioritizes the learner outcome of gaining an understanding of the contemporary politics of sustainability. He argues (2012) that the learner needs to become more alert to issues of inequality and social class; learning needs to be more firmly anchored in the realities of the dominant forms of unsustainable development and underdevelopment that shape the contemporary world; and more attention should be given to the struggles of the workers and citizens to introduce more sustainable alternatives, all of this calling for a critical pedagogy. To this we might add development of a capacity for self-reflexivity and the ability to evaluate the course, its content and delivery as well as the learner's own contribution to the learning nexus so that the course becomes self-reflexive for the teacher as well as the learner (Springett 2009). Such participatory methods, valuing students' input, provide an approach to ESD that may deliver education that is genuinely transformational.

Post-DESD expectations for education for sustainable development

So what can we expect of education for sustainable development post-2014? The major outcome of the DESD, as noted, is the plan for a Global Action Programme on Education for Sustainable Development (GAPESD), with the overarching goal 'to generate and scale-up action in all levels and areas of education and learning in order to accelerate progress towards sustainable development' (United Nations 2012; UNESCO 2013).

The goals comprise:

- advancing policy;
- transforming learning and training environments;
- building capacity of educators and trainers;
- empowering and mobilizing youth;
- accelerating sustainable solutions at the local level.

The scope of the Global Action Programme and the international involvement in preparing its goals appear impressive. However, there are questions about its implementation: will structural and institutional impediments curtail its effectiveness? Will the GAPESD itself represent a form of institutional control over education for sustainable development, determining the social politics of how the ESD agenda is set? Robottom (2013: 161), focusing on teacher professional development, notes that the DESD 'is marked by vigorous attempts to impose centrally developed curriculum packages designed for universal implementation'.

What would we hope for from UNESCO's major input into ESD? Will the Global Action Programme confront the 'big issues' of sustainability and unsustainability, the interconnectedness of the institutional, environmental, social and economic imperatives highlighted in Chapter 1? We might hope that the curricula will address the tough reality of unsustainability and encourage reflection on fundamental questions about the capitalist economy of consumerism and its impact on our ways of being, asking, for example: 'How Much is Enough?' (Durning 1992; Skidelsky and Skidelsky 2012), and 'To Have or To Be?' (Fromm 1976) – that is, the eternal philosophical question: 'How to live?' Learners need to be encouraged to envision what a sustainable political economy would look like if it were both socially and economically sustainable, meeting the needs of all of the world's people while conserving the means and conditions of production – in other words, as noted earlier, to assume a transformational role and to envision the moral economy of social justice, citizenship and sustainability, based in social democracy (Huckle 1996). An examination of the political abuse of language would be important – the semiotic conquest of the language and agenda of 'sustainable development' that has led to the appropriation of the term to suit corporate or political interests. We might look for more emphasis on community-led and grass-roots initiatives, as exemplified by the Alternative Treaties, to counterweigh some of the constraints that the formal sector of education currently suffers from and promotes.

In these post-Gutenberg times, the digital revolution, for all its manifold drawbacks, offers opportunities for a 'republic' of sustainable development educators and learners to emerge, free from some of the current constraints on ESD and able to broaden the conversation to include much wider and more diverse audiences – a movement perhaps akin to that of the popular, vernacular movements of the 1950s and 1960s that fed into the formalization of environmental education. It follows that different ontological, epistemological and pedagogical perspectives would be rife, along with matters of quality control of content and delivery, of measurement, assessment and evaluation – of 'control' *per se*. The scope for a more interactive and critical curriculum, drawing on some of the themes cited in this chapter and available to a wide community, is considerable. Will it emerge to drive the much-needed revolution in education for sustainable development? Importantly, can the DESD and its outcomes provide the necessary impetus?

Notes

1 This includes outputs from all of the major UN conferences on environment, development and sustainable development since 1972 (UNCHE 1972; UNCED 1992; UNWSSD 2002; UNCSD 2012).
2 Buckminster Fuller's *World Game*, 1961, Stewart Brand's *The Whole Earth Catalogue*, 1968–1972, and Paolo Soleri's *arcologies* are other possible precursors of the formal EE movement.
3 These can be accessed in full at: http://habitat.igc.org/treaties/at-05.htm.

References

Alternative Treaty on Environmental Education for Sustainable Societies and Global Responsibility (1992). http://habitat.igc.org/treaties/at-05.htm (accessed 25 July 2013).
Anderson, P. (2014) Diary. *The London Review of Books*, 36(2): 39.

Apple, M. W. (1979) *Ideology and Curriculum*. London: Routledge and Kegan Paul.

Becker, E. (1999) Fostering transdisciplinary research into sustainability in an age of globalization: a short political epilogue. In E. Becker and T. Jahn (eds) *Sustainability and the Social Sciences: A Cross-Disciplinary Approach to Integrating Environmental Considerations into Theoretical Reorientation*. London: Zed Books, pp. 59–73.

Becker, E., Jahn, T., Stiess, I. and Wehling, P. (1997) *Sustainability, A Cross-Disciplinary Concept for Social Transformations*. Management of Social Transformation Policy Papers, 6, Paris: UNESCO.

Beder, S. (1997) *Global Spin: The Corporate Assault on Environmentalism*. Melbourne: Scribe Publications.

Beder, S., Varney, W. and Gosden, R. (2009) *This Little Kiddy Went to Market: The Corporate Capture of Childhood*. Sydney: University of South Wales Press.

Carson, R. (1962) *Silent Spring*. New York: Fawcett Crest.

Collini, S. (2003) HiEdBiz: A review of the UK Government White Paper 'The Future of Higher Education'. *London Review of Books*, 25(21): 3–9.

Collini, S. (2010) 'Browne's Gamble': Review of 'Securing a Sustainable Future for Higher Education: An Independent Review of Higher Education Funding and Student Finance' by Lord Browne et al. *London Review of Books*: 32(21): 23–25.

Corcoran, P. B. (2009) 'Foreword'. In P. Jones, D. Selby and S. Sterling (eds) *Sustainability Education: Perspectives and Practice Across Higher Education*. London: Earthscan, pp. xiii–xvi.

Corcoran, P. B. and Wals, A. E. J. (2004) *Higher Education and the Challenge of Sustainability: Problematics, Promise, and Practice*. Dordrecht: Kluwer Academic Publishers.

CRE-COPERNICUS (1994) *The University Charter for Sustainable Development*. Geneva: CRE. Available at: www.iisd.org/educate/declarat/coper.htm (accessed 13 June 2013).

Durning, A. T. (1992) *How Much is Enough? The Consumer Society and the Future of the Earth*. Washington, DC: The Worldwatch Institute.

Fien, J. (1993) *Education for the Environment: Critical Curriculum Theorising and Environmental Education*. Melbourne: Deakin University.

Fromm, E. (1976) *To Have or to Be? The Nature of the Psyche*. New York: Harper and Row.

HEFCE (Higher Education Funding Council for England) (2008) *Report: The Future of Higher Education*. London: DoE.

Huckle, J. (1996) Realizing sustainability in changing times. In J. Huckle and S. Sterling (eds) *Education for Sustainability*. London: Earthscan, pp. 105–119.

Huckle, J. (2012) Towards a greater realism in learning for sustainability. In A. E. J. Wals and P. B. Corcoran (eds) *Learning for Sustainability*. Wageningen: Academic, pp. 35–48.

Huckle, J. (2013) Eco-schooling and sustainability citizenship: exploring some issues raised by corporate sponsorship. *The Curriculum Journal*, 24(2): 206–223.

Huckle, J. and Sterling, S. (eds) (1996) *Education for Sustainability*. London: Earthscan.

IUCN (International Union for the Conservation of Nature) (1971) Education and Environment. *Papers of the Zurich Conference of December, 1971*.

Jones, P., Selby, D. and Sterling, S. (2009) *Sustainability Education: Perspectives and Practice Across Higher Education*. London: Earthscan.

Jones, D. R. (2012) Embodying Tian Tao in the 'Biophilic University'. *Journal of Corporate Citizenship*, Summer: 159–173.

Kearins, K. and Springett, D. V. (2001) Educating for sustainability; developing critical skills. *Journal of Management Education*: 27(2): 188–204.

Lucas, A. M. (1979) *Environment and Environmental Education: Conceptual Issues and Curriculum Implications*. Melbourne: Australian International Press and Publications.

Luke, T. W. (1999) Training eco-managerialists: academic environmental studies as a power/knowledge formation. In F. Fisher and M. Hajer (eds) *Living with Nature: Environmental Discourses as Cultural Politics*. Oxford: Oxford University Press, pp. 103–120.

Maher, M. (1985) Censorship, consensus and challenge – environmental education in schools in Australia. *Social Alternatives*, 5(2): 23–26.

Martin, S. and Jucker, R. (2005) Educating earth-literate leaders. *Journal of Geography in Higher Education*, 29(1): 19–29.

McKibbin, R. (2010) Nothing to do with the economy. *London Review of Books*: 32(22): 18 November: 12–13.

O'Connor, J. (1998) *Natural Causes: Essays on Ecological Marxism*. New York: Guilford.

Orr, D. (1992) *Ecological Literacy: Education and the Transition to a Post-Modern World*. Albany, NY: SUNY Press.

Orr, D. (1994) *Earth in Mind: In Education, Environment, and the Human Project*. Washington, DC: Island Press.

Parks, T. (2013) Literature and bureaucracy. *New York Review of Books Newsletter*, 4 December, 2013.

Peoples' Sustainability Treaty on Higher Education Towards Sustainable Development. Rio+ 20, 2012. Treaties @ Rio+20 (accessed 13 July 2013).

PRME (United Nations Principles for Responsible Management Education) (2007).

Robottom, I. (2013) Changing discourses in EE/ESD: a role for professional self-development. In R.B. Stevenson, M. Brody, J. Dillon and A.E.J. Wals (eds) *International Handbook on Research on Environmental Education*. New York and London: AERA and Routledge, pp. 156–162.

Roome, N. J. (2005) Teaching sustainability in a global MBA: Insights from the OneMBA. *Business Strategy and the Environment*: 14(3): 160–171.

Rousseau, J-J. (1979) *Emile: or, On Education*, Trans. A. Bloom. New York: Basic Books.

Selby, D. (2006) The catalyst that is sustainability: bringing permeability to disciplinary boundaries. *Planet*, 17: 57–59.

Skidelsky, R. and Skidelsky, E. (2012) *How Much Is Enough? Money and the Good Life*. New York: Other Press.

Slaughter, S. and Rhoades, G. (2004) *Academic Capitalism and the New Economy: Markets, State, and Higher Education*, Baltimore, MD: Johns Hopkins University Press.

Spangenberg, J. H. (1995) The linkage of economy, environment and social organization in the concept of sustainability. *Discussions on Sustainable Production and Consumption in Europe: Report of the United Nations Environment Programme*. Geneva: UNEP/ROE, pp. 49–56.

Springett, D. V. (2005) Education for sustainability in the business studies curriculum: a call for a critical agenda. *Business Strategy and the Environment:* 14(3): 146–159.

Springett, D. V. (2006a) Contesting the business case for sustainable development: A New Zealand perspective. In R. Welford, P. Hills and W. Young (eds) *Partnerships for Sustainable Development: Perspectives from the Asia-Pacific Region*. Hong Kong: The University of Hong Kong, pp. 33–52.

Springett, D. V. (2006b) Managing the narrative of sustainable development: 'discipline' of an 'inefficient' concept. *International Journal of Green Economics*, 1(1 –2): 50–67.

Springett, D. V. (2006c) Structural limits to sustainable development: managers and progressive agency. *International Journal of Innovation and Sustainable Development*: 1(1): 127–152.

Springett, D. V. (2009) Education for sustainability in the business studies curriculum: ideological struggle. In P. Jones, D. Selby and S. Sterling (eds) *Sustainability Education: Perspectives and Practice Across Higher Education*. London: Earthscan, pp. 75–92.

Springett, D. V. (ed.) (2013) Editorial essay: critical perspectives on sustainable development. *Sustainable Development*: 21(2): 73–82.

Springett, D. V. and Kearins, K. (eds) (2001) Gaining legitimacy: sustainable development in business school curricula. *Sustainable Development*, 9(4): 213–221.

Springett, D. V. and Kearins, K. (eds) (2005) Education *for* sustainability in the business studies curriculum: a call for a critical agenda. *Business Strategy and the Environment:* 14(3).

Stapp, W. B. (1969) The concept of environmental education. *Journal of Environmental Education*, 1(1): 30–31.

Sterling, S. (1996) Education in change. In J. Huckle and S. Sterling (eds) *Education for Sustainability*. London: Earthscan, pp. 18–39.

Sterling, S. and EDET (1992) *Good Earth-Keeping: Education, Training and Awareness for a Sustainable Future*. London: UNEP-UK.

Stevenson, R. B., Brody, M., Dillon, J. and Wals, A. E. J. (2013) *International Handbook on Research on Environmental Education*. New York and London: AERA and Routledge .

Sultana, R. G. (1989) Are there any critical educators out there? Perspectives on teachers and transformation. *Critical Pedagogy Networker*, 2(4): 1–8.

Trainer, T. (1990) Towards an ecological philosophy of education. *Discourse*, 10(2): 92–117.

UK Government (2010) *Securing a Sustainable Future for Higher Education: An Independent Review of Higher Education Funding and Student Finance* (The Browne Report). Available at: www.independent.gov.uk/browne-report, (accessed 17 June 2013).

ULSF (1990) *The Talloires Declaration: 10 Point Action Plan*. Available at: www.ulsf.org/programs_tlloires_td.html (accessed 13 June 2013)

UNCHE (United Nations Conference on the Human Environment) (1972) *The Stockholm Declaration*. New York: UN.

UNCSD (United Nations Conference on Sustainable Development *Rio+20*). Rio de Janeiro, (2012).
UNWSSD (United Nations World Summit on Sustainable Development). Johannesburg, (2002).
UNEP (2007) *The United Nations Decade of Education for Sustainable Development (2005–2014)*. Available at: www.unep.org/training/programmes/undesd.asp (accessed 17 June 2013).
UNESCO (2004) *United Nations Decade of Education for Sustainable Development (2005–2014): Draft International Implementation Scheme*. Paris: UNESCO.
UNESCO (2007) *The UN Decade of Education for Sustainable Development (DESD, 2005–2014): The First Two Years*. Paris: UNESCO.
UNESCO (2009a) *Education for Sustainable Development: United Nations Decade (2005–2014)*. Paris: UNESCO. Available at: http://portal.unesco.org/education/en/ev.php-URL_ID+34756_DO_TOPICandURL=201.html (accessed: 13 June 2013).
UNESCO (2009b) *Bonn Declaration*. Available at: www.esd-world-conference-2009.org/fileadmin/download/News/BonnDecalarationFinal.pdf (accessed: 13 June 2013).
UNESCO (2013) *Report of the Hundred and Ninety Second Session (192/EX) of the Executive Board*. Paris: UNESCO, 31 July, 2013.
UNESCO-UNEP (1975) *The Belgrade Charter: A Global Framework for Environmental Education*. Washington, DC: US Government Printing Office.
UNESCO-UNEP (1978) *The Tbilisi Declaration: Toward an Action Plan: A Report on the Tbilisi Intergovernmental Conference on Environmental Education*. Washington, DC: US Government Printing Office.
United Nations (2012) *Shaping the Education of Tomorrow*. 2012 Report on the UN Decade of Education for Sustainable Development. New York: UN.
Wals, A. E. J. and Corcoran, P. B. (eds) (2012) *Learning for Sustainability*. Wageningen: Academic.
Ward, B. (1966) *Spaceship Earth*. New York: Columbia University Press.
WCED (World Commission on Environment and Development) (1987) *Our Common Future: The Report of the World Commission on Environment and Development*. Oxford: Oxford University Press.
Wheeler, D., Zohar, A. and Hart, S. (2005) Educating senior executives in a novel strategic paradigm: early experiences of the Sustainable Enterprise Academy. *Business and the Environment*, 14(3): 172–185.
Willmott, H. (1994) Management education: provocation to a debate. *Management Learning*: 25: 105–136.

PART III

Environmental dimensions of sustainable development

7

BIODIVERSITY AND SUSTAINABLE DEVELOPMENT

Stewart Lockie and Hedda Ransan-Cooper

Introduction

At face value, the importance of biological diversity to sustainable development is obvious. Beyond the intrinsic value we ascribe to living organisms and assemblages, biodiversity contributes to numerous ecosystem processes that support ecological, economic and social well-being. Biodiversity enhances the ability of ecosystems – including heavily modified ecosystems such as those found in farms, gardens, cities and towns – to cope with climatic and environmental shocks. Biodiversity supports food security by providing raw genetic material for improved crop and livestock varieties. Biodiversity provides opportunities for indigenous and other communities to cultivate market niches based on traditional knowledge and livelihood practices. Indeed, biodiversity and the ecosystem processes in which it is implicated provide a host of services to people that would otherwise require expensive technological and financial inputs. These include the purification of water and air; the provision of food, fibre, timber and fuel; the mitigation of floods, drought, disease; and so on. In more ways than we yet understand, biodiversity is central to the sustainability of human societies and economies.

According to Rockström et al. (2009), current rates of species extinction – a proxy for biodiversity loss – lie somewhere in the range of 100–1000 times historical rates. Biodiversity decline, they argue, threatens to shift the balance of other key Earth-system processes including climate change; pushing ecosystems towards tipping points – periods of rapid transformation from one state to another – that could profoundly compromise the capacity of those ecosystems to support human welfare (Rockström et al. 2009). It follows from this that reversing current rates of biodiversity loss and building biodiversity-enhancing practices into systems of production and consumption ought to be the focus of concerted political and policy attention. As the Convention on Biological Diversity's *Global Biodiversity Outlook 3* put it: 'protection of biodiversity should be seen as a prudent and cost-effective investment in risk-avoidance for the global community' (CBD 2010: 11).

Evidence to date, however, suggests that while the importance of investing in biodiversity is acknowledged by governments and multilateral institutions, action to preserve and enhance biodiversity is either insufficient or ineffective. At the first Rio Earth Summit in 1992, two legally binding agreements were opened for signature: the United Nations Framework Convention on Climate Change and the Convention on Biological Diversity (CBD).

At Rio+10 in 2002, agreement was reached to target significant reductions in biodiversity loss at the global, regional and national levels. But by 2010, it was evident that these targets would not be reached. The major drivers of biodiversity loss – habitat change, over-exploitation, pollution, invasive alien species and climate change – were intensifying while measures to implement the CBD were too small in scale to counteract them (CBD 2010).

As it is not possible within the scope of one chapter to offer comprehensive analyses of relevant policy frameworks and their successes and failures in relation to biodiversity, the emphasis in this chapter will be on how biodiversity governance frameworks reflect and recast the idea of sustainable development. It will begin by introducing the concepts of sustainability and biodiversity – along with their relationships – in more detail before outlining some of the major approaches to biodiversity management and regulation.

Defining sustainable development

The concept of sustainable development, as defined in the 1987 Brundtland Report, attempted to reconcile the ways in which economic activity is organized with the often competing needs of reversing environmental degradation and promoting human rights and poverty alleviation (WCED 1987). Meeting the needs of people living in the present without compromising the ability of future generations to meet their own needs has proven a compelling and enduring idea. But moving from general principles of sustainability to concrete actions has always proven difficult. The core principles of sustainability – intra-generational and inter-generational justice – raise numerous and often difficult questions. We are not always sure of the consequences of human actions. Attempts to implement sustainability are often characterized by debate over how cautious to be in the face of uncertainty, along with conflicting views over what we should be protecting and how much to prioritize the long-term benefits of environmental protection and resource conservation relative to the immediate benefits of resource exploitation. Decisions about sustainability must either accommodate multiple viewpoints, values and interests or they must force some people to compromise. Too often – as the environmental justice movement has demonstrated – it is those who are already socially and economically marginalized who are forced to do the compromising (Agyeman and Evans 2004).

Despite these difficulties, the ideas of sustainability and sustainable development provide useful concepts for discussing the goals and outcomes of environmental and social interventions. Further, by speaking to how we should live in the world, sustainability and sustainable development become more than concepts or ideas. They become a sort of bridge connecting our thinking and planning about the future to actions and consequences embedded in material ecosystem and social processes. The materiality, or concreteness, of sustainability is always present as a potentially countervailing force to those who seek to promote their own narrow interests; constraining and shaping the possibilities available to people in a number of important ways. Drawing on Lockie (2012), it is argued here that the pursuit of sustainable development thus imposes at least three inter-related sets of demands.

First, *sustainability demands learning*. As global environmental change illustrates, the temporal and spatial dynamics of human-nature interactions are characterized by processes of discontinuous change, interactive effects and unanticipated consequences (Lockie 2014). Maintaining a favourable environment for humans in the long term can never be about maintaining steady-state ecosystems, communities or economies (Steffen et al. 2007). Nor can it be about continuing to plan on the basis of current knowledge and institutional arrangements for environmental governance. Today's knowledge of Earth-system processes and other socio-ecological assemblages will necessarily be proven incomplete and outmoded as species and ecosystems – along with human communities and institutions – evolve in potentially unpredictable ways. In practice, this would be about re-designing our institutions to build in ongoing learning, as well as the ability to be flexible in light of new knowledge and understanding. The future must be planned but, even more so, it must be learned (see also Tàbara 2014).

Second, *sustainability demands deliberation; that is, reasoned and truthful communication and discussion about important issues open to all those potentially affected by that issue* (see Dryzek and Stevenson 2011). This is not simply a matter of peoples' rights to participate in democratic decision-making. Nor, for that matter, is it simply a matter of capturing local or indigenous knowledge. As important as these are (Magnani 2012), deliberation as demanded by sustainability is also a matter of recognizing that the human environment is a shifting terrain of knowledge, values, interests, aspirations and coalitions. As environmental disputes, planning exercises, management regimes etc. play out, multiple stakeholders are brought into contact. The knowledge, values and aspirations that people bring to any environmental governance process or conflict are always potentially redefined through their interaction with others. Ideas and understandings can shift, new interest groups form, and points of agreement and conflict change. Participatory deliberation is thus fundamental to understanding and responding to the dynamic ways in which social networks, understandings and priorities are constructed and re-constructed through processes of social-ecological change (Lockie 2007).

Third, *sustainability demands accountability*. It is not enough to implement new programs of action. Our planning and learning towards the future must be evaluated. We must distinguish – both in *prospect* and *retrospect* – between appropriate and inappropriate, successful and unsuccessful, good and bad, attempts to assemble future social-ecologies. Numerous institutional arrangements have been implemented throughout human history to impose such accountability (for example, property rights and responsibilities, pollution licensing, production standards etc.). Sustainability demands that critical scrutiny, through learning and deliberation, of these arrangements be extended and intensified (Dryzek and Stevenson 2011). In particular, it demands that scrutiny be focused on the distributive impacts of socio-ecological interventions across both space (intra-generational accountability) and time (inter-generational accountability).

Comprehending biodiversity

The CBD defines biodiversity as 'the variability among living organisms from all sources ... and the ecological complexes of which they are part: this includes diversity within species, between species and of ecosystems' (UN 1992: 3). This establishes three main levels at which biological diversity is relevant:

1 Genetic (or infraspecific/intraspecific) diversity refers to genetic variance *within* a species.
2 Species (or interspecific) diversity refers to variance *between* species.
3 Ecosystem diversity refers to variance in the communities, or assemblages, of living organisms and non-living ecosystem components (minerals, energy, water, nitrogen etc.) present in a given geographic area.

Human societies benefit in a multitude of ways from ecosystem services provided by biodiversity. The Millennium Ecosystem Assessment (2005) categorized these as:

- *Supporting services*: processes such as primary productivity, the formation of soil and the recycling of nutrients, which, in themselves, provide the basis for all other ecosystem services.
- *Provisioning services*: tangible products that can be sourced from ecosystems including food, fibre, water and fuel.
- *Regulating services*: processes that act to regulate climate and disease, mitigate floods, purify water, etc.
- *Cultural services*: the provision of nonmaterial benefits such as aesthetic, recreational, educational and spiritual values.

Diversity at a range of biological, spatial and temporal scales is associated with a variety of benefits to humans. However, it is the relationships between diversity and ecosystem processes – not the absolute level of genetic, species and ecosystem diversity *per se* – through which these benefits are delivered. As an indicator of ecosystem health it is thus necessary to supplement *absolute biodiversity* with the concept of *functional biodiversity:* that is, diversity within groups of organisms (such as bacteria and fungi) that perform ecosystem level functions (such as decomposition), which provide, in turn, ecosystem goods or services (such as nutrient cycling and the detoxification of chemical or biological hazards) (see Swift et al. 2004; Hillebrand and Matthiessen 2009; Altieri and Rogé 2010). Changes in absolute biodiversity may, therefore, have widely divergent impacts on ecosystem processes depending on how they affect diversity within particular functional groups. In fact, the number of species needed within any one functional group to provide essential ecosystem processes and services may be relatively small in the short-term (Swift et al. 2004). Further, biodiversity at the micro-scale is often highly variable due to the dynamic nature of environmental conditions that influence species behaviour and the ability of many species to move and colonize new ecological niches (Zimmerer 1994).

Absolute biodiversity has been proven essential to long-term ecosystem stability (Hillebrand and Matthiessen 2009) but changes in absolute biodiversity can be misleading when measured at an exclusively micro-scale (Zimmerer 1994).

Equally important in comprehending biodiversity is an understanding of how ecosystem processes are shaped in both planned and unplanned ways (Swift et al. 2004; Altieri and Rogé 2010). Commonly used distinctions between 'wild' and 'endemic' biodiversity, on the one hand, and 'cultivated' or 'exotic' biodiversity, on the other, can draw attention away from the functional relationships between domesticated and non-domesticated species at a variety of scales. Farms, for example, can be described as agroecosystems in which some elements of biodiversity are planned – as farmers consciously manipulate both domesticated and non-domesticated species in pursuit of desired ecosystem services – and in which other aspects of biodiversity are unplanned and perhaps not even known (see Altieri 1999).

The concepts of functional and planned biodiversity have a number of implications for sustainable biodiversity management and policy:

- Conservation of existing biodiversity is a necessary, but insufficient, step towards sustainable biodiversity management. New 'diversities' must be planned and implemented at a variety of spatial and temporal scales in order both to reverse current levels of species extinctions and to implement more sustainable approaches to human development.
- Promoting diversity without consideration of the functional relationships between groups of species may lead to poor targeting of management effort (Swift et al. 2004). It may, for example, be more important to preserve or enhance a small number of species or ecosystem fragments for which few functional substitutes are available in order to support key

ecosystem processes, than to preserve or enhance other species and/or more widely dispersed ecosystems.

- The concept of functional biodiversity suggests a shift from thinking about organisms in terms of niche specialisation and stability to thinking about them in terms of adaptability and dispersal (Zimmerer 1994). One of the more obvious conclusions to draw from this is that protected areas (such as national parks, biosphere reserves, marine protected areas, etc.) intended to conserve wild or endemic biodiversity must be large enough to allow species to migrate and evolve in response to both short- and long-term disturbances ranging from wildfire and pest invasions to climate change.
- Less obvious, perhaps, is the need to ensure those who depend on cultivated biodiversity are able to share genetic resources. Many farmer plant and animal breeders, for example, value regular access to fresh genetic material and happily creolize 'traditional' and 'modern' varieties. They, and others, prefer plant and animal varieties adaptable across a range of environmental conditions over varieties dependent on uniformly favourable soil, water and other conditions for their productivity (Zimmerer 1994, 2003; Wood and Lenné 1997; Carpenter 2005).
- The concepts of planned and unplanned biodiversity focus attention on the potentially positive relationships between cultivated and wild biodiversity. They highlight the need to think not only about how biodiversity can be protected *from* agriculture, forestry and other human uses but about how these activities can be managed to ensure biodiversity delivers services for a range of natural resource uses including habitat and species conservation (Vandermeer and Perfecto 2007). In light, for example, of evidence that even intensive agricultural systems derive measurable economic benefits from relatively 'natural' landscape features (Omer et al. 2010) opportunities clearly exist to design agroecosystems in ways that support wild biodiversity.
- Finally, both wild and cultivated biodiversity is supported by landuse diversity at greater spatial scales. Ecologically and culturally, the 'natural' unit for the management of planned biodiversity is not the protected area or the field but the more difficult to define unit of the landscape (see Zimmerer 2006). Attempts to conserve and enhance biodiversity are more likely to be successful in landscapes characterized by mosaics of land use – including relatively natural ecosystems (Vandermeer and Perfecto 2007). Connectivity between habitat types provides for species migration and increases the capacity of predator populations to respond to increases in pest numbers.

Convention on Biological Diversity (CBD)

As a multilateral framework convention, the Convention on Biological Diversity established an institutional structure to support international cooperation along with general and flexible obligations for member states to implement through national laws and policies (McGraw 2002). Explicitly reflecting the concept of sustainable development, the CBD aims to ensure: (1) conservation of biodiversity; (2) sustainable use of its components; and (3) fair and equitable sharing of the benefits arising from the utilization of genetic resources (UN 1992: 3). Given the prominence afforded to issues such as poverty eradication and capacity building at the 1992 Rio Earth Summit the goals of managing biological resources sustainably and equitably for human benefit may seem sheer common sense; as self-evidently desirable ambitions in the pursuit of win–win sustainable development outcomes. But as McGraw (2002) points out, no other international agreements – including those on climate change – so strongly reflected the interests of developing countries. Drawing on their collective custodianship of an estimated 80 per cent of the world's biodiversity, developing countries were able to assert sovereign rights to biological resources within their own borders and counter attempts to negotiate a treaty focused solely on biodiversity conservation.

As a framework convention which imposes no binding conditions on signatory governments the CBD is often criticized as a 'toothless tiger'. Jacquemont and Caparrós (2002: 176, italics in original), for example, argue that as a document declaring 'how parties *should* act rather than how they *must* act', the Convention has little more to rely on than the good faith of signatories. It is true that the CBD does allow parties to negotiate ancillary annexes and protocols containing more precise and binding conditions. However, those negotiated to date – the Cartagena and Nagoya Protocols – are limited in focus and scope when compared with the comprehensive ambitions of the Convention. The Cartagena Protocol on Biosafety, adopted in 2000, aims to manage risks to biodiversity and human health arising from the handling, transport and use of living modified organisms developed through modern biotechnology. The Nagoya Protocol on Access and Benefit Sharing, adopted in 2010, responds to concerns that the CBD was being used, against its intention, to 'lock up' biological resources by establishing clearer and more transparent arrangements for accessing genetic resources and sharing the benefits of their exploitation.

Despite these limitations, myriad other agreements, programs and processes have been linked in some way to the CBD and the conceptual framework it provides for integrating these within an overarching ecosystems approach to conservation. In fact, the inclusivity and comprehensiveness of the Convention has led to fears it will become unduly complex or collapse under its own weight (McGraw 2002). This has not, of course, happened. Indeed, in 2010, the Conference of the Parties to the CBD adopted a new strategic plan along with associated goals and targets intended to guide not only signatory governments and ancillary agreements to the Convention but the entire United Nations system. Rather than attempting to deal with every potentially relevant policy and program we will focus in the rest of this chapter on the biodiversity and sustainability implications of two relatively novel and globally-oriented initiatives, REDD/REDD+ (Reducing Emissions from Deforestation and forest Degradation) and IPBES (International Panel on Biodiversity and Ecosystem Services).

Reducing Emissions from Deforestation and forest Degradation: REDD and REDD+

The Reducing Emissions from Deforestation and forest Degradation Programme (REDD+) was launched in 2008 as an implementation mechanism of the United Nations Framework Convention on Climate Change. It aims, specifically, to provide a mechanism for developing countries to earn carbon credits in exchange for halting deforestation. As an umbrella programme, it includes a number of initiatives including the Forest Carbon Partnership Facility (FCPF) and Forest Investment Program (FIP), hosted by the World Bank (UN-REDD 2014). As such, the '+' is intended to recognize the importance of thinking beyond reducing deforestation and to consider the role of conservation, sustainable management of forests and enhancement of forest carbon stocks in reducing emissions. More recently, there have been calls and concrete proposals for expanding the remit of REDD+ to integrate biodiversity conservation and promote win-win outcomes for biodiversity and climate change mitigation (Gardner et al. 2012). Positive outcomes are not, however, inevitable. REDD+ projects could, for example, lead to unintentional biodiversity loss through the displacement of deforestation into other areas or the redirection of funds from other conservation objectives (Phelps et al. 2012). More broadly, REDD+ projects must meet a number of requirements if they are to ensure any kind of sustainable development. Gupta (2012) argues that REDD+ will create lose-lose scenarios for local people unless projects do the following:

- address the underlying drivers of deforestation (which relates to *learning*);
- ensure full participation of actors at all scales of the process (which relates to *deliberation*); and
- provide co-benefits and safeguards necessary to protect the rights of local communities (which relates to *accountability*).

The potential for lose-lose outcomes through failure to meet these criteria will intensify, Gupta (2012) argues, if developed countries fail to maintain their commitments to global climate change mitigation and thus the resources necessary to effectively implement REDD+ activities. With this in mind, the following sections will examine evidence of learning, deliberation and accountability in REDD+.

Learning

Planning, monitoring and assessing REDD+ activities in relation to biodiversity necessitate institutional dynamics and processes that foster ongoing learning. The challenges faced in undertaking such activities for biodiversity include selecting which aspects of biodiversity to conserve and monitor, challenges of attributing changes to REDD+ and limited resources available for biodiversity monitoring (Dickson and Kapos 2012). A number of scientists and practitioners have put forward proposals to respond to these challenges. One solution involves synthetic and interdisciplinary data analysis to feed into multi-user, multi-scale modelling programs. Ghazoul et al. (2010) propose a comprehensive trade-off analysis incorporating assessment of the less tangible costs and benefits such as downstream economic values of current land use. This analysis would be presented in a fairly sophisticated format (though user-friendly to the computer-literate) which could be continuously updated with new information, variables and computation scripts from end-users and experts. Dickson and Kapos (2012) similarly propose developing clear conceptual models and theories of change to determine attribution to REDD+ that relies on a range of data for causal modelling. Other authors have suggested spatial analysis of carbon and biodiversity trade-offs to feed into selection of specific REDD+ activities (Gardner et al. 2012). While these exercises appear to allow for open-ended addition of emerging information, experiences in REDD+ implementation to date provide some cautionary tales which are discussed below.

Deliberation

Incorporating biodiversity indices into planning is unlikely to be effective without the participation of local communities in planning, assessment and monitoring. By-passing them through sole reliance on sophisticated technologies such as metabarcoding (e.g. Ji et al. 2013) raises a host of risks, not least an incomplete understanding of social and economic impacts. In assessing changes in land-use, consideration should be given to the multiple government policies that do not always prove amenable to forest users' participation in planning and monitoring. For instance, there is evidence that smallholder farmers in Laos have been excluded from participating in REDD+ planning, in large part because of unresolved land tenure issues (Fox et al. 2013). Similarly in the much publicized case of the expulsion of local communities in REDD+ areas in Tanzania, Burgess et al (2013), argue that this eviction was precipitated by the application of the Forest Act 2002 by the government, rather than the World Wildlife Fund for Nature (WWF) partnered REDD+ activity as was originally intimated. In addition to access rights, other institutional change may be required to ensure the sustainability of forest livelihoods and, by extension, local biodiversity, including access to technology, capital, markets, labour, and knowledge (Ribot and Peluso 2003 in Fox et al. 2013). Ghazoul et al. (2010) emphasize the need for a multi-disciplinary and multi-sectoral process in assessing REDD+ activities. This would reflect the need for learning and deliberation that is still lacking in REDD+ implementation to date.

In regards to community involvement in biodiversity monitoring, Danielsen and Adrian (2013) in their review of community participation in carbon monitoring for REDD+ found that national implementers have not shown genuine commitment to fully involve local communities. This was despite evidence of local communities having the capacity to do the monitoring in a way that was cost-effective. Incorporating biodiversity concerns within REDD+ will require engagement from multiple sectors that actively engages local communities. Technocratic expert knowledge is currently drowning out other forms of knowledge in modelling and planning exercises. Two barriers to this might be national and sub-national governments that do not have a culture of participatory processes of governance and the dominance of Western scientific framing of biodiversity within REDD+ forums of decision-making, at the expense of local understandings. While the rhetoric within REDD+ encourages local participation, part of the problem is that REDD+ governing organizations shape who can participate, and the form of that participation (Thompson et al. 2011). In this way, it is still possible for blame deforestation on local communities while downplaying the level of responsibility held by other stakeholders.

Accountability

A lack of participation and deliberation among concerned actors, mainly rural people, raises critical questions about the accountability processes within REDD+. While justifications of REDD+ emphasize the equitable distribution of benefits, these are operationalized through a process that utilizes market-based benefit distribution and which may not align with the interests of poor and indigenous peoples (Ghazoul et al. 2010: 397). This has the potential to exacerbate existing inequalities. Rather than reducing poverty, seen as one of the co-benefits, a review of REDD+ activities in the Asia Pacific found that they have exacerbated existing inequities by concentrating resources among powerful political and economic actors (Barr and Sayer 2012). This is unsurprising when 'thus far efforts at aligning the interests of various REDD+ stakeholders remain principally focused on those stakeholders engaged and comfortable with measures and governmental structures common to the Global North' (Thompson et al. 2011: 108). Ghazoul et al (2010: 397) 'plead for more realism' about the unintended effects when REDD+ is introduced into complex local contexts, in particular with the potential to result in inequitable distribution of costs and benefits. A number of solutions have been proposed in response to these accountability issues. While Barr and Sayer (2012) focus on the distribution of economic benefits, Kanowski et al. (2011: 111) argue that progress can be made by 'supporting implementation of existing national and sub-national forest policies in ways that are consistent with the principles of good forest governance'. It is implementation, they argue, not legislation that forest-rich developing countries are lacking. They propose to allow REDD+ arrangements to emerge organically, largely from the bottom-up, within a sufficiently but not overly-defined international framework. Finally, Thompson et al. (2011) argue that the best way to enable this alignment is to carefully consider how the participation of affected communities is facilitated in the REDD+ process, both to ensure that the voices of a wide range of affected people might be heard in this process, and to make a significant effort to make participation as unconstrained as possible, so as to hear the real concerns and needs of these communities as these programs and projects move forward.

International Panel on Biodiversity and Ecosystem Services (IPBES)

The Intergovernmental Panel on Biodiversity and Ecosystem Services (IPBES) is a recently established platform for supporting the global community (international institutions and national governments) in their efforts to reduce global biodiversity loss. What IPBES will or should deliver is still a matter of vigorous debate. However, it does appears that a technocratic understanding of biodiversity is coming to dominate in which biological diversity and the services it provides are measured and modelled principally in relation to their economic exchange value. As with REDD+, there are concerns that this commodified framing of biodiversity fails to meet the three demands of sustainability. Multiple challenges for IPBES remain including identifying organization of the assessment process and connecting policy makers with IPBES' work. Underlying these challenges is a tension between identifying and promoting 'universal values' so that global agreements can move forward, versus the need to incorporate the multiple and conflicting values that are inherent in efforts to reduce biodiversity loss.

Learning

There is ongoing debate about what kind of learning needs to happen for IPBES to be an effective institution for the project of reducing biodiversity loss. Perrings et al. (2011) argue for a closer integration between science and policy-making processes across several domains. In particular, Perrings et al. hone in on what they believe to be the core business of the IPBES: assessment of biodiversity conservation. This might come in the form of integrated models of social and environmental change that are capable of providing conditional predictions of the impacts on biodiversity of different policies (see also Larigauderie and Mooney 2010; Duraiappah and Rogers 2011). Yet as Turnhout et al. (2013) argue, matching science too closely with policy demands narrowing the scope of investigation to a set of utilitarian rationalities around market value that may be driving biodiversity loss in the first place. Instead, Turnhout et al. (2013) suggest integrating ongoing learning about the variable examples of human–nature entanglements within a paradigm of 'living with' biodiversity. These avenues would avoid creating singular measures to represent social relationships with biodiversity and ensure a more inclusive approach that would not marginalize relationships outside of existing policy framings of the relationship between people and biodiversity. There is a tension between calls for the knowledge gathered by IPBES to be universal, and a reality check that scientific biodiversity knowledge is too often seen as 'universally representative, as neutral, as singular and as directly communicative from science to policy' (Turnhout et al. 2013). In order to meet the deliberative demand of sustainability, learning within IPBES must go beyond conventional understandings of biodiversity assessment in order to create the space for the kinds of broad-based decision-making processes needed for effective conservation practices (Funtowicz and Ravetz 1993; Robertson and Hull 2001 in Turnhout et al. 2013). As Vohland et al. (2011: 1192) argue:

> The IPBES should and must avoid linear constructions, and right from the beginning start as a communication tool across different scales and being explicit concerning

> uncertainties. IPBES should avoid the trap to overemphasize current, but limited knowledge and should facilitate social learning and identify critical knowledge gaps.

To this, we would add any assessment that excludes other forms of knowledge risks falling into the trap of not capturing the underlying drivers of biodiversity loss and, just as importantly, opportunities for conservation and restoration (see Duraiappah and Rogers 2011).

Deliberation

Just as narrow conceptions of biodiversity inhibit learning, they also have implications for deliberation. If the dominant framing of biodiversity as an ecosystem service measured in economic terms is maintained then economic values will almost inevitably be prioritized over less tangible or measurable values in decision-making (Turnhout et al. 2013). Granjou et al. (2013) argue that a regulatory form of science based on indicators, databases and computer projections seems to be winning out as the required science for biodiversity; 'steamrolling', in the process, indigenous and experiential knowledge. Contrary to this, they argue that: 'Knowledge established across all scales (especially the knowledge of local and indigenous peoples) and validated in multiple ways must be eligible for inclusion in IPBES processes.'

Certainly, some efforts have been made to incorporate local and indigenous knowledge in biodiversity assessments, even if only at the margins (Turnhout et al. 2013). In scaling such efforts up, it is critical, according to Turnhout et al., that such knowledges are not simply co-opted and integrated into mainstream knowledge production systems. Local and indigenous knowledge stripped of its connection to specific people and values cannot lead to truly deliberative outcomes.

Accountability

While many scientists writing about IPBES are concerned about the potential politicization of assessment findings (e.g. Duraiappah and Rogers 2011; Vohland et al. 2011), the solution need not be an exclusive focus on peer-reviewed scientific work. Deliberative processes have considerable potential as a means both to incorporate local and indigenous knowledge in assessments and also to evaluate the policy implications of assessment findings (Vohland et al. 2011). IPBES cannot be policy-neutral since it must by its own institutional make-up accommodate the needs of disparate governments and their constituents and non-government stakeholders. To be consistent with sustainable development, however, it needs to build in ongoing scrutiny of the distributive impacts of policy interventions across both space (intra-generational accountability) and time (inter-generational accountability).

Conclusion

As this chapter has argued, it is not diversity *per se* that delivers ecosystem services necessary for sustainable development but the functional relationships between groups of organisms. Promoting biodiversity-friendly practices without consideration of functional relationships and what they mean for natural resource use and management may lead to sub-optimal sustainability outcomes. At the landscape level, biodiversity has considerable potential to contribute to sustainable development through mosaics of modified and relatively natural ecosystems. Connectivity between habitat types provides for species migration and increases the capacity of predator populations to respond to increases in pest numbers. Still, much is unknown about the optimal mix of farmed agroecologies, commercial forests, urban areas and so on relative to comparatively natural ecosystems within landscapes. This creates a strong argument for research into the contribution of relatively natural ecosystem components within predominantly modified landscapes and the degree to which endemic biodiversity may purposefully be built into those landscapes without compromising productivity or, in fact, while lifting it. And it creates a strong argument to keep scaling up national and international efforts to monitor biodiversity in forums such as the IPBES. Sustainable development demands learning.

At the same time though, the complex mix of stakeholders and property rights implicated in landscape-scale management means that research into ecosystem processes needs to be backed up with the development of robust and participative planning institutions and processes, still currently lacking in many arenas discussed in this chapter. In the case of IPBES, technocratic language and knowledge remains dominant, reducing the scope of policy action. As with other dimensions of sustainable development, sustainable biodiversity management demands deliberation.

There is a pressing need to balance regulatory systems that protect native biodiversity *from* human use of resources with systems that focus on what native biodiversity can do *for* sustainable development. Currently, there is an enormous regulatory blind spot at both the national and multilateral levels in relation to functional relationships between landscape diversity, the role of agriculture and other resource uses in maintaining that diversity, and the services diversity provides. Binding biodiversity protocols are limited in scope and highly dependent on how they are utilized within national regulatory regimes. Indeed, it can be argued that the most significant programmes linking biodiversity with landscape-level management are those intended primarily for the management of other environmental issues including greenhouse gas mitigation. Within programs like REDD+ biodiversity is always likely to be de-prioritized relative to dimensions of global environmental change. In this respect, sustainable development demands accountability.

References

Agyeman, J. and Evans, B. (2004) 'Just sustainability': the emerging discourse of environmental justice in Britain? *The Geographical Journal*, 170(2): 155–164.

Altieri, M. (1999) The ecological role of biodiversity in agroecosystems. *Agriculture, Ecosystems and Environment*, 74(1–3): 19–31.

Altieri, M. and Rogé, P. (2010) The ecological role and enhancement of biodiversity in agriculture. In S. Lockie and D. Carpenter (eds) *Agriculture, Biodiversity and Markets: Livelihoods and Agroecology in Comparative Perspective*. London: Earthscan, pp. 15–32.

Barr, C. M. and Sayer, J. A. (2012) The political economy of reforestation and forest restoration in Asia–Pacific: critical issues for REDD+. *Biological Conservation* 154: 9–19.

Burgess, N. D., Mwakalila, S., Munishi, P., Pfeifer, M., Willcock, S., Shirima, D. and Marchant, R. (2013) REDD herrings or REDD menace: response to Beymer-Farris and Bassett. *Global Environmental Change*, 23(5): 1349–1354.

Carpenter, D. (2005) The in situ conservation of rice plant genetic diversity: a case study from a Philippine barangay. *Agriculture and Human Values*, 22(4): 421–434.

CBD (Convention on Biological Diversity) (2010) *Global Biodiversity Outlook* 3. Montréal.

Danielsen, F. and Adrian, T. (2013) Community monitoring for REDD+: international promises and field realities. *Ecology and Society*, 18(3): 41.

Dickson, B. and Kapos, V. (2012) Biodiversity monitoring for REDD+. *Current Opinion in Environmental Sustainability*, 4(6): 717–725.

Dryzek, J. and Stevenson, H. (2011) Global democracy and earth system governance. *Ecological Economics*, 70:1865–1874.

Duraiappah, A. K. and Rogers, D. (2011) The Intergovernmental Platform on Biodiversity and Ecosystem Services: opportunities for the social sciences. *Innovation: The European Journal of Social Science Research*, 24(3): 217–224.

Fox, J., Castella, J.-C. and Ziegler, A. D. (2013) Swidden, rubber and carbon: can REDD+ work for people and the environment in Montane Mainland Southeast Asia? *Global Environmental Change*. doi: 10.1016/j.gloenvcha.2013.05.011.

Funtowicz, S. O. and Ravetz, J .R. (1993) Science for the post-normal age *Futures*, 25(7): 739–755.

Gardner, T. A., Burgess, N. D., Aguilar-Amuchastegui, N., Barlow, J., Berenguer, E., Clements, T. and Vieira, I. C. G. (2012) A framework for integrating biodiversity concerns into national REDD+ programmes. *Biological Conservation*, 154: 61–71.

Ghazoul, J., Butler, R. A., Mateo-Vega, J. and Koh, L. P. (2010) REDD: a reckoning of environment and development implications. *Trends in Ecology and Evolution*, 25(7): 396–402.

Granjou, C., Mauz, I., Louvel, S. and Tournay, V. (2013) Assessing Nature? The genesis of the Intergovernmental Platform on Biodiversity and Ecosystem Services (IPBES). *Science Technology and Society*, 18(1): 9–27.

Gupta, J. (2012) Global forest and REDD+ governance: win–win or lose–lose? *Current Opinion in Environmental Sustainability*, 4(6): 620–627.

Hillebrand, H. and Matthiessen, B. (2009) Biodiversity in a complex world: consolidation and progress in functional biodiversity research. *Ecology Letters*, 12: 1405–1419.

Jacquemont, F. and Caparrós, A. (2002) The Convention on Biological Diversity and the Climate Change Convention 10 years after Rio: towards a synergy of the two regimes?, *Review of European Community and International Law*, 11(2): 169–180.

Ji, Y., Ashton, L., Pedley, S. M., Edwards, D. P., Tang, Y., Nakamura, A., Kitching, R., Dolman, P., Woodcock, P., Edwards, F. A., Larsen, T. H., Hsu, W. W., Suzan, B., Hamer, K. C., Wilcove, D. S., Bruce, C., Wang, X., Levi, T., Lott, M., Emerson, B. C. and Yu, D. W. (2013) Reliable, verifiable and efficient monitoring of biodiversity via metabarcoding. *Ecology Letters*, 16: 1245–1257.

Kanowski, P. J., McDermott, C. L. and Cashore, B. W. (2011) Implementing REDD+: lessons from analysis of forest governance. *Environmental Science and Policy*, 14(2): 111–117.

Larigauderie, A. and Mooney, H. A. (2010) The Intergovernmental science-policy Platform on Biodiversity and Ecosystem Services: moving a step closer to an IPCC-like mechanism for biodiversity. *Current Opinion in Environmental Sustainability*, 2(1–2): 9–14.

Lockie, S. (2007) Deliberation and actor-networks: the 'practical' implications of social theory for the assessment of large dams and other interventions. *Society and Natural Resources*, 20(9): 785–799.

Lockie, S. (2012) Sustainability and a sociology of monsters. *Sociologica*, 2: 1–13.

Lockie, S. (2014) Climate, scenario-building and governance: comprehending the temporalities of social-ecological change. In S. Lockie, D. Sonnenfeld and D. Fisher (eds) *The Routledge International Handbook of Social and Environmental Change*. London: Routledge: pp. 95–105.

McGraw, D. (2002) The CBD: Key characteristics and implications for implementation. *Review of European Community and International Law* 11, (1): 17–28.

Magnani, M. (2012) The green energy transition. sustainable development or ecological modernization? *Sociologica*, 6: 1 –25.

Millennium Ecosystem Assessment (MEA) (2005) *Ecosystems and Human Well-Being: Current State and Trends: Findings of the Condition and Trends Working Group*. Washington, DC: Island Press.

Omer, A., Pascual, U. and Russell, N. (2010) The contribution of biodiversity to modern intensive farming systems. In S. Lockie and D. Carpenter (eds) *Agriculture, Biodiversity and Markets: Livelihoods and Agroecology in Comparative Perspective*. London: Earthscan: pp. 117–135.

Perrings, C., Naeem, S., Ahrestani, F. S., Bunker, D. E., Burkill, P., Canziani, G., Thomas Elmqvist, T., Fuhrman, J. A., Jaksic, F. M., Kawabata, Z., Kinzig, A., Mace, G. M., Mooney, H., Prieur-Richard, A., Tschirhart, J. and Weisser, W. (2011) Ecosystem services, targets, and indicators for the conservation and sustainable use of biodiversity. *Frontiers in Ecology and the Environment*, 9(9): 512–520.

Phelps, J., Friess, D. A. and Webb, E. L. (2012) Win–win REDD+ approaches belie carbon–biodiversity trade-offs. *Biological Conservation*, 154: 53–60.

Rockström, J., Steffen, W., Noone, K., Persson, Å., Chapin, S., Lambin, E., Lenton, T., Scheffer, M., Folke, C., Joachim Schellnhuber, H., Nykvist, B., de Wit. C., Hughes, T., van der Leeuw, S., Rodhe, H., Sörlin, S., Snyder, P., Costanza, R., Svedin, U., Falkenmark, M., Karlberg, L., Corell, R., Fabry, V., Hansen, J., Walker, B., Liverman, D., Richardson, K., Crutzen, P. and Foley, J. (2009) A safe operating space for humanity. *Nature* 461: 472–4.

Steffen, W., Crutzen, J. and McNeill, J. R. (2007) The Anthropocene: are humans now overwhelming the great forces of Nature? *Ambio*, 36(8): 614–21.

Swift, M., Izac, A. and van Noordwijk, M. (2004) Biodiversity and ecosystem services in agricultural landscapes: are we asking the right questions? *Agriculture, Ecosystems and Environment*, 104: 113–134.

Tàbara, J. D. (2014) Social learning to cope with global environmental change and unsustainability. In S. Lockie, D. Sonnenfeld and D. Fisher (eds) *The Routledge International Handbook of Social and Environmental Change*. London: Routledge: pp. 253–265.

Thompson, M. C., Baruah, M. and Carr, E. R. (2011) Seeing REDD+ as a project of environmental governance. *Environmental Science and Policy*, 14(2): 100–110.

Turnhout, E., Waterton, C., Neves, K. and Buizer, M. (2013) Rethinking biodiversity: from goods and services to 'living with.' *Conservation Letters*, 6(3): 154–161.

UN (United Nations) (1992) *Convention on Biological Diversity. Concluded at Rio de Janeiro on 5 June 1992.* Nairobi: United Nations Environment Program.

UN-REDD. (2014) UN-REDD Programme FAQs. FAO, UNDP, and UNEP. Retrieved March 21, 2014. Available at: www.un-redd.org/UNREDDProgramme/FAQs/tabid/586/language/en-US/Default.aspx

Vandermeer, J. and Perfecto, I. (2007) The agricultural matrix and a future paradigm for conservation. *Conservation Biology*, 21(1): 274–277.

Vohland, K., Mlambo, M. C., Horta, L. D., Jonsson, B., Paulsch, A. and Martinez, S. I. (2011) How to ensure a credible and efficient IPBES? *Environmental Science and Policy*, 14(8): 1188–1194.

WCED (World Commission on Environment and Development) (1987) *Our Common Future, Report of the World Commission on Environment and Development.* Published as Annex to General Assembly document A/42/427, Development and International Co-operation: Environment.

Wood, D. and Lenné, J. (1997) The conservation of agrobiodiversity on-farm: questioning the emerging paradigm. *Conservation Biology*, 6: 109–129.

Zimmerer, K. (1994) Human geography and the 'new ecology': The prospect and promise of integration. *Annals of the American Association of Geographers*, 84 (1): 108–125.

Zimmerer, K. (2003) *Political Ecology: An Integrative Approach to Geography and Environment-Development Studies* (with T. J. Bassett). New York: Guilford Publications.

Zimmerer, K. (2006) Geographical perspectives on globalization and environmental issues: the inner-connections of conservation, agriculture and livelihoods. In K. Zimmerer (ed.) *Globalization and New Geographies of Conservation*. Chicago: The University of Chicago Press, pp. 1–44.

8
WATER AND SUSTAINABLE DEVELOPMENT

Naho Mirumachi

Introduction

The management of water resources exposes many of the challenges of sustainable development as a concept and practice. Freshwater is a vital natural resource for human life. However, as societies have developed, water resources have been extracted and utilised to the extent where trade-offs with damage to the natural environment are increasingly evident. As a general trajectory, Allan (2001) highlighted that as industrialisation progresses, there are increases in the abstraction of water resources. Water retaining infrastructure is developed through massive engineering projects of dams, barrages, piped networks and irrigation canals. After this phase of intense exploitation, a more reflexive mode of water utilisation takes place, with focus on efficient and environmentally conscious ways of managing the resource – at least in theory (ibid.). The tipping point to this more reflexive phase is where sustainable development of water resources becomes particularly relevant in policy discussions. To what extent is water abstraction acceptable? Sustainable development of water resources for whom? How can we understand the implications of water use on the sustainable development of other natural resources such as land and forests? Moreover, it could be argued that sustainable development could and should prevent the exponential growth of water resources so that no tipping point need be reached in the first place.

While the hydrological cycle ensures water as a renewable resource, freshwater is more limited in quantity than saline water. Of the quantity available, 97.5 per cent is saline water, while only 2.5 per cent is freshwater (UNEP 2002). Moreover, this limited amount of water is stored in ice caps and glaciers, posing issues of access. We rely on rivers, lakes and groundwater resources for multiple uses, ranging from agriculture to tourism. Often, these bodies of water are shared between different water users both within and across states. For example, there are 263 international transboundary surface water basins (UN Water 2008). Considering that water is vital for human and ecosystem health, it is not only quantity but also quality of the freshwater resources that matter to sustainable development.

Noting the transboundary nature of many freshwater bodies, the chapter aims to understand the ways in which water and sustainable development have been understood in global and national policy discussions. In this regard, rather than examining the traditional engineering perspectives of improving infrastructure, technology and services, the analysis focuses on the socio-economic and ecological aspects of water resources management, or what is loosely termed as the 'soft path' (Brooks et al. 2011). The chapter first examines the various initiatives to mainstream discussions of sustainable development. These initiatives highlight why water is a problem and the potential solutions within a sustainable development paradigm. This analysis is followed by a brief assessment of how water institutions have developed in response to sustainable development discourse. The framing of water issues within sustainable development discourses throws up problems of 'participation' for better decision-making. To this end, the next section critically discusses the meaning of participation for sustainable water resources. There are also emerging policy concepts and ideas such as water security, the water–food–energy nexus, water security and green economy. The following section analyses them to understand the new (and potentially old, recurring) issues of water and sustainable development. Here, the intention is to provide an exploratory analysis of these policy developments considering their emerging nature, rather than a rigorous assessment of their effectiveness. The chapter concludes by emphasising the political challenge of achieving sustainable development of and through water resources.

Sustainable development and water scarcity

Water resources have featured prominently in global discussions on sustainable development from an early stage. The first political forum on sustainable development at a global scale was the United Nations Conference on Environment and Development (also known as the Earth Summit) in 1992. As a first of its kind, the Earth Summit developed the Agenda 21 as a way of achieving sustainable development, with some action dedicated to water resources. The Agenda 21 emphasised water scarcity as a major issue, as well as issues of water quality (UN 1992a). Throughout this document, the linkages of water with other sectors were underscored with mention made of food production, ecosystems and sanitation. The Dublin Statement on Water and Sustainable Development (hereinafter the Dublin Statement) fed into shaping the discourse on water within a sustainable development context. The Dublin Statement (UN 1992b: n.p.) considered 'scarcity and misuse of freshwater [as] a serious and growing threat to sustainable development and protection of the environment'. As 'a finite and vulnerable resource', efficient management was necessary by treating it as an economic good (ibid.).

These political commitments acknowledged the important role water plays in sustainable development. However, this discourse of water and sustainable development homogenises the problem of water scarcity, when in fact the causes of scarcity are not uniform and not simply a matter to be solved through mechanisms to deal with economic goods. Across the world, agriculture uses between 70–90 per cent of water resources, while domestic use is marginal in comparison, consuming approximately 10 per cent (WWAP 2009). The problem of water scarcity for agriculture needs to be considered in conjunction with how water resources are abstracted, while as the problem of water scarcity for domestic use brings about a different issue of agency in access and provision of clean water.

Turning first to the issue of water for agriculture, this early discourse of water and sustainable development lacks differentiation between different kinds of water, and how they are used. As a simple shorthand for differentiating freshwater resources, the terms blue, green and grey water are often used.[1] Blue water refers to the freshwater bodies such as rivers, lakes and aquifers. Green water is soil moisture, vital to vegetation growth. Grey water refers to the quantity of water needed to treat water quality degradation, often from industrial processes. It has been argued that intensive and extensive irrigation that extracts blue water from the natural environment runs the risk of rivers running dry and with ecosystem services degraded within the basin (Allan 2011).

However, a more pressing issue that has received less attention is green water management. Understanding the vital role of green water is important because it is used over 2.5 times more than blue water, and 80 per cent of land used for agriculture relies on this particular type of water (Falkenmark and Rockström 2006). In other words, rainfed agriculture matters. Nonetheless, green water is not accounted for well, and often taken for granted in policy discussions. Thus, sustainable development, particularly in the developing world, requires management mechanism that takes into consideration the value of precipitation that provides green water (Falkenmark and Rockström 2010). The innovation in water footprint calculations helps promote the importance of understanding green water. Blue, green and grey water inputs to grow a crop or to manufacture a product are calculated as part of its water footprint. Water footprints give an indication of the quantity of water being used to produce a particular crop or product, but also the kind of water and its source (Hoekstra et al. 2011; Zhang et al. 2013). This tool, while certainly not a panacea for water scarcity in itself, illustrates to water users and decision-makers how consumption of products (and thus water resources) can have implications for water availability in a globally unevenly distributed situation. Rather than a narrow perspective on water as an economic good, considering better practices in rainfed agriculture and consumption patterns of agricultural products, underlined by lifestyle choices, is more fruitful.

Now turning to the issue of domestic water, framing water within the context of sustainable development as an issue of scarcity throws light on who is responsible for ensuring sustainable development. This aspect is particularly relevant for domestic water use, especially as urban and peri-urban populations grow. While water consumption for drinking and sanitation is smaller than that of agricultural activities, ensuring water quality and reliability of access to water is important. Providing safe water was traditionally seen as the role of the state, but formal public provision of water is not the only means or even an option available in urban and peri-urban areas. As evidenced by the existence of water vendors and community-led initiatives in developing countries, the political economy of domestic water supply involves mechanisms beyond the public sector, presenting a complex landscape of actors and power (e.g. Kjellén 2000; Bakker et al. 2008; Ahlers et al. 2013; Zug and Graefe 2014).

Water scarcity in the urban and peri-urban areas is thus influenced by socio-economic capacities of individuals and communities, not by the existence and level of infrastructure and formal water provision services *per se* (Bakker 2010). Water scarcity affects the poor more while the rich can find alternative means of securing access to water. In these circumstances, treating water as an economic good is highly contentious. The privatisation of water supply and provision has been one of the most notable developments in the water sector in the 1990s. Coupled with neoliberalism, privatisation of water resources was to provide efficiency, much more than what the state could do in providing these vital services. However, the track record of such privatisation has been patchy and the role of private sector has been heavily critiqued, especially in developing country contexts (e.g. Prasad 2006; Budds and McGranahan 2003; Araral 2009; Wu and Ching 2013). Even though Agenda 21 calls for the inclusion of a wide set of actors, private sector participation has been highly contentious in solving this particular problem of 'scarcity'.

Sustainable development and water institutions

With the Rio+20 United Nations Conference on Sustainable Development in 2012 marking two decades since the establishment of the global political agenda on sustainable development, it is worthwhile noting the extent to which various initiatives on water have been set up. The Earth Summit certainly stimulated a growth in global water initiatives. There are now more fora, campaigns and professional organisations that deal with global water issues than before

(Varady et al. 2008). The global water policy community has established key fora such as the World Water Week in Stockholm and the World Water Forum. These fora continue to grow in size, attracting not only high-level political figures but also businesses and NGOs. In addition, international agencies such as the UN organisations have raised the profile of water through various conferences and declarations. Consequently, there are 11 major declarations from 1972 to 2010 (Mount and Bielak 2011).[2]

The increase of global water initiatives shows that there is growing awareness of water issues. But a critical analysis provides some insight on their relevance. Varady et al. (2008) found that the increase of global water initiatives has resulted in a situation where there are overlaps between various organisations and mandates. At the same time, they argue that there are no coherent ways of accounting for the effectiveness of these initiatives. Mount and Bielak (2011) conducted a qualitative study on key terms used in the 11 UN declarations to see how the discourse of water has changed over time. Their findings show that there is a patchy take-up of issues such as water scarcity, water quality and human health across these declarations. In particular, they found that water scarcity tends to be framed in terms of drinking water scarcity. This study exposes problems such as water quality and health being acknowledged as key issues but only dealt with in a nascent manner.[3] Crucially, Mount and Bielak (2011) argued that declarations may simply be 'shallow words' engaging in water issues in a superficial manner, missing an opportunity to learn from previous declarations for better effectiveness. Where there is declining public expenditure on water services and challenges to stimulating investments in the water sector (WWAP 2009), it could be questioned whether numerous global water initiatives are best ways to utilise limited resources.

Participation for sustainable development of water resources

Noting the ways in which water issues touch upon other domains of economic activity and development concerns, a key outcome of the sustainable development discussions in the early 1990s was the recognition of an integrated approach to water and development. The Dublin Statement is a milestone in this regard, recognising the importance of integrated planning and management, which is also reflected in the Agenda 21 (UN 1992a; 1992b). In reality, various forms of integrated water management had already existed in these initiatives. Some argue that the US government had already practised a version of integrated water management through the development of the Tennessee Valley Authority in 1933 (Biswas 2004; Snellen and Schrevel 2004). The Tennessee Valley Authority, while having a political objective to address the Great Depression, also aimed to utilise water and other related resources. The 1977 United Nations Water Conference in Mar del Plata argued the need to recognise the various water uses, which national governments should coordinate, which can be interpreted as a form of integration (Snellen and Schrevel 2004). However, the Dublin Statement drew clear connections between different water uses and their effects and economic development more robustly. Importantly, the Dublin Statement called for better decision-making that involves a wide range of stakeholders.

Inheriting the principles of the Dublin Statement, the Ministerial Declaration of The Hague on Water Security in the 21st Century (hereinafter the Hague Declaration) set forth a new framework that the water sector could adopt and practise (WWC 2000). Tailored more towards management, this framework of Integrated Water Resources Management (IWRM) provides ways of practising sustainable development. The Global Water Forum, which has taken a leadership role in advancing IWRM globally, defined the concept as 'a process which promotes the coordinated development and management of water, land and related resources, in order to maximise the resultant economic and social welfare in an equitable manner without compromising the sustainability of vital ecosystems' (GWP 2000: 22). IWRM is thus concerned with three aspects: (1) to consider issues of social equity between different water users; (2) to identify the economically efficient ways of managing the resource; and (3) to promote sustainability of the ecosystem. Effectively, IWRM is an ambitious way 'to address (simultaneously!) two highly complicated and complex problem sets; sustainable development and cross-sectoral planning' (Jeffrey and Gearey 2006: 2).

IWRM is founded upon the idea that participatory decision-making is necessary and vital. This concept indicates that sustainable development of water resources is a deliberative process. Top-down decision-making would not be sufficient and the inclusion of previously marginalised water users necessary. This means that not only large water users, such as the agricultural water users, but also those working to conserve wetlands and other ecosystems, for example, must take part. IWRM calls for an understanding of the various values of water for different users and uses embodied in the inclusive, participatory process.

However, this theory of IWRM has not translated to practice well. Despite the very wide take-up of IWRM by many national governments, it has been subject to heavy criticism as being: unrealistic in its principle making implementation difficult, particularly in developing countries (Biswas 2004; 2008; Pegram et al. 2013); predictive without regard to local contexts in which water use is practised (Lautze et al. 2011); and so ambiguous that stakeholders can '[misuse] the concept as a smoke screen to camouflage other agendas and objectives' (Molle 2008: 136). For the purposes of space, this chapter will not detail the deficits of IWRM but rather focus on the ways in which participation within IWRM for sustainable development is challenging.

Implementing IWRM requires major institutional reform in many countries, particularly developing countries to recognise rights, rules and procedures for new forms of decision-making. Moreover, this decision-making needs to take into account the sectoral links for example between water and land management, and water resources management and energy governance (Horlemann and Dombrowsky 2012). Within the inclusive decision-making process, rules and expectations of water resources use and allocation need to be worked out. However, there will be stakeholders who engage for the first time or have had little previous interaction. For example, at the community level, those involved in fisheries and forestry management may need to exchange views on priorities over water resources without any shared history of working together. At the national level, ministries with different bureaucratic incentives such as energy and agriculture will need to consult each other.

Participation thus presents a problem of trust and time. Building up trust between those who do not have shared expertise and experience is likely to take time. Power differences between these stakeholders set the dynamics of engagement. Developing a culture of inclusive, participatory decision-making requires a mix of capacity building, institutional development and financial resources. Consequently, participation *does* come at a cost for many stakeholders financially and capacity-wise, with no guarantee for consensus in decision-making (Mirumachi and van Wyk 2010). This conundrum underscores how timelines for successful IWRM through inclusive participation is in tension with day-to-day management practices and policy cycles. The iterative process of deliberative engagement spans over the long term, while water is used daily and monitoring and evaluation of water policies are done in a much shorter time frame.

It can be said that IWRM adopts an 'instrumental rationality' to participation, prioritising the importance of data and information for better decision-making (Molle 2008: 133). The implication is that IWRM risks posing an apolitical understanding of the nature of participation and decision-making. Many of the empirical work on (the failure of) IWRM point out that deciding the balance between efficiency, equity and ensuring ecosystems is complex and challenging because of the very vested interests of stakeholders and the entrenched socio-economics that support difficult-to-change institutions (e.g. Funke et al. 2007; Agyenim and Gupta 2012; Hirsch 2012). The failure to grapple with the politics of sustainable development and integration across sectors is also noticeable in UN water initiatives with underlying tones of technocratic approaches. The initiatives have featured existing technology as a means of managing water issues, undermining the socio-political challenges of sustainable development of water resources (Mount and Bielak 2011).

An entangled nest of ideas: water security, water–food–energy nexus and the green economy

In parallel with the existing and ongoing efforts at IWRM, there is a set of new, emerging policy discussions that can be argued as taking up the spirit of sustainable development within the water sector in various forms. Water security is a concept that is gaining traction in global water policy circles. In conjunction with this concept, the water–food–energy nexus is becoming a common phrase among governmental actors, as well as non-governmental actors, such as international food and beverage businesses (see WEF 2011). Water in the green economy is another related discussion that is taking place in light of Rio+20 agendas. As will be shown in further detail below, these three concepts deal with sustainable development of water resources *and* water resources management for sustainable development.

Water security was highlighted in the Hague Declaration in 2000 as a key challenge of the new century. Nonetheless, more than a decade on, water security is still a loosely used term without a clear definition. The UN agencies involved in water issues acknowledged the under-developed dimensions of water security and presented a 'working definition':

> Water security is defined here as the capacity of a population to safeguard sustainable access to adequate quantities of acceptable quality water for sustaining livelihoods, human well-being, and socio-economic development, for ensuring protection against water-borne pollution and water-related disasters, and for preserving ecosystems in a climate of peace and political stability.
>
> *(UN Water 2013: 1)*

This definition underlines how water can be an input to sustainable development. A recent compilation of studies on water security showed that it is a broad concept that defies a single definition but is characterised by environmental sustainability (Zeitoun et al. 2013). Water security is regarded as a key consideration for Sustainable Development Goals to follow the Millennium Development Goals (UN Water 2013).

Water security not only makes explicit the linkage of sectors but also spatial scales at which water is used and managed. Thus, consideration is needed to the question of how water use at a particular scale by one group of stakeholders could threaten the water security of another at a different scale (Zeitoun 2011). The concept of risk is also associated with water security. Grey and Connors (2009) noted how water-related risks vary between different water users, the environment and the economies that depend on the resource. In this sense, water security can be interpreted to be about resilience and adaptive capacity in a way that IWRM did not discuss.

While the working definition of water security may provide contours to the concept, the way to practise water security is even less evident at this stage (see Lankford et al. 2013). One suggestion is to improve the economic diversity so that economies are not subject to direct impacts from water scarcity, droughts and other threats to availability (Grey and Sadoff 2007). In this regard, the idea of virtual water trade has been argued as a way in which water scarce countries import food and other products without having to deplete water resources within their territories (Allan 2001). This suggestion goes well beyond the domain of water resources management and poses challenges of macro-economy and other development options for decision-makers.

However, these suggestions on the wider political economy do not explicitly discuss dimensions of ecosystems and their role in water security. One policy response that makes an explicit consideration on ecosystems can be found in a recent framework presented by the ADB (2013). To deal with 'environmental water security' that ensures healthy ecosystems and water systems, a multi-pronged approach encompassing both economic incentives and institutional development was recommended. This requires implementing mechanisms such as payment for ecosystem services, better technology and information systems to address degradation of watersheds. At the same time, institutions need to be in place to make measures work and this approach points to the importance of water rights. Nonetheless, this framework by the ADB is based upon IWRM as a way to liaise across sectors. Even though IWRM has been promoted as good practice since the Hague Declaration, this mode of management may not be sufficient for water security, especially in light of the limitations discussed above.

While still an emerging trend, it is important to note that there are some progressive approaches to address the gaps in IWRM for water security. One such approach is positioning natural infrastructure central to practices of water resources management. Natural infrastructure or ecosystems that have a function to store water, a buffer against floods are actively valued and used in providing benefits to water quantity and quality issues (Coates and Smith 2012). For example, within a river basin, maintaining adequate river flows throughout the year not only ensures a healthy environment but also provides benefits to the stability of economic activities relying on the flows such as energy production and water supply for communities (Tickner and Acreman 2013). However, as Tickner and Acreman noted, mainstreaming this approach will take political will and again raises the issue of a conducive institutional landscape.

To understand the complexities of water security, the water–food–energy nexus is gaining attention. The World Economic Forum was the first major international organisation to shed light on this new concept in their annual meeting in 2008. The nexus concept goes beyond the water sector and includes discussions on how the energy sector uses water to produce and distribute energy, how food security can be enhanced (or threatened) by water resources. Thus, the nexus concept can be understood as a new way to interpret the sustainable development of water resources in a broader scope, not necessarily tied to hydrological basins or to the mandate of national governments or river basin organisations.

Perhaps the reason for the attention to this nexus concept is that it can bring to the table a broad range of actors in a way that IWRM has not done. While there is some evidence that oil and gas businesses have a low awareness of IWRM and have not applied IWRM to their actual practices (Romer 2013), major companies such as Shell are interpreting what the nexus would imply for their business operations (Castelein 2011; Shell 2013). In addition, with this concept, existing gaps in data and knowledge are coming to light, for example, on the extent to which the water sector uses energy to abstract, provide and treat water resources (Rothausen and Conway 2011). The water–food–energy nexus is a good reminder of how integration is important but difficult. The concept does act as a common language to re-attempt a meaningful discussion on integration of sectors in a way that is not prescriptive.

However, the assumptions of this concept are based on scarcity. The nexus concept equates water security with water supply security (Hoff 2011). The concept contributes to the discourse of water and development in a way that foregrounds the threat of water resources failing to meet the demands of human and economic activity. The nexus highlights increasing population, urbanisation, climate change and globalisation as crucial reasons that call for ensuring sufficient water supply, food and energy (ibid.). This narrative has neo-Malthusian undertones without differentiating rigorously the way in which scarcity is produced and sustained. The water–energy–food nexus currently seems to have best value as an inclusive phrase for different stakeholders with varying interests. Concrete policy frameworks utilising this concept will have to engage with the very messy politics of prioritising and qualifying natural resources needs and interests of multiple stakeholders.

These discussions of water security and the water–food–energy nexus are couched within the broader agenda of sustainable development in the post Rio+20 era. The idea of striving towards a green economy implies that growth is possible so long as it does not break the ecological thresholds (UNDESA 2012). Eco-efficiency in water resources management and sustainable infrastructure are promoted as a way of reducing environmental burdens but meeting water demands, especially for domestic water use (UNESCAP 2007). Green growth is discussed by promoting eco-efficient water infrastructure that reduces the environmental burdens. The water–food–energy nexus is posited as a way to catalyse green growth with policies working to address issues of social justice and appropriate infrastructure investment, and promoting resource efficiency (UNESCAP 2013).

However, it is worthwhile questioning the extent to which changes to practice will actually happen in the planning, construction and operation of 'eco-efficient' or 'sustainable' infrastructure. In the context of water security, new infrastructure is justified because 'hindering water development could well lead to stagnant or falling incomes and environmental and social harm all the same' (Grey and Sadoff 2007: 566). But this approach may cast new infrastructure as 'green' investments at the risk of depoliticising trade-offs between development and the environment, and prescribing ecological limits in a utilitarian manner. Critical perspectives are necessary to ensure that the green economy discourse does not simply mask the specific contentions between various actors, reducing itself to a 'totalising metaphor' of consent on problems relating to the environment (Bourke and Meppem 2000: 38).

Conclusion

The management and governance of water resources have received much attention in relation to sustainable development. The global policy community has been instrumental in shaping water issues in global agendas and numerous water-specific initiatives. The discourse of water and sustainable development has evolved to emphasise the multiple links of water with other resources. The new, emerging concepts of water security, nexus and green economy may provide opportunities to engage with sustainable development in different ways. However, sustainable development of water resources is inherently political and past experiences have shown that an understanding of the socio-economic conditions that can enable 'participation' and 'integrated management' is necessary. While policy innovation is welcome, the entangled nest of ideas relating to water security, nexus and green economy may well be self-reinforcing mechanisms of current water resources management practices if the socio-economic bottlenecks are not fully recognised, and sustainable development may remain elusive.

Notes

1 See Gawel and Bernsen (2011) for a critique of these terms.

2 Forerunners of the Earth Summit include the 1972 Stockholm Declaration of the United Nations Conference on the Human Environment, the 1977 United Nations Water Conference – Resolutions (or the Mar Del Plata Resolutions) and the 1990 New Delhi Statement.

3 The 2002 World Summit on Sustainable Development and the Plan of Implementation that was an outcome of this meeting do engage with the issue of water, sanitation and health.

References

ADB (Asian Development Bank) (2013) *Asian Water Development Outlook 2013: Measuring Water Security in the Asia and the Pacific*. Manila: ADB.

Agyenim, J. B. and Gupta, J. (2012) IWRM and developing countries: implementation challenges in Ghana. *Physics and Chemistry of the Earth, Parts A/B/C*, 47–48: 46–57.

Ahlers, R., Schwartz, K. and Perez Guida, V. (2013) The myth of 'healthy' competition in the water sector: the case of small-scale water providers. *Habitat International*, (38):175–182.

Allan, J. A. (2001) *The Middle East Water Question: Hydropolitics and the Global Economy*. London: I.B. Tauris.

Allan, J. A. (2011) *Virtual Water: Tackling the Threat to Our Planet's Most Precious Resource*. London: I.B. Tauris.

Araral, E. (2009) The failure of water utilities privatization: synthesis of evidence, analysis and implications. *Policy and Society*, 27(3): 221–228.

Bakker, K. (2010) *Privatizing Water: Governance Failure and the World's Urban Water Crisis*. Ithaca. NY: Cornell University Press.

Bakker, K., Kooy, M. and Shofiani, N. E. and Martijn, E. (2008) Governance failure: rethinking the institutional dimensions of urban water supply to poor households. *World Development*, 36(10): 1891–1915.

Biswas, A. K. (2004) Integrated water resources management: a reassessment. *Water International*, 29(2): 248–256.

Biswas, A. K. (2008) Current directions: integrated water resources management: a second look. *Water International*, 33(3): 274–278.

Bourke, S. and Meppem, T. (2000) Privileged narratives and fictions of consent in environmental discourse. *Local Environment*, 5(3): 299–310.

Brooks, D. B., Brandes, O. M. and Gurman, S. (eds) (2011) *Making the Most of the Water We Have : The Soft Path Approach to Water Management*. London: Routledge.

Budds, J. and McGranahan, G. (2003) Are the debates on water privatization missing the point? Experiences from Africa, Asia and Latin America. *Environment and Urbanization*, 15(2): 87–114.

Castelein, A. (2011) Shell and the water-energy-food nexus. *OECD Global Forum on Environment*, 26 Oct 2011.

Coates, R. and Smith, M. (2012) Natural infrastructure solutions for water security. In R. Ardakanian and D. Jaeger (eds) *Water and the Green Economy: Capacity Development Aspects*. UN Water Decade Programme on Capacity Development, Bonn.

Falkenmark, M. and Rockström, J. (2006) The new blue and green water paradigm: breaking new ground for water resources planning and management. *Journal of Water Resources Planning and Management*, 132(3): 129–132.

Falkenmark, M. and Rockström, J. (2010) Building water resilience in the face of global change: from a blue-only to a green-blue water approach to land-water management. *Journal of Water Resources Planning and Management*, 136(6): 606–610.

Funke, N., Oelofse, S. H. H., Hattingh, J., Ashton, P. J. and Turton, A. R. (2007) IWRM in developing countries: lessons from the Mhlatuze Catchment in South Africa. *Physics and Chemistry of the Earth, Parts A/B/C*, 32(15–18): 1237–1245.

Gawel, E. and Bernsen, K. (2011) The colour of water: what does it tell us about scarcity? *GAIA-Ecological Perspectives for Science and Society*, 20(4): 224–228.

Grey, D. and Connors, G. (2009) The water security imperative: We must and can do more. Stockholm World Water Week. Available at: www.worldwaterweek.org/documents/WWW_PDF/Resources/2009_19wed/0903_Grey_Connors_The_Water_Security_Imperative_FINAL_PRESS.PDF (accessed 25 March 2014).

Grey, D. and Sadoff, C. (2007) Sink or swim? Water security for growth and development. *Water Policy*, 9(6): 545–571.

GWP (Global Water Partnership) 2000, *Integrated Water Resources Management*. Stockholm: Global Water Partnership.

Hirsch, P. (2012) IWRM as a participatory governance: framework for the Mekong River Basin? In J. Öjendal, S. Hansson and S. Hellberg (eds) *Politics and Development in a Transboundary Watershed: The Case of the Lower Mekong Basin*. London: Springer Verlag, pp. 155–170.

Hoekstra, A. Y., Chapagain, A .K., Aldaya, M. M. and Mekonnen, M. M. (2011) *The Water Footprint Assessment Manual: Setting the Global Standard*. London: Routledge.

Hoff, H. (2011) *Understanding the Nexus. Background Paper for the Bonn 2011 Conference: The Water, Energy and Food Security Nexus*. Stockholm: Stockholm Environment Institute.

Horlemann, L. and Dombrowsky, I. (2012) Institutionalising IWRM in developing and transition countries: the case of Mongolia. *Environmental Earth Sciences*, 65(5): 1547–1559.

Jeffrey, P. and Gearey, M. (2006) Integrated water resources management: lost on the road from ambition to realisation? *Water Science and Technology*, 53(1):1–8.

Kjellén, M. (2000) Complementary water systems in Dar es Salaam, Tanzania: The case of water vending. *International Journal of Water Resources Development*, 16(1): 143–154.

Lankford, B., Bakker, K., Zeitoun, M. and Conway, D. (eds) (2013) *Water Security: Principles, Perspectives and Practices*. London: Routledge.

Lautze, J., de Silva, S., Giordano, M. and Sanford, L. (2011) Putting the cart before the horse: water governance and IWRM. *Natural Resources Forum*, 35(1): 1–8.

Mirumachi, N. and van Wyk, E. (2010) Cooperation at different scales: challenges for local and international water resource governance in South Africa. *The Geographical Journal*, 176(14): 25–38.

Molle, F. (2008) Nirvana concepts, narratives and policy models: insights from the water sector. *Water Alternatives*, 1(1): 131–156.

Mount, D. C. and Bielak, A. T. (2011) *Deep Words, Shallow Words: An Initial Analysis of Water Discourse in Four Decades of UN Declarations*. Hamilton, Ontario: UNU-INWEH.

Pegram, G., Li, Y., Quesne Le. T., Speed, R., Li, J. and Shen, F. (2013) *River Basin Planning: Principles, Procedures and Approaches for Strategic Basin Planning*. Paris: UNESCO.

Prasad, N. (2006) Privatisation results: private sector participation in water services after 15 years. *Development Policy Review*, 24(6): 669–692

Romer, R. (2013) Can the concept of Integrated Water Resource Management (IWRM) positively contribute to the oil and gas sector? Master's dissertation, King's College London.

Rothausen, S. G. S. A. and Conway, D. (2011) Greenhouse-gas emissions from energy use in the water sector. *Nature Climate Change*, 1(4): 210–219.

Shell (2013) Energy-water-food. Available at: www.shell.com/global/environment-society/environment/water-food.html (accessed 25 March 2014).

Snellen, W. B. and Schrevel, A. (2004) *IWRM: For Sustainable Use of Water. 50 Years of International Experience with the Concept of Integrated Water Management. Background Document to the FAO/Netherlands Conference on Water for Food and Ecosystems*. Rome/the Hague: FAO/Netherlands Conference on Water for Food and Ecosystems.

Tickner, D. and Acreman, M. (2013) Water security for ecosystems, ecosystems for water security. In B. Lankford, K. Bakker, M. Zeitoun and D. Conway (eds) *Water Security: Principles, Perspectives and Practices*. London: Routledge: pp. 130–147.

UN (United Nations) (1992a) *Agenda 21*. United Nations Conference on Environment and Development, Rio de Janeiro, Brazil, 3–14 June 1992.

UN (United Nations) (1992b) *The Dublin Statement on Water and Sustainable Development*. Dublin: International Conference on Water and the Environment.

UNDESA (United Nations Department of Economic and Social Affairs) (2012) *A Guidebook to the Green Economy: Issue 1: Green Economy, Green Growth, and Low Carbon Development. History, Definitions and a Guide to Recent Publications*. New York: UNDESA.

UNEP (United Nations Environment Programme) (2002) *Global Environmental Outlook 3: Past, Present and Future Perspectives*. Nairobi: UNEP.

UNESCAP (2007) *Sustainable Infrastructure in Asia: Overview and Proceedings*. Bangkok: UNESCAP.

UNESCAP (United Nations Economic and Social Commission for Asia and the Pacific) (2013) *Water, Food and Energy Nexus in Asia and the Pacific*. Bangkok: UNESCAP.

UN Water (2008) *Transboundary Waters: Sharing Benefits, Sharing Responsibilities*. Available at www.unwater.org/downloads/UNW_TRANSBOUNDARY.pdf. (accessed 25 March 2014).

UN Water (2013) *Water Security and the Global Agenda: A UN-Water Analytical Brief.* Hamilton. Ontario: UNU University.

Varady, R.G., Meehan, K., Rodda, J., McGovern, E. and Iles-Shih, M. (2008) Strengthening global water initiatives. *Environment: Science and Policy for Sustainable Development,* 50(2) (March/April): 19–31.

WEF (World Economic Forum) (2011) *Water Security: The Water-Energy-Food-Climate Nexus*. Washington, DC: Island Press

Wu, X. and Ching, L. (2013) The French model and water challenges in developing countries: evidence from Jakarta and Manila. *Policy and Society*, 32(2): 103–112.

WWAP (World Water Assessment Programme) (2009) *The United Nations World Water Development Report 3: Water in a Changing World*. Paris: UNESCO, and London: Earthscan.

WWC (World Water Council) (2000) *The Ministerial Declaration of The Hague on Water Security in the 21st Century*. The Hague: WWC.

Zeitoun, M. (2011) The global web of national water security. *Global Policy*, 2(3): 28–296.

Zeitoun, M., Lankford, B., Bakker, K. and Conway, D. (2013) Introduction: A battle of ideas for water security. In B. Lankford, K. Bakker, M. Zeitoun and D. Conway (eds) *Water Security: Principles, Perspectives and Practices*. London: Routledge, pp. 3–10.

Zhang, G. P., Hoekstra, A. Y. and Mathews, R. E. (2013) Water Footprint Assessment (WFA) for better water governance and sustainable development. *Water Resources and Industry*, 1–2: 1–6.

Zug, S. and Graefe, O. (2014) The gift of water: social redistribution of water among neighbours in Khartoum. *Water Alternatives*, 7(1): 140–159.

9
SUSTAINABLE ARCHITECTURE

Keith Bothwell

Introduction

This chapter outlines the characteristics of so-called sustainable architecture citing examples from current practice. 'So-called' because it should be established from the outset that it is very rare to find a truly sustainable building. Nearly every act of building damages the environment in some way: in excavating the site, the existing ecology is harmed; in moving materials, transport routes are polluted by noise and emissions; in providing heating or cooling, carbon dioxide is often released. All we can say with a modicum of certainty is that some buildings are more sustainable than others.

Contrary to popular perceptions, the greenest buildings are not usually those that wear their colour on their sleeves, in the form of solar panels, wind turbines or other *eco-bling*.[1] No, the most environmentally friendly buildings are usually quiet and unassuming in exploiting daylight, using natural ventilation and embracing other passive forms of environmental control. In this way they reduce the demand for energy that would otherwise be needed to run them on an hourly, daily and annual basis, minimising carbon emissions during their lifespan. In addition to the environmental and cost benefits, reducing demand for energy in buildings has three direct effects: (1) eliminating or requiring smaller mechanical service systems; (2) making the buildings themselves more robust and resilient, in that they require less heating or cooling; and (3) reducing the number of new power stations required to generate electricity.

The definition of what constitutes sustainable architecture will vary according to our perception of the environment to be sustained. The assumption here is that it is the broader global environment that is to be protected, and that the threats are those outlined in the Brundtland Report of 1987 (WCED 1987), as elaborated by Agenda 21.[2] Among a raft of aims, the need to protect biodiversity, to conserve resources and to limit pollution are put to the fore. More recent environmental summits have focused on the most pressing problem, which is to limit atmospheric carbon emissions. More sustainable buildings are characterised by their lower consumption of energy, materials, water and other resources and by their use of materials that have lower negative impacts on the natural environment.

Sustainable architecture is not a new phenomenon. Turn the clock back two hundred years – before the era when fossil fuels became available widely, cheaply, and in large quantities – and you find buildings that exhibit many of the characteristics that we see in the more sustainable buildings of today. Societies in the past operated within the capacity of the local environment to provide resources for the construction and operation of new buildings; and their environmental impact was generally felt locally (Fieldson 2004: 27). Look further back in time or further afield, to the multifarious forms of vernacular architecture that have evolved over centuries around the world to suit particular climates and cultures, and you can discover unique solutions in different indigenous communities that not only improve comfort in hostile environments, but that are beautiful in their own right (Rapoport 1969).

From this root, in vernacular buildings constructed prior to the Industrial Revolution, and from its other root in the counter-culture movement of the late 1960s, sustainable architecture has now grown to become mainstream. Building owners, architects, and even contractors, now vie to be recognised as the greenest or the most environmentally friendly.

Despite this, the claims made for sustainability by corporations and individuals are often poorly founded or exposed as *greenwash* – of suspect validity. Independently devised and administered assessment schemes have therefore been established to test environmental claims against a common code that both precedes and drives changes in legislation. Sustainability objectives are now entrenched in building regulations and government directives. The voluntary environmental assessment methodologies, such as BREEAM (Building Research Establishment Environmental Assessment System) and LEED (Leadership in Energy and Environmental Design), on which the new legislation is founded, are used to calibrate sustainability indicators against a set of common scales (BRE 2014). Although environmental assessment has now become commonplace, it is not very flexible. The methodologies employed do not tend to encourage the kind of innovative practice that is characteristic of the most advanced sustainable design, and which, by its very nature – at the vanguard of a rapidly evolving field – goes beyond the status quo.[3]

At the end of the chapter I probe possible new directions for sustainable architecture. Future scenarios must be seen in the context of the gauntlet set down by climate scientists, who assert that, in order to stabilise the climate, carbon emissions must be reduced by 80–90 percent compared to 1990.[4]

The challenge is huge and daunting, and it is very far from clear that the target will or even can be met. However, with the construction and use of buildings accounting for 50 per cent of all carbon emissions, there is little alternative but to try and rise to the challenge (BIS 2010). Acknowledging that most of the buildings standing in 40 years time have already been built, what is clear is that adaptation and retrofit must form a central part of the overall drive in creating the low carbon buildings of the future.

The roots of sustainable design

In exploring possible models for the low energy buildings of the future, architects have been looking to the past, both in the self-conscious tradition, as well as to vernacular architecture around the world. Among the vernacular body a large vocabulary of strategies has already evolved to deal with various environmental conditions in different regions, tuned to local climate and culture (Rapoport 1969; Behling and Behling 2000).

In the hot dry region of the Middle East, thick-skinned buildings with small windows are tightly packed together, forming narrow streets and courtyards, to prevent the sun from beating down on them. The earth or masonry walls provide high thermal mass, which stabilises the temperatures inside, so that they are lower than the ambient external temperature during the heat of the day. Plants and fountains in courtyards further contribute to improving comfort by lowering the air temperature through evaporation (Oliver 2003).

In marked contrast, in the tropical climate of Indonesia, houses are raised on stilts with perforate walling of open louvres. This maximises the potential for breezes, which are the only respite from the hot humid atmosphere. Light coloured roofs with large overhangs reflect or exclude sunlight, which would otherwise exacerbate the uncomfortable conditions inside (Pearson 1989: 69).

In Scandinavia, houses are optimally buried into a south-facing slope, to protect against the cold north winds, and have windows facing south to bring in warming and welcome sunlight. Thick walls and roofs of thatch or turf help to insulate the interior from the bitter cold during the long winters (ibid.).

The lessons learned in obtaining comfort in climatic extremes can be applied to new buildings in various regions. In temperate zones, for example, which have to cope with cold winters and hot summers, the passive solar strategies inherent in the Scandinavian example can be adopted in winter, by using thick insulation and south-facing glazing. For summer comfort, the high thermal mass materials of the Middle East example can be reinterpreted in concrete to stabilise temperatures, and with solar shading to exclude sunlight. Some examples later help to illustrate the possibilities.

Designers today, however, must be careful when adopting or adapting vernacular modes of construction. Although methods of environmental control in traditional buildings certainly improved conditions internally, they would rarely achieve the standards of comfort that we expect today. Traditionally, people in cold climates still needed to dress in thick clothes, and their houses, or part of them only, would be heated for limited periods. Similarly, buildings in hot climates would not achieve the low temperatures provided by air-conditioning systems today. Traditional vernacular buildings in general were often very energy inefficient by today's standards.

Also, the technologies that have evolved over many centuries in different climates and cultures may not be easy to fully understand. Misunderstandings may arise because local modes of building are often informed by social, religious or practical factors in addition to the desire for comfort in a hostile environment. Social hierarchies and ritual customs, or religious practice, can require particular orientations or room arrangements and so determine the building layout (Rapoport 1969; O'Cofaigh et al. 1996: 1–2). The limited availability of construction materials, or traditions employing particular building crafts and skills, can often trump a strategy that might otherwise prioritise comfort in response to adverse climatic conditions.

Despite these limitations, vernacular buildings also exhibit other characteristics that we associate with some enthusiasts building sustainably today; they are usually built of natural materials obtained in the locality, which are often renewable, biodegradable, and non-toxic – for example thatch or timber or clay – and use the skills of the owner or local community.

In the 1950s, in the United States, Victor Olgyay, together with colleagues at Princeton, formalised the science of analysing climates, and developed methodologies for designing buildings that respond to climate in a positive way – taking advantage of its beneficial effects and expressing the systems of environmental control in the architecture. Some of these methods were published in his seminal book *Design with Climate* (1963). His approach marked a distinct change from the prevailing 'design against climate' approach, which used energy hungry air-conditioning or heating systems to fight against the ambient temperature within glass buildings designed in the International Style, whatever the region or climate.[5]

The more astute colonial builders also realised that exporting building typologies that had evolved in Europe and transplanting them to Africa and India did not produce the most comfortable buildings! At the Building Research Station in the UK, founded in 1921, a colonial liaison section was established in 1948, later becoming the tropical division. Like Olgyay in the USA, they began to bring scientific method to the tasks that indigenous people had understood over centuries through intuition and tradition. BRS later evolved into the Building Research Establishment (BRE), the body that has pioneered the standardisation of environmental assessment internationally.

The functional lessons of environmental control and material use are only part of what vernacular architecture can teach us. Bernard Rudofsky was one of the first to awaken Western architects to the poetic beauty of an architecture without architects (1964) and to building traditions that had developed unconsciously, in contrast to the self-conscious methods employed by professional architects.

By the late 1960s, a counter-culture movement had emerged that challenged the established order on several fronts: political, cultural, social, and environmental. Environmental concerns were triggered by signs of degradation caused by the untrammelled use of chemicals (Carson 1962), the destruction of natural habitats and perceptions of the increasing scarcity of resources (*The Ecologist* 1972).

The environmental strand of the movement began to envisage models of living that would cope with the uncertain future that seemed to be round the corner. With shortages of oil a realistic prospect and shortages of most raw materials predicted (Ward and Dubois 1973), incorrectly as it happened, many thought that the solution lay in becoming self-sufficient – in energy, food, and other resources. Those that were well prepared would survive the feared apocalypse that could occur at any moment. The autonomous house emerged as one model to achieve this. The house on its own plot would be self-sufficient in energy for heating and hot water, for cooking fuel and food and water. The building, its systems and the land would provide all the everyday needs of a family. It was a dream (or nightmare depending on your point of view) that was attempted by a few pioneers.

At Cambridge University in 1971, Alexander Pike created the concept of the Autarkic House, a prototypical autonomous house, with solar heating, wind turbine on the roof to generate electricity, and digester to convert sewage to methane gas for heating and cooking (Vale and Vale 2000). Working on Pike's team, Brenda Vale began to publish academic papers setting out the technical specifications for the autonomous systems that would comprise the required technology. In 1974 she and her husband Robert published their seminal book *The Autonomous House*, but it took nearly twenty years before they implemented the ideas in practice – in their own home in Southwell, Nottinghamshire – the first autonomous house in the UK. In the USA, Steve Baer built a solar house – comprising polyhedral 'zomes' – with recycled oil drums placed behind a glazed wall that used the sun to heat water.

These early pioneers inspired some enthusiastic followers around the world from the mid-1970s onwards. These included Lucien Kroll in Belgium, Architype and Feilden Clegg in the UK, Thomas Herzog and Gunter Behnisch in Germany, Sim van der Ryn in the USA, and Glen Murcutt in Australia. Some common principles of sustainable design that began to emerge from this disparate group of architects are summarised in Table 9.1.

Current practice

It has taken some 40 years since the pioneering work of the Vales and others to arrive at a point now when environmental requirements are commonplace criteria within every architect's brief. Sustainable design has moved from its associations with 'alternative' lifestyles in the 1970s to a niche professional area in the 1980s and 1990s, to become mainstream from the turn of this century onwards.

Table 9.1 Five principles of sustainable design

1. Working in cycles, like natural ecosystems, to minimise or eliminate waste and cause minimal damage to natural ecosystems – in contrast to the linear processes characteristic of the industrial revolution;
2. Economy of means – using as little material as possible;
3. Materials selected preferentially to be: (a) least toxic; (b) least processed; and (c) least travelled, especially if heavy (after Robert Vale);
4. Passive design – getting the building fabric itself to do most of the work in controlling temperature and ventilation;
5. Designing buildings that people want and appreciate and understand – involving the user in the design, construction and post-completion stages.

Leading architects and engineers in the field, such as Thomas Herzog, Max Fordham and Ken Yeang, are of one view regarding the starting point for sustainable design: that the primary and initial focus should be for the building itself to control the internal environment, passively (Bothwell 2011: 70). Passive environmental control techniques, that in the past were the only choice for improving comfort, are now being relearned.

The headquarters building for Wessex Water near Bath is a showcase for these passive strategies (see Figure 9.1). In office buildings the major energy uses are for lighting and cooling. Bearing this in mind, the architect Rab Bennetts has very carefully choreographed the building elements to maximise the free use of natural light and to keep the building cool (Hawkes 2000).

The office wings are kept narrow and have high ceilings, to bring daylight deep into the interior. The ceilings are painted white and are uncluttered so as to efficiently reflect natural light inwards. External walls are proportioned to optimise the ratio of glazing to solid insulated elements, such that the total energy cost, balancing heat losses and light gains through the glazing, is minimised.

In addition to admitting high levels of daylight the shallow building depth assists with natural cross ventilation across the office wings. The exposed solid concrete elements in the ceiling, which form the structure of the floor above, act as a thermal flywheel, absorbing heat gains from people and computers during the day, and releasing them at night when cool outside air is passed underneath to purge them (Hawkes 2000).

Unwanted solar gains are particularly problematic in office buildings because they exacerbate the high *casual* heat gains arising from people, light fittings, computers and other equipment. Until recently this overheating problem would have been simply and swiftly banished by the installation of an energy hungry air-conditioning system. But the Wessex Water building is carefully designed to avoid this. It is orientated with the main façades facing north and south. This enables the south façade to be easily shaded by shallow overhangs and simple louvres. The north façades, which receive sunlight only in the summer, are shaded by a line of deciduous trees planted parallel to the building, that obstruct the low altitude sunlight in early morning and late afternoon. In winter when the trees have shed their leaves, daylight from the sky can easily penetrate past the bare branches to illuminate the interior.

In this building, a very careful consideration of building form (narrow plan with high ceilings), orientation (east–west linear wings), materials (concrete ceilings, light coloured), and façade proportions (glazing vs. solid) all combine to reduce energy use and increase comfort.

Although exemplary in passively controlling the internal environmental conditions, Bennetts Associates go further than this in their efforts to minimise the overall environmental impact. They have selected a combined steel and concrete floor structure, which ensures that the materials are lighter than on earlier projects which employed only solid concrete, thus reducing the

Figure 9.1 Wessex Water building, Bath, by Bennetts Associates Architects: south elevation

embodied energy in both manufacture and transportation. Moreover, recycled railway sleepers have been crushed to provide the aggregate for the new concrete ceiling elements. Bath stone – locally sourced to minimise transport impacts – forms the walls of the western wing of the building that houses a social 'street' for the employees. Further environmental measures include recovering rainwater for reuse, using solar panels to heat water, and selecting indigenous plants for the landscaping to encourage local fauna.

Many of these features and characteristics are not overtly green, and most people on seeing it would not immediately recognise this as an environmentally sound building. Although it looks much like any other office block, albeit a very elegant one, when it was completed in 2000, it was lauded as the lowest energy office building in the UK, exhibiting most of the typical characteristics of sustainable buildings (see Table 9.2).

Table 9.2 Typical characteristics of sustainable buildings

- Low energy consumption in use (well insulated, passively controlling temperature, light and ventilation)
- Low embodied-energy materials used in construction
- Low environmental damage materials used in construction (low toxicity, renewable materials, ...)
- Maintaining and enhancing biodiversity
- Reducing the need for travel (green travel plans, near transport hubs if large numbers of people using building)
- Conserving, recovering and reusing water
- Drainage treated on site using natural processes (reed beds)
- Long lived (beautiful, popular and/or pleasant places to live and work, that people want to keep, durable)
- Multi-use (buildings that combine various functions and/or that can be used for longer period of the day, week, year)

The costs of constructing a more sustainable building can be little more than building a conventional one, and sometimes even less, depending on the base case against which it is compared (Rehm and Ade 2013). A survey of buildings in California has reported that the typical construction cost premium for building green is 2 per cent but that the financial benefits are almost ten times this premium: 'The financial benefits of green buildings include lower energy, waste, and water costs, lower environmental and emissions costs, and lower operations and maintenance costs and savings from increased productivity and health'(Kats 2003: 85).

However, the calculated benefits are those that accrue to the people of California as a whole, rather than just the owners of buildings (ibid.). In the UK, the additional costs of constructing the most exemplary sustainable buildings are calculated at between 1 and 7 per cent, depending on the building type. In the most sophisticated building types, such as healthcare buildings, the premium is much lower (Cyril Sweett and BRE Trust 2005).

The social street in the Wessex Water example represents a further characteristic of the most sustainable buildings. Buildings that are loved or appreciated by people, where users have a role in the design or buildings that 'belong' in some sense to them, and that are comfortable to be in, are likely to be well-maintained and cared for into the future.

The BedZed community in south London was a test-bed for many sustainable design principles and technologies. It combines two distinct building types – housing and offices – to achieve the optimal passive design for each and to enable people to live close to their work. Arranged in rows aligned east–west, the houses are located on the south side of each block with large windows to receive sunlight in winter. The offices nestle along the north sides, to protect them from solar gains, but gain plenty of daylight from north-facing rooflights (Long 2001).

At Freiburg, in southern Germany, a similar community is emerging in the Vauban district. The city itself has ambitious objectives for public transport and low energy buildings. The solar community and *solar-ship* development combines housing with commercial uses to achieve a symbiotic relationship between the two – the housing benefitting from solar gains, and the commercial uses from daylight (see Figure 9.2). Overall its highly insulated passive solar houses are net exporters of energy – generating electricity from the photovoltaic panels on their roofs. The residents participated in the design of the housing so achieve a high sense of 'ownership' (Guzowski 2010).

This public-spirited approach can also be extended to tall buildings. Norman Foster challenged the established typology of the skyscraper – normally a stack of identical office floor plates – with his tower for the Hong Kong and Shanghai Bank in Hong Kong in 1985. First, the

Figure 9.2 Solar Community and Solar-ship mixed use development in Freiburg, Germany, by Rolf Disch Solar Architecture

ground level was given over entirely to the public, with the building raised on columns so that people could wander under and into the building via escalators starting in the street. He introduced sunlight reflected off a giant mirror hung outside the building and then bounced this down the atrium space in its centre. His Commerzbank in Frankfurt was similarly innovative, incorporating sky gardens – multi-storey atrium spaces with trees and other planting – that bring natural light deep into the building, provide ventilation, and create interactive social spaces. The façades are doubled up to form a buffer zone between inside and outside, that pre-heats air in winter and removes excess heat in summer, avoiding the need for full air-conditioning.

Some of the ideas for reducing the need for air-conditioning, which evolved in these earlier skyscraper projects were incorporated in the design of the 'Gherkin' – the office building for Swiss Re in London. Designed to be naturally ventilated, the tower has spiral atrium spaces winding their way round the building. Opening windows (a rarity in tall buildings) allow fresh air to directly enter the atrium spaces and thence to the adjoining offices (Ritchie et al. 2004). Unfortunately the tenants of the building are so sensitive to the possibility that others might overhear their corporate secrets through the open windows, that they do not use the natural ventilation systems and have installed air-conditioning instead!

Building users are the one factor that architects and designers cannot control, yet they generally account for the huge discrepancy between energy predictions and actual consumption levels. With the increasing complexity of building servicing systems and controls, there is much evidence that even building managers do not understand how many buildings are supposed to work! A hiatus often occurs between the original design strategy and the everyday operation of the building.

Under 'design and build' contracts (popular with some clients), the concept architects and engineers are not involved in the detailed design, which is carried out by a range of often poorly coordinated sub-contractors, under the direction of a main contractor. Systems may end up competing against each other, so that automatic vents are opening to cool a building when the users turn up the thermostat. Surprising as it may seem, this type of problem is commonplace. The message to take from this is plain – keep the building as simple as possible, communicate clearly between all parties, and tell the users how to operate the building.

One approach that may help to address this problem is the Passivhaus standard, which is emerging as a new model for sustainable design. Originally developed for houses in the climate of northern Europe, it has now evolved to encompass any building type in any climate. Passivhaus emerged in Germany in the 1990s, following the exhaustive analysis of actual performance data on a large number of dwellings. The originators of the standard, Wolfgang Feist and Bo Adamson, sought to fully account for, and model, all the subtle variables that affect energy consumption. Passivhaus accounts only for energy consumption and human comfort, excluding all other environmental impacts (Cotterell and Dadeby 2012: 19). Nevertheless, it is increasingly being used as the benchmark against which other environmental standards are compared. Passivhaus buildings are very highly insulated, air-tight and have mechanical ventilation heat recovery systems. These ventilation systems warm incoming air in winter using heat recovered from the vitiated air, and can be 80–90 per cent efficient.

Homes built to Passivhaus standards will incur much lower installation costs for the small heating systems that may still be required, but additional costs for the higher specification of insulation, windows and air-tightness. Net increases in construction cost are in the region of five percent, but can be balanced against far greater levels of comfort and very much lower fuel bills (ibid.).

Codes and methodologies

In response to wildly inconsistent environmental claims made by the building industry, environmental assessment systems have been established. The UK Building Research Establishment (BRE) launched the world's first environmental assessment system for buildings in 1990. The method, titled BREEAM (BRE Environmental Assessment Method), originally laid out guidelines for the evaluation of office buildings.

The BREEAM system endeavoured to embrace all environmental impacts caused by buildings. Its aims were to mitigate the impact of buildings on the environment; to enable buildings to be recognised according to their environmental benefits; to provide a credible label for buildings; and to stimulate demand for sustainable buildings (BRE 2014).

Environmental issues are only included in BREEAM if they meet specific criteria. They must be significant and offer worthwhile reductions in environmental impact, be assessable at the relevant stage in the building's life, be based on scientific evidence wherever possible, exceed the demands of law and legislation, and be achievable.

One of the objectives of environmental assessment is to challenge the market to provide innovative solutions that minimise the impact of buildings. This objective and the criterion that the system must exceed legislation create paradoxes. If the standards set have any validity, then they will, before too long, be incorporated into legislation (as they have been with respect to housing in the UK) and the method will therefore no longer surpass those required by regulations. The objective to stimulate innovative solutions is difficult to achieve. By its very nature, the method, within each specific issue, has to describe particular standards, targets and criteria for verification. This process can only be designed when the construction technologies employed are established, tested, and familiar, i.e. when they are no longer innovative.

Table 9.3 BREEAM categories of environmental impacts included in the Code for Sustainable Homes (CSH)

Category	*Points available*
Energy and CO_2	36
Health and well-being	14
Ecology	12
Management	10
Water	9
Materials	7
Waste	6
Pollution	3
Surface water run-off	2

Note: These categories have varied over the evolution of the method and vary according to building type.

A case arises when evaluating the use of straw, an increasingly common building material. Straw bales are a low cost, very low impact building material, that use an otherwise waste material, lock up carbon dioxide, and provide high levels of insulation. However, they are not listed in the schedule of BREEAM-approved materials, so cannot currently contribute positively to a rating.

For ease of assessment and to prioritise certain fields, each issue is placed within a particular category (see Table 9.3). These categories have changed as the system has developed and as it has been applied to different building types. Each issue is assigned a number of points and each category is weighted differently, depending on its perceived importance. For example, the category Energy and CO_2 emissions is weighted far more strongly than those for Waste or Ecology. This reflects the consensus on what is the most pressing environmental problem to solve – global warming. Because regulations are being improved in the wake of environmental assessment initiatives, the bar for environmental assessment systems themselves is also being raised. Thus, a rating of, say, Excellent today is much more difficult to achieve than the same rating ten years ago.

In the United States, the LEED system has evolved with a scale that has Platinum as the top rating. Unlike BREEAM, which is validated and controlled by a charitable trust, LEED is managed by a trade association, the Green Building Council. The Green Building Council comprises architects, engineers, contractors and others in the building industry. In Australia they use GreenStar, and in Singapore the BCA Green Mark system. International versions of BREEAM and LEED are also validated for different countries around the world.

All environmental assessment systems use life cycle assessment methodologies that take into account the environmental impacts that occur at all stages of a building's life, from construction, everyday use and maintenance, to refurbishment and eventual demolition. This is sometimes referred to as 'cradle-to-grave' analysis. However, Braungart and McDonough (2002) have extended this concept to 'cradle-to-cradle' such that the materials at the end of the building's life are considered not to be waste materials for recycling but valuable resources that could be 'upcycled' to achieve a higher value in their next incarnation. Some materials, such as timber flooring boards, can be clamped into position without nails, such that they can be simply disassembled to be reused for a future project (Liddell 2008).

Environmental assessment systems have done much to encourage consideration of sustainability criteria and to set standards against which achievements can be measured and projects compared. Many clients and their design teams have been encouraged to have their buildings assessed in the knowledge that this raises the prestige of their organisations. The Wessex Water building achieved a BREEAM Excellent rating when it was completed in 2000 and the Singapore Library by Ken Yeang achieved BCA Green Mark Platinum rating in 2005.

Ken Yeang is an architect who has been at the forefront in exploring new directions for green architecture over several decades. His Roof-Roof house of 1985 used the building elements to control the climate. It is named after its double roof, the outer one of which shades the lower terrace from the heat of the tropical sun, so that it can be used for recreation next to a swimming pool. The upper roof is perforated with louvres which are specially angled and orientated to allow through the low morning sun but to exclude the searing midday and evening sun. The pool, located on the east side to face the prevailing winds, also cools the air, through evaporation, before it enters the building. Walls on the south side direct wind to cool the dining area (Hart 2011).

An air-cooling pool is also deployed on the roof of his Menara Mesingiaga tower in Kuala Lumpur. Cylindrical in form, the building façades are partially covered in solar shading panels, which flow round the building in a pattern that follows the sun's path around the sky. The lift tower is located on the south side to shade the building. The upper louvred roof canopy allows for future photovoltaics and the stepped façade provides terraces for people as well as shading for the floors below (ibid.).

In spite of these pioneers, and the stimulus provided by environmental assessment methods, when looking at the building stock as a whole, progress has been slow and incremental. The overall environmental impact of buildings has been little affected and it is becoming apparent that fundamental and systemic changes are needed to achieve the carbon reductions that are necessary.

Future directions

Retrofit

One systemic change required will be the retrofit of the existing building stock, to raise its energy efficiency closer to current standards. Most of the buildings that will exist in 2050 were constructed prior to 1970, when energy efficiency standards were low. As well as bringing environmental benefits for society at large, with lower carbon emissions, retrofit will improve comfort for building users and reduce energy bills – a triple-win situation. However, to obtain the necessary reductions in CO_2 emissions 'deep retrofit' solutions are required and the difficulties encountered in achieving this are significant.

Pioneering work has been done, some funded directly by governments, to assess the feasibility of rolling out retrofit on a wide scale. Despite some encouraging results in terms of energy reductions it seems unlikely that retrofit can meet the carbon targets set for the building sector. There are a great many 'hard to treat' properties – such as historic buildings where the appearance cannot be changed, or buildings that have physical restrictions which, for example, prevent the application of insulation materials – and that can only receive rudimentary improvements. The process of deep retrofits is often very disruptive, requiring occupiers to move out during building works, adding the rent for temporary accommodation to the very high cost of construction works. Costs for whole house retrofits are predicted to come down to between on average £25,000–£30, 000 after experience has been gained, but these costs will take very many decades to recoup in terms of reduced energy bills.

The task is also gargantuan. In the UK housing sector alone there are 26 million homes, and if they are all to be treated by the year 2050, that will require them to be retrofitted at the rate of more than 700,000 per year. As this is seven times the rate that new houses are currently being constructed, it is questionable whether the building industry has the capacity to address the task, let alone the finance necessary to fund it.

Biomimicry

Integrated and holistic changes are beginning to emerge in the design of new buildings. One of the underlying concepts guiding sustainable architecture is that of biomimicry – modelling building designs on natural ecological systems. People have been inspired to copy natural examples from the earliest days. When the ecological design field began to emerge in the 1960s the technical means available to architects lacked the sophistication and subtlety to reflect the complexity of plants and animals. However, with the advanced computer software and manufacturing methods that are now available and our increasing understanding of biological systems, it is becoming possible to mimic the behaviour of some natural processes quite accurately.

As his œuvre has developed, Ken Yeang's buildings have become literally as well as metaphorically greener. Yeang's early ideas have evolved into a formally structured approach to architectural design founded on the concept of ecomimesis. Buildings, for Yeang, should not just be based on ecological principles or incorporate plant life, they should actually become 'constructed living systems' in their own right. Like naturally occurring ecosystems, they will produce no wastes, but recycle everything within a closed-loop system.

Yeang's new buildings now incorporate planting snaking up the façades. These form miniature green ecosystems of plants, insects and animals (Figure 9.3). A key requirement is that they must stretch continuously from the ground all the way up round the building, so that species, carefully selected to be compatible with indigenous ones in the area, can easily migrate. The vertical green eco-infrastructure is then networked into the green infrastructure of the city. The EDITT building shown here generates electricity, collects and purifies rainwater, and processes wastes into biogas and fertilisers (Hart 2011).

Zooming out to the larger scale of the city district, the concept of continuous productive urban landscapes (CPULs) has been put forward as a model for sustainable urban development (Viljoen 2005). Linear green corridors are created, using existing parks, vacant sites and street edges to form a continuous habitat for plants and animals. These corridors include water catchment reservoirs and waste treatment systems, cycle routes, leisure areas and allotments, all connected together and extending through the city.

CPULs are seen one solution to the high cost of food, particularly in poorer urban communities such as those in Cuba, where vacant city plots are converted into market gardens on a commercial basis. The land is tilled by hand and has a very high yield (ibid.: 153).

Food grown near to where people live cuts out the storage and distribution processes and transport that would otherwise consume fossil fuels. Perhaps more importantly, it brings people together into communities that might otherwise never have arisen – communities that work together to make compost, to plant seeds, and to harvest the crops and celebrate together when they have done so! These productive urban landscapes enhance the ecological value of cities, bringing in insects and birds and other fauna and flora. The heat island effect is also reduced by lowering temperatures in summer (ibid.).

Biomimicry is developing from the imitation of nature in formal terms, to the direct application of biological systems to control sunlight and generate energy in buildings. The

Figure 9.3 EDITT tower project, Singapore, by Ken Yeang

Source: T.R. Hamzah & Yeang Sdn. Bhd. (2014)

BIQ apartment building in Hamburg, which opened in 2013, uses algae in glass tanks on the south-facing façades to perform several functions. The algae-filled tanks restrict light penetration so act as a solar filters or solar shades (Figure 9.4). The system works by introducing nutrients and carbon dioxide, which is pulsed into the tanks at regular intervals. Algae is extracted on a regular cycle and fermented in a biogas plant which produces methane to power the building. Solar panels generate heat that is stored in brine-filled boreholes beneath the building, to be reused later (Wurm 2013: 90–95).

Conclusion

We have seen a variety of approaches to the design of a more-sustainable built environment. The trend has been away from the self-sufficient autonomous house with its hard technology *eco-bling* that pioneered the sustainable architecture movement, to the widespread adoption of passive design. This recognises the paramount importance of reducing the demand for energy in the first place. Only then, if at all, should *eco-bling* be added to supply energy, and even then it is more efficient to locate this in large arrays rather than on individual buildings.

The trend is now away from the design of the individual building towards a mixed-use and multiplex approach, identifying the mutually beneficial needs of different building types.

These kinds of symbiotic relationships characterise the more holistic strategies now being adopted for sustainable development in cities, where buildings and the urban landscape between them form a continuous system – a network of interconnected hard and soft technology elements. Biotechnology systems are beginning to offer many interesting solutions for energy supply, environmental control and waste treatments.

Systemic changes will be needed too in the way that we live and work in cities, so that we reduce the need for energy and resources, for travelling, and for heating and cooling our buildings, and for growing food. It seems possible that these changes will result in significant changes in lifestyles – to a more cooperative and community-based way of living – in contrast to the more individual lives that most in the developed world currently enjoy.

Some environmentalists have argued that individual small-scale efforts to reduce energy are pointless in the face of the threat of global warming. However, it is this author's view that in the battle to create the more sustainable buildings of the future – and it will indeed be a battle, for the effort required will be comparable to waging a war – we will need to fight on all fronts at the same time. This is not to say that new avenues, in terms of technologies or strategies, will not open up, but we cannot depend on encountering a technological panacea within the short time that remains available.

How all this can be funded is beyond the scope of this chapter, but it seems likely that, although sustainable new buildings can be seen to pay for themselves, markets alone will have insufficient motive to invest in large-scale retrofit, due to the huge costs and lengthy payback periods involved. Government subsidies or incentives are likely to be the only way to significantly reduce carbon emissions from the currently existing stock, which will still comprise the majority of buildings in 2050. Decarbonising the electricity supply itself must also form part of the mix (DECC 2010).

We have seen that the route to a more sustainable architecture has been to a large extent a journey of rediscovery – rediscovering old ways of achieving comfort in hostile environments, using materials frugally, efficiently and simply, and employing technology only when it really helps and when people can fully understand it. Although new technologies are emerging that have extraordinary potential, we may well find that the past remains the best guide to our future.

Figure 9.4 BIQ building, Hamburg, by Arup, exploits algae in façade

Source: Arup Deutschland GmbH, Colt International GmbH and SSC GmbH).

Notes

1 Eco-bling is a term coined by Doug King to describe low-performing renewable energy technologies installed on buildings. The shortcomings of various technologies classed as eco-bling are discussed in Liddell (2008 [2013]).
2 Agenda 21 is the plan agreed at the UN Conference on Environment and Development (UNCED) held in Rio de Janeiro in 1992. The Agenda 21 plan identified four primary areas for action: (a) the social and economic dimensions; (b) the conservation and management of resources; (c) strengthening major groups (children, youth, women, NGOs, local authorities, indigenous peoples); and (d) the means of implementation.
3 Rick Wheal (2013), an engineer specialising in environmental assessment, at leading global engineering company Arup, has criticised BREEAM for being too inflexible.
4 The UK government target of 80 per cent reductions in CO2 compared to 1990 levels, is highly ambitious but reflects the level of change advised as necessary by a consensus of climate scientists and even so is still lower than that advocated by some scientists and environmentalists, who suggest that we need a reduction target of ninety percent or higher. See also: DECC (2010) *2050 Pathways Analysis*.
5 The International Style, which developed out of the Modern Movement in architecture, was adopted by a generation of architects who built glazed slab and tower blocks in all parts of the world, irrespective of the local climate. The movement was inspired by Mies van der Rohe and Le Corbusier. Le Corbusier at the time advocated a universal house for all climates: 'only one house for all countries, the house of exact breathing' ([1930] 1991), although he later adopted a more climate-inflected approach.

References

Behling, S. and Behling, S. (2000) *Solar Power: The Evolution of Sustainable Architecture*. London: Prestel.

BIS (Department for Business Innovation & Skills) (2010) *Estimating the Amount of CO2 Emissions That the Construction Industry Can Influence*. London: UK Government 10/1316.

Bothwell, K. (2011) The architecture of the passively tempered environment. In S. Lee (ed.) *Aesthetics of Sustainable Architecture*. Rotterdam: 010 Publishers, pp. 66–79.

Braungart, M. and McDonough, W. (2002) *Cradle To Cradle: Remaking the Way We Make Things*. New York: North Point Press.

BRE (2014) *BREEAM UK New Construction: Technical Manual* SD5076: 0.1 (DRAFT) – 2014. Watford: BRE Global.

Carson, R. (1962) *Silent Spring*. Harmondworth: Penguin.

Cotterell, J. and Dadeby, A. (2012) *The Passivhaus Handbook: A Practical Guide to Constructing and Retrofitting Buildings for Ultra-Low Energy Performance*. London: Green Books.

Cyril Sweett/BRE Trust (2005) *BREEAM: Putting A Price on Sustainability*. Watford: BRE Trust.

DECC (Department of Energy and Climate Change) (2010) *2050 Pathways Analysis*. London: DECC.

The Ecologist (1972) *Blueprint for Survival*. Harmondsworth: Penguin.

Fieldson, R. (2004) Architecture & Environmentalism: Movements & Theory in Practice. *Forum (Ejournal)*, 6(1): 21–33.

Guzowski, M. (2010) *Towards Zero Energy Architecture: New Solar Design*. London: Laurence King.

Hart, S. (2011) *Eco Architecture: The Work of Ken Yeang*. Chichester: John Wiley and Sons.

Hawkes, D. (2000) The flow of ideas: Bennetts Associates in Bath. *Architecture Today*, 113: 60–76.

Kats, G. (2003) *The Costs and Financial Benefits of Green Buildings: A Report to California's Sustainable Building Task Force*. Sustainable Building Taskforce.

Le Corbusier ([1930] 1991) *Précisions on the Present State of Architecture and City Planning* (English Translation). Cambridge. MA: MIT Press.

Liddell, H. (2008) *Eco-Minimalism: The Antidote to Eco-Bling*, 2nd edn. (2013) London: RIBA Publishing.

Long, K. (2001) BedZed: case study part one – green and pleasant land. *Building Design*, 1473: 12–13.

O'Cofaigh, E., Olley, J. and Lewis, O. (1996) *The Climatic Dwelling*. London: James and James.

Olgyay, V. (1963) *Design with Climate*. Princeton, NJ: Princeton University Press.

Oliver, P. (2003) *Dwellings: The Vernacular House Worldwide*. London: Phaidon.

Pearson, D. (1989) *The Natural House Book*. London: Conran Octopus.

Rapoport, A. (1969) *House Form and Culture*. Englewood Cliffs, NJ: Prentice Hall.

Rehm, M. and Ade, R. (2013) Construction costs comparison between 'green' and conventional office buildings. *Building Research and Information*, 41(2): 198–208.

Ritchie, I. et al. (2004) Foster's 30 St Mary Axe Tower. *Architecture Today*, 149: 54–66.

Rudofsky, B. (1964) *Architecture Without Architects*. Albuquerque, NM: University of New Mexico Press.

Vale, R. and Vale, B. (2000) *The New Autonomous House*. New York: Thames and Hudson.

Viljoen, A. (2005) *Continuous Productive Urban Landscapes: Designing Urban Agriculture for Sustainable Cities*. Oxford: Architectural Press.

Ward, B. and Dubois, R. (1973) *Only One Earth*. Harmondsworth: Penguin.

WCED (World Commission on Environment and Development) (1987) *Our Common Future (The Brundtland Report)*. Oxford: Oxford University Press.

Wheal, R. (2013) There is more to sustainability than a building's environmental impact: BREEAM doesn't go far enough: truly great buildings make society better by adding to the area. *The Guardian* sustainable business blog, Available at: www.theguardian.com/sustainable-business/blog/sustainability-building-environmental-impact?CMP=twt_fd (accessed 13 December 2013).

Wurm, J. (2013) Developing bio-responsive façades: BIQ House – the first pilot project. *Arup Journal*, 48(2): 90–95.

10
SUSTAINABLE DESIGN
Concepts, methods and practices

Martina Maria Keitsch

Introduction

The concept of sustainable development has undergone huge transformations since its first definition by the World Commission on Environment and Development (also known as the Brundtland Commission) as: 'development that meets the needs of the present without compromising the ability of future generations to meet their own needs' (1987: 46). Since then, sustainable development has required a continually revised understanding of many issues, while missing knowledge has to be identified and innovation must take place when new challenges emerge. In industrial design, sustainable development is strongly coupled with the terms 'sustainable consumption and production' which were introduced by the 2002 Johannesburg World Summit on Sustainable Development:

> Fundamental changes in the way societies produce and consume are indispensable for achieving global sustainable development. All countries should promote sustainable consumption and production patterns, with the developed countries taking the lead and with all countries benefiting from the process ... Governments, relevant international organizations, the private sector and all major groups should play an active role in changing unsustainable consumption and production patterns.
>
> *(2002: 14)*

The frameworks of the Johannesburg World Summit and the Annex 2 of the Rio Declaration 2005 (Universal Design for Sustainable and Inclusive Development) have been adopted by the sustainable design community ever since. According to these frameworks, a working definition of sustainable design might be: 'taking all ecological, social and economic concerns into account in product and service systems, meeting the needs of the present without compromising the ability of future generations to meet their own needs' (Keitsch 2011).

This definition implies considering various technical and functional levels such as minimizing the negative environmental impact by enhancing efficiency and moderating the use of materials, energy, and development space. Measures and tools to relate the design solution to the climate, the region and cultural conditions seem equally important. In order to establish

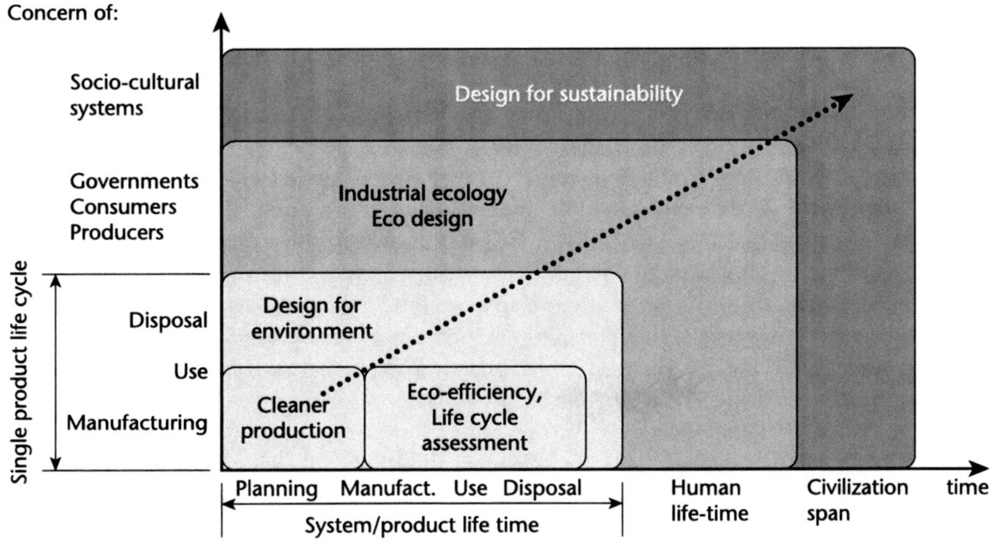

Figure 10.1 Successive changes in industrial design

Source: Keitsch (2011).

harmonious interactions between users and products or services, good form-giving is essential too: 'green' products and services should be well designed, easy to use and beautiful.

The chapter gives an overview of changes in industrial design towards sustainability, indicated in Figure 10.1. It will discuss main concepts, methods and practices in sustainable design from its start with cleaner production strategies in the 1980s, via life-cycle assessment and design for the environment until the turn of the millennium, to current eco-design and design for sustainability approaches.

A new and promising facet in sustainable design concepts is that greater emphasis is today placed on a 'user-centred approach' and on ways to elaborate solutions with involved stakeholders. The chapter concludes with a discussion on future opportunities and challenges for sustainability in industrial design and an overview of how design for sustainability concepts can, besides having ecological advantages, work as catalysts for the advancement of social sustainability – guided by the principle that a design solution is not truly considered sustainable until it is accepted by the users.

The infancy of sustainability approaches in industrial design

The history of sustainable development started at least two decades before Brundtland. By the late 1960s and early 1970s ideas about progress, growth, equity and resources had developed in this new direction (Du Pisani 2006). Environmental concern was triggered by the fear that economic growth might endanger the survival of the human race and the planet, and was expressed by authors such as Glick: 'if we continue our present practices we will face a steady deterioration of the conditions under which we live' (Glick, cited in Dubos et al. 1970: 2). In 1972, the United Nations Conference on the Human Environment recognized that:

> In our time, man's capability to transform his surroundings, if used wisely, can bring to all peoples the benefit of development and the opportunity to enhance the quality of

> life. Wrongly or heedlessly applied, the same power can do incalculable harm to human beings and human environment.

And further, 'To defend and improve the human environment for present and future generations has become an imperative goal for mankind' (Article 3).

However, the association of sustainability with industrial design only began in the mid-1980s, when the US and European manufacturing industry initiated cleaner production strategies (e.g. Frosch and Gallopoulos 1989). Successively, international agreements and national incitements stimulated the design of low energy products and novel ways of recycling or reusing by-products (waste). At the same time, the United Nations Environment Programme began to work on approaches to prevent pollution from occurring in the first place. The resulting strategy, Cleaner Production, is an essential part of the Sustainable Production and Consumption Policy and defined by the UNEP as follows: 'We understand Cleaner Production to be the continuous application of an integrated, preventive strategy applied to processes, products and services in pursuit of economic, social, health, safety and environmental benefits' (UNEP 1999). The strategy adopts, among other things, the precautionary principle, the preventive principle and the integration principle (*Clean Production Action* 2009) and covers areas such as energy efficiency, multilateral environmental agreement targets, and sustainable products.

In industrial design, cleaner production means taking into account the energy and material requirements for manufacturing, the use and the reparability, remanufacturing and recyclability of products. From the early 1990s, industrial designers working with Cleaner Production started to pay attention to the reduction of negative impacts along the life-cycle of a product – from the extraction of raw materials to its ultimate disposal. In 1988, a revised life-cycle methodology emerged, contributing to both exact eco-impact analyses of products and to improved product solutions. The Society of Environmental Toxicology and Chemistry defined life-cycle assessment (LCA) in 1993 as:

> An objective process to evaluate the environmental burdens associated with a product, process or activity by identifying and quantifying energy and materials used and wastes released to the environment, to assess the impact of those energy and materials uses and releases on the environment, and to evaluate and implement opportunities to affect environmental improvements. The assessment includes the entire life cycle of the product, process or activity, encompassing extraction and processing of raw materials, manufacturing, transportation and distribution, use/reuse/maintenance, recycling and final disposal.

In concert with incorporating environmental concerns into service solutions, Design for Environment (DfE) evolved out of product life cycle assessment in the early 1990s (United States Environmental Protection Agency). DfE developers apply LCA to all potential environmental implications of a product or a service being designed, energy and materials used; manufacture and packaging; transportation; consumer use; reuse or recycling and disposal. DfE tools enable consideration of these implications at every step of the production process from chemical design, process engineering, procurement practices, and end-product specification to post-use disposal. The DfE approach also enables designers to consider traditional design issues of cost, quality, manufacturing process, and efficiency as part of the same decision system. In an applied context, Design for Environment has, for example, been part of the Xerox industrial design since 1990, when the company started a five-year effort to create waste-free factories including

90 per cent minimum reduction in solid waste to landfills, air emissions, hazardous waste, and process wastewater discharges (Azar et al. 1995). The company's interest in DfE in the 1990s evolved in parallel with an increased consumer demand for 'green' design, i.e. the fabrication of environmental-friendly products (Unger and Eppinger 2011) and both created a 'second wave' of sustainable design (Bhamra and Lofthouse 2007) expressed in concepts as eco-design and industrial ecology (IE).

The second wave: eco-design and industrial ecology

In its initial phase, DfE and the emerging eco-design concept comprised mainly quantitative and empirical methods within a defined problem solving setting. Improvement strategies concentrated on a life-cycle optimization of material and energy flows within a system of production and consumption. In the DfE branch, as well as in early industrial ecology, normative questions such as whether developers and designers need a certain ethical attitude towards the environment or the consumer were not considered relevant (Opoku and Keitsch 2006). However, towards the millennium shift, many designers and developers started to realize that eco-design solutions may easily be lost by inappropriate production and consumption activities at other levels. To some extent, eco-design contributed, for example, to persuade consumers to sustain unfair economic wealth. These insights contributed to an attempt to define designers' tasks in terms of their contribution to sustainable societies (Madge 1997). Ehrenfeld summarizes this attempt as twofold: to realize eco-technical principles such as low material-energy intensity and high regenerative demands through products and service solutions and to respond to users' and societies' needs: 'The key to sustainability will be a balance between devices and a modified consumption ... and products and services that can transparently restore the human capability for caring and coping in all dimensions of life' (2008: 123, 124). In 2009, the eco-design concept eventually reached top-level political consciousness and the European Parliament established a framework for eco-design requirements for energy-related products:

> 'Ecodesign' means the integration of environmental aspects into product design with the aim of improving the environmental performance of the product throughout its whole life cycle ... The ecodesign of products is a crucial factor in the Community strategy on Integrated Product Policy. As a preventive approach, designed to optimize the environmental performance of products, while maintaining their functional qualities, it provides genuine new opportunities for manufacturers, consumers and society as a whole.
>
> *(Ecodesign Directive 2009/125/EC Article 2, 23 and Article 5)*

The EU eco-design framework defines conditions and criteria for all energy-related products in the residential, tertiary, and industrial sectors and implementing measures are being developed to define the product requirements for each product group.

Today, eco-design can be broadly characterized by two branches: a technology-oriented branch, and a society-oriented branch (Keitsch 2012a). The technology-oriented branch is, among others, developing tools to allow quick estimations on how to minimize the impact on the environment, e.g. the EcoDesign strategy wheel (Delft Design Guide) or Eco-it, a DfE and eco-design software. The society-oriented eco-design branch appears partly in Ehrenfeld's sense (e.g. Manzini 2003) and partly as an ethical call for design responsibility, aiming to raise designers' awareness and commitment to change society for the better, as, for example, in Papanek's work:

> There are professions more harmful than industrial design, but only a very few . . . by creating whole new species of permanent garbage to clutter up the landscape, and by choosing materials and processes that pollute the air we breathe, designers have become a dangerous breed . . . In this age of mass production when everything must be planned and designed, design has become the most powerful tool with which man shapes his tools and environments (and, by extension, society and himself). This demands high social and moral responsibility from the designer.
>
> *(Papanek 1991: ix)*

The concept of industrial ecology (IE) is traditionally closely linked to DfE and eco-design. Some authors claim that eco-design provides the setting for IE (Dale 2001) while others see IE as background for design over the life-cycle of products and processes within the framework of sustainable development (e.g. Indigo Development, see also Figure 10.2). The main objective of IE is to tackle environmental challenges attached to production, consumption and recycling processes of industrial products. The field is explained as the multidisciplinary study of industrial systems and economic activities, and their links to natural systems (Graedel and Allenby 2010). Conceptually, IE perceives units, processes and industries as interacting systems rather than isolated components: 'This systems-oriented vision accepts the premise that industrial design and manufacturing processes are not performed in isolation from their surroundings, but rather are influenced by them and, in turn, have influence on them' (Graedel and Allenby 1995: xix, 9).

The philosophy of IE is based on the assumption of interdependence between human-made and non-human-made systems and the matching of selected principles of natural ecological

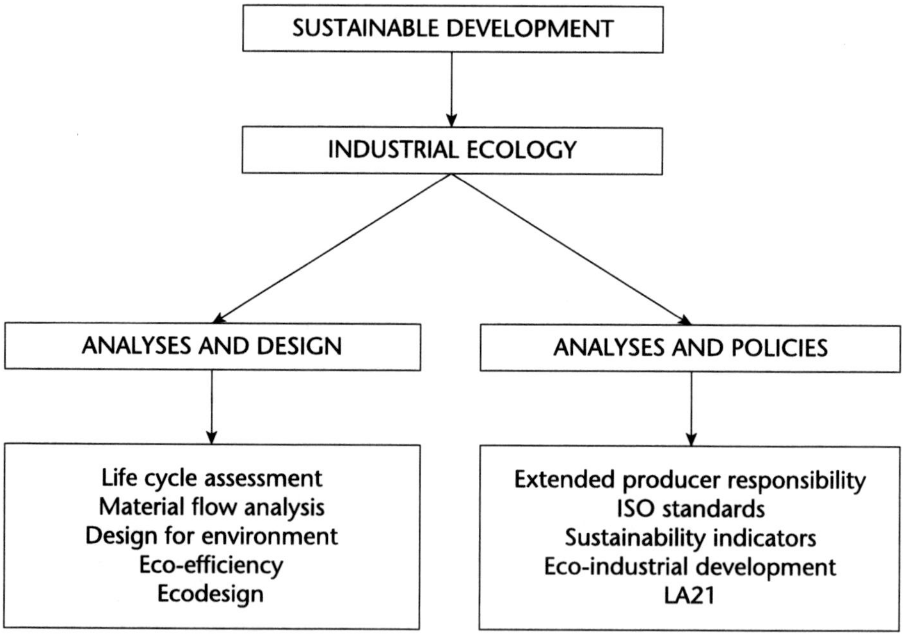

Figure 10.2 Locating eco-design in industrial ecology

Source: Keitsch (2012c).

systems to industrial contexts. Due to this assumption, the IE concept also achieved the status of being a multidisciplinary field bridging the gap between the natural sciences, social sciences and the humanities, even if this might not have been the intention of its founders:

> Industrial Ecology is the objective, multidisciplinary study of industrial end economic systems and their linkages with fundamental natural systems. It incorporates, among other things, research involving energy supply and use, new materials, new technologies and technological systems, basic sciences, economics, law, management, and social sciences. Although still in the development stage, it provides the theoretical scientific basis upon which understanding, and reasoned improvement, of current practices can be based. Oversimplifying somewhat it can be thought of as 'the science of sustainability.' It is important to emphasize that industrial ecology is an objective field of study based on existing and technological disciplines, not a form of industrial policy or planning system.
>
> *(Allenby, cited in Opoku and Keitsch 2006)*

Consequently, approaches to activate research on the socio-political implications of IE are still feeble. Socio-political issues in IE appear, for example, by relating energy and material flows to the social settings in which they occur (Boons and Howard-Grenville 2009) and by thematizing stakeholder participation (Ehrenfeld 2008). The latter includes questioning and interpretations of production and consumption values and creates a continuous broadening of scope beyond the rather simplistic notions of environmental technology and cleaner production in the previous decade (Madge 1997). Mostly, the technological importance of IE is, however, still emphasized while the concept shares several characteristics with the technology branch of eco-design.

A status quo appraisal of sustainable design

The sustainable design concepts presented in this chapter mirror to a certain degree the development of the sustainable development concept in general. Systematically, current sustainability approaches in industrial design can be illustrated by different implementations levels (Figure 10.3).

Didactically, Figure 10.3 is translated into three questions, which students in the design curriculum should relate to (Keitsch and Bjørnstad 2010):

1 Does the solution contribute environmentally to a sustainable development?
2 Does the solution promote new products and services?
3 Does the solution contribute to new sustainable consumption practices?

Meeting these questions in a design assignment, the most frequent student solutions relate to the micro implementation level, i.e. to analyze and improve the material and energy used in products. Students tend to dive here into the details of the main product. The material focus results, for example, in recycle solutions to reduce the amount of garbage. The students reuse/redesign materials often to less functional but witty objects. Example 1 in Figure 10.4 is a good illustration of redesign of thrown-away furniture, where the students use existing materials to make new objects. Some students also rethink the user's hunger for renewal. Instead of proposing new products with small changes, they focus on the history the objects have been a part of. That means living with the same objects but looking at them in a new light. Not through repair or redesign, just through storytelling. This reflective approach is illustrated in

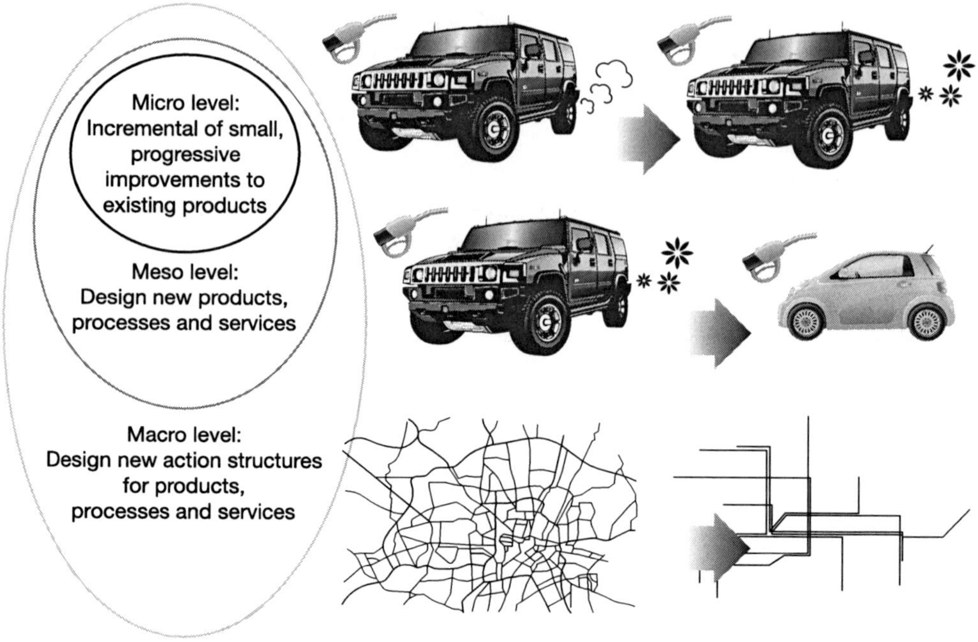

Figure 10.3 Three different implementation levels for sustainability in industrial design

Source: Keitsch (2011).

example 2 in Figure 10.4. A few students focus on a macro level in the form of new action structures or change of consumption practices. Example 3 in Figure 10.4 shows Niteo, a solar lamp and a charging station for small electrical devices. Niteo converts chemical energy, available in a bio-convertible substrate, directly into electricity. The main considerations of this solution were the aesthetic appearance and the cultural integrability of the product, i.e. its capability of being integrated in a specified cultural context thereby contributing to overall sustainability. Additionally, the student drafted how the distribution was planned and that the local craftsman, here from Nepal, gives the exterior form and expression.

Historically, in the first phase of sustainable design, after Brundtland, solutions concentrated primarily on ecological strategies and improvements and conservation of natural surroundings. Nature was regarded and employed as the most important source for inspiration and ecology

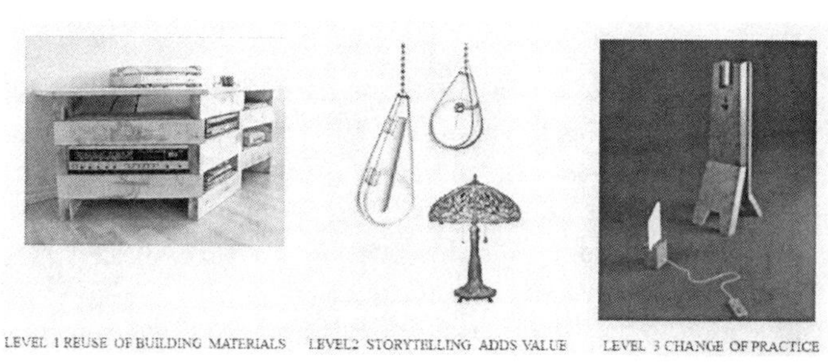

Figure 10.4 Examples, Master's student course

Source: Keitsch (2011).

and engineering provided descriptive, scientific approaches. However, the following decades made it clear that these disciplines have no normative basis to offer for decision-making. The ethical thinking needed to figure out sustainable solutions (Jonas 1984) cannot be learned from nature. It must be developed in parallel with the human self-realization. Authors claimed further that sustainable principles, indicators and strategies should be grounded in a holistic philosophy that includes both non-material aspects of the human–nature relationship and material requirements (Naess 1989). In this context, social sustainability, which promotes social interaction and cultural enrichment, received a lot of attention at the end of the millennium:

> Social Sustainability . . . is related to how we make choices that affect other humans in our 'global community' – the Earth. It covers the broadest aspects of business operations and the effect that they have on employees, suppliers, investors, local and global communities and customers. Social sustainability is also related to more basic needs of happiness, safety, freedom, dignity and affection.
>
> *(Green Team, weblog)*

Like environmental sustainability, social sustainability strives to take future generations into consideration, and to live with the awareness that human actions make an impact on others and the world at large.

Participation in society is an overall goal of social sustainability and can be viewed from perspectives such as social integration, personalization and appropriateness (Vavik and Keitsch 2010). This means, for example, treating all groups with dignity and respect; incorporating opportunities for choice and the expression of individual preferences; and respecting and reinforcing cultural values and the social and environmental context of any project. Today, many people experience information and communication technologies as barriers to participation. One reason for that may be that political bodies relate participation as a strategy of empowering less to individual conditions than to social processes. One social sustainability design approach to meet these challenges is the 'Dialogue Café'. The idea behind Dialogue Café is to facilitate communication between people from all walks of life, across the world, to address social, environmental and economic issues ranging from youth literacy and job skills needed for the twenty-first century to urban development. The cafés bring ordinary people together to share common interests and concerns. They are linked by life-size, high-definition video screens, the sound allowing people from different cities and cultures to talk and meet despite being located on different sides of the world. The Dialogue Café concept gives people the opportunity to be directly involved in creating solutions in their communities – solutions that need not be isolated and can be shared. A broad dialogue of a diverse group of people can exponentially expand our collective ability to solve problems and innovate as a global community. The cafés are bottom-up movements that complement the tradition of addressing sustainability issues from the top.

Reflecting these new perspectives, sustainable design approaches of the new millennium and its first decade attempted a transition towards socio-cultural sustainability and stakeholder participation including what Knight calls a 'broadening of scope in theory and practice' (2009: 4). McLennan expresses this transition programmatically: 'Sustainable design starts with the understanding that the purpose of our design is to create physical artefacts that benefit people' (2004: 5).

Currently, user involvement in sustainable design is motivated by two factors: a general increase on a user-focus in the design community (Lee et al. 2008) and the concept of 'people-centred sustainable development', introduced in 1995 by the Copenhagen Declaration on Social Development:

> We commit ourselves to promoting and attaining the goals of universal and equitable access to quality education, the highest attainable standard of physical and mental health, and the access of all to primary health care, making particular efforts to rectify inequalities relating to social conditions and without distinction as to race, national origin, gender, age or disability.

It is important to note here that the interpretation of 'user' has changed significantly in the design community over the last decades and that this change influences methods and results of user involvement for sustainable design as well. While the early 1970s and 1980s highlighted physical needs (e.g. Dreyfuss 1967; 2003) and introduced ergonomics as an important consideration for design, the early 1990s, with Krippendorff (1989), for example, started to focus increasingly on social and symbolic needs, extending the concern of designers to cognitive and emotional constraints and social interactions when using a product.

Recent concepts in sustainable design can broadly be categorized within three areas. The first one, sustainability and user involvement, is best represented by Ezio Manzini and his 'Sustainable everyday life' concept. Manzini's research focuses on foresight, creativity and interaction: 'Indeed, we cannot act in a forward-looking way if we are unable to imagine a state in which we could potentially live in a different and more attractive way than now' (Manzini and Jégou 2003: 13). Methodologically, Manzini combines a natural science and engineering-oriented approach (technology sphere) with social constructivism (society sphere). His 2006 article, 'Design, ethics and sustainability', also emphasizes the role of the designer in society:

> Conceiving and proposing products, services and lifestyles, designers play an important role and consequently have an equally important responsibility in generating social expectations in terms of wellbeing . . . Of course designers have no means of imposing, for good or bad, their point of view on others. But they do have the tools to operate on the quality of things, and their acceptability, and therefore on the attraction of the scenarios of wellbeing they help to generate.
>
> *(ibid.: 2)*

Practically, Manzini presents guidelines in the form of two fundamental principles for designers: low material-energy intensity and high regenerative potential. These principles are very much in line with the eco-technical part of sustainable development. However, he connects these principles with personal and social well-being: 'The concept of well-being is the most basic set of visions and ideas that legitimate socially and ethically the same existence of the production and consumption system' (Manzini 2003: 1). Building scenarios for sustainable well-being is (again) a social task for designers: 'Goal: we have to conceive scenarios of wellbeing in which the overall quality of the context of life has to be considered, in which the physical and social common goods are regenerated and where contemplative time has its place' (ibid.: 7).

The idea of creative communities, where stakeholders interact locally in daily life is the most significant feature of Manzini's concept:

> There is, in my view, a new model of organizing society and the production and consumption and whatever. When I use the words small, open, local and connected, this is my way of telling the story . . . For me, dealing with the needed sustainable changes that are mainly cultural and behavior change, the pivotal moment has been when I moved from saying 'What can I do to help people change behavior?' toward the discovery that a lot of people (even if they aren't yet so visible) had already

> changed, and in a good way, their behaviors. And that therefore, the right question is: 'What can I do to trigger and support these new ways of thinking and doing? How can I use my design knowledge and tools to empower these grass-roots social innovations?'
>
> *(Manzini 2011)*

Manzini's work summarizes some of the most recent ideas in sustainable design with an activist agenda for designers and stakeholders (Fuad-Luke 2009) and the attitude that sustainable design will not only meet the triple bottom line of ecological, economic and social sustainability, but contribute simultaneously to human well-being and civic stability (ibid.: 25). Here, interaction with stakeholders and mutual responsibility is the focus of the design work, instead of proclaiming a solipsistic individual ethos and a 'genius' design philosophy.

The second area in recent sustainable design concepts attempts to integrate elements of social practice theory into design research and practice, which are seen as a supplement to earlier 'social engineering' views that attempt to 'control or change behaviour' through physical, technological and cognitive interventions (Keitsch 2012b). In social practice, theory 'practice' is exemplified through single activities such as cooking, travelling, working, and so on (Reckwitz 2002). A practice is regarded as a significant unit for inquiries – in opposition to, for example, structuration theories which focus on general elements of social interactions. In aiming at empowering, educating and motivating consumers towards sustainable activities, novel design concepts (e.g. Gronow and Warde 2001; Shove 2003; Patterson 2006) take especially everyday practices into consideration. Everyday practices are seen as repetitive, routine and mundane activities and closely connected to common socio-cultural understandings about 'right' and 'wrong' ways of doing things (Gram-Hanssen 2008) and an analysis of everyday practices relating to socio-cultural identity development is significant for sustainable design in terms of product and service development.

The third area in sustainable design concepts is biocentric approaches, which have come forward in context with Arne Naess' 'gestalt' concept (1989). For Naess, the joy, when aesthetically experiencing nature's 'gestalt', triggers empathy with other living beings. The fact that every organism is part of a whole becomes realizable through experiencing the gestalt. Naess' gestalt ontology supports a moderate, aesthetically motivated biocentrism, based on the awareness for everyday experiences and different ways of communication about sustainable ways of living. As Goldsmith points out:

> There is a tendency in design that comes from a desire to appear objective and 'scientific' to try and quantify each aspect of design, from square footage of area, to kW of cooling. Extending even to our own field of sustainable design we take the science of ecology and use it to define the ecosystems we build in with terms like solar inputs and types of waste outputs. This is all in an effort to make the art of design seem more legitimate in a world that values quantification above appreciating the gestalt of a design's function. In Naess' essay, 'The Place of Joy in a World of Fact', he condemns this view and asks us not to try and reduce our experience to a simple knowledge of the basic physical realities of our surrounding world, but to appreciate them for their experiential reality of sounds, sights, smells, and feelings.
>
> *(2009: 4)*

Obviously, the aesthetic implications of Naess' gestalt ontology appeal to creative and innovative methods within the design process and therefore contain interesting material for the future development of sustainable design concepts, but are, in their current state, sketches rather than fully developed concepts since their methodological consequences and applications have not yet been examined thoroughly within in the design community.

Future opportunities and challenges for sustainability in industrial design

Considering the designer's role as mediating between 'what is possible by nature and our knowledge from the natural science on the one hand and of what is accepted or wanted by society on the other' (Hermansen 2006), an opportunity for future design research and education lies in the development of methodologies and design solutions which combine social, technological and aesthetic aspects. In terms of sustainable design research, a combined methodology can contribute with both ecological and technological know-how, *and* with methods and tools to advance social sustainability and social inclusion. Based on my own research and education practice, the following guidelines for future sustainable design within such a holistic framework can be outlined:

- The onsets for sustainable design strategies are *real-world challenges*.
- *User and stakeholder involvement* are fundamental attributes of meaningful sustainable product design solutions.
- Facilitating an *interdisciplinary experience* that includes comprehensive learning opportunities for different stakeholders is essential.

Meeting some of these guidelines, Morelli's work (2007) is a good example of how to create cross-cutting values by combining sustainable design strategies with social entrepreneurship within a food delivery system to activate elderly people. Social, technological and aesthetic aspects interact in this system on:

> [S]emi-finished platforms meant to organize material and immaterial flows, specify roles and competences, and possibly generate new knowledge that some actors (such as service providers or institutions) may add to their existing competences. The generation of a solution platform therefore is the basis for the design process.
>
> *(ibid.: 15)*

As this example illustrates, meeting sustainable development provides opportunities and new roles for industrial design in form of collaboration and ways of networking. Involvement of local users, stakeholders from municipalities and regions seem important when thinking about the industrial design contribution to sustainability. Some methods applied in these arenas are based on traditional product development strategies, while others originate in the natural and empirical sciences or deal with users, life styles and life quality on a social science foundation. One challenge for future research and education activities is to specify which methods are applicable and what their use implies for 'design for a sustainable society'. Figure 10.5 gives an overview of different methods available in design for sustainability.

Level	Tools
1. Micro level: Analyze and improve products, processes and services.	– design for the environment, life cycle assessment, material flow analysis dematerialization, energy effectiveness – material recycling, material exchange, material intensiveness – improvement of service, process and distribution and product chain oriented strategies
2. Meso level: Design new products, processes and services	– biomimicry, nature aesthetics – design semantics, product language, personas, narratives – universal and participatory design – emotional design
3. Macro level: Design new action and infrastructures	– user-driven innovation – ethics for the environment (analytical tool) – intellectual property management – social metabolism – sustainable production and consumption mechanisms – strategic sustainable development (stakeholder theory)

Figure 10.5 Methods for sustainability in industrial design

Source: Keitsch (2011).

Conclusion

> There are no passengers on Spaceship Earth. We are all crew.
>
> *(Marshall McLuhan 2005)*

The designers of tomorrow are likely to act in markets characterized by crises, innovation and constant variation, in professions undergoing continuous change, and hence they need to be competent learners. The biggest challenge for future sustainable design curricula comprises today in the systematization and the further development of methods. Methods for sustainability in industrial design are still cook-bookish. Even on the macro level when focusing on user activities, experiences, emotions or social surroundings, methods often look like directions for use rather than representing systematic and reflective steps towards improved practice. However, development and application of methods are only as good as the understanding of the theory behind them, and another challenge for future sustainable design is to generate knowledge on the relationships between sustainable development concepts, their analysis, with help of methods, and their 'translation' (Verganti 2003) into products and services. The tasks of design students usually include idea generation, concept development, strategic design, project planning, and project management. Besides applying the methods available, students should become familiar with the area of sustainable design thinking. As long as integrated models for sustainable design are still few (Wigum 2004; Morelli, 2007; Hussain 2011), theories and methods from other disciplines have to be utilized as well (see Figure 10.5). The future of design curricula is to graduate reflexive and skilful practitioners with a fundamental understanding of sustainability principles, capable of working in multidisciplinary teams, and aware of the contexts and systems, in which design acts. Augmented insights into responsible, acceptable and comprehensive design strategies will then contribute to pursue paths of innovation for products, services and structures for a sustainable society.

Design is implicated in the world in its actions and words – design practice is social practice. When design meets future sustainable design challenges, a systemic approach is required that joins the forces of different disciplines and stakeholders (Watson 2002; Innes 1995). A forthcoming contextualized, sustainable design practice comprises at least two components: First, developing profound situational knowledge when dealing with local sustainable problems and circumstances and, second, realizing workable, 'satisfycing' (a term coined by Herbert Simon 1956: 129, 136) solutions that are acceptable for the majority of involved stakeholders while considering the specific surroundings and conditions. Furthermore, future practitioners should be able to communicate with their surroundings – not only instrumentally about what is possible to achieve and how, but also ethically about what is worth achieving and why.

References

Azar, J., Berko-Boateng, V., Culhns, P., deJong, E., George J. and Hilbert H. (1995) Agent of change: Xerox Design-for-Environment Program. In *Proceedings of the 1995 IEEE International Symposium Electronics and the Environment*, 1–3 May 1995, Orlando, Florida.

Bhamra, T. and Lofthouse, V. (2007) *Design for Sustainability: A Practical Approach*. Aldershot: Gower.

Boons, F. and Howard-Grenville, J. (eds) (2009) *The Social Embeddedness of Industrial Ecology*. Cheltenham: Edward Elgar.

Clean Production Action (2009) Available at: www.cleanproduction.org/library/Factsheet1CleanProduction.pdf (accessed 18 March 2013).

Copenhagen Declaration on Social Development (1995) Commitment 6. Available at: www.un.org/documents/ga/confl66/aconfl66-9.htm, (accessed 18 March 2013).

Dale, A. (2001) *At the Edge: Sustainable Development in the 21st Century*. Vancouver: UBC Press.

Delft Design Guide. Available at: http://wikid.eu/index.php/EcoDesign_strategy_wheel, (accessed 18 March 2013).

Dubos, R., Cole, L. C., Jacobs, J., Carter, L. J., Temko, A., Bowen, W. and Wylie, P. (1970) *The Environmental Crisis*. Washington, DC: United States Information Service.

Dreyfuss, H. (1967) *The Measure of Man: Human Factors in Design*. New York: Whitney.

Dreyfuss, H. (2003) *Designing for People*. New York: Allworth Press.

Du Pisani, P. A. (2006) Sustainable development: historical roots of the concept. *Environmental Sciences*, 3(2): 83–96.

Ecodesign Directive 2009/125/EC of the European Parliament and of the Council. Available at: http://eur-lex.europa.eu/LexUriServ/LexUriServ.do?uri=OJ:L:2009:285:0010:0035:EN:PDF, (accessed 18 March 2013).

Eco-it Available at: www.pre-sustainability.com/eco-it (accessed 18 March 2013).

Ehrenfeld, J. (2008) *Sustainability by Design*. New Haven, CT: Yale University Press.

European Parliament, Directive 2009/125/EC of the European Parliament and of the Council of 21 October 2009 establishing a framework for the setting of ecodesign requirements for energy-related products. Available at: http://eur-lex.europa.eu/legal-content/EN/ALL/?uri=CELEX:32009L0125.

Frosch, R. A. and Gallopoulos, N. E. (1989) Strategies for manufacturing. *Scientific American*, 261(9): 94–102.

Fuad-Luke, A. (2009) *Design Activism*. London: Earthscan.

Glick, M. (1970) *The Environmental Crisis*. In R. Dubos, L. C. Cole, J. Jacobs, L. J. Carter, A. Temko, W. Bowen, P. Wylie (eds). Washington, DC: United States Information Service.

Goldsmith, D. (2009) Biocentric Development ethics. In *SASBE2009 3rd CIB International Conference on Smart and Sustainable Built Environments*, 15–19 June 2009. Delft. Available at: www.sasbe2009.com/proceedings/documents/SASBE2009_paper_BIOCENTRIC_DEVELOPMENT_ETHICS.pdf (accessed 8 February 2012).

Graedel, T. E. and Allenby, B. (1995) *Industrial Ecology*. Upper Saddle River, NJ: Prentice-Hall.

Graedel, T. E. and Allenby, B. (2010) *Industrial Ecology and Sustainable Engineering*. Upper Saddle River, NJ: Prentice Hall.

Gram-Hanssen, K. (2008) Consuming technologies: developing routines. *Journal of Cleaner Production*, 16: 1181–1189.

Green Team, Word Press Weblog. Available at: http://greenteamdw.com/social_sustainability.htm (accessed 22 October 2009).

Gronow, J. and Warde, A. (eds) (2001) *Ordinary Consumption*. London: Routledge.

Hermansen, J. (2006) Industrial ecology as mediator and negotiator between ecology and industrial sustainability. *Progress in Industrial Ecology: An International Journal*, 3(1/2).

Hussain, S. (2011) Designing for and with marginalized people in developing countries: efforts to undertake a participatory design project with children using prosthetic legs in Cambodia. PhD thesis, NTNU, Trondheim, Norway: Tapir Trykk.

Indigo Development, *Industrial Ecology*. Available at: www.indigodev.com/IE.html#WhyIE, (accessed 18 March 2013).

Innes, J. (1995) Planning theory's emerging paradigm: communicative action and interactive practice. *Journal of Planning Education and Research*, 14(3): 183–189.

Jonas, H. (1984) *The Principle of Responsibility: In Search of an Ethics for the Technological Age*. Chicago: University of Chicago Press.

Keitsch, M. (2011) Sustainable product design background, tools and solutions. Inaugural lecture 18 March 2011, Department for Product Design: Norwegian University of Science and Technology.

Keitsch, M. (2012a) Sustainability in industrial design: concepts, challenges and opportunities. *Sustainable Development: New Research, Economic Issues, Problems and Perspectives*. New York: Nova Science Publishers.

Keitsch, M. (2012b) Sustainable design: a brief appraisal of its main concepts. *Sustainable Development*, 20(3): 180–188.

Keitsch, M. (2012c) Industrial ecology and sustainable design. Lecture, 22 November, Department for Product Design, Norwegian University of Science and Technology.

Keitsch, M. and Bjørnstad, N. (2010) Ethics in product design curriculum: an example from the Oslo School of Architecture and Design. In *Proceedings from the 12th International Conference on Engineering and Product Design*: NTNU Trondheim.

Knight, A. (2009) Hidden histories: the story of sustainable design. *ProQuest Discovery Guides*. Available at: www.csa.com/discoveryguides/discoveryguides-main.php (accessed 2 January 2012).

Krippendorff, K. (1989) On the essential context of artifact or on the proposition that 'design is making sense (of things)'. *Design Issues*, 5(2): 9–39.

Lee, Y., Bichard, A. and Coleman, R. (2008) *Designing with Users, How?* Royal College of Art Helen Hamlyn Centre. Available at: www.hhc.rca.ac.uk/cms/files/2.pdf (accessed 18 March 2013).

McLennan, J. (2004) *The Philosophy of Sustainable Design*. Kansas City, MO: Ecotone.

McLuhan, M. Statement of 1965, quoted from *Paradigms Lost: Learning from Environmental Mistakes, Mishaps and Misdeeds* (2005) by Daniel A. Vallero: 367. Available at: http://en.wikiquote.org/wiki/Marshall_McLuhan (accessed 14 January 2014).

Madge, P. (1997) Ecological design: a new critique. *Design Issues*, 13(2), Summer.

Manzini, E. (2003) Scenarios of sustainable well-being. *Design Philosophy Papers*: Issue 1, Available at: http://changedesign.org/Resources/Manzini/Manuscripts/ManziniScenarios.pdf (accessed 18 March 2013).

Manzini, E. (2006) *Design, Ethics and Sustainability, Guidelines for a Transition Phase*. Available at: www.dis.polimi.it/manzini-papers/06.08.28-Design-ethics-sustainability.doc (accessed 3 January 2012).

Manzini, E. (2011) *Design for Social Innovation: An Interview with Ezio Manzini*. Shareable net. Available at: http://shareable.net/blog/design-for-social-innovation-an-interview-with-ezio-manzini (accessed 18 March 2013).

Manzini, E. and Jégou, F. (2003) *Sustainable Everyday, Scenarios of Urban Life*. Milan: Ambiente.

Morelli, N. (2007) Social innovation and new industrial contexts: can designers 'industrialize' socially responsible solutions? *Design Issues*, 23(4): 3–21.

Naess, A. (1989) *Ecology, Community and Lifestyle*. New York: Cambridge University Press.

Naess, A. (2005) *The Selected Works of Arne Naess: The Place of Joy in a World of Fact*. London: Springer, pp. 2371–2382.

Opoku, H. N. and Keitsch, M. M (2006) Une approche objective de la durabilité? Théorie des implications scientifiques et politiques de l'écologie industrielle. [An Objective Approach to

Sustainability? Theory of Science and Political Implications of Industrial Ecology]. *Ecologie et Politique*, 32/2006, Paris, ISBN:2-84950-084-4, ISSN:1166–3030.

Papanek, V. (1991) *Design for the Real World: Human Ecology and Social Change*, 2nd edn. London: Thames and Hudson.

Patterson, M. (2006) Consumption and everyday life. In A. Elliott (ed.) *The New Sociology*. London: Routledge.

Reckwitz, A. (2002) Toward a theory of social practices: a development in culturalist theorizing. *European Journal of Social Theory*, 5: 243.

Report of the World Summit on Sustainable Development (2002) Johannesburg, South Africa, 26 August–4 September 2002, III. Changing unsustainable patterns of consumption and production. Available at: www.johannesburgsummit.org/html/documents/summit_docs/131302_wssd_report_reissued.pdf, (accessed 19 March 2013).

Rio Declaration (2005) *The Rio Declaration: Universal Design for Sustainable Inclusive Development*. Available at: www.rollingrains.com/archives/000306.html (accessed 19 March 2013).

Shove, E. (2003) *Comfort, Cleanliness and Convenience: The Social Organisation of Normality*. Oxford: Berg Publishers.

Simon, H. A. (1956) Rational choice and the structure of the environment. *Psychological Review*, 63(2): 129–138.

Society of Environmental Toxicology and Chemistry (SETAC) (1993) *Guidelines for Life-Cycle Assessment: A Code of Practice*. Brussels: Society for Environmental Toxicology and Chemistry. Available at: www.canadianarchitect.com/asf/perspectives_sustainibility/measures_of_sustainablity/measures_of_sustainablity_lca.htm (accessed 19 March 2013).

The Dialogue Café. Available at: www.dialoguecafe.org/ (accessed 29 November 2013).

UNEP (United Nations Environment Program) Declaration of the United Nations Conference on the Human Environment (1972). Available at: www.unep.org/Documents.Multilingual/Default.asp?documentid=97&articleid=1503.

UNEP (United Nations Environment Program) (1999) *International Declaration on Cleaner Production*. Available at: www.ourplanet.com/imgversn/104/declare.html, (accessed 19 March 2013).

UNEP (United Nations Environment Program) International Declaration on Cleaner Production. Available at: www.unep.org/resourceefficiency/Portals/24147/scp/cp/network/pdf/english.pdf (accessed 14 October 2014).

Unger D. and Eppinger, S. (2011) Improving product development process design: a method for managing information flows, risks, and iterations. *Journal of Engineering Design*, 22(10): 689–699.

United States Environmental Protection Agency. Available at: www.epa.gov/dfe/pubs/about/history.htm (accessed 21 March 2013).

Vavik, T. and Keitsch, M. (2010) Exploring relationships between universal design and social sustainable development: some methodological aspects to the debate on the sciences of sustainability. *Sustainable Development*, 18(5).

Verganti, R. (2003) Design as brokering of languages: Innovation strategies in Italian firms. *Design Management Journal*, 14(3).

Watson, V. (2002) Do we learn from planning practice? The contribution of the practice movement to planning. *Theory Journal of Planning Education and Research* 22, 178–187.

Wigum, K. S. (2004) Human and ecological problem solving through radical design thinking; analyses and development of design theory and design framework based on long term human needs and ecological sustainable principles. PhD thesis, NTNU, Trondheim, Norway: Tapir Trykk.

World Commission on Environment and Development (1987) *Our Common Future*. Oxford: Oxford University Press.

11

IS MANAGING ECOSYSTEM SERVICES NECESSARY AND SUFFICIENT TO ENSURE SUSTAINABLE DEVELOPMENT?

Mark Mulligan and Nicholas J. Clifford

Refining the concept of ecosystem services

Ecosystem services flow from stocks of natural capital and provide benefits to humanity, for example, the carbon sequestration of forests that regulates global atmospheric composition and thus climate; the clean, fresh water flowing from natural landscapes and provided to dams and irrigation projects downstream and the flood storage capacity of wetlands that regulates floodwaters upstream of flood-prone urban areas. These services and the natural capital stocks from which they are derived are critical to the life-support functions of the Earth and contribute to human welfare in direct and indirect ways (Costanza et al. 1997). Ecosystem services are variously classified (see Fisher et al. 2009) including by the Millennium Ecosystem Assessment (MEA) (2005) into provisioning, regulating, supporting and cultural services. Provisioning services include the provision of food, timber, textiles and water, regulating services provide regulation against hazards (such as floods and droughts). Cultural services are the non-material aesthetic, recreational, spiritual and health benefits provided by nature. Supporting services support the aforementioned through, for example, maintenance of soil fertility. Ecosystem services are considered to be fundamentally dependent upon biodiversity (Hooper et al. 2005; Balvanera et al. 2006; Tilman et al. 2006). The term ecosystem services is used for both goods (provisioning services) and services (regulating, cultural and supporting services).

The sustainability of ecosystem service provision is threatened by human impacts on the environment. While these impacts are necessary to provide a number of the provisioning services, e.g. agriculture for food and deforestation for timber, these interventions by a given beneficiary can negatively impact the same services available to other beneficiaries or different services provided by the same landscape. These 'external' impacts of ecosystem service 'farming' are not accounted for in the economic system that drives most interventions in the environment and, as a result, these interventions can threaten the equity and sustainability of ecosystem service provision. These services have thus undergone various attempts at valuation, including economic valuation (Costanza et al. 1997) in the hope that their value can be better understood and so that 'market-based' mechanisms (Gómez-Baggethun et al. 2010) can contribute to better and more holistic management of ecosystem services. The cost and futility of replacing the services currently provided 'for free' by 'green' infrastructure with those engineered using grey infrastructure are often highlighted in this work.

Fundamental to ecosystem services is the understanding that the presence of an ecosystem with a particular suite of processes provides services that lead to benefits by a defined set of beneficiaries. The (mis-)management of these ecosystems can thus affect the benefits received from them now and in the future. This is, of course, very close to the principle that development can be sustainable or otherwise. The MEA (2005) concluded that humans have caused significant, irreversible biodiversity loss through extensive and rapid ecosystem alteration for human development in the last 50 years. This has led to improved human well-being and economic development for many, but has cost the degradation of many ecosystem services, and this is likely to continue unless ecosystem services management are embedded in environment and development policies, institutions, and practices with a stronger sustainability focus.

Environmental services vs. ecosystem services

To date the terms 'environmental services' and 'ecosystem services' have been used as synonyms, although Mulligan et al. (2013) ascribe specific meaning to each. For Mulligan et al. (2013), environmental services are a function of the broader environment (including climate and terrain) and thus not manageable at the typically local to regional policy and land management scales. Ecosystem services are, however, a service provided by the ecosystem on the ground (vegetation, soil, wetlands, etc.) and thus can be manipulated by farmers, conservationists or others for both positive and negative ecosystem service delivery outcomes.

Cloud forest example

For example, the abundant water resources coming from headwater catchments in the humid tropics (see Saenz and Mulligan 2013) are largely a function of the fact that tropical mountains receive a lot of rainfall and are subject to low ambient temperatures and low solar radiation, all as a function of their elevation. These are environmental services that are outside of the control of a land manager. On the other hand, cloud-affected forests that occur in some of these mountain zones receive additional inputs of water through the capture of passing ground level cloud (fog) as cloud water interception (Bruijnzeel et al. 2011). This additional water is not captured when cloud-affected forests are replaced by shorter stature land cover such as pasture-lands: this extra input of water is thus an ecosystem service that can be managed by managing land use. In managing ecosystem services we must therefore focus on managing the manageable: the ecosystem services and not the environmental services that are outside of the control of the typical decision-maker. Just because a cloud-affected forest occurs in a wet climate does not mean the forest produces all of the water received.

River example

The amount of water present in rivers is largely a function of the magnitude and distribution of rainfall in its flow above and below ground to the river network, and then transmission along the network conditioned by the network geometry and associated storages and transmission losses. The magnitude and distribution of rainfall, the nature of subterranean aquifers and the form and geometry of the river network are environmental processes that have little to do with the presence of specific ecosystems or land covers. The much smaller fluxes of rainfall interception, evapotranspiration and infiltration into soil are associated with ecosystem structure.

The key factors controlling river flow can thus be considered environmental services that are not easily managed (or mis-managed) by human activity, rather than ecosystem services which can be managed.

Table 11.1 provides a more comprehensive list of the ecologically dependent goods and services associated with river systems. It is clear that a gradient exists between generic and specific processes, components and services, and that, despite the longer listing here of services, many of these are directly manageable, or at least, subject to manipulation in an effort to effect a desired response in ecosystem behaviour. Crucially, some of the entries in fact depend on

Table 11.1 Ecologically dependent functions, goods and services of rivers

Functions	*Ecosystem processes and components*	*Goods and services*
Regulation functions	Maintenance of essential ecological processes and life-support systems	
Waste treatment	Role of vegetation and biota in removal or breakdown of discharges to rivers	Pollution control Reduction in full treatment costs
Nutrient regulation	Role of biota in storage and recycling of nutrients (N&P)	Maintenance of water quality Reduction of algal blooms
Biological control	Population control through trophic relationships	Balanced native populations Control of pest numbers (e.g. European carp)
Habitat functions	Providing habitat for native plants and animals	
Refuges	Suitable living space for native plants and animals	Maintenance of biodiversity Sources for re-colonisation Minimum population support
Nurseries	Suitable reproduction habitat	Maintenance of population numbers Natural recruitment
Complexity	Variety of niches to support complex communities	Resilient food webs Diverse ecosystem structure supporting long-term stability
Vertical structure	Floodplain inundation and riparian growth	Vertical habitat, especially in arid zones Connected zones throughout catchments
Connectedness	Migration and dispersal throughout catchments	Catchment-wide maintenance of ecological communities via channels and riparian corridors
Production functions	Provision of natural resources	
Genetic resources	Genetic material, evolution and adaptation flexibility in native plants and animals	Adaptation to changed conditions because of use or climate change Chemical models and tools Test and assay organisms
Recreation	Sport fishing, aquarium plants	Populations with sufficient production for harvesting
Food	Commercial fishing and aquaculture	Harvestable populations Source material for aquaculture

(Continued)

Table 11.1 (Continued)

Functions	*Ecosystem processes and components*	*Goods and services*
Raw materials	Conversion of solar energy into biomass for human construction and other uses	Specialist riparian species, e.g. river red gum
Functions	Ecosystem processes and components	Goods and services
Information functions	Providing opportunities for education and cognitive development	
Aesthetic value	Attractive landscapes	Enjoyment of scenery
Recreation	Variety in riverine landscapes	Travel and ecotourism Outdoor sports
Culture	Traditional people's values and significance	Understanding the place and its value for long-term human habitation
Art	Natural features with artistic value	Nature as motive in books, film, painting, folklore, national symbols, advertising, and so on
History	Variety of features with value	Historical development of the country via rivers
Science and education	Variety in nature with scientific and educational value	Use of natural systems for education Use of nature for scientific research

human agency – they are, in a sense, hybrid products of natural and modified systems; many are now subject to local manipulation, with less reliance on bounding, natural environmental controls.

The Brisbane Declaration on Environmental Flows, Freshwater Systems and Environmental Sustainability (2007) further emphasises the dynamic and hybrid nature of the environment-ecosystem services gradient. Climate change and human intervention have increased the pace and scale of ecosystem degradation in response to changing environment at ever-increasing rates, but with recognition of this, have also facilitated the scope and ambition of freshwater protection and remediation efforts. A key issue, then, arises as to the degree to which potential services are realised, and how improved management might lead to further realisation of this potential

Potential vs. realised ecosystem services

Ecosystem services are, by definition, those services that are realised as benefits; but not all potential services are realised, and it is important to understand the distribution of potential ecosystem services as well as realised services since the addition of people, infrastructure or agriculture to an area soon realises more of the potential services.The relationship between potential and realised services differs between service types. For carbon storage and sequestration, all potential service is realised since all carbon storage and sequestration benefits the global carbon balance and thus the global beneficiaries of a regulated climate. For water provisioning services, as Table 11.1 illustrates, while the presence of a particular ecosystem can lead to the delivery of more or better quality water downstream, this potential service is not realised as a benefit unless that water is used directly by populations, infrastructure or agriculture downstream or indirectly through its support of fisheries, etc. If there are few people and little human development downstream, the realised service will be a fraction of the potential service. Similarly for hazard mitigation services to be realised, there needs to be exposure to risk and the provision by ecosystems of hazard mitigation potential (e.g. wetlands providing storage that mitigates flood risk downstream). If the risk of flood does not exist in the area of the wetlands, or if there is no human exposure to any risk that does exist, then the potential hazard mitigation is never realised. The cultural service of nature-based tourism has potential where high aesthetic value, well-preserved, rare, species-rich and/or dramatic environments exist but it is only when these environments are (easily) accessible to an interested population with disposable time, income and means of travel that this service is realised.

Ecosystem dis-services

We cannot discuss ecosystem services without also highlighting that ecosystems are not always good for us: globally more people die from wild species (most often diseases) than of all other causes combined (Dunn 2010). So-called ecosystem dis-services are thus 'functions of ecosystems that are (or are perceived) as negative for human well-being' (Lyytimäki and Sipilä 2009). These ecosystem dis-services can be classified as:

1 Ecosystems negatively impacting human health, for example, wetlands providing habitat for malarial mosquitoes. Pathogens and the vectors that carry them are most speciose in the same tropical megadiversity countries in which most species occur and on which international conservation agendas are most focused. However, the dis-service (disease prevalence) is not greatest in the most pristine, diverse habitats but rather in disturbed habitats. According to Dunn (2010), we appear to make habitats worse for us in terms of their dis-services, i.e. agricultural land harbours more pathogens and their vectors than more pristine environments (Schmidt and Ostfeld 2001; Vanwambeke et al. 2007). Or maybe this is a case of already potential dis-services becoming realised in the presence of greater human populations.
2 Species causing damage to production such as crop and livestock damage by pests and wild animals (De Boer and Baquete 1998; Rao et al. 2002).
3 Species generating nuisance (DeStefano and Deblinger 2005), natural areas that generate feeling of fear, presence of large carnivores that cause a feeling of insecurity, and insects that cause discomfort.

We may also consider a series of environmental dis-services over which we have little control, such as meteorological extremes leading to floods, droughts, freezes and heat waves; coastal surges; volcanic eruptions and earthquakes. In some cases, ecosystem dis-services may be an economically more viable reason for conserving wild lands than are the services (Dunn 2010). Moreover, sustainable development must involve the management for sustainable ecosystem service provision and sustainable ecosystem dis-service minimisation.

Ecosystem service paradoxes for conservation

Conservationists expect ecosystem services to deliver significant conservation benefits with most of the large international conservation NGOs working and publishing on applications of the concept towards their conservation agendas. Unlike many other conservation prioritisations based on taxon-specific biodiversity (Important Bird Areas, IBAs; Birdlife International 2012), or endemism (Endemic Bird Areas, EBAs; Birdlife International 2005), wilderness areas

(Sanderson et al. 2002), high biodiversity threatened areas (Conservation International's hotspots; Myers et al. 2000), uniqueness of habitat (WWF's Global200 ecoregions; Olson et al. 1998), ecosystem service approaches prioritise the utility value of the services provided, not just the existence value of those services. Thus an area with very high potential service provision is not of high ecosystem service value unless those services are realised.

Deforestation leads to greater ecosystem services

Paradoxically for the conservation organisations, the ecosystem service value of a forest can be increased by its deforestation. While this may reduce its value to global beneficiaries (for carbon sequestration and biodiversity), the consequent increase in local population, infrastructure and agriculture, increases the proportion of potential services for water provision and hazard mitigation as well as a range of other provisioning and regulating services that are realised. A remote forested wilderness provides few locally realised ecosystem services, whereas the same geographical extent of forest upstream of a city can provide similar globally realised carbon and biodiversity services as well as significant locally realised water, hazard mitigation and nature-based tourism services, among others. The ecosystem services framework will certainly help protect peri-urban environments and the watersheds of dams (Saenz and Mulligan 2013) but will do little to protect the most remote, speciose wilderness areas of the world where the realised value of the goods (oil, minerals, forest plantations, agriculture) generated by conversion will invariably be greater than the realised value of the ecosystem to its remote users.

River restoration science and emerging intervention practice

The increasingly widespread practice of river restoration provides a further illustration of the paradoxes arising from management intervention crossing the environmental-ecosystems continuum. River restoration is itself a dynamic, evolving and global environmental intervention practice, which has multiple objectives, only some of which are focused on ecosystem improvement (Smith et al. 2014). Moreover, only some restoration interventions can be clearly framed in terms of a close match between the type of restoration activity and environmental context and controls (Smith et al. 2013), and even the abiotic (hydrological and geomorphological) principles which are assumed to control the ecological performance of the intervention are frequently of questionable robustness (Clifford et al. 2008; Clifford 2012). River restoration is, then, at best an immature and uncertain science (see Darby and Sear 2008). From an ecological and ecosystems point of view, the large majority of documented case studies illustrate failure rather than success (Ormerod 2004): 'restoring' the physical abiotic conditions in a river less frequently lead to predicted, desired ecological benefits: rather, invasive and exotic species exploit the new habitat more quickly and more productively, whether plants or fish. Such lack of success exemplifies a further paradox: that an increasingly popular environmental intervention seems to lack a reproducible science base, evaluated against a clear metric of environmental and ecosystem value. The paradox might partially be resolved when considering that many 'restorations' lie, in reality, on a spectrum of management intervention more appropriately characterised as 'rehabilitation' or 'remediation' where the management intervention either returns the trajectory of the system towards an original or to a new ecosystem state, as measured in terms of biomass and structure (Bradshaw 1996).

Use of the term trajectory is itself of significance, since the time frame over which success or failure is measured also becomes crucial. Given also that river restoration is increasingly undertaken as part of a community-building citizen and participatory science agenda (Clark 2002;

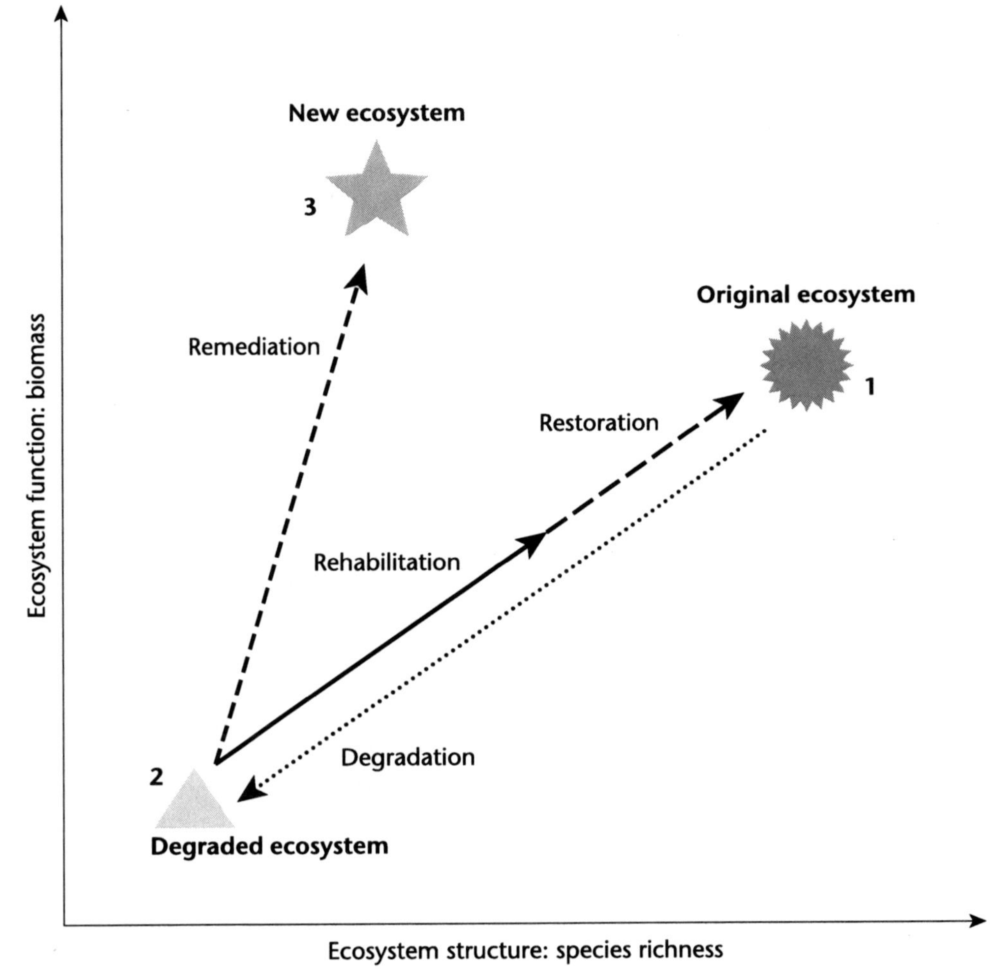

Figure 11.1 Underlying principles of restoration

Source: Bradshaw (1996), Figure 1. *Can. J. Fish. Aquat. Sci.* Vol. 53 (Suppl. 1), 1996 (modified by Breen and Walsh 1996 in Rutherfurd et al. 1999).

Clifford 2012) then, as discussed above and illustrated in Figure 11.1, both the range of services arising from, and the associated metrics of valuation associated with, any intervention are also subject to change, evolution and to diversification away from narrower concerns with the fundamentals of ecosystem dynamics. Intervention into ecosystems is thus subject to multiple uncertainties transcending the traditionally 'scientific'.

Necessary for sustainable development?

To be truly sustainable, development must be environmentally, economically, socially and politically sustainable. The ecosystem services concept allows us to break the sustainable development problem down into a series of services for which we can develop management strategies and policies that are designed to ensure that the ecosystem services are – and continue to be – provided as development progresses. The ecosystem structures and processes which help deliver each service – and the dependence of beneficiaries on the benefits supplied – can be studied. Development can then be managed to provide the necessary resource without undermining this service. In theory, service levels can then be monitored to ensure that the management objectives are met.

Technological vs. ecosystem-based development

In most cases ecosystem services can be delivered by the natural green infrastructure or the same services can be engineered through so-called 'grey' infrastructure. For example, a seasonally regulated flow regime can be achieved by catchment management that retains forests and other well-managed lands to encourage infiltration and slow seepage of water into sub-surface flows that contribute better to dry season baseflows. Alternatively, where this regulation service is no longer provided by the ecosystem, dams can be engineered to store wet season flows and thus maintain water supplies in the dry season. Maintaining green or developing grey infrastructure both have associated costs and political constraints. To maintain catchment infiltration rates by retaining forest lands, there is an opportunity cost to agricultural development. To maintain infiltration under agriculture requires careful land management (terracing, tillage) and this has associated economic costs (but also potential co-benefits for agricultural productivity). Alternatively, the building of dams incurs significant initial build costs and continuous maintenance costs, alongside co-benefits in the development of new fisheries, recreational areas and hydropower sources, for example. These costs and benefits are not simply economic but also political.

The relative cost-effectiveness of green vs. grey infrastructure will depend upon their relative requirements for land (land use cost), labour and financing require as well as their effectiveness at maintaining the (ecosystem) service of interest under normal and abnormal (extreme) conditions. Green infrastructure tends to require less initial investment and lower maintenance costs and institutional capacity (it largely 'looks after itself') but may require significantly more land and could be less effective at maintaining particular services than the grey equivalent. The extent to which green or grey is better will depend on local availability of land, finance, land and institutional and organisational capacity. Existing green infrastructure may not always be in the places that the services provided are used i.e. it may provide potential but not realised services. Where services are required (e.g. upstream of urban areas subject to flooding), if green infrastructure such as wetlands providing flood storage do not already exist, we have the option of developing new green infrastructure (restoring the green infrastructure that has been removed) or building new grey infrastructure. Design 'with nature' (McHarg 1971) is likely to be more sustainable than design without it. Although there is an increasing body of literature on green infrastructure, this is largely focused on providing recreational services within cities and management of urban drainage (Williamson 2003; Benedict and McMahon 2006; Wise 2008; Pincetl 2010). Much less is written on rural green infrastructure and the balancing of green and grey infrastructure (Kambites and Owen 2006). Here we discuss examples of managing ecosystem services through green and grey infrastructure from both a field and a modelling context.

Water: grey to green infrastructure in Kumasi, Ghana

The nearly 17m-tall Owabi Dam near Kumasi, Ghana, was built between 1928 and 1932 (Tetteh et al. 2004) to supply water to the growing city of Kumasi that had a population of nearly 24,000 in 1921. Under-estimation of the city's growth rate and under-investment in pipeline networks led to significant lack of supply and resulting water-related conflict as the city's

Figure 11.2 The now-urbanised catchment of the Owabi Dam (shadings represent elevation) as described by the WaterWorld model (www.policysupport.org/waterworld)

Source: Background imagery from Google Earth, DigitalGlobe.

population (estimated at 75,000 by 1951) continued to grow (McCaskie 2009). By 1957, the dam's catchment area had become an illegal building site and was eventually designated as city electoral wards 21 and 22. By 2005, Kumasi's population was 1.4–2 million. An inspection in 2003 also revealed that the Owabi Dam was near to collapse (McCaskie 2009)

The dam now supplies only 20 per cent of Kumasi's needs as the city, now Ghana's second city, has grown to a population of 2–3 million and has spread to cover almost all of the dam's catchment. The nearby Barekese Dam supplies much of the remaining water demand, though the supply situation is far from optimal. The Owabi forest reserve around the dam is posited to help secure the catchment's water resources and prevent sedimentation but the reality is that with an almost entirely urban catchment (see Figure 11.2), the reservoir is now highly prone to sedimentation and the forest reserve is unlikely to affect this since sediment originating in the urbanised catchment will enter the reservoir through the rivers and the forest will do little to reduce this. The forest reserve may, however, reduce wastewater contamination in what would otherwise be urban land.

Circumstances change: just because a dam is built for water supply does not mean it has to always be so. Thinking more broadly through an ecosystem service lens, perhaps it is better to let this reservoir fill with sediment as an urban wetland that forms part of the city's sanitation system and an urban recreational asset and focus resources that would have been used to dredge this reservoir on management of the dominantly rural catchment of the Barekese Dam in the north to increase its contribution to supply from 80 to 100 per cent. The urbanisation of the Owabi

Dam catchment is a clear example of how not to develop sustainably. Replacing natural ecosystems with poorly managed agriculture and urban areas, alongside poor wastewater management practices, significantly reduces the capacity of the reservoir to supply high quality water. Allowing this to happen at the same time that demand for water increases dramatically is particularly dangerous. However, given the illegal nature of much of the urbanisation, the huge rate of urban growth and the desperate poverty of many of the incoming migrants, it is unclear how this situation could have been avoided through a greater focus on development through an ecosystem services lens. Development in Kumasi has been sustainable to the extent that the huge population growth rate has been sustained, even with little attention to the implications for hydrological ecosystem service provision. Sustainability so far has been propped up by grey infrastructure development (of the Barekese reservoir). A more environmentally sustainable alternative may have been to continue to protect the Owabi catchment, but then where would the nearly 3 million people have lived and what would have been the political ramifications? Ecosystem service management is necessary to sustain development but in cases like this - where change is rapid and massive - it is not sufficient and sustained development can only be achieved through the management of grey infrastructure.

Water treatment vs. eco-efficient agriculture

The necessity of managing ecosystems for improved water quality is critical if the world's increasingly urban populations are to be provided with sufficient quality of water. Some 84 per cent of the population in more developed regions and 57 per cent in less developed regions are expected to live in urban areas by 2025 (Pacione 2009). Whether we manage the hydrological services provided to these cities through investment in surrounding green infrastructure (forest protection and eco-efficient agricultural techniques, see Keating et al. (2010) or grey infrastructure (water treatment), depends on the scale of eco-efficiency required to have an impact on the points at which urban supplies are sourced. This is determined at least in part by the distribution of peri-urban land uses. In Figure 11.2 we use the WaterWorld model (Mulligan 2013) and in particular its human footprint on water quality (HF) metric (Mulligan 2009) which examines the potential contamination of water based on the distribution of rainfall to human (polluting) land and natural (non-polluting) land covers. HF calculates the percentage of water in each pixel that fell as rain on potentially polluting land uses (cropland, pasture, urban, roads, mining, oil and gas) upstream and thus the HF index varies from 0–100 per cent.

By applying this metric to interventions in different contexts, we can assess the extent to which these interventions are effective at improving water quality and some of the trade-offs associated with their implementation. We examine three interventions (water treatment, eco-efficient agriculture and agricultural set-aside) for two urban settings, the city of Cali, Colombia, located in the highly agricultural Cauca Valley, and the city of Kathmandu in Nepal. The study area for Nepal is a one degree square tile centred on 27.5N,85.5E and the study area for Colombia is a one degree square tile centred on 3.5N,-76.5W. The land cover and use context for these complex catchments are shown in Figures 11.3 (a) and (b). Both urban areas are surrounded by a cropland mosaic with some forest and non-forest natural land. Cali also has nearby area of intensive pasture. Protected areas can be found near to both cities. These catchments are also highly variable in all of the climatic, land cover and use, terrain and population datasets that are used by WaterWorld.

The eco-efficient agriculture scenario is generated by reducing the unit-area footprint of all agricultural pixels from their default of 1.0 to 0.5, assuming reduced inputs of fertiliser, pesticides

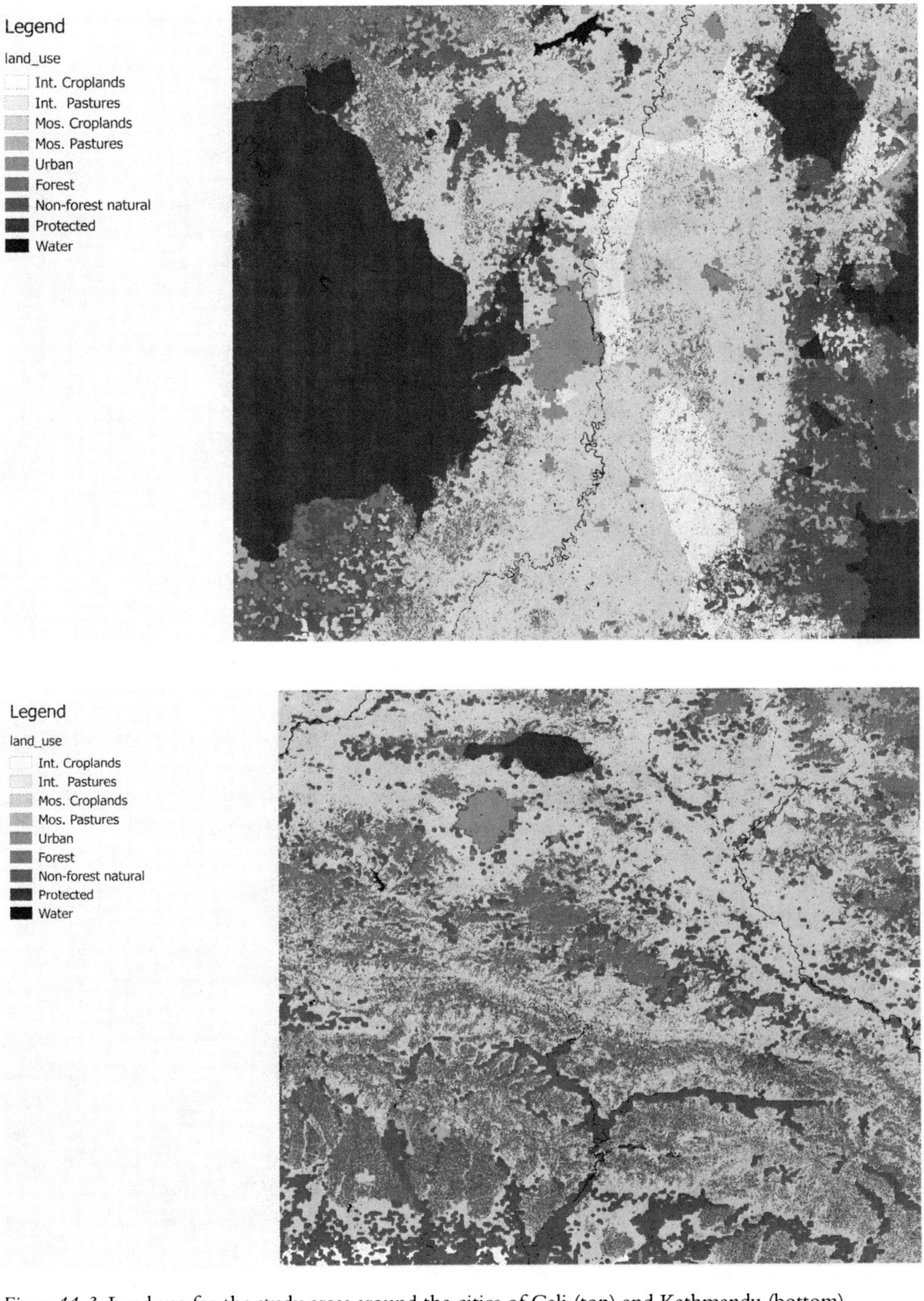

Figure 11.3 Land use for the study areas around the cities of Cali (top) and Kathmandu (bottom)

Note: Int = intensive, Mos = mosaic.

Table 11.2 Impacts of scenarios for ecosystem services management for water quality in Kathmandu, Nepal, and Cali, Colombia

	Land use cost (fraction of area)	*(Change in) HF in all areas (%)*	*(Change in) HF in urban areas (%)*	*Population with improved water quality*	*Population with reduced water quality*	*(Change in) population exposed to HF>50%*
Kathmandu						
Baseline	n/a	18%	61%	n/a	n/a	30000
Eco-efficient agriculture	64%	–7.1%	–0.49%	2.7M (42K/%)	0	–4800
Agricultural set-aside	22%	–2%	–0.044%	2900 (131/%)	340	–460
Water treatment	n/a	n/a	n/a	n/a	n/a	–3700
Cali						
Baseline	n/a	31%	75%	n/a	n/a	16000
Eco-efficient agriculture	61%	–14%	–14.4%	1.2M (20K/%)	0	–11000
Agricultural set-aside	17%	–1.7%	–1.6%	72000 (4200/%)	14000	–100
Water treatment	n/a	n/a	n/a	n/a	n/a	–2900

and herbicides. The water treatment scenario is represented as an improvement in water quality by 100 per cent for all cells with population density greater than 10,000 persons/km^2 because water treatment is assumed to be present in urban areas only for the baseline. The agricultural set-aside scenario converts agriculture to protected forest on steep (>15 degrees), wet (>2000 mm/year rainfall) slopes. Full details of the WaterWorld scenario generator used for these scenarios can be found in Mulligan (2014) and van Soesbergen and Mulligan (2014).

We can see from the results of this analysis (Table 11.2) that: (1) different interventions to improve water quality have different impacts on water quality; (2) the same intervention can have different impacts on urban vs. rural populations; (3) the same intervention can have different impacts at different sites; and (4) the agricultural set-aside scenario even leads to decreased water quality for some beneficiaries (because of reduced runoff – and thus reduced contaminant dilution – due to increased forest cover). The 'land use cost' of the intervention measured as the land area over which it needs to be applied and the effectiveness of that spend (measured as the population with improved water quality per unit cost) vary between interventions at the same site and between the same intervention at different sites. The most effective green infrastructure intervention is eco-efficient agriculture in Cali and in Kathmandu though the difference between the two green infrastructure interventions varies between the two sites. This means that even for simple ecosystem service management interventions there are no simple rules of thumb concerning which intervention is most effective, since this depends on the specific biophysical and socio-economic context including the spatial configuration of land uses and interventions in relation to the distribution of potential beneficiaries (population and urban areas). As a result detailed spatial analysis – case-by-case – is necessary to manage even single ecosystem services.

Sufficient for sustainable development?

We have discussed, with examples, whether and how ecosystem service management is necessary for sustainable development; we now examine whether sustainability can be achieved through ecosystem service management alone. We first examine the difficulties of accounting for the trade-offs between services when intervening to manage a single service and then examine the implications of these difficulties for sustainable development through the management of ecosystem services.

Bundles of services and trade-offs

In Table 11.3 we summarise some of the other ecosystem services and beneficiaries that will be affected by the interventions described. These are calculated by using the footprint of each intervention (the areas where the intervention occurs) to mask baseline maps for each of these properties and calculating the sum of the property within the intervention's footprint. Carbon storage is mapped after Saatchi et al. (2011); carbon sequestration is after Mulligan (2009); cropland and pasture productivity combine Mulligan (2009), Ramankutty et al. (2008) and Mulligan (2013); population is after LandScan™ (2007) and water quantity is according to the WaterWorld water balance (wind-driven rainfall plus fog and snowmelt minus actual evapo-transpiration).

We can see that the different interventions aimed at improving water quality have very different footprints and impacts on water quality (Table 11.3) but also directly affect the environment of different numbers of people, of productive land and of other ecosystem services (Table 11.2). The eco-efficient agriculture intervention, for example, is enacted over a very large

Table 11.3 Ecosystem services that may be affected by footprint of water quality service management interventions

	Carbon storage (% of total)	*Carbon sequestration (% of total)*	*Cropland productivity (% of total)*	*Pasture productivity (% of total)*	*Population*	*Population (% of total)*	*Water quantity (% of total)*
Kathmandu							
Eco-efficient agriculture	45 (0.7)	51 (0.8)	100 (1.56)	100 (1.56)	2200000 (34375)	46.81 (0.73)	50 (0.78)
Agricultural set-aside	18.57 (0.84)	18 (0.82)	12.31 (0.56)	13.85 (0.63)	320000 (14545.45)	6.81 (0.31)	21.67 (0.98)
Water treatment	0.06 (0)	0.1 (0)	0.15 (0)	0.03 (0)	230000 (0)	4.89 (0)	0.1 (0)
Cali							
Eco-efficient agriculture	42.11 (0.69)	56.04 (0.92)	100 (1.64)	100 (1.64)	920000 (15081.97)	26.29 (0.43)	42.86 (0.7)
Agricultural set-aside	23.16 (1.36)	16.48 (0.97)	4.36 (0.26)	5.71 (0.34)	25000 (1470.59)	0.71 (0.04)	24.64 (1.45)
Water treatment	0.03 (0)	0.07 (0)	0.13 (0)	0.11 (0)	4.86 (0)	4.86 (0)	0.05 (0)

Note: Figures in brackets are variable per unit land use cost of the intervention.

area of agricultural land. It thus affects a much greater population (47 per cent in the Kathmandu area and 25 per cent in the Cali area) than the set-aside or water treatment interventions. This is clear in the per-unit intervention area population affected of 34,000 for eco-efficient agriculture around Cali vs. 14,500 for agricultural set-aside (though in the case of water quantity populations downstream of the footprinted area must also be considered as they are affected by water quality). The populations affected differ between cities according to the land-use footprint of the interventions and the population distributions. The intervention may have positive or negative effects on the population aside from its effects on water quality (through, for example, reducing demand for water, energy and transportation of agricultural inputs which reduces the pressure on these services for other uses).

The interventions also have different footprints on the agricultural production landscape. Eco-efficiency is clearly targeted on agriculture so affects 100 per cent of cropland and pasture productivity. The effect on productivity may be positive or negative depending on the outcome of the eco-efficient techniques – which are unknown here – but which will affect much of the productive land in one way or another. Agricultural set-aside is focused on steep wet slopes and thus affects much less of the population and agricultural land (which do not tend to occupy such areas). However, per-unit area this intervention has a greater potential for impact on carbon storage and sequestration than the eco-efficient agriculture intervention, since set-aside is focused on areas with higher storage and sequestration. In both cases, agricultural set-aside has a lower footprint but a higher per-unit area water quantity that could be affected by the intervention (again because of the focus on steep, wet slopes in which the higher rainfall leads to a higher water balance).

Table 11.3 helps us to understand the trade-offs and the potential risks for other elements of sustainability of interventions associated with the management of one ecosystem service. The potential impacts on other services depend upon the spatial targeting of the intervention and the spatial relationships between biophysical and socio-economic characteristics of the region – and thus differ between these two regions. Those risks may be positive or negative (i.e. co-benefits of the intervention may accrue or the intervention may lead to degradation of other ecosystem services or components of human well-being).

The grey infrastructure intervention here (water treatment) has a land footprint of close to zero and thus leads to very small changes in all of the examined services. Because water treatment is targeted on populated areas, some populations are directly affected, i.e. water treatment will create a significant impact on the landscape in the areas where treatment plants are built; these are very small in relation to the other interventions which have large footprints and thus great potential for co-benefits or unforeseen dis-benefits of the intervention applied. Because of these trade-offs, the complexity of managing all services that are required for true sustainability is likely to be beyond our current analytical capability. Ecosystem services thus provides the framework for sustainability but only if we have full understanding of how to manage these services holistically and sustainably.

Conclusion: ecosystem services as a tool for sustainable development

The ecosystem services lens can help connect the benefits received from nature by people (and the contribution to well-being that accrues) with development or conservation interventions in the landscape that may impact those benefits (positively or negatively). It thus provides the potential for developing an operational framework for sustainable development through the assessment and management of ecosystem services. Realising this potential is fraught with difficulties that result from our lack of data on and understanding of: (1) the geographical distribution of ecosystem services; (2) the processes that drive these services; (3) the benefits that they provide and the contribution that these benefits make to well-being in different societal groups; (4) the impact of development and conservation upon these services and their sustainability, and perhaps most importantly within the context of sustainable development; (5) the interactions and trade-offs for other ecosystem services that results from interventions targeted at the management of one service.

Ecosystem services thinking has some contradictions with sustainable development, for example, increases in realised ecosystem service provision can be achieved through population growth, infrastructural and socio-economic development that create new beneficiaries that did not exist before. This increases ecosystem service provision – and may do so sustainably – but at the cost of biodiversity and other natural capital that may not provide a direct service and is thus not accounted for in the ecosystem services framework.

Ecosystem services can be sustained through the management of green infrastructure, the development of grey infrastructure or both. Green infrastructure is environmentally more sustainable since it is inherently 'self-managing' but socio-economically placing large areas of land under set-aside, for example, may not be socio-economically as sustainable as, for example, building a water treatment plant. This may be true both in terms of the much higher land-use cost of the green infrastructure intervention and because of the associated potential risk of dis-benefits for other ecosystem services in the intervened areas. Where co-benefits can be achieved, the green infrastructure intervention will be more sustainable but ensuring that only co-benefits result from an intervention is difficult.

Though the concepts and the rhetoric are well developed, we remain very naïve in our ability to measure, understand and map even single baseline ecosystem service, even less of understanding the impacts of management interventions and background scenarios for (climate) change, for example. Sustainable development requires the concurrent management of multiple ecosystem services that are relied on in different ways by many different socio-economic groups and affected in complex ways by management interventions. We are a very long way from being able to achieve that. But do we really need to or can we achieve sustainable development through high-level interventions focused on the precautionary principles and on basic changes in behaviour necessary for sustained development? We argue that in most cases keeping an eye on the big picture of sustainability will get us further than the micro-management of ecosystem services, at least until we really know what and how to micro-manage. Ecosystem service thinking has its real value in the analysis of simpler, specific interventions for managing specific services in specific places (for example, assessing green vs. grey infrastructure approaches to controlling sedimentation of a dam) rather than in advising the much broader goals of sustainable development.

References

Balvanera, P., Pfisterer, A. B., Buchmann, N., He, J. S., Nakashizuka, T., Raffaelli, D. and Schmid, B. (2006) Quantifying the evidence for biodiversity effects on ecosystem functioning and services. *Ecology Letters*, 9(10): 1146–1156.

Benedict, M. A. and McMahon, E. T. (2006) *Green Infrastructure: Linking Landscapes and Communities*. Washington, DC: Island Press.

Birdlife International (2005) *Endemic Bird Areas*. Digital database. www.birdlife.org

Birdlife International (2012) *Important Bird Areas*. Digital database. www.birdlife.org

Bradshaw, A. D. (1996) Underlying principles of restoration. *Canadian Journal of Fisheries and Aquatic Sciences*, *53*(S1), 3–9.

Brisbane Declaration (2007) The Brisbane Declaration: Environmental Flows Are Essential for Freshwater Ecosystem Health and Human Well-Being. Declaration of the 10th International River Symposium and International Environmental Flows Conference, 3–6 September 2007, Brisbane, Australia. Available at: www.eflownet.org/download_documents/brisbane-declaration-english.pdf.

Bruijnzeel, L.A., Mulligan, M. and Scatena, F.S (2011) Hydrometeorology of tropical montane cloud forests: emerging patterns. *Hydrological Processes* 25(3): 465–498.

Clark, M. J. (2002) Dealing with uncertainty: adaptive approaches to sustainable river management. *Aquatic Conservation: Marine Freshwater Ecosystems*, 12: 347–363. doi: 10.1002/aqc.531.

Clifford, N. J. (2012) River Restoration: widening perspectives. In M. Church, P. M. Biron and A. G. Roy (eds) *Gravel-Bed Rivers: Processes, Tools, Environments*. Chichester: John Wiley & Sons, Ltd.

Clifford, N. J., Acreman, M. C. and Booker, D. J. (2008) Hydrological and hydraulic aspects of restoration uncertainty for ecological purposes. In S. Darby and D. Sear (eds) *River Restoration: Managing the Uncertainty in Restoring Physical Habitat*. Chichester: John Wiley & Sons, Ltd.

Costanza, R., d'Arge, R., De Groot, R., Farber, S., Grasso, M., Hannon, B. and Van den Belt, M. (1997) The value of the world's ecosystem services and natural capital. *Nature*, 387(6630): 253–260.

Darby, S. and Sear, D. (eds) (2008) *River Restoration: Managing the Uncertainty in Restoring Physical Habitat*. Chichester: John Wiley & Sons, Ltd.

De Boer, W. F. and Baquete, D. S. (1998) Natural resource use, crop damage and attitudes of rural people in the vicinity of the Maputo Elephant Reserve, Mozambique. *Environmental Conservation*, 25(03), 208–218.

DeStefano, S., and Deblinger, R. D. (2005). Wildlife as valuable natural resources vs. intolerable pests: a suburban wildlife management model. *Urban Ecosystems*, 8(2), 179–190.

Dunn, R. R. (2010). Global mapping of ecosystem disservices: the unspoken reality that nature sometimes kills us. *Biotropica*, *42*(5), 555-557.

Fisher, B., Turner, R. K. and Morling, P. (2009) Defining and classifying ecosystem services for decision making. *Ecological Economics*, 68(3): 643–653.

Gómez-Baggethun, E., De Groot, R., Lomas, P. L. and Montes, C. (2010) The history of ecosystem services in economic theory and practice: from early notions to markets and payment schemes. *Ecological Economics*, 69(6): 1209–1218.

Hooper, D. U., Chapin Iii, F. S., Ewel, J. J., Hector, A., Inchausti, P., Lavorel S., Lawton J. H. et al. (2005) Effects of biodiversity on ecosystem functioning: a consensus of current knowledge. *Ecological Monographs*, 75(1): 3–35.

Kambites, C. and Owen, S. (2006) Renewed prospects for green infrastructure planning in the UK 1. *Planning, Practice & Research*, 21(4): 483–496.

Keating, B. A., Carberry, P. S., Bindraban, P. S., Asseng, S., Meinke, H. and Dixon, J. (2010) Eco-efficient agriculture: concepts, challenges, and opportunities. *Crop Science*, 50(Supplement_1): S-109.

LandScan™ (2007) *Global Population Database 2007*. Oak Ridge, TN: Oak Ridge National Laboratory. Available at www.ornl.gov/landscan/.

Lyytimäki, J.and Sipilä, M. (2009) Hopping on one leg: the challenge of ecosystem disservices for urban green management. *Urban Forestry & Urban Greening*, 8(4), 309–315.

McCaskie, T. (2009) 'Water wars' in Kumasi, Ghana. In F. Locatelli and P. Nugent (eds) *African Cities: Competing Claims on Urban Spaces*. Leiden: Brill, pp. 135–155.

McHarg, I. (1971) *Design with Nature*. Cambridge MA: MIT Press.

MEA (Millennium Ecosystem Assessment) (2005) *Ecosystems and Human Well-Being: Synthesis*. Washington, DC: Island Press.

Mulligan, M. (2009) *Global Mean Dry Matter Productivity Based on SPOT-VGT* (1998-2008). Available at: www.ambiotek.com/dmp.

Mulligan, M. (2013) SimTerra: A consistent global gridded database of environmental properties for spatial modelling: landsat tree cover. Available at: http://www.policysupport.org/simterra [based on Sexton, J. O., Song, X.-P., Feng, M., Noojipady, P., Anand, A., Huang, C., Kim, D.-H., Collins, K.M., Channan, S., DiMiceli, C. and Townshend, J.R.G. (2013) Global, 30-m resolution continuous fields of tree cover: Landsat-based rescaling of MODIS Vegetation Continuous Fields with lidar-based estimates of error. *International Journal of Digital Earth*, 130321031236007. doi:10.1080/17538947.2013.786146.

Mulligan, M. (2014) *WaterWorld Model Documentation*. Available at: http://www.policysupport.org/waterworld.

Mulligan, M., Silvia B., Juan Sebastian, L. and Jorge, L. (2013) Policy support systems for the development of benefit sharing mechanisms for hydrological ecosystem services: application of WaterWorld and RIOS to the Daule Water Fund. In J. Martin-Ortega, B. Ferrier, I. Gordon and S. Khan (eds) *How Can an Ecosystem Services Approach Help Address Global Water Challenges*? Cambridge: Cambridge University Press.

Myers, N., Russell, A., Mittermeier, C. G., Mittermeier, Gustavo A., da Fonseca, B. and Kent J. (2000) Biodiversity hotspots for conservation priorities. *Nature*, 403: 853–858.

Olson, D. M., Dinerstein, E., Wikramanayake, E. D., Burgess, N. D., Powell, G. V. N., Underwood, J. C., D'amico, J. A., Itoua, I., Strand, H. E., Morrison, J. C., Loucks, C. J., Allnutt, T. F., Ricketts, T. R., Kura, Y., Lamoreux, J. F., Wettengel, W. W., Hedao, P. and Kassem, K. R. (1998) Terrestrial ecoregions of the world: a new map of life on Earth. A new global map of terrestrial ecoregions provides an innovative tool for conserving biodiversity. *BioScience*, *51*(11), 933–938.

Ormerod, S. J. (2004) A golden age of river restoration science? *Aquatic Conservation: Marine and Freshwater Ecosystems* 14(6): 543–549.

Pacione, M. (2009) *Urban Geography: A Global Perspective*. New York: Taylor & Francis US.

Pincetl, S. (2010) From the sanitary city to the sustainable city: challenges to institutionalising biogenic (nature's services) infrastructure. *Local Environment*, 15(1): 43–58.

Ramankutty, P. et al. (2008) Farming the planet: 1. Geographic distribution of global agricultural lands in the year 2000. *Global Biogeochemical Cycles*, 22, GB1003 doi:10.1029/2007GB002952.

Rao, K.S., Maikhuri, R.K., Nautiyal, S. and Saxena, K.G. (2002) Crop damage and livestock depredation by wildlife: a case study from Nanda Devi Biosphere Reserve, India. *Journal of Environment Management*, 66: 317–327.

Rutherfurd, I., Abernthy, B. and Prosser, I. (1999) Stream erosion. In S. Lovett and P. Price (eds) *Riparian Land Management Technical Guidelines*, Volume 1: *Principles of Sound Management*. Land and Water Resources Research and Development Corporation: Canberra, Australia, pp. 61–78.

Saatchi, S., Harris, N. L., Brown, S., Lefsky, M., Mitchard, E. T., Salas, W., Zutta, B. R., Buermann, W., Lewis, S. L., Hagen, S., Petrova, S., White, L., Silman, M., Morel, A. (2011) Benchmark map of forest carbon stocks in tropical regions across three continents. *Proceedings of National Academy of Sciences USA*.108(24): 9899–9904.

Saenz, L. and Mulligan, M. (2013) The role of cloud affected forests (CAFs) on water inputs to dams. *Ecosystem Services*, 5: 69–77.

Sanderson, E. W., Malanding J., Levy, M. A., Redford, K. H., Wannebo, A. V. and Woolmer, G. (2002) The human footprint and the last of the wild. *Bioscience*, 52(10): 891–904.

Schmidt, K. A. and R. S. Ostfeld (2001) Biodiversity and the dilution effect in disease ecology. *Ecology* 82: 609–619.

Smith, B., Clifford, N. and Mant, J. (2013) Analysis of UK river restoration using broad-scale data sets. *Water and Environment Journal*. DOI: 10.1111/wej.12063.

Smith B., Clifford, J. and Mant J. (2014) The changing nature of river restoration. *WIREs Water* 2014. doi: 10.1002/wat2.1021.

Tetteh, I. K., Frempong, E. and Awuah, E. (2004) An analysis of the environmental health impact of the Barekese Dam in Kumasi, Ghana. *Journal of Environmental Management*, 72(3): 189–194.

Tilman, D., Reich, P. B. and Knops, J. M. (2006) Biodiversity and ecosystem stability in a decade-long grassland experiment. *Nature*, 441(7093): 629–632.

van Soesbergen, A. and Mulligan, M. (2014) Modelling multiple threats to water security in the Peruvian Amazon using the WaterWorld Policy Support System. *Earth Systems Dynamics*. 5: 55–65.

Vanwambeke, S. O., Lambin, E. F., Eichhorn, M. P., Flasse, S. P., Harbach, R. E., Oskam, L., Somboon, P. (2007) Impact of land-use change on dengue and malaria in northern Thailand. *EcoHealth* 4, 1: 37–51.

Williamson, K. S. (2003) *Growing with Green Infrastructure*. Doylestown, PA: Heritage Conservancy.

Wise, S. (2008) Green infrastructure rising. *Planning*, 74(8): 14–19.

12

CONSERVATION, SUSTAINABILITY AND ECONOMIC GROWTH

William M. Adams

Introduction

In 1973, the US environmental organization, the Conservation Foundation and the International Union for Conservation of Nature (IUCN) published a book giving ecological guidelines for development planning, *Ecological Principles for Economic Development* (Dasmann et al. 1973). This book encapsulated the concern on the part of conservationists and ecologists, growing since the end of the Second World War, about the impacts of economic change, particularly in the developing world (Adams 2009). It grew from a conference in 1968, which rehearsed a catalogue of environmental problems associated with or caused by economic development: its proceedings were published in the same year as *The Careless Technology: Ecology and International Development* (Farvar and Milton 1973).

Ecological Principles for Economic Development was originally intended to provide the basis for approaches to economic development that were compatible with conservation and ecology, a forerunner of the idea of sustainable development. However, in practice, it simply set out ecological concepts 'useful in the context of development activities', focusing on particular activities (tourism, agriculture and river basins, Dasmann et al. 1973: vi). Despite the evidence of serious environmental impacts of development (Farvar and Milton 1973), its argument was upbeat: development planners needed ecology 'to make sure of success' (Dasmann et al. 1973: 21); the application of ecology would enhance development's goals, and if the 'lessons' of ecology were ignored, 'entirely unexpected consequences can often result from what are intended to be straightforwardly beneficial activities' (ibid.).

This was not a novel argument: in 1864, George Perkins Marsh had written in a similar vein: 'the ravages committed by man subvert the relations and destroy the balance which nature had established between her organized and her inorganic creations' (Marsh 1864: 42). Since before the days of Marsh, conservationists have been equivocal about economic development. On the one hand, the conservation movement was founded by people opposed to the destruction of nature, and economic development (especially industrialization, urbanization and intensive agriculture) that were (and are) the chief engines of human impact, the main fabricators of what we now come to call the Anthropocene era (Crutzen 2002). On the other hand, economic development in the twentieth century seemed an unstoppable force, moreover one that underpinned the world from which those conservationists came, and on which they depended for life, livelihood and community. Dasmann et al. tried to ride the tiger of economic development, not opposing it but attempting to steer it. Rather vainly, they placed their faith in the power of science and rationality, saying that development might be justified if environmental costs were outweighed by benefits, but that the decision 'should never be taken blindly' (Dasmann et al. 1973: 21–22).

These debates continue. Recently, analysts of conservation have drawn attention to the growing influence of neoliberalism within conservation. Büscher (2008) found conservation biologists all too eager to reinvent their field to fit 'neoliberal win–win visions'. Since 2008, the neoliberalization of conservation has extended, and the application of market-based approaches has become fundamental to the conservation of nature (Büscher et al. 2012). As capitalism has 'grabbed' the green agenda (Corson et al. 2013), capitalism has increasingly been seen as the key to ecological sustainability (Igoe et al. 2010).

MacDonald (2010) argues that the view, common since the 1960s, that the environmental movement stands in opposition to the values, approaches and mission of businesses, and the agenda of capitalist growth, is misplaced. He suggests 'Biodiversity conservation has never really driven environmental agendas. Rather it has been an instrument in much larger political projects such as nationalism, colonialism and capitalism' (2010: 516). In as much as he may be held to be correct (and the histories remain to be explored in detail), the accelerating intensity of attempts to restructure conservation on rational lines, copying capitalist industrial models, is perhaps not too surprising.

The conservation movement was built within the frame set by the western industrial and consumption models that dominated the nineteenth and twentieth centuries. Refreshed by ongoing processes of neoliberalization, these same models now look set to dominate the twenty-first century. Contemporary conservation ideas and practice are being reworked by neoliberalism, but have also been shaped in the past by the growth imperative of colonial and post-colonial developmentalism and globalized concern about poverty and sustainability.

This chapter considers the close and paradoxical relations between conservation and economic growth through the long twentieth century. Then it analyses the established dependence of conservation on market-based strategies with built-in high throughputs of energy and materials. Finally, it explores the possibility of conservation strategies that embrace degrowth, and considers the transitions in scale, definitions of nature, priorities, forms of organization and democratic control that such a model would demand.

Conservation and Romanticism

While the informal history of conservation is long, its formal history begins in the second half of the nineteenth century, when nature or wildlife conservation in the modern sense developed as an essentially Romantic opposition to the effects of modernity: urbanization, industrialization, and capitalism (Adams 2004).

Capitalism contains its own power and logic, the rational mastery of the market driving the restructuring of society and nature as it 'continuously gnaws away at the resource base that sustains it' (Pepper 1993: 92). Linked to capitalism are the development and application of science and technology, formal hierarchical organisation and a formal legal system (Murphy 1994). The efficient mastery of nature was a central principle of rationalization in both capitalist and state socialist models of development. Both showed scant recognition that nature was not infinitely plastic, malleable to meet human demands (ibid.). From the sixteenth century, scientific knowledge of nature had underpinned imperial imagination and ambition and allowed the exploitation (or 'government') of nature (Drayton 2000). Scientific mastery of nature also formed part of a doctrine of improvement under which people and nature alike were reorganized in the common good. Governance in the modern state incorporated this vision of nature understood and ordered for social benefit (Scott 1998). Thus the application of science to woodland management in eighteenth-century Prussia involved a critical narrowing of vision and simplification, the rendering of the diversity of trees and other plants and the people who had interests in them legible to a bureaucratic process. Under this scientific management regime, the productivity of forests became susceptible to measurement and calculation as science was applied to the efficient management of nature. Simplification allowed 'a high degree of schematic knowledge, control and manipulation' (Scott 1998: 11). This applied to both societies and nature.

The 'return to nature' was one of the great roots of Romanticism (Veldman 1994). In the UK, environmental amenity organizations such as the Commons, Open Spaces and Footpaths Society, the National Trust and the Society for the Promotion of Nature Reserves were established in the three decades from 1880–1915, to protect 'unspoiled' land from urban or commercial use as nature reserves or open space. What was possibly the first nature reserve not for hunting purposes, established by the eccentric Charles Waterton on his Yorkshire estate, was preserved as an island of nature surrounded by polluted industrial landscapes. Indeed, the rural idyll of Tolkein's Shire is recognized as forming part of a tradition of Romantic environmentalist opposition to modernity, rationality and industry (Veldman 1994.)

There was also an element of Romanticism in the concern of the 'penitent butchers' of the Society for the Preservation of the Wild Fauna of the Empire (SPWFE), who lobbied the British Government for game reserves in colonial Africa (Prendergast and Adams 2003, Adams 2004). However, there was also class-based special pleading in their concerns about the depredations of their un-sporting colleagues, and the threat of natives hunting for trade or the pot, from the patrician landowning interest of big game shooting (MacKenzie 1988, Neumann 1996).

Conservation and imperialism

Conservation practice may have in part evolved as a reaction to the impacts of rationalization in metropolitan capitalism, but conservation soon evolved to embrace a rational approach to the enumeration and preservation of non-human life. Colonial conservation policy can be understood in terms of the attempts of the colonial state to render landscapes and people 'legible' to its regimes of registration, calculation and discipline. In the British Empire, discourses of conservation, environmentalism and betterment served as what Foucault (1975) describes as 'political technologies', allowing political issues such as the control and use of land to be translated into technical issues, where formal science could be drawn upon to diagnose health and prescribe treatment (Mackenzie 2000). The apparent impartial objectivity of science allowed landscapes to be assessed and (at least in theory) to be managed (ibid.: 217).

Thus, Bryant (1997) describes the rationalizing impact of scientific forestry in Burma in the nineteenth century, which involved the laying down and enforcement of a bureaucratic and legal regime and the establishment of reserved forests. Similarly, Neumann (2001) describes the creation and management of the Selous Game Reserve and Liwale District in colonial Tanzania in similar rationalizing terms, with attempts to confine animals (particularly elephants) to the first, and people to the second. 'Conservation' policy in fact comprised the creation of a new order for both nature and human society, in the name of colonial 'civilization'.

US national parks, colonial game reserves and UK parks were all aspects of the rationalizing project of the modern state. In colonial Africa, Game Reserves and especially National Parks fitted into a division of landscape between settler and native, wild and sown, commercially developed and preserved, resource-rich and supposedly natural. The application of ecology to planning (for example, in Uganda in the 1940s) represented one aspect of the second colonial occupation of development, and conservation had a specific (if modest) place in that conceptual and physical dispensation.

The same rational ordering of nature, and the symbolic positioning of nature as at the same time available for exploitation and (in specified zones) set aside from that development was obvious in the rise of the late nineteenth-century conception of conservation in the USA as rational resource use. George Perkins Marsh's *Man and Nature* (1864), with its rational critique of irrational human over-demand on 'wild' or disordered nature, had a huge readership. Vast areas of land in the American West had been annexed by the state, surveyed on a geometric grid under various Land Ordinances 1794–1796, and held for the public good for the resources they contained (Meine 2004).

The US conservation movement at the end of the nineteenth century (epitomized by Gifford Pinchot, trained at Yale in the traditions of German forestry) called for those lands and resources to be managed wisely to sustain their output (Hays 1959). The conservation provisions of the Progressive Era in the USA included the creation of a national system of Forest Reserves (1873), the Bureau of Reclamation (1902) and the US Forest Service (1905). In this rationalist mode, conservation was 'the use of the earth and all its resources for the enduring good of men' (Worster 1985: 266), its essence, 'rational planning to promote efficient development and use of natural resources . . . a political system guided by the ideal of efficiency and dominated by the technicians who could best determine how to achieve it' (Hays 1959: 2).

Under utilitarian conservation, nature was 'not to be preserved, but actively manipulated by scientifically trained experts to improve and sustain yields. Those yields were to be harvested and processed efficiently, and economic gains allocated equitably' (Meine 2004: 19). The idea of conservation as rational resource use became established in US public policy, inspired by the capitalist model of the intense pursuit of economy and efficiency, and the eradication of waste, for example, in prairie livestock raising and Chicago's slaughter and meat packing industry (Cronon 1991).

Through the first three decades of the twentieth century, the idea of conservation as rational use of living resources was backed by an increasing range of sciences, such as fisheries, wildlife management and population biology (Elton 1927; Leopold 1933). These ideas were the precursors of conservation's attempt to influence development planning in the 1970s (e.g. Dasmann et al. 1973), of the World Conservation Strategy (1980), and eventually the mainstream of sustainable development (Adams 2009).

Biodiversity in sustainable development

The biodiversity conservation movement had an important role in the emergence of ideas of sustainability in the 1970s. Conservationists turned their backs on the zero growth movement of the 1960s and 1970s (e.g. Mishan 1967; Daly 1973) in an energetic search for a 'third way' between zero and boundless economic growth, a path apparently made possible by the elastic concept of sustainable development (Adams 2009). This idea, first formulated in the preparations for the Stockholm Conference in 1972, was developed in the World Conservation Strategy (IUCN 1980). This argued that conservation was essential to human survival, and that development should be seen as 'a major means of achieving conservation, rather than an obstruction to it' (Allen 1980: 7). It proposed that national strategies should be written to review development objectives in the light of the conservation objectives.

Biodiversity had a smaller role in the proposals of the Brundtland Commission in 1987, which criticized attempts to defend the environment 'in isolation from human concerns'

(WCED 1987: xi). However, debate at Rio in 1992 not only made sustainable development an inextricable part of international political discourse for the next two decades, but it locked biodiversity into place as an integral part of that mission. Soon after publication of the World Conservation Strategy in the mid-1980s, IUCN, WWF, UNEP the World Resources Institute and the World Bank began to discuss a draft 'conservation convention'. The idea was endorsed at the Second World Congress on National Parks in Bali, and between 1988 and 1992 there was sustained pressure for a convention, culminating in a *Global Biodiversity Strategy* (WRI et al. 1992). Formal negotiations began in 1990, but the Convention on Biological Diversity (CBD) eventually agreed at Rio was broader than its advocates had planned, also addressing bioprospecting and biotechnology (Chatterjee and Finger 1994). Nonetheless, the CBD has become the centrepiece of international conservation policy, setting targets for slowing and stopping biodiversity loss (re-setting these in 2011 when the originals were missed), and for the coverage of terrestrial and marine protected areas (17 per cent and 10 per cent of the Earth respectively (www.cbd.int/2011-2020/goals)).

Conservation, growth, capitalism

The insertion of biodiversity conservation into the mainstream approach to sustainability has had profound effects on conservation ideas and practice. The price paid was adoption of a model of human development that made no attempt to challenge the need for economic growth. Biodiversity conservation, empowered from the 1980s by the new 'mission-driven' discipline of conservation biology (Meine et al. 2005), adopted a top-down science-driven strategy that increasingly divorced nature conservation from broader environmentalism. Conservation focused on the protection of endangered species and habitats, applying new technologies of remote sensing and geographic information science to the selection of protected areas, and harnessing increased resources (particularly from the private philanthropy of the global super-rich, Holmes 2012) to their defence.

Outside protected areas, 'community-based' conservation and natural resource management allowed conservation organizations to access development funds targeted to the delivery of environmental sustainability (Adams and Hulme 2001). It was increasingly argued that conservation should be 'incentive-driven' (Hutton and Leader-Williams 2003), delivered as a by-product of attempts to meet the livelihood needs and economic development objectives of local communities (Hutton et al. 2005). On this fertile ground the ideas of 'direct payments' for conservation (Ferraro and Kiss 2002), and then payment for ecosystem services (Redford and Adams 2009) began to flourish.

With the rapid economization of conservation thought and practice following the Millennium Ecosystem Assessment in 2005, there was also an increasing engagement with for-profit business. The Rio Conference had been a critical landmark in corporate engagement with environmentalism: the World Business Council for Sustainable Development (WBCSD, founded in 1990) played an important role, and corporations funded a fifth of the costs of the secretariat (Chatterjee and Finger 1994).

International business used Rio to present itself as a central part of the solution to environment and development problems: the oxymoron of 'green capitalism' was coined, and strongly promoted (Utting 2002). Over the same period, the private sector also became a fundamental part of conservation ideas, practice and businesses (MacDonald 2010).

Following Rio, biodiversity conservation became an important channel of the neoliberalization of environmentalism (Corson et al. 2013). Nature is now routinely framed in terms of monetary value (Roth and Dressler 2012). Its conservation is effected through a complex network of public-private-state partnerships (MacDonald 2010). Nature is increasingly commodified and financialized, as new strategies of accumulation are developed (Büscher and Arsel 2012). Büscher et al. (2012) argue that under neoliberal conservation, nature is seen to be conserved and not destroyed through the expansion of capitalism: nature is saved by the market, not destroyed by it; effective conservation positively demands commodification (the creation of elements of conserved nature that can be bought and sold, from the carbon in forest trees to a timeshare in a protected area eco-lodge). The growing 'economy of repair' seeks to compensate for unsustainable use in one place by conservation or sustainable practices somewhere else (Fairhead et al. 2012).

Conservation's market dependence is now widely accepted. Revenues from tourism are now essential to the conservation of many rare species (Buckley 2012), and the travel, hospitality and wildlife viewing aids industries advertise heavily in conservation magazines. Many conservation organizations are dependent on rich donors and corporations, for core and programme funds (Holmes 2012). These sources of revenue depend on economic activity, and it is not surprising to find the dependence of conservation on economic growth explicitly identified: an *Economist* magazine special report on biodiversity in 2013 evoked the idea of an 'environmental Kuznets curve' to argue that (contrary to environmentalist and popular belief) 'more growth, not less, is the best hope for averting a sixth great extinction' (*Economist* 2013).

Conservation and degrowth

Neoliberal conservation has not gone unchallenged among conservationists. Opposition takes a variety of forms. Some criticisms have focused on the way that commodification and monetization miss critical values of nature, for example, the aesthetic (McCauley 2006), and the potential for framing devices such as ecosystem services to narrow conservation options (Vira and Adams 2009). There is now a considerable literature on the complex interplay of biodiversity in ecosystem services (Mace et al. 2012), and on the valuation of 'cultural services', yet the dissatisfaction of conservationists with the analytical treatment of nature in monetary terms, and the creation of market instruments and products to allow nature to be bought and sold, continues (Sandbrook et al. 2013). Others have pointed out the way a close engagement between conservation organisations and for-profit businesses restricts what conservationists can achieve (e.g. Robinson 2012): support, reputation and freedom of action play off against each other in complex and often unrecognized ways. There are many critics of the corporate style of large international conservation organizations, and their dependence on donations from corporations (and the millionaires who have profited from their growth).

While there is dissatisfaction with conservation's unthinking endorsement of economic growth, path-dependence is powerful (Adams 2010). The constraint of operating within the evolving scaffolding of corporate relations has left conservation unable to challenge capitalism, or the growth agenda. Despite the manifest impacts of the energy and material resources of growing economies (Orr 2007), conservationists have found it difficult to challenge conservation's own progressive neoliberalization, its capture by capitalism (cf. Corson et al. 2013). Biodiversity conservation organisations are not prominent among degrowth actors (Demaria et al. 2013): a degrowth-based conservation has not yet been articulated. Attempts to do so run the risk of intellectual ridicule since, like degrowth itself, such ideas run counter to much theory and practice in conservation. What would a conservation strategy that took degrowth seriously look like? Here I outline four possible elements of a degrowth-based conservation.

The first element is the most approachable, although the least adequate, and it consists of the pursuit of radical efficiency in the area of energy and material consumption in the practice of conservation. The pursuit of efficiency and effectiveness has been a clarion call within science-based biodiversity conservation for several decades. Primarily, effort has been focused on prioritization (where should efforts be focused, for example in 'hotspots' or other areas?), and at cost-effectiveness of different strategies or ways of organizing. However, this effort of self-improvement could be harnessed to other metrics, for example, reducing the carbon footprint of conservation activities (for example, air travel). Some conservation organizations are starting to address their carbon footprint (e.g. CCI-CCF Carbon Management Task Force 2012), however, the sector as a whole is no better (and in some instances worse) than the for-profit corporate sector, whose shareholders (spurred on by environmental organizations) demand change. As an industry, conservation faces various constraints on its own 'greening': globally distributed workforces, extensive operations on the ground in remote areas, and funding streams dependent on supporters who demand to travel to see dwindling stocks of rare nature on the other side of the globe. Greater efficiency in energy and material consumption is certainly possible for conservation, but the strategy falls far short of the embrace of the principles of degrowth.

The second element of a degrowth-based conservation strategy might be individual disconnection and lifestyle transformation. McPherson (2012) advocates a return to the land and self-sufficiency as an appropriate response for conservationists faced by the unsustainability of the growth economy. His solution smacks of survivalism (a cabin in the desert), and invites criticism as excessively Romantic: a residential retreat from the world may be attractive but also as artificial as Thoreau's sojourn at Walden Pond. Nonetheless, there is a clear challenge for conservationists to extend their concern about biodiversity loss to clear lifestyle commitments: indeed, the lack of such a commitment smacks of double standards, or a failure to analyse the ecological basis for modern industrial subsistence. Concern about produce certification, and a measure of voluntary simplicity, form part of many conservationists' life choices, although by no means all: longline tuna, farmed prawns, salmon and meat are on the menu at many conservation meetings. Moreover, the desire of many conservationists to 'get away' from consumer society often involves air travel to far-flung places: few conservationists seem to have a coherent policy on air travel for pleasure. There is no easy and guaranteed route to a low-impact lifestyle, but clearly biodiversity conservationists have a particular responsibility to consider their role in joining and advocating changes in the metabolism of their societies to benefit biodiversity.

The third element in conservation under degrowth might involve an element of restructuring. In the twentieth century, conservation developed as a science-driven mission, developing centrally agreed strategies, overseen by a panopticon of expertise: literally in the form of technologies such as remote sensing, geographic information science, and genetic barcoding of nature, and figuratively in the endless lists of the rare and near-extinct, the assessment of risk and the prioritization of action, enforced by appropriate authorities from above through coerced behaviour (Peluso 1993). Instead, under degrowth, perhaps conservation would be seen as a distributed social practice, something that is not enforced, but which emerges from the decisions of citizens, an expression of a democracy that embraces both the human and the non-human (cf. Asara et al. 2013).

Fourthly, and finally, conservation under degrowth might involve the re-imagination of nature. Conservation to date has been powered by a sense of nature as pristine, standing threatened but essentially unchanged in a world increasingly transformed by human consumption. But this metaphor of the 'naturalness' of nature is problematic, for human transformations are profound and universal, not least through anthropogenic influences on climate change. Kareiva et al. (2007) speak of the 'domestication of nature', and Marris (2011) of the challenge of saving nature in a 'post-wild world'. The idea of a balance of nature, and of ecosystems in equilibrium, has given way to an understanding that ecosystems are dynamic, subject to changes in state at a variety of scales. Ecosystem restoration needs to become a central plank of conservation (alongside protection), but ecosystems are ecological hybrids not 'natural' habitats. Future ecosystems will be novel in their make-up, and will respond to climatic and other factors driven by human demands in novel ways. Novel ecosystems need novel conservation strategies (Seastedt et al. 2008), more open to different complexions of human and non-human natures.

Conclusion

For much of the last seven decades, conservationists have seen themselves as part of a broader environmental movement. Increasingly, however, they have moved into a separate space, seeking to protect nature in particular places (where its pre-human attributes are still strongest, and its diversity greatest), but failing to address the implications of economic growth for biodiversity loss. They are treating symptoms not causes, and moreover as they engage in neoliberal strategies they are seeking to use the engine of capitalism (that has driven the destruction) to save the remainder. This is a strange and short-sighted strategy.

To change it, conservation itself must change, and its idea of the nature it seeks to protect must change. Orr (2003: 950) argues that 'the preservation of diversity will require a different manner of thinking that runs counter to much of conventional wisdom, including that described as environmental'. The transformation required in conservation thought and practice is profound, and has barely begun.

References

Adams, W. M. (2004) *Against Extinction: The Story of Conservation*. London: Earthscan.

Adams, W. M. (2009) *Green Development: Environment and Sustainability in a Developing World*. London: Routledge.

Adams, W. M. (2010) Path dependence in conservation. In N. Leader-Williams, W. M. Adams and R. J. Smith (eds) *Trade-offs in Conservation: Deciding What to Save*. Oxford: Wiley-Blackwell, pp. 292–310.

Adams, W. M. and Hulme, D. (2001) Conservation and communities: changing narratives, policies and practices in African conservation. In D. Hulme and M. Murphee (eds) *African Wildlife and Livelihoods: The Promise and Performance Of Community Conservation*. London: James Currey, pp. 9–23.

Allen, R. (1980) *How to Save the World: Strategy for World Conservation*. London: Kogan Page.

Asara, V., Profumi, E. and Kallis, G. (2013) Degrowth, democracy and autonomy. *Environmental Value*, 22(2013): 217–239.

Bryant, R. L. (1997) *The Political Ecology of Forestry in Burma 1824–1994*. London: Hurst & Company.

Buckley, R. (2012) The tourist trap. *New Scientist*, 216(2868): 28–29.

Büscher, B. (2008) Conservation, neoliberalism, and social science: a critical reflection on the SCB 2007 Annual Meeting. *Conservation Biology*, 22: 229–231.

Büscher, B. and Arsel, M. (2012) Neoliberal conservation, uneven geographical development and the dynamics of contemporary capitalism. *Tijdschrift voor Economische en Sociale Geografie*, 103(2): 129–135.

Büscher, B., Sullivan, S., Neves, K., Igoe, J. and Brockington, D. (2012) Towards a synthesized critique of neoliberal conservation. *Capitalism, Nature, Socialism*, 23: 4–30.

CCI-CCF Carbon Management Task Force (2012) *Reducing the Carbon Footprint of Conservation Organisations*. Cambridge: Cambridge Conservation Forum.

Chatterjee, P. and Finger, M. (1994) *The Earth Brokers: Power, Politics and World Development*. London: Routledge.

Corson, C., MacDonald, K. I. and Neimark, B. (2013) Grabbing 'green': markets, environmental governance and the materialization of natural capital. *Human Geography*, 6: 1–15.

Cronon, W. (1991) *Nature's Metropolis: Chicago and the Great West*. New York: W. W. Norton.

Crutzen, P. J. (2002) Geology of mankind: the Anthropocene. *Nature*, 415: 23.

Daly, H. E. (1973) (ed.) *Towards a Steady-State Economy*. New York: W. H. Freeman.

Dasmann, R. F., Milton, J. P. and Freeman, P. H. (1973) *Ecological Principles for Economic Development.* Chichester: Wiley.

Demaria, F., Schneider, F. Sekulova, F. and Martinez-Alier, J. (2013) What is degrowth? From an activist slogan to a social movement. *Environmental Values*, 22: 191–215 .

Drayton, R. (2000) *Nature's Government: Science, Imperial Britain and the 'Improvement' of the World.* New Haven, CT: Yale University Press.

The Economist (2013) Hang on: more growth, not less is the best hope for averting a sixth great extinction. *Economist*, 14 September 2013, p. 1.

Elton, C. S. (1927) *Animal Ecology*. London: Sidgwick and Jackson.

Fairhead, J., Leach, M. and Scoones, I. (2012) Green grabbing: a new appropriation of nature? *The Journal of Peasant Studies*, 39(2): 237–261.

Farvar, M. T. and Milton, J. P. (eds) (1973) *The Careless Technology: Ecology and International Development.* London: Stacey.

Ferraro, P. J. and Kiss, A. (2002) Direct payments to conserve biodiversity. *Science*, 298: 1718–1719.

Foucault, M. 1975. *Discipline and Punish: the Birth of the Prison.* Paris: Gallimard (in translation 1997 Allen Lane, London).

Hays, S. P. (1959) *Conservation and the Gospel of Efficiency: The Progressive Conservation Movement, 1890–1920.* Cambridge, MA: Harvard University Press.

Holmes, G. (2012) Biodiversity for billionaires: capitalism, conservation and the role of philanthropy in saving/selling nature. *Development and Change*, 43: 185–203.

Hutton, J., Adams, W. M. and Murombedzi, J. C. (2005) Back to the barriers? Changing narratives in biodiversity conservation. *Forum for Development Studies*, 32(2): 341–370.

Hutton, J. M. and Leader-Williams, N. (2003) Sustainable use and incentive-driven *conservation*: realigning human and conservation interests. *Oryx*, 37: 215–226.

Igoe, J., Neves, K. and Brockington, D. (2010) A spectacular eco-tour around the historic bloc: theorising the convergence of biodiversity conservation and capitalist expansion. *Antipode*, 42:486–512.

IUCN (1980) *The World Conservation Strategy*. International Union for Conservation of Nature and Natural Resources, United Nations Environment Programme. Geneva: World Wildlife Fund.

Kareiva, P., Watts, S., McDonald, R. and Boucher, T. (2007) Domesticated nature: shaping landscapes and ecosystems for human welfare. *Science*, 316: 1866–1869.

Leopold, A. (1933) *Game Management*. New York: Scribner's.

McCauley D. J. (2006) Selling out on nature. *Nature*, 44327–44338.

MacDonald, K. I. (2010) The devil is in the (bio)diversity: private sector 'engagement' and the restructuring of biodiversity conservation. *Antipode*, 42: 513–550.

Mackenzie, A. F. D. (2000) Contested ground: colonial narratives and the Kenyan environment, 1920–1945. *Journal of Southern African Studies*, 26: 697–718.

MacKenzie, J. M. (1988) *The Empire of Nature: Hunting, Conservation and British Imperialism.* Manchester: Manchester University Press.

McPherson, G. (2012) Going back to the land in the age of entitlement. *Conservation Biology*, 25: 855–857.

Mace, G. M., Norris, K. and Fitter, A. H. (2012) Biodiversity and ecosystem services: a multilayered relationship. *Trends in Ecology & Evolution*, 27: 19–26.

Marris, E. (2011) *Rambunctious Garden: Saving Nature in a Post-Wild World.* London: Bloomsbury.

Marsh, G. P. (1864) *Man and Nature; Or, Physical Geography as Modified by Human Action.* New York: Scribner's (Harvard University Press, 1965).

Meine, C. (2004) Correction Lines: *Essays on Land, Leopold, and Conservation.* Washington DC: Island Press.

Meine, C., Soulé, M. and Noss, R. F. (2005) '"A mission-driven discipline": the growth of conservation biology'. *Conservation Biology* 20: 631–651.

Millennium Ecosystem Assessment (2005) *Ecosystems and Human Well-Being: Synthesis.* Washington, DC: Island Press.

Mishan, E. (1967) *The Costs of Economic Growth.* Harmondsworth: Penguin Books.

Murphy, R. (1994) *Rationality and Nature: A Sociological Inquiry into a Changing Relationship.* Boulder, CO: Westview Press.

Neumann, R. P. (1996) Dukes, Earls and ersatz Edens: aristocratic nature preservationists in colonial Africa. *Environment and Planning D: Society and Space*, 14: 79–98.

Neumann, R. P. (2001) Africa's 'last wilderness': reordering space for political and economic control in colonial Tanzania. *Africa*, 71: 641–665.

Orr, D. W. (2003) Diversity. *Conservation Biology*, 17(6): 948–951.

Orr, D. W. (2007) Optimism and hope in a hotter time. *Conservation Biology*, 21: 1932–1935.

Peluso, N. (1993) Coercing conservation: the politics of state resource control. *Global Environmental Change*, 3: 199–217.

Pepper, D. (1993) *Eco-Socialism: From Deep Ecology to Social Justice*. London: Routledge.

Prendergast, D. K. and Adams, W. M. (2003) Colonial wildlife conservation and the origins of the Society for the Preservation of the Wild Fauna of the Empire (1903–1914). *Oryx*, 37: 251–260.

Redford, K. H. and Adams, W. M. (2009) Payment for ecosystem services and the challenge of saving nature. *Conservation Biology*, 23: 785–787.

Robinson, J. G. (2012) Common and conflicting interests in the engagements between conservation organizations and corporations. *Conservation Biology*, 26: 967–977.

Roth, R. J. and Dressler, W. (2012) Market-oriented conservation governance: the particularities of place. *Geoforum*, 43: 363–366.

Sandbrook, C., Fisher, J. and Vira, B. (2013) What do conservationists think about markets? *Geoforum*, 50: 232–240.

Scott, J. C. (1998) *Seeing Like a State: How Certain Schemes to Improve the Human Condition Have Failed*. New Haven, CT: Yale University Press.

Seastedt, T. R., Hobbs, R. J. and Suding, K. N. (2008) Management of novel ecosystems, are novel approaches required? *Frontiers in Ecology and the Environment*, 6: 547–553.

Utting, P. (ed.) (2002) *The Greening of Business in Developing Countries: Rhetoric, Reality and Prospects*. London: Zed Books, for the United Nations Research Institute for Social Development.

Veldman, M. (1994) *Fantasy, the Bomb and the Greening of Britain: Romantic Protest, 1945–1980*. Cambridge: Cambridge University Press.

Vira, B. and Adams, W. M. (2009) Ecosystem services and conservation strategy: beware the silver bullet. *Conservation Letters*, 2: 158–162.

WCED (1987) *Our Common Future*. The Brundtland Report. Oxford: Oxford University Press, for the World Commission on Environment and Development.

Worster, D. (1985) *Nature's Economy: A History of Ecological Ideas*. Cambridge: Cambridge University Press.

WRI, UNEP, UNDP (1992) *Global Biodiversity Strategy: Guidelines for Action to Save, Study, and Use Earth's Biotic Wealth Sustainably and Equitably*. Washington, DC: World Resources Institute.

PART IV

Social dimensions of sustainable development

13
SUSTAINABLE DEVELOPMENT
Environmental justice and sustainability

Robert William Collin and Robin Morris Collin

Introduction

Contemporary inequity and distributional disparity pose a fundamental challenge to sustainable development. When sustainable development fails or ignores challenges based upon contemporary gender, race or ethnic disparities in income, health, housing, transportation and employment, these disparities will undermine successful development. Sustainability is difficult without repairing and restoring inherited and contemporary disparities which are inevitably reflected in ecosystems and environmental damage. The challenge of sustainable development is honest recognition of the historical roots of our current environment crisis as a critical leverage point for strategic change in how communities develop.

These disparities are destabilizing our climate, our economies, and our communities. The lack of balance in a given ecosystem generally decreases its resiliency. The disparities left in the wake of racism, colonialism, industrialism, are destabilizing the ecosystems on which all life depends (Millennium Ecosystem Assessment 2005). Destabilization is a reality reflected in the environment. The consequences of unstable and collapsing ecosystems are also famines, wars, droughts and floods, lost lives and livelihoods. The combination of economic deprivation and environmental degradation creates increasing poverty and environmental devastation. These downward spirals will transcend gender, class, and race.

Environmental justice and sustainability: reshaping economies for equity and ecosystem health

Environmental justice refers to the movement to redress disproportionate adverse impacts on vulnerable populations. Environmental racism refers to the constellation of public policies that intentionally imposed the risks and harms of development, including waste and toxic pollution, disproportionately on people of color, poor communities, working people, women and children. These policies used these communities as sinks and buffers for the hazardous wastes and pollution by-products of development without allowing them to partake of the wealth generated.

The environmental justice movement challenges these policies and practices and the contemporary disparities that are now etched into the landscape of our environment and communities. Environmental justice also challenges the lack of equal access to the benefits of nature and environmental experiences on the part of poor communities and communities of color. These benefits include physical and psychological health, the ability to support one's life and family, the ability to practice spirituality, human autonomy including family planning, dignity and virtue.

Justice and the environment

Sustainability will require us to confront the damage to our ecosystems caused by our choice of development modality. Slavery, genocide, colonialism, industrialism, and exploitation of limited natural resources are part of those development choices. Sustainability will require us to address disparities that exist because of this development model and its history, and revisit deliberate public policy decisions to sacrifice certain groups and communities for development in the quest for a better life for the majority.

Today's local environmental reality is powerfully linked with other global realities, including growing economic inequality. Resolving these issues will require acknowledging and resolving the entrenched heritage of inequality that has left some communities and some people exposed to hazardous waste and toxic conditions and deprived of the benefits of access to nature and politically unable to access environmental policy making. This heritage has also left communities (even in wealthy nations, like the USA) deprived of knowledge about the natural environment, without technical ability to access information about conditions in their own place on Earth, and without the means to engage powerful development decisions and decision-makers.

Building sustainable communities with capacity for resilience is not only a matter of equitable disaster planning and equitable relief provision when disaster strikes. Building sustainable communities with capacity for resilience requires an intentional public policy of restoration and reparation countering the dangers and harms left from prior development policies.

Development dialogues

Many wealthy nations developed through the conquest of foreign lands and peoples, albeit with much variation. Industrialization, commercialization, and fossil fuels followed global conquests creating the modern consumer economies of scale that we know today. The rapid depletion of resources, extractions, depletions and waste of a consumer-driven economic system have overwhelmed the ecosystems which balance and restore our natural resources. As population increases and more countries follow this model, environmental impacts will increase, impacting global environmental conditions such global warming, climate change, and rising ocean levels.

All development is context-driven, as is sustainable development. Growth means different things to different nations. In nations facing a health crisis from obesity-related illnesses, growth means radically different things from nations struggling to feed their people. Also, the power and role of the government in a given country differ greatly, including officially sanctioned corruption. Many countries struggle with the economic consequences of militarism, genocide, rape, near perpetual conflict, the lack of sustainable infrastructure, poverty and environmental degradation. These contexts will require contemporary sustainable development to face practical and moral intervention without relativism or apology.

The fact of growing global inequity of wealth creates poverty-driven consequences in all nations. The gap between rich and poor people within nations, as well as between nations, accelerates the trajectory of desperation that continues practices, such as hazardous waste disposal and dangerous extraction industries that lead to ecosystem degradation as well as human health impacts. The claims that poverty and inequity make upon our ecosystems contribute to the cumulative destabilization of those ecosystems as they become less and less able to absorb, cleanse and restore balance to the underlying air, water, and land systems. While industrialized countries historically have placed the most devastating burdens on our ecosystems through an economic system that encourages externalities such as waste and pollution, as well as poverty, growth in less developed countries that follows the same trajectory of fossil fuel dependences will increase ecological degradation.

Environmental justice is the robust demand for redress of inequities to women, children, people of color, and the poor in ways that will require actual restoration of our environment and its ecosystems. Fundamental changes in the way development operates, including the deeply subjective strata of world-views such as authoritarianism, sexism, racism, and values such as greed must be addressed. The fundamental promise of development is a better quality of life for the majority of people on Earth who are people of color, the poor, women and children.

The privilege paradox

Being born into a place to live, work, play, worship, and learn free from increasing ecological contamination and the fear of health-threatening toxicity is a privilege enjoyed by fewer and fewer sentient beings. Regardless of the rationalization for that privileged position, its ecological impact is no longer sustainable, even if political and social structures have not yet changed. The canaries in the coalmine – the environmentally exposed communities and other vulnerable beings – suffer first and worst. Over time, public health erosion transcends race, gender, class and nationality. Human communities will suffer regardless of wealth because we are joined and interdependent on ecosystems that all beings depend on to live.

Privilege supports and preserves unsustainable modes of living, working, and even thinking. For example, the illusion of racial preferences, which is scientifically unfounded, allows white privilege in the USA to be unconnected to the consequences of their conduct for other people whom they do not have to encounter or engage. As noted by one researcher in this area:

> The idea of race exists because people give it a particular meaning, a meaning that changes with tie, place, and circumstances. But one constant remains—the privileging of whiteness through different devices, social pattern, and even laws. This racial positioning is maintained in part through an unwritten rule that it cannot be discussed. In fact, the corollary rule mandates that we talk about social desire for equality while avoiding an examination of white privilege or any other privilege.
>
> *(Wildman 1996)*

Feeling unconnected to consequences of actions enables a full range of irresponsible, dangerous, and unexamined conduct towards people and ecosystems.

Public health: inequity made visible

Public health impacts are part of the development context for sustainable development as much as roads, schools, dams, and harbors. Science argues about cause and effect, industry hides them under the mask of "trade secrets," and their vectors remain shrouded in mystery. Public health impacts range from decreased sperm counts, early onset of menses, endocrine disrupters, asthma, birth defects, and other human reactions to environmental stressors. Technology may soon be able to determine chemical load to an individual body. Technology is also developing ways for individuals to contribute to real-time public health data. For example, in San Francisco,

California, inhalers for asthmatics were fitted with a Geographic Positioning System. Real and trend data emerge over time as to which places are hard to breathe in. While this allows those who have access to it to take preventative measures, it also indicates the physical location of environmental impacts and public health vectors. This data can be overlaid with race and class data to reveal distributions of environmental burdens and benefits. As technology increases the ability to measure local health impacts, the line between public and private health becomes blurred. This information will increasingly be part of community-driven decisions on sustainable development.

Intergenerational justice and justice to contemporaries: what's fairness got to do with it?

The classic definition of sustainable development comes from Gro Harlem Brundtland, MD, former prime minister of Norway. Her report for the United Nations, *Our Common Future*, was issued in 1987 – the same year as *Toxic Waste and Race*, a landmark study of the distribution of waste in the United States. Brundtland's iconic definition of sustainable development is development that allows contemporaries to meet their needs without compromising the ability of future generations to meet their needs. The *Toxic Waste and Race* study found that hazardous landfills, controlled and uncontrolled, were in African American communities 99.9 percent of the time, a 1 in 10,000 chance of being random. Hundreds of studies generally confirm that race is the prevailing dynamic in propinquity to industrial type land uses, even more of a factor than income. The *Toxic Waste and Race* study was conducted by the United Churches of Christ in 1987, verified by a leading accounting firm, and repeated 20 years later with even more pronounced results (United Church of Christ, *Toxic Wastes and Race at Twenty 1987–2007*, available at: www.ucc.org/assets/pdfs/toxic20.pdf.). How can we achieve intergenerational fairness without engaging the disparities and needs of contemporaries?

Intergenerational fairness is the idea that contemporary generations should leave to future generations the same quantity and quality of environmental resources, including biodiversity and ecosystem services. Yet, the impact of waste and pollution is discounted when it is imposed upon people, communities and nations. Too often our economic decisions have discounted the value of contemporary lives without political power. The environmental justice movement challenges decisions that arrogate the value of present-day decisions to the powerful few, and discount future risks and harms of these decisions to the many affected by them. When job blackmail, and fossil fuel economies are the only opportunities available, contemporaries will take that opportunity, at the greatest risk to all future generations.

Sustainable development requires an intergenerational focus looking backwards as well as forwards. Past environmental impacts are part of the contours of today's sustainable development including considerations such as carrying capacity. Exposure of past acts of oppression and environmental impact will reveal contemporary privilege. And they will be contentious.

The sustainable development choice: utilitarianism and fairness

Public policy decisions of the past have often been predicated on the philosophy of doing the greatest good for the greatest number, maximizing utility. This way of thinking has elevated financial interests in economic decisions above other social values. Utilitarianism has justified certain areas, and certain groups of people as acceptable sacrifice zones even if they did not consent to – or even participate in – the decision. By contrast, John Rawls asks in *A Theory of Justice* (1971) what decisions we would make if we could not be sure of the conditions of the lives we would actually come to live. What decisions would we make if we did not know whether we would be born African or European, male or female, rich or poor? From this vantage that he calls the "original position," he posits that just and fair principles would be those we choose for ourselves from behind this so-called "veil of ignorance" as to our ultimate position in life.

Utilitarian approaches to environmental regulation yielded toxic hotspots that increase in ecological pervasiveness. Over time, as toxic hotspots increase, ecosystems degrade, and climate change increases, the greatest good for the greatest number yields the least good for the least number. This is because of our ecological interdependence. Contrary to the assumptions of the model, we are only as resilient as our weakest most toxic link. Over time, utilitarianism short-sightedness poisons the Earth and ultimately threatens all life that depends on our existing ecosystems.

The greatest good for the greatest number reflects an unimplemented aspiration. It was not implemented because it was not actually for the greatest number, considering the numbers of people and sentient beings that were excluded from our policies, procedures or even consciousness. Utilitarianism does not encourage inclusion of affected subpopulations in development decisions. In many countries, affected subpopulations compose the majority of total population: women, children, people of color, and the poor. Excluding these subpopulations excludes the most affected populations, and often the most vulnerable ones. Accumulating effects, accurate baselines and knowledge thereof, expose the weaknesses of this value choice in sustainable development.

Even if we were able to immediately achieve radical resource efficiency, change to renewable and free energy, net zero buildings, zero waste manufacturing, and toxin-free products, sustainability would still require us to address the disparities that exist today because of our history, and deliberate public policy decisions to sacrifice certain groups and communities to development. Could we ignore the destroyed ecosystems in our cities, the poisons in our oceans and freshwater sources, the mountains of waste and hazards that are here now as a result of the past? With global urbanization, rising ocean levels and unknown amounts of ocean dumping, it will be difficult to ignore these dynamics. They are the backdrop to sustainable development.

Our futures are linked together by the environment we share locally and globally. Nature is indifferent to social status or wealth. So if collapse of the ecosystems comes from the developed nations or the developing nations, fault will not change the result and wealth may only postpone those consequences, at best, not change them.

The meaning of justice

Justice has many definitions, including normative, procedural, distributive, corrective and social justice. Environmental justice encompasses all of them (Kuehn 2000). Environmental justice represents the culmination and continuing accumulation of injustice in housing, education, employment, municipal services, and transit. One prominent example is waste disposal. In the USA, most controlled and uncontrolled hazardous waste sites were in African American communities. There over 100 studies exploring whether race or income plays a causal role. Most studies in the USA conclude that the substantial cause is race.

As corrective justice, environmental justice seeks redress for disproportionate adverse impacts. Environmental justice as distributive justice focuses on disproportionate adverse environmental impacts on vulnerable populations. As a matter of normative justice, environmental justice demands that no community bear a disproportionate share of risk and harm or deprivation of benefits. As a matter of procedural justice, environmental justice demands the right to participate and consent to decisions that will impose risks and harms on vulnerable already burdened communities and people.

Corrective justice is fairness in the way damages inflicted on individuals and communities are compensated and punishments for law breaking are assigned. Compensatory justice seeks reparation and restoration of losses that the wrongdoer has caused. Corrective justice speaks to the need for environmental reparations in many marginalized communities. Environmental enforcement and compliance data in the USA show that fines for the same environmental acts are higher when white communities are harmed. In urban areas, often associated with greater populations of mixed races, clean-up standards of polluted land are often to industrial levels, not residential standards. The lack of environmental enforcement and compliance and the continued lower standards for clean-up provide the backdrop of the environmental injustice from a corrective justice perspective. To achieve corrective justice, communities will need a broader engagement regime covering more environmental impacts, environmentally effective enforcement, and much higher cleanup standards.

Distributive justice is fairly distributed outcomes rather than a process for arriving at such outcomes. This involves addressing the disproportionate public health and environmental risks borne by people of color and lower incomes, and is achieved by lowering risks, not shifting or equalizing current risks. As a normative matter, no community should bear these disproportionate risks. Procedural justice is a function of the manner in which a decision is made, the fairness of the decision-making process, rather than on its outcome. A community's judgment about whether a decision is just is significantly influenced by the perceived fairness of procedures leading to that outcome. Procedural justice is a fundamental role of state and rule of law. Participation is part of a fair procedure. Procedural fairness generally requires actual notice as a preliminary step.

All these kinds of justice reveal how unfair environmental practices affect people and the environment. The most practical remedy is that of procedural justice. Through this mechanism the venues for inclusion of a broader public are developed. Procedural justice helps sustainable development by revealing lost or hidden environmental impacts, as well as past human injustices.

Environmental justice in international law: the Aarhus Convention

Environmental information moves sustainable development to implementation. Accurate information about environmental impacts is necessary for sustainable development. When place-based knowledge about environment impacts emerges, it reveals history about how the people who live there were treated in the past. As this knowledge emerges, it shows how present-day decisions continue to contribute to past environmental impacts, and how they accumulate at exponential rates. Real-time environmental monitoring is now possible and this evolving state of knowledge will uncover more past and present environmental inequities.

The people most impacted by resource and environmental decisions are often historically oppressed people. Armed with knowledge of these impacts, they are highly motivated to participate in the decisions that affect them. Their participation is both a matter of substantive and procedural justice. Evolving environmental information and inclusive procedures lead to environmental justice issues. Policies of sustainable development that fully incorporate environmental justice issues will be more effective in the formation and implementation by local populations because they may find creative place-based solutions in which the majority of local people are willing to invest their efforts.

These policy principles are recognized internationally in the Aarhus Convention, focused on information, public participation, and justice. The Aarhus Convention provides an example of integrating sustainable development and environmental justice. It uses the power of accurate environmental information. The United Nations Economic Commission for Europe Convention on Access to Information, Public Participation in Decision-Making and Access to Justice in Environmental Matters was adopted on 25 June 1998, in Aarhus, Denmark. It provides a comprehensive approach to information, public participation, and access to justice. It is a model policy for nations, regions, urban habitats, and communities.

The Aarhus Convention implements Principle 10 of the Rio Declaration on Citizen Participation. Signatories must ensure access to environmental information held by public authorities. This information includes environmental information, economic analysis, and conditions related to human health, safety, conditions of life, cultural sites, and built structures. Affected persons and their organizations may comment on activities including development proposals. They may also participate in plans, programs, and policies concerning the environment. Finally, members of the public may challenge these decisions.

"Environmental information" means any information in written, visual, aural, electronic or any other material form on the state of elements of the environment, such as air and atmosphere, water, soil, land, landscape and natural sites, biological diversity and its components, including genetically modified organisms, and the interaction among these elements. The environmental information also includes factors, such as substances, energy, noise and radiation, and activities or measures. Other information includes administrative measures, environmental agreements, policies, legislation, plans and programs, affecting or likely to affect the elements of the environment. This broad approach is very useful for sustainable development, and will highlight environmental justice issues in these powerful venues.

Economic analyses and assumptions used in environmental decision-making, including cost-benefits, and the values placed on present and future human life are also disclosed. This is important for sustainable development because of issues of intergenerational equity. Some of these issues are discussed in other chapters in this book.

Environmental decision-makers is a term used broadly. Private, corporate, and public decisions are all included. Past, present, and future environmental impacts are included. Implicit, quiet, private, non-disclosed, privileged, and secret environmental impacts are included. This range of environmental decision-making is necessary for sustainable development, and will more fully illuminate environmental justice issues.

The human dimensions of environmental information are important for environmental justice. The Aarhus Convention discloses information about the state of human health and safety, conditions of human life, cultural sites and built structures. These are important issues for many oppressed communities because these consequences are at crisis stages for them, and their indigenous cultural institutions are the only ones that have helped them to survive, and to be resilient. By including these issues, participation of these communities in decision-making is increased.

Further, the Convention differentiates between "the public," meaning one or more natural or legal persons, and, in accordance with national legislation or practice, their associations, organizations or groups. This is a general definition. The Aarhus Convention also addresses "*the public concerned*," meaning the public affected or likely to be affected by, or having an interest in, the environmental decision-making; for the purposes of this definition, non-governmental organizations promoting environmental protection and meeting any requirements under national law are deemed to have an interest.

This broad definition allows non-governmental organizations and communities to contribute their knowledge. In this process they may learn of the environmental benefits and burdens for the first time. They may learn of other regions facing similar issues. They learn about accumulating present-day impacts and their public health consequences. This shared, growing, and intense concern mobilizes participants towards environmental justice.

A powerful question is how to incorporate this information into the functioning of the state. The Aarhus Convention gives a structure in which to do so. Each Party to the Convention must take the necessary legislative, regulatory and other measures, including measures to achieve compatibility between the provisions implementing the information, public participation and access-to-justice provisions in this Convention. Enforcement measures to establish and maintain a clear and transparent and consistent framework to implement the provisions of this Convention are specifically required. Parties are specifically required to ensure that officials and authorities assist and provide guidance to the public in seeking access to information, in facilitating participation in decision-making and in seeking access to justice in environmental matters. The freedom of access to environmental information based on justice is a very strong environmental justice interest, followed closely by participation in these decisions. This acknowledges entrenched environmental inequities. Those most oppressed are those least able, for whatever reason, to participate in environmental decision-making. The Aarhus Convention specifically provides for that.

To overcome these social obstacles the Aarhus Convention ensures public access to information by requiring public access to information without the requirement of stating an interest, and it provides for direct electronic access through public telecommunications networks. Where the information is not easily publicly accessible by direct electronic means, each Party ensures that its competent authority provides that information by any other effective means, as soon as possible and at the latest within one month after the request has been submitted. Some general principles of inclusion provide a policy outline. Access to this information is free of charge, except for a charge for reproducing and mailing the specific information. For many oppressed groups this is an obstacle to participation. Where the information is not easily publicly accessible by direct electronic means, and at times when the costs are too high for the public, electronic access in publicly accessible locations is required.

Sustainability and environmental justice: the US context

The history of environmental injustice can often be traced back to the colonial experience. The USA is no exception. Before European conquest, the North American continent was sparsely populated, and its ecosystems and natural resources were abundant. Colonial expansion searched for gold, silver, tillable land, and furs and pelts to trade just as contemporary corporate ventures search the Earth for rare metals and objects of trade. Industrialization as a method of production has contributed further to the voracious appetite for resources, including labor. This model of development reoriented the continent toward short-term profit maximization making the wealthy elite of slave owners and traders. It also led to loss of top soil land resources during the Dust Bowl era, toxification of the Mississippi Delta, loss of biodiversity and diminution of all these natural assets. In the process, settlers destroyed the lives and livelihoods of indigenous peoples. Colonialism and industrialism allowed the benefits of capitalism to be captured and retained by a few, and allowed the costs of waste, pollution, and public health to be externalized onto the public. This is the equivalent of modern-day pattern of privatization of profits and socialization of losses. Having successfully externalized these costs to increase profit maximization, these costs now accrue to the detriment of global ecosystems and local communities.

In the USA, African slaves had no protection from the law. They had no rights to live, marry, learn to read, vote, or participate in government. After slavery ended, racial oppression continued in housing, education, land use, municipal service provision, and employment. Over time, these places of concentrated Africanity are still underserved, undercounted, and the site for concentrated sites of locally unwanted land uses. One of the most unwanted land uses is hazardous waste landfills, which is part of a growing, robust waste trade. *Toxic Waste and Race*, the 1987 study cited earlier, confirmed that hazardous US landfills, controlled and uncontrolled, were overwhelmingly located in African American communities 99.9 percent of the time, a 1 in 10,000 chance of being random. Hundreds of studies generally confirm that race is the prevailing dynamic in propinquity to industrial type land uses, even more of a factor than income.

The dynamic, continuous and growing characteristic of these impacts is that they accumulate, and bio-accumulate with environmental and epigenetic results. In Southern California, whites have a 1 in 7 cancer risk compared to Latino people who have a 1 in 3 risk. Over time pollution will saturate the ecosystem and spread impacts to other areas. Air pollution moves or stays with the wind, water pollution moves from waste water to drinking water, and the land becomes toxic, leaching into water, blowing into the air with wind.

The problematical role of the academy in environmental justice

Environmental justice challenges core values and the political economy of higher education. Environmental justice communities are often uncomfortable in higher education venues. Prominent US universities were involved in the extermination of indigenous peoples and the enslavement of African people from the seventeenth to nineteenth centuries. The first universities were intended to convert native populations to Christianity and played an institutional role in slavery (Wilder 2013). As these universities became established, the actual number of African or indigenous students plummeted. Wealth for the early universities came in part from the slave trade. Many universities and academics provided intellectual cover for racism in the study of science and presumed racial inferiorities and qualities. Faculty Abolitionists were highly discouraged. Even the bodies of slaves were used in research universities and medical schools for the students. The scientific defense of slavery came from these universities and continued in the nineteenth century. Institutionally, many of these universities are today places of privilege with limited access for oppressed and marginalized people. This fundamental schism is part of the institutional context for environmental justice issues in the USA now.

Against this background, universities often are inhospitable to the needs and claims of subordinated populations, perpetuating a legacy of colonial privilege clothed in post-colonial relativism.

Sustainability and environmental justice: the urbanization context

By 2030, 60 percent of the world will be living in urban settlements. In developed nations, 84 percent of our population will be living in cities. Environmentalism does not deal with either fact very well, as a matter of history or contemporary paradigm. In 1970, the US Environmental Protection Agency (EPA) was formed by President Nixon. It was formed to administer the recently developed environmental laws. 1970 was two years ago after Martin Luther King had been killed, six years since John F. Kennedy was assassinated, five years since the Civil Rights Act was signed, four years since the Voting Rights Act was signed. But the leadership of the EPA intentionally disengaged the issues of cities, civil rights, and poverty. This early disassociation from social justice formed a mental paradigm that dealt with wild places and wild things, not communities, and cared more for endangered species than endangered humans. This set early environmentalists on an anti-urban course. This paradigm paints cities as sources of waste and pollution. This paradigm leads to demonizing cities and their inhabitants who are disproportionately people of color. The statistics on future urbanization make it clear that this negative paradigm is unsustainable. We must embrace urbanization and explore ways in which it can preserve wild areas and improve quality of life and resilience for all beings. Urbanism is the new hope for human sustainability.

The context of sustainable development is an expanding and urbanizing population with rapid globalization. Any attempt at implementation reveals areas of cumulative environmental and public health impacts. Cumulative impacts are not only a threat to ecosystem-based sustainability posed by past accumulation, but also by the continued and usually increased impact. The problem of shifting environmental baselines is an issue here because, by failing to have an ecological baseline, we are underestimating environmental impacts and accumulating impacts. If a particular place or population is the site of accumulated and accumulating environmental and public health impacts, then both ecosystem and people need to be engaged for sustainable development because the lack of knowledge about this will erode ecosystem diversity and resiliency. The challenge to sustainable development is to engage past, present and near future environmental and public health impacts.

Sustainability and environmental justice: conflict management

Conflict in sustainable development is inevitable. The inescapable revelations about privileged positions and fairness discussed above will form a critical part of the future dialog of sustainable development. Exclusions imposed by raw power have run their dangerous course with nature. Social expectations and behaviors will need to adapt to ecological conditions. As inclusionary dialogues grow, privileges will be directly challenged, capitalism, racism, misogyny, greed and hypocrisy will find challenges in inclusionary dialogues.

A characteristic of modern environmental issues is the increased level of controversy. This is due in part to radically inadequate information about environmental conditions, environmental impacts, and community conditions and community impacts. Better data will not necessarily avoid controversy, but it will decrease epistemological uncertainty. A big part of inadequate data is the problem of generationally shifting environmental baselines to measure environmental impacts. Incomplete baselines, and usually no baselines, are the norm for environmental impact assessment. While advances in environmental modeling can fill in some information gaps, they are not reality.

Even our heuristic regarding environment differs greatly by race and gender. Some of these perceptions are borne of a cultural or community context. As new groups participate in processes of sustainable development, they will bring their perceptions of "environment" to the risk assessments. Another characteristic of modern environmental issues that fuels controversy is that values are in dispute. Values become explicit in the way choices are made when basic information is unknown. For many national economies, profit has emerged as a proxy for social good. Proponents of happiness measures rather than currency measures of development point out that increasing ecological and community health impacts contribute to currency measures of growth, but not health or happiness, especially over time (see Gross National Happiness Research). Further, if most benefits, including profits are captured by a very small part of the population, economic growth will not result in increased quality of life for most people. Analysis of profit as a proxy for social good reveals itself to be a heuristic for the least good for the majority and for the ecosystems that support us all.

Other characteristics of modern environmental decisions and policy are that they are global in scale, and known to be long term in impact, for example, nuclear wastes. In addition, delay in decision-making is costly. Inclusion challenges the urgency of decision-making on perceived risks.

An environmental restoration and reparations solution

The general arguments for reparations for African Americans are well developed in the USA. Past injustices remain intractably visible in the persistent and shocking gaps in health, income, education, justice, and basic urban fabric; constant over time, pervasive, predictable, and lethal despite the good intentions of individuals. Reparations, procedural and substantive, to an oppressed people, represent a bridge between sustainable development and environmental justice. To the extent that these social injustices are not etched into our landscapes, ecotones, and bioregions because of intentional human policies, reparations to some communities will benefit entire ecotones or bioregions. For example, in a region with a history of dumping toxic chemicals in an African American community, the worst risks to the regional water are from sites within that community. The location and status of toxic sites are important to regional water quality programs because wastes can migrate. Making environmental reparations to community in the form of waste detection, clean-up, adaptive reuse, and environmental monitoring will benefit the water quality of the whole region. Water quality issues affect everyone, and water quality in urban areas is directly related to waste management, and waste clean-up.

Environmental reparations may enlist the support of local people united by a collective memory that transcends generations. When tracking chemicals and wastes, there is no better watchful eye than the local neighborhood. Another example is found in underground storage tanks, either never regulated or forgotten; they will be remembered by the people who have lived, worked, and played there. The location and contents of waste storage and transfer sites are fundamental components of any policy of sustainable development. Sustainable development will need inclusionary urban environmental planning processes that incorporate urban community monitoring, neighborhood capacity building, and commitments to include those most affected.

Environmental Preservation Districts: a proposal

We have proposed Environmental Preservation Districts as reparations to both land and people in the USA. Land as reparations is not a new idea. Former colonies have reasserted these types of claims at the World Conference on Racism in 2001. The USA withdrew from this conference when the African delegates called upon the USA to make restitution for the slave trade.

Preservation districts are not a radical concept. In the USA, an entire legal and policy framework at the local, state, and federal level exists to implement historic preservation districts. Historic Districts establish criteria for the built environment. The purposes and goals of Historic Districts animate their processes. Their goals are the cultural preservation of a particular land use. Their processes include an Architectural Review Board that enforces the criteria for the district. There are well over 35,000 historic listings on the US National Register of Historic Places. Federal law requires federal agencies to take historic resources into account if an environmental impact assessment is performed. In the USA, Historic Districts represent the leading edge of governmental land use actions that greatly restrict the use of private property.

Environmental Preservation Districts would ecologically and culturally restore ecosystems and communities. Their purpose would be restoration, reparation and acknowledgment of damage done in the name of progress borne by the Earth and its most vulnerable people. The processes that implement this purpose are environmental justice principles. Environmental Preservation Districts would require ecosystem restoration actions just as architecture restoration actions are required in a Historic District. These actions would require review by an Environmental Review Board, just as an Architectural Review Board does in a Historic District. And just as a land use plan considers build out based on every land use zone's maximum density, sustainable development would consider carrying capacity analyses of an ecosystem. Environmental Preservation Districts would help establish urban environmental baselines, and provide a platform for grassroots community involvement and grassroots sustainable development. These ideas for reparation and investment zones are easily adapted to the international context, and justified by the same principles of justice and self-interest.

Conclusion

For sustainable development to be actually implemented in an environmental context, it will need to be fair to all people. Although "fairness" is a malleable term, it generally means increased participation and other principles ensconced in the Aarhus Convention. Most people seek environmental restoration as a way to partially remedy past and present environmental impacts. Models of sustainable development will unavoidably incorporate public participation processes. As these processes increasingly include communities which have been disproportionally burdened by environmental decisions, the processes of community involvement will include community goals of environmental restoration to partially remedy past and present environmental impacts. Sustainable development seeks to mitigate future environmental impacts, which is difficult to do if waste streams destroy ecosystems. New inclusionary dialogs are controversial and unavoidable before they are collaborative and consensual. These dialogs face community demands for reparations for past and present disproportionate environmental impacts before any active engagement with mitigation of future environmental impacts takes place in reality. These dialogs also include institutionalized resistance to justice from traditional environmental decision-makers. Impatience with cultural histories, confusion with differing ideas of "environment" and perceptions of risk, ignorance of the requirements of procedural justice, and different value structures are also a part of this challenging dialogue. Sustainable development processes are a meaningful evolution in environmental policy that bring in controversies in a meaningful way, and in this way address local and global issues of disproportionate environmental benefits and burdens.

References

Gross National Happiness Research. Available at: www.grossnationalhappiness.com (accessed 5 March 2014).

Kuehn, R. R. (2000) A taxonomy of environmental justice. *Environmental Law Reporter*, (September) (30): 10681.

Millennium Ecosystem Assessment (2005) *Ecosystems and Human Well-Being: Synthesis*. Washington, DC: Island Press.

Rawls, J. (1971) *A Theory of Justice*. Cambridge, MA: Belknap Press.

Wilder, C. S. (2013) *Ebony and Ivy: Race, Slavery, and the Troubled Histories of America's Universities*. New York: Bloomsbury Press.
Wildman, S. M. (1996) *Privilege Revealed: How Invisible Preference Undermines America*. New York: New York University Press.

14
INDIGENOUS PERSPECTIVES OF SUSTAINABILITY AND A HUMAN RIGHTS APPROACH TO SUSTAINABLE DEVELOPMENT

Oscar A. Forero

Introduction

On 13 September 2007, the United Nations General Assembly adopted the Declaration on the Rights of Indigenous Peoples (DHRIP). Regarding the promotion of human rights of Indigenous Peoples, the declaration is an outstanding achievement that rewards the intensive work of many indigenous leaders and human rights' activists. As it will be unveiled in this chapter, the issue of the human rights of Indigenous Peoples is closely related to conservation of biological diversity and sustainable development (SD). Not surprisingly, many of the leaders and activists who celebrated the UN Declaration on 13 September were also present three years later, on 29 October 2010, celebrating the adoption of the Nagoya Protocol on access to Genetic Resources and the Fair and Equitable Sharing of Benefits Arising from their Utilization to the Convention on Biological Diversity (CBD 1992).

To someone unfamiliar with the history of the struggle that Indigenous Peoples have endured in gaining recognition and implementation of their human rights, a synergetic approach between conservation, sustainable development and indigenism may appears obvious. However, a synergetic approach did not develop naturally. Diverse ideologies and geo-political aims have been competing against each other with reference to the understandings of 'ethnicity', 'identity', 'conservation' and 'sustainability', and about 'who must be' and 'who is' in charge of the sustainable development projects in indigenous territories or affecting in some way their livelihoods.

In pursuit of the recognition and implementation of their human rights, Indigenous Peoples needed to engage with national and supra-national organisations to define sustainability strategies and the sustainable development implementation agenda. However, engagement with the SD agenda has not always been enough to realise the rights of Indigenous Peoples. The engagement with the implementation of so-called sustainable development policies and programmes in indigenous territories has proved to be a very contentious and divisive issue.

This chapter will review the contribution of Indigenous Peoples to the transformation of the sustainable development concept and its practices. It will reflect on the ethical, legal and managerial synergies as well as the tensions that occurred when trying to implement SD policies and programmes with Indigenous Peoples or in their territories, and how these issues have been addressed. Indigenous Peoples have fought hard to make it obligatory under national and international laws that biodiversity conservation and sustainable development projects in their territories could only be attempted when these initiatives unequivocally endorse the complete implementation of their human rights as individuals and as peoples. There has been some progress towards this goal, but there remain difficult challenges ahead. By discussing how Indigenous Peoples have dealt with the challenges posed by the sustainable development paradigm, this chapter will also contribute to the on-going discussion that links management of SD to implementation of human rights.

Historical context: the lasting legacy of colonialism and imperialism

Colonisation and imperialism were complex processes that involved a military strategy, but also the dismantling of indigenous ideologies, the erosion of the cultural values and the identities of Indigenous Peoples, and the imposition of colonial or imperial ideologies. This process of cultural defoliation involved the promotion of Eurocentric views of the world and of the position and role of Europeans and their descendants in conquered territories.

The European political landscape was transformed during the Enlightenment era in the eighteenth century. Rousseau's *Social Contract* (1762) inspired the French Revolution and decisively influenced the Declaration of Independence by the United States of America. Such political change did not imply the end of slavery and servitude *per se*; neither did it mark the end of racism or discrimination against Indigenous Peoples. However, they reflected ideological changes taking place in Europe that were to influence the governmental institutions of nascent nation-states and of new empires.

The governmental institutions that surged following the Enlightenment varied in accordance to the geo-politics of empire and to local political context. In the Americas, political liberalism initially embraced and projected in the constitutions of the new nations Rousseau's idea of the 'noble savage'. In some cases the constitutions of these new nation-states explicitly forbade and condemned slavery, nevertheless discrimination and slavery still continued in practice.

Ideas of race and practices of racism were next to be influenced by evolutionism. The rough translations of natural evolution theory into the socio-political sphere as 'Survival of the Fittest' (Spencer 1864) suited European imperialism. Humanity's evolution, Morgan proposed, progressed from the savage state to barbarians and from there to civilisation (Morgan 1877).

Unlike in the Americas, decolonisation of most of Africa, Australia, Oceania and Asia was not to happen until the twentieth century in the aftermath of the Second World War. The encounter of Europeans with so many peoples and such cultural diversity posed a problem for the empire. Indeed, the first challenge posed to the anthropological discipline, when it was established, was to produce a rational explanation of cultural diversity. 'Cultural evolutionism' was the first anthropological theory.

The first critique of cultural evolutionism was formulated by Franz Boas, 'the Father of American Anthropology' at the beginning of the twentieth century. Boas agreed with the theory of natural selection, however, he argued that comparative studies of the human process of adaptation have yet to be documented and thus cultural evolutionism, as it was formulated then, was only speculative (see Boas 1940).

The ideas of race, evolution, progress, civilisation and development that served European imperialism and informed the constitutions and institutions of emergent de-colonised states, first, in the Americas and later in the Asian-Pacific region, Australasia and Africa, were essentially Eurocentric. Although they replaced the ideology of a divine right to enslave non-European peoples and helped the advance of political liberalism, they did not represent the end of racism and discrimination. The roots of paternalism in the Americas and those who continued to promote the domination of Indigenous Peoples everywhere else used cultural evolutionism as a reasonable justification for imperialism.

The making of sustainable development

Problematically, the ideas and the ideology of development were from the outset linked to evolutionism and Social Darwinism. The scientists of the Enlightenment era assumed that there were no limits to development except those posed by ignorance and obscurantism. In their view, science and technology would liberate humanity from most ordinary tasks, giving humankind the time and space to engage in more creative and challenging enterprises. This conception of development proved to be quite damaging to life systems, as living organisms were considered only as resources, with a comparable value to that of inert beings used in production processes. Arguably, it also affected socio-cultural systems, as many indigenous traditions considered the biosphere to be a living entity, and even elevated it to the sacred, with humans responsible for its care. Such traditions akin to religious practices were all considered superstitions to be overcome by rationalism. Such a perspective fuelled a type of industrialism, and social organisation that deemed indigenous knowledge systems to be backward, irrational and in need of reform.

In the 1970s, Georgescu-Roegen argued that the economic process requires the use of energy and therefore it has an entropic cost. He argued that following the two laws of thermodynamics implied that future life forms could not have high quality energy to use in the same quantities as they are used at present. The flaw in Georgescu-Roegen's argument is that, though it is not infinite, solar energy is a very stable source. Nevertheless, his questioning of the efficiency of industrial and economic activities had an impact on the development ideology, particularly in relation to the precarious management of non-renewable resources (Georgescu-Roegen 1971).

Georgescu-Roegen effectively put into question the implied ethics of governmental regimes that allow current generations to take decisions over the management of resources and services provided by the biosphere, when such decisions will negatively affect the 'development' possibilities left to future generations. If development implies a reduction of possibilities for future generations, then sustainable development: a development 'that meets the needs of the present without compromising the ability of future generations to meet their own needs' (United Nations 1987: 8), would be unrealisable.

It is clear that the SD concept evolved out of an ethical framework and not from a reductionist scientific one. The SD paradigm aims to establish some limits to human progress, but not principally from a purely materialistic perspective. The adaptive efforts of human beings to very different natural environments have resulted in diverse and interdependent bio-cultural modes of development that rely as much on ethical and aesthetic considerations as on technological innovation. The SD paradigm in this way responds to the errors of a scientistic approach. I argue that it is precisely because 'sustainable development', conceptually and in practice involves value judgements and ethics that Indigenous Peoples have engaged with the discussions and process of implementation of SD.

Given that the concept of development was from the outset linked to evolutionism and Social Darwinism, Indigenous Peoples have good reason to be suspicious of it. However, if Indigenous Peoples could reconsider development, discuss its values, virtues and shortcomings, then they would be more inclined to engage in the policy-making process and in development projects.

Economics imperative

Regarding development, economics is arguably the most politically influential discipline. Nationally and globally 'economic development' has scarcely been challenged as the unique way to deal with the problem of poverty (Sachs 1992). Economists have gained influence across all major governmental supranational institutions. The economic discipline has also positioned itself above all other social sciences in establishing means and measures of development. The discourses and performance of economists have sought to maintain roles of dominance and control through claims of scientific neutrality (Escobar 1995).

In the 1970s some analysts started to assess the work of development economists. In Latin America, the *Comisión Económica para América Latina* (CEPAL, Economic Commission for Latin America) challenged orthodox international economics by pointing out that lack of capital was related to the deterioration in terms of trade. CEPAL influenced changes in development policy during the 1970s and 1980s, but economists continued to develop policies conceiving of societies as mere subjects of development. This dominance of modern economics meant that many other existing conversations or models were appropriated, suppressed or overlooked (Escobar 1995), something that indigenous organisations have been highlighting for decades.

On the road to Rio (the 1992 United Nations Conference on Environment and Development) where the CBD text was to be agreed, civil society organisations, particularly those promoting biodiversity conservation and Indigenous Peoples' rights, articulated a more decisive critique of the economic imperative of the sustainability agenda. Conservationists condemned governments that were putting the interests of multinationals over those of their nations. Indigenous Peoples' organisations highlighted how the violence of these nation states targeted Indigenous Peoples disproportionally compared to the rest of the population. Indigenous Peoples highlighted that conflicts invariably related to the confrontation between the government elite implementing economic policies, and ethnic minorities legitimately protecting their ways of life, their ancestral territories and their human rights.

Although coming from different angles and pursuing different interests, academics, conservationists and Indigenous Peoples' organisations formed coalitions to make themselves heard during the Earth Summit in Rio. Morale was high, particularly among Amerindian movements, which had worked hard to promote devolution of government to indigenous peoples in entitled indigenous territories.

In 1989, the International Labour Organisation 169 Convention on the Rights of Indigenous and Tribal Peoples was opened for ratification. This boosted the morale of indigenous organisations worldwide. It proved that making alliances with other social movements at local and international level was a political strategy that had paid off. Notorious for pursuing an internationalisation strategy were the Zapatistas from the Mexican Chiapas (Collier 1994; Cleaver 1998); the Bolivian indigenous organisation that organised the insurrection of April 2000 against the privatisation of water services (*The Economist*, 10 February 2000); and a media team that documented a two-year struggle in the Colombian courts that the Uwa people went through to prevent extraction of oil in their ancestral land (David Lopez 2003). However, there were indigenous leaders who remained unconvinced of the merits of endorsing the sustainable development agenda.

Indigenous Peoples' experiences of the encounter with some of the biodiversity conservation organisations were complex. For instance, many of the biodiversity conservation areas and National Parks Systems of developing nations in the Americas copied the US legal framework and attempted to follow the management regime of protected areas (PA) in North America. However, the socio-political and bio-geographical contexts of most of the mega-diverse developing countries (i.e. Mexico, Colombia, Brazil, etc.) were very different to those of the USA. In Africa, the situation was worse, where many Indigenous Peoples had been forced out of their territories to make way for conservation areas (Cernea and Guggenheim 1993; Cernea 1996–1998; 1999).

Antagonism between some biodiversity conservation organisations and Indigenous Peoples emerged from an *a priori* assumption held by some conservation NGOs and environmental scientists, who were certain that they were better qualified than Indigenous Peoples to manage conservation areas. Indigenous Peoples, for their part, considered they were not only better equipped for the job, but also argued it was their right to manage their territories, whether they held the complete legal entitlements, as these territories had been taken illegitimately in the first place.

Historically, the so-called scientific based, and thus supposedly neutral, managerial regimes that were imposed in indigenous territories through the creation of many national parks and conservation areas did not consider traditional knowledge practices or the rights of Indigenous Peoples. It was not until 1997 at the first Latin American Congress of Parks and Protected Areas (in Santa Marta in Colombia) that governmental and conservation NGOs acknowledged that there was a problem with conservation regimes that ignored the rights of Indigenous Peoples. It was also noted that many of the management plans of conservation areas failed to consider the traditional knowledge of biodiversity even when such areas were located in indigenous territories or bordering with them (Ministerio del Medio Ambiente 1998a: 1998b).

Sustainable development lost in translation

Indigenous leaders, even those who had been educated in 'western schools', found it very difficult to understand the whole jargon used by a new breed of specialists in 'sustainable development': suitability, sustainability, development, poverty line, biodiversity, ecosystems, project, planning, progress, SD, empowerment, capacity building, etc. Indeed, in the name of sustainable development, diverse and even antagonistic social actors promoted social interventions in the territories of Indigenous Peoples. Suspiciously, however different their perspectives were, these social actors deployed similar discursive formations. This both intrigued and increased the scepticism of the SD paradigm among Indigenous Peoples.

When the traditional authorities and other members from communities requested translation, interpreters found it extremely difficult to do so and some went on to question the rationale of translating such an evolving and ambiguous terminology. To illustrate, while working with indigenous organisations in Northwest Amazonia, I witnessed interpreters arguing that translating the jargon of conservation NGOs and government representatives was as complicated as trying to explain to non-indigenous peoples the relationship of Indigenous Peoples to their territories. The anxiety expressed by interpreters reflected the lack of terminology (in Spanish and Portuguese, in this case) to refer to conceptions of indigenous territoriality and the equivalent lack of terminology in indigenous languages to express new terms used by development and conservation specialists (Forero 2003).

The last two decades of the twentieth century saw an increase in SD projects and rapid urbanisation. The associated environmental, social and public health problems were the object of study and research. New understandings about the relationship between social and biological systems came about. There was passionate research to uncover the links between environmental, social and cultural systems and also to define temporal and spatial relations that link the welfare of humanity to that of the biosphere. Such research led to the Gaia theory (Lovelock and Watson 1983), the hypothesis of Planet Earth as an entire living entity, and corroboration that human intervention in the biosphere has transformed the planet's climate and therefore impacted on the three systems in an unprecedented scale. This increased complexity made it hard for the public to understand the science and the more so in translation and dialogue with Indigenous Peoples, each one who had their own system of knowledge and epistemology.

Many of the scientists and academics with experience of working with Indigenous Peoples in development projects agreed with them that new pedagogies and improved communication systems were required for meaningful participation. Some were critical of governments and industries that promoted their own understanding of development and sustainability through the education systems offered to Indigenous Peoples, a process they denounced as 'cultural defoliation' of developmental education (Ke-Zerbo et al. 1997). The educational process that promoted development pursued the goal of modernising indigenous societies and reaching cultural homogenisation. National education systems and programs rarely considered the process of bio-cultural reproduction (Reid 1995). Human development was in the hands of specialists who proceeded independently of cultural diversity and with disregard for non-Western systems of knowledge.

By the end of the 1980s, some education experts, indigenous leaders and human rights advocates began proposing 'holism' and 'multi-disciplinary' approaches as an alternative to the reductionist approach to development and developmental education. Economist Manfred Max-Neef proposed 'Human Scale Development: An Option for the Future' (Max-Neef 1986; Max-Neef et al. 1987; 1989) as a new development paradigm. Max-Neef had worked in the private sector and as a lecturer in Economics at Berkeley. He went on to work in development projects with FAO-UNO and provided advice to the Organisation of American States (OAS). After reflecting on his own experiences and conducting economic assessment of the effects of development projects across continents, Max-Neef concluded that the conventional development model had failed to reduce poverty and instead the national debt of developing countries had increased. Not only that, externalities (i.e. the cost of pollution) had been passed on to impoverished peoples. Max-Neef argued that the development policy had proved to be biased and that the debates surrounding development were made by technocrats who were ignorant and uninterested in the cultures of the people involved in development (Max-Neef 1986).

During this time (the 1980s), anthropologists and sociologists who were critical of the industry and government top-down approach in development proposed 'participatory action research' (PAR) methodologies as an alternative (Fals Borda 1981; 1986). Sociologist Orlando Fals-Borda argued that the peoples for whom the SD projects were supposedly designed, ought to participate not only in the implementation phase that had been devised elsewhere, but instead ought to work with scientists and experts throughout the processes of investigation and in the development of the technologies and political strategies of SD. Ultimately, he argued, it was the local people who ought to decide implementation priorities and the methods of assessing sustainability and the suitability of projects (Fals Borda 1981; 1986; Fals Borda and Rahman 1991).

The ideas of 'Human Scale development' (Max-Neef 1986; Max-Neef et al. 1987; 1989) and 'participatory action research' (Fals Borda 1981; 1986; Fals Borda and Rahman 1991) resonated well with those of Schumacher's book, *Small Is Beautiful* (1973). It could be argued that the three theorists only highlighted the obvious but they did it eloquently, in a way that captured the public imagination. Common to all of their proposals was, first, that well-being is not about the accumulation of material wealth but instead is about creating solutions or satisfiers to finite needs. And, second, that well-being encompasses cultural understandings of how a person can realise their potential. Therefore, the satisfying strategies for the development of individuals and communities should be defined by them and not by external agents, least of all development experts judging from a distance, who were ignorant or oblivious to traditional knowledge.

Anthropologists working in the developing world were also critical of a type of fieldwork experience that justified objectifying the peoples they worked with as part of the academic endeavour. Some argued that 'taking distance' or 'not going native' should not imply that they should not assume the responsibilities and commitments that anthropologists do acquire by being guests and forging alliances with the peoples they work with. Furthermore, many anthropologists working in development were committed to the development and implementation of the human rights of Indigenous Peoples. In terms of the research practices they were already engaged in, a few years later, this was named 'engaged anthropology' (Rappaport 1995).

Sustainable development and the recognition of the human rights of Indigenous Peoples

The United Nations Organisation was initially unconcerned with the rights of Indigenous Peoples. Up until the 1960s there was uncertainty among UN members whether such rights ought be a UN concern at all. Indigenous Peoples were implicitly considered along with other minorities that were vulnerable or subject to discrimination. In 1971, on his own initiative, Augusto Willemsen Diaz, a Guatemalan lawyer working for the UN, proposed that the rights of Indigenous Peoples should be studied separately (Barsh 1994). At the time, two important organisations appeared: the International Work Group on Indigenous Affairs (IWGIA) (1968) and Survival International (1969). They alerted the public to the threats that many Indigenous Peoples were facing. They documented the genocide and the ethnocide that was happening in the Amazon basin and were effective at raising the public concern (Sanders 1989; Barsh 1994). In South America, representatives of Indigenous Peoples and anthropologists working with them voiced their concerns at a symposium organised on the issue of discrimination and racism against Indigenous People. The meeting produced the 1971 Declaration of Barbados.

Despite public concern, the calls from academics and lobbying from Indigenous Peoples themselves, it was not until 1982 that the UN finally decided to establish the Working Group on Indigenous Populations (Working Group). The Working Group was effectively composed of five members of a sub-commission on human rights that represent the five geo-political regions of the world.[1] Since its establishment the Working Group liaised well with representatives of Indigenous Peoples.

To the Working Group, Indigenous Peoples' organisations delivered the same message that they had delivered to environmentalists who have networked with them in preparation for Rio (UNCED): Indigenous Peoples consider that the most effective way of protecting both their territories and livelihoods was through political devolution and by obtaining legal entitlement to their territories. Without recognition of their right to self-determination, Indigenous Peoples considered they were prevented from engaging effectively in biodiversity conservation or sustainable development efforts.

Environmentalists have as their priority to stop the more destructive and disturbing development initiatives. And though, as described above, conservationists remained critical of the managerial capacities of Indigenous Peoples, the majority of organisations in the environmental movement saw the merit in the argument that protection of cultural and biological diversity could be achieved by working together with Indigenous Peoples towards this common goal. It comes as no surprise then that the dialogue between indigenous organisations and environmentalists initially focused on identifying what steps were required to overcome mistrust between them. The issue of ineffective communication preventing dialogue came up frequently when governmental and non-governmental organisations attempted to engage Indigenous Peoples in sustainable development.

The pivotal moment that facilitated opening up the dialogue between indigenous organisations, the environmental movement and governments came when the ILO 169 agreement on the rights of indigenous and tribal peoples was opened for ratification in 1989. By 1991, two of the so-called mega-diverse countries, Mexico and Colombia, had ratified the treaty. The cornerstone upon which all the provisions of ILO 169 are based is meaningful consultation and participation. ILO 169 was the first legally binding international instrument that recognised the right of Indigenous Peoples to self-determination. The Indigenous Peoples as signatory parties were now in a position to demand implementation. But importantly, Indigenous Peoples from non-signatory countries benefited as well, since the provisions of the ILO 169 served as a benchmark. ILO 169 provided further impetus to the UN Working Group discussing the text of the UN Declaration of Human Rights of Indigenous People.

The last decade of the twentieth century saw Indigenous Peoples' organisations worldwide highlighting that prior informed consent was not possible without effective translation and communication as specified in ILO 169. All stakeholders involved in SD, whether government, industry, NGOs or charities, began recognising that collaboration with Indigenous Peoples was possible only when mechanisms to monitor the implementation of policy development and activities of SD projects were agreed with the Indigenous Peoples. In other words, they started to publicly accept that Indigenous Peoples were in the right when demanding legal reassurances that the SD agenda could not be defined *a priori*, and that governance of ecosystems services would not be informed by scientific advisers alone, but that it would give due consideration to traditional knowledge and uphold the human rights of Indigenous Peoples throughout.

Despite the political and legal advances facilitating alliances between Indigenous People and environmentalists, some expert advisers, such as conservation biologists, tended to replicate the message that 'pristine environments' were vulnerable to human intervention, what Stott later called 'hegemonic mythmaking' (Stott 1999). Some conservationists vehemently argued that the intervention of locals went against scientific advice. Such 'expert advice' continued to promote a biodiversity conservation policy that was in direct contradiction to the rights of Indigenous Peoples (West and Brechin 1991). During the 1992 IUCN World Conservation Congress, held in Caracas, a group of anthropologists and development specialists working closely with Indigenous Peoples in Latin America helped recognised indigenous leaders to get into the venue of the Congress to express their anger against biodiversity conservation policy that blatantly contradicted the human rights of Indigenous Peoples.

Indigenous Peoples' representatives who made it to Caracas also argued that there were alternatives to 'Conservation without People' and to 'Development without Traditional Knowledge'. They proposed endorsing a paradigm that promoted innovation based on traditional knowledge, and biodiversity conservation management regimes inclusive of traditional institutions of indigenous and peasant societies. The movement towards biodiversity conservation management regimes that were respectful of Indigenous Peoples' rights had the backing of important academic figures as well, such as Richard E. Schultes, one of the founding fathers of ethno-botany, and who had been working with Indigenous Peoples since the 1950s. For decades, Schultes had called attention to the fact that traditional knowledge was key to effective conservation policy and that it was disappearing at the same pace as biodiversity: 'Much of this precious knowledge is disappearing faster even than the trees in many regions where forest devastation is rife. Its loss will be disastrous for the progress of humanity as a whole' (Schultes 1991: 264).

Schultes went on to propose that Indigenous Peoples should indeed be compensated somehow for their work as conservationists (Schultes 1992; 1994). Ethno-scientists working in pedology, zoology, ichthyology, entomology and forestry all confirmed that indigenous knowledge in all of these areas was vast, diverse and highly relevant to conservation programs. During the first International Meeting of the Society of Ethno-Biology in 1988 in Belem du Para, ethno-biologists, including representatives from 16 different ethnic groups, reported on exhaustive research confirming that Indigenous Peoples' managerial regimes of habitats and ecosystems were highly sophisticated and that in most cases it was the scientists who needed to catch up. Darrell Posey coordinated efforts for the ample distribution of the 'Declaration of Belem' which specified the responsibilities of scientists in addressing the needs of local communities and acknowledged the central role of Indigenous Peoples in all aspects of global planning (Posey and Dutfield 1996). The Belem Declaration set an important precedent as for the first time a scientific body recognised the obligation to compensate Indigenous Peoples for the utilization of their knowledge.

No doubt the combined efforts of ethno-scientists, anthropologists, indigenous organisations and progressive biodiversity conservation NGOs working closely with Indigenous People influenced the negotiations of the CBD (1992). Article 8j of the CBD states:

> Each contracting Party shall, as far as possible and as appropriate:
>
> Subject to national legislation, respect, preserve and maintain knowledge, innovations and practices of indigenous and local communities embodying traditional lifestyles relevant for the conservation and sustainable use of biological diversity and promote their wider application with the approval and involvement of the holders of such knowledge, innovations and practices and encourage the equitable sharing of the benefits arising from the utilization of such knowledge innovations and practices.

Addressing concerns of implementation

Currently there are only four countries in the world that are non-signatories of the CBD: Andorra, Iraq, Somalia and the USA. All other countries have been legislating for implementation the CBD. There is great diversity in how governments do this. Countries very rich in biological diversity are often also the richest in terms of cultural diversity. In terms of implementing Article 8j, such bio-cultural diversity makes it very difficult to unequivocally determine which knowledge 'belongs' to which specific 'Indigenous People'. Even if adequate procedures were in place to determine ownership of systems of knowledge, it would remain a challenge to monitor how specific innovations have indeed been developed upon such knowledge and then to enforce 'benefit sharing'. Indigenous Peoples' organisations are aware of the difficulty and have proposed mechanisms to conduct participatory research or allow data gathering, and ways to monitor research and development activities. There is also continuing dialogue about what constitute benefits and which are the adequate mechanisms to allow its sharing. Indigenous organisations have become better at drafting protocols, getting agreements, signing contracts and in pursuing compensation through the courts.

The UN Permanent Forum has hosted numerous fora for Indigenous Peoples' representatives and human rights experts to discuss which factors determine an acceptable SD paradigm for Indigenous Peoples. The main factor without which no SD paradigm is acceptable continues to be the recognition of the right of self-determination. Article 3 of the UN Declaration of Human Rights of Indigenous People (2007) states: 'Indigenous people have the right to self-determination. By virtue of that right they freely determine their political status and freely pursue their economic, social and cultural development.'

Article 32 of the Declaration further specifies that Indigenous Peoples have the right to establish and prioritise development strategies in their territories, that any project affecting their lands or territories should get their prior and informed consent; and that when development affects their resources, the State is obligated to provide a mechanism for just and fair redress and is also obligated to mitigate any adverse impacts of any development.

Besides upholding the right to self-determination, Indigenous Peoples have specified some other key factors that make the SD paradigm acceptable as follows (UN Permanent Forum on Indigenous Issues 2010):

- That any type of productive activity should be assessed in terms of its contribution to bettering quality of life and not just in terms of economic benefits.
- That development happens only when human and Earth interactions are in harmony with nature's well-being or the well-being of 'Mother Earth'.
- That sustainability is enacted when the integrity of indigenous government is preserved or enriched.

Following this discussion at the UN Permanent Forum, some recommendations were issued regarding research and development activities developed with Indigenous Peoples or affecting the territory of Indigenous Peoples (UN Permanent Forum on Indigenous Issues 2010):

- When research refers to knowledge of indigenous people, the interest, expertise and experience of indigenous people must be central to the methodology.
- State, supranational organisations and other interest groups must recognise the struggle of indigenous people in cohabiting with larger market-driven society. The State must protect indigenous governments and accommodate to indigenous economic and education systems; and also respect and protect the cultural and spiritual practices that define the relations of the territory (including natural resource) and Indigenous Peoples.
- Any development must serve to recover, reconstruct or strengthen indigenous identities; any development should concur with conceptions of well-being and sustainability as defined by indigenous people themselves.

It should be noted that these three recommendations derive from the effective implementation of the right to self-determination. In addition, they foreground a fundamental indigenous conception of the SD paradigm, the non-utilitarian and indeed non-human-centred relationship of indigenous peoples to their territories, which comprises the biosphere. Indeed, the relations that indigenous peoples have with the planet, what they consider the world, are not human-centred. It is a 'perspectival vision of the world' (Århem 1990), 'by "perspectival" vision of the world I mean that it appreciates the world under different perspectives and from the point of view of different beings/seers' (ibid.: 119, author translation). Humans, animals and plants are involved in the same eco-system; they each have their own perspective of the world, and all these perspectives are equally important and equally powerful in the care of the world.

There are two major unresolved issues concerning the implementation of the rights of Indigenous Peoples and the implementation of acquired rights. The two relate to extracting indigenous knowledge without informed consent. One way in which this is happening is by incorporating indigenous environmental classification systems into maps using geographical information systems (GIS) (Forero 2011; 2012). The other is 'biopiracy', the misappropriation of biological resources and traditional knowledge (Dutfield 2000; 2004; Sheridan 2005); that later becomes the basis for applications for patent rights in a variety of fields including cosmetics, medicine and new biotechnologies (Shiva 1997; Robinson 2010).

There are important biodiversity hotspots that are part of indigenous entitled land, or are recognised as both indigenous reserve and as a protected area. Not surprisingly some of the best preserved habitats and ecosystems are considered sacred places by the indigenous inhabitants. These often are places of contemplation, prayer or sites where offerings are made or rituals are performed. Any research activity, encompassing recording of any type, including use of hand-held GPS and digital cameras must not take place in a sacred site unless it is agreed to by the Indigenous Peoples, and carried out when they specify and in the manner they indicate. IUCN has gone a long way since the Santa Marta Congress referred to above. IUCN now recognises the rights of Indigenous Peoples and is working with indigenous organisations to ensure full implementation within protected areas. IUCN's Task Force on Cultural and Spiritual Values of Biodiversity in conjunction with indigenous organisations and in collaboration with UNESCO's Man and the Biosphere Programme, has produced the Guidelines for Protected Area Managers (Wild and McLeod 2008), which has proved to be a very valuable tool for both managers and indigenous communities that currently work together caring for sacred sites.

I have argued in the past that contravening the rights of Indigenous Peoples through mapping also occurs when no epistemological translation is attempted through a cartographic project, or when such translation occurs but there is no acknowledgement of the indigenous or local contribution (Forero 2012). Nevertheless, effective hybrid-management encompasses epistemological translation, and participatory GIS mapping has proven to be an effective tool to accomplish it. It is therefore advised that in all projects adopting participatory GIS, a memorandum and/or agreement should be signed before the project development with specifications on how monitoring processes would take place. It is also advisable to keep a record of the mapping project that should be properly archived to facilitate further reflection and monitoring (Forero 2012).

Regarding the problem of biopiracy, in 2010, the United Nations CBD adopted *The Nagoya Protocol on Access to Genetic Resources and the Fair and Equitable Sharing of Benefits Arising from their Utilization*, known as the Nagoya Protocol. This new protocol establishes that those seeking to conduct research and development on genetic resources and traditional knowledge must seek prior informed consent from both the relevant government(s) and from indigenous and local communities concerned and establish a benefit-sharing agreement on mutually agreed terms (Hamilton 2006; Buck and Hamilton 2011; Nijar 2011; Oliva 2011; Soares 2011). In addition to the Nagoya Protocol, the World Intellectual Property Organization (WIPO) has established an Intergovernmental Committee on Intellectual Property and Genetic Resources, Traditional Knowledge and Folklore (Dutfield 2004; Coombe 2005). Member states of WIPO are presently negotiating the draft of what may become a new international treaty to address the intellectual property dimensions of genetic resources, traditional knowledge and folklore (Oldham et al. 2013).

In the Americas, representatives of social movements, Indigenous Peoples and human rights activists have been proposing for some time that addressing these issues is indispensable to a SD paradigm as conceived by Amerindians (Coombe 2005). At this moment in time indigenous organisations are well prepared in terms of conceptual understanding of an acceptable SD paradigm for Indigenous Peoples. They have also organised globally to further advise implementation of the Declaration (DHRIP), the CBD and the Nagoya protocol; however, it remains problematic that legitimate indigenous organisations are underfunded.

The problem is accentuated by the high cost of opening and maintaining meaningful participation in research and development projects that make use of indigenous taxonomies. It has been assumed that Indigenous Peoples currently have the power, instruments and resources to protect and develop traditional knowledge practices and to translate them into research inputs ready for use. This is, however, not the case. The Global Taxonomy Initiative under the

Convention on Biological Diversity increasingly recognises that Indigenous Peoples require support in conserving and making their taxonomic knowledge available on terms that recognise and are respectful of their rights (Conference of the Parties; COP Decision IX/22 and X/39). Governments would need not only to adopt measures to provide conditions of reasonable certainty for the complete implementation of the rights of Indigenous Peoples but also provide adequate funding (Oldham et al. 2013). At present these conditions are yet to be met; until then, Indigenous Peoples will be unable to fully participate in advancing taxonomic knowledge. As a consequence, they are not yet able to benefit economically from innovations based on their traditional knowledge.

Conclusion

From the outset, Indigenous Peoples were sceptical about the merits of the concept and practices proposed as part of a sustainable development paradigm. In this chapter we have examined the historical factors that shaped the scepticism of Indigenous Peoples. These factors relate to the terrible legacies of colonialism and imperialism (i.e. dehumanisation, slavery and servitude) and to reductionist scientism, upon which ill-conceived theories (Social Darwinism, evolutionism) promoted or did not dispute discriminatory, racist or paternalistic policies.

It has been argued in this chapter that the inherent contradictions, the openness and vagueness of the sustainable development concept, are what in fact made it of interest to Indigenous Peoples engaging with the SD discussions, and attracted them to collaborate in SD research and practices. Indigenous Peoples have made immense and decisive contributions to the transformation of the SD paradigm. On the one hand, they have exposed the fallacy of meaningful participation without the complete implementation of human rights and, in the case of Indigenous Peoples, principally the right to self-determination. On the other hand, they have developed a critique of anthropocentric notions of development. They have made it clear that for Indigenous Peoples all other beings sharing the planet hold perspectives and exercise some agency. Human beings have an extended capacity and power, which makes humankind all the more responsible for the care of the biosphere (Mother Earth). This resonates well with mother ecological science and with those critical of the reductionist scientism approach to development.

The joint labour of civil society organisations promoting the human rights of Indigenous Peoples has paid off, as we now have a series of international treaties entering into force that have incorporated and developed most of the concerns that have made Indigenous Peoples sceptical of SD. However, there are pressing problems relating to the full implementation of these international instruments; the lack of commitment from many of the signatory parties is reflected in poor funding and indecisive political action.

Note

1 The African Group, the Asia-Pacific Group, the Eastern European Group, the Latin American and Caribbean Group (GRULAC), and the Western European and Others Group (WEOG).

References

Århem, K. (1990) Ecosofía Makuna. In F. Correa. (ed.) *La Selva Humanizada*. Bogotá, ICAN, FEN, CEREC. 1: 105–122.

Barsh, R. L. (1994) Indigenous Peoples in the 1990s: from object to subject in International Law. *Harvard Human Rights Journal*, (7): 33–86.

Boas, F. (1940) *Race, Language, and Culture*. New York: Macmillan.

Buck, M. and Hamilton, C. (2011) The Nagoya Protocol on access to genetic resources and the fair and equitable sharing of benefits arising from their utilization to the Convention on Biological Diversity. *Review of European Community & International Environmental Law*, 20: 47–61.

CBD (Convention on Biological Diversity) (1992) Concluded in Rio de Janeiro on 5 June 1992. Registered ex officio with Annexes on 29 December 2003.

Cernea, M. M. (1996–1998) *Resettlement and Development* (published in China, vol. I and II).

Cernea, M. M. (ed.) (1999) *The Economics of Involuntary Resettlement.* Directions in Development series. Washington, DC: World Bank.

Cernea, M. M. and Guggenheim, S. (1993) *Anthropological Approaches to Resettlement: Policy, Practice, Theory.* Boulder, CO: Westview Press.

Cleaver, H. (1998) The Zapatistas and the electronic fabric of struggle [Online]. Available at: https://webspace.utexas.edu/hcleaver/www/zaps.html (accessed 14 September 2013). First published in 1998 in John Holloway and Eloína Peláez (eds) *Zapatista! Reinventing Revolution in Mexico.* London: Pluto Press.

Collier, G. (1994) *Basta! Land and the Zapatista Rebellion in Chiapas.* Oakland, CA: Institute for Food and Development Policy.

Coombe, R. J. (2005) Protecting traditional environmental knowledge and new social movements in the Americas: intellectual property, human right, or claims to an alternative form of sustainable development. *Florida Journal of International Law*, 17: 115.

David Lopez, C. (2003) Desplazamiento Forzado: Conflicto U'wa Dissertation. National University of Colombia in Medellin. Online library. http://agora.unalmed.edu.co/desplazados/canal3/proyectos/2003-01/individual/Desplazamiento%20forzado%20Conflicto%20Uwa.pdf (accessed 14 September 2013).

Declaration of Barbados (1971) Available at: www.nativeweb.org/papers/statements/state/barbados1.php (accessed 23 March 2014).

Dutfield, G. (2000) Bioprospecting or biopiracy? *BIOFUTUR*, 42–45.

Dutfield, G. (2004) *Intellectual Property, Biogenetic Resources, and Traditional Knowledge.* London: Earthscan.

The Economist (2000) Water war in Bolivia. The Americas section, 10 February.

Escobar, A. (1995) *Encountering Development: The Making and Unmaking of the Third World.* Princeton, NJ: Princeton University Press.

Fals Borda, O. (1981) The challenge of action research. In *Development: Seeds of Change.* no.1. Roma. 1981: 55–61.

Fals Borda, O. (1986) La investigación-acción participativa: Política y epistemología. In Á. G. Camacho (ed.) *La Colombia de hoy.* Bogotá: Cerec, pp. 21–38.

Fals Borda, O. and Rahman, M. A. (1991) *Action and Knowledge: Breaking the Monopoly with Participatory Action Research.* New York: Apex Press.

Forero, O. A. (2003) A political ecology of Northwest Amazonia. PhD dissertation, Imperial College of Science, Technology and Medicine, University of London.

Forero, O. A. (2011) Digital technology uses for sustainable management of natural resources in multicultural contexts. *Development in Practice*, 21(6): 822–833.

Forero, O. A. (2012) Mapping in epistemological translation: revising the critique of GIS (Geographical Information Systems) as an instrument of cultural assimilation. *Human Geography*, 5(3): 32–49.

Georgescu-Roegen, N. (1971) *The Entropy Law and the Economic Process.* Cambridge, MA: Harvard University Press.

Hamilton, C. (2006) Biodiversity, biopiracy and benefits: what allegations of biopiracy tell us about intellectual property. *Developing World Bioethics*, 6(3): 158–173.

International Labour Organisation (1989) C169 Indigenous and Tribal Peoples Convention. June. English Translation online. Available at: www.ilo.org/wcmsp5/groups/public/—ed_norm/—normes/documents/publication/wcms_100897.pdf.

Ke-Zerbo, J., Kane, C. H. Archibald, J. et al. (1997) Education as main instrument of cultural defoliation. In M. Rahnema and V. Bawtree (eds) *The Postdevelopment Reader.* London: Zed Books.

Lovelock, J. E. and Watson, A. J. (1983) Biological homeostasis of the global environment: the parable of Daisyworld. *Tellus B*, 35(4): 284–289.

Max-Neef, M. (1986) *Economía Descalza. Señales desde el Mundo Invisible.* Stockholm, Nordan.

Max-Neef, M., Elizalde, A. and Hopenhayn, M. (1987) *Human Scale Development: Conception, Application and Further Reflections.* New York: Apex Press.

Max-Neef, M., Elizalde, A., Hopenhayn, M., Herrera, F., Zemelman, H., Jataba, J. and Weinstein, L. (1989) Human scale development: an option for the future. *Development Dialogue Journal*, 1.

Ministerio del Medio Ambiente (1998a) *Diagnóstico Regional y Estrategias de Desarrollo de las Areas Protegidas de América Latina*. Conference: Primer Congreso Latinoamericano de Parque Nacionales y Otras Areas Protegidas, Santa Marta, Colombia. Bogota DC: Ministerio del Medio Ambiente.

Ministerio del Medio Ambiente (1998b) *Memorias del Primer Congreso Latinoamericano de Parque Nacionales y Otras Areas Protegidas*. Conference: Primer Congreso Latinoamericano de Parque Nacionales y Otras Areas Protegidas, Santa Marta, Colombia. Bogota DC: Ministerio del Medio Ambiente.

Morgan, L. H. (1877) *Ancient Society or Researches in the Lines of Human Progress from Savagery through Barbarism to Civilization*. Marxist Internet Archive Reference Archive. Available at: www.marxists.org/reference/archive/morgan-lewis/ancient-society/ (accessed 14 September 2013).

Nagoya Protocol on Access to Genetic Resources and the Fair and Equitable Sharing on Benefits Aarising from their Utilization to the Convention on Biological Diversity (2010) Text and Annex. (2010) Secretariat of the Convention on Biological Diversity: Montreal. ISBN: 92-9225-306-9.

Nijar G. S. (2011) The Nagoya Protocol on Access and Benefit Sharing of Genetic Resources: Analysis and Implementation Options for Developing Countries. South Centre and CEBLAW.

Oliva, M. J. (2011) Sharing the benefits of biodiversity: a new international protocol and its implications for research and development. *Planta Med* 77: 1221–1227.

Oldham, P., Hall, S. and Forero, O. A. (2013) Biological diversity in the patent system, in Press, *PLOS ONE*. Accepted for publication 17 Sept. 2013.

Posey, D. and Dutfield, G. (1996) *Beyond Intellectual Property: Traditional Resource Rights for Indigenous Peoples and Local Communities*. Ottawa: International Development Research Centre.

Rappaport, R. (1995) Disorders of our own. In S. Forman (ed.) *Diagnosing America: Anthropology and Public Engagement*. Ann Arbor, MI: The University of Michigan Press, pp. 235–294.

Reid, D. (1995) *Sustainable Development. An Introductory Guide*. London: Earthscan.

Robinson, D. F. (2010) *Confronting Biopiracy: Challenges, Cases and International Debates*. London: Earthscan.

Rousseau, J. J. (1762) *The Social Contract, or Principles of Political Right*. Trans. G.D.H. Cole, Public Domain.

Sachs, W. (1992) Poor not different. In P. Ekins and M. Max-Neef (eds) *Real-life Economics: Understanding Wealth Creation*. London: Routledge.

Sanders, D. (1989) The UN Working Group on Indigenous Populations. *Human Rights Quarterly*, 11(3): 406–433.

Schultes, R. (1991) Ethnobotany and technology in the Northwest Amazon: example of partnership. *Environmental Conservation*, 18(3).

Schultes, R. (1992) Ethnobotany and technology in the Northwest Amazon: a partnership. In M. Plotkin and L. Famolare (eds) *Sustainable Harvest and Marketing of Rain Forest Products*. Washington, DC: Island Press, pp. 7–13.

Schultes, R. (1994) The importance of ethnobotany in the environmental conservation. *American Journal of Ethnobotany in Environmental Conservation*.

Schumacher, E. R. (1973) *Small is Beautiful: A Study of Economics as if People Mattered*. New York: Blond and Briggs.

Sheridan, C. (2005) EPO NEEM patent revocation revives biopiracy debate. *Nature Biotechnology*, 23: 5 May: 511–512.

Shiva, V. (1997) *Biopiracy: The Plunder of Nature and Knowledge*. Boston, MA: South End Press.

Soares, J. (2011) The Nagoya Protocol and natural product-based research. *ACS Chemical Biology*, 6: 285–289.

Spencer, H. (1864) *The Principles of Biology*. London: Williams and Norgate.

Stott, P. (1999) *Tropical Rain Forest: A Political Ecology of Hegemonic Mythmaking*. London: IEA Studies on the Environment, No. 15.

United Nations (1987) *Report on the World Commission Environment and Development: Our Common Future*. Transmitted to the General Assembly as an Annex to document A/42/427. http://conspect.nl/pdf/Our_Common_Future-Brundtland_Report_1987.pdf (accessed 17 October 2014).

United Nations General Assembly (2007) *UN Declaration on the Rights of Indigenous Peoples*. New York: United Nations.

UN Permanent Forum in Indigenous Issues (2010) *Los pueblos indigenas en sus propias voces*, 19 to 30 of April, New York. Available at: www.un.org/es/events/indigenousday/pdf/indigenous_culture_identity_sp.pdf (accessed 14 September 2013)

West, P.C. and Brechin, S.R. (eds) (1991) *Resident Peoples and National Parks*. Tucson, AZ: University of Arizona Press.

Wild, R. and McLeod, C. (eds) (2008) *Sacred Natural Sites: Guidelines for Protected Area Managers*. Task Force on the Cultural and Spiritual Values of Protected Areas in collaboration with UNESCO's Man and the Biosphere Programme. Gland, Switzerland: IUCN. http://data.iucn.org/dbtw-wpd/edocs/PAG-016.pdf (accessed 30 July 2012).

15
THE POLITICS OF SUSTAINABLE CONSUMPTION

Emma Hinton

Introduction

Despite decades of political support for sustainable consumption, contemporary consumption remains unsustainable. A combination of increasing consumer demand and rising global populations drives global consumption and production patterns that exceed the Earth's carrying capacity, leading to a situation known as 'global ecological overshoot' (Bond 2005; Global Footprint Network 2013). This unsustainable trend is not solely due to the rapid economic development and growing populations of newly industrialised countries, such as China and India: developed countries share responsibility. Taking the UK as an example, household expenditure doubled between 1968 and 2000 while the proportion of this concerning the satisfaction of basic needs (such as clothing, food and housing) declined to approximately a third; over this period, the greenhouse gas (GHG) emission intensity of this consumption increased by over a third (Jackson and Papathanasopoulou 2008). Although GHG emissions from production in the UK are decreasing as a result of increasingly efficient domestic production and the shift to a service-based economy, the rising emissions associated with UK consumption are driven by the increasing consumption of imported products, especially from non-OECD countries (Baiocchi and Minx 2010; Barrett et al. 2013). There are also problems of equity: while some people live in poverty and fail to meet their basic needs, others are able to consume profligately, yet the negative environmental consequences of consumption tend to fall disproportionately on those that consume the least.

The term 'sustainable consumption' was coined in the context of international sustainable development governance, but the politics of sustainable consumption is not limited to this forum. Working with the distinction between 'weak' and 'strong' forms of sustainable consumption (Fuchs and Lorek 2005; Lorek and Fuchs 2013), this chapter explores the politics of sustainable consumption that have emerged in a range of settings, with a particular focus on how this plays out in the UK, concluding with some reflections on the extent to which these constructions of sustainable consumption might be 'properly-' or 'post-political' (e.g. Mouffe 2005; Swyngedouw 2005).

The multiple forms of sustainable consumption politics

It is only recently that the politics of consumption and production has become aligned with discourses of sustainability and sustainable development: in the UK, historical precedents include the co-operative movement in the nineteenth century; the sufficiency discourses promoted during and after the Second World War (discussed in Chapter 19 in this volume); the counter-cultural movements that promoted simple living during the 1960s; alternative consumerism in the 1970s; and the green consumerism of the latter part of the twentieth century, with its concerns about animal welfare, acid rain, the hole in the ozone layer and global warming (Clarke et al. 2003; Purvis 2003; Barnett et al. 2005; Lang and Gabriel 2005; Jackson 2006).

Like these historical precedents, sustainable consumption politics today are not driven solely by formal government policies and governance fora. Sustainable consumption politics can be understood as a form of 'green-' or 'eco-governmentality' (Barnett et al. 2005; Rutherford 2007; Paterson and Stripple 2010; Hinton 2011): through this theoretical lens, power is understood to flow not just through state-exercised disciplinary power but also through rationalities and technologies of government circulated by a range of agents seeking to coerce and persuade us to govern our conduct in particular ways (e.g. Foucault 2001; Miller and Rose 2008). A range of stakeholder groups including quasi-autonomous non-governmental organization (quangos), third sector organisations (TSOs), businesses, industry and individuals are involved in constructing, influencing and circulating expressions of sustainable consumption, employing rationalities and technologies of government that seek to intervene in the 'politics of lifestyle' (Giddens 1991), where sustainable consumption constitutes one way among many by which individuals in late modernity may choose to define themselves. A burgeoning cultural politics of sustain-able consumption has developed, manifesting in self-help books, lifestyle television shows, magazine and newspaper articles and celebrity endorsements (Clarke et al. 2007; Thomas 2008; Boykoff and Goodman 2009; Littler 2009; Goodman 2010; Hinton and Goodman 2010), where TSOs increasingly incorporate these rationalities and technologies into their advocacy (Hinton 2011). In addition to encouraging us to engage in formal politics in the form of participating in peaceful protests and signing petitions, TSOs also seek to engage us in acts of political consumerism such as boycotts and buycotts, encouraging us to consider the politics embedded in particular products, such that our consumption choices become transformed into a kind of individualised collective action and where statistics on the sales of particular products may be used by third sector intermediaries to lobby for change (Micheletti 2003; Clarke et al. 2007).

Although these multiple manifestations of sustainable consumption politics draw together a range of rationalities and technologies of government and ways of constructing the problems of and solutions to consumption issues, one particular construction of sustainable consumption dominates. This mainstream discourse is discussed next.

Mainstreaming weak sustainable consumption

The mainstream sustainable consumption discourse has been characterised as 'weak', unable to deliver environmentally, socially and economically sustainable consumption (Fuchs and Lorek 2005; Hobson 2013; Lorek and Fuchs 2013). Weak forms of sustainable consumption are framed as seeking to green the status quo, relying upon increasing resource efficiency and technological innovations delivered within a framework of continuing economic growth. In contrast, strong forms demand a radical reorganisation of society, emphasising sufficiency, problematising economic growth and calling for some combination of the production and consumption of eco-efficient products within the formal marketplace and exchange outside this. Whereas strong forms seek to address issues of justice, the rebound effect and overall limits, weak forms are characterised as overlooking these issues and trusting in technological solutions and market approaches to deliver sustainability. Human ingenuity is central to both forms: it is required to deliver technological solutions in weak forms, while in strong forms it is also needed to drive social innovation. Whereas weak sustainable consumption tends to be top-down, strong forms are more bottom-up (Akenji 2014). This characterisation of weak and strong sustainable consumption echoes the long-standing opposition between proponents of ecological modernisation (with their focus on increasing the efficiency of existing systems while conceding that some transformations in how these are organised may be necessary) and those in favour of 'demodernisation' (holding that fundamental institutional reorganisation is essential for long-term sustainability), discussed in Mol and Spaargaren (2000).

The success of the weak sustainable consumption discourse is strongly linked to international governance organisations (IGOs) such as the UN, the OECD, the IIED, UNDESA and UNEP, which have taken the lead in co-ordinating international sustainable consumption governance (Fuchs and Lorek 2005). Their interest in supporting economic growth is rooted in the desire for economic recovery following the Second World War (Redclift 1996). It was in this context that over-consumption was first discussed in the international policy arena, at the UN International Scientific Conference on the Conservation and Use of Resources held in New York in 1949 (Jackson 2006). Here, delegates agreed that it would be possible to both meet demand from and deliver improved living standards to a growing global population through increasingly resource-efficient production driven by technological change (United Nations 1949). The UN Conference on the Human Environment, held in Stockholm in 1972, also emphasised the role of technology in sustainable resource management and called for communication initiatives aimed at individuals, communities and businesses to support this. 'Eco-efficiency' entered the discourse following the inception of the World Business Council for Sustainable Development in 1990 (Schmidheiny 1992), created in order to represent businesses at the UN Conference on Environment and Development (UNCED, or 'Earth Summit') held in Rio de Janeiro in 1992. It was at the UNCED that the term 'sustainable consumption' was first declared an international policy objective, formalised in *Agenda 21* (United Nations 1992). This called for increasing levels of consumption for those whose needs were not currently met alongside increasing the eco-efficiency of consumption for the rest of the world, framing sustainable consumption as compatible with economic growth.

Subsequent IGO activity – and the national policies of signatory governments – have focused on operationalising the ambitions for sustainable consumption set out in *Agenda 21*. The UN Commission on Sustainable Development was established in order to monitor progress on commitments made at the UNCED and launched an international work programme on changing production and consumption patterns in 1995. Progress was revisited in 1997 at a 'special session' of the UN General Assembly held in New York ('Rio +5') and again in 2002 at the World Summit on Sustainable Development held in Johannesburg ('Rio +10'). The resulting *Johannesburg Plan of Implementation* called upon signatories to develop 10-year frameworks of programmes to implement sustainable consumption and production, but was only included after much debate (Fuchs and Lorek 2005). The 'Marrakech Process' – a bottom-up, multi-stakeholder process – was subsequently initiated at the International Expert Meeting in Marrakech in 2003 in order to drive forward the development of these framework programmes, tailored to regional needs, consolidating international commitments to weak sustainable consumption by emphasising growth and voluntarism (Hobson 2013). A review of the framework programmes produced by Finland, Sweden and the UK – who drove the initiative – found that they all emphasise efficiency (though Sweden also considers sufficiency) and that 'on the whole, government commitment to the programmes is limited, and clear targets, timetables and resources are mentioned only occasionally' (Berg 2011: 9). Even so, UNEP considered Finland's and the UK's national plans to be ideal models to be emulated by other nations (Bentley 2008) and the *10-Year Framework of Programmes on Sustainable Consumption and Production Patterns* (10YFP) was adopted by Heads of State at the UN Conference on Sustainable Development in Rio de Janeiro in 2012 ('Rio +20'). In the context of the economic recession experienced by many developed countries since 2008, it is perhaps unsurprising that this summit once again emphasised the need for growth: one of the conference themes was 'a green economy in the context of sustainable development and poverty eradication' (United Nations 2011). Ultimately, Rio +20 failed to reconcile these aims and the resulting document has been 'dubbed "lame even by the standards of international diplomacy"' (Tukker 2013: 278).

Although IGOs have been instrumental in mainstreaming weak sustainable consumption, there have been some attempts to include stronger articulations. The original definition of sustainable consumption in *Agenda 21* called for lifestyle change among those who consume the most, though this was dropped from subsequent international policy proclamations (Jackson 2006); it also encouraged signatories to consider rethinking the need for economic growth and measuring progress and prosperity in alternative ways, of which there has been limited progress so far. Later, UNEP reviewed progress on sustainable consumption and produced its *Consumption Opportunities* report (Manoochehri 2001). In this, it argued for encouraging debate within society as to whether existing levels of consumption deliver a desirable quality of life, alongside action within government (focused on changing infrastructures and choice editing) and industry (dematerialisation). However, this report 'was widely ignored for a decade, even by UNEP itself' (Lorek and Fuchs 2013: 40).

What might account for this difficulty in incorporating stronger forms of sustainable consumption into international governance? The problem may lie in the comparative lack of 'leadership, vision and resources' for sustainable consumption and production in contrast to the climate change agenda, for example (Berg 2011: 17). It may be because IGOs are comparatively weak actors in global governance: they are often institutionally weak, operating with limited resources and dependent on resources from governments and businesses, and as such they are strongly influenced by vested interests (Fuchs and Lorek 2005). It may also be due to 'the institutional embedding of sustainable consumption governance' in ministries and departments whose interests were formerly, or still are, focused on the production side, related to the early focus on the environmental impacts of production (Lorek and Fuchs 2013: 40). The international policy-making system may contribute to the continued success of weak sustainable consumption: the UN 'is still largely based on the 20th century top-down decision-making philosophy of "analyze, decide, instruct" (cf. Hajer, 2011). All views must be accommodated and hence, programs will usually be based on the lowest common denominator' (Tukker 2013: 277). Tukker goes on to suggest that an alternative system driven by bottom-up initiatives put into practice by industry, civil society and others may be more likely to produce radical change and get past the current incremental, 'win–win' approach.

The relationship between consumption and economic growth is at the heart of the weak vs. strong sustainable consumption debate. The following sections consider the extent to which different manifestations of sustainable consumption – green and ethical consumerism, voluntary simplicity and anti-consumption – can be considered weak or strong forms, before going on to consider the different kinds of roles implied for sustainable consumers within these discourses.

Green and ethical consumerism

Green consumerism and ethical consumerism encourage the consumption of specific types of products: those with environmental or ethical credentials, respectively. It is a flourishing business in the UK, though it still accounts for a relatively small proportion of the market. In 2013, total sales of low carbon, environmental and renewable energy products (including within the supply chain) were valued at £109 billion (Defra 2013); while The Co-operative group, which provides a more comprehensive measure that considers ethical finance, household goods, food and eco-travel, valued the market at £47.2bn in its 2012 report, an increase of £11.7bn since the recession began in 2008 (The Co-operative Group 2012).

The mainstream policy framing of sustainable consumption seeks to encourage only a limited form of green consumerism, primarily focused on the purchase of resource-efficient products; the consumption of other kinds of 'green' product – such as those which have been organically produced – and products that have been ethically produced tend to circulate outside policy, in third sector advocacy and within the cultural politics of sustainable consumption.

Resource-efficient green consumerism can be understood to be a weak form of sustainable consumption. It aligns with the ecological modernisation paradigm, where 'more production and consumption ... does not have to imply more environmental devastation' (Mol and Spaargaren 2000: 36). However, the extent to which this avoidance of environmental devastation is possible without also addressing overall levels of consumption has been called into question (Carolan 2004; Bond 2005). Increasing levels of green consumption can precipitate a 'rebound effect': an analysis of European consumption and production found that any environmental gains due to increased efficiency were offset by growth in levels of consumption (Watson et al. 2011). Different goods and services place different amounts of pressure on different ecosystem services, which cannot always be addressed by improving resource efficiency (Barrett and Scott 2012). A focus on eco-efficiency can obscure other social and environmental impacts associated with 'green' products. Renewable energy technologies provide an interesting example: successive IPCC reports and climate policies frame renewable energy technologies as an important means of decarbonising the economy, mitigating climate change and delivering energy security, and encouragements to consume energy from renewable sources have become a common feature of sustainable consumption advocacy (Hinton 2011). However, the production of this 'clean' energy may be associated with negative social and environmental impacts: for example, solar photovoltaic panels are associated with considerable environmental and health hazards during production and disposal, which tend to be concentrated in less developed countries such as China and India (Silicon Valley Toxics Coalition 2009; Gottesfeld and Cherry 2011).

In contrast, in ethical consumerism, concern for social and economic sustainability is emphasised over any environmental benefits. Arguably, the consumption of fairly or ethically traded products constitutes a strong form of sustainable consumption in that it seeks to deliver change in the ways in which production is organised. Emerging from social movement activity, related certification schemes 'seek to transform traditionally exploitative global production and trade relations' through 'new producer/distributor relationships that challenge the distribution of value' (Low and Davenport 2006: 315). However, the success of this 'counter-hegemonic project' (ibid.) has been called into question. Goodman outlines 'fair trade's Faustian Bargain':

> with mainstreaming and the increasing quality of its products has come market growth and more money going back to poor and relatively marginalized farmers. But all of this

> has transpired at the cost of bringing in the 'unsavories' of super-markets, greater barriers to entry to fair trade producers and a growing opaqueness to its transparency.
> *(Goodman 2010: 110)*

Similarly, participation in organic certification schemes can have excessive social and economic costs for producers, where schemes impose high financial and bureaucratic demands on producers in order to guarantee quality, create value and so drive the market (Guthman 2007).

Voluntary simplicity and anti-consumption

Whereas green and ethical consumerism encourage the consumption of particular kinds of sustainable products typically provided through the mainstream marketplace, voluntary simplicity and anti-consumption imply more radical change, aligning with sufficiency and stronger forms of sustainable consumption.

Voluntary simplicity has been described as 'living in a way that is outwardly simple and inwardly rich' (Elgin and Mitchell 1977: 13), where personal qualities and benefits (such as personal growth, fulfilment, creativity, independence, self-reliance, health, authenticity) are cultivated through frugal consumption, self-sufficiency and small-scale, decentralised organisation. It is not anti-capitalist or anti-consumption: voluntary simplifiers consume durable, resource-efficient, simply made, repairable and reusable – including second-hand – products while reducing their overall levels of consumption, sharing products and producing their own (Elgin and Mitchell 1977; Shaw and Newholm 2002). Voluntary simplifiers may only make changes to some of the products they buy or they may change careers and accept lower wages, downsize their homes or even live communally in intentional 'new consumption communities' (Bekin et al. 2005). Whereas downshifting is a more limited, self-centred variant, voluntary simplicity entails a greater withdrawal from a conventional consumerist lifestyle (Shaw and Newholm 2002, discussed in Bekin et al. 2005).

In contrast, anti-consumerism seeks to bring about wider social and political change but, as with voluntary simplicity, there is no single way in which this is to be done. It is a manifestation of political consumerism, motivated by the politics embedded in products, encompassing any acts of consumption avoidance (of products, brands or even consumer culture) associated with some form of 'reasons against' their consumption that may be ethical or environmental, concerned with resistance (resisting some dominating force, such as a multinational corporation) or symbolism (avoiding looking thrifty by not shopping in a particular place) (Chatzidakis and Lee 2012). In Littler's (2005) review of the cultural politics of anti-consumerism, which focused on related discourses circulating in selected books (*No Logo* by Naomi Klein and *Globalisation: Take it Personally* by Anita Roddick) and campaigns (Reverend Billy's Church of Stop Shopping and Adbusters' *Buy Nothing Day*), she argues that anti-consumerism is not 'monolithic': 'the type of consumer and anticonsumer being imagined, the role of activism in cultural and social change, and the scenarios imagined as happening after the boycott can all vary substantially' (Littler 2005: 242). Whereas Anita Roddick envisages change as being driven by a combination of individual consumption choices, limited activism and legal changes, Naomi Klein emphasises the need for change in global laws driven by social movements, while Adbusters seeks to encourage discursive and ideological change driven by coalitions.

Citizenship and the sustainable consumer

Participation in sustainable consumption suggests an expression of some form of citizenship: one that focuses upon sustainability as a socio-political goal and that acts upon perceived rights and responsibilities that can be performed in a range of political spaces including private spaces of consumption, interactions in virtual space or engagements with democratic political institutions. In weak sustainable consumption, rational consumers are responsible for becoming suitably informed about the availability and impacts of different products, driving the market for sustainable products, effectively voting for change through their purchases. In strong sustainable consumption, individuals have a role in driving not just this market but also more radical change in the economy, with responsibility for some combination of becoming informed about alternative means of consuming, shifting at least some of their personal consumption outside the formal marketplace and supporting ideological and political change.

The extent to which sustainable consumption constitutes an appropriate form of citizenship has been called into question (Hobson 2002; 2008; Barnett et al. 2005; Clarke et al. 2007; Johnston 2008) but arguably, the outcome of such arguments depends on which form of sustainable consumption is in question – weak or strong – and which model of citizenship it is being compared against. Critiques have tended to focus on the weak form constructed in sustainable consumption governance, noting that the extent to which change is possible is limited by the products that are made available and consumers' ability to access them, where such expressions of citizenship inevitably reinforce norms of neoliberal consumption (Smith 2000; Slocum 2004; Seyfang 2005; Clarke et al. 2007). Yet strong sustainable consumption overcomes these criticisms to some extent, since it also includes consumption outside the formal marketplace and encourages more radical change to modes of economic organisation.

Of the various conceptualisations of environmental citizenship that have been developed (for an overview, see, for example, Hinton 2013), post-cosmopolitan ecological citizenship (Dobson 2003; 2006; 2007) would seem to be a particularly appropriate model with which to conceptualise the roles and responsibilities of sustainable consumers. This recognises the globalised nature of political processes, relations of production and consumption and environmental problems, and on this basis transnational civil society constitutes the political community in question. All forms of consumption are relevant in post-cosmopolitan ecological citizenship, in contrast to 'sustainability citizenship' or 'green civic republicanism' where only active and 'mindful' forms of consumption – for example, those that deliberately attempt to address some form of inequality, injustice or environmental impact – count. Here, through every act of consumption, citizens are responsible for any associated impacts and the inequity of their distribution, where responsibility is produced through transnational, asymmetrical bonds of obligation linking consumers with producers. The inclusion of all forms of consumption, not just that of products marketed as being sustainable in some way, provides a means of addressing the criticism that sustainable consumption (understood in that particularly weak form) is only accessible by those who can afford to consume those products, which still tend to carry a price premium.

The extent of a citizen-consumer's obligation can be conceptualised in terms of the quantity of ecological space that their consumption occupies, which can be quantified in the form of an ecological footprint. When this reveals that the consumer citizen has exceeded their fair share of ecological space, consumer citizens act upon virtues of justice, care and compassion in order to rectify this. This emphasis on footprinting provides a means of apportioning responsibility more fairly among consumers: levels of consumption within industrialised countries like the UK are unevenly distributed (Bond 2005) and so it would be unfair to apportion responsibility equally among all UK citizens. However, relying on the ecological footprinting device to apportion responsibility may be problematic. These tools are not neutral and their representation of consumption is inevitably both partial and simplified, based on a top-down, expert selection of which aspects of consumption to include and what values to apportion them (Marres 2008; Collins et al. 2009; Hinton and Goodman 2010; Hinton 2013). In order for footprinting to function as a fair means of allocating responsibility, there must be greater transparency and democratic agreement concerning the methodology and datasets informing these tools. Even so, footprinting may fail to adequately capture consumption outside the formal marketplace since this is comparatively difficult to trace. Neither does footprinting make clear where the negative impacts of consumption take place (Bond 2005), nor does it capture the conditions of production for each individual product that is consumed, where the social is included only in terms of exposure to environmental impacts.

Dobson acknowledges that 'individual room for ecological space manoeuvre is limited by living in a society which operates at a high level of systemic ecological space occupancy' (2009: 136) and suggests that post-cosmopolitan ecological citizenship should be combined with other forms of environmental citizenship, combining action in the private and the public sphere and including taking action to alter constraining systems and 'the institutional structures that underpin and serve to reproduce the injustice' (Dobson 2007: 281). Models of consumer citizenship assume that citizen-consumers are relatively free to intervene in some way in unsustainable consumption when driven to do so by bonds of obligation and feelings of responsibility; however, this may not be sufficient to drive individual action in every case and even if it were, the extent to which it is appropriate to rely upon individuals to drive structural change has been called into question. These points are considered in the next section.

Consumer agency

Individualist and structuralist paradigms have dominated environmental research since the 1970s (Spaargaren 2011). Jackson summarises their differences as follows:

> In the first perspective, enlightened consumers are free to choose pro-environmental behaviours – assuming that they possess appropriate beliefs or attitudes; in the second, consumers may be 'locked in' to consumption choices by a variety of external conditions ranging from genetic conditioning to economic necessity, social expectation, accessibility constraints and the 'creeping evolution of social norms'.
>
> *(Jackson 2005: 24)*

While individualist approaches place too much responsibility on individual citizen-consumers to drive social change, structuralist approaches afford them too little, conceptualising social change as being driven by the top-down provision of products and infrastructures (Spaargaren 2011).

Theories of social practice provide an alternative understanding of the role of citizen-consumers in delivering social change, and this approach is gaining in prominence in consumption research. This provides a means of disrupting the 'structure-actor dualism' (Giddens 1984) and as such, an emphasis on delivering change in the lifestyles (understood as collections of practices) of citizen-consumers need not be dismissed as being trivial or individualistic (Spaargaren and Oosterveer 2010). Attending to practices constitutes:

> a more balanced approach which pays attention to both agency and structure, which makes room for (combining) both bottom-up and top-down dynamics of change, and which recognises the mutual influencing and co-shaping of human actors on the one hand and objects and technological infrastructures on the other.
>
> *(Spaargaren 2011: 815)*

Here, agency is conceptualised as being distributed between consumers, the forms of know-how and skills associated with doing things in particular ways, the materials involved (understood in a socio-technical sense) and the practices themselves (Shove 2010). Practices change when some or all their constituent elements change, which may be enabled or constrained by a host of factors including the location of the practice within a particular person's life, their home, or the association of a practice with a particular group of people or way of living (Shove et al. 2012). While Dobson's articulation of post-cosmopolitan ecological citizenship requires individualist attention to personal footprints, a practice-informed approach would seek to reduce the size of the footprints of practices (Spaargaren 2011). A practice-informed approach may have greater potential to support the kind of radical societal transformations that strong forms of sustainable consumption demand, since they refocus attention on 'how the contours and environmental costs of daily life evolve' (Shove 2010: 1277).

Are the politics of sustainable consumption 'properly-' or 'post-political'?

Critiques of the various articulations of sustainable consumption often focus on the extent to which these approaches may be able to deliver the kinds of change that are understood to be necessary. The literature on 'post-politics' developed by Chantal Mouffe, Erik Swyngedouw and Slavoj Žižek (see, for example, Mouffe 2005; Swyngedouw 2005; 2007; 2009; 2010) provides a further lens through which to consider the adequacy of these approaches. According to this literature, contemporary politics is understood to be post-political: 'debate, disagreement and dissensus [are replaced] with a series of technologies of governing that fuse around consensus, agreement, accountancy metrics and technocratic environmental management' (Swyngedouw 2009: 601). Consensus is prized and typically founded upon moral and scientific arguments, where the interests of those stakeholders involved in establishing this consensus are backgrounded. There is little room for radical points of view, and idealised conceptualisations of community and sociability are at the core. In contrast, the properly political condition welcomes dissensus and agonistic debate. Instead of reinforcing or at least working within the existing neoliberal capitalist order, a 'proper' politics would encourage the contestation and radical reshaping of existing systems of thought, provision and politics.

The mainstream, weak form of sustainable consumption politics would seem to constitute exactly the kind of post-political condition described by Swyngedouw (2009). This consensus position has been reinforced through successive IGO summits and national policies. The emphasis is technocratic, focused on eco-efficiency. Accountancy metrics include sustainable development indicators and footprinting tools applied at the national and individual levels. Consumers are encouraged to respond to moral and scientific arguments about the consequences of their consumption and accept responsibility to change; where this change consists of consuming more, as with green or ethical consumerism, this supports the existing neoliberal capitalist order. Although radical change is expected to be driven by grassroots activity (for example, in the literature on degrowth), it is difficult for TSOs (like IGOs, as discussed earlier) to diverge from the mainstream consensus on sustainable consumption. Those TSOs that rely upon external funding and/or public support in order to pursue their sustainable consumption advocacy may pursue mainstream, weaker forms based on the knowledge that stronger articulations are less 'fundable' and popular, such that TSOs may conceal their interests in strong sustainable consumption, constructing an advocacy discourse that backgrounds dissensus in order to guarantee organisational sustainability (Hinton 2011). However, even strong sustainable consumption has a post-political character where this speaks to communitarian and social ideals: grassroots community-oriented activity such as Transition Initiatives focus on community-level action, and intentional communities of voluntary simplifiers promote communal living as an ideal.

However, sustainable consumption politics may also incorporate some properly political aspects. Although the literature on post-politics tends to privilege political activity within national and international governance and government, sustainable consumption politics extends beyond these fora: its political spaces are not limited to those provided via democratic institutions. This wider range of activity incorporates some challenges to the neoliberal capitalist order, where consumption shifts outside the formal marketplace and either is reduced overall or achieved through alternative systems of provision. This variability in articulations of sustainable consumption, with their interests in alternative modes of production, of living and of organising society and the economy represent a challenge to the mainstream consensus. Advocates' use of virtual space mediated by web 2.0 technology provides opportunities for cultivating dissensus and encouraging debate as to what counts as sustainable consumption, as well as facilitating the performance of sustainable consumption in less mainstream ways, supporting local-level organisation and community exchange and encouraging the sharing of lived experiences of different kinds of consumption (Hinton 2011).

Conclusion

In conclusion, then, contemporary sustainable consumption politics has the potential to deliver a change to patterns of consumption and production that are equitable and just, and which stay within the Earth's carrying capacity. However, the extent to which the current mainstream articulation of sustainable consumption can achieve this has been called into question and more radical change is almost certainly required, involving some combination of efficiency and sufficiency (e.g. Lorek and Fuchs 2013). Yet individuals, TSOs and IGOs are limited in their ability to drive this change.

In the short term, policy-makers should shift their focus from the models of behaviour change that are grounded in economics and psychology that currently dominate, and should take seriously alternative conceptualisations of agency and appropriate action such as those grounded in theories of social practices and socio-technical transitions (Shove 2010; 2012; Shove and Walker 2010). Measures of progress should take into account forms of consumption outside the formal marketplace, however difficult this may be, or at least acknowledge that purchases are only a partial representation of sustainable consumption activity. It should be easier to distinguish between sustainable products – understood more broadly than eco-efficient products, or those produced through some form of ethical or environmental certification scheme – and unsustainable counterparts, while recognising that consumption practices are not (always) economically rational and driven by the availability of information.

Over the longer term, structural change is required to deliver strong sustainable consumption, which must be achieved through governance mechanisms (Lorek and Fuchs 2013). Rather than a continuing commitment to the current neoliberal capitalist order, sustainable consumption may require an alternative form of capitalism. This could perhaps be driven by prosumption (Ritzer and Jurgenson 2010; Büscher and Igoe 2013): 'prosumer capitalism' would be characterised by 'a trend toward unpaid rather than paid labor [*sic*] and toward offering products at no cost', where 'the system is marked by a new abundance where scarcity once predominated' (Ritzer and Jurgenson 2010: 13). Alternatively, 'post-consumerism' may follow consumerism as the next phase of economic organisation, which 'will need to entail clever combinations of the following: urban agriculture, individual and communal provisioning, labor [*sic*] reskilling, infrastructural retrofitting, low-carbon technologies, carbon rationing, and hyperconnected modes of social interaction' (Cohen 2012: 118). Maintaining the status quo is not a viable option in the face of the continued social and economic inequity and environmental harm associated with contemporary consumerism: continued commitment to weak sustainable consumption politics may simply serve to 'sustain the unsustainable' (Blühdorn 2007).

References

Akenji, L. (2014) Consumer scapegoatism and limits to green consumerism. *Journal of Cleaner Production*, 63: 13–23.

Baiocchi, G. and Minx, J. C. (2010) Understanding changes in the UK's CO_2 Emissions: a global perspective. *Environmental Science & Technology*, 44(4): 1177–1184.

Barnett, C., Cloke, P., Clarke, N. and Malpass, A. (2005) Consuming ethics: articulating the subjects and spaces of ethical consumption. *Antipode*, 37: 23–45.

Barrett, J., Peters, G., Wiedmann, T., Scott, K., Lenzen, M., Roelich, K. and Le Quéré, C. (2013) Consumption-based GHG emission accounting: a UK case study. *Climate Policy*, 13(4): 451–470.

Barrett, J. and Scott, K. (2012) Link between climate change mitigation and resource efficiency: a UK case study. *Global Environmental Change*, 22(1): 299–307.

Bekin, C., Carrigan, M. and Szmigin, I. (2005) Defying marketing sovereignty: voluntary simplicity at new consumption communities. *Qualitative Market Research: An International Journal*, 8(4): 413–429.

Bentley, M. (2008) *Planning for Change: Guidelines for National Programmes on Sustainable Consumption and Production*. New York: United Nations Environment Programme.

Berg, A. (2011) Not Roadmaps but toolboxes: analysing pioneering national programmes for sustainable consumption and production. *Journal of Consumer Policy*, 34(1): 9–23.

Blühdorn, I. (2007) Sustaining the unsustainable: symbolic politics and the politics of simulation. *Environmental Politics*, 16(2): 251–275.

Bond, S. (2005) The global challenge of sustainable consumption. *Consumer Policy Review*, 35: 38–44.

Boykoff, M. T. and Goodman, M. K. (2009) Conspicuous redemption? Reflections on the promises and perils of the 'Celebritization' of climate change. *Geoforum*, 40: 395–406.

Büscher, B. and Igoe, J. (2013) 'Prosuming' conservation? Web 2.0, nature and the intensification of value-producing labour in late capitalism. *Journal of Consumer Culture*, 13(3): 283–305.

Carolan, M. S. (2004) Ecological modernization theory: what about consumption? *Society & Natural Resources: An International Journal*, 17(3): 247–260.

Chatzidakis, A. and Lee, M. S. W. (2012. Anti-consumption as the study of reasons against. *Journal of Macromarketing*, 33(3), 190–203.

Clarke, D., Doel, M. A. and Housiaux, K. L. (2003) *The Consumption Reader*. London: Routledge.

Clarke, N., Barnett, C., Cloke, P. and Malpass, A. (2007) Globalising the consumer: doing politics in an ethical register. *Political Geography*, 26: 231–249.

Cohen, M. J. (2012) Managing cultural dissonance in the transition to a postconsumerist future. In *SCORAI Europe Workshop Proceedings: First Trans-Atlantic SCORAI Workshop*. Presented at the Sustainable Consumption During Times of Crisis, Bregenz, Austria, pp. 107–124.

Collins, A., Cowell, R. and Flynn, A. (2009) Evaluation and environmental governance: the institutionalisation of ecological footprinting. *Environment and Planning A*, 41: 1707–1725.

Defra (2013) *Sustainable Development Indicators*. London.

Dobson, A. (2003) *Citizenship and the Environment*. Oxford: Oxford University Press.

Dobson, A. (2006) Ecological citizenship: a defence. *Environmental Politics*, 15: 447–451.

Dobson, A. (2007) Environmental citizenship: towards sustainable development. *Sustainable Development*, 15: 276–285.

Dobson, A. (2009) Citizens, citizenship and governance for sustainability. In W. N. Adger and A. Jordan (eds) *Governing Sustainability*. Cambridge: Cambridge University Press, pp. 125–141.

Elgin, D. and Mitchell, A. (1977) Voluntary simplicity. *Strategy & Leadership*, 5(6): 13–15.

Foucault, M. (2001) *Power: The Essential Works of Michel Foucault 1954–1984*. London: Allen Lane.

Fuchs, D. and Lorek, S. (2005) Sustainable consumption governance: a history of promises and failures. *Journal of Consumer Policy*, 28: 261–288.

Giddens, A. (1984) *The Constitution of Society: Outline of the Theory of Structuration*. Cambridge: Polity Press.

Giddens, A. (1991) *Modernity and Self-Identity: Self and Society in the Late Modern Age*. Cambridge: Polity Press.

Global Footprint Network (2013) Earth Overshoot Day 2013.

Goodman, M. K. (2010) The mirror of consumption: Celebritization, developmental consumption and the shifting cultural politics of fair trade. *Geoforum*, 41: 104–116.

Gottesfeld, P. and Cherry, C. R. (2011) Lead emissions from solar photovoltaic energy systems in China and India. *Energy Policy*, 39: 4939–4946.

Guthman, J. (2007) The Polanyian way? Voluntary food labels as neoliberal governance. *Antipode*, 39(3): 456–478.

Hajer, M. (2011) *The Energetic Society. In Search of a Governance Philosophy for a Clean Economy*. The Hague: PBL Netherlands Environmental Assessment Agency.

Hinton, E. (2011) Virtual spaces of sustainable consumption: governmentality and third sector advocacy in the UK. PhD thesis. King's College London.

Hinton, E. (2013) Citizenship. In C. Death (ed.) *Critical Environmental Politics*. London: Routledge, pp. 31–40.

Hinton, E. D. and Goodman, M. K. (2010) Sustainable consumption: developments, considerations and new directions. In M. Redclift and G. Woodgate (eds) *International Handbook of Environmental Sociology*, 2nd edn. Cheltenham: Edward Elgar, pp. 245–261.

Hobson, K. (2002) Competing discourses of sustainable consumption: does the 'Rationalisation of lifestyles' make sense? *Environmental Politics*, 11: 95–120.

Hobson, K. (2008) Reasons to be cheerful: thinking sustainably in a (climate) changing world. *Geography Compass*, 2: 199–214.

Hobson, K. (2013) 'Weak' or 'strong' sustainable consumption? Efficiency, degrowth, and the 10 Year Framework of Programmes. *Environment and Planning C: Government and Policy*, 13.

Jackson, T. (2005) *Motivating Sustainable Consumption: A Review of Evidence on Consumer Behaviour and Behavioural Change*. Guildford: University of Surrey.

Jackson, T. (2006) Readings in sustainable consumption. In *The Earthscan Reader in Sustainable Consumption*. London: Earthscan, pp. 1–24.

Jackson, T. and Papathanasopoulou, E. (2008) Luxury or 'lock-in'? An exploration of unsustainable consumption in the UK: 1968 to 2000. *Ecological Economics*, 68(1–2): 80–95.

Johnston, J. (2008) The citizen-consumer hybrid: ideological tensions and the case of Whole Foods Market. *Theory and Society*, 37: 229–270.

Lang, T. and Gabriel, Y. (2005) A brief history of consumer activism. In R. Harrison, T. Newholm, and D. Shaw (eds) *The Ethical Consumer*. London: Sage, pp. 29–53.

Littler, J. (2005) Beyond the boycott: anti-consumerism, cultural change and the limits of reflexivity. *Cultural Studies*, 19(2): 227–252.

Littler, J. (2009) *Radical Consumption: Shopping for Change in Contemporary Culture*. Maidenhead: Open University Press.

Lorek, S. and Fuchs, D. (2013) Strong sustainable consumption governance – precondition for a degrowth path? *Journal of Cleaner Production*, 38: 36–43.

Low, W. and Davenport, E. (2006) Mainstreaming fair trade: adoption, assimilation, appropriation. *Journal of Strategic Marketing*, 14: 315–327.

Manoochehri, J. (2001) *Consumption Opportunities – Strategies for Change: A Report for Decision-Makers*. Geneva: UNEP.

Marres, N. (2008) The making of climate publics: eco-homes as material devices of publicity. *Distinktion*, 9: 27–45.

Micheletti, M. (2003) *Political Virtue and Shopping: Individuals, Consumerism, and Collective Action*. New York: Palgrave Macmillan.

Miller, P. and Rose, N. (2008) *Governing the Present*. Cambridge, MA: Polity Press.

Mol, A. P. J. and Spaargaren, G. (2000) Ecological modernisation theory in debate: a review. *Environmental Politics*, 9(1): 17–49.

Mouffe, C. (2005) *On the Political*. London: Routledge.

Paterson, M. and Stripple, J. (2010) My space: governing individuals' carbon emissions. *Environment and Planning D-Society & Space*, 28: 341–362.

Purvis, M. (2003) Societies of consumers and consumer societies: cooperation, consumption and politics in Britain and continental Europe c. 1859–1920. In D. Clarke, M. A. Doel, and K. M. L. Housiaux (eds) *The Consumption Reader*. London: Routledge, pp. 69–76.

Redclift, M. (1996) *Wasted: Counting the Costs of Global Consumption*. London: Earthscan.

Ritzer, G. and Jurgenson, N. (2010) Production, consumption, prosumption: the nature of capitalism in the age of the digital 'prosumer'. *Journal of Consumer Culture*, 10(1): 13–36.

Rutherford, S. (2007) Green governmentality: insights and opportunities in the study of nature's rule. *Progress in Human Geography*, 31: 291–307.

Schmidheiny, S. (1992) *Changing Course: A Global Business Perspective on Development and the Environment*. Cambridge, MA: MIT Press.

Seyfang, G. (2005) Shopping for sustainability: can sustainable consumption promote ecological citizenship? *Environmental Politics*, 14: 290–306.

Shaw, D. and Newholm, T. (2002) Voluntary simplicity and the ethics of consumption. *Psychology & Marketing*, 19: 167–185.

Shove, E. (2010) Beyond the ABC: climate change policy and theories of social change. *Environment and Planning A*, 42: 1273–1285.

Shove, E. (2012) Putting practice into policy: reconfiguring questions of consumption and climate change. *Contemporary Social Science*, 1–15.

Shove, E., Pantzar, M. and Watson, M. (2012) *The Dynamics of Social Practice: Everyday Life and How it Changes*. London: Sage.

Shove, E. and Walker, G. (2010) Governing transitions in the sustainability of everyday life. *Research Policy*, 39: 471–476.

Silicon Valley Toxics Coalition (2009) *Toward a Just and Sustainable Solar Energy Industry*. A Silicon Valley Toxics Coalition White Paper.

Slocum, R. (2004) Consumer citizens and the Cities for Climate Protection campaign. *Environment and Planning A*, 36: 763–782.

Smith, S. J. (2000) Citizenship. In R. J. Johnston, D. Gregory, G. Pratt, and M. Watts (eds) *The Dictionary of Human Geography*. Oxford: Blackwell, pp. 83–84.

Spaargaren, G. (2011) Theories of practices: agency, technology, and culture: exploring the relevance of practice theories for the governance of sustainable consumption practices in the new world-order. *Global Environmental Change*, 21(3): 813–822.

Spaargaren, G. and Oosterveer, P. (2010) Citizen-consumers as agents of change in globalizing modernity: the case of sustainable consumption. *Sustainability*, 2: 1887–1908.

Swyngedouw, E. (2005) Governance innovation and the citizen: the Janus face of governance-beyond-the-state. *Urban Studies*, 42: 1991–2006.

Swyngedouw, E. (2007) Impossible 'sustainability' and the postpolitical condition. In R. Krueger and D. Gibbs (eds) *The Sustainable Development Paradox: Urban Political Economy in the United States and Europe*. New York: The Guilford Press, 13–40.

Swyngedouw, E. (2009) The antinomies of the postpolitical city: in search of a democratic politics of environmental production. *International Journal of Urban and Regional Research*, 33: 601–620.

Swyngedouw, E. (2010) Apocalypse forever? Post-political populism and the spectre of climate change. *Theory, Culture & Society*, 27: 213–232.

The Co-operative Group (2012) *Ethical Consumer Markets Report*. Manchester: The Co-operative Group.

Thomas, L. (2008) Alternative realities: downshifting narratives in contemporary lifestyle television. *Cultural Studies*, 22: 680–699.

Tukker, A. (2013) Knowledge collaboration and learning by aligning global sustainability programs: reflections in the context of Rio+20. *Journal of Cleaner Production*, 48: 272–279.

United Nations (1949) *The Proceedings of the United Nations Scientific Conference on the Conservation and Utilization of Resources*. New York: UN Department of Economic Affairs.

United Nations (1992) *Agenda 21*. New York: United Nations.

United Nations (2011) Objective and Themes [Online]. *Rio +20 - United Nations Conference on Sustainable Development*. Available at: www.uncsd2012.org/objectiveandthemes.html (accessed 20 November 2013).

Watson, D., McKinnon, D., Bjørn, A., Stenbæk Hansen, M., Wittmer, D., von Geibler, J., Saurat, M., Schütz, H., Tobias, S., Zoboli, R., Marin, G., Mazzanti, M., Volpi, M., Beretta, I. and Dal Negro, L. (2011) *Progress in Sustainable Consumption and Production in Europe: Indicator-based Report*. Copenhagen: European Topic Centre on Sustainable Consumption and Production, No. 1/2011.

16
SUSTAINABLE TOURISM DEVELOPMENT

Tony Johnston

Introduction

Lest we forget at the outset of this chapter, tourism is invasive, insidious and destructive. No other industry has the ability to spread its tentacles into the most remote corners of the planet with the speed, force or power of tourism. Yet tourism is a seductive industry which promises much by way of development potential. As a result, there is hardly a location on Earth which has not been commodified by the industry, as planners, developers and governments seek to use tourism to generate wealth and employment.

The industry's ability to infiltrate is equally evident with the provision of ever new products, which commodify phenomena as diverse as conflict, poverty, delicate and pristine environments and the body, for example. As Duffy (2013) notes, tourism is adept at creating all manner of must-see and must-do commodities – strikingly illustrated by 'last-chance' and 'doom tourism' products, which offer the chance to see vanishing landscapes, seascapes and species before they become extinct (Lemelin et al. 2010).

In response to the tourism industry's growth and infiltration, a more critical tone has underpinned tourism scholarship in recent years (Bianchi 2009), ranging from research on tourism epistemologies (Ateljevic et al. 2007) to specific work on, for example, tourism and the environment (Duffy 2013), ecotourism and poverty (Butcher 2011) and tourism and peace (Blanchard and Higgins-Desboilles 2013). Although broadly speaking, tourism remains firmly rooted in an applied business agenda, there is doubtless an increasing number of tourism academics turning their attention to the intersection of the industry with global imbalances; climate change, poverty, human rights and environmental protection are among some of the themes regularly under examination in contemporary literature. From this body of work, the recognition that tourism has 'worldmaking' potential has emerged (Hollinshead 2009); it is an industry with transformative powers. In the developing world, the transformative potential of tourism is clear. Mitchell and Ashley (2010) state, for example, that international tourists are better at spending money in the developing world than aid agencies, spending \$295 billion in 2007 – three times the level of official development assistance.

Nonetheless, the choice of sinister vocabulary to open this chapter is deliberate. Tourism *is* insidious by nature, and has frequently exacerbated rather than eliminated global inequalities. It is for this reason the industry is worthy of inclusion in a compilation on sustainable development. We must acknowledge that tourism is a deeply invasive phenomenon, and, as it continues to expand in the developed and developing world, with new products and destinations constantly emerging in response to globalisation pressures, increased competition, new consumption patterns and the sustainable development agenda, critical reflection is needed on the academy's role in the global policies and patterns which shape the industry.

To review these challenges, this chapter presents a chronology of tourism development theory, followed by a reflection on new agendas in sustainable tourism development research and a concluding discussion on the who, what, where and how of sustainable tourism development research. First, to construct a chronology of sustainable tourism development, the following section is structured loosely around a globalisation, development and networks of power framework, as devised by Mowforth and Munt (2009). This framework affords the flexibility to consider how current and forthcoming global sustainable development policies, agendas and industry actions may configure the contribution tourism makes to sustainable development in the coming years. Throughout, the chapter draws upon secondary and comparative scholarship, namely current industry statistics, policy and NGO strategy documents and academic interpretation and discourse of both industry and policy.

Globalisation, development and networks of power

Tourism is a major contributor to the world economy and an industry which continues to expand, with almost consistent year-on-year growth since the 1950s. Some context-setting statistics include international tourist arrivals topped one billion in 2012 (Figure 16.1) for the first

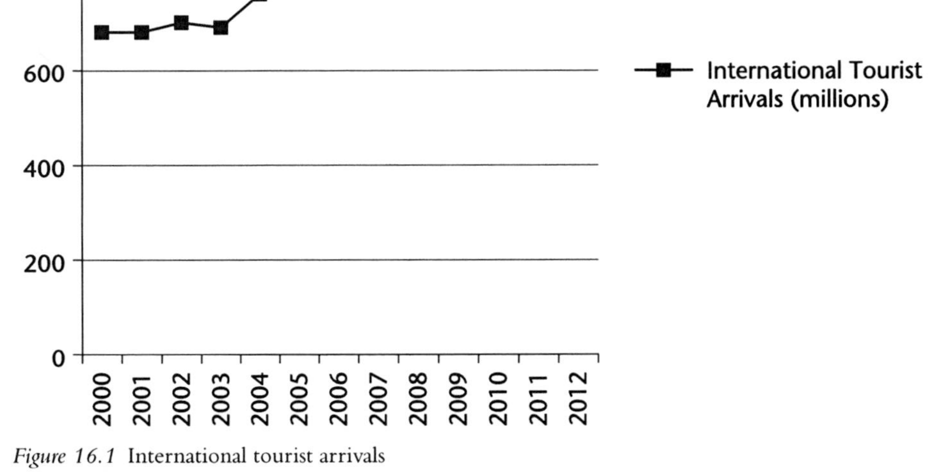

Figure 16.1 International tourist arrivals

Source: UNWTO (2013b).

time, with the United Nations World Tourism Organisation (UNWTO) subsequently recording 1,087 million international arrivals in 2013 (UNWTO 2014). This figure is expected to continue growing over the next two decades, reaching 1.8 billion international arrivals by 2030 (UNWTO 2013b). Such an increase would represent a 2.2 per cent growth in arrivals in the developed world and a 4.4 per cent growth in the developing world. This growth has been clearly evident in the developing world in recent years. In 2013, for example, Africa saw an increase of 6 per cent in international arrivals, equivalent to 3 million more tourists and reaching a new record of 56 million international arrivals (UNWTO 2014).

In financial terms, international tourism receipts in 2012 were recorded at US$1,075 billion, with notable increases in the developing world. International tourist expenditure in Africa rose in 2012, for example, with tourists spending $26.1 billion, up from $23.5 billion in 2011. Asia and the Pacific witnessed a similar increase, hosting 16 million more tourists, representing a 7 per cent increase (UNWTO 2013b). But arrivals and expenditure figures in recent years reflect a longer trend of growth in the industry, especially in the developing world. International arrivals in the world's least developed countries increased by an average of 11 per cent annually between 1990 and 2009 (UNDP 2011).

In addition to these figures, international arrivals and receipts are dwarfed by domestic tourism figures, which are estimated to range from 5 billion to 6 billion tourists in 2012. Tourism as an industry overall is estimated to support approximately 9 per cent of global GDP, through direct and induced impact, support 1 in 11 jobs worldwide and account for 6 per cent, or $1.3 trillion of world exports (UNWTO 2013b). While this list of figures may overwhelm, managing such unparalleled growth represents the first major challenge to sustainable tourism development.

Second, in terms of adopting Mowforth and Munt's (2009) framework, the figures outlined primarily originate from a desire to develop tourism at national levels; the industry specifically features in many countries' national development strategies in both the developed and developing world. But despite positive global economic figures, neither growth in arrivals or expenditure tell much about the impacts of tourism at ground level. Thailand, to illustrate the point, is often examined in tourism literature because of the state's neoliberal tourism agenda (Mowforth and Munt 2009). Arrivals in Thailand almost doubled between 2004 and 2012, from 11,650,703 to 22,303,065, contributing 7.3 per cent of the country's GDP in 2012 and directly creating 5.2 per cent of total employment (World Travel and Tourism Council 2013). Such figures and success stories, which dominate political tourism decision-making, say almost nothing beyond the historical transformation of the industry's economic contribution, and even there they reveal little. To counter the Thai statistics, for example, Mowforth and Munt (2009) point to the brutal destruction of Thailand's beaches and islands, caused by a tourism industry which lacks control, displays utter disregard for the environment and has turned the coast into a male fantasy theme park. The need to curtail such impacts is clear and if tourism is to be used as a development vehicle, increased criticism of the industry's value is needed in practitioner circles.

Third, in terms of relationships of power, Mowforth and Munt (2009) note, that despite sustained levels of growth in global tourism, change occurs rapidly, with volatility, vulnerability and resilience configuring the structure of the industry, due to its interconnected nature and exposure to external influences. China, in particular, illustrates volatility in tourism. Now the top spender in international tourism – an arguably unimaginable scenario as recently as the early 1990s – Chinese travellers spent a record $102 billion on international tourism in 2012, up 37 per cent from 2011 (UNWTO 2013b). However, tourism volatility is most frequently considered negatively, and especially in the context of economic, environmental and political shocks. Tourism in the Lebanon, for example, declined 18 per cent in 2012 over 2011 as a result of the civil war in neighbouring Syria (UNWTO 2013b), while the Philippines is likely to feel the impact of the 2013 Typhoon Haiyan for many years. Yet tourism is also highly resilient. Average annual growth in international arrivals for the decade 2000 to 2010 was 3.4 per cent (World Travel and Tourism Council 2011), despite the decade including a number of environmental, economic and political global shocks, including the World Trade Center attack in New York in 2001, the war in Iraq, the SARS crisis, the 2004 Asian Tsunami, the global financial crisis in 2008 and the Avian Influenza Pandemic in 2009. The decade saw emerging markets grow strongly (5.6 per cent) even outpacing advanced economies, which grew at 1.8 per cent (World Travel and Tourism Council 2011). In the decade overall, tourism made a direct contribution to global GDP of 9.7 per cent.

Further to globalisation, development theory and networks of power discourse, the configuration of academic and practitioner trajectories in sustainable tourism development research is compounded by semantics. Even the meaning of 'sustainable tourism development' has long been contested in academia; with many adapting it for their own specific needs. Garrod and Fyall (1998: 199) noted for example that, 'defining sustainable development in the context of tourism has become something of a cottage industry in the academic literature of late', a phenomenon which has largely remained unchanged a decade and a half later. Similar challenges exist in practitioner and private enterprise circles, where abuse of the term 'sustainability' is rife, arguably to the point of it losing all meaning. Industry greenwashing, for example, is now one of the most popular research areas in sustainable tourism development (Mowforth and Munt 2009) in response to the increasing misuse of the label. Organisations of all types in the tourism industry, from community-based ventures to local accommodation providers to global airlines, hotel groups and agents, are lining up to highlight their responsible approach to the economy, environment and society. Ryanair is 'Europe's Greenest Airline' (Ryanair 2013), the Hilton Group proudly promotes its Green Certified Hotels (Hilton 2013) and the Greenwashing report (Totem 2013) states that almost 150 green tourism certification schemes exist worldwide. There appears to be recognition that it pays to look green.

Finally, 'sustainable tourism' is a very different phenomenon to 'sustainable tourism development'. Sustainable tourism is centred on the viability of the tourism industry, with much use of the term centred on the balance of tourism and its impacts. In essence, sustainable tourism attempts to find a trade-off in its activities which help sustain the industry. This could be, for example, sustaining tourism as an economic activity through wage and supply chain negotiations. However, such initiatives may run contrary to development initiatives; sustaining the tourism industry through low wages, for example, could be argued to be against the United Nations Millennium Development Goal of eradicating extreme poverty.

A chronology of sustainable tourism development

With United Nations independent experts calling for the post-2015 development agenda to focus on equality, social protection and accountability (United Nations 2013), it seems an appropriate temporal juncture for academia and policy to pause and reflect on the achievements of the sustainable tourism development agenda over the past six decades. The last 60 years have witnessed enormous growth in tourism; spreading new wealth – but also new complexities – to all corners of the world. Great increases in the numbers of international tourists, their pattern of travel and their volume of spending, the emergence of new markets and the segmentation of industry products are among some of the key topics dominating industry discourse. Coupled with this, the rise of service economies, the dedifferentiation of work, changing structures in tourism supply chains and the democratisation of travel are all shaping why, how, where and when people travel.

Historically, tourism development theories which interrogate the potential of the industry to address global imbalances, have largely mirrored broader development paradigms (Telfer and Sharpley 2008; Mowforth and Munt 2009). A strong counter-argument exists, however, that sustainable tourism development did not fully embrace the principles and objectives of sustainable development until recently, instead retaining a primarily economic perspective (Sharpley 2000). To document this evolution, a chronology of sustainable tourism development is discussed, tracing the industry's perceived impact from primarily economic to its current broader intersection with key global issues. The industry has long been mooted as a potential driver of 'development', frequently critiqued chronologically against the structures of modernisation, dependency, neoliberalism and alternative modes of development theory, arriving at an impasse or period of 'post-development'. Each of these paradigms is addressed in turn to allow for a chronological approach to understanding current discourse on sustainable tourism development.

From modernisation to new horizons

Global attention on tourism and development is often situated as originating in the 1950s, beginning with a 'modernisation' period but dominated by Western growth models. Economic growth was the ultimate aim of the modernisation period, with a focus on trickle-down benefits, impulses and growth poles. The modernisation period provided a road map for 'traditional' or 'backward' societies to progress (Mowforth and Munt 2009: 32), generally along a traditional to modern continuum (Telfer and Sharpley 2008). The modernisation period was primarily theorised within economic frameworks by academics who sought to document and explain the impact of the imposition of Western economic principles on the undeveloped world; a world, Mowforth and Munt (2009) note, which was juxtaposed against the developed world.

The potential of tourism to act as a development vehicle remained firmly rooted in economic discourse for a significant period of time. Sharpley (2000: 4) argued that at the turn of the millennium, tourism development theory remained embedded in early modernisation theory, with tourism-induced growth strategies linked to economic notions, such as 'foreign exchange earnings, the multiplier concept and backward linkages throughout the economy'. This prevalence of economic discourse should perhaps not be surprising; tourism is an industry after all, and exists primarily to drive profits and not social or environmental change. However, despite the dominance of economic models in early tourism development theory, there appears to have been a shift in both private enterprise and policy aims over the past decade, as will be demonstrated presently.

To continue the chronology, in the 1960s, dependency theory arose in critique of the preceding modernisation period, rejecting the view that society progresses through a hypothetical traditional to modern continuum of development. As a result, underdevelopment was theorised as the outcome of domination and exploitation by developed countries. Dependency theory recognised this dominance, arguing that third world countries were not simply traditional societies or primitive versions of their Western counterparts, instead positing that underdeveloped countries have unique features and structures of their own, which configure their economy, society and environment. Essentially therefore, dependency theory proposed, not that a country would move through a hypothetical continuum, but instead offered suggestions as to why modernisation theories could or would fail to materialise.

It has been argued that dependency theory provides a useful framework for exploring the negative impacts of tourism development (for a lengthy discussion, see Mowforth and Munt 2009). In particular, the theory has been proposed as useful for exploring those impacts which arise as a result of the domination held by the industry over a destination, especially in relation to profits, leakages and networks of power. To counter such claims, it could be stated that the value of conceptualising sustainable tourism development within a dependency framework is diminishing as a result of rising globalised trade and communication and the interconnected nature of global environmental challenges, such as climate change. Nonetheless, the value of the dependency model can clearly be seen in the relationship between Western external ideals and localised tourism planning, where cultural imperialism transplants Western-based agencies modes of thinking onto third world economies. Reducing such dependency by increasing self-reliance and developing community capacity is one of the key objectives of sustainable development, and a notion discussed at length in recent years in tourism academia (for examples, see Honey 2008; Moscardo 2008; Aref 2011).

By the 1970s, development policies had returned to classical economic theories, suggesting that state intervention restricted, rather than furthered, development goals, and in particular the economic aims of private enterprise. Proponents argued that government intervention in the market resulted in inefficiencies and that free market capitalism would only flourish with market deregulation and privatisation. Such principles were driven by powerful global actors including governments, financial institutions, including the International Monetary Fund and the World Bank, and private corporations which variously provided grants, structural adjustment lending programmes (SALPs) and donor assistance to recipient countries with the agreement that regulatory procedures would be relaxed or removed. While such SALPs ultimately failed to decrease poverty in many cases, the impressive growth figures associated with tourism in this period made it an attractive development option for governments.

It could be suggested that the promise of tourism to alleviate poverty and address resource concerns emerged in this period, and as such, the 1970s saw many countries adopt tourism into national growth strategies. As a result, an era of neoliberalism was ushered in, with deregulation, privatisation and wealth creation configuring the industry. Although most tourism development chronologies move quickly through this neoliberalism 'decade' to a period of alternative development around the 1980s, as with modernisation theory, much contemporary commentary on tourism development is still situated within neoliberal paradigms. In addition, in recent years, academics have reconfigured neoliberal tourism development discussion to question cause and effect. Duffy (2013), for example, has argued that tourism is not just *reflective* of neoliberalism, but is in fact a core *driver* of neoliberalism, given that it is one of the processes which allows neoliberal norms to globally disseminate, through the movement of people, capital and ideas. And, further to tourism's ability to simply spread the principles of neoliberalism, the industry even facilitates neoliberal agendas by creating commodities to counter the environmental, economic and social crises which it created in the first place. As a blunt example, tourism has, on one hand, through its rapid global growth, contributed to climate change and melting polar ice caps, but on the other hand, as an industry it has responded in kind through the creation of new Arctic and Antarctic cruise tourism products, namely 'last chance tourism'.

However, despite the prevalence of neoliberal critique in contemporary tourism development discourse, the apparent failure of mainstream economic growth-driven models purported in the 1970s and 1980s resulted in a search for a new development paradigm. Alternative models of development were proposed, which moved away from Western and institutional driven modes towards community-based or bottom-up approaches. The principles of the alternative development movement ultimately became close to synonymous with sustainable development, given its environmental ethic, its advocacy of decentralisation and its inclusion of issues such as gender equality, empowerment, poverty alleviation, environmental protection and conflict resolution (Sharpley 2009). In tourism, the change was particularly evident, as concern shifted from the economy towards the environment, humanity and society. Alternative tourism strategies emerging at the time included ecotourism, community-based tourism and pro-poor tourism (PPT), among others, with the general premise of all being that, as these were a departure from previous mass tourism models, they must bring greater benefits and have lower negative impacts than their predecessors.

Quite simply, alternative tourism development's principal objectives involved developing tourism that 'is appropriate to local environmental, social and cultural values' (Sharpley 2009: 43). While such aims themselves are admirable, in recent years alternative modes of development in tourism have been heavily criticised, given that, just like their predecessors, alternative tourism models also rely on international markets and environmental exploitation. Duffy (2013: 609), for example, argues that 'there is little difference between various forms of "alternative tourism" (such as ecotourism) and mass tourism', given that both are interlinked with global capitalism. In the case of ecotourism, the connection is striking; nature is conserved primarily for its market value (Honey 2008; Duffy 2013). Other critics of alternative tourism development models have pointed to semantics difficulties (Meyer 2012); for example, the term 'community-based tourism', pointing to the challenges of even establishing what a community is, before getting to the more pertinent question of who benefits from such ventures.

Despite the tensions in temporally situating sustainable tourism development, there is no doubt that in recent years academic literature has switched focus from analysis of solely economic impacts towards the role of tourism development in peace building, poverty eradication, establishment and protection of workers' and human rights, resource use, environmental change and many other global imbalance issues, which tie more directly with the sustainable development agenda than the previous primarily economic perspective of tourism. The intersection between tourism and conflict provides an example of the potential of the new agenda.

The 'First Global Conference: Tourism: A Vital Force for Peace' was held in Vancouver in 1988, a conference which subsequently drove an enthusiasm among academics that tourism could play a role in sustainable development after conflict. While this interest diminished throughout the 1990s, there has been a recent resurgence in interest in tourism's potential in peace building (Pernecky 2010), which must be welcomed considering the scale, impact and number of ongoing conflicts worldwide. Authors have posited that tourism development after conflict has the capacity to normalise society and bring economic benefits (Causevic and Lynch 2011) and even (re)establish a positive destination image (Hall 2002). Studies exploring tourism's complex relationship with peace and conflict in Cambodia (Winter 2007), Rwanda (Friedrich and Johnston 2013; Hohenhaus 2013) and Northern Ireland (McDowell 2008) are among some of the many publications to emerge examining aspects of post-conflict tourism development in recent years. Proponents point to the success of tourism in several post-conflict countries, particularly Northern Ireland, Croatia and Bosnia-Herzegovina, as evidence that tourism can intersect and further development goals beyond simple economic benefits.

Tourism after conflict poignantly illustrates the intersection between development and society, as has been argued, to sensationalise, trivialise and spectacularise war, on one hand (Sharpley and Stone 2009; Bowman and Pezzullo 2009), but spread important genocide prevention messages on the other (Charlesworth 1996; MacDonald 2006). Indeed, the notion that tourism has a role to play in resolving, or exacerbating, conflict has been institutionalised in academia; various bodies and publications, such as the International Institute for Peace through Tourism (founded 1986, IIPT 2014) and the *Journal of Tourism and Peace Research* (published since 2010) are but some of the many conducting research on these topics. Much academic research has queried the role of tourism in post-conflict society (Winter 2007; McDowell 2008) and such research complements the long-standing private consultancy sector's interest in the intersection (D'Amore 1988). However, whether or not the industry contributes positively to conflict resolution and peace appears to depend primarily on local variables.

Returning to the broader analysis of sustainability, despite suggestions that a search for a new paradigm is ongoing, the alternative development agenda remains particularly evident in the industry; the tourism industry generally appears to recognise the rewards which come with responsibility and implementation of ethical standards in tourism development. However, recognition is most probably based on the economic rewards arising from consumer perceptions in many cases. While such recognition could result in economic greenwashing in some cases, the less cynical would suggest it more likely comes from a recognition that resources are limited and that sustainable tourism and sustainable tourism development are not necessarily incompatible. For example, the World Travel Market (WTM) in London, one of the world's biggest tourism industry trade fairs, holds an awards ceremony on its WTM World Responsible Tourism Day, during their annual meeting (World Travel Market 2013). These awards include recognition for work on local economies, child protection, water conservation and wildlife protection. Other organisations, such as the International Tourism Partnership (ITP), which proclaims itself as 'The voice for environmental and social responsibility in the hospitality industry', conduct similar schemes (International Tourism Partnership 2013). In 2013, the ITP launched guidance for hotels on addressing human trafficking in addition to its carbon emissions reduction collaborations and water scarcity research initiatives. In 2013, Tourism Concern, the tourism NGO, launched petitions to tackle what they describe as an alarming rise in orphanage volunteer tourism (Tourism Concern 2013). Others have similar rights-based focuses: Skal International, for example, a global tourism trade association with over 20,000 members, repeatedly raise human rights issues in their publications. Recent signs of recognition of this breadth of possibilities among practitioners include the creation of a United Nations' World Tourism Organisation Global Code of Ethics for Tourism (GCET) (UNWTO 2013c), or Tourism Concern's specific campaign on Ethical Trekking, for example (Tourism Concern 2014). However, such codes have existed for decades, and, when examined, have rarely been shown to have the desired effect. Hall (2010), for example, examines the 1992 Convention on Biological Diversity, noting that few countries have successfully implemented the guidelines with relation to tourism. Su, Hall and Ozanne (2013) note a similar situation in relation to implementation of codes in Taiwanese hotels.

To conclude, various other lens have been proposed to situate sustainable tourism development, particularly in recent years as the period of alternative development is subjected to critique in search of a new paradigm. Sharpley (2000), for example, suggests examining tourism's impact against the sustainable development fundamental principles of holism, futurity and equity. Mowforth and Munt (2009), as noted previously, structure the discussion of tourism development impacts against theories of globalisation, development and networks of power, but also when they resolve that, given there is no all-encompassing definition of the sustainable development concept anyway, propose that tourist activities can be individually examined against a set of sustainability criteria: society, environment, economy, education, local participation, conservation and culture. However, which approach has the most value remains to be seen.

Is there an academy-practitioner divide?

While the sustainable tourism development agenda has broadened to incorporate issues such as conflict, its main support in policy circles remains linked to its poverty alleviation potential, albeit that conceptualisations of poverty have long moved away from reductionist and income-based principles towards those which incorporate environmental security, equality and human rights. Despite this widened agenda, there is little consensus on the actual impact of so-called 'pro-poor tourism' in the developing world (Mitchell and Ashley 2010). Like 'sustainable development', understanding of the term 'pro-poor tourism', its tourism offspring, is contested among academics (Meyer 2012). The term is even further contested between academics and practitioners, who are constrained by their own job targets; university research audits, on one hand, on the ground destination impacts, on the other. As a result, sustainable tourism development research represents a significant theory and practice divide and it is crucial for the credibility of future research that attempts are made to close this gap.

The divide exists for a number of reasons. Academic interest in sustainable tourism development research has tended to explore social, cultural and environmental impacts, tourism structures and processes, spatial analysis, tourism and conservation, community-based tourism and alternative tourism development paradigms. While this broad range of themes is not without merit, it has been criticised for some fundamental failings. Mitchell and Ashley (2010) pointed to the academy's failure to study the economic impact of tourism on the beneficiaries themselves, the development of pro-poor research in silos and the disappointing levels of attention given by academics to differentiating tourism segments. The body of sustainable tourism development research as a whole has largely ignored local voices, the private sector and the tourist experience, focusing instead much more prominently on policy and impacts (Meyer 2012). In recent years, however, research has started to incorporate local voices, with Troung et al. (2014), for example, researching local perceptions on pro-poor tourism in Vietnam, and Akyeampong (2011) examining local expectations of tourism in Ghana. Despite such publications, the majority of work in the field remains structural in nature, and the neglect of local voices will likely take some years to redress. Further to these criticisms, it could be argued that a significant proportion of academic pro-poor tourism research is narrow in scope, focusing on case studies, which are almost exclusively negative in nature and frequently highly dubious of tourism's development potential. A further criticism by Peeters (2012) brings us back to a key underpinning philosophy of sustainable development; noting that while it is easy to be attracted to the promises of pro-poor tourism, we must consider it within the context of finite resources. How can tourism eliminate poverty, on one hand, yet reduce its environmental impact, on the other?

Practitioners have been more supportive of the potential of tourism to develop sustainably. Tourism can help countries 'to combat poverty, diversify their economies and pursue pro-poor inclusive growth strategies' (UNDP 2011: 6). The industry is frequently thus situated, primarily because it 'is consumed at the point of intervention, even low-skilled workers in remote areas can become tourism exporters' (ibid.: 4). Such views provoke regular criticism, however, from both within and outside practitioner circles. There has been caution among policy-makers, especially with the acknowledgement that tourism is not a panacea for development challenges. In academia, Mitchell and Ashley (2010) point, for example, towards the validity of policy research, noting that 'grey literature' must be read with scepticism, given its lack of peer review. Further to this, several have argued the incompatibility of mass tourism and environmental protection (Gössling et al. 2013; Hall et al. 2013). Peeters (2012: 143) additionally notes the physical environment can be neglected in tourism development discourse, arguing, for example, that 'large scale PPT is strongly incompatible with the desire to avoid dangerous climate change'. Finally, in a criticism which could apply to both academics and practitioners, the term 'pro-poor tourism' itself could be criticised, given that the word 'poor' has negative connotations and is unlikely to endear itself to consumers, businesses or local populations.

While the tone in the academic literature has become increasingly critical in recent years, it has long been argued by academics, that for practitioners, much project work in tourism development is constrained by clearly defined parameters as opposed to the more general and idealistic world-changing notions available to academics (Jenkins 1999; Meyer 2012). This very point threatens the sustainable development potential of the industry; much sustainable tourism development research is not conducted for altruistic purposes. However, levying such an accusation against practitioners would be unfair; as Meyer (2012) notes, academics and policy-makers are just as acutely aware of the restrictions, barriers and challenges which constrain their work.[1] Perhaps any criticism would be better levied against the academy which has failed to adequately lead in relation to the development potential of the industry, suggest mechanisms for removing practitioner barriers, or adequately drive change in private enterprise or consumption habits.

Given the ever increasing spatial and societal reach of tourism, as noted in the introduction, we must therefore question who has the responsibility to direct future agendas, minimise negative impact and realise the potential of the industry. In essence, how can the process of tourism development be made more sustainable? This has long been an issue in tourism academia. In 1999, for example, Jenkins suggested that tourism academia rarely influences tourism planning or development and that consultancy work, if carried out by academics, is usually derived from experience and is methodologically standardised. However, optimism has appeared in recent years. Hall and Brown (2012) note that there has been a welcome increase in the volume of self-critical voices in tourism academia, which reflect on the sociology of tourism academia and tourism academia successes to date, which propose methods to reduce the academy–practitioner divide and particularly the physical and institutional barriers which knowledge transfer faces.

With regards to tourism synergy barriers, it is vital to find the common ground between the academy and practitioners, but it must be acknowledged that the nature of tourism as a phenomenon means it attracts a diversity of stakeholders, which is in itself likely to be a barrier to sustainable development. Goeldner and Ritchie (2008) note that there is a fragmentation of tourism studies, which is informed by more than 20 disciplines. However, such a range of informant disciplines is both a strength and weakness of the discipline, as noted by McKercher (2009), and, as demonstrated in this very Handbook, is no different from the subject of sustainable development itself. Further to this, even greater breadth exists, in the industry when compared to academia. Although bringing these disparate interests together is fraught with challenges, it is clear at least that most stakeholders suggest that tourism, if conducted through appropriate policy frameworks, a dynamic private sector, responsible consumers and altruistic research, can translate policy measures into a sustainable development tool (Mitchell and Ashley 2010; UNDP 2011; Scheyvens 2012), an environmental conservation tool (Honey 2008) and contribute to the normalisation of society after conflict (Causevic and Lynch 2011).

In terms of bridging the academy–practitioner gap, it must be noted that critical voices in the literature increasingly identify both tourism consultants and academics as having self-interests rather than consultee interests at heart (Hall and Brown 2012; Meyer 2012). At best, write Hall and Brown, the tourism consultant brings much-needed expertise and experience, but at worst 'may parachute in and helicopter out with insensitivity to and of ignorance of local cultures' (2012: 230). For Hall and Brown, this self-interest arises from developed world administrations' desire to use employment measures as indicators of success, changing universities from institutions with high moral authority into mechanistic skills training agencies. As a result, original thinking has been given a back seat, with employability, research audits and income generation, for example, some of the key phenomena driving the higher education agenda. The market-like behaviours which configure academia (Rhoades and Slaughter 2004) have further resulted in universities reflecting the incompatibility of business need for profit and sustainability. This is of course, as opposed to driving any significant change.

Outlook

Highlighting the gaps is but a small step and addressing the divide must be a critical concern. Several solutions have been proposed; albeit they are largely practical, as opposed to conceptual in nature. These include increasing and deepening collaboration opportunities between researchers and practitioners, improving practitioner access to published research and increasing the frequency and quality of jointly developed projects which involve academics, practitioners and local voices. Meyer (2012) suggests that there are a number of intervention points, including what academics teach and what they research. One of the most salient points made in relation to this debate refers to the publication of research, by both academics and practitioners. For both to speak to each other more directly, practitioners need improved access to academic journals and conferences, while academics need improved access to grey literature, and what is often client-confidential industry research.

Overall, there is some cautious optimism in the literature, particularly in terms of who is conducting tourism research. Ryan (2009) points to the volume of non-native English-speaking contributors in *Tourism Management*, one of the top-ranked tourism journals. However, many of these papers are positivist in orientation and do not challenge global hegemony. From a practitioner perspective, there is some cause for optimism; in 2014, for example, the UNWTO hosted a 'Bridging Theory and Practice' conference in Mexico (UNWTO 2013d), aimed to improve the ability of 'stakeholders to foster innovation in their approach to the development process'. However, the great question remains of whether or not increased influence of practitioner perspectives will actually lead to more sustainable forms of tourism development.

Going forward, it may also be useful if academics and practitioners further explore the notion that sustainable tourism development should not be thought of as a goal; given the volume of stakeholders in the industry, it is unlikely that consensus could ever be found on what constitutes sustainable development. Instead it may be beneficial to consider sustainable tourism development as a process which can lead to change or reduced impact and improvements in the industry. True sustainable tourism development needs academics, policy-makers, consumers and academics who recognise the oxymoronic nature of sustainable tourism growth and understand the dynamism of economy, society and environment. Future growth in industry should focus primarily on the value of experience for both host and guest, and not on visitor numbers or expenditure. This is evident to some extent in industry, which often awards certification based on improvements and not already established norms.[2]

Finally, though this chapter provides only a snapshot of the fragmented, but arguably continuous, nature of the sustainable tourism development discourse, it would be remiss to conclude without acknowledgement of the importance of the consumer voice in destination sustainability. There is clearly a need to confront industry with demands for greener service; a triple bottom line has been proposed and critiqued which protects socio-cultural and environmental interests as well as the business need for economic success. Williams and Ponsford (2009) have argued that this notion will become more important in future; the preservation of destinations within a wider global context of diminishing quality suggest tourists will be influenced by environmental standards. However, as tourists are primarily driven by price, Hall (2013) has suggested that a suite of approaches is needed to modify tourist behaviour towards a more sustainable form of tourism consumption. Such approaches include nudging, social marketing, education and market-based solutions. Such notions highlight the complexity of tourism, arguing that there is a growing need, on one hand, for new tools and technologies to facilitate consumer understanding of tourism supply chains, environmental impact and rights issues, and, on the other, a need for proposals which reduce attitude–actions gaps in place consumption. Given the increases in international tourist arrivals noted throughout, it is anticipated that this will continue to be a flourishing area of academy and practitioner research in future.

Notes

1 For an example, see the United Nations World Tourism Organisation 'Sustainable Tourism-Eliminating Poverty initiative', or ST-EP, (UNWTO 2013a), which acknowledges and attempts to overcome the limitations of tourism in eradicating extreme poverty.
2 For an example, see 'A Simple User's Guide to Certification for Sustainable Tourism and Ecotourism' (The International Ecotourism Society, n.d.), which describes how the ISO 14001 standard for environmental management systems is awarded due to year-on-year improvements and not pre-established achievements.

References

Akyeampong, O.A. (2011) Pro-poor tourism: residents' expectations, experiences and perceptions in the Kakum National Park area of Ghana. *Journal of Sustainable Tourism*, 19(2): 197–213.

Aref, F. (2011) Barriers to community capacity building for tourism development in communities in Shiraz, Iran. *Journal of Sustainable Tourism*, 19(3): 347–359.

Ateljevic, I., Pritchard, A. and Morgan, N. (2007) *The Critical Turn in Tourism Studies: Innovative Research Methodologies*. Oxford: Elsevier.

Bianchi, R. (2009) The 'critical turn' in tourism studies: a radical critique. *Tourism Geographies*, 11(4): 484–504.

Blanchard, L. and Higgins-Desboilles, F. (2013) *Peace through Tourism: Promoting Human Security Through International Citizenship*. London: Routledge.

Bowman, M. S. and Pezzullo, P. C. (2009) What's so 'dark' about 'Dark Tourism'?: Death, tours, and performance. *Tourist Studies*, 9(3): 187–202.

Butcher, B. J. (2011) Can ecotourism contribute to tackling poverty? The importance of 'symbiosis'. *Current Issues in Tourism*, 14(3): 295–307.

Causevic, S. and Lynch, P. (2011) Phoenix tourism, post-conflict tourism role. *Annals of Tourism Research*, 38(3): 780–800.

Charlesworth, A. (1996) Teaching the Holocaust through landscape study. In R. L. Millen (ed.) *New Perspectives on the Holocaust, A Guide for Teachers and Scholars*. New York: New York University Press.

D'Amore, L. (1988) Tourism; a vital force for peace. *Tourism Management*, 9(2): 151–154.

Duffy, R. (2013) The international political economy of tourism and the neoliberalisation of nature: challenges posed by selling close interactions with animals. *Review of International Political Economy*, 20(3): 605–626.

Friedrich, M. and Johnston, T. (2013) The memorialisation and commodification of the Rwandan genocide. *Journal of Tourism & Cultural Change*, 11(4): 302–320.

Garrod, B. and Fyall, A. (1998) Beyond the rhetoric of sustainable tourism? *Tourism Management*, 19(3): 199–212.

Goeldner, C. R. and Ritchie, J. R. B. (2008) *Tourism: Principles, Practices, Philosophies*, 10th edn. Toronto: Wiley and Sons.

Gössling, S., Scott, D. and Hall, C.M. (2013) Challenges of tourism in a low-carbon economy. *WIRES Climate Change*, 4(6): 525–538.

Hall, C. M. (2010) Tourism and the implementation of the Convention on Biological Diversity. *Journal of Heritage Tourism*, 5(4): 267–284.

Hall, C. M. (2013) Framing behavioural approaches to understanding and governing sustainable tourism consumption: beyond neoliberalism, 'nudging' and 'green growth'? *Journal of Sustainable Tourism*, 21(7): 1091–1109.

Hall, C. M., Scott, D. and Gössling, S. (2013) The primacy of climate change for sustainable international tourism. *Sustainable Development*, 21(2): 112–121.

Hall, D. (2002) Brand development, tourism and national identity: the re-imaging of former Yugoslavia. *The Journal of Brand Management*, 9(4/5): 323–334.

Hall, D. and Brown, F. (2012) 'Post colonialism', responsibility and tourism academics: where's the connection? In T.V Singh (ed.) *Critical Debates in Tourism*. Bristol: Channel View, pp. 228–233.

Hilton (2013) Think trees: Green-certified hotels [Online]. Available at: http://doubletree3.hilton.com/en/about/greenhotels.html (accessed 20 December 2013).

Hohenhaus, P. (2013) Commemorating and commodifying the Rwandan genocide: memorial sites in a politically difficult context. In E. Frew and L. White (eds) *Dark Tourism and Place Identity*. London: Routledge, pp. 142–155.

Hollinshead, K. (2009) The 'worldmaking' prodigy of tourism: the reach and power of tourism in the dynamics of change and transformation. *Tourism Analysis*, 14(1): 139–152.

Honey, M. (2008) *Ecotourism and Sustainable Development: Who Owns Paradise?* Washington, DC: Island Press.

IIPT (International Institute for Peace through Tourism) (2014) Report. [Online] Available at: www.iipt.org/ (accessed 20 March 2014).

International Tourism Partnership (2013) Human trafficking [Online]. Available at: www.tourismpartnership.org/what-we-do/key-issues/human-trafficking (accessed 20 December 2013).

Jenkins, C. L. (1999) Tourism academics and tourism practitioners: bridging the great divide. In D. G. Pearce and R.W. Butler (eds) *Contemporary Issues in Tourism and Development*. London: Routledge, pp. 52–63.

Lemelin, H., Dawson, J., Stewart, E., Maher, P. and Lueck, M. (2010) Last-chance tourism: the boom, doom, and gloom of visiting vanishing destinations. *Current Issues in Tourism*, 13(5): 477–493.

Macdonald, S. (2006) Mediating heritage: tour guides at the former Nazi Party rally grounds, Nuremberg. *Tourist Studies*, 6(2): 199–238.

McDowell, S. (2008) Selling conflict heritage through tourism in peacetime Northern Ireland: transforming conflict or exacerbating difference? *International Journal of Heritage Studies*, 14(5): 405–421.

McKercher, B. (2010) The state of tourism research: a personal reflection. *Tourism Recreation Research*, 34(2): 135–142.

Meyer, D. (2012) Pro-poor tourism: is there actually much rhetoric? And, if so, whose? In T.V. Singh (ed.) *Critical Debates in Tourism*. Bristol: Channel View, pp. 132–136.

Mitchell, J. and Ashley, C. (2010) *Tourism and Poverty Reduction: Pathways to Prosperity*. London: Earthscan.

Moscardo, G. (ed.) (2008) *Building Community Capacity for Tourism Development*. Wallingford: CABI.

Mowforth, M. and Munt, I. (2009) *Tourism and Sustainability, Development, Globalisation and New Tourism in the Third World*, 3rd edn. London: Routledge.

Peeters, P. (2012) Pro-poor tourism, climate change and sustainable development. In T.V. Singh (ed.) *Critical Debates in Tourism*. Bristol: Channel View, pp. 141–144.

Pernecky, T. (2010) The being of tourism. *The Journal of Tourism and Peace Research*, 1(1): 1–15.

Rhoades, G. and Slaughter, S. (2004) Academic capitalism in the new economy: challenges and choices. *American Academic*, 1(1): 37–59.

Ryan, C. (2009) Editorial: thirty years of tourism management. *Tourism Management*, 26(5): 657–662.

Ryanair (2013) Ryanair and the environment [Online]. Available at: www.ryanair.com/en/about/ryanair-and-the-environment (accessed 20 December 2013).

Scheyvens, R. (2012) Pro-poor tourism: is there value beyond the rhetoric? In T.V. Singh (ed.) *Critical Debates in Tourism*. Bristol: Channel View, pp. 124–132.

Sharpley, R. (2000) Tourism and sustainable development: exploring the theoretical divide. *Journal of Sustainable Tourism*, 8(1): 1–19.

Sharpley, R. (2009) *Tourism Development and the Environment: Beyond Sustainability?* London: Earthscan.

Sharpley, R. and Stone, P. R. (2009) (Re)presenting the macabre: interpretation, kitschification and authenticity. In R. Sharpley and P. R. Stone (eds) *The Darker Side of Travel: The Theory and Practice of Dark Tourism*. Bristol: Channel View Publications, pp. 109–128.

Su, Y.-P., Hall, C. M., and Ozanne, L. (2013) Hospitality industry responses to climate change: a benchmark study of Taiwanese tourist hotels. *Asia Pacific Journal of Tourism Research*, 18(2): 92–107.

Telfer, D. J. and Sharpley, R. A. (2008) *Tourism and Development in the Developing World*. London: Routledge.

The International Ecotourism Society (n.d.) *A Simple User's Guide to Certification for Sustainable Tourism and Ecotourism* [Online]. Available at: www.ecotourism.org/certification-and-standards (accessed 20 December 2013).

Totem (2013) TotemTourism GREENWASH Report [Online]. Available at: www.totemtourism.com/sustainable-tourism-reports-and-masterclasses.html (accessed 20 December 2013).

Tourism Concern (2013) Orphanages [Online]. Available at: www.tourismconcern.org.uk/orphanages.html (accessed 23 December 2013).

Tourism Concern (2014) Ethical trekking [Online]. Available at: www.tourismconcern.org.uk/ethical-trekking.html (accessed 23 March 2014).

Troung, V. D., Hall, C. M. and Garry, T. (2014) Tourism and poverty alleviation: perceptions and experiences of poor people in Sapa, Vietnam. *Journal of Sustainable Tourism*, DOI: 10.1080/09669582.2013.871019.

UNDP (United Nations Development Programme)(2011) Tourism and poverty reduction strategies in the integrated framework for least developed countries. Discussion Paper [Online]. Available at: http://unwto.org/sites/all/files/pdf/undp_discussion_paper_tourism_and_poverty_reduction_strategies_in_the_integrated_framework_for_least_developed_countries.pdf (accessed 20 December 2013).

United Nations (2013) The Right to Equality in Post-2015. A speech by John Hendra in Oslo [Online]. Available at:www.unwomen.org/en/news/stories/2013/6/the-right-to-equality-in-post2015-a-speech-by-john-hendra-in-oslo/ (accessed 20 December 2013).

UNWTO (2013a) Sustainable tourism: eliminating poverty [Online]. Available at: http://step.unwto.org/content/background-and-objectives (accessed 20 December 2013).

UNWTO (2013b) UNWTO World Tourism Barometer [Online]. Available at: http://mkt.unwto.org/en/barometer (accessed 20th December 2013).

UNWTO (2013c) Global Code of Ethics for Tourism [Online]. Available at: http://ethics.unwto.org/en/content/global-code-ethics-tourism (accessed 20 December 2013).

UNWTO (2013d) Innovation in tourism: bridging theory and practice [Online]. Available at: http://know.unwto.org/event/call-papers-2nd-unwto-global-knowledge-network-forum-innovation-tourism-bridging-theory-and-pr (accessed 20 December 2013).

UNWTO (2014) International tourism exceeds expectations with arrivals up by 52 million in 2013 [Online]. Available at: http://media.unwto.org/press-release/2014-01-20/international-tourism-exceeds-expectations-arrivals-52-million-2013 (accessed 20 March 2014).

Williams, P. W. and Ponsford, I. F. (2009) Confronting tourism's environmental paradox: transitioning for sustainable tourism. *Futures*, 41: 396–404.

Winter, T. (2007) *Post-Conflict Heritage, Postcolonial Tourism: Tourism, Politics and Development at Angkor.* London: Routledge.

World Travel and Tourism Council (2011) Travel and tourism 2011 [Online]. Available at: www.wttc.org/site_media/uploads/downloads/traveltourism2011.pdf, (accessed 20 December 2013).

World Travel and Tourism Council (2013) Travel and tourism economic impact, Thailand 2013 [Online]. Available at: www.wttc.org/site_media/uploads/downloads/thailand2013.pdf, (accessed 20 December 2013).

World Travel Market (2013) WTM Responsible Tourism Day [Online]. Available at: www.wtmresponsibletourism.com/ (accessed 20 December 2013).

17

FOOD AND SUSTAINABLE DEVELOPMENT

How should we feed the world?

Colin Sage

Introduction

The food system represents one of the principal challenges for moving societies toward a more sustainable form of development. Accumulating scientific evidence is demonstrating that what we eat has a significant bearing on the global environment. Whether through emissions of greenhouse gases, the drawing down of freshwater stocks or impacts upon biological diversity, food production and supply have a host of consequences for resources, ecological services and waste sinks worldwide. Yet at the same time it is becoming apparent that agriculture is increasingly vulnerable to processes of environmental change and the depletion of resources. Events over the past decade – marked by rising and volatile global food prices – have given cause to believe that production systems may be reaching resource limits and therefore are in need of an urgent rethink. It might be argued that never has the issue of sustainable development been more needed in relation to our food supply than at present.

How we will feed the world in the decades ahead is becoming a highly contested arena of competing visions but one where *sustainability* is frequently cited in the discourses of opposing protagonists. On the one hand, there remains a hugely powerful status quo that regards the current predicament of global malnourishment as vindication for the rejuvenation of an agri-industrial model that we might label as *productivism*. This paradigm extols the merits of next generation biotechnology and nanotechnology to deliver greater output (by between 70–100 per cent) in order to feed a projected population of 9 billion by 2050 (Beddington 2010; Scrinis and Lyons 2010; Tester and Langridge 2010). While the emphasis remains on technological solutions and market-driven innovations, an important strand of this approach ('sustainable intensification') argues that greater agricultural productivity could be achieved with reduced environmental impacts (Royal Society 2009; Garnett and Godfray 2012).

A different vision for feeding the world places much greater emphasis on sustainable development principles. Here, it is recognized that a more fundamental set of changes are required than tinkering around with technical efficiencies. Perhaps the most comprehensive case for a change of direction has been set out by the International Assessment of Agricultural Knowledge, Science and Technology for Development (IAASTD 2009). The reports, which resulted from a multi-stakeholder process involving over 400 scientists and 100 countries over three years, ultimately argued that industrial agriculture alone would not resolve the problems of hunger and poverty and was incapable of adapting to the environmental challenges that lay immediately ahead. As it so bluntly noted: 'Business as usual is no longer an option' (2009: 3). Here, sustainability goals are placed in the context of multiple uncertainties, changing environmental conditions and poor nutrition and food quality. While the IAASTD findings have been subject to marginalization in mainstream agricultural policy circles (Feldman and Biggs 2012), the process has arguably served to open a space for wider deliberation around food and sustainable development. Most especially, debate has helped to make clear that sustainability considerations can no longer be confined to the realm of agricultural policy alone but must firmly embrace matters of consumption.

This chapter addresses the urgency of developing a whole food systems analysis to the way in which we feed ourselves now and into the future. Such an approach reveals just how tightly coupled the food system has become, not only with environmental systems across a range of scales, but also with corporate control. These latter connections are conspicuous and are deepening throughout the length of the food chain: from the corporate seed and agri-chemical interests that are extending intellectual property rights over the basic building blocks of life, through to the efforts of big food in reshaping consumption patterns in poor and middle-income countries throughout the world. Setting out a sustainable alternative, then, is not simply a matter of restoring some basic ecological and social principles to food: it is about speaking truth to power.

The chapter first establishes how we might approach the notion of sustainability in relation to food before going on to trace the development of the global agri-food system. It then proceeds to explore some fundamental issues around the sustainable production and, then, the sustainable consumption of food. It will be argued that any hope that we might have of achieving sustainability within the global food system as a whole requires challenging prevailing assumptions about consumers' rights to 'cheap' food and to the maintenance of current 'Western-style' dietary practices. For it is now well established that the low price paid by consumers for their food conceals huge externalities up and down the supply chain (Pretty et al. 2005; Carolan 2011). Moreover, one of the most problematic food categories is livestock products, and the chapter will explore the implications of rising consumption of meat and dairy produce in middle-income countries.

Ultimately, the contemporary global food system cannot be regarded as a success when there are around one billion people hungry and malnourished, a further one billion or more regarded as over-nourished (and overweight), and where health services around the world are dealing with rising levels of diet-related ill-health. A system that has achieved the massification of food by focusing upon throughput is creating an indelible legacy of ecological disruption and high levels of waste; landlessness and social injustice; and a burden of nutritional insecurity and malnourishment. How we feed the global population in the decades ahead *really is* a matter for debate.

Food and sustainability

It is straightforward to assemble a list of the multiple first-order environmental impacts associated with food production: deforestation and land use change; loss of biological diversity; soil erosion; freshwater depletion and contamination; climate change as well as other forms of pollution to air. There are also economic threats to the survival of farms and rural communities unable to maintain livelihoods as a consequence of agricultural policies that encourage scale expansion, labour saving and the extraction of value from local economies. Itemizing such impacts reveals how many diverse sub-systems are threatened to varying degrees according to the different ways used to produce many kinds of food.

One approach to conceptualizing sustainability is to view these different sub-systems as constituting a relative equilibrium held within an arrangement of functional integrity; that is, threats to any one of these sub-systems represent a threat to total system sustainability. Indeed, Thompson cautions against tampering with any functioning sub-system for fear that it might 'upset the complex interconnection of the whole' (2010: 22). This relative equilibrium approach, where elements are held together within a notional 'balance of nature', represents one approach in sustainability thinking but is now increasingly displaced. Arising from work in ecology, the concepts of resilience and stability have become more widely employed and inform the notion of 'complex adaptive management of social-ecological systems'. As Folke has observed, 'managing for resilience enhances the likelihood of sustaining desirable pathways for development in changing environments where the future is unpredictable and surprise is likely' (2006: 254).

Given the range and scale of the environmental and developmental challenges faced by the global agri-food system – as well as the conspicuous failure of so many policy interventions to date (e.g. the 1996 World Food Summit goal of cutting by half the number of malnourished people by 2015, or the Millennium Development Goals) – it is clear we need a different approach to global target setting than that which has prevailed hitherto. Moreover, if sustainability is to become a genuine part of a new global food equation, then complexity, dynamism and resilience will become critical concepts. These are terms which are central to an approach developed by Leach et al. (2010). Their approach explicitly rejects standard equilibrium thinking and the kinds of interventions that follow from it, one where blueprint models, such as those comprising 'magic bullet' technologies, could be rolled out from the laboratory to the field. Rather, by highlighting the interactions between different systems (social, ecological, technological) that occur across multiple scales (global, national, local) and play out in different ways in particular contexts, their approach is alert to longer-term stresses and disruptive shocks originating from diverse sources. The key to this is not always seeking to control and eliminate a problem but developing the capacity of a system to adapt to its occurrence.

For example, modern agriculture has come to rely upon applications of chemical pesticides to control outbreaks of crop pests and this has brought in its wake damage to human health and natural resources as well as pest resurgence arising from complex ecological feedbacks. In this respect integrated pest management practices have become a proven and sustainable alternative. A second example might be with regard to changing weather systems including climate drying that requires more profound forms of adaptation, including changing cropping systems, farming practices and the development of non-agricultural strategies. Here, a complex adaptive approach demonstrates flexibility but also alerts us to the many different ways in which people understand system functions and value different outcomes pursuing even contrasting pathways by which to achieve them.

At the time of writing, the Report of Working Group II of the IPCC's Fifth Assessment Report had just been published (IPCC WGII 2014). Of greatest media attention have been its warnings about future food supply with the Report highlighting the likely effects of climate change over coming decades for crop yields. It notes how across tropical and temperate regions temperature increases of 2°C or more over late twentieth-century levels will reduce yields by about 2 per cent per decade. This is particularly worrying given that a large proportion of the world's calories are provided by a small number of staple crops. Of the 10,000 plant species that have been used for human food since the origin of agriculture, only 150–200 species have been commercially cultivated, of which only four – rice, wheat, maize and potatoes – supply 50 per cent of the world's energy needs, while 30 crops provide 90 per cent (Hunter and Fanzo 2013). Consequently, the capacity of the global food system to produce sufficient calories rests heavily upon the performance of a small number of staple crops under changing climatic conditions. For the IPCC Report goes on to note, first, the likelihood of increased variability between regions, with some – especially in the tropics – expected to experience significantly falling yields (of >25 per cent) by 2060; and, second, the greater risks associated with extreme weather events (including flood and drought), both in terms of frequency and magnitude, which are likely to disrupt the stability of food supply arrangements (IPCC WGII 2014).

Such scenarios underline how all aspects of food security – availability, accessibility, utilization and price stability – will be affected by climate change and explains why there is increasing emphasis on adaptation with a view to ensuring greater resilience to these multiple and diverse threats. Under these circumstances it is difficult to see how the model of productivism represents an appropriate way forward for the global agri-food system, for the drive to double food production is unlikely to result in significantly fewer food insecure and hungry people. Yet before we can make the case for a food system that is underpinned by sustainability principles, it is first necessary to trace the technological basis of modern agriculture.

The rise of modern agricultural production

Since the Neolithic Revolution some 12,000 years ago, humans have been engaged in transforming natural habitats and utilizing resources in attempts to extend and intensify agricultural production. Subsequent waves of technological innovation involving mechanical, chemical and biological engineering have all contributed to rising levels of productivity. During the late seventeenth, eighteenth and early nineteenth centuries, a series of innovations took place across Europe, largely centred upon new rotations with the elimination of fallowing, that resulted in an overall doubling – and more – of agricultural production (Mazoyer and Roudart 2006). From the first half of the nineteenth century, industry began to produce a new range of equipment, with all-metal construction replacing wooden contraptions, and mechanical aids greatly saving on labour time. While these innovations were developed to improve animal-drawn cultivation, the development of steam engines had greater importance in relation to transportation than in aiding the performance of field tasks. First, trans-Atlantic steamships and the expansion of the railways enabled Chilean nitrates and Peruvian guano to be distributed in Europe at much lower cost such that increasing use of soil amendments served to enhance yields. Yet, at the same time, these same modes of transport also served to bring to European markets wheat, wool and meat from the new territories of European colonization, often at prices well below the costs of production in Europe.

But it was the twentieth century that witnessed the greatest changes in the world's agri-food economy, a transformation most vividly explained by Mazoyer and Roudart in their encyclopaedic account of the development of world agriculture. Their argument is that the astonishing increases in agricultural productivity in the second half of the twentieth century, in particular, set it apart from any earlier phase of human history. They distinguish between a number of discrete but inter-connected technological developments involving: *motorization* (the development of the internal combustion engine within increasingly powerful tractors and engines fuelled by oil); *mechanization* (increasingly complex and effective machines); *chemicalization* (synthetic fertilizers and pesticides), as well as associated developments in plant and animal breeding. To take just one example here, consider the extraordinary transformation of the food system which resulted from Fritz Haber's invention to synthesize atmospheric nitrogen to ammonia, work that was designed to produce TNT as an aid for Germany's 1914 war effort. Long recognized as the single most limiting factor in plant growth, the ability to make nitrogen available in the soil – previously performed through crop rotations involving legumes – was to have huge consequences for food output. Industrial production of chemical fertilizers, together with the development of fertilizer-responsive, high-yielding varieties of seed, has led Vaclav Smil to argue that up to half of the present population of the world today owes its existence to the availability of synthetic nitrogen (Smil 2000).

Within the regions of industrialized agriculture, this combination of technological developments resulted in a ten-fold increase in grain yields due to fertilizers and plant breeding, and a more than ten-fold increase in cultivated area per worker due to motor-mechanization (Mazoyer and Roudart 2006). Such productivity increases led to a strong reduction in real agricultural prices – in the order of two to four times depending upon the product during the second half of the twentieth century. Inevitably the majority of farms impoverished by this dramatic decline in prices and incapable of competing on this treadmill have simply disappeared. It is little wonder that the numbers employed in agriculture in these industrialized regions fell to below 5 per cent of the total working population.

It is this history of scientific and technological innovation in agriculture that has enabled the world to produce enough food by volume of crops to meet the needs of 10 billion people today. And to be clear: that one billion remain malnourished and deeply food insecure is not a consequence of a Malthusian failure of output; it is a failure of entitlements, the claims of the poor to secure access to food (Sen 1981). Yet, the impacts on the environment arising from this model of production have been multiple and diverse, and extend well beyond the matter of land use change with the resulting loss of important habitats and biological diversity. For example, the *chemicalization* aspect noted by Mazoyer and Roudart, which caused such devastation to wildlife that it became the subject of Rachel Carson's *Silent Spring* (1962), has still left a legacy of persistent organic pollutants even in those countries which abide by strict controls over pesticide applications. And while regulations were introduced in the decades since Carson's publication with a resulting flattening of the market for pesticides, at least in the OECD countries, this only served to encourage the agri-chemical corporations to move into control over seeds, especially genetically modified (GM) ones (Dinham 2005).

Moreover, the energy demand of agriculture has continued to rise not only from the expanding use of ever more powerful machinery, but also as a consequence of increasing production of chemical fertilizer, which correlates closely with world population growth. During the twentieth century the world's cultivated area increased by about one-third and with average yields rising four-fold total output increased by almost six times. According to Smil, 'This gain has been due largely to a more than eightyfold increase of external energy inputs, mostly fossil fuels, to crop cultivation' (2000: 4). While these energy subsidies have performed a number of important functions, above all, they have underpinned the supply of energy-intensive nitrogen fertilizers. Today, fertilizer production alone accounts for about 1.1 per cent of global energy consumption (Dawson and Hilton 2011). However, with 90 per cent of the cost of nitrogen fertilizer determined by the price of natural gas, rising energy prices translate directly into higher fertilizer prices. Between 2005 and 2008 the price of fertilizer increased five-fold, rising at an even sharper rate than the cost of food (UK Government Office for Science 2011). This inevitably had a huge impact on farmers, especially those in the South.

If higher energy prices are a consequence of tightening oil markets, then it is unsurprising that there should be an interest in the production of biofuels as an alternative to liquid petroleum. However, this process begins to demonstrate how the pursuit of value and profit in agriculture can lead to the abandonment of 'feeding the world' in favour of 'fuelling our cars'. The development of energy sources from biomass, particularly potential food crops such as sugar cane, maize and oil palm, has arguably further cemented the interlocking of food and energy markets.

Seeking to replicate the success that Brazil has had with the distillation of ethanol from sugar cane stretching back to the 1970s, the United States rapidly developed an infrastructure during the first decade of the twenty-first century to utilize maize. In 2000, ethanol production in the USA accounted for just 6 per cent of maize output, but rose to 38 per cent by 2010 (Cassidy et al. 2013). By 2010, the combined amount of maize and sugar cane from the United States and Brazil respectively amounted to 460 million tonnes of biofuel feedstock, or 6 per cent of global crop production by mass (ibid.). This represented a 450 per cent increase in biofuel output between the years 2000 and 2010, mostly through the use of human edible crops. In contrast, while the EU's Renewable Energy Directive sets mandatory targets for achieving the utilization of renewable energy sources in the transport sector (10 per cent by 2020), ostensibly in order to reduce greenhouse gas emissions, it limits the contribution of food-based biofuels to 5 per cent. And while scientific research is developing 'second generation' cellulosic biofuels and even third generation using algae, the short to medium term looks set to remain dominated by sugar cane and maize (for ethanol) and palm and other vegetable oils (biodiesel). While acknowledging the essential fungibility of agri-commodities such as these, this process demonstrates how the food needs of the poor are subordinated to the energy demands of the more powerful. It also looks set to continue to drive the process of 'land-grabbing' in the South as powerful states and corporations engage in land-leasing and other investment opportunities in pursuit of their own food and energy security (Cotula et al. 2011; Sage 2013).

Overall, then, we can begin to understand why the IAASTD report argued that 'the current agricultural knowledge, science and technology model requires revision' (IAASTD 2009: 3). This model is responsible for producing around one-third of global greenhouse gas emissions and is contributing to the process of climate uncertainty; though delivering growing volumes of available food calories, these are increasingly derived from a limited number of globally important cereal and oil crops such that diets worldwide are becoming more homogeneous (Khoury et al. 2014) and food supplies more vulnerable to instability; and, not least, global calorie availability could be increased by as much as 70 per cent by shifting crops from animal feed and biofuels directly to human consumption (Cassidy et al. 2013). These are strong reasons to support the case for moving toward a more sustainable agriculture.

Sustainable food production

Taking stock of the major challenges faced by the global agri-food system, most especially those presented by climate change, freshwater depletion and the consequences of tightening energy markets, is leading many to believe that we need to move away from the productivist model and its certainties about outputs. For the goal is no longer simply one of maximizing productivity but to optimize it across a far more complex landscape of production, rural development, environmental and social justice outcomes (Pretty et al. 2010). Moreover, this will require a fundamental break with the central role accorded to 'magic bullet' technologies and scientific innovations developed in research laboratories and regarded as suitable blueprints for driving change in diverse regions of the world. Rather, it will require working through context-specific pathways that combine particular social, technological, ecological and other elements prevailing within each area. It means, above all, working with small-scale farmers who make up the overwhelming majority of the world's food producers and who are best placed to deliver required outputs while sustaining ecosystem functions.

Replacing the dominant model of productivism which has been underpinned by some of the scientific and technological achievements outlined above, with one which we might call agricultural sustainability represents nothing less than a fundamental paradigm shift. Yet while Kuhn's account of scientific revolutions demonstrated that replacing one paradigm with another was a multi-generational process, particularly when stakes are high, we do not have such time on our side. Fortunately, increasing numbers of transdisciplinary scientists recognize the urgency of embracing the core principles of this emerging paradigm that might be summarized as:

- *ecologically sound*: integrating natural processes such as nutrient cycling, nitrogen fixation, soil regeneration and pest management and by minimizing the use of non-renewable inputs (pesticides and fertilizers);
- *economically viable*: that farms produce sufficient food output capable of supporting the livelihoods of those engaged in production, but also recognize their multifunctional role as environmental stewards and as economic actors within local and regional economies;
- *socially just*: those who produce food have rights to land, to appropriate technical support and to market opportunities; and this enhances social capital, self-reliance and growing cooperation in pursuit of food security for all (Sage 2012).

These principles for a sustainable agriculture are common to a wide range of initiatives that have spread over the past quarter-century all around the world, in the countries of the Global North and the Global South, from some of the richest to some of the poorest, in rural areas and, increasingly, in cities. Although increasingly visible, they can hardly be called 'new' initiatives as their principles and practices long precede the appearance of productivist agriculture. Moreover many different labels are used to describe them: agroecological, organic, or biological farming; low external input and sustainable agriculture (LEISA); while more unorthodox approaches include biodynamic farming and permaculture. All, however, share a vision of 'farming with nature' by recycling, conserving and minimizing resource use.

One of the less obvious but critical dimensions of building sustainable food production is recovering the link with good nutrition. The Green Revolution model, that particular application of productivism to some parts of the developing world endowed with good land and irrigation and best able to take advantage of high-yielding varieties of seed and agri-chemicals, was concerned principally with raising calorie output through two cereal crops: wheat and rice. While it was successful in this objective, it resulted in a number of unanticipated consequences. One was the clear evidence of micronutrient deficiencies as plant diversity was eliminated in favour of generating market-bound single commodity surpluses. Evidence of widespread dietary deficiencies, for example, in iron, iodine, and vitamin A, have brought forth various public and private interventions aimed at fortification (McEwan et al. 2013), nutrient supplement programmes and other forms of technical 'fixes' (such as Golden Rice which has been genetically engineered in order to contain a higher beta carotene content that can be converted into vitamin A in the body).

It is now well established that good nutrition is provided by dietary diversity: a greater range of plant material in the human diet is more likely to meet all the micro-nutrient needs of the body. Yet the worldwide expansion of a small number of commodity crops for the global agri-food system has led to the displacement of a huge stock of less commercial but culturally and nutritionally important plant (and animal) species (Hunter and Fanzo 2013). Neglected by mainstream agricultural science and extension systems as 'traditional' and unimportant, such 'underutilized' crops may play a vital role not only in delivering nutrients especially to poorer households, but may aid in the process of agricultural adaptation to climate change. In many parts of the world, farmers have developed an extraordinary diversity of local varieties, or landraces, that have co-evolved through interactions with wild species and through adaptation with changing farming conditions. While they represent a vital stock of biological assets, the knowledge held by local farmers responsible for the selection and breeding of this material is inseparably connected.

This is why, finally, one is reluctant to speak of sustainable food production as if it were simply a set of narrow technical procedures to be followed, much like the certification standards for conventional organics. Increasingly it represents something more than that: not least, the aspirations of a wider agrarian movement not just for the Right to Food, but for the right to feed oneself (McEwan et al. 2013). Under the banner of food justice for all, the notion of food sovereignty has spread around the world; from the fields occupied by the small-farmer movement La Via Campesina to activists working in the community gardens of poor urban neighbourhoods in North America. Food sovereignty presents a powerful counter-hegemonic perspective that not only insists upon food being treated as a basic human right but proclaims the right of peoples to define their own agriculture (Sage 2014a). It captures the very spirit of what a sustainable food system should represent.

Sustainable food consumption

It might be argued that making a distinction between production and consumption is a fallacious construction that sustainable thinking would avoid. Perhaps we should regard production and consumption as existing on a continuum, or as a nexus, in which performances and responsibilities are held to account. As it is, food provides an especially interesting lens through which to think about sustainable consumption, one that offers a means to go beyond narrowly eco-efficiency criteria in shopping choices (Goodman et al. 2010). Unlike compact fluorescent light bulbs or hybrid cars, food is 'good to think, as well as to eat', and has the power to convene many different perspectives, issues and questions: where, how and by whom was this food produced? Food, unlike other products, entangles us in webs of relations with distant others: those who harvest our coffee beans, pack those green beans, and winch those nets. Food should do this in a way that buying trainers does not because of its essential materiality: it derives from ecological processes managed by other people, however remote from us, and given that we ingest this material into our bodies, we place trust in them that it will not make us sick. Clearly, it should give us cause to think about what we put into our mouths and the grounds on which we choose between different foods.

Thinking sustainably about our food has developed as part of a *moral turn* that has sought to interrogate the logic and practices of the conventional agri-food system and to develop alternative strategies and practices of its own. This process has been immeasurably aided by the succession of food safety failures that have significantly undermined trust and confidence in the mainstream food system from the 1980s onward. Besides outbreaks of pathogens such as *Listeria*, *Salmonella* or *E.coli* in a variety of livestock products, consumer confidence was most severely damaged by the BSE (bovine spongiform encephalopathy) episode. While governments eventually put in place measures to restore confidence, principally through the creation of food safety authorities, such episodes helped to create the conditions for some people to look more actively for traceability and other direct assurances about the quality of their food. A number of different schemes and initiatives have emerged in response, including: animal welfare-friendly, fair trade, organic, foods of designated origin and, above all, locally produced. Most of these now form part of what has been loosely labelled alternative food networks (AFN).

The value of AFNs is their ability to demonstrate that food markets are not the result of some 'invisible' hand external to the social world, but result from the active construction of networks by actors in the food chain. The shorter this chain – that is the fewer intermediaries between producer and consumer, but also the more geographically proximate – the greater the possibility for remoralizing and resocializing food. In other words, our decisions on food are taken out of the highly individualized way in which consumers make personal choices within the range offered by supermarkets and are instead brought more fully into the civic arena where matters of public good are given due weight and consideration. Ideally, this encourages a more reflexive and critical judgement about the relative desirability and quality of different food products, and offers the basis for more collective solutions to build local food systems for community development. Illustrations of this can be found within the more successful community-supported agriculture schemes in North America, or in the solidarity purchase groups (GAS) flourishing across Italy (Grasseni 2013).

As we have argued above, a sustainable food system will not be achieved only through technology-centred changes in the realm of agriculture: it will require massive strides towards changing the configuration of consumption too. Fortunately, food has the capacity to engage people that other aspects of life do not. For example, growing edible plants presents a low entry threshold: it does not require pre-existing knowledge or significant resources, only motivation and some helpful advice. Food serves as a social lubricant, aiding connectivity; bringing people together to work collectively in community gardens creates opportunities to engage in reflection on the injustices of the food system as well as to partly rectify our alienation from nature. Growing food has the potential to help re-establish a relationship between humans and the biophysical environment by re-integrating intellectual and human labour (McClintock 2010). If we can recover a sense of the link between ecological and human health, we might not only improve our dietary health but cease to be so complacent about the environmental costs of producing our cheap food (Carolan 2011). Growing food, in short, opens a space to challenge the mainstream food system by offering a more equitable, sustainable and socially empowering alternative. But if we are to be truly serious about sustainability, then assumptions about maintaining our dietary preferences will need to be challenged, as the next section of the chapter outlines.

The place of meat in sustainable diets

Recent years have seen increasing attention given to the environmental consequences of the rising farm animal population worldwide, in particular its substantial contribution through greenhouse gas emissions to global climate change (Stehfest et al. 2009; Nordgren 2012; Weis 2013). At the same time, other work has sought to explore awareness of eating practices involving animal-derived foods and how these are shaped by consideration of environmental or animal welfare concerns (cf. Cole et al. 2009; Miele and Evans 2010; Evans and Miele 2012). Gradually, a body of work is emerging that problematizes meat consumption practices and seeks to explore options for lowering demand for animal products in high-income countries (Sage 2014b). The challenges are considerable, not least because our societies appear to be 'locked into' consumption patterns that are reinforced by powerful advertising messages despite the persistence of negative health and environmental outcomes (Frank 2007).

Meat is, and has long been, a deeply culturally embedded food, though the quantities consumed in the Global North and, increasingly across the rapidly developing economies of the Global South, are quite novel. While there is a case that the poorest societies in the South should have room to increase consumption as a means to alleviate malnourishment, it is clear that in the North aggregate levels should fall significantly – by at least 30 per cent – in the interests of environmental and human health. Meat production has tripled in volume worldwide since the 1970s; it has grown by more than one-fifth since 2000; and it is expected to double by 2050 (FAO 2009). Per capita meat consumption now averages 41.2 kg per year, up from

30 kg in 1980. However, there remains considerable disparity across the world: in India just 5.8 kg of meat are eaten per person per year whereas the USA accounts for almost 127 kg per person. Consumption of animal products, including milk and eggs, has grown most quickly in China where around 60 kg of meat are consumed annually per capita, a rate that has grown by four times since 1980 and by 50 per cent since 1995 (ibid.). Underpinning all of this, of course, are farmed animals, principally cattle, pigs and chickens that together account for 88 per cent of all animal flesh by volume (Weis 2007). In 2005, more than 55 billion farm animals were slaughtered, a more than five-fold increase in four decades. Today more than 40 per cent of all meat production worldwide is produced by factory farms, a production model that illustrates the almost complete globalization of the industrial grain–livestock complex (ibid.).

But it is with regard to environmental impacts that the aggregate effect of meat consumption is causing rising concern. In the first place this has to do with the growing volumes of cereals and oil seeds produced for dedicated use in the animal feeds sector, to be converted into meat and other livestock products. Livestock now account for over 75 per cent of all agricultural land, including pasture and rangeland, with over one-third of global arable land given over to the production of animal feeds, which account for 24 per cent of global crop production by mass. However, as feed crops are dense in both calories and protein content, feed crops represent 36 per cent of global calorie production and 53 per cent of global plant protein production (Cassidy et al. 2013). Yet the conversion of plant to animal protein is inefficient so that, of the 36 per cent of crop calories consumed by animals, only 4 per cent is available to humans through the consumption of animal products. Moreover, on a global basis, almost three-quarters of maize production is used to feed animals, leaving less than a quarter of global maize calories to be consumed as either plant or animal products (ibid.).

There is a second way in which meat and dairy products are labelled as foods carrying the greatest environmental burden (Tukker et al. 2006). Livestock are estimated to account for around 37 per cent of anthropogenic methane, 65 per cent of nitrous oxide and 9 per cent of carbon dioxide, that together constitute 18 per cent of all greenhouse gas emissions, a share greater than the transport sector worldwide (Steinfeld et al. 2006). Robert Goodland has challenged these FAO figures, arguing that the methodology used failed to develop a true whole life-cycle estimate of GHG emissions attributable to livestock and that livestock products actually account for at least 51 per cent of annual worldwide anthropogenic GHG emissions (Goodland and Anhang 2009; Goodland 2014). If Goodland is correct, given the prevailing scientific understanding of the need for abatement measures that would avoid serious climatic perturbation, how are we to achieve stabilization of the global climate system, if animal numbers further increase? Intensive livestock farming also gives rise to other significant waste streams to air (e.g. ammonia), land and water resulting in loss of environmental quality (CIWF 2008), as well as huge demands on depleting freshwater resources.

The expansion of the global food economy which has done so much to transform dietary patterns has come to associate meat consumption with progress, wealth and status. As countries become more integrated into the world economy, their dietary patterns converge with 'increased consumption of meat and meat products, dairy products, edible oil, salt and sugar, and a lower intake of dietary fibre' (Hawkes 2006: 3). Global dietary patterns are changing as a consequence of complex social and economic processes, including: increased urbanization, greater market penetration by foreign retail and food service chains and brands, the expansion of advertising and mass media, and highly competitive prices. However, this process of Nutrition Transition (Popkin 2005) where Western-style highly processed products comprising higher levels of meat intake displace long-established dietary patterns should not be regarded as inevitable or necessarily desirable. Changing diets are also being reflected in changing patterns of body composition and as Rayner and Lang (2012) highlight, mass population weight gain and obesity are a worldwide phenomenon that is entirely modern and is adding a new disease burden to health services.

Yet, the pressing question remains: to what extent can Western dietary norms be maintained in the West, let alone extended to the rest of the world without imperilling planetary limits? In less than 50 years the world has not only achieved a high level of meat consumption: it has cemented almost universal expectations about meat consumption that will be catastrophic to maintain but very hard to change (Roberts 2008). As we have seen, meat consumption practices appear to be closely anchored to cultural traits, even if the quantities consumed are entirely modern. This makes it extremely difficult to devise and implement pathways to lower levels of consumption.

Conclusion

The chapter has discussed a range of issues entangled within a consideration of food and sustainable development, but makes no claim to being complete or comprehensive. It has highlighted some of the ways in which the contemporary food system has a significant bearing on the global environment, not least through emissions of greenhouse gases. At the same time, different agricultural systems around the world are demonstrating increasing vulnerability to environmental change, most especially the diverse effects arising from a warming climate.

How we are to feed the world going forward is a highly contested debate with a great deal at stake. By maintaining a focus on output and the need to feed a global population of 9 billion by 2050, productivism possesses the Malthusian trump card. Yet if we are to enquire more deeply, as we should when speaking of sustainability, into matters of ecological integrity, social justice and nutritional security for all, it is clear that present arrangements must change: fundamentally and quickly. For the present system not only fails to feed 1 billion people, it is responsible for the malconsumption – if the clinical data are correct – of at least 1 billion more. If human well-being is a matter for sustainability, then we need to rectify the way in which people are fed. As Burlingame notes: 'The era of industrial agriculture emerged in the twentieth century and environmental sustainability was uncoupled from human health' (2014: 1).

There can be no better reminder of the alternative ways that we could feed the world if we look more closely at the amount of land dedicated to the production of meat and to biofuels. Leaving to one side any moral arguments about meat consumption, it is instructive to learn how much grain and oil seed crops are grown to feed animals: 36 per cent of total calorie production from crops. If, as Cassidy et al. speculate, we were to divert entirely the crops currently grown for feed and biofuels, this would increase global calorie availability by 70 per cent, sufficient to potentially feed an additional 4 billion people. Even if we choose to continue to eat meat, switching from grain-fed beef to pork or poultry would also achieve significant savings, given the higher levels of metabolic efficiency of those animals. Moreover, and perhaps surprisingly for those who regard meat as a necessary source of protein, is that shifting all crop production to direct human consumption would also double protein availability (Cassidy et al. 2013).

Finally, how we will feed the world sustainably is a political question that will require attention to the balance of power within the existing food system. Powerful corporations exercise effective oligopolies at each stage of the food chain, from control of seeds to retail sales (Hendrickson and Heffernan 2007). Recovering responsibility for how we feed ourselves is an axiomatic requirement of a more sustainable arrangement, wherein people begin to redefine themselves not as supermarket customers or consumers but as food citizens engaged, with others, in a new civic endeavour to build a sustainable food system.

References

Beddington, J. (2010) Food security: contributions from science to a new and greener revolution. *Philosophical Transactions of the Royal Society B*, 365: 61–71.

Burlingame, B. (2014) Grand challenges in nutrition and environmental sustainability. *Frontiers in Nutrition*, 1(3): 1–2.

Carolan, M. (2011) *The Real Cost of Cheap Food*. London: Earthscan.

Carson, R. (1962) *Silent Spring*. London: Hamish Hamilton.

Cassidy, E., West, P., Gerber, J. and Foley, J. (2013) Redefining agricultural yields: from tonnes to people nourished per hectare. *Environmental Research Letters* 8. http://dx.doi.org/10.1088/1748-9326/8/3/034015 Open access.

CIWF (Compassion in World Farming) (2008) *Global Warning: Climate Change and Farm Animal Welfare*. Godalming, Surrey: CIWF.

Cole, M. Miele, M. and Hines, P. (2009) Animal foods and climate change: shadowing eating practices. *International Journal of Consumer Studies*, 33: 162–167.

Cotula, L., Vermeulen, S., Mathieu, P. and Toulmin, C. (2011) Agricultural investment and international land deals: evidence from a multi-country study in Africa. *Food Security*, 3: S99–S113.

Dawson, C. and Hilton, J. (2011) Fertiliser availability in a resource-limited world: production and recycling of nitrogen and phosphorus. *Food Policy*, 36: S14–S22.

Dinham, B. (2005) Corporations and pesticides. In J. Pretty (ed.) *The Pesticide Detox: Towards a More Sustainable Agriculture*. London: Earthscan, pp. 55–69.

Evans, A. and Miele, M. (2012) Between food and flesh: how animals are made to matter (and not matter) within food consumption practices. *Environment and Planning D: Society and Space*, 2012(30): 298–314.

FAO (Food and Agriculture Organisation) (2009) *The State of Food and Agriculture: Livestock in the Balance*. Rome: FAO.

Feldman, S. and Biggs, S. (2012) The politics of international assessments: the IAASTD process, reception and significance. *Journal of Agrarian Change*, 12(1): 144–169.

Folke, C. (2006) Resilience: the emergence of a perspective for social-ecological systems analyses. *Global Environmental Change*, 16: 253–267.

Frank, J. (2007) Meat as a bad habit: a case for positive feedback in consumption preferences leading to lock-in. *Review of Social Economy*, LXV(3)L 319–348.

Garnett, T. and Godfray, C. (2012) *Sustainable Intensification in Agriculture: Navigating a Course Through Competing Food System Priorities*. Food Climate Research Network and the Oxford Martin Programme on the Future of Food, University of Oxford, UK.

Goodland, R. (2014) A fresh look at livestock greenhouse gas emissions and mitigation potential in Europe. *Global Change Biology*. DOI: 10.1111/gcb.12454.

Goodland, R. and Anhang, J. (2009) Livestock and climate change: what if the key actors in climate change were pigs, chickens and cows? *World Watch*, November/December 2009. Washington, DC: Worldwatch Institute, pp. 10–19.

Goodman, M., Maye, D. and Holloway, L. (2010) Guest editorial. *Environment and Planning A*, 42: 1782–1796.

Grasseni, C. (2013) *Beyond Alternative Food Networks: Italy's Solidarity Purchase Groups*. London: Bloomsbury Publishers.

Hawkes, C. (2006) Uneven dietary development: linking the policies and processes of globalization with the nutrition transition, obesity and diet-related chronic diseases. *Globalization and Health*, 2(4). Available at: www.globalizationandhealth.com/content/2/1/4) open access.

Hendrickson, M. and Heffernan, W. (2007) Concentration of agricultural markets. Unpublished paper, Department of Rural Sociology, University of Missouri, Columbia, MO.

Hunter, D. and Fanzo, J. (2013) Introduction: agricultural biodiversity, diverse diets and improving nutrition. In J. Fanzo, D. Hunter, T. Borelli, and F. Mattei (eds) *Diversifying Food and Diets: Using Agricultural Biodiversity to Improve Nutrition and Health*. London: Routledge, pp. 1–13.

IAASTD (International Assessment of Agricultural Knowledge, Science and Technology for Development) (2009) *Synthesis Report: A Synthesis of the Global and Sub-Global IAASTD Reports*. Washington, DC: Island Press.

IPCC (Intergovernmental Panel on Climate Change) WGII AR5 (2014) *Climate Change 2014: Impacts, Adaptation, and Vulnerability: Summary for Policymakers*. www.ipcc-wg2.gov/AR5 (accessed 2 April 2014).

Khoury, C., Bjorkman, A., Dempewolf, H., Ramirez, J., Guarino, L., Jarvis, A., Riesenberg, L. and Struik, P. (2014) Increasing homogeneity in global food supplies and the implications for food security. *PNAS*. DOI: 10.1073/pnas.1313490111.

Kuhn, T. (1996) *The Structure of Scientific Revolutions*. Chicago: University of Chicago Press.

Leach, M., Scoones, I. and Stirling, A. (2010) *Dynamic Sustainabilities: Technology, Environment, Social Justice*. London: Earthscan

McClintock, N. (2010) Why farm the city? Theorizing urban agriculture through a lens of metabolic rift. *Cambridge Journal of Regions, Economy and Society*, 3: 191–297.

McEwan, M., Prain, G. and Hunter, D. (2013) Opening a can of mopane worms: can cross-sectoral partnerships leverage agricultural biodiversity for better quality diets? In J. Fanzo, D. Hunter, T. Borelli, and F. Mattei (eds) *Diversifying Food and Diets: Using Agricultural Biodiversity to Improve Nutrition and Health*. London: Routledge, pp. 207–228.

Mazoyer, M. and Roudart, L. (2006) *A History of World Agriculture: From the Neolithic to the Current Crisis*. London: Earthscan.

Miele, M. and Evans, A. (2010) When foods become animals: ruminations on ethics and responsibility in care-*full* practices of consumption. *Ethics, Place and Environment*, 13(2): 171–190.

Nordgren, A. (2012) Meat and global warming: impact models, mitigation approaches and ethical aspects. *Environmental Values*, 21: 437–457.

Popkin, B. (2005) Using research on the obesity pandemic as a guide to a unified vision of nutrition. *Public Health Nutrition*, 8(6A): 724–729.

Pretty, J., Ball, A., Lang, T. and Morison, J. (2005) Farm costs and food miles: an assessment of the full cost of the UK weekly food basket. *Food Policy*, 30: 1–19.

Pretty, J., Sutherland, W., Ashby, J., Auburn, J., Baulcombe, D., Bell, M., Bentley, J., Bickersteth, S., Brown, K., Burke, J., Campbell, H., Chen, K., Crowley, E., Crute, I., Dobbelaere, D., Edwards-Jones, G., Funes-Monzote, F., Godfray, C., Griffon, M., Gypmantisiri, P., Haddad, L., Halavatau, S., Herren, H., Holderness, M., Izac, A-M., Jones, M., Koohafkan, P., Lal, R., Lang, T., McNeely, J., Mueller, A., Nisbett, N., Noble, A., Pingali, P., Pinto, Y., Rabbinge, R., Ravindranath, N.H., Rola, A., Roling, N., Sage, C., Settle, W., Sha, J.M., Shiming, L., Simons, T., Smith, P., Strzepeck, K., Swaine, H., Terry, E., Tomich, T., Toulmin, C., Trigo, E., Twomlow, S., Vis, J.K., Wilson, J. and Pilgrim, S. (2010) The top 100 questions of importance to the future of global agriculture. *International Journal of Agricultural Sustainability*, 8(4): 219–236.

Rayner, G. and Lang, T. (2012) *Ecological Public Health: Reshaping the Conditions for Good Health*. London: Routledge.

Roberts, P. (2008) *The End of Food: The Coming Crisis in the World Food Industry*. London: Bloomsbury.

The Royal Society (2009). *Reaping the Benefits: Science and the Sustainable Intensification of Global Agriculture*. Policy document 11/09. London: The Royal Society.

Sage, C. (2012) *Environment and Food*. London: Routledge

Sage, C. (2013) The inter-connected challenges for food security from a food regimes perspective: energy, climate and malconsumption. *Journal of Rural Studies*, 29(1): 71–80.

Sage, C. (2014a) The transition movement and food sovereignty: from local resilience to global engagement in food system transformation. *Journal of Consumer Culture*, 14(2): 254–275.

Sage, C. (2014b) Making and un-making meat: cultural boundaries, environmental thresholds and dietary transgressions. In M. Goodman and C. Sage (eds) *Food Transgressions: Making Sense of Contemporary Food Politics*. Farnham: Ashgate, pp. 181–203.

Scrinis, G. and Lyons, K. (2010) Nanotechnology and the techno-corporate agri-food paradigm. In G. Lawrence, K. Lyons and T. Wallington (eds) *Food Security, Nutrition and Sustainability*. London: Earthscan, pp. 252–270.

Sen, A. (1981) *Poverty and Famines: An Essay on Entitlement and Deprivation*. Oxford: Clarendon Press.

Smil, V. (2000) *Feeding the World: A Challenge for the Twenty-First Century*. Cambridge, MA: MIT Press.

Stehfest, E., Bouwman, L., van Vuuren, D. et al. (2009) Climate benefits of changing diet. *Climatic Change*, 95: 83–102.

Steinfeld, H., Gerber, P., Wassenaar, T., Castel, V., Rosales, M. and Haan, C. de (2006) *Livestock's Long Shadow*. Rome: Food and Agriculture Organisation. Available at: www.fao.org/docrep/010/a0701e/a0701e00.HTM.

Tester, M. and Langridge, P. (2010) Breeding technologies to increase crop production in a changing world. *Science*, 327: 818–822.

Thompson, P. (2010) What sustainability is (and what it isn't). In S. Moore (ed.) *Pragmatic Sustainability: Theoretical and Practical Tools*. London: Routledge, pp. 16–29.

Tukker, A., Huppes, G., Guinée, J., Heijungs, R., de Koning, A., van Oers, L., Suh, S., Geerken, T., Van Holderbeke, M., Jansen, B. and Nielsen, P. (2006) *Environmental Impact of Products (EIPRO): Analysis of the Life Cycle Environmental Impacts Related to the Total Final Consumption of the EU25*. IPTS/ESTO, European Commission Joint Research Centre, Brussels. Available at: http://ec.europa.eu/environment/ipp/pdf/eipro_report.pdf.

UK Government Office for Science (2011) *Foresight: The Future of Food and Farming. Challenges and Choices for Global Sustainability*. London: TSO.

Weis, T. (2007) *The Global Food Economy: The Battle for the Future of Farming*. London: Zed Books.

Weis, T. (2013) *The Ecological Hoofprint: The Global Burden of Industrial Livestock*. London: Zed Books.

PART V

Economic dimensions of sustainable development

18

ECOLOGICAL ECONOMICS AND SUSTAINABLE DEVELOPMENT

Building a sustainable and desirable economy-in-society-in-nature

Robert Costanza, Gar Alperovitz, Herman E. Daly, Joshua Farley, Carol Franco, Tim Jackson, Ida Kubiszewski, Juliet Schor and Peter Victor

Introduction

The current mainstream model of the global economy is based on a number of assumptions about the way the world works, what the economy is, and what the economy is for (Table 18.1). These assumptions arose in an earlier period, when the world was relatively empty of humans and their artifacts. In this context, built capital was the limiting factor, while natural capital was abundant. It made sense not to worry too much about environmental "externalities," since they could be assumed to be relatively small and ultimately solvable. It also made sense to focus on the growth of the market economy, as measured by gross domestic product (GDP), as the primary means to improve human welfare. And it made sense to think of the economy as only marketed goods and services and to think of the goal as increasing the amount of these goods and services produced and consumed.

Now, however, we live in a radically different world that is relatively full of humans and their built capital infrastructure. In this new context, we have to reconceptualize what the economy is and what it is for. We have to first remember that the goal of the economy should be to sustainably improve human well-being and quality of life, and that material consumption and GDP are merely means to that end, not ends in themselves. We have to recognize, as both ancient wisdom and new psychological research tell us, that too much of a focus on material consumption can actually reduce our well-being (Kasser 2002). We have to better understand what really does contribute to sustainable human well-being and recognize the substantial contributions of natural and social capital, which are now the limiting factors to improving that well-being in many countries. We have to be able to distinguish between real poverty, in terms of low quality of life, and merely low monetary income. Ultimately we have to create a new vision of what the economy is and what it is for, and a new model of the economy that acknowledges this new "full-world" context and vision.

Some argue that relatively minor adjustments to the current economic model will produce the desired results. For example, they argue that by adequately pricing the depletion of natural

Table 18.1 The basic characteristics of the current economic model, the green economy model, and the ecological economics model

	Current Economic Model	*Green Economy Model*	*Ecological Economics Model*
Primary policy goal	*More:* Economic growth in the conventional sense, as measured by GDP. The assumption is that growth will ultimately allow the solution of all other problems. More is always better.	*More but with lower environmental impact:* GDP growth decoupled from carbon and from other material and energy impacts.	*Better:* Focus must shift from merely growth to "development" in the real sense of improvement in sustainable human well-being, recognizing that growth has significant negative by-products.
Primary measure of progress	GDP	Still GDP, but recognizing impacts on natural capital.	Index of Sustainable Economic Welfare (ISEW), Genuine Progress Indicator (GPI), or other improved measures of real welfare.
Scale/carrying capacity/role of environment	Not an issue, since markets are assumed to be able to overcome any resource limits via new technology, and substitutes for resources are always available.	Recognized, but assumed to be solvable via decoupling.	A primary concern as a determinant of ecological sustainability. Natural capital and ecosystem services are not infinitely substitutable and real limits exist.
Distribution/ poverty	Given lip service, but relegated to "politics" and a "trickle-down" policy: a rising tide lifts all boats.	Recognized as important, assumes greening the economy will reduce poverty via enhanced agriculture and employment in green sectors.	A primary concern, since it directly affects quality of life and social capital and is often exacerbated by growth: a too rapidly rising tide only lifts yachts, while swamping small boats.
Economic efficiency/ allocation	The primary concern, but generally including only marketed goods and services (GDP) and market institutions.	Recognized to include natural capital and the need to incorporate the value of natural capital into market incentives.	A primary concern, but including both market and nonmarket goods and services, and effects. Emphasis on the need to incorporate the value of natural and social capital to achieve true allocative efficiency.
Property rights	Emphasis on private property and conventional markets.	Recognition of the need for instruments beyond the market.	Emphasis on a balance of property rights regimes appropriate to the nature and scale of the system, and a linking of rights with responsibilities. Includes larger role for common-property institutions.
Role of government	Government intervention to be minimized and replaced with private and market institutions.	Recognition of the need for government intervention to internalize natural capital.	Government plays a central role, including new functions as referee, facilitator, and broker in a new suite of common-asset institutions.
Principles of governance	*Laissez-faire* market capitalism.	Recognition of the need for government.	Lisbon principles of sustainable governance.

Source: Adapted from Costanza et al. (2014a).

capital (e.g. putting a price on carbon emissions) we can address many of the problems of the current economy while still allowing growth to continue. We call this approach the "green economy" (GE) model (see Table 18.1). Some of the areas of intervention promoted by GE advocates, such as investing in natural capital, are necessary and we should pursue them. However, we do not agree that they are sufficient to achieve sustainable human well-being. We need a more fundamental change, a change of our goals and paradigm.

Both the shortcomings and the critics of the current model are abundant. A coherent and viable alternative is sorely needed. *Our aim here is to sketch a framework for a new model of the economy based on the world-view and principles of ecological economics* (Costanza 1991; Costanza et al. 1997; Daly and Farley 2004). These include the following ideas:

1. Our material economy is embedded in society which is embedded in our ecological life-support system, and that we cannot understand or manage our economy without understanding the whole, interconnected system.
2. Growth and development are not always linked and that true development must be defined in terms of the improvement of sustainable human well-being, not merely improvement in material consumption.
3. A balance of four basic types of assets (capital) are necessary for sustainable human well-being: built, human, social, and natural capital (financial capital is merely a marker for real capital and must be managed as such).

We also accept that growth in material consumption ultimately is unsustainable because of fundamental planetary boundaries (Rockström et al. 2009) and, further, that such growth is or eventually becomes counterproductive (uneconomic) in that it has negative effects on well-being and on social and natural capital (Costanza et al. 2014b).

There is a substantial and growing body of new research on what actually contributes to human well-being and quality of life. While there is still much ongoing debate, this new science clearly demonstrates the limits of conventional economic income and consumption in contributing to well-being. For example, economist Richard Easterlin has shown that well-being tends to correlate well with health, level of education, and marital status and shows sharply diminishing returns to income beyond a fairly low threshold (Easterlin 2003). Economist Richard Layard argues that current economic policies are not improving well-being and happiness and that "happiness should become the goal of policy, and the progress of national happiness should be measured and analyzed as closely as the growth of GNP (gross national product)" (Layard 2005).

In fact, if we want to assess the "real" economy—all the things that contribute to real, sustainable, human well-being—as opposed to only the "market" economy, we have to measure and include the nonmarketed contributions to human well-being from nature; from family, friends, and other social relationships at many scales; and from health and education.

Doing so often yields a very different picture of the state of well-being than may be implied by growth in per capita GDP. Surveys of people's life satisfaction, for instance, have been relatively flat in the United States and many other developed countries since about 1975, in spite of a near doubling in per capita income.

A second approach is an aggregate measure of the real economy that has been developed as an alternative to GDP called the Index of Sustainable Economic Well-Being (ISEW) or a variation called the Genuine Progress Indicator (GPI). The GPI attempts to correct for the many shortcomings of GDP as a measure of true human well-being. For example, GDP is not only limited—measuring only marketed economic activity or gross income—it also counts all of this activity as positive. It does not separate desirable, well-being-enhancing activity from undesirable, well-being-reducing activity. An oil spill increases GDP because someone has to clean it up, but it obviously detracts from society's well-being. From the perspective of GDP, more crime, sickness, war, pollution, fires, storms and pestilence are all potentially good things, because they can increase marketed activity in the economy.

GDP also leaves out many things that *do* enhance well-being but are outside the market, such as the unpaid work of parents caring for their own children at home, or the nonmarketed work of natural capital in providing clean air and water, food, natural resources, and other ecosystem services. And GDP takes no account of the distribution of income among individuals, even though it is well known that an additional dollar of income produces more well-being if one is poor rather than rich.

The GPI addresses these problems by separating the positive from the negative components of marketed economic activity, adding in estimates of the value of nonmarketed goods and services provided by natural, human, and social capital, and adjusting for income-distribution effects. Comparing GDP and GPI for the United States, shows that, while GDP has steadily increased since 1950, with the occasional dip or recession, GPI peaked in about 1975 and has been flat or gradually decreasing ever since (Talberth et al. 2007). The United States and several other developed countries are now in a period of what might be called uneconomic growth, in which further growth in marketed economic activity (GDP) is actually reducing well-being, on balance, rather than enhancing it.

A new model of the economy consistent with our new full-world context would be based clearly on the goal of sustainable human well-being. It would use measures of progress that openly acknowledge this goal (e.g. GPI instead of GDP). It would acknowledge the importance of ecological sustainability, social fairness, and real economic efficiency.

A framework for an ecological economy

Elsewhere (Costanza et al. 2014a; Costanza and Kubiszewski 2014) we have described in detail a vision of what a new economy-in-society-in-nature might look like. A number of other groups, for example, the Great Transition initiative (www.gtinitiative.org) and the Future We Want (www.futurewewant.org), have performed similar exercises. All are meant to reflect the essential broad features of a better, more sustainable world, but it is unlikely that any particular one of them will emerge wholly intact from efforts to make human civilization sustainable. For that reason and because of space limitations, we will not describe those visions here. Instead we want to lay out what we believe are the changes in policy, governance and institutional design that will be required to achieve any of these sustainable and desirable futures.

The key to achieving sustainable governance in the new, full-world context is an integrated approach—across disciplines, stakeholder groups, and generations—based on the paradigm of "adaptive management," whereby policy-making is an iterative experiment acknowledging uncertainty, rather than a static "answer." Within this paradigm, six core principles (the Lisbon principles) embody the essential criteria for sustainable governance(Costanza et al. 1998) and the use of common natural and social capital assets:

Principle 1: Responsibility. Access to common asset resources carries attendant responsibilities to use them in an ecologically sustainable, economically efficient, and socially fair manner. Individual and corporate responsibilities and incentives should be aligned with each other and with broad social and ecological goals.

Principle 2: Scale-matching. Problems of managing natural and social capital assets are rarely confined to a single scale. Decision-making should: (1) be assigned to institutional levels that maximize ecological input; (2) ensure the flow of information between institutional levels; (3) take ownership and actors into account; and (4) internalize social costs and benefits. Appropriate scales of governance will be those that have the most relevant information, can respond quickly and efficiently, and are able to integrate across scale boundaries.

Principle 3: Precaution. In the face of uncertainty about potentially irreversible impacts to natural and social capital assets, decisions concerning their use should err on the side of caution. The burden of proof should shift to those whose activities potentially damage natural and social capital.

Principle 4: Adaptive management. Given that some level of uncertainty always exists in common asset management, decision-makers should continuously gather and integrate appropriate ecological, social, and economic information with the goal of adaptive improvement.

Principle 5: Full cost allocation. All of the internal and external costs and benefits, including social and ecological, of alternative decisions concerning the use of natural and social capital should be identified and allocated, to the extent possible. When appropriate, markets should be adjusted to reflect full cost.

Principle 6: Participation. All stakeholders should be engaged in the formulation and implementation of decisions concerning natural and social capital assets. Full stakeholder awareness and participation contribute to credible, accepted rules that identify and assign the corresponding responsibilities appropriately.

The following are examples of world-views, institutions and institutional instruments, and technologies that can help move us toward the new economic paradigm. The list is divided into three primary sections: (1) respecting ecological limits; (2) protecting capabilities for flourishing; and (3) building a sustainable macro-economy.

Respecting ecological limits

Once society has accepted the world-view that the economic system is sustained and contained by our finite global ecosystem, it becomes obvious that we must respect ecological limits. This requires that we understand precisely what these limits entail, and where economic activity currently stands in relation to them.

A key category of ecological limit is dangerous waste emissions, including nuclear waste, particulates, toxic chemicals, heavy metals, greenhouse gases, and excess nutrients. The poster child for dangerous wastes is greenhouse gases, as excessive stocks of greenhouse gases in the atmosphere are disrupting the climate. Since most of the energy currently used for economic production comes from fossil fuels, economic activity inevitably generates flows of greenhouse gases into the atmosphere. Ecosystem processes such as plant growth, soil formation, and dissolution of CO_2 in the ocean can sequester CO_2 from the atmosphere. However, if flows into the atmosphere exceed flows out of the atmosphere, then atmospheric stocks will accumulate. This represents a critical ecological threshold for flows, and exceeding it risks runaway climate change with disastrous consequences. At a minimum then, for any type of waste where accumulated stocks are the main problem, emissions must be reduced below absorption capacity.

Current CO_2 stocks are well over 400 parts per million (ppm), and there is already clear evidence of global climate change in current weather patterns. Moreover, the oceans are beginning to acidify as they sequester more CO_2. Acidification threatens the numerous forms of oceanic life that form carbon-based shells or skeletons, such as molluscs, corals, and diatoms. In short, the weight of evidence suggests that we have already exceeded the critical ecological threshold for atmospheric greenhouse gas stocks (Rockström et al. 2009). This means that we must reduce flows by more than 80 percent or increase sequestration until atmospheric stocks are reduced to acceptable levels. If we accept that all individuals are entitled to an equal share of CO_2 absorption capacity, then the wealthy nations would need to reduce net emissions by 95 percent or more.

Another category of ecological limit entails renewable resource stocks, flows, funds and services. All economic production requires the transformation of raw materials provided by nature, including renewable resources (for example, trees). To a large extent, society can choose the rate at which it harvests these raw materials, i.e. cuts down the trees. Whenever extraction rates of renewable resources exceed their regeneration rates, stocks will decline. Eventually, the stock of trees (the forest) will reach a point at which it is no longer capable of regenerating. So the first rule for renewable resource stocks is that extraction rates must not exceed regeneration rates, thus maintaining the stocks to provide appropriate levels of raw materials at an acceptable cost.

However, a forest is not just a warehouse of trees, it is an ecosystem that generates critical services, including life support for its inhabitants. These services are diminished when the structure is depleted or its configuration changed. So another rule for guiding resource extraction and land use conversion is that they must not threaten the capacity of the ecosystem fund to provide essential services. Our limited understanding of ecosystem structure and function, and the dynamic nature of ecological and economic systems, mean that this precise point may be difficult to determine. However, it is increasingly obvious that the extraction of many resources to drive growth has already become uneconomic. Rates of resource extraction must therefore be reduced to below regeneration rates in order to restore ecosystem funds to desirable levels.

Protecting capabilities for flourishing

In a zero-growth or contracting economy, working-time policies that enable equitable sharing of the available work are essential to achieve economic stability and to protect people's jobs and livelihoods. Reduced working hours can also increase flourishing by improving the work/life balance, and there is evidence (Durning 1992; Schor 2005) that working fewer hours can reduce consumption-related environmental impacts. Specific policies should include greater choice for employees about working time; measures to combat discrimination against part-time work as regards grading, promotion, training, security of employment, rate of pay, health insurance, etc.; and better incentives to employees (and flexibility for employers) for family time, parental leave, and sabbatical breaks (Jackson 2009).

Systemic social inequality can likewise undermine the capacity to flourish. It expresses itself in many forms besides income inequality, such as life expectancy, poverty, malnourishment, and infant mortality (Acemoglu and Robinson 2009). Inequality can also drive other social problems (such as over-consumption), increase anxiety, undermine social capital, and expose lower income households to higher morbidity and lower life satisfaction (Jackson 2009).

The degree of inequality varies widely from one sector or country to another. In the civil service, military, and university sectors in the United States, income inequality ranges within a factor of 15 or 20. Corporate America has a range of 500 or more. Many industrial nations are below 25 (Daly 2010).

A sense of community, necessary for democracy, is hard to maintain across such vast income differences. The main justification for such differences has been that they stimulate growth, which will one day filter down, making everyone rich. In our full world, with its steady-state or contracting economy, this is unrealistic. And without aggregate growth, poverty reduction requires redistribution. Fair limits to the range of inequality need to be determined, i.e. a minimum income and a maximum income (ibid.). Studies have also shown that the majority of adults would be willing to give up personal gain in return for reducing inequality they see as unfair (Fehr and Falk 2002; Almås et al. 2010). Redistributive mechanisms and policies could include revised income tax structures, improved access to high quality education, anti-discrimination legislation, implementing anti-crime measures and improving the local environment in deprived areas, and addressing the impact of immigration on urban and rural poverty (Jackson 2009). New forms of cooperative ownership (as in the Mondragón model) or public ownership, as is common in many European nations, can also help constrain internal pay ratios.

The dominance of markets and property rights in allocating resources also can impair communities' capacity to flourish. Private property rights are established when resources can be made "excludable," i.e. one person or group can use a resource while denying access to others. However, many resources essential to human welfare are "non-excludable," meaning that it is difficult or impossible to exclude others from access to them. Examples include oceanic fisheries, timber from unprotected forests, and numerous ecosystem services, including the waste absorption capacity for unregulated pollutants.

Absent property rights, resources are "open access"—anyone may use them, whether or not they pay. However, individual property rights owners are likely to over-exploit or under-provide the resource, imposing costs on others, which is unsustainable, unjust, and inefficient. Private property rights also favor the conversion of ecosystem structure into market product, regardless of the difference in contributions that ecosystems and market products have on human welfare. The incentives are to privatize benefits and socialize costs.

One solution to these problems, at least for some resources, is common ownership. A commons sector, separate from the public or private sector, can hold property rights to resources created by nature or society as a whole and manage them for the equal benefit of all citizens, present and future. Contrary to wide belief, the misleadingly labeled "tragedy of the commons" (Hardin 1968) results from no ownership or open access to resources, not common ownership. Abundant research shows that resources owned in common can be effectively managed through collective institutions that assure cooperative compliance with established rules (Pell 1989; Feeny et al. 1990; Ostrom 1990).

Finally, flourishing communities will be supported and maintained by the social capital built by strong democracy. A strong democracy is most easily understood at the level of community governance, where all citizens are free (and expected) to participate in all political decisions affecting the community. Broad participation requires the removal of distorting influences like special interest lobbying and funding of political campaigns (Farley and Costanza 2002). The process itself helps to satisfy myriad human needs, such as enhancing the citizenry's understanding of relevant issues, affirming their sense of belonging and commitment to the community, offering opportunity for expression and cooperation and strengthening the sense of rights and responsibilities. Historical examples (though participation was restricted to elites) include the town meetings of New England or the system of the ancient Athenians (Prugh et al. 2000; Farley and Costanza 2002).

Building a sustainable macro-economy

The central focus of macro-economic policies is typically to maximize economic growth; lesser goals include price stabilization and ensuring full employment. If society instead adopts the central economic goal of sustainable human well-being, macro-economic policy will change radically. The goal will be to create an economy that offers meaningful employment to all, that balances investments across the four types of capital to maximize well-being. Such an approach would lead to fundamentally different macro-economic policies and rules.

A key leverage point is the current monetary system, which is inherently unsustainable. Most of the money supply is a result of fractional reserve banking. Banks are required by law to retain a percentage of every deposit they receive; the rest they loan at interest. However, loans are then deposited in other banks, which in turn can lend out all but the reserve requirement. The net result is that the new money issued by banks, plus the initial deposit, will be equal to the initial deposit divided by the fractional reserve. For example, if a government credits $1 million to a bank and the fractional reserve requirement is 10 percent, banks can create $9 million in new money, for a total money supply of $10 million. In this way, most money is today created as interest-bearing debt. Total debt in the United States, adding together consumers, businesses, and the government, is about $50 trillion dollars. This is the source of the national money supply.

There are several serious problems with this system. First, it is highly destabilizing. When the economy is booming, banks will be eager to loan money and investors will be eager to borrow, which leads to a rapid increase in money supply. This stimulates further growth, encouraging more lending and borrowing, in a positive feedback loop. A booming economy stimulates firms and households to take on more debt relative to the income flows they use to repay the loans. This means that any slowdown in the economy will make it very difficult for borrowers to meet their debt obligations. Eventually some borrowers will be forced to default. Widespread default eventually creates a self-reinforcing downward economic spiral, leading to recession or worse.

Second, the current system systematically transfers resources to the financial sector. Borrowers must always pay back more than they borrowed. At 5.5 percent interest, homeowners will be forced to pay back twice what they borrowed on a 30-year mortgage. Conservatively speaking, interest on the $50 trillion total debt of the United States must be at least $2.5 trillion a year, one-sixth of our national output.

Third, the banking system will only create money to finance market activities that can generate the revenue required to repay the debt plus interest. Since the banking system currently creates far more money than the government, this system prioritizes investments in market goods over public goods, regardless of the relative rates of return to human well-being.

Fourth, and most important, the system is ecologically unsustainable. Debt, which is a claim on future production, grows exponentially, obeying the abstract laws of mathematics. Future production, in contrast, confronts ecological limits and cannot possibly keep pace. Interest rates exceed economic growth rates even in good times. Eventually, the exponentially increasing debt must exceed the value of current real wealth and potential future wealth, and the system collapses.

To address this problem, the public sector must reclaim the power to create money, a constitutional right in the United States and most other countries, and take away from the banks the right to do so by gradually moving towards 100-percent fractional reserve requirements.

A second key lever for macro-economic reform is tax policy. Conventional economists generally look at taxes, although necessary, as a significant drag on economic growth. However, taxes are an effective tool for internalizing negative externalities into market prices and for improving income distribution.

A shift in the burden of taxation from value added (economic goods, such as income earned by labor and capital) to throughput flow (ecological bads, such as resource extraction and pollution), is critical for shifting towards sustainability (Daly 2010). Such a reform would internalize external costs, thus increasing efficiency (Daly 2008). Taxing the origin and narrowest point in the throughput flow, for example, oil wells rather than sources of CO_2 emissions, induces more efficient resource use in production as well as consumption, and facilitates monitoring and collection. Such taxes could be introduced in a revenue-neutral way, for example, by phasing in resource severance taxes while phasing out regressive taxes such as those on payrolls or sales.

Taxes should also be used to capture unearned income, or rent, in economic parlance. Green taxes are a form of rent capture, since they charge for the private use of resources created by nature. However, there are many other sources of unearned income in society. For example, if a government builds a light rail or subway system—more sustainable alternatives to private cars—adjacent land values typically skyrocket, providing a windfall profit for landowners. New technologies also increase the value of land, due to its role as an essential input into all production (Gaffney 2009). Because the supply of land is fixed, any increase in demand results in an increase in price. Landowners therefore automatically grow wealthier independent of any investments in the land. High taxes on land values (but not on improvements to land, such as buildings) allow the public sector to capture this unearned income. Public ownership through land trusts and other means also allows for public capture of the unearned income and eliminates any reward from land speculation, thus stabilizing the economy.

Tax policy can also be used to reduce income inequality, which can have pernicious effects on human well-being.

There is also a strong correlation between tax rates and social justice (see Figure 18.1). High tax rates that contribute to income equality appear to be closely related to human well-being. This suggests that tax rates should be highly progressive, perhaps asymptotically approaching 100 percent on marginal income. The measure of tax justice should not be how much is taxed away, but rather how much income remains after taxes. For example, hedge fund manager John Paulson earned $4.9 billion in 2010 (Goldstein 2011). If Paulson had to pay a flat tax of 99 percent, he would still retain nearly $1 million per week in income.

Other policies for achieving financial and fiscal prudence will almost certainly be required as well. Our relentless pursuit of debt-driven growth has contributed to the global economic crisis. A new era of financial and fiscal prudence needs to do the following: increase the regulation of national and international financial markets; incentivize domestic savings, for example, through secure (green) national or community-based bonds; outlaw unscrupulous and destabilizing market practices (such as short selling); and provide greater protection against consumer debt (Jackson 2009). Governments must pass laws that restrict the size of financial sector institutions, eliminating any that impose systemic risks for the economy.

Finally, as alluded to above, we need to improve macro-economic accounting, by which we mean replacing or supplementing GDP as the prime economic indicator. GDP does, however, belong as an indicator of economic efficiency. The more efficient we are, the less economic activity, raw materials, energy, and work it requires to provide satisfying lives. When GDP rises faster than life satisfaction, efficiency declines. Our goal should be to minimize GDP, subject to maintaining a high and sustainable quality of life.

Is a sustainable civilization possible?

The very brief sketch we have presented here of a sustainable and desirable "ecological economy," along with some of the policies we think would be required to achieve it, begs the important question of whether these policies taken together are consistent and whether they are sufficient to achieve the goals we have articulated. Can we have a global economy that is not growing in material terms but that is sustainable and provides a high quality of life for most (if not all) people? Several lines of evidence suggest that the answer is yes.

The first comes from history. Achieving long-lasting, zero- or low-growth, and desirable societies has been difficult—but not unheard of. While many historical societies have collapsed

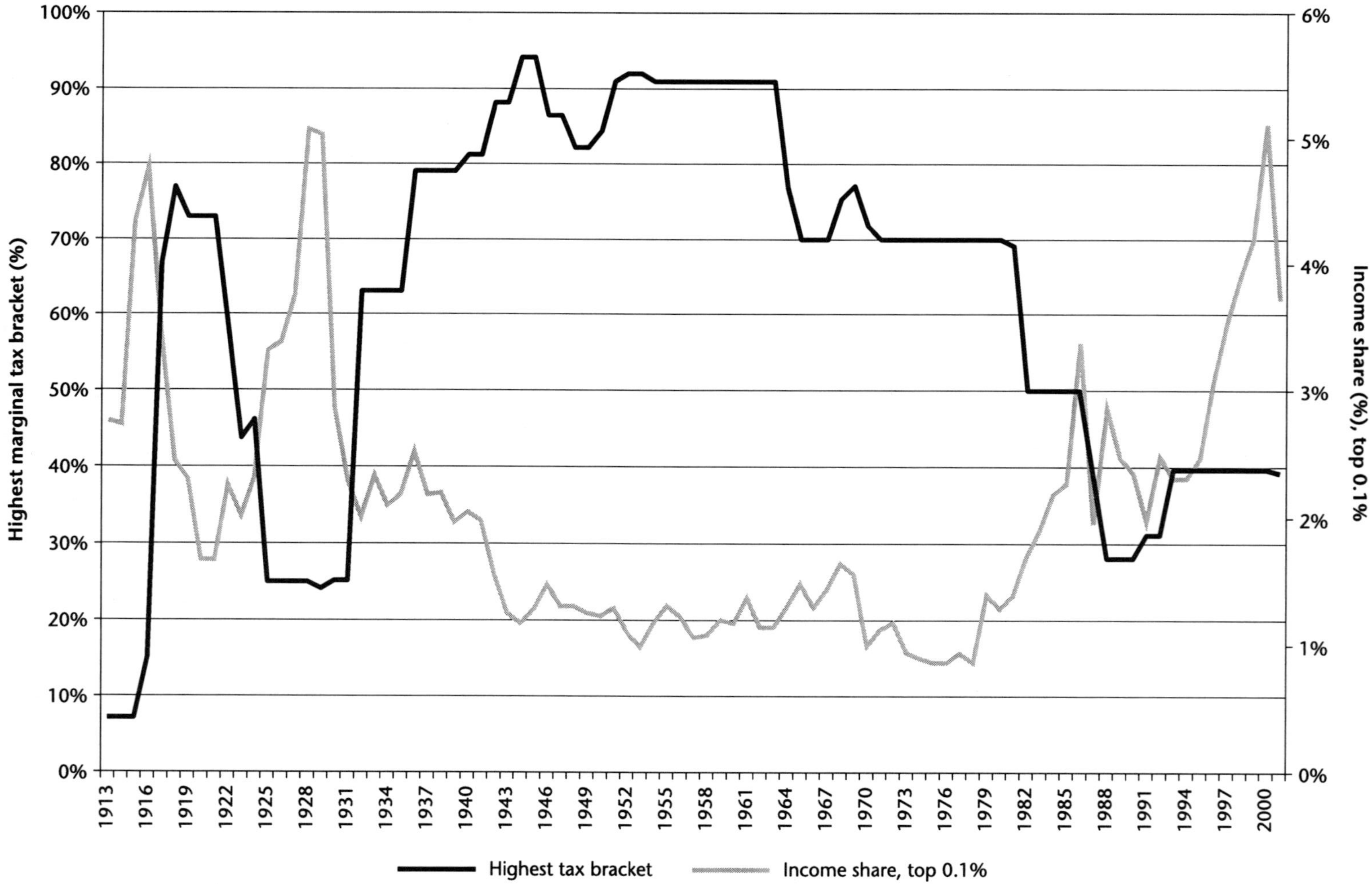

Figure 18.1 Time series of income in the highest tax bracket in the U.S. (black) and income share in the top 0.1% of households (grey) from 1913 to 2002

Source: Daly and Farley (2004).

(Diamond 2005; Costanza et al. 2007), and many of them were not what we would call "desirable," there have been a few successful historical cases in which decline did not occur, including the following (Weiss and Bradley 2001; Diamond 2005):

- Tikopia Islanders have maintained a sustainable food supply and non-increasing population with a bottom-up social organization.
- New Guinea features a silviculture system more than 7,000 years old with an extremely democratic, bottom-up decision-making structure.
- Japan's top-down forest and population policies in the Tokugawa-era arose as a response to an environmental and population crisis, bringing an era of stable population, peace, and prosperity.

A second line of evidence comes from the many groups and communities around the world that are involved in building a new economic vision and testing solutions. Here are a few examples:

- Transition town movement (www.transitionnetwork.org)
- Global EcoVillage Network (www.gen.ecovillage.org)
- Co-Housing Network (www.cohousing.org)
- Wiser Earth (www.wiserearth.org)
- Sustainable Cities International (www.sustainablecities.net)
- Center for a New American Dream (www.newdream.org)
- Democracy Collaborative (www.community-wealth.org)
- Portland, Oregon, Bureau of Planning and Sustainability (www.portlandonline.com/bps/)

All of these examples embody the vision, world-view, and policies we have elaborated to some extent. Their experiments collectively provide evidence that the policies are feasible at a smaller scale. The challenge is to scale up some of these models to society as a whole, and several cities, states, regions, and countries have made significant progress along that path, including Portland, Oregon; Stockholm and Malmö, Sweden; London, UK; the states of Vermont, Washington, and Oregon in the United States; Germany, Sweden, Iceland, Denmark, Costa Rica and Bhutan.

A third line of evidence for the feasibility of our vision is based on integrated modeling studies suggesting that a sustainable, non-growing economy is both feasible and desirable. These include studies using such well-established models as World3, the subject of *The Limits to Growth* (Meadows et al. 1972) and other more recent books, and the Global Unified Metamodel of the BiOsphere (GUMBO) (Boumans et al. 2002).

A recent addition to this suite of modeling tools is LowGrow, a model of the Canadian economy that has been used to assess the possibility of constructing an economy that is not growing in GDP terms but that is stable, with high employment, low carbon emissions, and high quality of life (Victor and Rosenbluth 2007; Victor 2008). LowGrow was explicitly constructed as a fairly conventional macro-economic model calibrated for the Canadian economy, with added features to simulate the effects on natural and social capital.

LowGrow includes features that are particularly relevant for exploring a low/no-growth economy, such as emissions of carbon dioxide and other greenhouse gases, a carbon tax, a forestry sub-model, and provision for redistributing incomes. It measures poverty using the UN's Human Poverty Index. LowGrow allows additional funds to be spent on health care and on programs for reducing adult illiteracy and estimates their impacts on longevity and adult literacy.

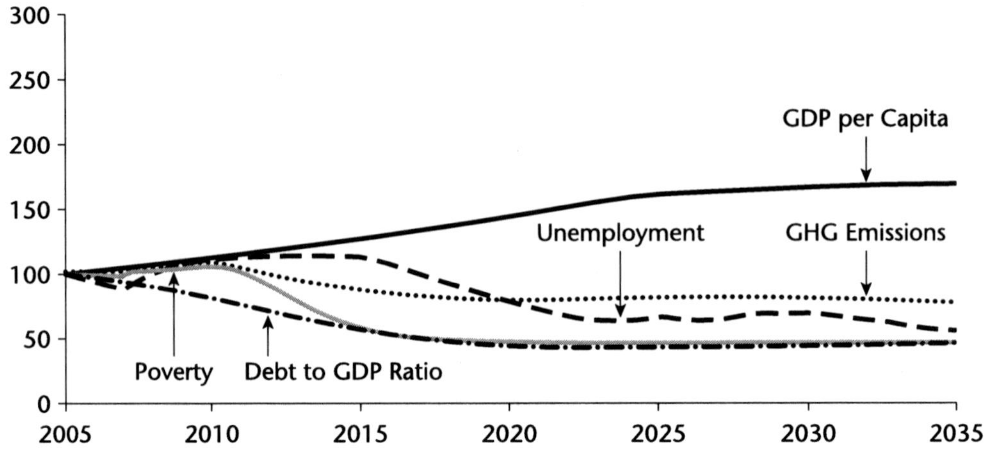

Figure 18.2 A low-/no-growth scenario

Source: Victor (2008).

A wide range of low- and no-growth scenarios can be examined with LowGrow, and some (including that shown in Figure 18.2) offer considerable promise.

Compared with the business-as-usual scenario, in this scenario, GDP per capita grows more slowly, leveling off around 2028, at which time the rate of unemployment is 5.7 percent. The unemployment rate continues to decline to 4.0 percent by 2035. By 2020 the poverty index declines from 10.7 to an internationally unprecedented level of 4.9, where it remains, and the debt-to-GDP ratio declines to about 30 percent and is maintained at that level to 2035. Greenhouse gas emissions are 31 percent lower at the start of 2035 than 2005 and 41 percent lower than their high point in 2010. These results are obtained by slower growth in government expenditures, net investment, and productivity; a positive net trade balance; cessation of growth in population; a reduced workweek; a revenue-neutral carbon tax; and increased government expenditure on anti-poverty programs, adult literacy programs, and health care. In addition, there are more public goods and fewer positional (status) goods, through changes in taxation and marketing; limits on throughput and use of space through better land use planning and habitat protection and ecological fiscal reform; and fiscal and trade policies to strengthen local economies.

These are precisely the policies that we have elaborated in the previous sections of this chapter. No model results can be taken as definitive, since models are only as good as the assumptions that go into them. But what World3, GUMBO, and LowGrow have provided is some evidence for the *consistency* and *feasibility* of these policies, taken together, to produce an economy that is not growing in GDP terms, but that is sustainable and desirable.

This chapter offers a vision of the structure of an "ecological economics" option and how to achieve it—an economy that can provide nearly full employment and a high quality of life for everyone into the indefinite future while staying within the safe environmental operating space for humanity on Earth. The policies laid out here are mutually supportive and the resulting system is feasible. Due to their privileged position, industrial countries have a special responsibility for achieving these goals. Yet this is not a utopian fantasy; to the contrary, it is business as usual that is the utopian fantasy. Humanity will have to create something different and better—or risk collapse into something far worse.

Acknowledgements

This chapter is adapted from a report commissioned by the United Nations for the 2012 Rio+20 Conference. (Costanza et al. 2012) and a shorter version that appeared in the 2013 State of the World Report (Costanza et al. 2013).

References

Acemoglu, D. and Robinson, J. (2009) Foundations of societal inequality. *Science*, 326: 678–679.

Almås, I., Cappelen, A. W., Sørensen, E. Ø. and Tungodden, B. (2010) Fairness and the development of inequality acceptance. *Science*, 328: 1176–1178.

Boumans, R., Costanza, R., Farley, J., Wilson, M. A., Portela, R., Rotmans, J., Villa, F. and Grasso, M. (2002) Modeling the dynamics of the integrated earth system and the value of global ecosystem services using the GUMBO model. *Ecological Economics*, 41: 529–560.

Costanza, R. (1991) *Ecological Economics: The Science and Management of Sustainability*. New York: Columbia University Press.

Costanza, R., Alperovitz, G., Daly, H. E., Farley, J., Franco, C., Jackson, T., Kubiszewski, I., Schor, J. and Victor, P. (2012) *Building a Sustainable and Desirable Economy-in-Society-in-Nature*. New York: United Nations Division for Sustainable Development.

Costanza, R., Alperovitz, G., Daly, H. E., Farley, J., Franco, C., Jackson, T., Kubiszewski, I., Schor, J. and Victor, P. (2013) Building a sustainable and desirable economy-in-society-in-nature. *State of the World 2013: Is Sustainability Still Possible?*. Washington, DC: Island Press.

Costanza, R., Alperovitz, G., Daly, H. E., Farley, J., Franco, C., Jackson, T., Kubiszewski, I., Schor, J. and Victor, P. (2014a) *Building a Sustainable and Desirable Economy-in-Society-in-Nature*. Canberra, Australia, ANU Press.

Costanza, R., Andrade, F., Antunes, P., Van Den Belt, M., Boersma, D., Boesch, D. F., Catarino, F., Hanna, S., Limburg, K., Low, B., Molitor, M., Pereira, J. G., Rayner, S., Santos, R., Wilson, J. and Young, M. (1998) Principles for sustainable governance of the oceans. *Science*, 281: 198–199.

Costanza, R., Darge, R., De Groot, R., Farber, S., Grasso, M., Hannon, B., Limburg, K., Naeem, S., Oneill, R. V., Paruelo, J., Raskin, R. G., Sutton, P. and Van Den Belt, M. (1997) The value of the world's ecosystem services and natural capital. *Nature*, 387: 253–260.

Costanza, R., Graumlich, L., Steffen, W., Crumley, C., Dearing, J., Hibbard, K., Leemans, R., Redman, C. and Schimel, D. (2007) Sustainability or collapse: What can we learn from integrating the history of humans and the rest of nature? *Ambio*, 36: 522–527.

Costanza, R. and Kubiszewski, I. (2014) *Creating a Sustainable and Desirable Future: Insights from 45 Global Thought Leaders*. Singapore: World Scientific.

Costanza, R., Kubiszewski, I., Giovannini, E., Lovins, H., Mcglade, J., Pickett, K. E., Ragnarsdottir, K. V., Roberts, D., De Vogli, R. and Wilkinson, R. (2014b) Time to leave GDP behind. *Nature*, 505: 283–285.

Daly, H. E. (2008) *Ecological Economics and Sustainable Development: Selected Essays of Herman Daly*. Cheltenham: Edward Elgar Publishing.

Daly, H. E. (2010) From a failed-growth economy to a steady-state economy. *Solutions*, 1: 37–43.

Daly, H. E. and Farley, J. (2004) *Ecological Economics: Principles and Applications*. Washington, DC: Island Press.

Diamond, J. (2005) *Guns, Germs, and Steel: The Fates of Human Societies*. New York: W. W. Norton.

Durning, A. (1992) *How Much Is Enough? The Consumer Society and the Future of the Earth*. New York: W. W. Norton.

Easterlin, R. A. (2003) Explaining happiness. *Proceedings of the National Academy of Sciences*, 100: 11176–11183.

Farley, J. and Costanza, R. (2002) Envisioning shared goals for humanity: a detailed, shared vision of a sustainable and desirable USA in 2100. *Ecological Economics*, 43: 245–259.

Feeny, D., Berkes, F., Mccay, B. J. and Acheson, J. M. (1990) The tragedy of the commons: Twenty-two years later. *Human Ecology*, 18: 1–19.

Fehr, E. and Falk, A. (2002) Psychological foundations of incentives. *European Economic Review*, 46: 687–724.

Gaffney, M. (2009) The hidden taxable capacity of land: enough and to spare. *International Journal of Social Economics*, 36: 328–411.

Goldstein, M. (2011) Paulson, at $4.9 billion, tops hedge fund earner list. *Reuters*.

Hardin, G. (1968) The tragedy of the commons. *Science*, New Series, 162(3859): 1243–1248.

Jackson, T. (2009) *Prosperity without Growth: Economics for a Finite Planet*. London: Earthscan/James and James.

Kasser, T. (2002) *The High Price of Materialism*. Cambridge, MA: The MIT Press.

Layard, R. (2005) *Happiness: Lessons from a New Science*. New York: The Penguin Press.

Meadows, D. H., Meadows, D. L., Randers, J. and Behrens, W. W. (1972) *The Limits to Growth*. Rome: Club of Rome.

Ostrom, E. (1990) *Governing the Commons: The Evolution of Institutions for Collective Action*. Cambridge: Cambridge University Press.

Pell, D. (1989) *Common Property Resources: Ecology and Community-Based Sustainable Development*. London: Belhaven.

Prugh, T., Costanza, R. and Daly, H. E. (2000) *The Local Politics of Global Sustainability*. Washington, DC: Island Press.

Rockström, J., Steffen, W., Noone, K., Persson, Å., Chapin, F. S., Lambin, E. F., Lenton, T. M., Scheffer, M., Folke, C., Schellnhuber, H. J., Nykvist, B., De Wit, C. A., Hughes, T., Van Der Leeuw, S., Rodhe, H., Sörlin, S., Snyder, P. K., Costanza, R., Svedin, U., Falkenmark, M., Karlberg, L., Corell, R. W., Fabry, V. J., Hansen, J., Walker, B., Liverman, D., Richardson, K., Crutzen, P. and Foley, J. A. (2009) A safe operating space for humanity. *Nature*, 461: 472–475.

Schor, J. B. (2005) Sustainable consumption and worktime reduction. *Journal of Industrial Ecology*, 9: 37–50.

Talberth, J., Cobb, C. and Slattery, N. (2007) *The Genuine Progress Indicator 2006: A Tool for Sustainable Develoment*. Oakland, CA: Redefining Progress.

Victor, P. A. (2008) *Managing Without Growth: Slower by Design, Not Disaster*. Cheltenham: Edward Elgar Publishing.

Victor, P. A. and Rosenbluth, G. (2007) Managing without growth. *Ecological Economics*, 61: 492–504.

Weiss, H. and Bradley, R. S. (2001) What drives societal collapse? *Science*, 291: 609–610.

19

SUSTAINABLE DEVELOPMENT AND THE ECONOMIC CRISIS UNDER AUSTERITY

The experience of the United Kingdom

Michael Redclift and Emma Hinton

The discussion of sustainable development was initially prompted by the report of the Brundtland Commission (WCED 1987; Redclift 1987, 2005) and focused upon the less developed world and the relations between the Global North and Global South. The mainstream sustainable development discourse, which originated in and was driven by developed countries, assumed that economic growth would continue unchecked and that it could be made sustainable by implementing changes in technology and policy which could reduce environmental externalities ('ecological modernisation'). In contrast, an alternative discourse, which circulated predominantly outside international governance institutions, understood one of the key problems to be the pressure placed on the environment by excessive consumption, particularly in the developed world, which could best be addressed by implementing 'limits to growth'. 'Sufficiency', according to the mainstream sustainability discourse, was linked to poverty and was confined to poorer, developing economies, largely in the form of attention to 'basic needs'. Yet sufficiency took on a more positive connotation within the alternative discourse: 'voluntary simplicity' found some support among a minority of the middle classes in the developed world (Elgin 1993). More recently, the financial problems experienced within many developed countries since 2008 present a new opportunity for sufficiency in the face of imposed austerity. Consumers with reduced disposable incomes are now often forced to 'do more with less' and the financial crisis has been used by some sustainable consumption advocates to attempt to persuade consumers to embrace sufficiency. The implications of economic austerity for the developed world, informed by experiences during and after the Second World War (Zweininger-Bargielowska 2002), are now being considered more seriously. However, the prevailing economic and political conditions then were radically different from those today.

This chapter builds upon work in sustainability, sustainable development and environmental security, and seeks to extend and develop our understanding of these ideas in the context of economic austerity in much of Europe and North America since the 'economic crisis' of 2008. It considers the principles and practices which underlie current attempts to make shifts in consumption and investment, to combat climate change and to reduce the negative impact of human activities on the natural environment, at a time when financial institutions are often constrained or febrile. It is suggested that the policy tools being developed to combat the current fiscal crisis are insufficiently linked to environmental challenges, to social agency and real-world experiences of environmental governance.

The chapter examines the different underlying models of individual and group behaviour favoured by governments, businesses and third sector organisations in Britain today, including regulation, market-based Green consumption and 'non-market'-based instruments. Each of these policy approaches is predicated on assumptions about human behaviour during a period of relative 'prosperity' between 1955 and the beginning of this century. Regulation assumes high levels of compliance and often involves 'regulatory capture' as the regulating agency becomes complicit with the regulated. Market-based models in turn usually assume that *levels* of personal consumption cannot be changed readily, while *forms* can be: fair trade, responsible travel, alternative food networks, etc. Finally, community-based, non-market models emphasise the need to manage insufficient resources (material and time) through barter, or the substitution of 'use values' for market activities (for example, community food banks, credit unions, allotments, Web communication and advocacy, Local Exchange and Trading Schemes (LETS) and recycling). In addition, many of the new forms of political association and networking are digital or 'virtual' in nature, and their implications for arriving at a better conceptual understanding are only beginning to be acknowledged (Redclift et al. 2011).

These concerns over underlying models suggest that we should re-examine the fragile basis for compliance in current public policy towards both the financial and environmental 'crises', and the future direction of alternative and 'oppositional' politics. It is clear that a world whose surpluses were generated by an expanding tax base and increasing private affluence can no longer be taken for granted. The chapter seeks to build on the sustainability research agenda by drawing on what we have learned about austerity and 'sufficiency' over half a century ago, as well as in recent decades. It is argued that the history of austerity policies in the past can provide insights for contemporary 'austerity' policies in the United Kingdom and more widely in Europe.

The economic 'crisis'

The discussion of sustainable development is necessarily linked today with the banking crisis that has affected most financial institutions since September 2007. In the UK, this led to the first economic downturn since the 1990s and the most serious economic recession since the 1930s. The 'toxicity' of many financial institutions was triggered by excessive lending in a number of countries including the United States, the United Kingdom, Spain and Ireland, especially on house purchases. This brought about a loss of confidence in the ability of the lending institutions to recoup their assets, and national governments acted to guarantee the private banking sector against a feared 'run on the banks'. These developments occurred within the context of relatively high personal (and institutional) indebtedness since the 1980s in many, though not all, OECD countries (Ferguson 2003).

The financial crisis has led to a reinvigoration of less mainstream articulations of what sustainable development might entail (see Chapter 15 in this volume), such as alternative modes of socio-economic organisation. Since the G20 meeting in April 2009, thousands of people – climate change campaigners, economic activists and ordinary members of the public – have taken to the streets to protest at the unsustainability of the current economic system in the face of climate change, and to call for radical change. The global 'Occupy' movement is a prominent example (though its focus is primarily on social and economic inequality, rather than environmental issues) and one which has strong links to anti-consumerism: Occupy Wall Street, conceived and promoted by the Adbusters Media Foundation in mid-2011, was one of the first Occupy protests to garner significant media attention. Some sustainable consumption advocates have referred to the financial crisis as a means for legitimating radical changes to personal consumption. The Energy Saving Trust (EST), a not-for-profit organisation operating in the UK to promote sustainable energy consumption, sought to engage the public via its 'Wartime Spirit' campaign in 2009. Referring to a survey it had commissioned of over 1,500 people, the EST found public support for wartime-era activities such as community-level resource management, sharing food or journeys, and for externally imposed limits or rations to help people to reduce their consumption. Phillip Sellwood, Chief Executive of the EST, suggested that the financial crisis presented an opportunity for the British public to embrace a 'wartime spirit' of voluntary thrift, sufficiency and austerity:

> We are certainly not advocating a return to rationing or indeed enforced personal daily allowances. However, if we could adopt just a few of the practices used during the war, such as recycling bath water for watering plants, then it would go a long way towards saving energy and reducing our carbon footprint ... We can now see an age of 'thrift being the new thrust' and 'frugality the new frontier'.
>
> *(EST 2009)*

This kind of sustainable consumption advocacy echoes the imposed austerity associated with the Second World War in some respects. Yet despite public support for enforced austerity today in some quarters, in light of the fiscal deficit, the 'new frontier' of frugality suggests conditions very different from those of 70 years ago.

At the same time a shift has been occurring in consumer policy, this time prompted by the much wider acknowledgement of the threat of global, anthropogenically-induced climate change following the publication of the series of IPCC Assessment Reports and the Stern Review on the Economics of Climate Change (Stern 2007). The need to pursue 'low-carbon' solutions to economic growth rapidly altered policy discourses surrounding consumption, and it has become an article of faith for public policy that economic growth is only tolerable if it does not exacerbate existing concentrations of greenhouse gases (GHGs) in the atmosphere. In 2008, the United Kingdom introduced its Climate Change Act, which established a very ambitious and legally binding target for GHG emission reductions of 80 per cent by 2050 compared to the 1990 baseline. This policy activity had been accompanied by sustained activity on the part of NGOs and others, including the series of Camps for Climate Action in the UK between 2006 and 2010, which lobbied and mobilised public support for urgent action on climate change and a new approach to economic organisation. Since 2009, however, the introduction of economic austerity policies in the United Kingdom, as elsewhere in Europe, has shifted attention away from climate change, framed as a future problem, and towards the distributional consequences of budget cuts at the national level in the present. The campaigns for environmentally sustainable policies are now waged against the drumbeat of enforced cuts in public expenditure and the need for private consumers to 'spend more' and stimulate economic growth with the promise that this will deliver private benefits in terms of increased employment opportunities, disposable income and quality of life, regardless of whether it is economically or environmentally sustainable in the longer term.

This prioritisation of growth regardless of its environmental costs is in marked contrast with the policy discourses governing sustainability just a few years ago, which sought to deliver a more sustainable form of growth by reducing environmental externalities. The pre-austerity perspective (before 2009) is seen clearly in the document which, more than any other, represents the high-water mark of free market environmentalism: the Stern Review. Stern (2007) wrote: 'The transition to a low-carbon economy will bring challenges for competitiveness but also opportunities for growth . . . Reducing the expected adverse impacts of climate change is therefore both highly desirable and feasible.' This quotation illustrates the way in which what had previously been viewed as a 'threat' could quickly become an 'opportunity', though the quotation fails to say for whom the opportunities exist. Unsurprisingly, the immediate responses to Stern (and the IPCC Fourth Assessment in 2007) were effusive and optimistic in tone. One commentator on business and the environment wrote:

> People would pay a little more for carbon-intensive goods, but our economies could continue to grow strongly . . . The shift to a low-carbon economy will also bring huge opportunities . . . Climate change is the greatest market failure the world has seen.
>
> *(Welford 2006)*

The characterization of climate change as a 'market failure' immediately offered economists, businesses and government a lifeline. Rather than necessitating expensive and comprehensive restructuring in systems of provision or even reduced volumes of production and consumption, Stern's neoclassical view that sustainability could be delivered through *increased* consumption of particular kinds of products, simultaneously feeding the economy, typifies the mainstream sustainable consumption discourse. In contrast, the attention given to the Fifth IPCC Report in 2012 was eclipsed by the perceived priority of engineering economic growth, at whatever cost to sustainability, through hydraulic fracturing (or 'fracking'), increased nuclear power capability and subsidies to first-time home buyers. The goal was to 'liberate' spending, rather than long-term sustainable investment, and to do so through stimulating consumption, especially on the High Street.

These developments in the UK economy and in public policy raise some awkward questions for the extent to which it will be possible to deliver sustainable consumption. If sustainable consumption is understood to be compatible with increasing levels of consumption, so long as this shifts to the consumption of less resource-intensive products – as per the mainstream sustainability discourse – then the current focus on increasing the consumption of any and all kinds of products in order to revive the economy may not deliver sustainability. If, instead, sustainable consumption necessitates frugality, thrift and a kind of voluntary austerity – key features of the alternative sustainable consumption discourse – then a focus on economic growth will be unsustainable whatever the short-term socio-economic benefits from addressing the economic downturn. It is pertinent to reflect that the rising levels of personal consumption in the UK in the latter half of the twentieth century, considered by some to have exceeded environmental limits, were driven by efforts to revive the national economy following a period of wartime and post-war austerity (1940–1960). The link between macroeconomic policy and sustainable consumption is discussed next.

Macroeconomic policy and sustainable consumption today

The contrasts between public policy today and prior to the 2008 'economic crisis' demonstrate how sustainable consumption has developed as a policy discourse during the last two decades. General optimism about the economy in the United Kingdom during the last decade coupled with an escalation in property prices had served to discourage saving (Bernthal et al. 2005; Braucher 2006) and increase consumption. At the same time the level of indebtedness had increased, even prior to the banking crisis of 2008/9. In a society in which increased equity in housing seemed assured and borrowing was easy, individuals were prepared to buy property to rent and re-mortgage their homes with apparent alacrity (Tucker 1991). More disposable income meant enhanced personal consumption, rather than saving, and *sustainable* consumption (or the consumption of more sustainable products) represented another consumer choice in a buoyant market. It was one way in which the citizen, passenger, or neighbour could be re-labelled as a 'customer', a discursive practice which had grown since the 1980s, and which drew attention to the ubiquity of market relations (Cross 1993; Cohen 2003). For Green and Left critics, it also represented a further step towards the privatization of people's lives and aspirations and the disarticulation of community and solidarity bonds.

Interest in sustainable consumption was fuelled by the expansion of credit and market opportunities (Bernthal et al. 2005). It consisted largely of widening consumer choice and making new or ethical products more available on the market rather than in comprehensively narrowing choice to fewer, more sustainable products and services. Progress towards sustainable consumption was quantified in terms of numbers of purchases of particular 'green' or 'ethical' commodities, where success was framed in terms of market share (Clarke et al. 2007). Although there has been some interest in 'choice editing' in policy circles (Sustainable Consumption Roundtable 2006), this has only had limited application to date, such as the phase-out of energy inefficient incandescent light bulbs in the EU and around the world.

Prior to the economic crisis, the rise in disposable income (for most consumers) was driven in part by increasing female participation in the labour force, facilitating wider social participation for the majority (but not all) of the population (Goodman and Redclift 1991). This model of rising consumption had also been associated with longer working hours, as Richard Titmuss had argued, to explain the apparent rise of the 'Affluent Society' in the late 1950s (Titmuss 1962) and captured more recently in the concept of 'time poverty' (de Graaf 2003). In addition, of course, the post-war generation of so-called 'baby-boomers', having paid off their mortgages, had surplus income with which to either consume more or to pass on to their children.[1] The model of growth at the dawn of the twenty-first century was one of enhanced personal consumption on the basis of negotiated debt.

This 'model' of 'stabilised' debt management and enhanced personal consumption might at first appear at odds with what we refer to as 'sustainable consumption', but in fact it was quite consistent with the individual consumer-based policy discourses of the last decade. The increased purchase of consumer goods and services which carry an 'environmental', 'natural' or 'ethical' imprimatur has been bolted on to a loosely regulated market that prioritised individual choice and profitability over more fundamental shifts in behaviour. The context for most sustainable consumption discourses during the last few years has elements which were consistent with credit expansion and indebtedness, rather than 'self-sufficiency' and deeper Green credentials (OECD 2002). In fact, the sustainable development discourses were several, and often mutually contradictory throughout the period in which the idea of green consumerism as 'sustainable consumption' became established.

Discourses of fear: climate and war

It is worth considering the strengths and weaknesses of campaigns to encourage austerity. Wartime rationing and austerity represented a very different challenge from that of today. The rise in personal consumption which marked the last half of the twentieth century has served to obscure the experiences of wartime and post-war rationing and scarcity which preceded it (Calder 1969; Hickman 1995; Briggs 2000; Gardiner 2004; Hennessy 2006). During that period of austerity, between 1940 and the end of rationing 15 years later, the British people became accustomed to scarcity, and to the imposition of an administrative edict governing what they could consume and how they could spend (Sissons and French 1964; Longmate 1971; Briggs 1975; Hennessy 1993). The time line begins with enforced wartime austerity in 1940, when Churchill took over the new Coalition Government, and continues through the impulse of the Beveridge Report and post-war shortages into the late 1950s and 1960s. With the arrival of relative prosperity, the era in which the British public had 'never had it so good', in Prime Minister Macmillan's words, the level of personal consumption took a dramatic turn. The Great Depression of the 1930s had come about as a result of insufficient demand, according to Keynes, and the creation of the Welfare State and the post-war planned economy were attempts to enhance security and increase economic stability through increased demand. By the 1960s, the improvement in household income levels and the pattern of economic growth suggested that the model had succeeded. There was no injunction for the public to spend until the late 1950s, because there was little to spend money on and the injunction to save during and after the Second World War was not only a moral one, it was a necessity, given the scale of government borrowing. In other respects, too, the new social order was manifesting social changes. Much of the appalling pre-war housing deficit, made worse by the bombing of cities, was beginning to be addressed by the early 1950s, and some areas of personal consumption, such as clothing and furniture, which had been rationed during the war, were beginning to be seen as market opportunities. The 'utility' brand introduced for clothes and furniture was making way for 'ready-to-wear' and the creation of 'wants' rather than the fulfilment of 'needs' by the mid-1950s. The legacy of the austerity years was that personal consumption was grounded in family and household security, for the first time. Personal credit was still largely a thing of the future, and the opportunities for savings were limited. Even in wartime Britain it was often difficult to distinguish between 'essential' and 'non-essential' items, as Juliet Gardiner shows in her excellent history of the Home Front, but this distinction was even more difficult to make in the succeeding period (Gardiner 2004).

The years of austerity laid the basis for modern consumer Britain, not simply in seeming to offer choice and individuality, where it had been absent, but also in helping to disseminate new social attitudes. The post-war consensus surrounding the British welfare state continued in the 1950s under the soubriquet of 'Butskellism', the hybrid name given by Norman Macrae to the common perspective of R. A. Butler and Hugh Gaitskell (Hennessy 2006: 211). The Welfare State was constructed on the twin pillars of sound Keynesian economics and Beveridge's attractive policies for comprehensive social security. It was established to meet need, and succeeded in doing so, but not everyone envisaged it as the launching pad for wholesale advances in personal consumption and credit, such as ensued from the 1960s onwards. It was a generation for which 'everything was achievable', and those achievements would not be put fully in jeopardy for another half-century, under the financial crisis heralded by a 'credit crunch', which began in the autumn of 2008 (ibid.: 27). Without the platform provided by the British Welfare State, it is difficult to imagine an exit from the siege economy of wartime, but wartime austerity was the platform on which unsustainable consumption was built in the last quarter of the century. It is something of a paradox, then, that the 'new' austerity practised by the UK Coalition Government (2010–2015) has been implemented largely through reforming (or 'demolishing') the Welfare State, rather than through increased taxation.

Voluntarism and rationing

The situation of consumers in 1940, or 1950 for that matter, was very different in most respects from that of today. For some UK consumers, the contemporary financial crisis has meant a reduction in disposable income and, consequently, limited opportunities for consumption, especially in the face of rising unemployment and the raft of changes to taxation and benefits introduced by the Conservative–Liberal Democrat coalition government that came into power in 2010 (the first since Churchill's). It is only for those who are still able to consume freely and who consume the most that 'voluntary simplicity', 'downsizing' or a 'lowered carbon footprint' are relevant: they are most able to participate in these activities and their participation is most likely to make a difference to the outcome (e.g. Bond 2005).

Consumer 'satisfaction' was an oxymoron until the late 1950s, when a new era of consumerism was made possible through mass production and indeed encouraged to support economic renewal after the war. Prior to this, in wartime, personal consumption and market choices were severely limited. Food production is a case in point: subject to rationing throughout and immediately after the Second World War, the British public were encouraged to 'make do' by avoiding waste and 'grow(ing) your own'. This has echoes in contemporary sustainable consumption discourses: many third sector advocates now call for consumers not just to buy more sustainable products, but also to engage in sufficiency by growing their own food either alone or in community gardens and farms, as well as reducing waste (Hinton 2011). The possibility of introducing a form of rationing has been seriously considered again recently in the UK, though this time for energy consumption. The concept of personal tradable emission quotas – a form of carbon rationing – gained some political support: it had been part of Green Party policy since the 1990s but more recently had the support of multiple Secretaries of State for the Environment under the Labour government, which commissioned a pre-feasibility study into the matter and included in the 2008 Climate Change Act a provision for the government to introduce such a scheme without further primary legislation (The Lean Economy Connection 2013). Government action on the subject has subsequently stalled, however, following the unfavourable cost-benefits analysis produced in the pre-feasibility study (ibid.). Frustrated by the apparent lack of political commitment to take radical action to tackle climate change, some activists attending the National Climate March in London in 2005 subsequently established a loose, national network of Carbon Rationing Action Groups (CRAGs), whose members voluntarily monitor and ration the carbon emissions associated with their domestic energy consumption and transport (Hinton 2011). In considering the potential for rationing to support contemporary sustainable consumption, it is worth revisiting the impact of rationing on post-war consumption in the UK. To what extent did the nation put on a united patriotic front to meet the economic challenges of war, and what consequences did this have for consumption over the longer term?

The nation's food supply had been seriously jeopardised by pre-war shifts in production: much of the land was under pasture and the animals were fed on imported fodder, so reversing the trend was not easy to undertake (Gardiner 2004). Under the Emergency Powers Act, the Ministry of Agriculture could requisition farms and intervene wherever farm production was unsatisfactory. In addition, the government controlled the slaughter of livestock and the price offered to producers. 'Luxury' crops, such as cut flowers, were forced out and a massive campaign was undertaken to grow more food on allotments and smallholdings. By 1942, it was estimated that 'over half the nation's manual workers had an allotment or garden', and by the end of the war probably one-tenth of total farm production came from allotments (Gardiner 2004: 166). By 1944, there were over half a million new allotments (Briggs 2000: 59). However, a closer look at this evidence suggests that the move to allotments was both more and less than an act of patriotic fervour. A survey in *The Economist* published in the same year showed that only one-fifth of allotment holders claimed to be working them to help the war effort. Over half said their main aim was to produce fresh food for themselves, family and friends, and about one-fifth cited 'fresh air' and the desire 'to save money' as their chief objectives. This suggests that 'a combination of public and private interest lay behind much voluntary, and even compulsory, war work' (ibid.: 59). Self-sufficiency was engineered by necessity in wartime, yet contributed to the well-being of individuals and their communities. It underlined the wartime propaganda that personal sacrifices would ultimately contribute to military victory.

The 'war economy' of 1940 is often viewed, with hindsight, as a successful attempt to galvanise people for a common cause, setting clear economic and social priorities and enlisting widespread public support for them, under a national Coalition Government. It is worth recalling the scope of this challenge, 'to direct the economy, straight and fast, towards the production of weapons' (Calder 1969: 69). In 1939, plans were laid for a three-year war: shipbuilding was to be doubled, two million more acres were to come under the plough, and imported raw materials were to come under the monopoly control of the government. The Ministries of Supply and Food used a system of 'controls' to manage production and control demand, working closely with the private sector trade associations. In the first few years of the war, the 'belt-tightening' was highly selective, and most people who could afford luxury goods obtained them easily (ibid.: 70). There was rapid inflation, especially of clothing and food, although most unfurnished accommodation was subject to rent controls. By the Spring of 1940 there was a real risk that inflation might trigger more wage pressure, and even strikes (such as happened in the still privatised coal industry).

This was the context in which rationing was introduced to the British consumer, initially on a very tentative basis, but later on an unprecedented scale. The evidence, from the Mass Observation archive and elsewhere is that the public were ready for it: 'people minded doing without their usual quantities less than they minded the unfairness which came with the shortages' (ibid.: 71). At the same time, in the early stages of the war, it proved difficult allocating labour to sectors where it was most needed, such as munitions production. There had been too few skilled workers during the period of re-armament in the late 1930s, and more labour was needed to replace those who were being called up into the forces. Even the full potential offered by women's employment, so obvious during the First World War, was only gradually re-acknowledged (Ciment and Russell 2007).

Voluntarism is an important element of contemporary sustainable consumption advocacy: consumers are encouraged to voluntarily change the ways they consume and are supported in these endeavours by encouragements from voluntary organisations (Hinton 2011). This emphasis on voluntary behaviour change has precedents in wartime discourses of sufficiency. According to popular myth, encapsulated in television programmes like *Dad's Army*, about the Home Guard, much of the 'success' on the Home Front can be attributed to ordinary people's willingness to work together, even if it often appeared eccentric. It is argued that, in combination with labour controls, wartime voluntarism succeeded in forging a war economy out of a domestic economy – saucepans were literally turned into Spitfires.

The evidence, however, is more mixed. The methods of 'command and control' exercised by the state in wartime were most effective in drawing out the public's full potential when they were linked to voluntary efforts. Government edicts did not receive immediate legitimacy, especially in the first year of the war, and several critical studies of morale such as the reports from the Mass Observation archive, suggest widespread public unease with the inefficiencies, and injustices, of controls (Calder 1969; 1992). People did acknowledge that changes in their work and daily life could also carry private advantages – this, perhaps, was an early precedent for Soper's 'alternative hedonism' (Soper 2008), which she proposes as a driver of sustainable consumption. As Asa Briggs has argued, the 'distinctively British combination of voluntary effort and compulsory service . . . has to be charted occupation by occupation, region by region', it was not self-evidently successful (Briggs 2000: 35). In fact, even mobilising women's labour on a voluntary basis was still inadequate for the war effort, and women were directed into jobs in 1941, the year in which civil defence also ceased to be voluntary. Again, contrary to the popular imagination, the industrial war effort effectively reached its apogee in 1943, two years before the war ended, and after this date a major preoccupation of the authorities was how to return men and women in the forces to civilian work. Demobilisation rather than mobilisation was the policy challenge. In some respects, the post-war years suggest that: 'the "war effort" deserved praise, but more than fifty years later it demands discussion as much as recollection and celebration. In some respects it left Britain less prepared for years of peace than its enemies' (ibid.: 35). One aspect of this was that the wartime deprivations also contributed to the demand for social improvement after the war.

If voluntarism is only a partial explanation of the public mood in wartime, and one that needs to be prised from its ideological wrappings, so do the successes of rationing. The war economy meant that resources of labour and capital were diverted from domestic production into the industries most directly employed in conflict. Food production needed to increase on the limited land base available to the British, to save on imports from North America, and to meet the ever increasing needs of the 'non-productive' sector represented by the war economy. The threat of famine, or its imminence, was not lost on political leaders, especially after the débâcle at the end of the Great War, when Britain had been forced to ration most food, with the exception of milk, vegetables and fish. During the winter of 1917–1918, food rationing had ensured adequate supplies of food to British households, though imports from the United States proved necessary in 1918 (Ciment and Russell 2007: 299).

Food rationing had been anticipated by most of the public before it was introduced during the Second World War. The National Identity Card and the Food Ration card were familiar staples of wartime Britain, which only ended in 1952 (for ID cards) and 1954 (for ration books). Peter Hennessy argues that 'selling rationing to the people during the war was the most successful Government public relations exercise' he ever encountered (1993: 47). The food rations were linked to recipes and good health, and cooking meals on limited resources was championed by radio celebrities, including Lord Woolton, the Food Minister and the 'Radio Doctor'. However, even Hennessy admits that 'there is a danger of compiling an over-rosy picture of genius and solidarity at the store and in the queue' (ibid.: 48). Food rationing enabled demand to be met by supply, ultimately through the introduction of a 'points system' introduced in 1941. As Gardiner commented, 'All rationing could do – and this was by no means negligible – was to ensure a fair distribution of basic items, be they food or clothing' (2004: 177). The existence of the ration also drew attention to those who were able to flout the rules, through wealth or criminality, and as such probably fuelled the feelings about inequality which helped to bring the Labour Government to power in 1945. The great success of rationing was to 'bring the battle front' into the home, putting women, particularly, into the 'front line' (ibid.: 181).

Wartime rationing was supplemented by campaigns to reduce waste. Richard Hoggart commented in the 1980s that the folk memory of people who had lived through the war was infected with 'the built-in rules of thumb of the permanent siege economy' (quoted by Hennessy 1993: 308). 'There is still,' he wrote, 'behind every dealing with money and things, the fear and the hatred of waste.' That old phrase, 'you'll pay for this', is joined by 'it's a sin and a crime to be so wasteful', 'fancy good food being thrown away', 'waste not, want not', and dozens of similar expressions, all of which express the fear of excess. These ingrained attitudes and values reflect the fact that rationing, of petrol, clothes, furniture and food was not a wartime phenomenon alone. In fact, there was no easing of rationing until 1949, and in 1947, two years after the war ended, it was at its worst. It was to be several years before children saw for the first time 'the first pineapples and bananas, the first washing machine, the first television set. The world opening before us was not a pale imitation of one we had lost, but a lucky dip of extraordinary things we had never seen' (Susan Cooper, quoted by Hennessy 1993: 309). Thus the austerity associated with the war years was followed by conspicuous over-consumption, a type of lifestyle that was newly available to generations that had grown used to the tight rationing of resources.

What do these experiences of wartime austerity suggest for contemporary sustainable consumption efforts in the context of enforced austerity? For those with increasingly limited incomes following the economic crisis and the package of austerity measures subsequently introduced by the UK government, opportunities to consume in the same volumes as before have diminished. This might be expected to have had a negative impact on the consumption of sustainable products, since these often carry a price premium. Perhaps the current experience of austerity could encourage consumers to both question the current economic system and to become habituated to consuming less, supporting sufficiency and, consequently, sustainable consumption (Hinton and Goodman 2010). However, this may be an over-simplification, as Evans (2011) argues: consumers may respond to limited incomes by enacting thrift (restraining expenditure but maintaining consumption and the ethics of care for those within a person's social network that this performs) rather than developing frugality (where the emphasis is on restraining consumption in response to moralistic impulses). According to Evans, while frugality can support sustainable consumption, thrift may not; and it may take more than the current economic downturn for the majority of consumers to question both their own ethical and moral engagements in consumption and the economic system that demands unceasing growth. Further, a school of thought within environmental psychology posits that though sustainable forms of consumption behaviour might develop in response to some external driver, once that driver is removed, it is only those holding the 'right' attitudes and values that will sustain that behaviour, with the others reverting to prior unsustainable forms (e.g. Crompton 2010; Chilton et al. 2012). Contemporary austerity may not, therefore, contain within it the seeds for longer-term sufficiency and sustainable consumption for the majority of consumers.

Conclusion

This chapter has compared some aspects of the austerity programmes in Britain during the Second World War, and the subsequent decade, with contemporary measures to reduce consumption and enhance sustainability within a new climate of austerity. It has argued that during wartime both austerity and sufficiency were key planks in the policy discourse, and that they were the product of increased government powers, enhanced regulation and more emphasis on voluntary measures throughout the civilian population. This conjuncture was made possible by the threat of military defeat and, indeed in the first two or three years, of invasion and occupation by German forces. The moves to austerity and sufficiency gained considerable public support and were bound up with – though always capable of undermining – national morale. There is both circumstantial and documentary evidence that, provided the burden of wartime austerity was shared 'fairly', the public response was largely positive. The largely favourable response to the Beveridge Report, which was published in 1943, underlines this claim (Nicholson 1984). It is therefore tempting to infer that if the public accept the severity of the threat of the negative impacts associated with climate change and resource scarcity in contemporary Britain, they may also accept the need to implement sufficiency in their personal consumption.

The period of rationing and austerity led, in turn, to demands to widen social insurance, and improve health and life chances in the post-war world, of which the principal architects were Keynes and William Beveridge. During the 1950s, a broad consensus developed around policies designed to reverse pre-war social and economic conditions. The period of austerity and 'belt-tightening' was followed by one of affluence, in which personal consumption rose and personal security increased. Economic growth was increasingly harnessed to provide previously unseen levels of private affluence, and helped to fund improved social services. In time, the moves away from austerity not only increased levels of personal consumption, they also generated new levels of credit and debt, particularly associated with equity in house ownership and increased personal mobility. To some extent, then, the concern with environmental problems in the late 1950s and 1960s was associated with 'plenty', rather than 'scarcity', and policies came to reflect a concern with the situation of succeeding generations, rather than past ones. The drive for sustainability was linked to intergenerational equity and fears for the future became increasingly linked to issues like climate change, rather than military defeat.

In this sense the comparison between austerity Britain and the current challenge to 'decarbonise society' (Redclift 2009) are not so much historical parallels and contrasts as succeeding historical periods, linked inexorably by the experience of economic growth in the second half of the twentieth century, not only in the United Kingdom but throughout Western Europe. Wartime austerity and sufficiency (1939–1955) gave rise to enhanced levels of personal and family security (1956–1997) when sustainability was largely seen as a desirable rather than necessary policy goal. Heavy reliance on new forms of financial capital, increased dependence on housing equity and easy access to credit helped to precipitate both private and public sector indebtedness and a loss of confidence in the markets which had made the protracted economic 'boom' possible. At the same time, the dependence on hydrocarbons became linked with 'externalities', principally global warming. The subsequent period (2008 onwards) has been one in which increased insecurity, prompted by personal and sovereign debt, sits alongside calls for more sustainable behaviour in areas such as domestic energy consumption and for increased engagement in voluntarism in order to meet social need following the further rolling back of the state (the 'Big Society' advocated by British Prime Minister, David Cameron). At the same time, a suite of 'austerity' policies have been introduced both to cut public sector budgets in order to reduce the deficit and to support economic recovery by calling for increased spending and consumption.

The major driver now is climate change, but the imperatives, unlike those of wartime, are not so tangibly identified, and are often politically contested, not least because personal consumers are not forced by events to make the necessary economies. The links, however, are instructive: public policy in the United Kingdom has emphasised green consumption as a facet of the 'sustainable development' discourse, while refusing to acknowledge, for example, the importance of home ownership (over rental housing) as an essential element of the policy 'package'. The current policy dilemmas over sustainable development are a product of the past, as well as a mirror to past periods of real austerity, but they fail to problematize 'prosperity' in other than conventional terms and, as such, are inadequate in the face of both domestic and global challenges, notably of climate change.

Note

1 This interpretation is also consistent with a Regulation Theory approach, which helped to explain the ability of capitalism to stabilise itself in the 1970s and 1980s, but might also help explain the illusion of 'stability' during the long boom of the last decade (Aglietta 1976; Boyer 1990; Jessop and Ngai-Ling Sum 2006).

References

Aglietta, M. (1976) *A Theory of Capitalist Regulation: The United States Experience*. London: Verso.

Bernthal, M., Crockett, D. and Rose, R. (2005) Credit cards as lifestyle facilitators. *Journal of Consumer Research*, 32(1): 130–145.

Bond, S. (2005) The global challenge of sustainable consumption. *Consumer Policy Review*, 35(2): 38–44.

Boyer, R. (1990) *The Regulation School: A Critical Introduction*. New York: Columbia University Press.

Braucher, J. (2006) Theories of over indebtedness: interaction structure and culture. *Theoretical Inquiries in Law*, 7(2).

Briggs, A. (2000) *Go To It! Working for Victory on the Home Front 1939–1945*. London: Mitchell Beazley/ Imperial War Museum.

Briggs, S. (1975) *Keep Smiling Through: the Home Front, 1939–1945*. London: George Weidenfeld and Nicolson.

Calder, A. (1969) *The People's War: Britain, 1939–1945*. London: Pimlico.

Calder, A. (1992) *The Myth of the Blitz*. London: Pimlico.

Chilton, P., Crompton, T., Kasser, T., Maio, G. and Nolan, A. (2012) *Communicating bigger-than-self problems to extrinsically-oriented audiences*. Available at: www.wwf.org.uk/wwf_articles.cfm?unewsid=5641

Ciment, J. and Russell, T. (2007) *The Home Front Encyclopedia*, Volume One. Santa Barbara, CA: ABC-CLIO.

Clarke, N., Barnett, C., Cloke, P. and Malpass, A. (2007) Globalising the consumer: doing politics in an ethical register. *Political Geography*, 26(3): 231–249.

Cohen, J. (2003) *A Consumer's Republic: The Politics of Mass Consumption in Postwar America*. New York: Vintage.

Crompton, T. (2010) *Common Cause: The Case for Working with Our Cultural Values*. Godalming, Surrey: WWF-UK.

Cross, G. (1993) *Time and Money: The Making of Consumer Culture*. New York: Routledge.

de Graaf, J. (2003) *Take Back Your Time: Fighting Overwork and Time Poverty in America*. San Francisco: Berrett-Koehler.

Elgin, D. (1993) *Voluntary Simplicity: Towards a Way of Life That Is Outwardly Simple and Inwardly Rich*. New York: William Morrow.

EST (2009) Wartime Spirit. Press Release, Energy Savings Trust, Wartime Spirit campaign. London: Energy Savings Trust.

Evans, D. (2011) Thrifty, green or frugal: reflections on sustainable consumption in a changing economic climate. *Geoforum*, 42(5): 550–557.

Ferguson, N. (2003) The nation: true cost of hegemony: huge debt. *The New York Times*, 20 April.

Gardiner, J. (2004) *Wartime: Britain 1939–1945*. London: Headline Book Publishing.

Goodman, D. E. and Redclift, M. R. (1991) *Refashioning Nature, Food, Ecology, Culture*. London: Routledge.

Hennessy P. (1993) *Never Again: Britain 1945–1951*. New York: Vintage.

Hennessy P. (2006) *Having It So Good: Britain in the Fifties*. London: Allen Lane.

Hickman, T. (1995) *What Did You Do in the War, Auntie? The BBC at War 1939–1945*. London: British Broadcasting Corporation.

Hinton, E. (2011) Virtual spaces of sustainable consumption: governmentality and third sector advocacy in the UK. Unpublished thesis, King's College London.

Hinton, E. and Goodman, M. (2010) Sustainable consumption: developments, considerations and new directions. Working Paper, King's College London.

Jessop, B. J. and Ngai-Ling Sum (2006) *Beyond the Regulation Approach*. Cheltenham: Edward Elgar.

Longmate, N. (1971) *How We Lived Then: A History of Everyday Life During the Second World War*. London: Hutchinson.

Nicholson, N. (1984) *Harold Nicholson: Diaries and Letters, 1930–1964*. Harmondsworth: Penguin Books.

OECD (Organisation for Economic Cooperation and Development) (2002) *Towards Sustainable Household Consumption? Trends and Policies in OECD Countries*. Paris: OECD.

Redclift, M. R. (1987) *Sustainable Development: Exploring the Contradictions*. London: Routledge.

Redclift, M. R. (2005) Sustainable development (1987–2005): an oxymoron comes of age. *Sustainable Development*, 13: 212–227.

Redclift, M. R. (2009) The environment and carbon dependence: landscapes of sustainability and materiality. *Current Sociology*, 57(3): 368–383.

Redclift, M., Pelling, M. and Manuel-Navarrete, D. (2011) *Local Governance and Human Security in the Mexican Caribbean*. Cheltenham: Edward Elgar.

Sissons, M. and French, P. (1964) *The Age of Austerity*. Harmondsworth: Penguin Books.

Soper, K. (2008) Alternative hedonism, cultural theory and the role of aesthetic revisioning. *Cultural Studies*, 22(5): 567–587.

Stern, N. (2007) *The Economics of Climate Change: The Stern Review*. New York: Cambridge University Press.

Sustainable Consumption Roundtable (2006) *I Will If You Will: Towards Sustainable Consumption*. Sustainable Consumption Roundtable.

The Lean Economy Connection. (2013) *FAQs*. House of Commons All Parliamentary Group on Peak Oil and the Lean Economy Connection. Available at: www.teqs.net/faqs/ (accessed 23 December 2013).

Titmuss, R. (1962) *Income Distribution and Social Change*. London: Allen and Unwin.

Tucker, D. (1991) *The Decline of Thrift in America: Our Cultural Shift from Saving to Spending*. New York: Praeger.

WCED (World Commission on Environment and Development) (1987) *Our Common Future (The Brundtland Report)*. Oxford: Oxford University Press.

Welford, R. (2006) Comment. *International Journal of Innovation and Sustainable Development*, 21(4).

Zweininger-Bargielowska, I. (2002) *Austerity in Britain*. Oxford: Oxford University Press.

20

INDICATORS FOR SUSTAINABLE DEVELOPMENT

Joachim H. Spangenberg

Introduction

Sustainability indicators are technical means for monitoring trends relevant to sustainable development, and if combined with politically set targets, to assess distance to the target and the progress in getting closer to it. Obviously, the choice of targets and indicators is influenced if not determined by the sustainability concept that the respective agent holds and/or promotes, resulting in a diverse array of indicators and assumptions on which they rest. The two most important families of concepts are introduced in the second section of this chapter.

Indicators designed for different purposes will have different characteristics: if designed for government prioritising, they must help identify key drivers, while for administrators, a lot more details are required to plan concrete measures, and for civil society and the public at large, the number must be smaller. The actual choice of indicators reflects not only purposes and quality concerns as described in the third section, but what is included, and what is not, are a reflection of societal power relations: who decides what is monitored and how, who does the monitoring, or which actions are taken as the result of a certain outcome. The array of indicators from both families of concepts presented in the fourth and fifth sections illustrates this: the selection criteria and the indicators chosen are as distinct as their users and supporters. The final section discusses the role of indicators and offers a conclusion.

Thus, in order to measure sustainability, first, an operational concept of sustainability is needed, defining *what* to measure; the two main families of approaches are introduced in the next section. Then a methodology (indicators) has to be defined, standardising *how* to measure it, according to quality criteria which are presented subsequently. Finally, a selection of prominent indicators from both families is presented and discussed, and in the discussion data sources and limitations of the indicator approach are briefly presented.

Sustainability concepts

Essentially two families of world-views can be distinguished: one assuming that sustainability can be achieved by modifications of the existing system, the other not convinced of this possibility and calling for deep structural change. While the "modification camp" expects solutions from continued economic growth if only market adjustments are brought about by corrective policy frameworks, in particular from the internalisation of external cost (in this aspect, modificationists diverge from neoclassical economics), the "transformation camp" is suspicious about the possibility and desirability of continuous growth. Instead transformationists emphasise the need to manage and limit the physical or monetary scale of the global economy. These diverging world-views result in different factors being identified as critical and in need of being monitored, and consequently have different albeit overlapping suggestions regarding sustainability indicators, frameworks and indices.

Let us compare both camps to the original definition of sustainable development coined by the World Commission on Environment and Development, better known as the Brundtland Commission (WCED 1987: 43) "Sustainable development is development that meets the needs of the present without compromising the ability of future generations to meet their own needs. It contains within it two key concepts:

- the concept of needs, in particular the essential needs of the world's poor, to which overriding priority should be given; and
- the idea of limitations imposed by the state of technology and social organization on the environment's ability to meet present and future needs."

Their differences now become obvious. The "modification camp" is focused on the first key concept, meeting human needs (although the "overriding priority" of the needs of the world's poor is not always detectable), while the "transformation camp" emphasises the second key concept, that of "limitations". As these different world-views influence the perception of which problems are relevant, it is plausible and consistent that both camps have different priorities regarding the indicators or the aggregation method to be chosen. However, for both camps, a change of societal structures and economic processes is needed to make sure environmental concerns (and in the transformation camp, social and sometimes institutional ones as well) are properly taken into account.

In the following exploration of sustainable development indicators (SDI) both camps will be presented as archetypes, without discussing in any detail their internal modifications. Key suggestions from the mainstream modification camp will be described in historical sequence, and some of the alternatives suggested by the transformation camp as complements – a comprehensive analysis is beyond the scope of this chapter.

A commonality of both camps is that they want indicators to be effective tools, so most of the criteria regarding what makes a good indicator are respected by both camps. These criteria are elaborated in the next section.

What (are good) indicators?

Basic considerations

Different kinds of indicators can serve the main purposes of SDI, political guidance, summarising analysis and communication:

- *Nominal or binary indicators* can only assume one of two given values: a certain characteristic is either given or not (yes/no). They are only of limited value for the purpose of policy evaluation and steering, but are often the easiest to agree upon in policy-making.
- *Ordinal indicators* are based on qualitative concerns. They give information on the factor reported by locating it within a specific class of cases which would be considered better or worse than other classes, thus referring to a hierarchy of qualitative states.

- *Cardinal indicators* give quantitative information. This can be absolute or relative data on stocks or flows, or ratios of these. However, without an explicit target, the data remain quite meaningless.

Major systematic questions to be answered are:

- What is the maximum number of indicators that can simultaneously be applied in politics, given the complexity of the economic and social system and the resulting limits to steering capacity?
- What is the minimum number of indicators in order to properly reflect the key threats to sustainability, given in particular the complexity of ecological systems?
- To what extent will these indicators be better obtained by aggregating data or by systemic reasoning?
- Should the final result be a set of indicators or an aggregate index of sustainable development?
- Which then are the most suitable indicators for sustainable development planning, policies and monitoring?

Regarding the last question, it is improbable that for different functions of indicators (policy development, enforcement monitoring, state analysis), there is only one optimal system of indicators. Instead, different but mutually reinforcing systems may prove to be a more appropriate solution.

Indices can enhance the communicative capabilities of indicators, as long as their meaning is sufficiently clear. For instance, the GDP as an index adding up market activities must not be confused with an indicator of progress or human well-being; their correlation only holds up to a certain threshold (Max-Neef 1995). However, there is a downside to easier communication: simplification necessarily comes at the price of lost information. Furthermore, methodologically, building indices requires a standardised unit of measurement which does not exist in the case of incommensurable goods. Monetisation is used as a stand-in, but implies that no longer the goods but their prices are the object of observation. Normalisation, i.e. expressing an indicator as a share of an externally defined maximum value reduces transparency, as the reasoning for a certain scale is hidden behind a veil of ignorance to most users. Furthermore, having normalised results, they must be weighed – usually a subjective weight is attached, making the evaluator the final judge of the resulting advice. Finally, the aggregation procedure necessarily makes all individual indicators mutual substitutes: worsening of one indicator can be compensated by improvement of another. In policy planning this camouflage effect is hardly suitable. Aggregation is thus no problem for data with the same unit like Greenhouse Warming Potential or Ozone Depletion Potential, but becomes a risky undertaking beyond that level. Finally, regarding the minimum and maximum number of indicators, the jury is still out to find a final answer. In the meantime a pragmatic solution has been established: structuring indicator sets by introducing several hierarchical levels populated by increasing numbers of indicators made-to-order.

Indicator quality criteria

In order to be of use in the decision preparation, implementation and monitoring processes, indicators must fulfil a number of criteria that are discussed in this section. In decision preparation, they should be applicable to different policy scenarios and facilitate the comparison of their potential outcomes in order to help identify the policy options and future administrative initiatives best suited to yield the desired results. For policy implementation, they should be policy-oriented, operational, causality-oriented, and include a focus on links between policy fields. Monitoring is about observing change, rather than the status quo, implying repeated, if not regular or continuous observation or measuring. The high complexity of sustainable development processes, covering a number of otherwise politically separate dimensions and involving all sectors of society calls for indicators that can do the following:

- provide a reliable but easily understandable information base;
- help monitor the progress achieved;
- support communication with the public at large.

While, for reliability and accuracy of monitoring internationally applicable standards can be established, this is not the case for understanding and communication. The modes and media of communication within and between different groups of stakeholders (including government to citizens) are framed by the cultural and institutional context, and thus differ between countries. Even similar situations in objective terms can have strongly diverging meanings to the people experiencing them.

Indicators must be based on measurable or at least observable quantities in order to be useful. As such, they can be intensive or extensive properties, being either independent of or dependent on the size or volume of the system under consideration. For instance, the number of schools in a particular country or region has to be related to some meaningful extensive property, e.g. the number of people living in that region, in order to be an indicator of the provision of education. Similarly, the amount of waste generated is meaningless as economic indicator, if not put into relation to the activity generating the waste (resulting in an economic indicator for resource use efficiency, per product, per company, per business sector or for a regional/national economy), or to its environmental activity potential and the carrying capacity of the (local) environment, as an environmental one. The former can be measured in monetary or physical units, the latter requires biophysical characterisation (Falck and Spangenberg 2014).

The necessary key qualities of suitable indicators result from their purposes. To fulfil them, indicators need to be:

- *indicative*, i.e. an indicator must be truly representative of the phenomenon it is intended to characterise;
- *derived from a sound scientific basis*, which is a challenge in particular for interdisciplinarity;
- *relevant*, i.e. they have to cover crucial aspects of sustainable development;
- *transparent*, i.e. their selection, calculation and meaning must be obvious even to non-experts;
- *measurable*, i.e. they should be based as far as possible on data that are easy to access and to update. Such data do not necessarily have to be cardinal figures but can also be ordinal or nominal metrics.

To generate a simplified but sufficiently reliable description of reality, indicators must be:

- *reproducible*, to be endorsed by the relevant scientific and political communities;
- *robust*, i.e. immune against small variations in data and methodology not indicating a changing trend; and
- *general*, i.e. not specific for a single case but broadly applicable.

For successful monitoring, indicators must be:

- *sensitive*, i.e. react early and clearly to relevant changes in what they are intended to monitor.

For obvious reasons, it is neither necessary nor possible all the time to meet all these criteria to the same extent (for instance, the more robust an indicator is, the less sensitive it may be). As indicators that do not resonate with stakeholders will not be useful to them, an important element of indicator development is the elucidation of stakeholder needs. This is one reason why indicator development processes are usefully conducted as transdisciplinary processes. The resulting indicators can be meaningful if it is clear what they are intended to measure. Preferably, it would be "distance to target", the indicator giving alarm whenever this distance increases or the speed of overcoming it is reduced (performance indicators). Even if agreed quantitative targets are missing, a consensus on qualitative criteria may be possible, permitting progress to be monitored.

Some specific quality criteria apply to indicator systems. To provide a framework which helps structuring decision preparation, supports education and communication, and is a suitable basis for monitoring, indicator sets should do the following:

- consist of independent indicators, i.e. each indicator should be meaningful in itself;
- reduce complexity in a plausible and meaningful manner;
- be limited in number according to the purposes they are being used for.

Since these quality demands refer to the whole set of indicators, the development of indicator systems requires careful attention not only to the quality of the individual indicators, but to the system as such. Combining indicators with different strengths and weaknesses can thus lead to a balanced and meaningful system.

Modification indicators

The mainstream approach dominating the discourse for the last quarter century has thrived on an interpretation of development as GDP growth, and sustainability as greening that growth (distributional issues play a secondary role); this view determines the specific indicators and indices promoted.

The philosophical basis of the modificationists tends to be consequentialism, the view that normative properties depend on consequences, the paradigm case being classic utilitarianism. It claims that an act is morally right if and only if that act maximises utility, defined as pleasure, satisfaction, welfare or otherwise. As the moral stance of agents depends on the consequences of their actions, monitoring is essential for moral judgement, and the metrics chosen are decisive. The economics platform of the modificationists is usually environmental economics, an extension of neoclassical economics integrating nature and society as natural, human and social capital stocks into the economic models. Unsustainable development is then a misallocation of capital caused by a market failure; the latter is seen in the fact that environmental (rarely mentioned: social) damages are externalised, having no cost in the market system. Consequently, monetisation of such damages and their internalisation into the market system are considered the problem-solving strategy. What is disputed is the degree of substitutability between capital stocks: can man-made capital substitute for all natural capital, or must a critical natural capital be preserved (Noël and O'Connor 1998)?

Consequently, monetary measurements and indicators play a major role in the SDI developed by this camp. In particular, in international bodies like the UN and the OECD, they are blended with biophysical indicators partly originating from earlier traditions, partly from competing schools of thought including the transformationists.

Indicator systems

The OECD PSR indicator system

In the 1990s, the Pressure-State-Response (PSR) approach was developed by Statistics Canada, popularised by the OECD (1991; 1993) and shared by other international agencies, like UNstat or Eurostat, and was dominant in the international debate; several national governments (e.g. the Netherlands and Norway) built their indicator systems on a similar basis.

The WWF (1994) described the basic approach: "The PSR framework for indicator development is based on the concept of causality:

- human activities exert pressures on the environment;
- these pressures change the quality of the environment and the quality of natural resources (the "state" of the environment);
- society responds to these changes through environmental, general economic and sectoral policies (the societal "response"). Thus societal responses form a feedback loop to pressures through human activities. Indicators may be developed for each phase in the framework."

The PSR system had a number of limitations. Its focus was on environmental stresses which at a particular time had been of major (political) concern and thus data had been collected. Consequently most indicators monitored the state of the environment (forest decline, biodiversity, climate change), with a few pollutants and specific waste streams as the only output-focused issues, and inputs from the ecosphere not covered at all. Only the remaining stocks were seemingly of interest. This necessarily results in a very complex description, as each input and output has a wide range of environmental impacts, without identifying clear links between the driving forces and the environmental degradation they cause. Deriving responses from the selected states, i.e. the symptoms and episodic events, is necessary when acute crises require short-term curative politics, but not suitable to develop cause-oriented prevention and mitigation approaches. The PSR system is thus indicative of a kind of political "end-of-the-pipe-thinking".

The UNCSD indicators for measuring sustainability

Chapter 40 of Agenda 21 calls for the development and application of indicators which help evaluate the progress made towards sustainable development (UN 1993). So in its first session, the Commission for Sustainable Development (CSD) called for indicators to be integrated into the national reporting to the UNCSD, assessing progress towards sustainable development. UN bodies and external collaborators, coordinated by the Department for Policy Coordination and Sustainable Development (UNDPCSD), responded and developed an indicator system. They used the OECD PSR experience, but developed the system further by adding non-environmental dimensions of sustainability, resulting in the DSR (Driving force – State – Response) scheme. However, in doing so, the indicator set declined to address causality: the responses measured by the indicators proposed only occasionally referred to the driving forces identified (the same weakness prevails today, in the indicators suggested for the post-2015 Sustainable Development Goals). The system provided no advice which of the responses listed were considered effective in redirecting the driving forces and/or improving the state, in particular when considering the interdependencies with constraints in other sectors. In 1996, a list of 134 indicators, accompanied by 124 methodology sheets, were adopted by the CSD and published as the *Blue Book* (UNDPCSD 1996). The indicators were structured along the lines of Agenda 21, reporting chapter by chapter. The chapters were classified as belonging to the environmental, social or economic dimension of sustainable development, plus an institutional one inherent to but not explicit in Agenda 21 (Spangenberg et al. 2002). In this view – unlike the separate treatment of sustainable development and institutions *for* it in the 2012 Rio de Janeiro UNCSD conference – institutions are not external to but part of the sustainability transitions; they are institutions *of* sustainable development.

After a first revision in 2001 (UNDSD 2001), the second revision of the indicator set in 2007 abandoned the four-dimensional structure and eliminated the institutional indicators, some of them addressing power relations, from the set. The methods were harmonised with other reporting schemes and the CSD indicators were aligned with those developed to monitor the implementation of the Millennium Development Goals (MDGs) (UNDESA 2007). The flexible theme/sub-theme framework developed for this third set of CSD indicators has been taken up by most countries with adaptations, and is currently the dominant framework for national indicators of sustainable development, not least because UN Statistics started a capacity-building programme supporting the introduction of SDI.

Simultaneously to the work on the CSD indicators, UNDESA started a process to develop indicators monitoring changing consumption and production patterns (UNDESA 1998). They could have complemented the UN SDI set, making it more sensitive to developments in affluent countries than the current one. However, despite international discussions on the issue, endorsing the development of a sustainable consumption action plan at the Rio+10 Conference WSSD 2002 in Johannesburg, and the subsequent Marrakech Process, the Action Plan failed at CSD 19 in 2011 and was only endorsed by the 2012 UNCSD conference, however, without an attempt of indicator development.

Monetary measurement

In particular in the Anglo-Saxon countries, cost-benefit analysis (CBA) plays an important role in justifying policy decisions (in continental Europe, cost-effectiveness is more important: objectives are not identified based on cost-benefit ratios; the role of cost calculations is in deciding how a politically defined objective is realised). CBA is based on identifying all the efforts necessary for a certain measure and their cost, and comparing them to the benefits generated. For instance, when deciding to build a motorway, land, materials, labour, capital cost, etc. are counted and compared to benefits such as saving time and travel expenses through using a shorter route. All factors are monetised, and the cheapest solution is realised.

CBA requires the calculation of monetary cost for a variety of market and non-market goods. While for real goods traded in real markets, their prices describe costs and benefits, it is more difficult when future costs are to be assessed. Then prices for hypothetical goods are constructed based on real market values, e.g. to assess the cost of future damages, the assets lost and their expected future market prices are used (damage cost). Alternatively, the cost of measures necessary to avoid the same damage can be calculated (avoidance cost), if they are higher than the damage cost, prevention is considered uneconomic. The Total Economic Value (TEV) refers to all the value derived by people from an object, based on their current individual preferences and compared to not having it. The object may be an ecosystem, a man-made heritage resource or an infrastructure system, or anything else. It is calculated as the aggregate of use and non-use values, the latter, for instance, is the possibility of using a resource, though there is no plan for doing so (option value), or the enjoyment of a sunset. As sunsets are not traded on markets, it is not possible to calculate the value in the same way; instead the value is deduced from interviews (stated preferences: contingent valuation, choice experiments, etc., which however represent only an initial offer, not an equilibrium market price) and human behaviour (revealed preferences such as expenditure on travelling to a certain leisure site – travel cost). Here the prices of hypothetical goods in hypothetical markets are used as the basis of judgement. However, these methods are disputed as their results are hardly reproducible and depend on a wide range of factors strongly influencing the results (Spash 2008; Spangenberg and Settele 2010), a key reason why UN Stat accepts nothing but repair or restoration cost for inclusion in national accounting systems. Bequest value and existence value are other values in hypothetical markets, representing the satisfaction arising from knowing that an object exists without ever using it, or from knowing that future generations will have it as well (like polar bears – existence and bequest value are a reason for charitable donations). All these methods are used when calculating monetised sustainability indicators and indices. Some of the best known are:

- *The World Bank Capital Stock Approach*: In a fundamental sense, capital consists of any produced thing that can enhance a person's power to perform economically useful work; capital is an input in the production function. Four capital stocks are distinguished by the World Bank (World Bank 1997): man-made capital consisting of real capital (all already-produced durable goods such as machinery, equipment, infrastructure or any non-financial asset that is used in production of goods or services, and is not being consumed but depreciated in the production process) and financial capital, i.e. all forms of money and its equivalents used for production processes. Durable household goods are not capital as in the prevailing accounting system unpaid household labour using them productively is not accounted for, unless the household production generates market goods. In environmental economics, this standard definition of neoclassical economics is complemented by accounting for the stocks of Human Capital (intra-personal assets: personal skills, dedication, creativity, experience, but also health), Social Capital (interpersonal assets, e.g. trust, social security, justice, solidarity, institutions, including markets and law enforcement) and Environmental Capital (bio-geochemical systems and their components, including biodiversity; in the WAVES project, the World Bank promotes the monetisation of such assets). Capital stocks are measured in money units, making them mutual substitutes. For any object to count as an element of the respective capital stock, it must be used for productive work – unproductive nature or skills are not capital. Maintaining the sum of all capital stocks is the economic definition of weak sustainability; it requires investment to compensate for depreciation. However, how a capital stock can be returned to its pre-production state varies based on the type of capital involved, its specific form of depreciation and the corresponding investment needs.
- *Adjusted net savings* or *genuine savings* are derived from standard national accounting measures of gross national savings by making four types of adjustments:

  > First, estimates of capital consumption of produced assets are deducted to obtain net national savings. Then current expenditures on education are added to net domestic savings as an appropriate value of investments in human capital (in standard national accounting these expenditures are treated as consumption). Next, estimates of the depletion of a variety of natural resources are deducted to reflect the decline in asset values associated. Estimates of resource depletion are based on the calculation of

> resource rents. An economic rent represents the excess return to a given factor of production. Rents are derived by taking the difference between world prices and the average unit extraction or harvest costs (including a "normal" return on capital) with their extraction and harvest. Finally, pollution damages are deducted. Many pollution damages are local in their effects, and therefore difficult to estimate without location-specific data. Here we estimate health damages due to urban air pollution. As for global pollution damages, the estimates include damages from carbon dioxide emissions.
>
> *(World Bank 2010)*

- *Green Accounting*: the System of Environmental-Economic Accounting (SEEA) was developed, promoted and refined by UN Statistics in the 1990s, in broad consultation with national statistical offices and academia. It does not modify the System of National Accounts (SNA) (the basis of GDP calculations) but complements it by introducing satellite accounts which can be monetary or not. Separate sub-systems for water and energy have been developed. The latest version was introduced in 2013, and a second part dealing with the integration of biodiversity and ecosystem services, partly in monetary terms (Natural Capital Accounting) into the accounting system is still being tested.
- *Index of Sustainable Economic Well-Being (ISEW)* and *Genuine Progress Index (GPI)*: although developed as a means to illustrate the limits of monetisation (Daly and Cobb 1990), the ISEW and its successor, the GPI, have been calculated for a variety of countries in the North and the South. The indices take the GDP as their starting point, subtract the monetary value of "bads" like environmental pollution, resource depletion or the cost of climate change and add the monetary value of "goods" like unpaid work; the GPI includes some additional categories. A polarised income distribution reduces the ISEW; this may be one main reason for the limited support ISEW and GPI have received from the modification camp.

Mixed indicator sets

Indicator sets include monetary indicators combined with non-monetary ones (otherwise the results could have been added up into one index). One reason why this combination is predominant in national SDI systems is the public information demand: people do not want to know about the economic loss due to unemployment or air pollution, they want to know how many people are unemployed and what they breathe. Indicator systems are data-hungry; collecting and processing the data requires human and financial resources. The best-known indicator systems are:

- *The OECD PSR*: The PSR scheme popularised by the OECD was the starting point first for the UN DSR indicators and then for the DPSIR scheme (I = Impacts) used by the European Environment Agency and other bodies with good results (Stanners et al. 2007). By 1999, the OECD had developed a balanced set of sustainable development indicators and the OECD Environmental Strategy for the first decade of the twenty-first century was essentially a sustainability strategy, including indicators (OECD 1999; 2001). However, from the beginning of the new millennium and after intensive internal debates, the OECD decided to focus on its economic core, resulting in a less-profiled role in sustainability issues. Nonetheless the OECD developed and refined indicators on sustainable household consumption, decoupling of resource consumption and economic production, waste minimisation and more; the latest step being a set of Green Growth indicators for monitoring Green Growth strategies were developed in the wake of the 2012 UNCSD conference (OECD 2011a; 2011b). They are mostly composite indicators reflecting the resource efficiency of production, but do not refer to the environmentally decisive absolute amounts.

- *The Human Development Index (HDI)* is a composite index based on normalised scales of life expectancy, education (both not monetised), and income indices. Created by the Pakistani economist Mahbub ul Haq and the Indian economist Amartya Sen in 1990 and published by the United Nations Development Programme with the explicit aim "to shift the focus of development economics from national income accounting to people-centered policies" (UNDP 1992), it ranks countries according to their level of human development. Its results are strongly influenced by the level of GDP and per capita income. From time to time the index is updated and complemented by issue-specific modifications like a gender-adjusted or an inequality-adjusted HDI. In particular, in the South, the HDI and the Human Development Reports accompanying it are of high political relevance.
- *The UN Millennium Declaration* was adopted at the Millennium Summit in New York, September 2000. At its core are eight time-bound targets – with a deadline of 2015 – that have become known as the Millennium Development Goals. They range from halving extreme poverty via halting the spread of HIV/AIDS and providing universal primary education, to promoting gender equality and ensuring environmental sustainability. As they address the most pressing social sustainability issues, the indicators developed for that purpose have been integrated into the latest version of UNCSD SDI. In 2015 new targets will be set, merging the MDG agenda with the demand for globally applicable sustainable development goals as decided at the 2012 UNCSD conference in Rio de Janeiro. Monitoring indicators are under development, with strengthened applicability to affluent nations and thus enhanced political relevance, but with a strong focus on social issues at the expense of environmental ones.

The transformation approach

The minority approach has different roots in civil society (a strong group of development and environment NGOs, some trade unions, selected scientific representatives and organisations), but hardly support from international organisations, business and governments. Its historical roots go as far back as those of the mainstream camp. The philosophical basis leans on deontological ethics and morals; the rightness of an act has to be justified not by its outcomes as for consequentialists, but by its conformity to a moral norm. Probably the best-known example is Immanuel Kant's categorical imperative (Davidson 2013); for transformationists, justice and Human Rights play a crucial role.

Transformationists consider development as improving the quality of life. As long as livelihood improvements are dependent on income growth, they support it while emphasising the need for equitable distribution. While there is a strong correlation of life satisfaction and income below a threshold of about US$15,000/cap*yr, above it the correlation vanishes (Max-Neef 1995). Average income figures provide little information about how many people are living below the life satisfaction threshold.

The economics in this camp combine ecological, evolutionary, political, development, and traditional institutional economics with natural and social science research, with no comprehensive theory so far, but a sophisticated critique of the neoclassical/resource economics theories (Spash 2012). Thus indicator proposals from this camp tend to combine biophysical indicators with social and monetary ones; in particular the satisfaction of needs in the Brundtland sense is considered to be a multi-criteria objective, impossible to be measured in monetary terms (Max-Neef et al. 1989).

The perceived topology, whether the ecosystem is a part of the economy or vice versa, distinguishes the ontologies of both schools of thought. In a transformationist world-view, the ecosystem is not a part of the economy as the modificationists see it, but vice versa. Whereas the size of stocks and their accessibility are economic issues, ecology worries about resource flows, since these contribute to environmental impacts: limits, as defined by the Brundtland Commission, refer to flows rather than stocks. Thus, the environmental condition of sustainability is a physical steady-state system, with the smallest-feasible flows of resources at the (functionally, not geographically defined) input and output boundaries between the technosphere and the ecosphere leaving intact – for an infinite length of time – the stability of the internal evolutionary processes of the bio-physical ecosphere. An economic system is environmentally sustainable only as long as it is physically in a (dynamic) steady-state, i.e. the amount of resources used to generate welfare is permanently restricted to a size and a quality that do not over-exploit the sources, or over-burden the sinks, provided by the ecosphere.

The anthroposphere is considered an open, thermodynamic subsystem of the Earth with respect to materials and energy. Thus economic activities cannot escape the laws of nature, in particular, thermodynamics, while the environment does not follow the "laws" of neoclassical economic theory. Market clearance, with increasing supply triggering demand and increasing demand automatically leading to an increase of supply, does not apply to natural systems. Thus, sustainability policy has a focus on the specifics of the ecosystems providing services, including the limitations arising from their limited (re-)production capacities. The maximum continuously supportable rate of output has been called the *critical load*, and the maximum continuously supportable rate of flow, the *carrying capacity*.

The ecosphere, as well as the anthroposphere, is part of the Earth system which is – to all practical purposes – closed to flows of external matter but open to energy inputs, consisting mainly of solar radiation. It is primarily this window to energy inputs from space which provides room for a sustainable use of natural resources for humankind. Without this:

- human economies would have to continue to draw on the stock of natural resources (e.g. high grade ore, crude oil, fertile soil) or, from an energy viewpoint, they would continue to use up low-entropy resources which sooner or later (in the third millennium) would be exhausted;
- the immense (and rapidly increasing) flows of resources through the global economies would continue to lead to an increase in entropy, resulting in a variety of unpredictable and irreversible environmental impacts as planetary boundaries are crossed (Rockström et al. 2009). As a result of the destabilisation of ecological systems, this will include slow, long-term changes such as biodiversity loss and global warming, and short-term irregularities such as increasing top speeds of typhoons, high tides and extended drought periods combined with rivers flooding due to heavy precipitation. This tendency is threatening the life-support system of humankind. Consequently, physical measurement of resource consumption plays a key role in the sustainable development indicator portfolio of the transformation camp.

Physical measurement

- *Energy related*: Embodied energy (also known as emergy) is the sum of all energy consumed in the process of producing, distributing and maintaining a product. Calculating it distinguishes more and less energy-intensive products and consumption patterns, taking the energy consumed for imported raw materials or intermediate products into account. Exergy is an indicator describing the available energy inherent to a product, and thus the potential to actively interact with its environment. Exergy analysis is performed in the field of industrial ecology to use energy more efficiently, or to minimise the damage potential of waste to be released. Exergy is destroyed in such interactions (unlike energy which can only be transformed) and entropy is generated (Jørgensen 2010).

- *Material related*: Material flow analysis (MFA) is a tool to assess the physical consequences of human activities. Each use of materials has environmental impacts; while a small number of highly active substances are regulated under toxicity and similar regulation (e.g. heavy metals), and larger flows of medium-sized activity are regulated under environmental law (for instance, SO_2 or NO_x), the massive flows of low activity (exergy) substances have long escaped regulation, CO_2 being the most prominent example. MFA indicators can either refer to domestic or total material consumption (DMC or TMC), the latter including imports. While life-cycle assessments usually account for all the materials which enter the production process, material flow analysis accounts for all materials being activated, including drainage water or the overburden of mining. Depending on the substance mined and purified, the amount of unused material can exceed the material used by a factor of several thousand; a factor 10 is rather normal. The global amount of material activated is the total material requirement (TMR) of an economy, illustrating how its footprint is composed (Spangenberg et al. 1998). Due to data problems, the European Commission uses a simplified indicator, called raw material consumption (RMC) in monitoring its Resource Efficiency Strategy.
- *Land* is an absolutely limited resource, and scarce. Probably the best known indicator is the ecological footprint (Rees and Wackernagel 1996). It calculates the area of land needed for food, fuel and fibres, adding up real land use and land hypothetically needed to absorb carbon emissions from fuel consumption. While good for awareness raising, it is not helpful for planning processes due to the mixture of real and hypothetical land use. The EU uses indicators for the size of domestic land demand and the net actual global land demand of the EU, the latter called the "land footprint". The land use intensity is assessed by measuring the human appropriation of net primary production (HANPP), an indicator reflecting the disturbance effects of human interventions in natural landscapes (Haberl et al. 2007).
- *Biodiversity, ecosystems and their services* are essential bases for human civilisation. It took until 2006, 14 years after adopting the Convention on Biological Diversity (CBD) at the 1992 UNCED conference, until the Conference of Parties agreed upon indicators endorsed at COP 8 in 2006 (Decision VIII/8) after testing a preliminary set. The indicators chosen are a rather unsystematic mix of biological, socio-cultural and political indicators and indices from different DPSIR categories. For instance, pressures mentioned include nitrogen deposition and trends in invasive alien species, impacts are trends in abundance and distribution of selected species, change in status of threatened species, but also incidence of human-induced ecosystem failure and health and well-being of communities who depend directly on local ecosystem goods and services. The focus is on state indicators like trophic integrity and connectivity/fragmentation of ecosystems, but also the status and trends of linguistic diversity and numbers of speakers of indigenous languages, of access and benefit-sharing and of resource transfers. The only response indicator mentioned is coverage of protected areas – the disconnection between pressures and responses is obvious. Driving forces are not on the list: the list of indicators clearly misses basic quality standards; it is neither suitable for policy steering nor for monitoring policy implementation. The EU

SEBI biodiversity indicators (European Commission 2008) closely follow the UNCBD approach, with minor adaptations.

Subjective indicators

As for transformationists, quality of life is a predominant concern (as opposed to economic growth), subjective judgements play a major role, in particular for social sustainability (Spangenberg and Omann 2006). Nonetheless scholars have long been hesitant to develop subjective indicators as this seemed to be beyond the scope of "objective" science. Early proponents were long ignored (Veenhoven 1993) until a decade ago a book by Richard Layard (2005) managed to seize the attention of economists. In the meantime the research field has been established with its own methods, journals and international happiness databases (Veenhoven 2010), but – with the notable exception of the UK – a response in policy is only slowly emerging.

This is a pity as, on the one hand, enhanced life satisfaction is an important policy objective (surveys would serve that objective better, from a policy-making point of view, if they did not ask for the current level of happiness, but for the obstacles to being happy – then decision-makers could identify those obstacles in the political realm and act accordingly). On the other hand, implementing political decisions in democratic countries depends on the acceptance by the majority of people – so satisfaction with current politics is a major condition for successful sustainability policies. Subjective sustainability indicators will remain an issue for further research and development for the time being.

Limitations of indicator use and usefulness

While indicators are useful tools to reduce a complex set of diverse data, it should be kept in mind that every process of indicator selection or aggregation inevitably includes both a gain in clarity, but also a loss of information. Indicator sets must balance the needs to reduce complexity, be easily understandable, resonate with a clearly defined target audience, and be limited in number. Using indicators for policy planning provides new opportunities for transparency and efficiency, but also certainly generates new risks (Spangenberg 2009). Four key risks are:

1 The temptation to define easily achievable rather than adequate objectives, and to set targets derived from the desire to be able to deliver positive reports in the short term rather than reporting on substantial progress in the medium to long term.

   Response 1: A comprehensive and publicly known model of sustainability minimises this risk, as the lack of relevance of the indicators chosen is easily detectable. However, institutional assets such as freedom of speech are essential to transform this kind of insight into a political force.

2 The risk of focusing in a narrow-minded way on progress towards the indicators defined while neglecting other relevant trends. Some of these may emerge as a side-effect of the improvements achieved, others might emerge anew or pre-exist but become relevant or even dominant once the initial challenge is under control.

   Response 2: No system of indicators is set in stone or cast in iron – indicators reflect current priorities which may not only be different in different countries, but will also change over time (they should: no change in priorities would indicate in itself that the problem has not been solved). Regular revisions of indicators are necessary, updating the system according to the emerging trends identified by general monitoring, but not yet covered by the system of indicators.

3 Focusing on single issues as described by the indicators may lead to a neglect of the links between different dimensions of policy, with the trends in other indicators going unnoticed. So a juxtaposition of different sectorial politics could emerge, undermining the effectiveness of governing and governance.

Response 3: As long as the four dimensions of sustainable development are considered independently of each other, this is a serious risk. The concept of sustainable development must avoid such systemic blindness by integrated assessments.

4 The desire for positive news might lead to attempts to "cook the books", to hide negative results and generate positive reports without a substantial base. Hierarchical administrative systems, but also dependency on good records in the face of external shareholders, donors of money or voters create situations favouring such fraud. For instance, in the UK, the Blair government deleted those indicators showing negative trends from the reporting sheet, while in Germany reporting is done – laudably independently – by the statistical office, a body without any public resonance.

Response 4: Institutional innovations requested by Agenda 21 include access to information (so far mainly to environmental data; this needs to be extended to all information relevant to sustainable development), transparency, accountability and more participation of civil society. These measures also help to unearth hidden failures and avoid unjustified reports of success.

This makes it even more important to identify the most suitable indicators for a specific purpose and not only to focus on their respective strengths (i.e. making problems visible and proposed solutions comparable), but also to keep their limitations in mind while using them.

References

Daly, H. E. and Cobb, J. B. Jr. (1990) *For the Common Good: Redirecting the Economy Towards Community, the Environment and a Sustainable Future*. London: Green Print.

Davidson, M. D. (2013) On the relation between ecosystem services, intrinsic value, existence value and economic valuation. *Ecological Economics*, 95: 171–177.

European Commission (2008) *SEBI 2010 Biodiversity Indicators*. Commission Staff Working Document, accompanying document to the Communication from the Commission to the Council, the European Parliament, the European Economic and Social Committee and the Committee of the Regions: A mid-term assessment of implementing the EC biodiversity action plan, COM(2008) 864 final. Brussels: European Commission.

Falck, W. E. and Spangenberg, J. H. (2014). Selection of social demand-based indicators: EO-based indicators for mining. *Journal of Cleaner Production*, in press, DOI: 10.1016/j.clepro.2014.02.021.

Haberl, H., Erb, K. H., Krausmann, F., Gaube, V., Bondeau, A., Plutzar, C., Gingrich, S., Lucht, W. and Fischer-Kowalski, M. (2007) Quantifying and mapping the human appropriation of net primary production in earth's terrestrial ecosystems. *Proceedings of the National Academy of Sciences USA* 104(31): 12942–12947.

Jørgensen, S. E. (2010) Ecosystem services, sustainability and thermodynamic indicators. *Ecological Complexity*, 7(3), 311–313.

Layard, R. (2005) *Happiness: Lessons from a New Science*. New York: Penguin Press.

Max-Neef, M. (1995) Economic growth and quality of life: a threshold hypothesis. *Ecological Economics*, 15(2): 115–118.

Max-Neef, M., Elizalde, A. and Hopehayn, M. (1989) Human scale development. an option for the future. *Development Dialogue*, 1989(1): 7–80.

Noël, J.-F. and O'Connor, M. (1998) Strong sustainability: towards indicators for sustainability of critical natural capital. In S. Faucheux and M. O'Connor (eds) *Valuation for Sustainable Development: Methods and Policy Indicators*. Cheltenham: Edward Elgar, pp. 75–97.

OECD (1991) *Environmental Indicators. A Preliminary Set*. Paris: OECD.

OECD (1993) *Core Set of Indicators for Environmental Performance Reviews*. Paris: OECD.
OECD (1999) *Sustainable Development and its Economic, Social and Environmental Indicators*. ENV/EPOC/SE/CONF(99)7. Paris: OECD.
OECD (2001) *OECD Environmental Strategy for the First Decade of the 21st Century*. Paris: OECD.
OECD (2011a) *Towards Green Growth*. Paris: OECD.
OECD (2011b) *Monitoring Progress Towards Green Growth: OECD Indicators*. Council Paper C(2011)30. Paris: OECD.
Rees, W. E. and Wackernagel, M. (1996) *Our Ecological Footprint: Reducing Human Impact on Earth*. Gabriola Islands, BC: New Society Publishers.
Rockström, J., Steffen, W., Noone, K., Persson, Å., Chapin, F. S., Lambin, E. F., Lenton, T.M., Scheffer, M., Folke, C., Schellnhuber, H. J., Nykvist, B., de Wit, C. A., Hughes, T., van der Leeuw, S., Rohde, H., Sörlin, S., Snuder, P. K., Costanza, R., Svedin, U., Falkenmark, M., Karlberg, L., Corell, R. W., Fabry, V. J., Hansen, J., Walker, B., Liverman, D., Richardson, K., Crutzen, P. and Foley, J.A. (2009) A safe operating space for humanity. *Nature*, 461(7263): 472–475.
Spangenberg, J. H. (2009) Sustainable development indicators: towards integrated systems as a tool for managing and monitoring a complex transition. *International Journal of Global Environmental Issues*, 9(4): 318–337.
Spangenberg, J. H., Femia, A., Hinterberger, F. and Schütz, H. (1998) *Material Flow-based Indicators in Environmental Reporting*. Luxembourg: Office for Official Publications of the European Communities.
Spangenberg, J. H. and Omann, I. (2006) Assessing social sustainability: social sustainability and its multicriteria assessment in a sustainability scenario for Germany. *International Journal of Innovation and Sustainable Development*, 1(4): 318–348.
Spangenberg, J. H., Pfahl, S. and Deller, K. (2002) Towards indicators for institutional sustainability: lessons from an analysis of Agenda 21. *Ecological Indicators*, 2(1–2): 61–77.
Spangenberg, J. H. and Settele, J. (2010) Precisely incorrect? Monetising the value of ecosystem services. *Ecological Complexity*, 7(3): 327–337.
Spash, C. L. (2008) How much is that ecosystem in the window? The one with the bio-diverse trail. *Environmental Values*, 17(2): 259–84.
Spash, C. L. (2012) New foundations for ecological economics. *Ecological Economics*, 77, 36–47.
Stanners, D., Bosch, P., Dom, A., Gabrielsen, P., Gee, D., Martin, J., Rickard, L. and Weber, J.-L. (2007) Frameworks for environmental assessment and indicators at the EEA. In T. Hak, B. Moldan, and A.L Dahl, (eds) *Sustainability Indicators: A Scientific Assessment*. Washington, DC: Island Press, pp. 127–144.
UN (United Nations) (1993) *Earth Summit: Agenda 21, the United Nations Programme of Action from Rio*. New York: United Nations.
UNDESA (UN Department of Economic and Social Affairs) (1998) *Measuring Changes in Consumption and Production Patterns*, Report ST/ESA/264. New York: United Nations.
UNDESA (UN Department of Economic and Social Affairs) (2007*) Indicators of Sustainable Development: Guidelines and Methodologies*, 3rd edn. New York: United Nations.
UNDP (UN Development Program) (1992). *Human Development Report*. Oxford: Oxford University Press.
UNDPCSD (UN Division for Sustainable Development, Department of Policy Co-ordination and Sustainable Development) (1996) *Indicators of Sustainable Development, Framework and Methodologies*. New York: United Nations.
UNDSD Division for Sustainable Development. UN Department of Economic and Social Affairs (2001) *Indicators of Sustainable Development: Guidelines and Methodologies*, 2nd edn. New York: United Nations.
Veenhoven, R. (1993) *The Study of Life Satisfaction*. Rotterdam: Erasmus University.
Veenhoven, R. (2010) Greater happiness for a greater number: is that possible and desirable? *Journal of Happiness Studies*, 11: 605–629.
WCED (World Commission on Environment and Development) (1987) *Our Common Future (The Brundtland Report)*. Oxford: Oxford University Press.
World Bank (1997) *Expanding the Measure of Wealth: Indicators of Environmentally Sustainable Development*. Washington, DC: World Bank.
World Bank (2010) *Adjusted Net Saving: A Proxy for Sustainability*. Available at: http://web.worldbank.org/WBSITE/EXTERNAL/TOPICS/ENVIRONMENT/EXTEEI/0,,contentMDK:20502388~menuPK:1187778~pagePK:210058~piPK:210062~theSitePK:408050,00.html (accessed 15 May 2011).
WWF (World Wildlife Fund International) (1994) *Indicators for Sustainable Development* London: WWF.

21
SUSTAINABLE BUSINESS
A critique of corporate social responsibility policies and practices

Timothy Luke

Introduction

This chapter rethinks the policies and practices of corporate social responsibility (CSR) programmes since their emergence during the 1980s and 1990s in the USA. Many firms – both large and small enterprises – typically deploy sustainability rhetoric as part and parcel of their routine commercial agendas to demonstrate a willingness to engage in many community outreach, cultural sensitivity, and environmental justice practices that have been endorsed by local chambers of commerce as well as transnational lobbies for global corporations. These policies often are adopted as either tactical reactions or principled responses to ethical and political pressures put on the business sector by local, national, or global anti-corporate movements.

These political struggles with corporations stretch back to the 1960s, and the widespread acceptance of notions, like sustainable development with allied ideals like "fair trade," "child labor free," "no GMO ingredients," or "commodity stewardship certification," has become one of the most successful negotiated settlements between the private sector and the new social movements arising from post-1968 civil society. While there are very brittle aspects of the extremely weak interpretations of sustainability that are now deeply embedded in CSR business policies and practices, many nonetheless regard the acceptance of this weak baseline as a new ethical benchmark that is better than nothing at all. On the one hand, this point has some validity; yet, on the other hand, ratifying profit-driven agendas to strengthen the imperatives of "economic development" with such buttresses for "ecological sustainability" mystifies what sustainability should, or does, mean for business as commercial interests. The struggle to be more responsible ethical agents in society at large all too often does not really sit well with the relentless pursuit of seeing strong profits on firms' bottom lines.

Consequently, this chapter reassesses uncritical understandings of sustainability as they have been implemented in CSR policies and practices over the past generation. In conducting this assessment, however, the analysis, first, will not try to discover, once and for all, "what sustainability really is." Such ventures usually wander around everywhere, and then go nowhere at the same time. Instead, it will, second, express worries about the "sustainable enterprise" ethics at work behind both the green consumerism and green producerism of too many CSR schemes. And, third, it asserts the thin ethical consensus binding the difficult merger of sustainability and development inevitably ends up preserving not the Earth's ecologies, but rather the power, privilege, and position attained by businesses in developing their economic returns in competitive markets.

Profiling sustainability

In the process of establishing a profile for sustainability on today's continuously shifting market terrains, one can turn to the ethical discussions of rapid climate changes for initial insights. Flannery observes:

> Everyone knows what the solution is: we must begin to live sustainably. But what does that actually mean? "Sustainability" is a word that can mean almost anything to anyone. Whether used by cosmetics advertisers or fruit sellers, it is bandied about as if it were the essence of virtue. Yet so recent is the word that my spell-checker doesn't recognize it.
>
> *(2009: 3)*

His point is well taken, but despite his spell-checker's scope, "sustainable" came into use in English during the 1640s, and it often turned up in conservationist debates during late nineteenth and early twentieth centuries (Gottlieb 1993). Clearly, the concept has had a "utopian" dimension (Harlow et al. 2011), but it acquired quite "utilitarian" purposes during the Gilded Age's anxieties about resource depletion (Luke 1997). After the oil crises of the 1970s and 1980s, sustainability became associated with satisfying a national economy's needs for basic natural resources, and then sustaining continued access to those supplies for the firms using them without compromising their use by coming generations (WCED 1987). In terms of business ethics, a modicum of "community concern" or "social responsibility" in corporate headquarters for the adverse transaction costs and negative externalities generated by such industrial logistics has never been entirely ignored by business (Küpers 2011). Of course, some firms attend to these conservationist obligations to minimize environmental pollution and industrial waste better than most, but such ethical goals have concerned many business managers and owners at least since the Gilded Age and Progressive Era in the USA (Gottlieb 1993).

The decades during which prudent worries about the conservation of natural resources become a general alarm about the sustainability of the Earth *per se* come later (Jermier and Forbes 2003: 157–176). For businesses, this worry becomes a more focused problematic, first, as the overall levels of better material existence improved for some countries from the late 1940s to the early 1970s; and, second, as the possible survival of humanity as such came to be questioned worldwide during the Cold War. The ideals of "sustainable" development, then, crystallized several contradictory events and forces in the 1970s (UNEP 1972) that have yet to be fully sorted out (Blewitt 2008). At the same historical conjuncture, one sees thermonuclear weapons with the power to cause tremendous environmental destruction proliferating in great numbers, and the accelerated development of ballistic missiles to deliver such military nuclear payloads rapidly to targets all over the world.

Not surprisingly, corporate thinking about the sustainability of the Earth as a planetary system came into more common parlance with the "the Spaceship Earth" metaphor, which was popularized by many statesmen and scientists in the 1960s (Boulding 1966). US Ambassador to the United Nations, Adlai Stevenson (1965), delivered an address to the General Assembly noting, "We travel together, passengers on a little spaceship, dependent on its vulnerable reserves of air and soil." After using the idea in presentations for years, R. Buckminster Fuller expressed similar ideas in his 1963 book, *Operating Manual for Spaceship Earth*. In 1966, the internationally noted author, Barbara Ward, also released her book, *Spaceship Earth*, and so did the economist Kenneth Boulding in his essay, "The Economics of the Coming Spaceship Earth."

Recognizing this reality, more firms accepted measures of greater responsibility for their operations on Spaceship Earth by working with communities and other stakeholders (Freeman 1984) in ways that implicitly addressed caring for the so-called "triple bottom line" of "people, planet, profit" articulated during the 1990s (Elkington 1997). At the same time, scientists, naturalists and activists elaborated sustainability discourses to preserve the Earth for its own sake, although some acknowledged more serious attention must be given to economic growth to sustain the wayfarers of Spaceship Earth (Ward and Dubos 1972). Imperiled by willful neglect and/or careless ignorance, according to these defenders of the environment, too many of Earth's ecosystems had become overburdened by human overpopulation and destructive industries intent upon realizing short-term economic gain rather than conserving long-term ecological viability (Goldsmith et al. 1972).

The thrust of these debates followed insights from critical scientific experts, including Barry Commoner, *The Closing Circle: Nature, Man, and Technology* (1971), Paul Ehrlich, *The Population Bomb* (1968), or Donella Meadows et al., *The Limits to Growth* (1972). Their analyses were big picture overviews that tended to overlook how little of the material affluence that they saw as being so destructive had trickled down to the planet's poorer populations. Yet, their anxieties about limiting growth, controlling population, and closing nature/human/technology circles were clearly intended to preserve the many social advances that rapid economic growth already had delivered to affluent countries (Hirsch 1976).

A generation later, Commoner's *Making Peace with the Planet* (1990) ironically expresses this ambivalence very well by suggesting humanity has indeed won enough wealth from Nature to end its war on natural ecosystems as well as maintain the gains won from centuries of environmental destruction. Thus, sustainability policies came to focus on new terms – "deliberation, citizenship, even the rights of species – but they hid, or marginalized, the inequalities and cultural distinctions that had driven the 'environmental' agenda internationally" (Redclift 2005: 224). With these rhetorical twists-and-turns, the fundamental commitment to environmental conservation slipped into a grudging accommodation of CSR-driven agenda for preserving the more affluent economy and society that modernization had made possible. Still, early proponents of sustainability continued to seek the protection of the Earth from humanity for its own sake (Harlow et al. 2011), and not to accommodate the rhetorics for advancing clean, lean, corporate, green living (Horn 2006).

Another force behind the green CSR mess arose with the biodiversity protection regime, tied to the Convention of Biological Diversity, which was signed in 1992 (Luke 2000). This agreement, along with the trade-related aspects of intellectual property rights (TRIPS) protocols in the Uruguay Round of the GATT, the Kyoto Protocol on Climate Change, the ISO 14000 series for environmental management standardization, the Forest Stewardship Council (FSC) silvicultural certification regime as well as the creation of the Chicago Climate Exchange, the Emissions Marketing Association, and International Emissions Trading Association among other structural influences in the 1990s, pushed more environmental governance of sustainability matters into the private sector by legitimizing new investment criteria, trading schemes, labeling rules, production standards, commodity markets, and labor codes (Springett 2005: 271–281). While CSR programs continued to address more than just environmental concerns, these more explicit rules for corporate responsibilities institutionalized their sense of obligation to society vis-à-vis the environment (Clapp 1998; Werksman 1998; Cashore et al. 2004; Pulver 2007).

As sustainability became an imperative for all economies and societies in the 1990s, its supporters parted ways at the divide between "weak" versus "strong" sustainability

(Daly 1996: 77–78). "Weak sustainability" concentrates on maintaining the ability of society to appropriate and accumulate – through the use of existing human monetary and social capital, suppliers of labor, and stores of information – more man-made capital. Historically, as a complement to natural capital, monetary, social or cultural capital, weak sustainability proponents presume the wealth of nature will always exist in abundant pools of exploitable resources. "Strong sustainability," however, contests this traditional stance, doubting that accumulations of such man-made capital can substitute for natural capital. Without natural capital, there is no human capital of any type, because low, declining or no natural resources create conditions where human capital cannot be appropriated or accumulated. To sustain an economy of any type, strong sustainability directs humans first to preserve and protect their supplies of natural capital (Scruton 2012).

To explore these tensions more closely, one must look at the motives and machinations involved in managerial CSR programs rooted in sustainable development pledges to shareholders and stakeholders (Jermier et al. 2006; Springett 2006). These commitments often are part and parcel of a firm's implementation of responses for community outreach, social impact, cultural sensitivity or environmental regulation, which are undertaken in answer to local pressure, national legislation or global standards. All too often, this ensemble of practices is one of the most common modes of distributed collaborative governance for sustainability (Adiger and Jordan 2009). At the same time, it allows strains of weak sustainability thinking to become entrenched in many firms' CSR offices and operations as standard operating procedures. These very thin commitments to sustainability end up favoring, in turn, more developmentalist goals that limit the significance of what strong sustainability practices should, or could, mean in everyday corporate operations.

Sustainability as steady stability

Sustainability therefore has become a label for something many CSR offices favor, but no one is certain what this term exactly means. In everyday use, because of the ties to ethical consumerism, community outreach or ecological commerce (Hawken 2010), it commonly is now associated with policies and practices that are "green," or "clean," or even "lean," in the commerce of business and industry "operating" the Earth (Alley 2011). Nonetheless, its ambiguities or limits become more obvious when planners, entrepreneurs or chambers of commerce speak in all sincerity about expanding sustainable plastics sales, sustainable herbicide utilization or sustainable asphalt production, despite all of the good intentions in their CSR training. For environmentalists, who have vigorously opposed efforts to pave over the planet, dump more toxic chemicals into planted farmland or package more consumer goods in dangerous, unnecessary nonrenewable materials, these rhetorical uses of sustainability are astounding abuses for even what is becoming a "planet of slums" (Davis 2006).

John Stuart Mill in his *Principles of Political Economy* sketched a widely acknowledged precursor to business-based CSR efforts at sustainable development during the 1850s. Mill deemed his system the "stationary state" economy in which both zero population growth and capital accumulation would be reached; but, at the same time, he reasoned this "stationary condition of capital and population implies no stationary state of human improvement" (Mill 1909). While not quite like Marx's vision for the full attainment of complete communism, Mill's "stationary state" economy promised a comparable outcome, namely, the rich continuing opportunities for qualitative growth in the human condition that required very little quantitative growth to attain (Edwards 2010).

During the 1970s, Mill's insights were resurrected in a more elaborate fashion in Herman Daly's designs for an "SSE," or a "steady-state economy" (Daly 1977). Dismayed with how advanced industrial society's "growthmania" was creating neither security nor prosperity as it degraded Earth's complex atmospheric, lithospheric, hydrospheric, cryospheric, and biospheric systems, Daly with others sought an economy operating in a dynamic steady-state of input/output balances (Goodland et al. 1992). Rather than relentlessly pushing to maximize industrial output, consumption, higher profit, greater value, increased rent or monetary accumulation, the steady-state economy would have another goal as its guiding maxim, namely,

> Life, measured in cumulative person-years ever to be lived at a standard of resources use sufficient for a good life ... the SSE would go a long way toward maximizing cumulative life for all species by imposing the constraint of a constant throughput at a sustainable level, thereby halting the growing takeover of habitats of other species, as well as slowing the rate of drawdown of geological capital otherwise available to future generations.
>
> *(Daly 1996: 32)*

Conventionally, as Daly argues, it was the scarcity of human capital – monetary, social, and cultural – that limited growth. Today it is different. Man-made capital, acquired by destroying the environment, is now in high supply, but natural capital is declining or degrading. The limits on growth now are natural, because the availability of resources is dropping, or has even disappeared. No matter how many sawmills, timber lots or lumberyards one has, for example, these factors cannot create new trees and forests. Hence, "we have moved from a world relatively full of natural capital and empty of man-made capital (and people) to a world relatively full of the latter and empty of the former" (ibid.: 78). At this juncture, sustainability, as stable everyday CSR policy and practice, emerges as a decisive new set of managerial goals. Apprehensions about the stability of the Earth as a system of systems for providing ecological services are the marker of perceived new conditions of scarcity, and finding the means for containing such risk stirs the hunt for truly global environmental governance (Speth and Haas 2006).

Sustainability practices

The inclusion of stability-seeking sustainable development targets in CSR practices often are a feature of management's response to on-going criticism of the turmoil caused in markets and societies by commercial enterprise (Pulver 2007). Firms try to gain by challenging such resistance in an apparent stance of having an open debate, first, by dismissing certain critical claims as extremist or subversive and, second, by domesticating other critical assertions as constructive or supportive as they maneuver to normalize the real, or once, more radical aspirations for sustainability (Luke 1999). The economistic turn in ecological discourse during the 1990s and 2000s shifted corporate and scientific analyses towards an appraisal of environments as reserves of natural capital, sources for ecosystem services or stores of common-pool assets (Simon 1981; Smith 2011).

Conceding that earlier industrial market thinking misunderstood the co-evolving needs of the economy and ecology by ignoring the promise of natural capitalism, businesses' CSR units now work through plans based on biomimicry analysis, industrial metabolism or c2c design to harness sustainability to their companies' rhetoric and policy (Benyus 2002; Edwards 2005; Vogel 2005; Szasz 2007). While the notion of sustainability remains contested, CSR programs reveal how neoliberal firms, business journals, and university programs have captured sustainability as an ethical business principle. In turn, their institutional agendas are reshaping it to match development characteristics that perpetuate the pursuit of profit as cleaner, greener and leaner corporate activities that enable greater profitability through making production and consumption more rational (Dresner 2010; Rumpala 2011; Loftus 2012).

To the consternation of many average citizens who still seek unlimited abundance, sustainability, as an individual and collective good, has gotten a hard sell as a necessary move for society since the 1970s (Allen 1980; Bakker and Bridge 2006). Everyday invocations to the community "to reduce, recycle, and reuse" consumption of everyday vital necessities have rung in the public's ears now for decades. To soften what can be strident appeals, the social imperative is reduced to an individual purchasing decision. Whether one regards buying as "shopping for safety" (Szasz 2007), "green chic" (Matheson 2008), "cradle to cradle" (McDonough and Braungart 2002), or "green consumerism" (Luke 1997), each individual is urged to treat her or his everyday purchases as tactics to forestall climate change, push sustainability, and volunteer for simplicity in the marketplace (Rogers and Kostigen 2007). In different accents and dialects over time, producers and consumers in the USA have been told that "being Green isn't a fad . . . it's timelessly chic" so just "embrace the fabulousness of green living" (Matheson 2008: cover).

To this extent, selling green identities to some consumers has been a success, but its effectiveness is also severely limited. To cope with the risk society of second modernity (Beck 1992), ecological awareness has been reprocessed, like most ethical values in the capitalist marketplace, to survive as an individual taste rather than a social necessity. In other words,

> [E]nvironmental action has been a good idea to some, and annoyance to others. It has been a personal virtue, a cause, a rallying cry, a self-righteous plea, a haven for do-gooders and misfits. It has been a value preference, a lifestyle choice, a contest of lobbyists and litigators. More recently, it has been a product placement, a consumer choice, a marketing brand, a bandwagon to jump on and ride to ever-greater commercial glory.
>
> *(Princen 2010: 11)*

Sustainability is implied by these agendas; but, despite these turns in corporate brand marketing, environmental conditions materially have worsened. Being an "environmental protection agent" by changing incandescent light bulbs to CFL, picking plastic over paper, or recycling soda cans has come up short as the epitome of sustainable enterprise (Luke 1997).

Growth cannot solve all social problems, especially those it creates for itself as such. World economic growth has been, is, and will be (at least in the short run), advancing far beyond renewable carrying capacity. While its minimalist program of change might be an organizational transformation of sorts (Edwards 2009), the "sustainable development" of CSR offices continues in many ways to be policies for masking or mystifying environmental destruction. Since it does not mark the end of growth (Heinberg 2011), the stocks, services, and systems of natural capital (Luke 2009) are being depleted to the point that their on-going degradation truly should not continue. Such corporate work now has even become a special vocation, demanding a particular education to succeed.

The *Wall Street Journal* on Monday, June 25, 2012 ran a "Big Issues: The Journal Report", an eight-page special section entitled "Squaring Off on Education." With a color teaser panel on the front page above the headlines of the day, the reader was presented a question "Is College a Waste of Time and Money?," and a promise, "EDUCATION: A SPECIAL REPORT." After reading about the "pros vs. cons" on national testing standards, college financial aid, tenure for professors, legacy student admissions, and the financial pay-off of higher education, the reader could scan an eye-catching quarter page color ad. Headlined as "Graduate Programs in Emerging

Professions," Columbia University declared, "Before You Can Take on the World Evolving Challenges, You Need to Master the World's Emerging Professions." In addition to Actuarial Science, Bioethics, Construction Administration, Landscape Design, and Narrative Medicine, Columbia invited prospective students to investigate its Master of Science program in Sustainability Management.

The message here is clear. Sustainability has now developed itself into a highly professionalized industry. In turn, Sustainability Management addresses one of the world's most serious evolving challenges; it is an emerging profession with real prospects for career advancement, but this program – as the world worsens environmentally – will never be a waste of time and money (Martin and Samuels 2012) since it now requires hordes of thoroughly trained managers to be green to do good for corporations. At its inception as a new cultural value, sustainability typically was seen as antithetical to the work of trained professional managers. Indeed, sustainability was associated with hordes of grassroots countercultural, insurgent, and perhaps even revolutionary resistance movements against the everyday technocratic operations of the advanced industrial society that "old school-trained" professional managers were once educated to administer and maintain (Hilary 2013). So getting the word out to the would-be masters of such new emerging professions about the promise of Sustainability Management is a useful insight into a new interpretation of an older idea.

With CSR training, the gradual evolution of sustainable development increasingly has taken the ideas of sustainability to mean protecting the Earth for humanity based on a newfound faith in environmental goods and services as green capital for ecomanagerial command-and-control. As Goldsmith et al. (1972: 23) maintained, sustainability would arise from a steady-state economy, or "stable society" that might be "sustained indefinitely while giving optimum satisfaction to its members." At the same time, Meadows et al. regarded the optimal condition for human society to be that "condition of ecological and economic stability that is sustainable far into the future" (1972: 24). The valences of "stable," "steady-state," and "sustainable" are all close, but sustainable has been the concept that prevailed.

The utility of sustainability as a rhetorical bridge between a perceived corporate "mainstream," which was disinterested in and uncommitted to preserving sustainability *per se* in the business world, and a countercultural formation, which is rooted in "social change values" drawn from anti-commercial sustainable practices, is in many ways its central appeal (Jermier and Forbes 2003: 157–176). While the persistence of such 1960s-era terms of countercultural identification seems astounding four or five decades later, Edwards captures this policy contradiction accurately when he labels this ideological impulse "the Sustainability Revolution," asserting it is the optimal opportunity:

> to provide the context for dialogue and act as a catalyst for action . . . As an organizing principle, sustainability reflects the fundamental relationships that underlie ecological, economic, and social concerns. It offers the possibility of bringing social value values into the mainstream and pushing the mainstream toward sustainable practices.
>
> *(Edwards 2005: 133)*

Sustainability as a development practice, then, quickly has been transposed into double-entry registers of accountancy to husband original endowments of service, stock or system in the environment (Luke 2009: 129–159).

Anti-corporate social movements, which many firms once scorned, are now openly embraced as part of demonstrating a vital engagement with community groups and social responsibility (Jermier et al. 2006). Not only is the pursuit of quick profit praised for its usual economic benefits, maintaining more sustainable profit streams becomes even more advantageous ideologically in the long-term strategies of this or that firm, because green capitalism is adopted into many corporations' social responsibility programs. Demonstrating responsible concern for the community with lean, green and clean production systems also sells much better than ruthless self-service of narrow business interests (Hawken 2010). Having attained a position to control, if not dominate, profit-seeking, the ability to sustain these grids of greed now gains gracious ecological seals of approval by CSR programs deeming corporate routines as clean, lean or green.

Merging sustainability and development

Sustainable development now tends to be an ecological consciousness of, by, and for, the commanding heights of transnational businesses whose interest in global competitiveness, social responsibility, and total performance far exceeds that of most national, regional, and local firms. As David Cooperrider, founder and chair of the Center of Business as an Agent of World Benefit, Weatherhead School of Management, Case Western Reserve University, observes, key centers of global governance all have noted this fact. As a result, United Nations Secretary-General, Kofi Annan, asked Cooperrider and the Weatherhead School to explore all of the ins-and-outs of corporate social responsibility "to reconcile the forces of the private entrepreneurship with needs of the disadvantaged and the well-being of future generations" (Annan, cited in Laszlo 2008: 193). By 2007, 4,000 corporations, which mainly were multinational firms, were part of this United Nations-sponsored Global Compact to actualize a new corporate citizenship movement. Of course, these values then could serve as normative ideals for other smaller companies, but effectively adopting and implementing these values, even at low levels of commitment, is much easier said and done by bigger global firms.

The essential contestedness of these sustainability ideals in the corporate sector, despite all of the huzzahs in favor of its widespread acceptance and rising popularity, is betrayed by the narratives of management consulting tracts, like Chris Laszlo's *Sustainable Value: How the World's Leading Companies Are Doing Well by Doing Good*. A long-time advocate of corporate sustainability and social responsibility programs, Laszlo consulted Fortune 500 firms on the merits of turning "sustainability" to the advantage of business. While he never explicitly defines and defends his proposition, "doing well" suggests conventional business outcomes, like realizing shareholder value, enterprise growth targets, market dominance or bottom-line profits, and "doing good" using such strategies for "doing well" to build a "better world" by advancing the personal empowerment of employees, submitting financial practices to triple bottom-line accounting, and accepting sustainability as a core principle of corporate social responsibility. Yet, his case study for "the sustainable" is divided into third parts, and Part I, interestingly enough, "is a management fable about Deena, a young CEO, and the challenges she faces to profitably address her company's impacts on society and the environment" (Laszlo 2008: 21).

Two decades after the Brundtland Report (WCED 1987), then, a typical corporate manual for pursuing green business practices must reaffirm this moralizing mythos to map its normative agendas for business as well as outline factual case studies of best practices. Indeed, Laszlo notes in Part II how the global marketplace remains at odds over "doing good." Some mainstream business leaders "are successfully integrating sustainability into their core activities, not only from a sense of moral correctness, but because it makes good business sense" (2008: 21). Yet, other firms still take bad missteps, like Toyota's "push into large gas-guzzling SUVs in the same time-frame as their roll-out of the hybrid drivetrain" (ibid.: 22).

Admitting that the regulatory environment for auto sales in many countries necessitates twinning the sales of highly profitable large SUVs with marginally profitable hybrid compacts to hit corporate fleet fuel economy averages, Laszlo ignores the slow, small market adoption of hybrid cars. Nonetheless, Laszlo offers in Part III "a tool kit and process for mainstream business managers" to realize "how and where they can do well by doing good" (ibid.: 22). Laszlo's book is indeed a normative primer for young professionals aspiring to work with big firms as well as mainstream executives, who are eager to have "a positive image of the future" in which they can learn how environmental and social sustainability are realistic, effective, and credible inputs into better "job performance" (ibid.: 23) that stress CSR's triple bottom-line for society – people, planet, profits.

This celebration of environmental sustainability as the epitome of everyday performativity is underscored in the book's Foreword by Tyler J. Elm, Senior Director, Corporate Strategy & Finance, Wal-Mart Stores, Inc. Elm asserts businesses, like Wal-Mart, "are witnessing a metamorphosis in the role of business in society, with for-profit companies targeting many of the emerging social issues once reserved for the non-profit sector" (Elm, in Laszlo 2008: 18). While businessmen once resisted environmentalists' calls for reform, he affirms times have changed. The environmental challenges posed for corporate social responsibility must be recognized by innovative firms as "changes in the business activities required to deliver a winning value proposition," because – as Peter Drucker – argues "every single pressing social and global issue of our time is a business opportunity" (Elm, in Laszlo 2008: 19).

Green capitalism (Hawken 2010), as it is embedded in these terms of operation, is more than selling organic garden produce or handcrafted wood items at local farmers markets. Instead Cooperrider recommends sustainability to corporate strategists as the ultimate benchmark for product valorization in this century. Posed in near millenarian terms,

> We are on the eve of one of the greatest revolutions in management history, an era of deep-seated transformation, where "sustainable value creation" is and can emerge as the most powerful unifying thread for propelling industry-leading innovation in complete and simultaneous convergence with solutions to the call of our times.
>
> *(Cooperrider, in Laszlo 2008: 192)*

Without saying it as boldly as Charlie Wilson once pronounced about General Motors and America, sustainability strategies will ensure that what is good for the Fortune 500 is good for the Earth. Indeed, "Doing good and doing well is increasingly the smartest way to do business, if you have the knowledge and competencies to turn eco-imagination and social entrepreneurship into and innovation engine" (Cooperrider, in Laszlo 2008: 192). To the extent that they enhance profitability and innovation, a solid CSR program is every corporation's ultimate social responsibility.

This CSR impulse is neither entirely cynical nor merely symbolic. Allowing individuals and groups the legal latitude and institutional wherewithal to construct organizations that work like businesses without serving purely profit-seeking ends has been a pressure relief valve in the United States since its founding, but it clearly took hold strongly in the late nineteenth and early twentieth centuries with the acceptance of credit unions, non-profit 501c(3) corporations, and cooperatives. The new practices of "socially responsible investing" that encompass, but also exceed sustainability pursuits, are another sign of institutional elasticity at work today. Indeed, some states, beginning with Maryland in 2010, have gone so far as to pass legislation to charter "benefit corporations" (B corporations) that allow legal observance of "triple bottom-line" accounting for "people, planet, and profits," which traditional S, LLC or C corporations cannot easily attain. B corporations still can be taxed like either C or S corporations, but their instruments of corporate purposes, accountability, and transparency are pitched at triple bottom line accountancy. By 2013, the District of Columbia and 19 states, including among others California, Hawaii, Illinois, Maryland, New Jersey, New York, Pennsylvania, Virginia, Vermont, and Washington had enacted B corporation legislation.

While these juridico-legal shifts could be transformative, they also could regularize a set of highly greenwashed ecological modernization corporate strategies to inoculate firms against more careful review by highly skeptical consumers and suspicious publics. Socially responsible investment and enterprise is a new segment of the economy; yet, it is an adaptation to corporate social responsibility policies and programs to hitherto untapped market niches. A new accountability regime must co-evolve with B corporations, or legacy accountancy and auditing firms must develop new modes of responding to third party standards for public benefit, transparency, and environmental benefit. The cultural contingencies here are vast and untapped, but there is little to suggest that the agendas of ecological modernization, green capitalism or c2c design will not soon become the trusted *bona fides* of accountability for B corporations. Once cooperative third-party validators bless the avowed public purposes of sustainability and development, certain kinds of greenwashed, but still suspect, modes of advanced capitalist life will become even more entrenched and difficult to oppose.

Conclusion

Decades of spirited environmental agitation, intellectual debate, and even militant street fighting under conditions of advanced industrial capitalism, as big business schools and major industrial companies have activated CSR programs, now have been captured in pious accounts of how profitable this reborn mode of ecomodernization can become. CSR officers in financial and manufacturing firms alike, therefore, can transform what once might have been blessed as ordinary frugality, sensible design or alert management by a firm's board of directors or CEO into extraordinary campaigns of caring for the Earth. The *T. Rowe Price Investor* magazine's "Closing Bell" summary page in its September 2012 issue, for example, touts "The Growth of Sustainability" to clients, assuring them "more companies are developing a long-term strategic view of environmental impact of their products" (2012a: 26).

A green graphic accompanying the story stresses an ethic of "reduce-reuse-recycle" as it details how "The Car of Today Includes the Materials of Yesterday." By using recycled steel, plastic bottles, tires, blue jeans and cotton to build a new 2013 Ford's car body, dashboard, engine gaskets, carpet, and sound dampening, what was old and near worthless becomes new and quite profitable again. Sustainability, then, works on many levels, so both small and big businesses can link into these commodity chains. Still, the economistic turn given to sustainable development by big business is highlighted in the story's text:

> In the past, a product ended up in a landfill because manufacturers devoted little thought to sustainable design and practices – the pursuit of an entirely closed-loop process in which darts return to the Earth or become another, new product. Creating goods with minimal or no negative environmental and health impact has become the guiding principle of a growing number of companies ... Sustainability practices are becoming more than a way to develop brands and reputations – an increasing number of executives see them as providing operational and growth-oriented benefits that help cut costs and develop new markets and products.
>
> *(T. Rowe Price Investor 2012a: 26)*

Although the piece purports to focus on "the growth of sustainability," the real motive force behind this shift in manufacturing philosophy pivots on realizing the sustainability of corporate growth (Rogers 2010). To underscore this subconscious thrust in big businesses' nearly full spectrum engagement with sustainable development, another vignette in same *T. Rowe Price Investor* September 2012 issue is entitled, "Finding Sustainable Growth," which focuses on one of the firm's top managers for its successful Blue Chip Growth Fund. Never mentioning ecology, the environment or nature as such, the article underscores how the fund seeks steady, secure, and stable investments "that can maintain solid growth over long periods" (*T. Rowe Price Investor* 2012b: 6). If CSR programs with strict environmental policies function effectively, then these practices should move investors to own a "company that can consistently grow earnings at 15%" as opposed to buying "one growing at a 30% rate," which such blue chip capitalist growth managers do not "think is sustainable" (ibid.: 6). Here biomimicry reasoning comes full circle. Sustainability in the business world built by CSR programs allows for both the strong sustainability of natural ecosystems to ensure the weak sustainability of respectable return on investments year-in/year-out for shareholders.

That sustainability has morphed into a central thematic for CSR policies is not surprising given how a "sustainability industry" already was forming around the time of the Rio Earth Summit in 1992 (Yates 2012). Hence, one must ask very different questions about sustainability after the 1960s. Sustainability crystallizes:

> a point where in some way the certainties all mix together, the lights go out, night falls, people begin to realize that they act blindly and that consequently a new light is necessary, new lighting and new rules of behavior are needed.
>
> (*Foucault 2007: 142*)

Indeed, this is "the history of the present." As these policies and practices co-align for corporations, new problematizations take shape for businesses, and with them new strategies and tactics articulated in the overtly disciplinary discourses and strategic policy paybacks of corporate social responsibility programs.

In conclusion, sustainable development is an amorphous concept that many interests have embraced, especially since the end of the Cold War. As the trends in rapid climate change, loss of natural habitat, declining biodiversity, and human overpopulation continue to accelerate, the belief that industrial growth and economic development can easily be reconciled with the green values of sustainability is attractive. Nonetheless, "sustainable development," like "sustainability" *per se*, is another idea whose meaning is quite elusive. Its easy widespread acceptance suggests its elusive quality serves quite contradictory ideological ends, cultural needs, economic agendas or social goals. These contradictions paper over deeper conflicts as they build measures of thin weak consensus. Yet, this is a moment when solid strong consensus needs to be found about environmental protections so that the glaringly obvious, and now obviously worsening, environmental despoliation of the Earth might be checked, and then possibly reversed, rather than merely endured under green CSR policies that enable commercial practices leading to greater degradation.

References

Adiger, W. N. and Jordan, A. (eds) (2009) *Governing Sustainability*. Cambridge: Cambridge University Press.

Allen, R. (1980) *How to Save the World: Strategy for World Conservation*. London: Kogan Page.

Alley, R. B. (2011) *Earth: The Operators' Manual*. New York: W.W. Norton.
Bakker, K. and Bridge, G. (2006) Material worlds? Resource geographies and the 'matter of nature'. *Progress in Human Geography*, 30(5): 5–27. DOI: 10.1191/0309132506ph58809.
Beck, U. (1992) *Risk Society*. London: Sage.
Benyus, J. M. (2002) *Biomimicry: Innovation Inspired by Nature*. New York: Morrow.
Blewitt, J. (2008) *Understanding Sustainable Development*. London: Earthscan.
Boulding, K. (1966) The economics of the Coming Spaceship Earth. In H. Jarrett (ed.) *Environmental Quality in a Growing Economy*. Baltimore, MD: Resources for the Future/Johns Hopkins University Press, pp. 3–14.
Cashore, B., Auld, G. and Newsom, D. (2004) *Governing Through Markets: Forest Certification and the Emergence of Non-State Authority*. New Haven, CT: Yale University Press.
Clapp, J. (1998) The privatization of global environmental governance: ISO 14000 and the developing world. *Global Governance*, 4: 295–316.
Commoner, B. (1971) *The Closing Circle: Nature, Man, and Technology*. New York: Random House.
Commoner, B. (1990) *Making Peace with the Planet*. New York: Pantheon.
Daly, H. (1977) *Steady-State Economics*. San Francisco: W.H. Freeman Company.
Daly, H. (1996) *Beyond Growth: The Economics of Sustainable Development*. Boston: Beacon Press.
Davis, M. (2006) *Planet of Slums*. London: Verso.
Dresner, S. (2010) *The Principles of Sustainability*, 2nd edn. London: Earthscan.
Edwards, A. R. (2005) *The Sustainability Revolution: Portrait of a Paradigm Shift*. Gabriola Island, BC: New Society Publishers.
Edwards, A. R. (2010) *Thriving Beyond Sustainability: Pathways to a Resilient Society*. Gabriola Island, BC: New Society Publishers.
Edwards, M. (2009) *Organizational Transformation for Sustainability: An Integral Metatheory*. New York: Routledge.
Ehrlich, P. (1968) *The Population Bomb*. New York: Sierra Club-Ballantine Book.
Elkington, J. (1997) *Cannibals with Forks: The Triple Bottom Line of 21st Century Business*. Hoboken, NJ: John Wiley & Sons, Inc.
Flannery, T. (2009) *Now or Never: Why We Must Act Now to End Climate Change and Create a Sustainable Future*. New York: Atlantic Monthly Press.
Foucault, M. (2007) *The Politics of Truth*, ed. Sylvére Lotringer. New York: Semiotext(e).
Freeman, R. E. (1984) *Strategic Management: A Stakeholder Approach*. Boston: Pittman.
Fuller, R.B. (1963) *Operating Manual for Spaceship Earth*. New York: E. P. Dutton.
Goldsmith, E. et al. (1972) *Blueprint for Survival*. London: Penguin.
Goodland, R., Daly, H., El Serafy, S. and von Droste, B. (1992) *Population, Technology and Lifestyles: The Transition to Sustainability*. Washington, DC: Island Press.
Gottlieb, R. (1993) *Forcing the Spring: The Transformation of the American Environmental Movement*. Washington, DC: Island Press.
Harlow, J., Golub, A. and Allenby, B. (2011) A review of utopian themes in sustainable development discourse. *Sustainable Development*. DOI: 10.1002/sd.522.
Hawken, P. (2010) *The Ecology of Commerce: A Declaration of Sustainability*, rev. edn. New York: Harper Business.
Heinberg, R. (2011) *The End of Growth: Adapting to Our New Economic Reality*. Gabriola Island, BC: New Society Publishers.
Hilary, J. (2013) *The Poverty of Capitalism: Economic Meltdown and the Struggle for what Comes Next*. London: Pluto Books.
Hirsch, F. (1976) *Social Limits to Growth*. Cambridge, MA: Harvard University Press.
Horn, G. (2006) *Living Green: A Practical Guide to Simple Sustainability*. Topanga, CA: Freedom House.
Jermier, J. M. and Forbes, L. C. (2003) Organizational greening: critical issues. In M. Alvesson and H. Wilmutt (eds) *Studying Management Critically*. London: Sage, pp. 157–176.
Jermier, J. M., Forbes, L. C., Benn, S. and Orsato, R. (2006) The new corporate environmentalism and green politics. In S. Clegg, C. Hardy, T. Lawrence and W. Nord (eds) *Handbook of Organizational Studies*. London: Sage, pp. 618–650.
Küpers, W. N. (2011) Integral responsibilities for a responsive and sustainable practice in organization and management. *Corporate Social Responsibility and Environmental Management*, 18: 137–150.

Laszlo, C. (2008) *Sustainable Value: How the World's Leading Companies Are Doing Well by Doing Good.* Foreword P. J. Cescau and T. J. Elm, Afterword D. Cooperrider. Stanford, CA: Stanford University Press.

Loftus, A. (2012) *Everyday Environmentalism: Creating an Urban Political Ecology.* Minneapolis: University of Minnesota Press.

Luke, T. W. (1997) *Ecocritique: Contesting the Politics of Nature, Economy, and Culture.* Minneapolis: University of Minnesota Press.

Luke, T. W. (1999) *Capitalism, Democracy, and Ecology: Departing from Marx.* Urbana, IL: University of Illinois Press.

Luke, T. W. (2000) Rough road out of Rio: the right-wing reaction in the United States against global environmentalism. In N. Low, B. Gleeson, I. Elancer, and R. Lidskog (eds) *Consuming Cities.* London: Routledge, pp. 54–69.

Luke, T. W. (2009) Developing planetarian accountancy: fabricating nature as stock, service, and system for green governmentality. *Current Perspectives in Social Theory*, 26: 129–159.

McDonough, W. and Braungart, M. (2002) *Cradle to Cradle: Remaking the Way We Make Things.* San Francisco: North Point Press.

Martin, J. and Samuels, J. E. (2012) How colleges can bring sustainability to campuses. *The Chronicle of Higher Education*, July 23.

Matheson, C. (2008) *Green Chic: Saving the Earth in Style.* Naperville, IL: SourceBooks, Inc.

Meadows, D. et al. (1972) *The Limits to Growth: A Report of the Club of Rome's Project on the Predicament of Mankind.* New York: Universe Books.

Mill, J. S. (1909) Of the stationary state. *Principles of Political Economy*, 7th edn. London: Longmans. Available at: www.econlib.org.library/mill/m/pg1.html

Princen, T. (2010) *Treading Softly: Paths to Ecological Order.* Cambridge, MA: MIT Press.

Pulver, S. (2007) Making sense of corporate environmentalism: an environmental contestation approach to analyzing the causes and consequences of the climate change policy split in the oil industry. *Organization & Environment*, 20: 1–40.

Redclift, M. (2005) Sustainable development (1987–2005): an oxymoron comes of age. *Sustainable Development*, 13: 212–237.

Rogers, E. and Kostigen, T. M. (2007) *The Green Book: The Everyday Guide to Saving the Planet One Simple Step at a Time.* New York: Three Rivers Press.

Rogers, H. (2010) *Green Gone Wrong: How Our Economy Is Undermining the Environmental Revolution.* New York: Scribner's.

Rumpala, Y. (2011) 'Sustainable consumption' as a new phase in a governmentalization on consumption. *Theory & Society*, 40: 669–-699. DOI: 10-DO>/s11186-011-9153-5.

Scruton, R. (2012) *How to Think Seriously About the Planet: The Case for an Environmental Conservatism.* Oxford: Oxford University Press.

Simon, J. (1981) *The Ultimate Resource.* Princeton, NJ: Princeton University Press.

Smith, M. (2011) *Against Ecological Sovereignty, Ethics, Biopolitics, and Saving the Natural World.* Minneapolis: University of Minnesota Press.

Speth, J. and Haas, P. M. (2006) *Global Environmental Governance.* Washington, DC: Island Press.

Springett, D. V. (2005) Whom is sustainable development for? Unions and deliberative democracy. *Sustainable Development*, 13: 271–281.

Springett, D. V. (2006) Structural limits to sustainable development: managers and progressive agency. *International Journal of Innovation and Sustainable Development*, 1(1): 127–152.

Stevenson, A. (1965) Speech to UNESCO. Geneva, July 9.

Szasz, A. (2007) *Shopping Our Way to Safety: How We Changed from Protecting the Environment to Protecting Ourselves.* Minneapolis: University of Minnesota Press.

T. Rowe Price Investor (2012a) The growth of sustainability. (September): 26.

T. Rowe Price Investor (2012b) Finding sustainable growth. (September): 6.

UNEP (United Nations Environmental Programme) (1972) Declaration of the United Nations Conference on the Human Environment. Available at: www.unep.org/Documents.Multilingual/Default.asp?documentid=97&articleid=1503

Vogel, D. (2005) *The Market for Virtue: The Potential and Limits of Corporate Social Responsibility.* Washington, DC: Brookings Institution Press.

Ward, B. (1966) *Spaceship Earth.* New York: Columbia University Press.

Ward, B. and Dubos, R. (1972) *Only One Earth: The Care and Maintenance of a Small Planet*. London: Deutsch.

WCED (World Commission on Environment and Development) (1987) *Our Common Future (The Brundtland Report)*. Oxford: Oxford University Press.

Werksman, J. (1998) The clean development mechanism and unwrapping the Kyoto surprise. *Review of European Community and Environmental Law*, 7(2): 147–158.

Yates, J. J. (2012) Abundance on trial: the cultural significance of 'sustainability'. *The Hedgehog Review*, (Summer): 8–25.

22

URBAN TRANSPORT AND SUSTAINABLE DEVELOPMENT

Peter Newman, Anne Matan and James McIntosh

Introduction

The idea of sustainable development is highly relevant to the world's cities. Cities have been the major source of social and economic opportunity for the growing world population for around 8,000 years, but in the last century this has dramatically increased. In this period of industrialization and globalization, the world's cities have been creating opportunity at the expense of ecological footprint. Growing consumption of resources and the subsequent growth in wastes have had local, regional and global impacts (Newman and Kenworthy 1999). Today cities are responsible for around 40 per cent of the world's greenhouse gases (GHG). Thus the challenge of sustainable development in cities is how they can continue to play their historic role as providers of social and economic opportunity while reducing, not increasing, their ecological footprint. Put simply, the challenge to the world's cities is to reduce their ecological footprint while improving liveability (Newman and Kenworthy 1999, Newman 2006).

Transport is the fundamental technological force that shapes cities. As most ecosystems are shaped by certain limiting parameters such as their temperature, rainfall, or nutrients, cities are limited in size by their transport systems due to the Marchetti limit on travel time. As humans do not like to travel more than one hour a day on average (Zahavi and Ryan 1980; Marchetti 1994; Newman and Kenworthy 1999), cities have grown to be 'one hour wide'. Traditional Walking Cities were usually no more than 3–5 kilometres (km) across (as walking speeds are around 3–5 kilometres per hour (kmph)). The nineteenth- and early twentieth-century Transit Cities could spread out 20 km and followed the train and tram tracks (based on average tram and train speeds of 20 kmph). Once the car became the dominant force in cities, they could spread out more than 50 km (based on an average car travel speed of 50 kmph). The Automobile City was not tied to train and tram lines, nor to the time and speed limitations of walking, and cities were able to spread in every direction that a road could be built. Many cities developed around the transport technology and infrastructure requirements of cars to such a point that residents became dependent on using a car to access all their daily needs – known as *automobile dependence* (Newman and Kenworthy 1989; 1999).

All cities have combinations of these three city fabrics. No city has yet been found that is not shaped by these primary movement functions. Thus urban transport has a major role in shaping future cities to meet the multiple dimensions of sustainable development. The challenge for urban transport is to see how to enable the transport system and its associated urban form to facilitate the reduction in ecological footprint while enabling the city to improve its liveability. While this will undoubtedly involve a significant improvement in the technological efficiency of motor vehicles and also a greater use of more sustainable fuels, if the city continues to build in more and more car dependence, it will not address the issues of ecological footprint or enhanced liveability. There are many transport-based economic issues related to the inefficient use of land and infrastructure budgets as well as automobile congestion, urban sprawl, GHG emissions and health issues (Newman and Kenworthy 2011a; Trubka et al. 2010a; 2010b; 2010c). Automobile City expansion will mean cities are unable to achieve a more sustainable future (Asian Development Bank 2012; United Nations Human Settlements Programme 2013). Awareness of this has not been without contention as many commentators in automobile-dominated cities could not imagine a more liveable city (e.g. Gordon and Richardson 1989). However, the global debate has shifted to seeing how a more balanced city can be created where car use is not such a requirement for all trips and destinations (see above and Intergovernmental Panel on Climate Change (IPCC) 2007) in order to create outcomes that are more equitable, healthy and economic (Matan and Newman 2012; Matan et al. 2012; Newman and Matan 2012; Trubka et al. 2010a; 2010b; 2010c).

The next phase of urban development is therefore often described as a Polycentric City with a much greater role for the Walking City and the Transit City together with modifications to the Automobile City.

This chapter will look at the recent trends in urban transport and city development that suggest how these roles are beginning to transition from the less sustainable to the more sustainable, and how the changes can be accelerated and structured into three urban form typologies: the Walking City, the Transit City and the Automobile City.

The Walking City

Walking, until the popularity of motorized transport, has been the dominant form of transport in cities since urban settlements began (Kostof 1992; Newman and Kenworthy 1999; Crawford 2002; Newman 2003) and cities have traditionally developed around walking ('the slow pedestrian') as the dominant mode of transport (Burchard, 1957:112). Within this historic city type, all goods and services needed for daily life had to be within a walkable area, and, therefore, cities developed in quite dense and compact ways in order to facilitate this form of social and economic interaction. Modern cities are now redeveloping and restructuring their urban cores to be more walkable and vibrant in order to address the growing cultural and economic shift towards more sustainable and more urban lifestyles (Newman and Newman 2006; Brookings Institution Metropolitan Program 2008; Newman and Kenworthy 2011b). Many cities are seeking to attract educated residents to facilitate knowledge-oriented and services-oriented economic development and this happens best in Walking City fabric where face-to-face interactions are easy (Florida 2002; Gehl 2010). There is also a social equity motivation with the need to accommodate the car-less in such walkable urban centres.

The Walking City goes beyond providing basic pedestrian infrastructure to be more about creating cities that are attractive, liveable and equitable. Walkable urban environments need to be accessible, containing not only appropriate pedestrian infrastructure but also having the necessary urban destinations within close proximity (Forsyth and Southworth 2008; Matan 2011). This requires urban areas that are dense and compact with mixed land use and accessible public transport and public space, particularly green space (Saelens et al. 2003; Jackson 2003; Handy et al. 2005; Soltani 2006; Saelens and Handy 2008; Guo 2009; Ewing and Cervero 2010; Forsyth and Krizek 2010; Larco et al. 2011). Pedestrian infrastructure needs to be safe, barrier-free, pleasant and interesting, inviting people to walk. These features go beyond simply encouraging walking for transport purposes to include understanding and recognition of how people experience and use urban spaces and thus refocus transport planning within Walking Cities to suit people and their needs, rather than car-based mobility (Wunderlich 2008; Matan 2011).

The sustainability of the Walking City is well recognized. Walking is one of the healthiest ways to get around our cities for both public and environmental health (Newman and Kenworthy 1999; Huy et al. 2008; Pucher and Buehler 2010; Hoornweg et al. 2011; Newman and Matan 2012). Furthermore, walkable areas have been shown to have significant economic benefits, including increased real estate values (Sohn et al. 2012), increased productivity (Trubka et al. 2010c), reduced physical health costs (Frank et al. 2004; Trubka et al. 2010c; Litman 2012; Matan et al. 2012), reduced mental health costs (Stanley et al. 2011a; Stanley et al. 2011b), and reduced congestion-related costs, vehicle-related costs and reductions in roadway provision (see, for example, Sinclair Knight Merz and PricewaterhouseCoopers 2011). Walkable areas also enable a reduction in transport externalities such as noise and air pollution and GHG emissions (Rabl and de Nazelle 2012). This reduction in motorized traffic externalities in addition benefits pedestrians and cyclists, who can be exposed to high levels of air pollution in certain urban microenvironments of the Automobile City such as in busy street canyons (Kaur et al. 2007).

Globally there is a move towards reclaiming space that was for cars and car parking and to turn this space into spaces for people (Gehl 2010). This process can be seen in the pedestrianization of city centres, the implementation of bicycle ways and in the reduction of the provision of on and off street parking. The adaptation to Walking City design has been facilitated by the work of Danish academic, architect and urban designer Jan Gehl and Gehl Architects. Gehl is one of the most internationally recognized urban designers and has made substantial contributions in over 40 cities around the world, including in Copenhagen, Melbourne and New York (Matan 2011; Matan and Newman 2012; Gehl Architects 2013). Gehl has demonstrated that each improvement to the pedestrian environment results in an increase in the level of activity in the city spaces.

Perhaps the biggest current example of a city implementing sustainable streets and reclaiming public space is New York. To become a sustainable city and to accommodate an additional one million people by 2030, the City of New York and the Department of Transportation (NYDOT), headed by Commissioner Janette Sadik-Khan, hired Gehl Architects in 2007 to survey the pedestrian environment in New York. Unsurprisingly, the survey found that New York has many pedestrians, however, it also found that many of the footpaths were overcrowded, there were few places to sit, and although New York has many public places, many were difficult to access and exhibited an unwelcoming environment (as measured through numbers of youth and older users). It was determined that people were primarily walking only for transport purposes – they were on the streets to move quickly from A to B – rather than to spend time in the public realm.

Following the conclusion of the surveys, the City of New York and NYDOT have rapidly been implementing changes to the public realm and to the walking and cycling environment with the aim of using road capacity more efficiently. The most visible changes include new plazas throughout the city, most notably at Times Square, and the redevelopment of Broadway into a 'Boulevard' (New York City Department of Transport 2010). In addition, the City and NYDOT have been rapidly building cycle paths throughout the city. They completed 320 km of cycle ways between June 2007 and November 2009 with a plan to have nearly 3,000 km in their bicycle network, as well as extending footpaths and other pedestrian infrastructure throughout the city. Most of the changes have been quick and simple infrastructure changes focusing on repainting road surfaces and the redistribution of road space through bollards, planting boxes and fold-out chairs.

The closing of Broadway to cars at Times Square has been the most visible symbol of the city's pedestrianization. On 23 May 2009, Broadway was closed to through traffic at Herald Square between 47th and 42nd Streets initially as an experiment. This was made permanent in February 2010. The closure has resulted in a 'seven percent improvement in traffic flow' (Gehl Architects 2011: n.p.n.), with northbound taxi trips found to be 17 per cent faster after the Broadway shutdown (comparing Fall 2009 to Fall 2008) (New York City Department of Transport 2010; City of New York 2011). The closure has shown significant economic benefits to the businesses at Times Square, with 71 per cent projecting revenue increases after the closure (City of New York 2011).

The changes in New York did not happen smoothly, and created much controversy. The City and NYDOT persevered, however, and now the results are becoming evident. Throughout the project areas pedestrian numbers have increased, pedestrian injuries have fallen by 35 per cent and 80 per cent fewer pedestrians walk in the roadway in Times Square (Taddeo 2010; City of New York 2011). Between June 2007 and November 2009, cycling to work doubled in New York, with commuter cycling increasing by 35 per cent between 2007 and 2008 (New York City Department of Transport 2010). These changes to the city's multimodal transport system demonstrate how quickly changes can be made to improve the walkability and public realm, and to reclaim the Walking City from the automobile. The Commissioner explains these changes:

> Until a few years ago, our streets [in New York] looked the same as they did fifty years ago. That's not good business . . . We're updating our streets to reflect the way people live now. And we're designing a city for people, not a city for vehicles.
>
> *(Taddeo 2010: n.p.n.)*

The City of Melbourne shows perhaps the most dramatic results of all the Australian cities in illustrating how positive changes to the public realm can result in synergistic increases in walking and city life, offering 'a remarkable case study in an emerging pedestrian city, having shown some dramatic, positive change in its pedestrian character and public sphere in the relatively short span of twenty years' (Beatley and Newman 2009: 134). The City of Melbourne deliberately focused on restoring and strengthening the city's traditional grid pattern and redesigning footpaths and alleyways to create a walkable interesting urban environment. Two surveys (1993–1994 and 2004) measuring and monitoring the changes have been made by Gehl and the City of Melbourne, enabling a decade of work by the City to be evaluated. The surveys demonstrate that there have been:

- an increase in the number of people walking in the city centre. The number of pedestrians in the city centre on weekdays in the evening has increased 98 per cent (from 45,868 in 1993 to 90,690 in 2004), and daytime pedestrian traffic has increased by 39 per cent (from 190,772 in 1993 to 265,428 in 2004);
- an increase in public space by 71 per cent via creation of new squares, promenades and parks (from 42,260 m^2 in 1994 to 72,200m^2 plus Birrarung Marr Park's 69,200m^2 in 2004) and an increase in the number of people spending time in urban spaces;
- more places to sit and pause, with an increase in cafés and restaurants (from 95 in 1994 to 356 in 2004), a threefold increase in café seats outdoors (from 1,940 in 1993 to 5,380 in 2004) and an integrated street furniture collection;
- improved streets, including the revitalization of a network of lanes and arcades (Gehl Architects 2004).

These examples of Melbourne and New York illustrate the growth of the Walking City. There are many other examples around the world of this growing cultural and economic shift towards creating walkable urban cores and redistributing city space from automobiles to people, reinvigorating the liveability of the Walking City and at the same time reducing the ecological footprint.

The Transit City

Trends in car use and transit use are reversing globally with most developed cities showing peak car use and most cities in the developed and developing world are now rapidly growing in transit use, especially in rail (Newman and Kenworthy 2011b; Newman et al. 2013).

The biggest change in the economy during the period leading up to and including the period of car use decline and transit growth has been the digital transformation and the consequent knowledge/service economy. This has been a concentrating force in terms of city structure and fabric across the world's cities. Newman and Kenworthy (2011b) present new data on global cities showing a universal increase in urban density in the past decade or so, reversing over one hundred years of decline in most cities. The knowledge economy and digital jobs are focused in city centres, as these are where the creative synergies between people occur (Kane 2010). This has been best achieved in the old central business districts (CBDs) as well as the sub-centres based along transit lines. As shown above, the transformation of Walking Cities is well underway but so too is the transformation of the old inner suburbs based along tram lines or metros and the old rail corridors of centres strung along like pearls on a string. All these areas are where high intensity people-based activity gravitates such as large health and education facilities, enabling creative synergies between business people requiring especially intensive information technology (Kane 2010). Transit-oriented development (TODs) at all these centres has begun transforming the existing urban fabric and has become the basis for the revival of the Transit City.

As with many economic changes, there is also a cultural dimension to this change that perhaps explains the rapidity of the changes in transport observed by Newman et al. (2013) as well as the demographic complexion of the change. Young people (especially those involved in knowledge economy jobs) are moving to reduce their car use, with a significant trend in the reduction in those obtaining a driver's licence (0.6 per cent per annum), as they switch to alternative transport faster than any other group (Delbosc and Currie 2013; Metz 2013). This has been recognized by a few commentators and is related to the use of social media devices (Florida 2010; Metz 2013). While in transit or while walking, people are already connected by their smart technology phones and tablets, thus driving is less preferred as it is increasingly being outlawed to drive while using such devices. The Davis, Dutzik and Baxandall (2012) report shows that the mobile phone is a far more important device than a car for younger people and this is part of the cultural revolution that underlies the rail transit revolution. Baby-boomers (those born after the Second World War, from 1946 to 1964) gained freedom and connection with a car, Generation Ys (those born early 1980s to the early 2000s) are not needing one but like to save time on a fast train while constructively relating to their friends and work (Goodwin and Van Dender 2013).

The other expression of this change is that younger people are moving to live in the Walking City or Transit City, as these locations more readily enable them to express the kind of urban experience and culture that they aspire to (Florida 2010; Metz 2013). Thus they feed the market that enables the Transit City and Walking City renewal to continue.

Other parts of the economy such as manufacturing, small and large industry, freight transport and storage, have remained vehicle-based and are outside this new knowledge economy. It is expected that they will remain so, as they are also not where the growth in jobs or the growth in wealth is happening. Thus, the Automobile City economy and culture have become somewhat distinct from the new regenerated urban economy of knowledge/services and its basis in Walking and Transit City locations. In many cities, the Automobile City fabric is becoming significantly less wealthy than the Walking City and Transit City fabrics (Newman et al. 2009; Florida 2010; Glaeser 2011).

The rise of rail transit (as well as the reduction in per capita car use) can be explained by a combination of urban structural limits together with urban cultural and economic change that together enable us to see a different kind of urban future emerging. Cities that are responding to the powerful new agenda for building rail transit systems can enable this new, less car-dependent city to emerge. However, if a city does not adequately develop or build the rail infrastructure required, then it can easily miss out on this important social and economic change (Metz 2013). The biggest threat is if car-dependent cities do not recognize that the golden age of the car is over. Metz suggests that this transition, which is observable in most developed cities, could occur at a lower level of Gross Domestic Product (GDP) in most developing cities and thus enable a rapid global transition to reduced ecological footprints especially GHG from transport.

There are a few emerging trends in best practice for Transit Cities that can enable large and small cities to capitalize on the opportunities that are now presented by this global new world. These include:

1 *Integration of modes*. Rail is most effective when it is properly integrated with bus feed-in services to enable a broader catchment to be served. This is particularly evident in car-dependent cities, where rail cannot be served by just walk-on passengers. This requires ticket integration and fast and convenient transfer systems. Perth's Mandurah rail line (outlined in more detail below) illustrates this well with some 80 per cent of the ridership coming from bus transfers and only a very small percentage from Park and Ride, despite generous Park and Ride provision (McIntosh et al. 2011). The provision of bus right-of-way into stations is a critical part of enabling this integration. Of course, integration with bicycles is also an opportunity that offers huge rewards, as evidenced by looking at the surroundings of any Dutch or Danish railway station, or even the new, specially designed secure bike parking areas around São Paulo's commuter rail system or those in Seoul.

2 *Integration of land use*. Rail transit will be optimized if there is a chance to redevelop non-supporting land uses around the stations in order to enable more people to have easy access. Measuring this potential and making it part of the planning process seems to be an emerging standard practice (Bachels and Newman 2011; Renne and Curtis 2011). Where Park and Ride is needed, it should be integrated with attractive high density, mixed use development and not as vast swathes of bitumen, which destroy station environments (Schiller and Kenworthy 2011).

3 *Speed*. The value of travel time will not change much in this new world and must be central to how any rail system is designed. Giving reasonably long station distances and separate right-of-way is critical in order to enable speed that is competitive with the car (McIntosh et al. 2013). Light rail running on dedicated right-of-way, rather than on-street tram or bus options, will be mostly needed in car-dependent cities to compete with the car in speed.

4 *PPP (Private-Public Partnership) Procurement*. The delivery process can enable all of these options to be highlighted if procurement is based on a PPP process, as suggested by many

(e.g. Bottoms 2003; Infrastructure Australia 2012). The Gold Coast Light Rail provides the best example in Australia of how PPP approaches can be achieved in light rail and the new Manchester City Deal shows how rail PPPs can work in the UK. The full integration with land use remains to be done and is much more likely if land value capture (see below) is made part of the package.

5 *New assessment approaches for rail.* There are two major ways for the assessment of rail projects to be improved through the transport economic assessment process: recognizing the role of agglomeration economies in the Benefit-Cost Ratio (BCR) and recognizing the role of avoidable land development costs. Agglomeration economies are being included in transport BCRs since the Eddington Transport Study in the UK (Eddington 2006). The application of BCR and agglomeration economies in rail is considerably better than road projects as rail acts as a focusing feature that enables the synergies and clustering of knowledge economy productivity. The London Crossrail went from 1.5 to 3.0 in its BCR when agglomeration economies were added. Trubka (2011) has outlined the value of agglomeration elasticities for Australian cities. Even more significant (though rarely done) is the use of avoidable costs in assessment of transport. Rail and its focusing ability in land use can enable reductions in urban sprawl that invariably are heavily subsidized and have many external costs. Trubka et al (2010a; 2010b; 2010c) have shown considerable cost savings and health benefits from rail-oriented development as opposed to car-based development that can be included in any transport assessment.

6 *New approaches to funding rail through value capture.* Rail infrastructure increases land value due to its accessibility benefits (McIntosh et al. 2012). This increase in financial value can be captured and used to help fund the infrastructure. McIntosh et al. (2011) have shown that a five-step process can work in the following way:
   - a Accessibility benefits analysis to demonstrate the land area where owners will benefit most from the new infrastructure.
   - b Land value data collection of the differential between those areas varying in accessibility. This can be around 20–25 per cent for residential land values and over 50 per cent for commercial land values.
   - c Assessment of the various potential financing mechanisms available in the city through public and private value capture, e.g. government land and parking revenues.
   - d Economic and financial assessment of how much land value can contribute to the funding of the rail through a dedicated fund based on land value taxes that are going to increase due to the new rail system.
   - e Delivery through a planning mechanism and a fund established to bring it together, probably in a PPP as in the Manchester City Deal project.

7 If rail is going to continue to grow and car use to decline, then a range of sophisticated value capture mechanisms will be needed for each city to make the most of this opportunity for funding.

Perhaps the most significant trend in recent years in Australia and America following the lead of Europe has been the emergence of light rail as a solution in small car-dependent cities. Lobby groups in Australia have been actively pushing the political case for light rail in Canberra, Hobart, Bendigo, Darwin, Newcastle, Cairns, the Sunshine Coast and Parramatta. These cities are mostly well under 300,000 people, Canberra being the largest at a little over 300,000. Similar trends have been observed in the USA (Bottoms 2003).

There are 545 cities with light rail according to Wikipedia; from this there are now 118 cities with populations under 150,000 that have light rail or are constructing light rail. This appears to suggest that a changing appreciation of the value of light rail in small cities has occurred. The change is probably associated with the shift in value associated with the trends in peak car use, fuel prices, urban traffic speed trends and urban economic and cultural changes outlined above and in Newman et al. (2013).

The question needs to be asked whether light rail is likely to be a viable option for these small cities, since the traditional approach would suggest it was not. Bus options have long been considered the only viable option for small cities. However, the above dramatic turnaround in the fortunes of light rail may be indicating that a new era of desirability and viability for light rail in small cities is emerging. The case for these cities to be considered suitable for light rail is based on an understanding of what is likely to be causing the above trends in traditionally car-dominated cities, as well as some new options for assessing and funding light rail in such cities as the basis of regenerating or extending the Transit City in smaller cities.

The Automobile City

Newman and Kenworthy (1989) first coined the term automobile dependence in their book, *Cities and Automobile Dependence*. The data from 32 global cities provided urban metrics for their analysis, including:

- gasoline consumption;
- public and private transport system modal split;
- degree of infrastructure provision for the automobile (road supply and parking) relative to transit;
- a measure of urban density and of urban centralization.

Twenty years later the parameters are all showing that automobile dependence has begun to decline and perhaps we are witnessing its demise (Newman et al. 2013). The one-hundred year growth in the use of the automobile in cities appears to have plateaued and then declined across the world's developed cities (Goodwin and Melia 2011; Newman and Kenworthy 2011b; Gargett 2012). Demonstrations of how Automobile Cities are being restructured with rail transit are now being seen. This trend back to rail-based transit is perhaps to be expected in the relatively dense cities and in countries in Europe, the Middle East and Asia. However, perhaps the more surprising trends have been in the traditional car-dependent cities of the USA, Canada and Australia that were once only considered suitable only for bus transit in their suburbs but are now seeing a future based around rail down corridors deep into their traditional Automobile City fabric.

The beneficiaries from the investment in transit infrastructure in all cities are broad and in areas often not accounted for when deciding on whether to invest in new transit infrastructure. This is often the case in the Automobile City fabric where the key beneficiaries from the investment in transit include:

- land owners: due to increases in underlying land values;
- property developers: the potential increase in developed real estate values, faster sales rates and thus reduced holding costs, and lower construction costs due to reduced parking requirements, thus inducing urban infill and TOD;
- transport system users: a more efficient, less congested transport system results in less time spent in transit, allowing more time for other activities and better transit experience;

- business owners: increased economic activity due to improved accessibility for their customers and employees to their business, with workers arriving at work less stressed and more productive;
- Federal/State and Local Governments: due to increases in land property-based revenue from existing levies and taxes from increased land and property values;
- It is the transit beneficiaries who are driving the change away from the private vehicle to transit, and are helping reshape the centres and suburbs of the Automobile City.

The growth in public transport patronage has occurred for all transit modes, but the highest growth has been in urban rail systems (Newman et al. 2013). In Perth, Western Australia, the development of a fast rail system deep into car-dependent suburbs has been a major success and indicates the main elements necessary for the regeneration of the Automobile City fabric.

Perth's 72-km-long Mandurah Rail System opened in 2007. With a maximum speed of 137 kmph and an average speed of almost 90 kmph, this system acts more like a fast rail than a suburban rail system, which in Australia typically averages around 40 kmph for an all-stops services. The Mandurah rail line was very controversial when being planned as the urban areas served by the line are not typical of those normally provided with rail but instead were highly car-dependent scattered low density land uses. Nevertheless the rail line has been remarkably successful, carrying over 70,000 people per day (five times the patronage on the express buses it replaced) and has reached the patronage levels predicted for 2021 a decade ahead of time. The reasons for this success include well-designed interchanges, careful integration of bus services, the use of integrated ticketing and fares without transfer penalties and, crucially, the high speed of the system when compared to competing car-based trips. Perth's Mandurah rail line was the second in Australia to be implemented in the median of an existing freeway (after the section to the north of Perth). As a result, there is only limited pedestrian catchment along the alignment, and the patronage model for the Mandurah rail line is:

- 7 per cent pedestrian (walk-able) catchment;
- 85 per cent of the total patronage come from passengers that are dropped off and the feeder bus services; and
- 8 per cent of total patronage to come from the 5,260 park and ride bays.

This low pedestrian catchment/transfer-based patronage model for transit is a major shift for the roles of the different public transport modes, with the park and ride facilities and closely integrated bus interchanges designed to extend the rail line's catchments into the surrounding low density suburbs, using the regional bus network as a feeder service for areas that had previously been car-dependent. The other major difference to other public transport systems in Australia is that the public transport system was designed to be competitive with the private motor vehicle in both time and cost (generalized cost).

One of the most contentious debates in public transport planning is the role of transfer costs in deterring patronage due to time losses. This has been used to stop many rail projects (Hensher 1999, Currie 2009). The Mandurah rail line was designed to minimize transfer penalties through well-integrated bus interchanges and bus services, and as a result these are responsible for 85 per cent of the patronage, a figure much higher than for most rail systems. This seems to be acceptable to the patrons as the speed of the train means that the overall journey saves time compared to the private vehicle.

There would appear to be a lesson here for all rail planning but especially fast rail in car-dependent cities: it is essential to minimize transfer penalties and create speeds that mean the generalized costs of choosing to travel on fast rail are lower than the alternatives (car).

The Mandurah rail line maintains a strong focus on the competitiveness of the public transport against the private motor vehicle in a time and financial generalized cost model for access from the Mandurah suburbs to the Perth CBD and the rest of the rail network. This is illustrated by:

- the competitiveness of the train to the car in time due to the high speed of the trains (maximum speed 137 kmph) compared to the car (freeway speed limit 100 kmph), and due to the congested nature of the competing Kwinana Freeway, which is increasing with peak hour travel speeds being much lower than the theoretical speed limit;
- the introduction of the electronic ticketing system that enabled zero cost transfer between the bus and rail modes, hence removing any transfer cost penalty associated with transferring between modes;
- the frequency of the feeder bus services and the ease and speed of interchange between the bus and rail modes, minimizing the time penalty for transferring between modes;
- the majority of the feeder bus services that transfer to the rail stations do so very quickly and conveniently, and operate within the single transport ticketing zones, therefore do not add to the trip cost for the overall journey.

This model for the minimization of public transport generalized cost when compared to the private vehicle has enabled Perth's Mandurah rail line to be very competitive with the private vehicle in a region where the Mandurah rail line is located. This area is where the private vehicle has been historically extremely dominant due to low dwelling and population density, and long travel distances for the journey to work. The low generalized cost network design minimizes the time and financial cost for the multimodal trip and induces traditionally car-based ridership onto the transfer-designed feeder services to the stations, and this is the key success for the intermodal public transport model that operates for the Mandurah rail line.

The application of the Mandurah rail model to the design of high speed intra-city and regional rail for large, low density car-dependent cities has now been demonstrated. It shows that a viable alternative is possible to build into any Automobile City.

Recent studies have demonstrated that the land values associated with the Mandurah rail line have increased by over 28 per cent over a five-year period. This has been modelled to show that the rail line could have used value capture as a major means of creating finance for building the train service (between 40 and 60 per cent of the capital cost of the project could have been raised by this mechanism) (McIntosh et al. 2014). The land value increases also show why dense Transit City fabric is now being built into the Automobile City fabric and can be further anticipated as the market for these locations becomes more and more attractive. This indicates that the viability of building rail into Automobile City fabric can now be envisaged.

Conclusion

This chapter has shown that a major factor in the sustainable development of cities in the future will depend on the extent to which they can create or regenerate areas of Walking City and Transit City rather than areas of Automobile City. Economic change and cultural change seem to be now favouring this opportunity. Demonstrations are happening in cities of all kinds and it will only be the lack of growth opportunities or the legacy of institutional barriers that will prevent it from happening rapidly in cities across the world. Urban transport infrastructure changes can provide the fundamental transformative force in creating more sustainable development patterns in the world's cities.

References

Asian Development Bank (2012) Green urbanization in Asia. *Key Indicators for Asia and the Pacific 2012.* 43rd ed. Mandaluyong City: Asian Development Bank.

Bachels, M. and Newman, P. (2011) Transit orientated development. In R. Salter, S. Dhar, and P. Newman (eds) *Technologies for Climate Change Mitigation: Transport, TNA Guidebook Series.* Copenhagen: UNEP Riso Centre.

Beatley, T. and Newman, P. (2009) *Green Urbanism Down Under: Learning from Sustainable Communities in Australia.* Washington, DC: Island Press.

Bottoms, G. T. (2003) Continuing developments in light rail transit in Western Europe: United Kingdom, France, Spain, Portugal and Italy. *9th National Light Rail Conference.* Portland, OR: Transportation Research Board and APTA.

Brookings Institution Metropolitan Program (2008) The road . . . less traveled: an analysis of vehicle miles traveled trends in the U.S. *Metropolitan Infrastructure Initiative Series.* Washington, DC: Brookings Institution.

Burchard, J. E. (1957) The urban aesthetic. *The Annuals of the American Academy of Political and Social Science,* 314: 112–122.

City of New York (2011) *The City of New York* [Online]. New York: The City of New York. Available at: www.nyc.gov (accessed 9 February 2011).

Crawford, J. (2002) *Carfree Cities.* Utrecht: International Books.

Currie, G. (2009) Research perspectives on the merits of light rail versus bus. *BITRE Colloquium.*

Davis, B., Dutzik, T. and Baxandall, P. (2012) *Transportation and the New Generation: Why Young People are Driving Less and What it Means for Transportation Policy.* Washington, DC: Frontier Group and U.S. PIRG Education Fund.

Delbosc, A. and Currie, G. (2013) Causes of youth licensing decline: a synthesis of evidence. *Transport Reviews: A Transnational Transdisciplinary Journal,* 33: 1–20.

Eddington, R. (2006) *The Eddington Transport Study: The Case for Action: Sir Rod Eddington's Advice to Government.* London.

Ewing, R. and Cervero, R. (2010) Travel and the built environment. *Journal of American Planning Association,* 76: 265–294.

Florida, R. (2002) *The Rise of the Creative Class.* North Melbourne: Pluto Press.

Florida, R. (2010) *The Great Reset: How New Ways of Living and Working Drive Post-Crash Prosperity.* Toronto: Random House.

Forsyth, A. and Krizek, K. (2010) Promoting walking and bicycling: assessing the evidence to assist planners. *Built Environment,* 36: 429–446.

Forsyth, A. and Southworth, M. (2008) Cities afoot: pedestrians, walkability and urban design. *Journal of Urban Design,* 13: 1–3.

Frank, L. D., Andresen, M. A. and Schmid, T. L. (2004) Obesity relationships with community design, physical activity, and time spent in cars. *American Journal of Preventative Medicine,* 27: 87–96.

Gargett, D. (2012) Traffic growth: modelling a global phenomenon. *World Transport Policy and Practice,* 18: 27–45.

Gehl, J. (2010) *Cities for People.* Washington, DC: Island Press.

Gehl Architects (2004) *Places for People, Melbourne 2004.* Report for the City of Melbourne. Melbourne.

Gehl Architects (2011) Making cities for people. *Making Cities for People* [Online]. Available at: http://gehlarchitects.wordpress.com/ (accessed 9 February 2011).

Gehl Architects (2013) *Gehl Architects* [Online]. Copenhagen: Gehl Architects. Available at: www.gehlarchitects.dk (accessed 2 February 2011).

Glaeser, E. (2011) *The Triumph of the City, How Our Greatest Invention Makes Us Richer, Smarter, Greener, Healthier, and Happier.* Harmondsworth: Penguin Press.

Goodwin, P. and Melia, S. (2011) Three views on 'peak car', special issue on 'A future beyond the car'. *World Transport Policy and Practice,* 17: 3–6.

Goodwin, P. and Van Dender, K. (2013) 'Peak car': themes and issues. *Transport Reviews: A Transnational Transdisciplinary Journal*, 33: 243–254.
Gordon, P. and Richardson, H. (1989) Gasoline consumption and cities: a reply. *Journal of the American Planning Association*, 55: 342–345.
Guo, Z. (2009) Does the pedestrian environment affect the utility of walking? A case of path choice in downtown Boston. *Transportation Research Part D: Transport and Environment*, 14: 343–352.
Handy, S., Cao, X. and Mokhtarian, P. (2005) Correlation or causality between the built environment and travel behaviour? Evidence from Northern California. *Transportation Research Part D*, 10: 427–444.
Hensher, D. (1999) A bus-based transit way or light rail? Continuing the saga of choice versus blind commitment. *Road and Transport Research*, 8: 3–21.
Hoornweg, D., Sugar, L. and Gomez, C. L. T. (2011) Cities and greenhouse gas emissions: moving forward. *Environment and Urbanization*, 23: 207–227.
Huy, C., Becker, S., Gomolinsky, U., Klein, T. and Thiel, A. (2008) Health, medical risk factors, and bicycle use in everyday life in the over-50 population. *Journal of Aging and Physical Activity*, 16: 454–464.
Infrastructure Australia (2012) *Infrastructure Financing and Funding Reform*. Infrastructure Financing Working Group. Canberra: Infrastructure Australia.
IPCC (Intergovernmental Panel on Climate Change) (2007) *IPCC Fourth Assessment Report: Climate Change 2007. Contribution of Working Group III to the Fourth Assessment Report of the Intergovernmental Panel on Climate Change IPCC*. ed. B. Metz, O. R. Davidson, P. R. Bosch, R. Dave, and L. A. Meyer. Cambridge and New York: IPCC.
Jackson, L. (2003) The relationship of urban design to human health and condition. *Landscape and Urban Planning*, 64: 191–200.
Kane, M. (2010) The knowledge economy and public transport. In P. Newman and J. Scheurer (eds) *The Knowledge Arc Light Rail: A Concept for Delivering the Next Phase of Public Transport in Perth*. Perth: Parsons-Brinkerhoff-CUSP Discussion Paper, Curtin University.
Kaur, S., Nieuwenhuijsen, M. J. and Colvile, R. N. (2007) Fine particulate matter and carbon monoxide exposure concentrations in urban street transport microenvironments. *Atmospheric Environment*, 41: 4781–4810.
Kostof, S. (1992) *The City Assembled: The Elements of Urban Form Through History*. London: Thames and Hudson.
Larco, N., Steiner, B., Stockard, J. and West, A. (2011) Pedestrian-friendly environments and active travel for residents of multifamily housing: the role of preferences and perceptions. *Environment and Behavior*, X: 1–13.
Litman, T. (2012) *If Health Matters: Integrating Public Health Objectives in Transport Planning*. Australia: Victoria Transport Policy Institute.
McIntosh, J., Newman, P., Crane, T. and Mouritz, M. (2011) *Alternative Funding for Public Transport in Perth*. Perth: Committee for Perth and CUSP.
McIntosh, J., Newman, P. and Glazebrook, G. (2013) Why fast trains work: an assessment of a fast regional rail system in Perth, Australia. *Journal of Transportation Technologies*, 3: 37–47.
McIntosh, J., Newman, P., Scheurer, J., Wisdom, A. (2012) Initial assessment of the accessibility and new funding opportunities for the Doncaster Rail Project, City of Manningham, Melbourne [Online]. Available at: www.manningham.vic.gov.au/council/advocacy/doncasterrail/doncaster_rail.html?s=848374284 (accessed 19 March 2014).
McIntosh, J., Newman, P., Trubka, R. and Kenworthy, K. (2014) Framework for land value capture from the investment in transit in car dependent cities. Forthcoming, *Journal of Transport and Land Use*.
Marchetti, C. (1994) Anthropological invariants in travel behavior. *Technological Forecasting and Social Change*, 47: 75–88.
Matan, A. (2011) Rediscovering urban design through walkability: an assessment of the contribution of Jan Gehl. PhD thesis, Curtin University.
Matan, A. and Newman, P. (2012) Jan Gehl and new visions for walkable Australian cities. *World Transport Policy and Practice*, 17: 30–37.
Matan, A., Trubka, R., Newman, P. and Vardoulakis, S. (2012) Review of public health and productivity benefits from different urban transport and related land use options in Australia. Paper presented at The 5th Healthy Cities: Working Together to Achieve Liveable Cities Conference. Geelong.
Metz, D. (2013) Peak car and beyond: the fourth era of travel. *Transport Reviews: A Transnational Transdisciplinary Journal*, 33: 255–270.

Newman, C. E. and Newman, P. (2006) The car and culture,. In P. Beilhartz and T. Hogan (eds) *Sociology: Place, Time and Division*. South Melbourne: Oxford University Press.

Newman, P. (2003) Walking in historical, international and contemporary context. In R. Tolley (ed.) *Sustainable Transport: Planning for Walking and Cycling in Urban Environments*. Cambridge: Woodhead Publishing.

Newman, P. (2006) The environmental impact of cities. *Environment and Urbanisation*, 18(2): 275–295.

Newman, P., Beatley, T. and Boyer, H. (2009) *Resilient Cities: Responding to Peak Oil and Climate Change*. Washington, DC: Island Press.

Newman, P. and Kenworthy, J. (1989) *Cities and Automobile Dependence: An International Sourcebook*, Aldershot: Gower.

Newman, P. and Kenworthy, J. (1999) *Sustainability and Cities: Overcoming Automobile Dependence*. Washington, DC: Island Press.

Newman, P. and Kenworthy, J. (2011a) Evaluating the transport sector's contribution to greenhouse gas emissions and energy consumption. In R. Salter, S. Dhar, and Newman (eds) *Technologies for Climate Change Mitigation: Transport*. Riso: UNEP Riso Centre for Energy, Climate and Sustainable Development.

Newman, P. and Kenworthy, J. (2011b) 'Peak car use': understanding the demise of automobile dependence. *World Transport Policy and Practice*, 17: 31–42.

Newman, P., Kenworthy, J. and Glazebrook, G. (2013) Peak car use and the rise of global rail: why this is happening and what it means for large and small cities. *Journal of Transporation Technologies*, 3: 272–287.

Newman, P. and Matan, A. (2012) Human health and human mobility. *Current Opinion in Environmental Sustainability*, 4: 420–426.

New York City Department of Transport (2010) *New York City Department of Transport (DOT)* [Online]. New York: New York City Department of Transport. Available at: www.nyc.gov/html/dot/html (accessed 23 November 2010).

Pucher, J. and Buehler, R. (2010) Walking and cycling for healthy cities. *Built Environment*, 36: 391–414.

Rabl, A. and de Nazelle, A. (2012) Benefits of shift from car to active transport. *Transport Policy*, 19: 121–131.

Renne, J. and Curtis, C. (eds) (2011) *Transit Oriented Development: Making it Happen*. Aldershot: Ashgate Publishers.

Saelens, B. and Handy, S. (2008) Built environment correlates of walking: a review. *Medicine and Science in Sports and Exercise*, 40: S550–S567.

Saelens, B., Sallis, J. F. and Frank, L. (2003) Environmental correlates of walking and cycling: findings from the transportation, urban design, and planning literatures. *Annals of Behavioral Medicine*, 25: 80–91.

Schiller, P. and Kenworthy, J. (2011) Walk to transit or drive to transit? *Walk 21*. Vancouver, BC.

Sinclair Knight Merz and Pricewaterhouse Coopers (2011) *Benefits of Inclusion of Active Transport in Infrastructure Projects*. Queensland: Queensland Department of Transport and Mainroads.

Sohn, D. W., Vernez Moudon, A. and Lee, J. (2012) The economic value of walkable neighbourhoods. *Urban Design International*, 17: 115–128.

Soltani, A. (2006) How urban design affects personal activity and travel choice:an analysis of travel data from sample communities in Adelaide. Paper presented at 29th Australasian Transport Research Forum, Crowne Plaza Surfers Paradise, Gold Coast.

Stanley, J., Hensher, D., Stanley, J. and Vella-Brodrick, D. (2011a) Mobility, social exclusion and well-being: exploring the links. *Transport Research A*, 45: 789–801.

Stanley, J., Hensher, D. A., Stanley, J., Currie, G., Greene, W. H. and Vella-Brodrick, D. (2011b) Social exclusion and the value of mobility. *Journal of Transport Economics and Policy*, 45: 197–222.

Taddeo, L. (2010) The brightest: 15 geniuses who give us hope: Sadik-Khan: urban reengineer. *Esquire*. Hearst Digital Media.

Trubka, R. (2011) Agglomeration economies in Australian cities: productivity benefits of increasing urban density and accessibility. PhD thesis, Curtin University.

Trubka, R., Newman, P. and Bilsborough, D. (2010a) Cost of urban sprawl (2): greenhouse gases. *Environment Design Guide*, 84: 1–16.

Trubka, R., Newman, P. and Bilsborough, D. (2010b) Costs of urban sprawl (1): infrastructure and transport. *Environment Design Guide*, 83: 1–6.

Trubka, R., Newman, P. and Bilsborough, D. (2010c) Costs of urban sprawl (3): physical activity links to healthcare costs and productivity. *Environmental Design Guide*, 85: 1–13.

United Nations Human Settlements Programme (2013) Planning and design for sustainable urban mobility: global report on human settlements 2013. In UN-Habitat (ed.) *Global Report on Human Settlements*. Nairobi: United Nations Human Settlements Programme.

Wunderlich, F. M. (2008) Walking and rhythmicity: sensing urban space. *Journal of Urban Design*, 13: 125–139.

Zahavi, Y. and Ryan, J. M. (1980) Stability of travel component over time. *Transportation Research Record: Journal of the Transportation Research Board*, 750: 19–26.

23

CHINA'S TRANSITION TO SUSTAINABILITY

Which direction to take?

Arthur P. J. Mol

Introduction

China's unprecedented period of high economic growth over at least the last two decades has driven the country from a developing country in the 1980s towards being a new global superpower in the twenty-first century. This development process has far-reaching consequences not only for the Chinese economy but in every corner of its society. It is not just a state-directed economy turning into a successful market economic growth model, combined with the growing importance of the service and industrial sectors vis-à-vis the agricultural sector, increasing integration in the global economy, and growing inequalities among the various regions and classes in China. The transformation taking place in China today has an equally far-reaching impact on the relations between different government levels; on the multiple relations between China and the outside world; on the cultural diversification that is brought in via (new) media and international exchanges; on the openness, transparency and accountability of the political processes and the leaders; and on the activities and organizational structures of civil society, to name but a few. Hence, China is not just a transitional economy; it is a modernizing society in full transition.

This transitional society is faced with a rapidly changing environmental profile that reaches beyond its borders. Following rapidly increasing industrial production, expanding domestic consumption, growing imports of natural resources and growing exports of manufactured products, exponential growth of private-owned cars, expansion of road, rail and housing infrastructure and construction, to name but a few indicators, one should not be too surprised that China's domestic environment is rapidly deteriorating. In addition, and not unlike what most industrialized nations did before, China is increasingly searching the Southeast Asian region and the world for natural resources to meet its growth needs. Wood from Southeast Asia and Latin America, minerals from Africa and Australia, oil and energy from Sudan, the Middle East and Russia, and even crops such as grain and soy from various corners of the world, are complemented by increasing sulphur dioxide, greenhouse gas and small particulates emissions crossing borders, and deterioration of regional (and local) water quality and quantity. China's ecological shadow crosses its geographical boundaries. Historically, this process of 'conquering' environmental resources and quality beyond sovereign borders by an upcoming global power is nothing new. So-called environmentally unequal exchange was key in Japan's rise in the 1980s and 1990s, and that of the USA and European countries before that time (see Goldfrank et al. 1999; Mol 2011).

The sheer size of China, the unprecedented speed of its development and the truly global impact worry environmental advocates around the world, sometimes resulting in apocalyptic scenarios of the world's future following China's accelerated growth. Others are less worried about the environmental consequences of China's ascendance as world (economic) power, but primarily fear the undemocratic, authoritarian way through which China will address national and supranational sustainability challenges. Yet others point hopefully to the significant socio-technical innovations that China is currently developing and implementing in coping with the many sustainability challenges it is facing. Especially since the 10th Five-Year Plan (2001–2005) China's growing environmental commitment is now framed as a circular economy, a resource-conserving and environment-friendly society (You 2007), an ecological civilization (He et al. 2013) or ecological modernization (see China Centre for Modernization Research 2007).

This chapter investigates different strategies that are currently being debated and partly implemented on how China will and should handle the sustainability challenges it is facing. After reviewing the current state of and trends in China's environmental performance and profile, it formulates four ideal-typical discourses (in a Weberian (1969) sense) unfolding in the various debates and practices on sustainable development in China: (1) global expansionism with environmentally unequal exchange; (2) environmental authoritarianism; (3) reflexive ecological modernization; and (4) local environmental democracy. Each of the ideal-types is inherently logical, consistent and is to some extent reflected in (discursive) practices. Together these ideal-types form the contours of the discursive playing ground on which the discussions on China's sustainability and environmental constraints take place. But, as will be explained in the last sections, there is no dominant discourse or a simple relation between discourses and interests or ideological positions.

China's environmental profile

Although some popular media and scholars might want us to believe differently, China's changing environmental profile is not an evolutionary treadmill of ongoing environmental deterioration, leading the world into an environmental apocalypse. Information distortion, the discontinuities and inconsistencies in environmental statistics, limited data availability on emissions and resource use, and the absence of longitudinal environmental data should make us cautious in drawing any lasting conclusions about China's environmental performance. Still, the available data can provide a sense of developments in China's environmental profile and environmental performance over time. And the (still incomplete) evidence that emerges shows a complex picture: the (static) environmental quality and deterioration are very worrying, but some – though certainly not all – dynamic trends and relative environmental indicators (e.g. per capita, per unit GDP) provide more hopeful signs.

Over the past two decades all air emissions show a relative decline per unit of GDP, and many of them even witness decreases in absolute total emissions (He et al. 2012). Concentrations of sulphur dioxide, nitrogen oxides and carbon monoxide, and small particulates show an absolute decline in most major Chinese cities between the mid-1990s and 2000, but sometimes an increase again in the new millennium (Rock 2002; SEPA 2007). This is particularly the case with small particulates, which continue to be one of the key worries of urban environmental authorities in the second decade of this millennium. Chlorofluorocarbon (CFC) production as well as consumption – of key relevance for ozone layer depletion – shows continuing decreasing levels from the mid-1990s onwards, due to the closure of companies and a commitment to implement the Montreal Protocol. It is reported (but also contested) that emissions of carbon dioxide have fallen between 1996 and 2000, despite continuing economic growth (Sinton and Fridley 2001; 2003, Chandler et al. 2002), but agreement exists on the absolute increase of carbon dioxide emissions since then.

Following strong reforestation programmes and stringent deforestation monitoring, forest coverage shows a fabulous increase in the new millennium. Most other environmental indicators show a delinking between environmental impacts and economic growth (hence a relative decline of environmental distortion per unit of GDP). Many absolute environmental indicators (total levels of emissions; total energy use) show less clear signs of improvement. For example, water pollution in terms of biological oxygen demand stabilized in absolute amounts in the new millennium, but decreased per unit of GDP and also per capita (NSB/SEPA 2007; SEPA 2007).

More indirect indicators that also suggest relative improvements are the increase in governmental environmental investments (He et al. 2012) and the growth in (domestic and industrial) wastewater treatment plants during the last decade. In addition, exponential growth patterns of renewable energy production (wind, solar, hydro), the ongoing establishment and growth of new environmental NGOs, the establishment and growth of environmental departments at all levels of government and within an increasing number of private companies and organizations, the experimenting with new environmental policy instruments and strategies such as eco-cities and eco-provinces, environmental insurance, payments for ecosystem services, environmental evaluation systems for cadres (Wang 2013), and the growing environmental commitments in Five-Year Plans (Kostka and Mol 2013) and by the top leaders all provide hopeful signs for sustainability.

Obviously, these positive signs should not distract us from the fact that overall China remains heavily polluted; that emissions (think only of particles smaller than 2.5 micrometres in many cities) are more than incidentally above (and with environmental quality levels below) international standards; that in 2006 only 40 per cent of the municipal wastewater was treated before discharge (although 85 per cent of industrial wastewater, according to SEPA data); and that environmental and resource efficiencies in industrial and agricultural production, construction, and consumption are overall still rather low compared to those in, for instance, EU member states. Regardless of the relative environmental improvements that can be identified, China's absolute levels of emissions, pollution, resource extraction and environmental quality often do not meet international environmental, health and safety standards and fall significantly below the levels of the advanced industrialized countries.

But also with respect to these absolute performances quite some variation exists internally in China, between different regions, provinces, cities and counties. Variations also exist between economic sectors; consumption practices; classes, income groups and lifestyle categories; and domestic versus globally integrated entities. Eco-cities, organic products, an environmentally conscious urban middle class, green credit schemes, and poor farmers in the west of the country show a much better environmental profile than their polluting and high consuming counterparts.

Sustainability discourses on China

This contrasting and sometimes contradictory evidence feeds into a number of discourses on China's sustainability progress and challenges. We will elaborate on four ideal-typical discourses on how China can, will or should handle the domestic and global sustainability challenges it causes. Each discourse articulates a logical, consistent argumentation line, provides evidence that feeds the discourse and has a discourse coalition supporting and framing the discourse.

Global expansionism/global environmental injustice

This discourse is strongly based on the international literature on environmentally unequal exchange in the traditions of World Systems Theory and political economy (see Goldfrank et al. 1999; Mol 2011), and of especially US-based environmental social science studies on environmental (in)justice (e.g. Agyeman et al. 2003). The essence of this discourse is that eastern and urban China's unprecedented economic growth over the last two decades is only possible at the (environmental) cost of less advantaged regions, both within China as well as internationally. And the initiatives and strategies for greening the main production and consumption bases in rapidly developing China are only possible with major environmental and social costs in the peripheries of China and the world. China (especially the developed parts) manages to handle its environmental crises at the costs of other regions. Environmental sustainability in China is a zero sum game, with environmental winners and losers. Unequal economic and political relations within China as well as in the world economy result in the displacement and relocation of environmental 'bads' from the centre to the peripheries. China's increasing attempts to behave sustainably at home (in the developed eastern regions) comes with major environmental disruptions elsewhere. This discourse contrasts Beck's 'risk society' thesis (Beck 1986), in claiming that there is no equal distribution of environmental risks, neither within China nor across the globe. The advancement of an environmental agenda in China creates environmental injustice and it is the less fortunate (within China and internationally) that are victimized, in environmental and socio-economic terms.

The evidence of this sustainability strategy connects China to the peripheries of the global economy and to its domestic hinterland (Ma 2010; Liu 2013). The major improvements in China's reforestation programmes are especially possible through large-scale imports of unprocessed wood from, among others, Southeast Asian economies (Coxhead 2007). A major part of the renewable energy production comes with severe costs for China's neighbouring states, where large dams in cross-border rivers influence environmental conditions and economic possibilities downstream in other countries. Blue skies in the large Chinese cities are partly enabled and advanced by the relocation of polluting companies to less 'visible' and less well-connected locations in the rural peripheries of China, as was, for instance, strongly evidenced by the 2008 Olympic Games in Beijing (Mol 2010). Mining, non-food agriculture (e.g. for biofuel production) and oil exploration increasingly take place outside China, involving high local environmental costs and cases of 'land grabbing' (Moyo 2012). High speed train connections come at environmental costs and land confiscations for the marginalized people along the trajectories of these trails, while these trains do not stop in rural areas. Counterfeit products from China, with substandard environmental performances end up on the national and global peripheries (such as Sub-Saharan Africa), in exchange for natural resources from these peripheries that flow into the main production centres of the world, among which is China (Mol 2011). The operations of the Chinese (private and state-owned) firms in these peripheries come together with low labour and environmental standards and low transparency, negatively affecting local communities (e.g. Bräutigam 2009).

By the same token, the sustainability frontier of China is to be found among the urban high and middle classes in Eastern China. In China, organic and safe food products, advanced public transport, clean drinking water, environmental information and transparency, low-carbon and energy-efficient housing are especially available for the so-called 'top of the pyramid', but hardly for its base (see Kandachar and Halme 2008).

This discourse is a critical discourse, as most of its 'adherents' analyse these mechanisms of unequal exchange, environmental injustice and relocation of environmental problems to other countries or the domestic peripheries, but none of them interpret these mechanisms as the preferred strategy to be followed for long-term sustainability. In contrast to the next two discourses, this discourse is predominantly a descriptive analytical sustainability discourse of what is happening and what will happen when China safeguards its resource demand and domestic environmental quality, and hardly a normative prescriptive one that ought to be followed for China to enhance sustainability.

Authoritarian sustainability

Southeast Asian and East Asian countries are often interpreted in terms of authoritarian regimes, especially in comparison with their European counterparts. Mark Beeson (2010) applied Heilbroner's (1974) concept of environmental authoritarianism to analyse how Southeast Asian and East Asian countries are now developing policies and strategies to cope with growing sustainability challenges. The intensification of a range of environmental problems is addressed by these countries through the fortification of authoritarian state rule, limited participation by social actors, and the decrease in individual liberty. Countries such as China – but also Singapore, Malaysia and even Burma (Doyle and Simpson 2006) – are seen as more or less successful examples of such an environmental authoritarianism (Gilley 2012).

This notion and the practice of environmental authoritarianism feed into wider debates on the relationship between democracy and the environment, where numerous authors have taken different positions and provided contrasting evidence as to whether democratic systems and regimes perform better at coping with environmental crises than authoritarian ones. Sherman and Smith (2007) argue quite strongly that democracy has its limits when coping with the current climate crisis; Winslow (2005) disputes that to argue for why democracy is much better in protecting the environment than other regimes; while Buitenzorgy and Mol (2011) claim a kind of environmental Kuznets curve relationship between levels of democracy and environmental protection (see also Ward 2008; Wurster 2013).

The aggravating environmental crises in terms of increasing total emissions (especially greenhouse gases), species extinction, consumption and depletion of natural resources, and deteriorating environmental quality demand extraordinary measures and 'humanity will have to trade its liberty to live as it wishes in favour of a system where survival is paramount' (Sherman and Smith 2007: 4). Forms of 'good' authoritarianism are then justified where unsustainable ways of production and consumption are forbidden without too much participation by wide constituencies or the public. China is often taken as the key example of such forms of environmental authoritarianism. It is believed that China is already practising such a form of sustainability management successfully in its current methods of dealing with, for instance, climate change (Gilley 2012), and by the same token, it is well positioned to further develop this mode of sustainability management, given its political system, cultural roots and organization of the economy.

Evidence of the reality of this sustainable authoritarianism discourse on China is drawn from the successful way in which China could increase its renewable energy production in such a short time, to become a global leader in windmill and solar PV panel production (Santalco 2012). The so-called 'environmental storms', where in a short time Chinese state authorities closed down large numbers of heavy polluting companies, are used as another form of environmental authoritarianism, as are measures to rapidly introduce European car emission norms, measures to sideline every working day one-fifth of Beijing's car fleet, and the large-scale reforestation programmes to curb erosion and desertification (Zhang et al. 2008). These are all examples of stringent and drastic measures, taken and implemented in a short time by the state authorities, with a significant intervention in economic processes and citizens' lifestyles, and with limited or no public participation.

Within this environmental authoritarian discourse and related practices in China there are also nuances to be found. So-called consultative and deliberative environmental authoritarianism points to various developments in China where citizens are given wider influence to co-determine environmental developments, yet still within an overall authoritarian system. Public opinion surveys, the Chinese People's Political Consultative Conferences, intra-party consultation to appoint local party leaders (He and Thøgersen 2010) and a proposal for formal environmental litigation rights to (one) NGO (Zhang et al. 2013) are some mechanisms whereby local citizens and party members are consulted or can deliberate on various (pre-determined) choices. These mechanisms may ease some of the problems with environmental authoritarian rule, such as the short time horizons of eco-elites (Eaton and Kostka 2014) and the shortage of legitimacy. Hence, some rather use terms like 'fragmented authoritarianism' (Mertha 2009) or consultative authoritarianism (He and Thøgersen 2010), to indicate that various state and non-state actors do interact on environmental strategies and measures, be it within the confines of an determining authoritarian party-state.

Although this discourse can easily be identified, the discourse 'coalition' that identifies and articulates sustainable authoritarianism is far from unified and falls apart in distinct factions. One group of the actors pursuing this discourse perceives sustainable authoritarianism as the only viable route (for China) to cope with growing environmental crises. Only draconian measures taken by a 'non-corrupt and green state elite' will be able to turn China green; and this requires authoritarian rule without too much participation, transparency, and deliberations on legitimacy among wider constituencies, whether these are NGOs, citizens or other stakeholders. Others recognize environmental authoritarianism as China's current road to sustainability, but criticize such a model for the trade-off on democracy, participation, legitimacy, transparency, and minority interests. One cannot and should not exchange one value (democracy and participation) against another (environmental sustainability). Some even go one step further and question the long-term effectiveness and environmental performance of China's sustainability authoritarianism, exactly because in the end it lacks legitimacy, participation and support for the necessary draconian environmental measures, resulting in the destabilization of the country and the environmental ineffectiveness of measures. In that sense, Singapore, a small, relatively homogeneous and wealthy city-state with an often quoted successful environmental authoritarianism model, is different from China.

(Reflexive) ecological modernization

The third discourse on a Chinese transition to sustainability can be called reflexive ecological modernization. Ecological modernization frames emerged in the 1980s and 1990s in North-west Europe, to understand and interpret the emergence of new ideas and strategies in coping with environmental crises. Reactive state approaches using simple and standardized add-on technological approaches were replaced with a modernization of governance, in which new state approaches were complemented and combined with proactive market and civil society responses, aimed at redesigning socio-technical systems based on sustainability criteria (Spaargaren and Mol 1992; Jänicke 1993). In the 2000s, these ideas and strategies relocated to China where they form elements of a Chinese discourse on ecological modernization, first, in a more state-technocratic mode (Mol 2006; China Centre for Modernization Research, 2007; Zhang et al. 2007), but gradually also including more reflexive ecological modernization elements.

Ever since the establishment of the People's Republic of China in 1949 modernization in China has been related to 'catching up' with developed countries. In 1964, to catch up with the West, the Third National People's Congress set the objective of modernizing agriculture, industry, national defence, and science and technology, the so-called 'si ge xiandaihua' (Four Modernizations policy). In the late 1970s, Premier Deng Xiaoping combined achieving (by the middle of the twenty-first century) the Four Modernizations with 'open-door' market-oriented economic reforms. With these reforms, modernization took centre-stage in the political discourse in China, both as a slogan and as a task to be achieved. With the China Centre for Modernization Research (2007) report on ecological modernization, environmental sustainability was brought into this modernization perspective. The 2007 report identified the start of China's ecological modernization at the turn of the millennium, but draws a quite down-to-earth picture of China's environmental profile at that time. Based on 30 indicators, China ranked among the worst of all countries regarding ecological quality, ecological economy, and ecological society. China's ecological modernization strategy for coping with these sustainability challenges relies strongly on new technologies and the market. Advanced technological developments in industry, transport, ICT, agriculture and services, together with private companies and market-based policies are the core strategies for China's ecological modernization (e.g. Park et al. 2010; Zhu et al. 2011). Key examples of ecological modernization strategies are the circular economy (Mathews and Tan 2011), cleaner production, green credit schemes, low-carbon technologies, corporate social responsibility (CSR) and the like. As Zhang and colleagues (2007) noted, European elements of ecological modernization such as political modernization, sub-politics, deliberative politics, and the reinvention of environmental governance are mentioned less often, and neither are participation, civil society and NGO engagements, transparency and disclosure. In that sense, this Chinese ecological modernization discourse reflects what others have labelled a weak or technocratic form of ecological modernization (Christoff 1996).

Increasingly, this economic-technological ecological modernization discourse is being adapted by including more reflexive elements of ecological modernization. The limited successes of economic-technological trajectories in transforming production and consumption towards sustainability (caused by among others the Jevons' paradox,[1] problem displacement, unequal distributions for different social groups and locations), have resulted in stronger calls in China for more democratic forms of environmental governance, more countervailing powers from civil society, more transparency and disclosure, a greater role for NGOs and civil society. Within China, calls for and experimentation with participation, information disclosure, NGO development, partnerships, and media openness are particularly strong in the fields of environment and sustainability (Kostka and Mol 2013). This often also comes with ideas for new economic actors and mechanisms in the field of sustainability governance. These innovations widen the narrow technocratic ecological modernization towards more reflexivity: a wider debate with and involvement of (organized) citizens, consumers, and other interest groups in designing new approaches in sustainability governance, in order to 'tame the economic treadmill of unbridled economic growth'.

Evidence of such a more reflexive ecological modernization discourse is found in increasing demands by the urban middle class for environmentally friendly products such as safe, green and organic food, growing numbers of environmental NGOs also at provincial and local levels (Wu 2013), increasing environmental protests and citizen environmental complaints, more disclosure and transparency of environmental misbehaviour, increasing freedom in (old and new) media to report on environmental misbehaviour, and increasing possibilities of environmental participation in state governance (e.g. in public hearings (Zhong and Mol 2008) and even in law-making (Zhang et al. 2013)). This combines with a further role of market parties in environmental reforms, such as an emerging market for environmental liability insurance (e.g. Feng et al. 2014), green credit schemes (e.g. Aizawa and Yang 2010), environmental labelling and certification schemes (also with respect to export markets), reporting and disclosure obligations for companies (Mol et al. 2011), payment for environmental services, and new environmental partnerships between state agencies and market parties.

While evidence of such innovative approaches exists, some find the descriptive analysis of what actually takes place currently less convincing than the normative undertones of what ought to or is desired to happen with respect to reflexive ecological modernization. Hence, many scholars as well as many Western and Chinese environmental NGOs and activists follow such a discourse as the preferred strategy out of China's environmental crisis, but few dare to conclude that this will be the most likely route to turn rapidly developing China sustainable.

(Local) environmental democracy

The discourse on local environmental democracy is closely related to the reflexive variants of the discourse on ecological modernization. In this final discourse, the participation of citizen-consumers is seen as of crucial importance in bringing about sustainability in China. Local participation, involvement, co-decision-making and transparency are at the heart of ideas of environmental democracy. As such, this discourse opts for a broader definition of sustainability, beyond a narrow environmental connotation, and including elements of social sustainability, thus making it quite different from the first discourse. It emphasizes democracy and participation, rather than unequal distribution of environmental side-effects. In its articulation the discourse combines two elements.

First, it builds upon Western ideas that prevailed in the 1970s in influential publications such as *Small Is Beautiful*, and *Blueprint for Survival*. These decentralized and participatory ideas and initiatives of sustainable production and consumption to some extent still continue in contemporary industrialized society with regard to, for instance, urban agriculture, Local Exchange and Trading Schemes (LETS; Williams et al. 2001), and decentralized (bio)energy communities (Wüste and Schmuck 2012). A key element is the active participation of citizens-consumers in organizing sustainable practices. In China's environmental democracy discourse, this is combined with a second element: mounting calls for and practices of information disclosure and transparency, to further enable and empower citizens and consumers to participate in making society sustainable. This transparency turn is far from restricted to China, but is rather a wider global development (e.g. Fung et al. 2007; Mol 2008; Gupta and Mason 2014), though with particular relevance to, and articulation in, contemporary China. Especially in the environmental domain, China seems to witness increasing room for the media and the public to discuss and disclose unsound practices, and constitute a countervailing informational power against the mainstream (polluting and extracting) economy.

In China, this discourse is to be found particularly beyond the mainstream state and economic scholars and hegemonic actors, and more in the province of NGOs, critical academics, some of the state environmental staff, and small-scale economic initiatives. Local experiments, best practices, 'model' developments ('*shifan*') and examples, and pioneering initiatives are collected from all over China to illustrate that sustainable and participatory alternatives to the current large-scale marketized development paths do exist. For instance, with regard to food, the Beijing-based Donkey farm is famous, but increasingly there are also in many other major cities small farmers markets, food box schemes, pick-your-own-vegetables farms, alternative (non-mainstream) farmer cooperatives and the like which provide organic or green food directly to middle-class consumers (Song et al. 2013; Mol 2014). Also in other sectors (nature conservation, energy, ecotourism), local participatory developments are prevailing, sometimes closely connected to non-governmental organizations. The common denominator of all these initiatives is the desire to have more citizen-consumer participation in determining how production and consumption are organized, in order to reduce all kinds of 'side-effects'. Sometimes this discourse links up with traditional Chinese ideas and culture (e.g. Hong et al. 2013).

These local sustainability initiatives in what some call an alternative economy are complemented by increasing calls and the practice of environmental transparency and disclosure regarding mainstream economic developments. Especially the emerging environmental NGO community is calling for and developing initiatives on transparency and disclosure initiatives regarding environmental pollution and environmental quality (but less so yet on the environmental quality of products). The national Institute of Public and Environment works closely together with numerous local NGOs to feed a publicly accessible database on environmental quality and environmental polluters in a large number of cities. These NGO initiatives are to some extent backed by or flow over into state policies and practices, such as local deliberative democracy experiments (Fishkin et al. 2010) and the national Open Government Information Regulation (Mol et al. 2011). Still, overall it is a marginal discourse, both in terms of adherents and discourse coalition, as well as in (local) practices that illustrate the practical viability of this discourse in contemporary China.

Assessing environmental discourses

These four discourses provide the contours of environmental and sustainability debates regarding China's future. One cannot find or identify a unique set of Chinese actors behind each discourse, which vehemently criticize or ignore the other discourses. And one cannot place one discourse simply against the others; rather, each discourse elucidates specific discussion lines that run through debates on how China does or should tackle its sustainability crisis.

The global expansionism/global environmental injustice discourse brings to the fore the trade-off between environmental and social sustainability. This discourse highlights the unequal distribution of costs that comes along with domestic sustainable economic growth. And as such, it juxtaposes the interests of the major Chinese (extractive) industries, the sectoral ministries and China's upper class against the less well-off and resource-dependent people and sectors in China's peripheries, as well as in developing countries. The powerful economy-oriented players in the Chinese economy and state see an expansion of the inflow of natural resources as a vital element in making possible domestic sustainable development for the urban well-off and of safeguarding China's economic interests in a global economy. Critical international scholars and environmental justice advocates of the domestic – often rural – environmental victims form the critics in this discourse, often accusing the state-market complex in China regarding its domestic and international expansionist practices.

The authoritarian sustainability discourse and the reflexive ecological modernization discourse circle around the role of the Chinese environmental state. Contributors to these discourses are to be found in the major environmental interest representatives in state organizations, economic sectors and civil society. The Ministry for Environmental Protection and its provincial and local representatives; the growing economic sector of environmental industries, consultants, and green utilities; and a major group of the (domestic and international) environmental NGOs operating in China take different positions on what role the Chinese state – also vis-à-vis other governance actors – has to play in making China environmentally sustainable. It is not so much a debate on 'strong state' versus 'weak state', but rather a debate on a conventional authoritarian state versus a modern form of multi-actor governance. Dividing lines of supporters are not easy to predict and may run through organizations and interest positions, because often a significant ideological component is included. Major national and international oriented environmental non-governmental organizations (ENGOs) combine ideas and agendas on strong sustainability often with public participation, modern accountable governance, transparency of state and business environmental performances, further use of economic/market instruments, and hence articulate more often an ecological modernization discourse. But that is not necessarily the case with respect to smaller provincial and local ENGOs, which can be heavily dependent on and related to state authorities in their region (so-called government-organized NGOs, GONGOs). Local environmental state authorities, but also factions within the Ministry of Environmental Protection and within the Communist Party and its diverse organs can also articulate a strong authoritarian state in safeguarding environmental protection. These complexities regarding the state are also identifiable among international China watchers and commentators. While initially major international organizations (such as the World Bank, the EU, FAO) and international NGOs adhered to a (reflexive) ecological modernization discourse as China's way out of the environmental crisis, more recently nuanced authoritarian standpoints can also be identified, especially regarding climate change problems.

The final discourse further articulates the role of non-state actors, and especially civil society, in developing China's move towards sustainability. The modern institutions of state and market are distrusted as organizers of sustainability, as participants of this discourse coalition rely especially on local bottom-up initiatives and the empowerment of civil society locally. But, in contrast to the first discourse, marginalized groups are not emphasized nor carry this discourse, as it is much more grounded in the urban intellectual elite. It is typically a discourse without major national power brokers, without representatives of the national state and economic elites. Hence, (discursive) struggles around, for instance, the national Five-Year Plans or major new environmental and other policies typically involve especially the first three discourses, and less strongly the last one.

Epilogue

The increasing openness and room for deliberation, debate and public and media reporting in China, especially on the environment, accompany a growing debate on how China should cope with its mounting sustainability challenges in the coming years and decades. And this debate flourishes both within and outside China. In reviewing this debate, four discourses could be identified and have been introduced above. These four discourses are of course ideal-typical discourses, which together form the outer lines or contours of the discursive playing field on environment and development in China. In the specific discursive and material practices in contemporary China, one will seldom find these discourses and related practices in their ideal-typical form, in isolation. China is also too diverse and complex for one discourse to be applied and adhered to universally, even by one actor. Hence, some actors/organizations will celebrate the ecological modernization of renewable solar and wind energy in China, while by the same token condemning the environmental injustice that accompanies the production of these technologies for the domestic and world market in terms of labour standards and natural resource (rare earth) use. Others will celebrate '*shifan*', the local model best practices of sustainable villages, households, projects or organizations, while by the same token arguing to diffuse these model practices widely through centralized directives from the national government. This all makes the discursive field complex. Discourses are not easily related to or explained by merely (economic) interests, or class or ideological positions, though these positions definitely play their role for Chinese actors in advancing some discourses and not others.

While it is highly unlikely that in the near future any of these four discourses will obtain universal prevalence or dominance in turning China sustainable, it does not mean that these discourses – and the discursive struggles between them – are merely an academic exercise. In contemporary and rapidly transforming China, discourses on how to solve environmental crises do spill over into material and policy practices; and they do that with sometimes high velocity. The materialization of ecological modernization ideas of the circular economy in industry, of environmental transparency in (local) air quality policies and practices (IPE 2012) and of environmental authoritarianism in restricting EIA approval (Zhu et al. 2015) illustrate the practical relevance of discourses and discursive struggles in the sustainability governance of contemporary China. The difference between China and other industrialized countries is perhaps less and less related to the nature of the discourses, and more to the fact that none of these discourses has yet gained dominance in environmental reform. We can witness the materializations of all environmental discourses as environmental policies and practices, and lively debates on their strengths and weaknesses. Also in that sense, China is the environmental battlefield of the early twenty-first century.

Note

1 Jevons' paradox refers to the proposition that efficiency increases in resource use through technological progress tend to increase (rather than decrease) the rate of consumption of that resource (Alcott 2005).

References

Agyeman, J., Bullard, R. D. and Evans, B. (2003) *Just Sustainabilities: Development in an Unequal World*. London: Earthscan.

Aizawa, M. and Yang, C. (2010) Green credit, green stimulus, green revolution? China's mobilization of banks for environmental cleanup. *The Journal of Environment & Development*, 19(2): 119–144.

Alcott, B. (2005) Jevons' paradox. *Ecological Economics*, 54(1): 9–21.

Beck, U. (1986) *Risikogesellschaft. Auf dem Weg in eine andere Moderne*. Frankfurt: Suhrkamp.

Beeson, M. (2010) The coming of environmental authoritarianism. *Environmental Politics*, 19(2): 276–294.

Bräutigam, D. (2009) *The Dragon's Gift: The Real Story of China in Africa*. Oxford: Oxford University Press.

Buitenzorgy, M. and Mol, A. P. J. (2011) Does democracy lead to a better environment? Deforestation and the democratic transition peak. *Environmental & Resource Economics*, 48(1): 59–70.

Chandler, W., Schaeffer, R., Dadi, Z., Shukla, P.R., Tudela, F., Davidson, O. and Alpan-Atamer, S. (2002) *Climate Change Mitigation in Developing Countries: Brazil, China, India, Mexico, South Africa, and Turkey*. Arlington, VA: Pew Center on Global Climate Change.

China Centre for Modernization Research (2007) *China Modernization Report 2007: Study of Ecological Modernization*. Beijing: Beijing University Press (in Chinese).

Christoff, P. (1996) Ecological modernisation, ecological modernities. *Environmental Politics*, 5(3): 476–500.

Coxhead, I. (2007) A new resource curse? Impacts of China's boom on comparative advantage and resource dependence in Southeast Asia. *World Development*, 35(7): 1099–1119.

Doyle, T. and Simpson, A. (2006) Traversing more than speed bumps: green politics under authoritarian regimes in Burma and Iran. *Environmental Politics*, 15(5): 750–767.

Eaton, S. and Kostka, G. (2014) Authoritarian environmentalism undermined? Local leaders' time horizons and environmental policy implementation. *The China Quarterly*, 218: 359–380.

Feng Y., Mol, A. P. J., Lu, Y., van Koppen, C. S. A. and He, G. Z. (2014) The development of environmental pollution liability insurance in China: in need of strong government backing. *Ambio*, 43(5): 687–702.

Fishkin, J. S., He, B., Luskin, R. C. and Siu, A. (2010) Deliberative democracy in an unlikely place: deliberative polling in China. *B. Journal of Political Science*, 40: 435–448.

Fung, A., Graham, M. and Weil, D. (2007) *Full Disclosure: The Perils and Promise of Transparency*. New York: Cambridge University Press.

Gilley, B. (2012) Authoritarian environmentalism and China's response to climate change. *Environmental Politics*, 21(2): 287–307.

Goldfrank, W.L., Goodman, D. and Szasz, A. (eds) (1999) *Ecology and the World-System*. Westport, CT: Greenwood Press.

Gupta, A. and Mason, M. (eds) (2014) *Transparency in Global Environmental Governance: A Critical Perspective*. Cambridge, MA: MIT Press.

He, B. and Thøgersen, S. (2010) Giving the people a voice? Experiments with consultative authoritarian institutions in China. *Journal of Contemporary China*, 19(66): 675–692.

He, G. Z., Lu, Y., Mol, A. P. J. and Beckers, T. (2012) Changes and challenges of China's environmental management. *Environmental Development*, 3: 25–38.

He, G. Z., Zhang, L., Mol, A. P. J., Lu, Y. and Liu, J. (2013) Revising China's environmental protection law. *Science*, 341: 133.

Heilbroner, R. L. (1974) *An Inquiry into the Human Prospect*. New York: Norton & Norton.

Hong, G., Zhiyung, O., Chen, S. and van Koppen, C. S. A. (2013) Role of culturally protected forests in biodiversity conservation in Southeast China. *Biodiversity and Conservation*, 22(2): 531–544.

IPE (Institute of Public and Environmental Affairs) (2012) *Small Particles, Big Breakthrough: 2012 Urban Air Quality Information Transparency Index*. Beijing: IPE.

Jänicke, M. (1993) Über ökologische und politische Modernisierungen. *Zeitschrift für Umweltpolitik und Umweltrecht*, 16(2): 159–175.

Kandachar, P. and Halme, M. (eds) (2008) *Sustainability Challenges and Solutions at the Base of the Pyramid: Business, Technology and the Poor*. Sheffield: Greenleaf.

Kostka, G. and Mol, A. P. J. (2013) Implementation and participation in China's local environmental politics: challenges and innovations. *Journal of Environmental Policy and Planning*, 15(1): 3–16.

Liu, L. (2013) Geographic approaches to resolving environmental problems in search of the path to sustainability: the case of polluting plant relocation in China. *Applied Geography*, 45: 138–146.

Ma, C. (2010) Who bears the environmental burden in China?: an analysis of the distribution of industrial pollution sources. *Ecological Economics*, 69(9): 1869–1876.

Mathews, J. A. and Tan, H. (2011) Progress Toward a circular economy in China: the drivers (and inhibitors) of eco-industrial initiative. *Journal of Industrial Ecology*, 15(3): 435–457.

Mertha, A. (2009) 'Fragmented authoritarianism 2.0': political pluralization in the Chinese policy process. *The China Quarterly*, 200: 995–1012.

Mol, A. P. J. (2006) Environment and modernity in transitional China: frontiers of ecological modernisation. *Development and Change*, 37(1): 29–56.

Mol, A. P. J. (2008) *Environmental Reform in the Information Age: The Contours of Informational Governance*. Cambridge: Cambridge University Press.

Mol, A. P. J. (2010) Sustainability as global attractor: the greening of the 2008 Beijing Olympics. *Global Networks*, 10(4): 510–528.

Mol, A. P. J. (2011) China's ascent and Africa's environment. *Global Environmental Change*, 21(3): 785–794.

Mol, A. P. J. (2014) The role of transparency in governing China's food quality: a review. *Food Control*, 43: 49–56.

Mol, A. P. J., He, G. Z. and Zhang, L. (2011) Information disclosure as environmental risk management: developments in China. *Journal of Current Chinese Affairs*, 40(3): 163–192.

Moyo, D. (2012) *Winner Take All: China's Race for Resources and What It Means for the Rest of the World*. New York: Basic Books.

NSB/SEPA (National Bureau of Statistics/State Environmental Protection Agency) (2007) *China Statistical Yearbook on Environment 2006*. Beijing: SEPA.

Park, J., Sarkis, J. and Wu, Z. (2010) Creating integrated business and environmental value within the context of China's circular economy and ecological modernization. *Journal of Cleaner Production*, 18(15): 1494–1501.

Rock, M.T. (2002) Getting into the environment game: integrating environmental and economic policy-making in China and Taiwan. *American Behavioral Scientist* 45(9): 1435-1455

Santalco, A. (2012) How and when China will exceed its renewable energy deployment targets. *Energy Policy,* 51: 652–661.

SEPA (2007) *Report on the State of the Environment in China 2006.* Beijing: State Environmental Protection Agency.

Sherman, D. and Smith, J. W. (2007) *Climate Change Challenge and the Failure of Democracy.* Westport, CT: Praeger.

Sinton, J. and Fridley, D. (2001) Hot air and cold water: the unexpected fall in China's energy use. *China Environment Series* 4: 3–20.

Sinton, J. and Fridley, D. (2003) Comments on recent energy statistics from China. *Sinosphere,* 6(2): 6–11.

Song, Y, Qi, G., Zhang, Y. and Vernooy, R. (2013) Farmer cooperatives in China: diverse pathways to sustainable rural development. *International Journal of Agricultural Sustainability,* 14 (2): 95–108.

Spaargaren, G. and Mol, A. P. J. (1992) Sociology, environment and modernity: ecological modernization as a theory of social change. *Society and Natural Resources,* 5(5): 323–345.

Wang, A. L. (2013) The search for sustainable legitimacy: environmental law and bureaucracy in China. *Harvard Environmental Law Review,* 37: 365–440.

Ward, H. (2008) Liberal democracy and sustainability. *Environmental Politics,* 17(3): 386–409.

Weber, M. ([1949] 1969) *The Methodology of the Social Sciences.* New York: The Free Press.

Williams, C. C., Aldridge, T., Lee, R., Leyshon, A. et al. (2001) Bridges into work? An evaluation of local exchange and trading schemes (LETS). *Policy Studies,* 22(2): 119–132.

Winslow, M. (2005) Is democracy good for the environment? *Journal of Environmental Planning and Management,* 48(5): 771–783.

Wu, F. (2013) Environmental activism in provincial China. *Journal of Environmental Policy and Planning* 15 (1): 89–108.

Wurster, S. (2013) Comparing ecological sustainability in autocracies and democracies. *Contemporary Politics,* 19(1): 76–93.

Wüste, A. and Schmuck, P. (2012) Bioenergy villages and regions in Germany: an interview study with initiators of communal bioenergy projects on the success factors for restructuring the energy supply of the community. *Sustainability,* 4: 244–256.

You, M. (2007) Annual review of Chinese environmental law developments: 2006. *Environmental Law Reporter,* 37: 10836–10840.

Zhang, L., He, G. Z., Mol, A. P. J. and Zhu, X. (2013) Power politics in the revision of China's Environmental Protection Law. *Environmental Politics,* 22(6): 1029–1035.

Zhang, L., Mol, A. P. J. and Sonnenfeld, D. A. (2007) The interpretation of ecological Modernization in China. *Environmental Politics,* 16(4): 659–668.

Zhang, L., Tu, Q. and Mol, A. P. J. (2008) Payment for environmental services: the sloping land conversion program in Ningxia Autonomous Region of China. *China & World Economy,* 16(2): 66–81.

Zhong, L. and Mol, A. P. J. (2008) Participatory environmental governance in China: public hearings on urban water tariff setting. *Journal of Environmental Management,* 88(4): 899–913.

Zhu, Q., Geng, Y., Sarkis, J. and Lai, K.-H. (2011) Evaluating green supply chain management among Chinese manufacturers from the ecological modernization perspective. *Transportation Research Part E: Logistics and Transportation Review,* 47(6): 808–821.

Zhu, X., Zhang, L., Ran, R. and Mol, A. P. J. (2015), Regional restrictions on EIA approval in China: the legitimacy of environmental authoritarianism. *Journal of Cleaner Production* (forthcoming).

PART VI

Sustainable development: future challenges

24

AGROECOLOGY AS POST-DEVELOPMENT DISCOURSE AND PRACTICE

Graham Woodgate

Development, sustainable development and post-development

Regardless of political orientation, the clearest historical role of the modern state has been to promote or engender 'development' and enhance the social and economic well-being of its citizens. At one extreme, states have sought to do this by taking over ownership of the means of production (land and capital), organising labour and directing economic output to pre-determined end uses. At the other, they have promoted the institution of private property regimes and facilitated the free functioning of markets, on the pretext of ensuring the most efficient distribution of scarce goods among competing needs. Development as state practice is a particular feature of the twentieth century, exemplified in the Soviet Union's 'Five-Year Plans', Roosevelt's 'New Deal' policies for 1930s USA, the post-war European Recovery Programme or the Marshall Plan and, in terms of agriculture, the so-called Green Revolution of the 1940s to the 1970s. All of these development plans and programmes involved the mechanisation and industrialisation of production and were based on access to cheap and increasingly abundant fossil energy.

By the early 1960s, however, worrying accounts of the negative environmental and human health impacts of fossil fuel-driven industrialisation began to attract public attention: Rachel Carson's (1962) book, *Silent Spring*, for example, cast light on the negative ecological effects of chemical pesticides in agriculture. Then, at the beginning of the 1970s, the USA passed peak oil production, shortly after which the oil-rich Arab nations imposed an embargo on supplies to the USA, as a way of registering their protest at US support for Israel during the Yom Kippur War. This led to a quadrupling of the price of crude and effectively brought an end to the post-war economic boom. Prompted by peak oil and the emerging energy crisis, the Club of Rome commissioned a team of scientists to undertake an assessment of the future of humanity in the context of varying levels of natural resource availability, industrialisation, agricultural productivity, population control and environmental protection. The results of their computer modelling were published in Meadows et al.'s (1972) report, *Limits to Growth*, which cast serious doubt over the future of humanity, with two of the three scenarios generated predicting human population growth outstripping the planet's carrying capacity, leading to the collapse of civilisation before the end of the twenty-first century. The report's publication coincided with the 1972 United Nations Conference on the Human Environment, which concluded that the 'protection and improvement of the human environment is a major issue which affects the well-being of peoples and economic development throughout the world' (UNCHE 1972, Article 2) and presaged the founding of the United Nations Environment Programme (UNEP) in the same year.

Stagnating economic growth, the failure of state-led development and emerging environmental crises provided the context for the emergence of the concept of 'sustainable development', the most succinct and enduring definition of which was provided by the World Commission on Environment and Development (WCED) in its 1987 report, *Our Common Future*: sustainable development is development that meets 'the needs of present without compromising the ability of future generations to meet their own needs' (1987: 8). Given the conditions that stimulated the emergence of the concept, we might expect sustainable development to focus on social equality and ecological integrity, and propose limits to growth. Yet according to the report, the limits were not absolute and 'technology and social organisation [could] both be managed and improved to make way for a new era of economic growth' (ibid.). Thus, sustainable development brought developmentalism and environmentalism together in a marriage of capitalist convenience, initiating what Sachs (1991) critiqued as 'the story of a dangerous liaison' and Hildyard (1993) characterised as 'putting the foxes in charge of the chickens'.

While sustainable development sought to rekindle economic growth to fund a more ecological form of modernisation, a much more deep-seated disquiet with development *per se* prompted the appearance of post-development discourse. Esteva and Illich (1986: 4–5) claimed:

> Development signifies sacrificing possibilities, solidarity, traditional interpretations and customs, on the altar of the experts whose assessments are always changing. Development promotes getting rich but for the majority it only signifies the modernisation of their poverty and growing dependence on the guidance and administration of others.

Esteva further suggested that, in his native Mexico, one had either to be very rich or completely insensitive not to notice that 'development stinks' and that alternatives such as 'sustainable development' simply acted as a deodorant to mask its unpleasant odour (1987: 135). Thus, rather than suggesting further or alternative development, post-development sought to encourage thinking about alternatives to development.

Nederveen Pieterse offers a critical analysis of post-development, which he describes as 'a radical reaction to the dilemmas of development' that begins from the recognition 'that attaining a middle-class lifestyle for the majority of the world's population is impossible' (2010: 110). According to Nederveen Pieterse, post-development is characterised by the problematisation of 'poverty' and critiques of development as westernisation and of Enlightenment thinking and modern science as instruments of domination. Claiming that post-development essentialises 'development', he claims that this 'misrepresent[s] the history of development, . . . [and] underrates the dialectics . . . of motives and motions in modernity and development' (ibid.: 118–119). He further asserts that while post-development promotes indigenous knowledge and cultural diversity and opts for frugality and conviviality in place of consumerism and competition, it shares these positions with other critical views of development but ultimately fails to offer any clear alternatives: 'the general trend' he suggests 'is to stop at critique' (ibid.: 119).

This chapter takes issue with this view. One of post-development's best-known scholars, Escobar points out that he never conceived of the 'post' prefix as pointing towards a future in which liberalism, development and the state would cease to exist but to 'an era where development ceased to be the central organising principle of social life and which, even more, visualised such a displacement as already happening in the present' (2010: 12). For Escobar, 'the "post" signals the notions that the economy is not essentially . . . capitalist, societies are not naturally liberal, and the state is not the only way of instituting social power'. In what follows, I seek to reject neoliberal proposals for 'sustainable agricultural development' and to demonstrate the validity of Escobar's claim by examining 'transformative agroecology' (Méndez et al. 2013) as post-development discourse and practice.

From agricultural industrialisation to agroecology

Agriculture in whatever form represents an important and long-standing source of environmental change. Whereas anthropogenic global warming is popularly conceived as a consequence of the rapid escalation of carbon emissions from fossil fuel-driven industrialisation, there are those that claim the phenomenon began many thousands of years earlier. According to Ruddiman (2003), the advent and expansion of agriculture provoked a global mean temperature rise of almost 1°C prior to industrialisation, implying that what Crutzen and Stoermer (2000) dubbed the Anthropocene began not 200–300, but 5000–8000 years ago. While Ruddiman's hypothesis has gained significant support, it remains undeniable that the industrialisation of both manufacturing and agriculture in the last 200 years has resulted in a much accelerated process of global warming and in a great variety of additional, negative environmental and social impacts.

Hildebrand and Poey (1985: ix) suggest that the first major breakthroughs in agricultural productivity occurred 'with the development of hybrid maize in the 1930s, followed by the expanding use of complete fertilisers and improved weed and pest control technology following World War II'. The Green Revolution, as it became known, extended technological packages of hybrid seeds, synthetic fertilisers and chemical pesticides across the Third World. Under optimum conditions industrial technologies returned remarkable increases in production. At the same time, however, as numerous studies have demonstrated, increased productivity came at the cost of loss of environmental integrity, social justice and long-term ecological and economic viability (Carson 1962; Eckholm 1976; Repetto 1985; Wright 2005; Vandermeer and Perfecto 2013). Industrial agriculture and what McMichael (2009) calls the corporate food regime (government ministries, institutions of global governance and finance, agri-food transnationals, and agricultural research institutions) have: concentrated land ownership, marginalised and impoverished small-scale, family-based, community-oriented food production, degraded soils, depleted wild and agricultural biodiversity, polluted soils, water and the atmosphere, and transformed food from the most basic of human rights into globally traded commodities. In his final report to the UN General Assembly, the Special Rapporteur on the Right to Food called for the world's food systems to be radically and democratically redesigned to ensure the human right to adequate food and freedom from hunger, and called for an urgent shift to agroecological methods (de Schutter 2014).

In contrast to industrial agricultural development, agroecology begins not with the development of 'magic bullet' technological packages in the laboratory but with the agricultural practices of farmers in the field, seeking to learn from and build upon the ecological principles, social structures and place-based, bio-cultural knowledge that support long-term sustainable food and fibre production and vibrant rural communities. Transformative agroecology is pursued by coalitions of farmers and activist scientists in a significant and growing movement for food sovereignty. For Altieri and Toledo, agroecology represents a technical, epistemological and social revolution, which goes well beyond the precepts of sustainable development to 'directly challenge neoliberal modernisation policies based on agribusiness and agroexports' (2011: 587). It is to the three core dimensions of agroecological post-development discourse and practice (cultural practice, transdisciplinary science and social movement) that we now turn our attention.

Agroecology as agri-cultural practice

> We had long desired to stand face to face with Chinese and Japanese farmers; to walk through their fields and to learn by seeing some of their methods, appliances and practices. We desired to learn how it is possible after ... forty centuries, for their soils to be made to produce sufficiently for the maintenance of such dense populations.
>
> *(King 1911: 2)*

This short extract from F. H. King's seminal text, *Farmers of Forty Centuries* captures two of the central premises of agroecological practice. First, sustaining agri-cultures have been developed around the world as a result of centuries of experience living in and with nature. Second, the fundamental basis of all such agricultures is a living and healthy soil. Similar observations were made in another foundational volume, Howard's *Agricultural Testament* (1940), which resulted from his experiences as Imperial Economic Botanist to the Government of India during the first quarter of the twentieth century. Although Howard had been sent to India to introduce Western agricultural practices, he quickly concluded that he had more to learn from the Indian farmers. Echoing King (1911), Howard considered a healthy soil to be the basis of healthy plants, healthy livestock, nourishing food and healthy human populations.

The first indications of agriculture date back some 9000 years to the 'Fertile Crescent', where wheat, barley, goats, sheep and cattle were domesticated, while the earliest evidence for the use of draught animals and ploughs comes from the Mediterranean basin (Toledo and Barrera-Bassols 2008). The domestication, breeding, production and processing of crops, and the distribution and consumption of agricultural products have been accompanied and conditioned by place-based cultural learning and the establishment of a broad range of social institutions. Farmers have always experimented and the agroecosystems and agri-cultures they co-produce with nature can best be conceptualised as 'works in progress'. For most of its 9000-year history, agri-culture has expanded crop plant and animal diversity. Since the beginning of the twentieth century, however, industrialisation has wrought a great transformation of agroecosystems and agri-cultural practices: diversification has been replaced by homogenisation:

> [B]iodiversity loss due to ... chemically intensive monocultures is extraordinary ... Entire habitats and [associated] wild species ... have been lost or are on extinction trajectories ... and ... the current loss of biodiversity ... also erodes fundamental ecosystem services ... such as soil fertility, pollination and natural pest control.
>
> *(Barthel et al. 2013: 1145)*

Although industrial agriculture now occupies the majority of the world's best farmland, in the more isolated regions, traditional agri-cultures and agroecosystems still exist as reservoirs of biological and cultural diversity. These distinct agri-cultural landscapes

> [have] been maintained through a mosaic of management practices that have co-evolved in relation to local environmental fluctuations, and ... are carried forward by both biophysical and social features ... including: genotypes, artefacts, written accounts, as well as embodied rituals, art, oral traditions and self-organized systems of rules.
>
> *(ibid.: 1142)*

Toledo and Barrera-Bassols (2008) refer to these traditional agri-cultures as 'biocultural memory' and concur with Barthel et al. regarding their importance in terms of biodiversity conservation and future food security (see also IAASTD 2009 and UNCTAD 2013). Of some '1.5 billion smallholders, family farmers and indigenous people' that occupy around 350 million small farms, roughly 50 per cent employ agroecological practices representing 'a testament to the remarkable resiliency of traditional agroecosystems in the face of continuous environmental and economic change – while contributing substantially to food security at local, regional and national levels' (Altieri and Toledo 2011: 591).

Traditional agri-cultural practices based on soil health and crop and non-crop biodiversity display a number of properties that are of vital importance to future food security. First, low external input polycultures tend to be more energy efficient than high input industrial monocultures, as Pimentel et al. (1973) first noted in the context of concerns over food security during the 1970s energy crisis. Martínez-Alier (2011) points out that for most of its 9000-year history, agriculture was 'the energy sector', with energy returns on energy input ratios for systems using draught animals of circa 10:1 and for manual agriculture reaching as much as 30:1 (Wilken 1987). High external input, industrial agriculture, on the other hand, often requires 10 calories of fossil fuel energy to produce just 1 calorie of food, transforming agriculture from a net energy producer to a net energy consumer. Peasant and family farm polycultural agroecosystems also outperform monocultures in terms of productivity per unit area (Van der Ploeg 2013). Mesoamerican corn, beans and squash polycultures can produce almost twice as much food per hectare as industrial maize monoculture and twice as much organic residue for animal fodder and composting, thus obviating the need to purchase animal feeds and synthetic fertilisers (Altieri and Toledo 2011).

Another important characteristic of low-input, biodiverse, polycultural systems that integrate annual and perennial crops is that they tend to be carbon sinks rather than carbon emitters and thus have the potential for climate change mitigation (IAASTD 2009; UNCTAD 2013). Industrial agriculture, on the other hand, is a significant source of atmospheric carbon. In addition to climate change mitigation, diversified agroecosystems are more resilient to the increasingly severe and frequent extreme weather events that are associated with global warming. A survey of more than a thousand farms in Central America, reported by Holt-Giménez (2001), demonstrated that following the ravages of Hurricane Mitch in 1998, farms with biodiverse agroecosystems suffered significantly lower economic costs and recovered more rapidly than those where monocropping was prevalent, reflecting the inherent risk-mitigating character of agroecological production. As diversity confers resilience, in combination with traditional, place-based farmers' profound understanding of local ecological and social resources and relationships, it also imparts adaptability. Indeed, the many millions of traditional farms that continue to exist at the margins of the corporate food regime represent vital reservoirs of adaptive capacity that will be indispensable in the struggle to maintain global food security in the context of dwindling oil reserves and accelerated global warming (cf. Altieri and Toledo 2011; Barthel et al. 2013; IAASTD 2009; Martínez-Alier 2011; UNCTAD 2013). Recognition of traditional agri-cultural practice as 'agroecology in action' suggests traditional farms and farming communities should be the starting point for agroecology as science.

Agroecology as science

Wezel et al. (2009) claim that, from the first use of the term 'agroecological' in the late 1920s, the science developed through the intersection of agronomy and ecology. In the 1970s, the term 'agroecosystem' emerged in reference to the field-level research, gradually being extended to encompass entire food systems and, by the 1990s, 'agroecology' was also being used in reference to agrarian social movements and environmentally friendly agricultural practices. For Wezel et al., this broadening of the scope of agroecology is a source of confusion and a cause for concern. I would take issue with their analysis and conclusions. Focusing their analysis on the term 'agroecology', they miss the broader historical context from which agroecological science emerged. From its earliest origins, any agriculture that failed to recognise and abide by ecological guidelines was short-lived: King's (1911) *Farmers of Forty Centuries* were clearly agroecology practitioners. Similarly, Wezel et al. take no account of the numerous agrarian counter-movements that have accompanied the development of capitalist agriculture (more of which in the next section). Thus, their narrowly focused analysis leads to flawed conclusions and recommendations. As Eric Wolf noted in his Introduction to *Europe and the People Without History*, 'the world of humankind constitutes a manifold, a totality of interconnected processes, and inquiries that disassemble this totality into bits and then fail to reassemble it falsify reality' (1982: 3). If we focus on what is signified rather than the signifier, a very different story comes into view where the science emerges from practice and in support of movements for agrarian justice and food sovereignty.

Vandermeer and Perfecto (2013) describe traditional, place-based, agricultural knowledge as narrow but profound compared to the modern science of ecology, which they characterise as broad but comparatively shallow. Thus, they suggest that the role of scientific agroecology should be to inform synergistically 'the ongoing accumulation of knowledge inherent in the practices of small-scale farmers' (ibid.: 76). They further declare that both agroecological science and practice 'are given political life in the movement for food sovereignty' (ibid.: 77). Méndez et al. (2013) distinguish two major agroecological perspectives or 'agroecologies' that have emerged from the interplay of science and practice. In contrast to the interdisciplinary but top-down and apolitical 'agroecology-as-natural science' (ibid.: 12) that aims to develop recommendations and ecotechnological packages directed at the transformation of agricultural production (cf. Wezel et al. 2009; Tomich et al. 2011, *inter alia*), the version that Méndez et al. defend is transdisciplinary, participatory, politically engaged, and oriented toward social action focused on the transformation of agrifood systems toward the goal of food sovereignty.

By defining 'transdisciplinary approaches as those that value and integrate different types of knowledge systems ... [and challenge] conventional approaches to agricultural research that privilege Western epistemologies of knowledge production' (2013: 8), the 'transformative agroecology' proposed by Méndez and colleagues chimes with the 'decolonial projects' that Escobar (2010) heralds as evidence of post-development practice. One such decolonial project is underway at the Mayan Intercultural University of Quintana Roo, Mexico, where agroecological research and education proceed within a framework of 'interculturality', which provides 'a platform for knowledge exchange and collaboration under conditions of mutual respect between cultures and knowledge systems' (Méndez et al. 2013: 11–13). Transformative agroecology operates within a participatory action research (PAR; see Fals Borda 1985) framework to generate understanding of agri-food system issues in order to inform transformative social action. The co-production of knowledge and shared understanding by activist researchers and scientist farmers does not lead to the promotion of technological solutions, but rather the 'co-motion' (Esteva 1987: 149) of systemic strategies directed at establishing and reinforcing beneficial socio-environmental relationships. Such strategies seek: to reduce dependency on external inputs of commoditised knowledge and petrochemical technologies; to increase functional diversity; and to optimise productivity across provisioning, regulating, supporting and cultural ecosystem services. They also aim to enhance the quantity of energy output from each unit of energy input, to empower farmers and rural communities and to make a positive contribution to their goal of food sovereignty.

Transformative agroecology thus clearly strikes at the heart of the 'global food security' model promoted by the corporate food regime whose supporters, despite clear evidence to the contrary (Altieri and Toledo 2011; Van der Ploeg 2013), criticise agroecology as unable to produce sufficient food to feed the world's growing population. This censure rings somewhat hollow, however, as more and more ecotechnological fixes from agroecology-as-natural science are incorporated into industrial production systems. Detractors also criticise agroecology for not scaling up. In response, Holt-Giménez and Altieri (2013) point to the massive mobilisation of state and private capital that was required to globalise the Green Revolution and the significant efforts and resources that are currently being poured into the promotion of commercial bio- and eco-technologies. They further suggest that '[a]sking "Why can't agroecology scale up?" begs the question, "What is holding agroecology back?"' (2013: 93). Besides the vastly unequal funding received by 'transformative agroecology' revisionist 'agroecology-as-natural science' (cf. Wezel et al. 2009; Tomich et al. 2011) obscures agroecology's social context and neglects its political potential. It is to the politics of agroecology that we now turn our attention.

Agroecology as social movement

We have already indicated that what is signified by 'agroecology' is prefigured in traditional agricultural practices and the same is true for agrarian social movements. In this sense, transformative agroecology can be characterised as building a post-development political programme on pre-development discourse and practice. There are many parallels between the factors that animated early agrarian social movements and those associated with transformative agroecology today. Perhaps the clearest of these is access to land. From the thirteenth century, the enclosure of the open fields and commons as private sheep pastures in England denied ordinary people access to land and restricted their ability to feed themselves, their families and their communities. One of the earliest critiques of enclosure can be found in Thomas Moore's (1516) novel *Utopia*: 'Your sheep . . . which are usually so tame and so cheaply fed, begin now . . . to be so greedy . . . that they devour human beings themselves and devastate and depopulate fields, houses, and towns' (cited in Melville 1994: vi). In the fifteenth and sixteenth centuries, the problem became more acute, leading to numerous localised revolts and the coming together of the dispossessed into direct action movements to level the ditches and fences of the enclosures and invade and cultivate the land. Thus they challenged the most fundamental element of the emerging capitalist economy – private property.

> When men take to buying and selling the land . . . they restrain other fellow creatures from seeking nourishment from Mother Earth . . . so that he that had no land was to work for those . . . that called the Land theirs; and thereby some are lifted up into the chair of tyranny and others trod under the footstool of misery, as if the Earth were made for a few and not for all.
>
> *(Winstanley 1649, cited in Berens 1906: 70)*

The commoditisation of nature, beginning with land, has been central to the development of capitalism. From the early enclosure of the English commons, the development of capitalist agriculture and food production through the commoditisation of land, water and most recently biodiversity and knowledge, has provided the basis for the dispossession of small-scale farmers from biocultural resources that had been co-produced over generations of agri-cultural practice. The collapse of state-sponsored development and the return of economic liberalism in the 1980s, created the space and stimulus for a resurgence of peasant politics and direct action social movements (Peréz Vitoria 2005; Van der Ploeg 2009; Martínez-Torres and Rosset 2010). These new agrarian movements demand access to and invade unoccupied land and denounce the twenty-first-century phenomenon of international land-grabbing: foreign capital's rapid, large-scale acquisition of rights to vast areas in the South and the associated removal of peasant farmers (Magdoff 2013). They also protest against the environmental degradation caused by industrial production, promote agroecological alternatives, condemn the biopiracy of trans-national seed companies and proclaim land, water, seed, food, technological, and energy sovereignty.

In Brazil, the landless workers movement (MST; www.mst.org.br) like the Diggers and Levellers of England, came together in protest at the concentration of land in the hands of the few. Since 1984, the MST has led more than 2,500 land occupations, settling at least 350,000 families on somewhere in the region of 10 million hectares of land. They promote agroecological methods among their members and in 2006 established the Latin American School of Agroecology on MST land in the State of Paraná. They also run an agroecological seed network to facilitate food sovereignty. In Europe, the Campaign for Seed Sovereignty (www.seed-sovereignty.org) represents the interests of more than 30 national and sub-national organisations of small farmers and growers in 19 nations of the European Union, united in their struggle against EU legislation aimed at the standardisation and concentration of the seed market in the hands of a small number of seed industry corporations. At the plenary of the 5th European Seed Meeting 'Let's Liberate Diversity!', they issued the Graz Declaration, claiming '[e]ach human being has the right to live without hunger and to eat adequately. This human right includes access to productive resources, in particular seeds' (Seed Sovereignty 2010). In addition to the right to produce, save, re-sow and distribute crop seeds, the Declaration demands: the prohibition of genetic modification technologies in agriculture; the prohibition of patents on plants and animals; and a new agrarian policy, which promotes biodiverse, agroecological production. Movements to defend traditional agri-cultures and advance food sovereignty include food consumers as well as producers and have the capacity to mobilise vast numbers of people in opposition to the institutions of the global corporate food regime. On 25 May 2013, some two million people took part in hundreds of rallies across more than 50 countries in protest against the corporate seed giant Monsanto. 'March Against Monsanto' protesters call attention to the dangers posed by genetically modified food and the food giants that produce it.

Many national and regional agrarian organisations, confederations and social movements are members of the peasant and small-farmer International, La Via Campesina (www.viacampesina.org), which presents a clear, potent and unified challenge to the corporate food regime and its neoliberal discourse of 'sustainable development' and 'food security'. Martínez-Torres and Rosset (2010) trace the historical development of La Via Campesina (LVC) from the early coalescence of numerous peasant and small farmer organisations and confederations in Latin America. Established as a global social movement in 1993, during the 1990s, the movement's leaders gained access to international policy fora, rejecting NGO representation and making a space for authentic peasant voices to be heard. In the twenty-first century, LVC has taken on a global leadership role for agrarian struggles and positioned itself in opposition to the corporate food regime and neoliberal sustainable development. In short, 'peasants and family farmers have been able to build a structured, representative, and legitimate movement, with a common identity, that links social struggles on five continents' (ibid.: 150). In 20 years, LVC has grown to encompass around 150 local and national organisations in 70 countries, representing about 200 million small-scale farmers in their struggle to 'defend community-based agroecological farming as a cornerstone in the construction of food sovereignty' (www.viacampesina.org).

LVC introduced the concept of 'food sovereignty' at the World Food Summit in 1996, since when it has developed into 'a holistic and internally coherent alternative framework' (ibid.: 160). The political and practical goals of food sovereignty are summarised in LVC's 'Support the Fight for Our Future' campaign (LVC 2012):

- to advocate food sovereignty with global institutions and national governments;
- to make farmers' voices heard through enhanced communications;
- to cool the planet by expanding sustainable peasant agriculture through agroecology;
- to preserve biodiversity and defend seed sovereignty through support for farmer to farmer seed exchanges;
- to strengthen women's and youth leadership for food sovereignty;
- to increase the struggle to recover people's natural resources: land, water and seeds.

The successful organisation and global expansion of LVC and other food sovereignty movements, while building from local activism, have taken full advantage of the digital communications revolution. A simple internet search for 'food sovereignty' returns almost one million results. This vibrant and engaging internet presence includes social movement websites and social media pages containing the latest news of actions in defence of food sovereignty, declarations of political intent, explications of agroecological principles and access to peer-reviewed journal articles written by activist intellectuals and movement representatives. At the local level, LVC works with member organisations to facilitate agroecological knowledge exchange through farmer-to-farmer processes and has established continental-scale networks of trainers that organise regular encounters, to share and develop the agroecological approach to food sovereignty. In the face of global capital's relentless pursuit of profit through land-grabbing, displacement of small-scale producers, and the patenting of seeds, knowledge, and technologies developed over generations of farming practice, the second Americas Continental Encounter in 2011 issued a declaration:

> Agroecology is Ours and is Not For Sale. Peasant agriculture is part of the solution to the current crisis of the system. In this context we reaffirm that indigenous, peasant and family farm agroecology [can] feed the world and cool the planet.
>
> *(LVC 2011)*

This declaration is an unequivocal statement proclaiming the indivisibility of transformative agroecology as agri-cultural practice, science, and social movement.

Some final comments on agroecology as post-development discourse and practice

In recent years agroecology has been recognised as an important resource for confronting the food production, climate change and biodiversity conservation challenges of the twenty-first century. The 2009 International Assessment of Agricultural Knowledge, Science and Technology for Development acknowledges that:

> Current patterns of agricultural subsidies, international trade and related policy frameworks do not stimulate transitions toward . . . sustainable food and farming systems and have given rise to perverse impacts on natural resources and agroecologies as well as on human health and nutrition.
>
> *(IAASTD 2009: 4)*

It also recognises local agri-cultures as 'an extensive realm of accumulated practical knowledge and knowledge-generating capacity [with the] traditional knowledge, identities and practices of indigenous and local communities ... embodying ways of life relevant for conservation and sustainable use of biodiversity' (ibid.: 11). UNCTAD's 2013 Trade and Environment Review 'Wake Up Before It Is Too Late: Make Agriculture Truly Sustainable Now for Food Security in a Changing Climate' offers further endorsement of the productive, adaptive and climate change-mitigating potential of biodiverse, agroecological farming methods. For the most part, however, the validity of the claims of agroecology by institutions of the corporate food regime has been tacit and reflected in moves to co-opt agroecology-as-natural science and, at the margins, to engage in ecological input substitution.

The politics of agroecology and food sovereignty represent an explicit challenge to the corporate food regime's proposals for global food security, which call for a 70 per cent increase in global food production by 2050, to be achieved by a new, biotechnological, green revolution and the further enclosure of the agricultural commons (land, water, seeds, etc.) by international capital (Holt-Giménez and Altieri 2013). While the constitution of agroecology as post-development discourse, encompassing pre-development agri-cultural practice, transformative agroecological science, and agrarian social movements in pursuit of food sovereignty has led some commentators to claim that 'these varied meanings ... cause confusion' (Wezel et al. 2009: 503), for others, the assumption that the science of agroecology can be separated from its politics and practice is deeply problematic. Méndez et al. argue that 'a persistent depiction of agroecology as unclear explicitly ignores important aspects of its evolution', while portraying the approach as confusing 'justifies the application of narrow definitions ... favoured by those that view agroecology solely as a new form of scientific endeavour' (2013: 5). This reflects Sevilla Guzmán and Woodgate's concern that when the science of agroecology is separated from agricultural practice and movements for food sovereignty, its transformative potential is lost and agroecology becomes 'just another instrumental discipline in the continuing saga of capitalism's struggle to overcome its own internal contradictions' (2013: 43).

As McMichael (2007) has argued, the late twentieth- and early twenty-first-century return of peasant movements and politics (see also Peréz Vitoria 2005, and Van der Ploeg 2009) recasts development in at least four key senses. Resonating with post-development discourse, poverty is viewed as the result of unsustainable development rather than an original condition. The new, agroecology-endorsing social movements reject biotechnology and the new green revolution as the basis for achieving global food security, and offer a post-liberal proposal that peasant agri-cultures and agroecosystems are global goods that must be defended from enclosure and incorporation within global commodity markets. They challenge individualisation, reclaim the politics of solidarity and adhere to a pluriversal perspective, which makes room for other rationalities beyond the economistic perspective of neoliberalism. These politics conform to Escobar's post-liberal, post-capitalist, post-Enlightenment, and decolonial aspects of post-development discourse and practice.

In terms of meeting the nutritional requirements of a growing population, there is no great merit in sustainable development if it will not let go the apron strings of neoliberalism or recognise the unsustainability of transforming fossil fuels into food. Agroecology goes beyond technological packages to sustainable food and energy systems and beyond 'sustainable development' to the post-development politics of 'food sovereignty'. It is a post-liberal, post-capitalist, post-Enlightenment programme for establishing an enduring basis for the ongoing co-evolution of society and nature. Accepting nature as a social actor and societies as ecological agents and rejecting the exceptionalist assumptions upon which the entire Enlightenment project has been built requires us to acknowledge humanity's ecological embeddedness in nature and biological embodiment in a resource-hungry population of more than 7 billion people. Any pretence at achieving a liveable future must get beyond the whole idea of development based on easy access to cheap and abundant fossil fuels. With hindsight, nobody would have founded the 'consumer society' on subsidies from the geological past and loans from the ecological future. The corporate food regime has taken us so far past carrying capacity that virtually everything we do and eat today steals from future generations. This huge burden of ecological debt will eventually bankrupt industrial capitalism and demand new, post-liberal politics and economics. We have failed to recognise the Enlightenment we have been seeking, dazzled instead by the bright lights of technology. The political task ahead is not to facilitate neoliberal sustainable development but to manage the inevitable senescence, of the eco-illogical *ancien régime*.

References

Altieri, M. A. and Toledo, V. M. (2011) The agroecological revolution in Latin America: rescuing nature, ensuring food sovereignty and empowering peasants. *Journal of Peasant Studies*, 38(3): 587–612.

Barthel, S., Crumley, C. and Svedin,U. (2013) Bio-cultural refugia: safeguarding diversity of practices for food security and biodiversity. *Global Environmental Change*, 23(5): 1142–1152.

Berens, L. H. (1906) *The Digger Movement in the Days of the Commonwealth*. London: The Merlin Press.

Carson, R. (1962) *Silent Spring*. Boston, MA: Houghton Mifflin.

Crutzen, P. I. and Stoermer, E. F. (2000) The 'Anthropocene'. *IGBP Newsletter* 41: 12.

de Schutter, O. (2014) *Final Report of the Special Rapporteur on the Right to Food: The Transformative Potential of the Right to Food*. New York: United Nations. Available at: www.srfood.org/images/stories/pdf/officialreports/20140310_finalreport_en.pdf (accessed 21 March 2014).

Eckholm, E. P. (1976) *Losing Ground: Environmental Stress and World Food Prospects*. New York: Norton.

Escobar, A. (2010) Latin America at a crossroads: alternative modernizations, post-liberalism, or post-development? *Cultural Studies*, 24(1): 1–65.

Esteva, G. (1987) Regenerating people's space. In S. H. Mendlovitz and R. B. J. Walker (eds) *Towards a Just World Peace*. London: Butterworths, pp. 271–298.

Esteva, G. and Illich, I. (1986) El desarrollo: metáforo, mito, amenaza. In *Tecno-Política*. Mexico DF: Sorremans.

Fals Borda, O. (1985) *Conocimiento y Poder Popular*. Bogotá: Editorial Siglo XXI.

Hildebrand, P. E. and Poey, F. (1985) *On-Farm Agronomic Trials in Farming Systems Research and Extension*. Boulder, CO: Lynne Rienner

Hildyard, N. (1993) Foxes in charge of the chickens. In W. Sachs (ed.) *Global Ecology: A New Arena of Political Conflict*. London: Zed Books, pp. 22–35.

Holt-Giménez, E. (2001) Measuring farms' agroecological resistance to Hurricane Mitch. *LEISA*, 17: 18–20.

Holt-Giménez, E. and Altieri, M. A. (2013) Agroecology, food sovereignty, and the new green revolution. *Agroecology and Sustainable Food Systems*, 37(1): 90–102.

Howard, A. (1940) *An Agricultural Testament*. London: Oxford University Press.

IAASTD (International Assessment of Agricultural Knowledge, Science and Technology for Development) (2009) *Agriculture at a Crossroads: A Synthesis of the Global and Sub-Global IAASTD Reports*. Washington, DC: Island Press.

King, F. H. (1911) *Farmers of Forty Centuries or Permanent Agriculture in China, Korea and Japan*. Madison, WI: Democrat Publishing Co. Available at: https://archive.org/stream/farmersoffortyce00kinguoft#page/n7/mode/2up (accessed 27 July 2013).

LVC (La Via Campesina) (2011) American Continental Encounter of Agroecology Trainers. Available at: http://viacampesina.org/en/index.php/mainissues-mainmenu-27/sustainable-peasants-agriculturemainmenu-42/1083-finaldeclaration-of-the-2nd-continental-encounter-of-agroecology-trainers-in-laviacampesina (accessed 17 March 2013).

LVC (La Via Campesina) (2012) Support the fight for our future: time for food sovereignty is NOW! Available at: http://viacampesina.org/en/index.php/2-uncategorised/1351-support-the-fight-for-our-future-time-for-food-sovereignty-is-now (accessed 15 August 2013).

McMichael, P. (2007) Reframing development: global peasant movements and the new agrarian question. *Revista NERA*, 10(10): 57–71. Available at: www2.fct.unesp.br/nera/revistas/10/mcMichael.pdf (accessed 14 July 2013).

McMichael, P. (2009) A food regime genealogy. *Journal of Peasant Studies*. 36: 139–169.

Magdoff, F. (2013) Twenty-first-century land grabs: accumulation by agricultural dispossession. *Monthly Review*, 65(6). Available at; http://monthlyreview.org/2013/11/01/twenty-first-century-land-grabs (accessed 5 November 2013).

Martínez-Alier, J. (2011) The EROI of agriculture and its use by the Via Campesina. *The Journal of Peasant Studies*, 38(1): 145–160.

Martínez-Torres, M. E. and Rosset, P. M. (2010) La Vía Campesina: the birth and evolution of a transnational social movement. *Journal of Peasant Studies*, 37(1): 149–175.

Meadows, D. H., Meadows, D. L., Randers, J. and Behrens III, W. W. (1972) *Limits to Growth*. New York: New American Library.

Melville, E. G. K. (1994) *A Plague of Sheep: The Environmental Consequences of the Conquest of Mexico*. Cambridge: Cambridge University Press.

Méndez, V. E., Bacon, C. M. and Cohen, R. (2013) Agroecology as a transdisciplinary, participatory, and action-oriented approach. *Agroecology and Sustainable Food Systems*, 37(1): 3–18.

Nederveen Pieterse, J. (2010) *Development Theory: Deconstructions/Reconstructions*. London: Sage.

Peréz Vitoria, S. (2005) *Les paysans sont de retour*. Paris: Actes Sud.

Pimentel, D., Hurd, L. E., Bellotti, A. C., Forster, M. J., Oka, I. N., Sholes, O. D. and Whitman, R. J. (1973) Food production and the energy crisis. *Science*, 182: 443–449.

Repetto, R. (1985) *Paying the Price: Pesticide Subsidies in Developing Countries*. Washington, DC: World Resources Institute.

Ruddiman, W. F. (2003) The anthropogenic greenhouse era began thousands of years ago. *Climatic Change*, 61: 261–293.

Sachs, W. (1991) Environment and development: the story of a dangerous liaison. *The Ecologist*, 21(6): 252–257.

Seed Sovereignty (2010) *The Graz Declaration*. Available at: www.seed-sovereignty.org/PDF/GRAZ_EN_ Graz_declaration.pdf (accessed 15 October 2013).

Sevilla Guzmán, E. and Woodgate, G. (2013) Agroecology: foundations in agrarian social thought and sociological theory. *Agroecology and Sustainable Food Systems*, 37(1): 32–44.

Toledo, V. M. and Barrera-Bassols, N. (2008) *La Memorial Biocultural*. Barcelona: Icaria.

Tomich, T. P., Brodt, S., Ferris, H., Galt, R., Horwath, W. R., Kebreab, E., Leveau, J. H. J., Liptzin, D., Lubell, M., Merel, P., Michelmore, R., Rosenstock, T., Scow, K., Six, J., Williams, N. and Yang, L. (2011) Agroecology: a review from a global-change perspective. *Annual Review of Environmental Resources*, 36: 193–222.

UNCHE (United Nations Conference on the Human Environment) (1972) *Declaration of the United Nations Conference on the Human Environment*. Stockholm. Available at: www.unep.org/Documents. Multilingual/Default.asp?documentid=97&articleid=1503 (accessed 5 November 2013).

UNCTAD (United Nations Conference on Trade and Development) (2013) *Wake Up Before It Is Too Late: Make Agriculture Truly Sustainable Now for Food Security in a Changing Climate*. Geneva, Switzerland: UN Press.

Vandermeer, J. and Perfecto, I. (2013) Complex traditions: intersecting theoretical frameworks in agroecological research. *Agroecology and Sustainable Food Systems*, 37(1): 76–89.

Van der Ploeg, J. D. (2009) *The New Peasantries: Struggles for Autonomy and Sustainability in an Era of Empire and Globalization*. London: Earthscan.

Van der Ploeg, J. D. (2013) Peasant-driven agricultural growth and food sovereignty. *Food Sovereignty: A Critical Dialogue*. International Conference at Yale University, 14–15 September. Available at: www.yale.edu/agrarianstudies/foodsovereignty/pprs/8_van_der_Ploeg_2013.pdf (accessed 22 March 2014).

WCED (World Commission on Environment and Development) (1987) *Our Common Future*. New York: Oxford University Press.

Wezel, A., Bellon, S., Doré, T., Francis, C., Vallod, D. and David, C. (2009) Agroecology as a science, a movement and a practice: a review. *Agronomy for Sustainable Development*, 29: 503–515.

Wilken, G. C. (1987) *Good Farmers: Traditional Agricultural Resource Management in Mexico and Guatemala*. Berkeley, CA: University of California Press.

Wolf, E. (1982) *Europe and the People without History*. Berkeley, CA: University of California Press.

Wright, A. (2005) *The Death of Ramón González: The Modern Agricultural Dilemma*. Rev. edn. Austin, TX: University of Texas Press.

25

THE SOCIAL DIMENSION OF SUSTAINABLE DEVELOPMENT IN THE TOP EMITTING COUNTRIES' CLIMATE CHANGE POLICY

Marco Grasso

Introduction

Climate change is a major global concern for the international community that, given its urgency and dangerousness, needs to be addressed promptly. At the same time, decisions about climate change at every level are becoming more complex, and the current political impasse obliges a rethinking of approaches in order to undertake more effective action.

The main argument of this chapter is that the most useful overall strategy against climate change should be consistent with, and shaped around, the objectives of sustainable development. This chapter will not, however, analyse any particular notions of sustainable development *per se*, since other chapters in this Handbook abundantly cover this point. Rather, the present chapter assumes, consistently with the predominant view in the literature, that sustainable development should guide climate policy along three dimensions: environmental, economic and social. It is further argued that, in relation to climate change, these dimensions involve four issues: effectiveness, efficiency, equity and feasibility. The more that climate policy is consistent with such normative desiderata, the more it is expected to contribute to the advancement of sustainable development.

The aim of the chapter is to conduct a thorough investigation of the social dimension of sustainable development in relation to the major carbon-emitting countries, i.e. the equity and feasibility of their climate policy. In particular, after a section devoted to pointing out why climate policy should be guided by sustainable development, the chapter will investigate the social dimension of sustainability through specific assessment of the equity and political feasibility of the major emitters' climate policy. By way of conclusion, the chapter briefly describes some shared features of, and issues emerging from, the top emitters' climate policy as evidenced by the investigation of the social dimension of sustainability.

The urgency of climate change and the guiding role of sustainable development in climate policy

The 195 parties that signed the United Nations Framework Convention on Climate Change (UNFCCC) have committed themselves to reducing anthropogenic greenhouse gas (GHG) emissions and to stabilizing their concentrations in the atmosphere "at a level that would prevent dangerous anthropogenic interference with the climate system", as demanded by Article 2 of the UNFCCC. Yet, policy-makers are still "trying to figure out how specifically to do that" (Schmidt and Archer 2009: 1117). In fact, many countries call for warming to be limited to 2°C above pre-industrial levels, others to 1.5°C; some demand that global average per capita emissions be below 2 tonnes (t) carbon dioxide (CO_2). From a different perspective, a number of countries suggest stabilizing CO_2 concentrations in the atmosphere at 450, or 350, parts per million (ppm); other parties cast doubts on the utility of defining limits to temperature increases or to GHG concentrations and alternatively propose global pathways of GHG emissions reductions (UNFCCC 2009).

Nor has science thus far been able to provide a decisive definition of what constitutes "dangerous anthropogenic interference", because "such a definition is ultimately a normative decision" (Zickefeld et al. 2009: 16129). Nonetheless, some recent studies have set out new evidence with which to gain such an understanding. For instance, Hansen et al. (2008) argue that, to prevent the Earth from irreversible catastrophic effects, humanity should reduce CO_2 concentration in the atmosphere from its current 401.88[1] ppm to 350 ppm (it was about 280 ppm in the pre-industrial period (IPCC 2007)). A group of scientists (Allen et al. 2009) instead suggest focusing on a fascinating round number: one trillion tonnes, the upper limit to our cumulative CO_2 emissions over the period 1750–2100, in order for there to be a reasonable likelihood of limiting the temperature increase to 2°C above the pre-industrial level in 2100. In a companion study published in the same issue of *Nature*, Meinshausen et al. (2009) maintain that cumulative CO_2 emissions in 2050 are robust indicators of the probability that temperatures will be more than 2°C above the pre-industrial level by 2100. As pointed out by Meinshausen et al. (2009) and by Schmidt and Archer (2009), there is nothing special in such a target to suggest that lower warming levels would be safe for humankind.[2] The 2°C objective is an indication of the scale of the problem, which, given the wide and growing support gained in the political debate, as well as the increasing attention of climate science (Schellnhuber et al. 2006),[3] seems to have obtained the normativeness demanded by Zickefeld et al. (2009) in shaping understanding of what constitutes dangerous climate change, and, ultimately, "*significant* international legitimacy" (Moellendorf 2009: 249, emphasis in the original).

On different grounds, Caney (2009) argues that the definition of "dangerous anthropogenic interference" is a normative issue. However, he does not identify any quantitative thresholds of dangerousness, claiming instead that climate change becomes dangerous when it threatens human rights. On the basis of this approach, the chapter assumes normatively that the dangerousness of climate change mainly consists in climate policy not aimed at, and shaped by, sustainable development. Consistently with the seminal study by Adger et al. (2003), the chapter acknowledges that decisions relative to environmental issues should involve, as anticipated, questions of environmental effectiveness, economic efficiency, political feasibility and, broadly understood, equity.[4] These desiderata are constitutive of the environmental, economic and social dimensions of sustainable development. In regard to climate change, environmental effectiveness basically involves consistency with the long-term objective of stabilizing GHGs in the atmosphere at a non-dangerous level. Economic efficiency demands optimal climate policy, i.e. climate policy that achieves its goals at the least possible cost for society. Such policy requires minimization of the costs borne by all the subjects involved (regulators, industry, the public sector, individuals), through, in theory, equalization of their marginal abatement costs.

Turning to the social dimension of sustainable development, equity plays a major role as a unifying principle that facilitates collective action against climate change: the more that such action is informed by ethical considerations, the more it is likely to succeed (Gardiner 2004).

Equity, in fact, can persuade parties with conflicting interests to cooperate more closely on collective action. However, given the urgency of the climate crisis, also prompt action to combat the climate crisis is a fundamental component of the social dimension of sustainability in relation to climate change decision-making. The issue ultimately depends on the political feasibility of climate policy. Feasibility, in fact, determines the choice of strategies, plans, projects, instruments, and initiatives (Felder and Schleiniger 2002; Bennear and Stavins 2007), and it depends on the relationships among ideas, power and resources (Tanner and Allouche 2011). All in all, it seems that the inclusion of feasibility considerations requires understanding of the political economy of climate change, i.e. of the political, institutional, economic, cultural and scientific factors that affect climate policy.

The following sections will specifically focus on the social dimension of sustainability through analysis of the equity and feasibility of the major emitters' climate policy: two issues that are still relatively underexplored. By contrast, there is already an extensive literature scrutinizing the environmental effectiveness and economic efficiency of climate policy. Hence they will not be investigated here.

Two specifications are in order. First, the chapter will take the nation-state as its unit of analysis in investigating and assessing the selected dimensions of sustainable development. Despite the pervasiveness of climate change action at all governance levels, states have a predominant role in it. In fact, besides their primacy in international climate policy and politics, states have a moral role that is not limited to the promotion of virtuous behaviours – as, for instance, libertarian paternalism requires (see, for instance, Thaler and Sunstein 2003); rather, their role is to impose and enforce coercive actions. To be stressed is that this argument is not intended to downplay the role and importance of individuals' efforts to make their lifestyles less carbon-intensive; nor does it uncritically emphasize the necessity of a technocentric carbon-efficient society. It is in fact argued that individuals' behaviours alone, virtuous and necessary as they may be, are not enough to avoid and/or prevent climate change. The ambitious but inevitable objective set by the urgency and dangerousness of the climate crisis requires additional drastic measures on the part of collective actors – states in this case.

Second, in relation to the possible operationalization of international climate policy, it is useful to single out a group of countries small enough to avoid the unworkability of the UNFCCC's universal multilateralism and at the same time "sufficiently broad to exert leverage on the global situation" (Victor et al. 2005: 1821).[5] In this regard, climate governance scholars suggest that this group should be selected on the basis of its members' contributions to the problem (Carin and Mehlenbacher 2010). For instance, the top ten carbon emitters – including the European Union (EU) as a single emitter – account in cumulative (1990–2008) terms for 80 per cent of global emissions. They can thus constitute the coalition most appropriate to thoroughly address emission abatements and more generally the problems raised by climate change because such a group can in principle remedy the manageability/inclusiveness tension pointed out above and dramatically reduce transaction costs.[6]

Equity of the top emitters' climate policy

Equity, one of the core issues of the social dimension of sustainability, plays a crucial role in the climate crisis. Climate change is, in fact, still characterized by a condition of "structural" injustice (Okereke 2011: 131; Parks and Roberts 2010: 145) that by and large penalizes the vital interests of poor people and countries in favour of the trivial interests of the affluent world. Therefore, current climate policy necessarily needs to include issues of equity in order to be more widely acceptable (Grasso 2007). A very insightful perspective from which to assess equity at the international level in the context of climate change relates to the developed world's recognition of its carbon debt, i.e. the portion of the ecological debt ascribable to carbon-emitting activities, towards developing countries – as made clear by Davis and Caldeira (2010) and Peters and Hertwich (2008). Indeed, the developed world is offshoring its emissions to poorer countries (Roberts and Parks 2009). In fact, the relative decarbonization of wealthy economies is largely due to their emission transfers via international trade to poorer countries (Peters et al. 2011), whose emissions, conversely, have roughly doubled in the past twenty years (Hertwich and Peters 2008).

The interpretative frame of carbon debt seems particularly useful for understanding the ethical nature of climate change in the context of international-level sustainable development and in relation to top emitting countries. It, in fact, moves the discourse from the more abstract dimension of distributive justice to the pragmatic one of political justice. In practical terms, the chapter adopts a notion of carbon debt/credit based on the difference between territorial- and consumption-based emissions inventories: those countries with consumption-based emissions larger than territorial-based ones have a carbon debt, and vice versa, as shown for top emitters in Table 25.1.[7]

The dimension of equity intrinsic to the carbon debt can be usefully captured by a single indicator of multilateral and bilateral funding for adaptation, mitigation and reduction of emissions from deforestation and forest degradation (REDD). This is, in fact, an excellent proxy for the willingness of the developed world to recognize its carbon debt. In particular, equity requires that carbon debtors (the USA, Canada, the UK, Italy, the EU and Germany) should contribute to multilateral and bilateral climate funding in proportion to the relative sizes of their carbon debts. Therefore, in order to evaluate the ethical contents, i.e. the social dimensions of sustainable

Table 25.1 Top 10 emitters: carbon-exporting (E), carbon-importing (I) countries, the carbon credit/debt based on cumulative 1990–2008 territorial (T), consumption (C) emissions [carbon credit/debt = T – C], percentage of the carbon credit (+) debt (-) in relation to territorial cumulative emissions, and climate funding

Top emitter	*T Cum emissions* $MtCO_2$	*C Cum emissions* $MtCO_2$	*Carbon credit (+) and debt (–)* $MtCO_2$	*% Carbon credit/debt on total emissions*	*Funding Pledged (Mln. US$)*
China (E)	75,341	63,335	12,006	0.16	8.2
Russia (E)	31,371	27,916	3,455	0.11	3.5
India (E)	21,701	20,182	1,519	0.07	6.4
Japan (E)	23,914	23,239	675	0.03	15,277.3
US. (I)	103,700	109,385	–5,685	–0.05	2,398.8
Canada (I)	9,587	10,720	–1,133	–0.12	479.5
USA (I)	10,652	12,281	–1,629	–0.15	4,872.2
Italy (I)	8,458	9,917	–1,459	–0.17	60.0
EU* (I)	76,717	92,310	–15,593	–0.20	8,759.7
Germany (I)	16,459	19,913	–3,454	–0.21	2,204.6

Source: Elaboration on Peters et al. (2011); for funding pledged, Climate Funds Update (www.climatefundsupdate.org, accessed 3 July 2014).

Note: * Six EU member countries could not be included owing to lack of data: Bulgaria, Estonia, Latvia, Lithuania, Malta and Poland (whose contributions to climate funding are, however, very likely non-significant in absolute value).

development, of climate policy, the chapter checks the consistency of this provision with the realpolitik of climate finance for every debt-emitter. It ultimately looks for an acceptable degree of consistency between the emitter's contribution and the relative size of its carbon debt: the greater the consistency, the closer the adherence of the country's climate policy to equity.

More specifically, acknowledgement of the carbon debt is measured by the weight of climate funding in the monetized amount of the carbon debt. The monetization of the carbon budget is given by multiplying it by the average price of a tonne of carbon as specified by the prices of two Kyoto flexibility mechanism allowances implemented by the EU, the EUA and the CER (Certified Emission Reduction), whose daily average price amounts to 14.21 US$/tonne.[8] Accordingly, the UK is the only country among the debt-emitters acknowledging its climate debt, with pledges to climate finance that are more than twice the average pledges of the other top emitters. By contrast, Italy has the lowest contribution to climate finance, with pledges 97 per cent less than the debt-emitters' average. The two North American countries' pledges are two-thirds less than the average; those of the EU and Germany are respectively 49 per cent and 42 per cent below the average (see Table 25.2).

It should be noted that the notion of carbon debt adopted, as outlined above, determines the exclusive focus on the relative equity status of debt-emitters. It is, in fact, one of the possible indicators with which to assess the social sustainability of a country's climate policy, selected for the reason given above. However, this perspective provides a notion of relative equity calculated only on the basis of the specific situation of debt-emitters. This notion highlights their carbon debts acknowledgements and is ultimately important in ascertaining the social dimension of sustainability as understood here.

The outcomes of the application of this perspective may seem counterintuitive, since in absolute terms the contribution of every debt-emitter (and of other richer countries, also those not included among top emitters) is still largely insufficient (Grasso 2010: 71–88). However, the aim of the chapter is not to advance general considerations on the equity of top emitters' climate policy; rather, the chapter conducts a comparative exercise on only those subjects that, according to the notion of carbon debt adopted, are committed to providing climate finance, i.e. on the debt-emitters' acknowledgement of their climate debt *per se*. This standpoint, furthermore, implies the non-consideration as equity yardsticks of both the historical responsibility of debt-emitters and their ability to pay as determined by their GDPs.[9]

Overall, the UK shows greater acknowledgement of its carbon debts – as captured by a single indicator of multilateral and bilateral funding for adaptation, mitigation and REDD – than do

Table 25.2 Equity of debt emitters' climate funding

Top emitter	*Carbon debt ($MtCO_2$)*	*Monetized carbon debt (billion US$)*	*Current pledges (million US$)*	*Acknowledgment of carbon debt (% of pledges on monetized carbon budget compared to the average of debt-emitters)*
UK	1,629	23,148	8,233.4	315.5
Germany	3,454	49,081	2,434.0	–42.3
EU	15,593	221,576	9,754.2	–48.9
USA	5,685	80,783	2,398.8	–65.5
Canada	1,133	16,099	550.6	–60.2
Italy	1,459	20,732	60.0	–96.6

Source: Elaboration on Peters's et al. (2011) dataset; for funding figures, elaboration on Climate Funds Update (www.climatefundsupdate.org, accessed 3 July 2014).

the remaining debt-emitters (Canada, Italy, Germany, the USA and the EU). This ultimately reveals a high level of relative equity, understood as climate debt acknowledgement, among emitters characterized by a carbon debt, i.e. a solid approach to the social dimension of sustainable development. By contrast, Italy, which almost completely disregards climate finance, has the least socially sustainable approach to climate change. Among other debt-emitters, Germany and the EU show a relatively acceptable degree of equity, whereas North American countries still need to improve their carbon debt recognition, so that, according to this standpoint, the social dimension of their climate policy is still inadequate.

Feasibility of top emitters' climate policy

The assessment of the feasibility of the top emitters' climate policy requires the adoption of a prospective stance. This basically boils down to the following question: why do some countries have ambitious objectives in terms of climate policy, and others do not? The ex-ante standpoint of political feasibility concerns the concrete possibility that national climate policy can achieve the necessary support among policy-makers, civil society and industry so that the policy can be implemented. Political feasibility is indeed a very broad issue that by and large centres on the relationships among ideas, power and resources (Tanner and Allouche 2011) and involves national cultures and sensitivities, the role of science, as well as political, institutional and economic systems. It is therefore extremely difficult to reduce and dissolve the complexity and breadth of this soft perspective into a single hard yardstick. A realistic and useful approach for assessing the feasibility of climate policy consists in scrutinizing how related ideas, power and resources are conceptualized, negotiated and agreed, i.e. it consists in succinctly investigating the political economy of climate change.

Therefore, this section provides a concise overview of the major factors likely to drive top emitters' climate policy. According to the emerging literature on the political economy of climate change (e.g. de Serres et al. 2011; Steves et al. 2011), which largely draws on experiences of structural reforms around the world, such factors can be synthesized into the following main categories: (1) burdens; (2) public awareness; (3) democracy and institutional capacity; and (4) interest groups.

As regards the first category, it can be claimed – as also the literature on political science unambiguously points out (e.g. Dahl 1998: 145–165) – that the lower the burden of a policy, the more it is likely to succeed in the long term, at least in democratic societies. To this end, the chapter assumes that the main burden of climate policy relates to the cost associated with mitigation efforts (Nemet 2010). It should be noted that climate policy feasibility has been further weakened in the past few years by the global economic crisis, by the post-Copenhagen sense of disillusionment, and by a certain loss of credibility of climate science. All in all, the political feasibility of future mitigation action largely depends on the projected marginal cost of emission abatements (MACs) contextualized to the country's average welfare level. To this end, the absolute MACs are parameterized to countries' 2011 per capita GDP, US$ PPP. In particular, it is assumed, in line with the relevant literature, that the higher the MAC, the proportionally lower is the political feasibility of future mitigations (Goulder and Parry 2008; Bosetti and Frankel 2009). Table 25.3 reports the absolute and parameterized MACs for top emitters aggregated on a regional basis.

According to this evidence, India and China are the least willing to abate carbon emissions, whereas Russia, and to a lesser extent the EU and its members, are the most favourable to mitigation action. Canada, the USA and Japan lie somewhere in between, so that their incentive to emissions abatement cannot be clearly understood according to this category.

Table 25.3 Marginal abatement costs (MAC)

Top emitter	*MAC (2005 US$ per ton CO_2)*	*Parameterized MAC*
India	28.5	160.7
China	20.6	38.5
North America	40.7	18.5
Japan	45.0	13.4
EU and Members	29.6	7.8
Russia	15.7	2.1

Source: Elaboration on Morris et al. (2008). Calculated as average of 2010 MAC for the 7 (1, 5, 10, 20, 30, 40, 50 per cent) levels of abatement.

Also public awareness of the threat posed by climate change is expected to be an influential driver of stronger climate policy, given the extent to which governments, at least in democratic societies, respond to public pressure. The correlation between public knowledge and better climate policy is complex because it could include also the opposite direction, given that the latter can influence the former. However, with a crude simplification, the chapter assumes that the greater the awareness of the dangerousness of climate change, the stronger climate policy becomes. In particular, the World Values Survey provides important insights into the perception of the threat posed by climate change.[10] It makes it possible to identify three groups of top emitters with high, medium and low awareness of the climate crisis: (1) High: Canada, the EU, Italy, and Japan; (2) Medium: Germany, India, the USA; and (3) Low: China, Russia, and the UK. Consistent with the assumption adopted, group (1) High would be most likely to implement a courageous climate policy, followed by the other groups with decreasing likelihoods of introducing an effective climate policy.

It is further assumed, in line with most of the relevant literature, that democracies are more likely to provide environmental public goods like climate stability (e.g. McGuire and Olson 1996; Bernauer and Koubi 2009; Burnell 2012). Bernauer and Böhmelt (2013) empirically found that democracy has a positive effect on the performances of climate policy, and that democracies, also by virtue of their greater institutional capacity, can better participate in international environmental regime-making (e.g. Ward 2008; Bernauer et al. 2010; Neumayer 2002 empirically proved this claim). There are several indexes that measure the state of democracy at the country level: they by and large establish very similar rankings. The chapter uses the Economist Intelligence Unit Democracy Index, since it includes both indicators on the quality of democratic processes and on the institutional capacity to implement policies.[11] According to this index, Canada, Germany, the UK, the USA, and Japan are full democracies. Consequently, even if not expressly calculated by the index, also the EU can be considered as belonging to this category, similar to the majority of its most influential members. India and Italy are instead flawed democracies, whereas Russia and China are considered authoritarian regimes. As underlined above, in the current analysis, full democracies are those most likely to implement effective climate policy, as opposed to authoritarian regimes, whose climate policy is expected to be the least effective.

The strength of interest groups, and in particular the power of the carbon-intensive industry lobby, is probably the most important single determinant of climate policy. While the role of the carbon lobby is theoretically uncontroversial, in practice it is also the most difficult factor to identify, let alone to measure. In other words, the role of the carbon-intensive industry lobby can

Table 25.4 Shares of carbon-intensive industry in total GDP 2010 in US$ current prices

Top emitter	*Shares*	*% in comparison to average share*
China	0.407	+78
Russia	0.310	+36
Germany	0.237	+4
Canada	0.218	−5
Japan	0.214	−6
EU	0.203	−11
Italy	0.193	−15
India	0.181	−21
USA	0.163	−29
UK	0.157	−31

Source: Elaboration on UN Statistics, National Accounts Main Aggregates Database (http://unstats.un.org/unsd/snaama/introduction.asp, accessed 3 July 2014).

Table 25.5 Feasibility of climate policy in top emitters according to categories of factors

Top emitter	*Burdens*	*Public awareness*	*Democracy*	*Interest groups*
Canada	Medium	High	High	Medium
China	Low	Low	Low	Low
EU	High	High	High	Medium
Germany	High	Medium	High	Medium
India	Low	Medium	Medium	High
Italy	High	High	Medium	Medium
Japan	Medium	High	High	Medium
Russia	High	Low	Low	Low
UK	High	Low	High	High
USA	Medium	Medium	High	High

Source: Elaborations on tables and information related to the four categories of feasibility.

be only roughly captured: to this end, consistently with what was suggested by Steves et al. (2011), it is calculated as the share of carbon-intensive industries – manufacturing, mining and utilities – in the top emitters' GDPs (Table 25.4). The larger this share is, the greater the importance and weight of the carbon lobby in opposing actions against carbon-intensive activities, and the lower the eventual possibility of effective climate policy.

Overall, it seems possible to divide top emitters into three groups with diminishing likelihoods of implementing effective climate policy: (1) high carbon-intensive industry: China and Russia; (2) medium carbon-intensive industry: Germany, Canada, Japan, the EU, and Italy; and (3) low carbon-intensive industry: India, the USA, and the UK. In light of these considerations, an attempt is now made to answer the question posed at the beginning of this section. To do so, it is useful to refer to Table 25.5, which indicates for each top emitter the importance (low, medium, high) of the category of factors that favour the implementation of climate policy.

First, it seems evident that in both China and Russia the feasibility of climate policy is rather problematic, and that the scope for climate-effective policy is quite limited. On the other hand, the EU and to a lesser extent the UK are, according to the current analysis, the most proactive subjects in terms of climate policy. The situation of the other top emitters is more nuanced. Canada, Germany, Japan, Italy and the USA seem ready for more forceful climate policy, even if they are still encumbered by specific resistances, while India's climate policy is instead characterized by an apparently lower politically feasibility.

Conclusion: common threads and emerging issues

By way of conclusion it is worth synthesizing the outcomes of the assessment carried out on the social dimension of sustainability of top emitters' climate policy into a synoptic table (see Table 25.6) highlighting some common features of, and issues emerging from, top emitters' climate policy.

Table 25.6 Top emitters' social dimension of sustainable development

Top emitter	*Equity*	*Feasibility*
Canada	W	A
China	S	W
EU	A	S
Germany	S	A
India	S	W
Italy	W	A
Japan	S	A
Russia	W	W
UK	S	S
USA	W	A

Source: Author's conceptual elaboration on Tables 25.2–25.5.

Notes: Weak (W), Average (A), Strong (S).

First and foremost, it seems possible to cluster top emitters on the basis of their performances in the social dimension of sustainable development into two main groups: those which include at least one weak dimension of sustainable development, and those which do not. The first group includes Canada, China, India, Italy, Russia and the USA, four of which (China, India, Russia and the USA) are major actors in the current international arena. Their ambivalent acknowledgement of the social dimension of sustainability is rather worrisome and such countries may be major stumbling blocks to the development of sustainable international action against climate change, and ultimately of effective climate policy. The remaining top emitters, namely the EU, Germany, Japan and the UK, the second group, instead seem to have well-articulated awareness of the ethical dimension of climate change and a supportive political context – especially so the UK, whose climate policy, in fact, is highly consistent with the social dimension of sustainable development.

Second, to be stressed is the evidence on the social dimension of sustainability of top emitters highlighted in Table 25.6. In this regard, it seems possible to argue that political feasibility is the weakest component, whereas equity shows greater acknowledgement. It seems, therefore, that any future climate policy should pay extremely close attention to the political economy of climate change in order to prompt adequate solutions to the climate crisis.

Notes

1 As of July 2014: figure reported by CO_2 now based on 2014 NOAA-ESRL data (http://co2now.org/, accessed 2014).
2 In fact, Lumumba Di-Aping, the Sudanese Chair of the G77 and China group at the Copenhagen COP 15, compared the 2°C target indicated by the Copenhagen Accord to the Holocaust. "[This] is asking Africa to sign a suicide pact, an incineration pact in order to maintain the economic dependence of a few countries. It's a solution based on values that funnelled six million people in Europe into furnaces" (*The Guardian*, 19 December 2009) (accessed 2014).
3 According to Vaughan et al. (2009), the scientific prominence of the 2°C target is mainly due to studies that point out that the last interglacial (Eemian) was 1–2°C warmer than now, causing significant losses in the Arctic and Antarctic ice sheets with a consequent sea level rise of 4 ± 2 m.
4 Actually, Adger et al. (2003) introduce also a fourth question, i.e. 'political legitimacy'. For the purposes of this chapter, political legitimacy concurs with other normative ideals of justice to the social dimension of sustainable development, and will not be specifically analysed.
5 In the same vein, the Kyoto-like inclusion of additional countries would, in fact, be scarcely significant in terms of solving the problem, yet extremely onerous in terms of transaction costs and negotiation complexity (Victor 2006; Prins and Rayner 2007).
6 This coalition would include the United States (US) (22.1 per cent of global 1990–2008 cumulative emissions), the European Union (EU) (16.3 per cent), China (16.0 per cent), Russia (6.7 per cent), Japan (5.1 per cent), India (4.6 per cent), Germany (3.5 per cent), the United Kingdom (UK) (2.3 per cent), Canada (2.0 per cent), Italy (1.8 per cent). Data on emissions are calculated from the Global Carbon Budget 2012 (Le Quéré et al. 2012).
7 To be noted is that other schools of thought, especially in the developing world, put forward a different notion of carbon debt that refers to the overuse of the atmospheric capacity of absorbing GHG, i.e. to the greater historical contribution of the developed countries (for a thorough investigation of the ethical arguments backing the notion of carbon debt, see Pickering and Barry 2012: 671–677). The current choice of a more prudent account of the carbon debt is based on the non-dependency of the latter on any *a priori* ethical assumptions that artificially split (top) emitters into developed and developing countries with consequent *a priori* different moral duties and rights.
8 The market price of CO2 – 14.21 $/tonne – is calculated as the average of 2008–2013 (first semester until 30 June 2013) daily prices of two Kyoto flexibility mechanism allowances implemented by the European Union, the EUA (European Union Allowances) and the CER (Certified Emission Reduction). Data retrieved from: www.sendeco2.com/it/precio_co2.asp?ssidi=5.
9 Having specified this, however, extremely noteworthy is the conduct of Japan, which, though it belongs among the 'credit-emitters', has by far the largest absolute contribution to climate finance with US$16,614 million pledged (and over US$13,000 deposited). Similarly, the Non-Annex I countries (China and India) have always shown extreme sensitivity to equity concerns, given their systemic vulnerability to the structural injustice brought about by climate change. By contrast, Russia, the other Annex I top emitter, has never shown any real interest in equity, let alone advanced any ethical argument in negotiations, so that it is possible to envisage a nonchalant attitude towards this dimension of sustainable development.
10 See www.worldvaluessurvey.org (accessed 2014). The data used are from the fifth wave of the World Values Survey (WVS 5), in particular from question VIII, 'Environmental problems in the world: Global warming or the greenhouse effect'. The percentages of respondents in top emitters that believe that climate change is a very serious issue are the following: Canada 66.7 per cent, China 38.0 per cent, the EU 61.2 per cent, Germany 49.9 per cent, India 51.1 per cent, Italy 71.4 per cent, Japan 71.3 per cent, Russia 41.2 per cent, the UK 36.8 per cent, the USA 48.5 per cent.
11 See www.eiu.com/public/topical_report.aspx?campaignid=demo2010 (accessed 2014).

References

Adger, W. N. et al. (2003) Governance for sustainability: towards a 'thick' analysis of environmental decision-making. *Environment and Planning A*, 35: 1095–1110.

Allen, M. R., Frame, D. J., Huntingford, C., Jones, C. D., Lowe, J. A., Meinshausen, M. and Meinshausen, N. (2009) Warming caused by cumulative carbon emissions towards the trillionth tonne. *Nature*, 458: 1163–1166.

Bennear, L. S. and Stavins R. N. (2007) Second-best theory and the use of multiple policy instruments. *Environmental and Resource Economics*, 37(1): 111–129.

Bernauer, T. and Böhmelt, T. (2013) National climate policies in international comparison: the climate change cooperation index. *Environmental Science & Policy*, 25: 196–206.

Bernauer, T., Kalbhenn, A., Koubi, V. and Spilker, G. (2010) A comparison of international and domestic sources of global governance dynamics. *British Journal of Political Science*, 40(3): 509–538.

Bernauer, T. and Koubi, V. (2009) Effects of political institutions on air quality. *Ecological Economics*, 68(5): 1355–1365.

Bosetti, V. and Frankel, J. (2009) Global climate policy architecture and political feasibility: specific formulas and emission targets to attain 460 PPM CO_2 concentrations. The Harvard Project on International Climate Agreements, Discussion Paper 09-30.

Burnell, P. (2012) Democracy, democratization and climate change: complex relationships. *Democratization*, 19(5): 813–842.

Caney, S. (2009) Climate change, human rights and moral thresholds. In S. Humphreys (ed.) *Human Rights and Climate Change*. Cambridge: Cambridge University Press, pp. 69–90.

Carin, B. and Mehlenbacher, A. (2010) Constituting global leadership: which countries need to be around the summit table for climate change and energy security? *Global Governance: A Review of Multilateralism and International Organizations*, 16(1): 21–37.

Dahl, R. (1998) *On Democracy*. New Haven, CT: Yale University Press.

Davis, S. and Caldeira, K. (2010) Consumption-based accounting of CO_2 emissions. *Proceedings of the National Academy of Sciences USA*, 107(12): 5687–5692.

de Serres, A., Llewellyn, J. and Llewellyn, P. (2011) The political economy of climate change mitigation policies: how to build a constituency to address global warming? Economics Department Working Papers No. 887. Paris: OECD.

Felder, S. and Schleiniger, R. (2002) Environmental tax reform: efficiency and political feasibility. *Ecological Economics*, *42*(1): 107–116.

Gardiner, S. M. (2004) Ethics and global climate change. *Ethics*, 114: 555–600.

Goulder, L. H. and Parry, W. H. (2008) Instruments choice in environmental policy. *Review of Environmental Economics and Policy*, 2(2): 152–174.

Grasso, M. (2007) A normative ethical framework in climate change. *Climatic Change*, 81: 223–246.

Grasso, M. (2010) *Justice in Funding Adaptation Under the International Climate Change Regime*. Dordrecht: Springer.

Hansen, J. E., Sato, M., Kharecha, P., Beerling, D., Masson-Delmotte, V., Pagani, M., Raymo, M., Royer, D. L. and Zachos, J. C. (2008) Target atmospheric CO_2: where should humanity aim? *The Open Atmospheric Science Journal*, 2: 217–231.

Hertwich, E. G. and Peters, G. P. (2008) Carbon footprint of nations: a global, trade-linked analysis. *Environmental Science & Technology*, 43: 6414–6420.

IPCC (Intergovernmental Panel on Climate Change) (2007) *Climate Change 2007: Synthesis Report. Contribution of Working Groups I, II and III to the Fourth Assessment Report of the IPCC*. Cambridge: Cambridge University Press.

Le Quéré, C. et al. (2012) The global carbon budget 1959–2011. *Earth System Science Data Discussion*, 5: 1107–1157.

McGuire, M. and Olson, M. (1996) The economics of autocracy and majority rule: the invisible hand and the use of force. *Journal of Economic Literature*, 34(2): 72–96.

Meinshausen, M., Meinshausen, N., Hare, W., Raper, S., Frieler, K., Knutti, R., Frame, D. J. and Allen, M. R. (2009) Greenhouse-gas emission targets for limiting global warming to 2°C. *Nature*, 458: 1158–1162.

Moellendorf, D. (2009) Treaty norms and climate change mitigation. *Ethics & International Affairs*, 23(3): 247–265.

Morris, J., Paltsev, S. and Reilly, J. (2008) Marginal abatement costs and marginal welfare costs for greenhouse gas emissions reductions: results from the EPPA model. Report No. 164. Cambridge, MA: MIT Joint Program on the Science and Policy of Global Change.

Nemet, G. F. (2010) Cost containment in climate policy and incentives for technology development. *Climatic Change*, 103: 423–443.

Neumayer, E. (2002) Do democracies exhibit stronger international environmental commitment? A cross-country analysis. *Journal of Peace Research*, 39(2): 139–164.

Okereke, C. (2011) Moral foundations for global environmental and climate justice. *Royal Institute of Philosophy*, Supplement 69: 117–135.

Parks, B. C. and Roberts, J. T. (2010) Climate change, social theory and justice. *Theory, Culture & Society*, 27(2–3): 134–66.

Peters, G. P. and Hertwich, E. G. (2008) CO_2 embodied in international trade with implications for global climate policy. *Environmental Science & Technology*, 42(5), 1401–1407.

Peters, G. P., Minx, J. C., Weber, C. L. and Edenhofer, O. (2011) Growth in emission transfers via international trade from 1990 to 2008. *Proceedings of the National Academy of Sciences USA*, 108(21): 8903–8908.

Pickering, J. and Barry. C. (2012) On the concept of climate debts: its moral and political value. *Critical Review of International Social and Political Philosophy*, 15(5): 667–685.

Prins, G. and Rayner, S. (2007) Time to ditch Kyoto. *Nature*, 449: 973–975.

Roberts, J. T. and Parks, B. C. (2009) Ecologically unequal exchange, ecological debt, and climate justice: the history and implications of three related ideas for a new social movement. *International Journal of Comparative Sociology*, 50(3–4): 385–409.

Schmidt, G. and Archer, D. (2009) Too much of a bad thing. *Nature*, 458: 1117–1118.

Schnellnhuber, J. S., Cramer, W., Nakicenovic, N., Wigley, T. M. L. and Yohe, G. (eds) (2006) *Avoiding Dangerous Climate Change*. Cambridge: Cambridge University Press.

Steves, F., Treisman, D. and Teytelboym, A. (2011) Political economy of climate change policy in the transition region. In A. Chirmiciu and S. Fankhauser (eds) *The Low Carbon Transition*. London: European Bank for Reconstruction and Development (EBRD).

Tanner, T. and Allouche, J. (2011) Towards a new political economy of climate change and development. *IDS Bulletin*, 42(3): 1–14.

Thaler, R. H. and Sunstein, C. R. (2003). Libertarian paternalism. *American Economic Review*, 93(2): 175–179.

UNFCCC (United Nations Framework Convention on Climate Change) (2009) *Fulfilment of the Bali Action Plan and components of the agreed outcome (FCCC/AWGLCA/2009/4 (Part II))*. Bonn: UNFCCC.

Vaughan, N. E., Lenton, T. M. and Sheperd, J. C. (2009) Climate change mitigation: trade-offs between delay and strength of action required. *Climatic Change*, 96: 29–43.

Victor, D. G. (2006) Toward effective international cooperation on climate change: numbers, interests and institutions. *Global Environmental Politics*, 6(3): 90–103.

Victor, D. G., House, J. C. and Joy, S. (2005). A Madisonian approach to climate policy. *Science*, 309: 1820–1821.

Ward, H. (2008). Liberal democracy and sustainability. *Environmental Politics*, 17(3): 386–409.

Zickefeld, K., Eby, M. Matthews, H. D. and Weaver, A. J. (2009) Setting cumulative emissions targets to reduce the risk of dangerous climate change. *Proceedings of the National Academy of Sciences – USA*, 106(38): 16129–16134.

26

SUSTAINABLE DEVELOPMENT OR THE CREEPING INCUBATION OF DISASTER?

Raymond Murphy

The issue of sustainability implies a long-term perspective dealing with the needs of future generations as well as immediate needs. The Earth's population is increasing toward 9 billion and could easily exceed that figure. Formerly poor societies like Brazil, Russia, India, and China (the BRIC nations) are rapidly consuming more, and poor nations need economic growth to rise out of poverty. Wealthy societies have a culture of entitlement to high levels of consumption. Where will the resources and waste sinks come from to sustain this development over the long run? Some observers argue that 'sustainable development' is an oxymoron because its two terms are in opposition (Redclift 2005) and there are many indications that development is occurring at great environmental cost. This chapter will analyze the unmentionable possibility that the present path-dependent trajectory of development is leading to a slow-onset global degradation of the natural environment which provides essential services to humans, and is driving the creeping incubation of environmental problems that threaten disastrous unsustainability over the long run.[1] By long run, I mean the length of a human life of about a hundred years, which is not that far in the future on a historical scale and certainly not on an evolutionary scale but much further than economists and decision-makers typically consider.

Although the technologies that will exist a century from now are not known, using that ignorance as an excuse for blindly charging full-speed ahead and failing to mitigate scientifically documented dangers like anthropogenic climate change, deforestation, freshwater depletion, etc., makes no more sense than constructing unprotected buildings in earthquake zones, hurricane alleys, and flood plains. Threats to long-term sustainability can be foreseen, even if the specifics of timing, location, impact, etc., are unknown. Many disasters occur when hazards are known but preventive action is not implemented because of cost, hence disasters are the unpaid bills and debts of development (see Quarantelli 1998, for a debate about the definition of disaster, and Murphy 2006 and 2010, for an update and extension of the analysis). The possibility that disastrous degradation of the service-providing natural environment is occurring will be investigated and lessons will be learned from prior disaster incubation to enhance vigilance concerning warning signs, to avoid being misled by improvements that are only partial, temporary, or inadequate, and to lay the basis for action to increase long-term sustainability. The chapter's focus will be on how societies are reacting to cumulative, slow-onset anthropogenic environmental problems having significant time lags and geographical distances between causes and consequences, a reaction that has much in common with the incubation of disaster. It presents, in short, a self-denying prophecy.

Learning from past disasters

This chapter should not be misconstrued as fatalism. Development can be sustainable and disasters prevented or at least diminished if evidence of danger is heeded and action taken to minimize risk. In 1964, an earthquake followed by a tsunami struck Alaska, killing people and destroying villages. In 1989, the *Exxon Valdez* oil supertanker spilled 11 million gallons of crude oil, contaminating 1,000 miles of Alaskan shoreline and killing sea life (Hernan 2010). The Alaskan earthquake prompted increased awareness of vulnerability and led to improved warning systems, building codes, and disaster preparation. The oil spill also incited measures to enhance safety (Busenberg 1999). Disasters and fears of similar ones have been important sources of motivation to take preventive action, to increase the robustness of infrastructures and societies so that they can withstand disturbances, and to augment resilience so that societies can bounce back or up to better states after calamities. Learning lessons from previous disasters has been done even at great cost to prevent future repeat disasters. The 1952 storm surge that drowned 2,000 Dutch citizens incited the Netherlands to build an enormous system of dykes to protect against surges. Chronic flooding of the Canadian city of Winnipeg located on a flood plain prompted the construction of a river bypass that saved lives and property. Despite its huge cost, it saved money in the long run. The London fog of 1952 which killed 10,000 people led to the 1956 British Clean Air Act that reduced air pollution (Hernan 2010: 31–37). Disasters act as focusing events and as agenda-setting prompts that have the potential to raise prevention and preparation to higher levels (Kingdom 1995; Birkland 1997), much like coughing up blood is a focusing event that has the potential to convince smokers that smoking causes cancer and makes them reconsider stopping smoking. Rudel (2013) documented that local disasters incited defensive environmentalism and changes in practices to prevent future disasters, then hypothesized that those changes could be scaled up to more broadly based altruistic environmentalism. For example, the discovery of toxic waste under a school near Love Canal induced the United States to create a Superfund in 1984 to clean all contaminated sites and legislate control over toxic waste disposal. The potentially disastrous depletion of the ozone layer by chlorofluorocarbons (CFCs) was remedied by scientific monitoring of this problem that was invisible to the naked eye, which triggered successful lobbying of political leaders to eliminate CFCs, that then stimulated the development of technological alternatives. This involved international cooperation and the implementation of the Montreal Protocol whereby wealthy nations would replace CFCs and then transfer technology to developing nations. It showed how scientific risk assessment, political action, international cooperation, and technological innovation can prevent a looming disaster and make development sustainable even for global, delayed-action, harmful consequences of market-based technological innovation. When warning signs are acted upon, risk can be managed, disaster can be prevented and sustainability enhanced. The acute problem of disaster can be avoided if and only if the chronic and costly problem of monitoring and prevention of unsustainability is embraced (Tenner 1997).

Sustainability at risk

Threats to sustainability have resulted in the development of windmills in Spain, wave energy in Portugal, the world's biggest solar energy farm in Texas, electrified Bus Rapid Transit in Bogata, renewable energy in China, reductions in per barrel emissions from tar sands oil extraction in

Alberta, desalination producing fresh water in Saudi Arabia, nature reserves, etc. Underscoring demonstration projects like these is important to inspire hope, but it is nevertheless essential to keep in mind what is needed to make development sustainable and determine whether improvements meet the needs. Some researchers (Pielke 2010; Prins et al. 2010; Rayner 2010) talk about the ecological directions of change and transition to sustainable development, low carbon energy, decarbonization, dematerialization, and post-carbon societies as if these were happening. Is such optimistic talk warranted or premature? Whether the sum of local successes has the required scale and timeliness to make development sustainable on the planetary level remains doubtful. Accuracy requires assessing successes in the context of the cumulative harmful effects of overall development. Evidence of danger is often dismissed when it inconveniently conflicts with the pursuit of economic benefits, thereby resulting in disasters, even repeat disasters. It is necessary to see the real world for what it is rather than falling into Pollyannaish discourse or greenwashing. Rudel (2013: 2–3) is forced by the evidence to give an ambiguous answer to the question of whether practices will be reformed in time to avoid disastrous consequences of development: 'This book says "maybe yes"', which implies maybe no.

The cost of environmental disasters has increased exponentially as populations grow, become more affluent, and place expensive constructions in harm's way. The increasing use of centralized, tightly coupled technologies like electrical grids confers many benefits under normal conditions of nature and can be made robust to withstand foreseen abnormal disturbances, but if robustness-enhancing costs are refused or if disturbances exceed what is foreseen, the result is the propagation of disaster because of dependence on that infrastructure (Murphy 2009). Fatalities are highest in poor countries, which raises issues of environmental justice. Slow-onset environmental disasters are arguably most threatening in the long run – deforestation, desertification, anthropogenic global climate change, accumulation of nuclear waste and nuclear weapons (Davis 1998; Kondratyev et al. 2002; Del Moral and Walker 2007; Patt et al. 2009) – because distant future consequences are discounted and preventive action is refused due to cost.

Fossil fuels have powered modern development, hence their depletion and the pollution they cause are the principal threats to sustainability. The main recent inanimate energy innovations have not been renewable ones promoting sustainability, like fuel cells, cheap solar energy, storage of intermittent wind energy, and so on, but instead methods of extracting fossil fuels from bituminous sands, upgrading heavy oil, extracting tight oil by hydraulically fracturing shale, drilling in deepwater oceans, in Amazon rainforests, and in the Arctic made accessible by global warming, and liquefying natural gas, with the accompanying pollution. These innovations hasten the pace of depleting fossil fuels and contaminate land, water, and air. Many new extraction techniques use more fossil fuels and produce more greenhouse gas (GHG) emissions to extract a barrel of oil than pumping conventional oil from a well (Hughes 2009; Murphy 2011; Davidson and Andrews 2013), thereby accelerating depletion of these non-renewable resources and exacerbating climate change. Whereas the energy in a barrel of oil resulted in almost 100 barrels gushing out of a Saudi well in the 1960s, now that same amount of energy only results in four barrels extracted and upgraded from the Alberta bituminous sands (Hughes 2009). Net energy is declining rapidly. The pursuit of near-term market gains has resulted in market failure to foster long-term sustainability. Instead of banking fossil fuels in the ground until clean technologies are developed, there is a rush to combust them immediately. American oil abundance resulting from fracking is expected to peak in the 2020s and decline thereafter as economically retrievable sources are exhausted. The present extractive boom threatens to be followed by a bust of depleted non-renewable resources, carbonized atmosphere, acidified oceans, deforested land, and reduced biodiversity.

There is much evidence that the present fossil fuel path dependency is unsustainable over the long haul, partly because economically retrievable resources are finite (Hughes 2009), and partly because of pollution caused by combustion (Jaccard 2009). The Intergovernmental Panel on Climate Change (IPCC) recently released its fifth assessment report (IPCC 2013: SPM-7) concluding that:

> The atmospheric concentrations of carbon dioxide (CO_2), methane, and nitrous oxide have increased to levels unprecedented in at least the last 800,000 years. CO_2 concentrations have increased by 40% since pre-industrial times, primarily from fossil fuel emissions and secondarily from net land use change emissions. The ocean has absorbed about 30% of the emitted anthropogenic carbon dioxide, causing ocean acidification.

It concluded with great confidence that these changes were caused by human activities. They in turn lead to threats of what Hannigan (2012) aptly calls 'disasters without borders'.

There are huge problems of scale in transitioning to a post-carbon economy, namely, the enormous energy used and the tiny proportion now based on renewable sources. The International Energy Agency (IEA 2012) documented that increases in global energy demand have been met more by coal than by renewables over the last decade. Creating renewable energy displaces little fossil-fuel energy (York 2012) unless accompanied by measures to directly suppress fossil fuels. Since the greenhouse effect results from the absolute amount of carbon in the atmosphere where it remains for a century, and is indifferent to the proportion of renewables, it is worsening despite increases of the latter. The emergence of some renewable energy must not obscure the intensifying use of fossil fuel combustion to power economic growth. Latin (2012) argues persuasively that backloaded strategies based on incremental cuts to emissions, which defer significant reductions for decades, let anthropogenic global warming worsen and will prove too little too late. Yet backloaded strategies are the main ones being proposed because of resistance to frontloaded ones. The danger is that carbon will have been transferred from safe storage in the ground to the atmosphere with threatening consequences before technological and social solutions are implemented.

Threats to the sustainability of development are not only additive but also interactive. Constructing a nuclear reactor at Fukushima in the known path of tsunamis resulted in a near nuclear meltdown in 2011 and caused a leak of radioactive material and long-lasting contamination. It led Japan to use more fossil fuels, thereby worsening its emissions. Germany's planned elimination of nuclear energy will likely increase the combustion of fossil fuels to meet energy demand. Scarcity of fresh water in the Middle East is managed by desalination plants, but these combust fossil fuels to provide energy to desalinate water, thereby depleting a non-renewable energy source and causing more pollution. Vehicle fuel efficiency standards and reduced emissions downstream have been defeated by greater fossil-fuel energy combustion and emissions upstream in fossil-fuel extraction from tar sands, deepwater, and remote locations in the Arctic and the Amazon. Production of ethanol fuel takes land away from growing food. Threats to sustainability have proven to be a many-headed hydra: cutting off one head provokes the emergence of others.

Many proposals to make development sustainable involve wishful thinking. Giddens (2009) proposes indirect hope-based strategies whereby time-delayed environmental threats like climate change would be managed indirectly by making solutions converge with economic opportunities. He claims that European societies lead in mitigating climate change because they aimed for energy security and therefore developed renewable energy. But Giddens' analysis has been shown to be an oversimplification with the fear of disastrous energy scarcity after the formation of the OPEP cartel being significantly involved (Murphy and Murphy 2012). US energy security has been enhanced by developing new techniques for extracting fossil fuels. Near-term economic opportunities have often been achieved by creating long-term danger. Similarly the proposal of the Hartwell Group (Pielke 2010; Prins et al. 2010; Rayner 2010) for sustainable development is based on an almost magical faith in technological innovation to create abundant clean, cheap energy when needed. But the new energy sources that innovation has hitherto yielded have typically been polluting fossil fuels, and certainly have not been cheap. To steer innovation toward sustainability, Giddens (2009), the Hartwell Group (Prins et al. 2010), and Jaccard (2009) advocate carbon taxes beginning low, then doubling in ten years, and set upstream on extraction of fossil fuels. That argument is vulnerable to Latin's criticism that emissions would thereby only decrease after the atmosphere is loaded with carbon. Moreover carbon taxes have been rejected by most polluting countries (the USA, Canada, Australia, France) and are only accepted by populations when they are revenue neutral (British Columbia), thereby providing no funds to support sustainability innovation. Wished-for technological developments have often not succeeded (fuel cells for transportation), or have not developed in a timely manner (cancer cures), or have resulted in dangerous side-effects (nuclear energy). Hence inanimate energy remains expensive and based largely on non-renewable, polluting fossil fuels with threatening long-term consequences. Giddens' analysis constitutes a version of ecological modernization whereby ecological and economic goals are integrated to attain sustainable development (Mol et al. 2009). But this approach all too often uses misleading intensity-based indicators of improvement where absolute indicators are required. Fewer emissions per unit of gross domestic product (GDP) in a country or per barrel of oil extracted from tar sands are false positive indicators of improvement when emissions are increasing and the greenhouse effect is being made worse by more GDP or more barrels.

'Treadmill of production' (Schnaiberg 1980) and 'ecological rift' (Foster et al. 2010) theories contend that the unsustainability of the present development goes much deeper because these are inherent features of the capitalist market. Critical ecological theory (York et al. 2003) claims that environmental degradation is intrinsic to increased affluence and population growth. There is, however, no evidence that the market will be replaced by something better in the foreseeable future nor that affluence and population will be intentionally reduced. In their analysis of climate change, the Hartwell Group (Prins et al. 2010; Rayner 2010) postulates what Pielke (2010) calls an 'iron law' claiming that when populations have to choose between near-term economic benefits and mitigation of long-term environmental dangers, they always choose the former. These researchers assume it is impossible to decrease consumption even if it is unsustainable and leads to disaster, and the only way to promote sustainability is to innovate abundant clean, cheap energy. They correctly specify the difficulty of restraining consumption, but putting all bets on a quasi-religious blind faith in technological innovation borders on recklessness because technical solutions often have not appeared when needed.

Development has already caused local unsustainability. When Europeans discovered the Grand Banks of Newfoundland, codfish were abundant. By 1990, improvements in fishing technology and resulting overfishing had depleted the cod to such a degree that a moratorium on fishing two decades long has not resulted in the fish population bouncing back. The diversion of water from the Aral Sea to irrigate nearby land resulted in the degradation of that vast body of fresh water. In both cases, signs of disaster incubation were dismissed because caution would restrain economic activities. These examples indicate that extrapolations of sustainability from past well-being are dubious when economic development degrades the natural environment that renders us services.

Why are long-term threats not fostering sustainable development?

Disasters and fear of future ones have been strongly motivational encouraging the taking of preventive action even at great cost. However, most people have not yet experienced severe consequences that can be undisputedly attributed to long-term threats like global warming, biodiversity loss, deforestation, fresh water scarcity, nuclear waste accumulation, etc. Scientific evidence that these are occurring and will eventually produce calamities consists of projections very different from experience (Jasanoff 2010), and are predicted to happen in the distant future or in distant lands. Hence, these threats can easily be discounted by the companies and the people who are causing the problems and they can convince themselves the future will take care of itself. The time-delayed character and distant impacts as well as issues of scale on a huge planet lead populations and decision-makers to give priority to immediate economic growth over threats to long-term sustainability. For example, a time contradiction is evident between the gradual implementation of carbon taxes necessary to convince a reluctant population to accept them (and hence slow movement toward low-carbon energy) and the urgent requirement to stop transferring carbon from safe storage in the ground to the atmosphere where its accumulation causes global warming for a century, then descends to acidify the oceans. Time lags between causes and consequences are characteristic of most environmental problems.

Sustainable development requires a cultural shift from present near-term perspectives to long-term ones, as proposed in Adam's analysis of time. She argues that environmental problems result from the clash 'between divergent temporal systems – industrial as opposed to the rhythmicity of life and ecological relations' (Adam 1998: 16) and documents 'how the time characteristics of pollution – out-of-sync time-frames, time-lags, vastly expanded time-horizons, uncertainty and longevity of materials – are handled with political "short-termism", economic production for obsolescence' (Adam 1995: 9). This results in a contradiction with nature's cycles: 'whilst the socio-economic, scientific and political development is towards ever-faster change and "short-termism", actions required by environmental change need ever-longer time spans of reference and consideration' (ibid.: 136). For time-delayed anthropogenic threats that are scientifically foreseen but not immediately experienced, it is necessary to reflectively learn from the incubation of previous calamities in order to prevent the present incubation and future actualization of disastrous unsustainability.

The incubation of disaster: theory and experience

Turner and Pidgeon (1978) found that sudden technological disasters typically had an incubation period when prior experiences of well-being and economic pressures led to the extrapolation of assumptions of safety and the dismissal or ignorance of visible signs of impending disaster. Had the signs been heeded and appropriate action taken, the disasters could have been avoided. Hence it was the 'failure of foresight' that resulted in continuing inappropriate action during this incubation period and therefore in these 'man-made disasters'. Risk was underestimated, warning signs missed, preventive action not taken, and disaster experienced. A criticism of the study is that failure was determined in hindsight after the disastrous event was known. It is much more difficult to determine beforehand whether foresight is failing. Some disastrous events are unforeseeable, given the available knowledge at the time (Murphy 2009). Nevertheless, retrospective studies after disasters are important to document whether expectations were mistaken and to learn lessons to improve foresight and avoid future disasters. After all, 'unforeseeable' is the excuse of leaders to justify refusing to see the inconveniently foreseeable, for example, many studies foresaw the breach of the levees in New Orleans if hit by category 4 or 5 hurricanes, yet after Katrina struck, George W. Bush still claimed: 'I don't think anyone anticipated the breach of the levees' (*Ottawa Citizen* 2005).

Perrow (1984) documents how disasters in tightly coupled systems using dangerous materials or in dangerous locations result from minor, common human errors and foibles, hence he argued these should be called 'normal accidents'. He showed that industries in public view dealing with powerful clients, such as airlines, typically pay the cost of installing high reliability systems (LaPorte 1996; Weick et al. 1999), but those hidden from view, like tanker shipping, often become error-inducing systems that incubate disasters. Vaughan (1996: 380) concluded from her investigation of the *Challenger* Space Shuttle calamity that even the scientists at NASA, the pinnacle of applied scientific knowledge, who worried about the O-rings never 'thought that a complete ring burn-through was possible'. She called her analysis the sociology of mistake and the normalization of deviance, whereby signs of oncoming calamity were missed or seen as normal because of extrapolations from 25 successful launches. Clarke (1999) showed how risk analyses claiming safety deviated from available pre-disaster facts, and therefore called them 'fantasy documents'. Freudenburg et al. (2009: 163–164) documented how vulnerability to hurricanes in New Orleans was exacerbated by the exclusive focus on near-term economic benefits:

> Predictions of danger that were chillingly similar to what came to pass with Katrina were put forth repeatedly . . ., however, environmentally damaging projects such as MRGO have continued to be described as necessary 'for the good of the economy,' while risks of environmental harm have routinely been dismissed as something 'not to be feared'.
>
> *(ibid.: 163–164)*

Hence they entitled their study 'Catastrophe in the Making: The Engineering of Katrina and the Disasters of Tomorrow'. Mulvihill and Ali (2007) demonstrated that the accumulation of manure from factory farming combined with assumptions of infinite supply of groundwater and cost cutting of inspections resulted in the E-coli contamination of the water supply in a Canadian town of 4,800 people, killing seven and making 2,500 ill with bloody diarrhea.

Immediate economic benefits lead companies, governments and populations to underestimate risk. BP claimed a week before the Deepwater Horizon blowout that its technology, including the blowout preventer, was 'fail-safe'. A few days before the disaster, the government regulator, the U.S. Minerals Management Service, gave the oil rig a passing grade for safety. The 2010 blowout in the Gulf of Mexico showed that the blowout preventer was not safe, that the company's initial estimate of the oil spill of 1,000 barrels of oil per day underestimated the spill rate by a factor of 60 for a total spill of 4.9 million barrels, that its spill recovery plan claiming the capacity of removing 490,000 barrels a day was a vast overestimation compared to the 67,500 barrels per day it managed to recover, and that inspections by government regulators were inadequate (Freudenburg and Gramling 2011). BP's Oil Spill Response Plan was an example of a 'fantasy document'. Both the company and the regulator had been cutting corners on safety. As happens often when a regulated industry is assumed to be economically beneficial but is complex or located in inaccessible locations, there is 'regulatory capture' (Stigler 1971; Levine and Forrence 1990; Laffont and Tirole 1991) whereby the regulator becomes dependent on the industry for information and personnel, and shares similar priorities.

After a disaster, or when new technology is first used, there is heightened vigilance to ensure safety. But as time goes by, there is typically an 'atrophy of vigilance' (Freudenburg 1992) and creeping complacency, particularly concerning rare events, even if these are high impact. This intensifies as operators get away with less costly and less onerous safety measures. The very fact that the Space Shuttle and deepwater oil rigs functioned without exploding, and oil tankers carried Alaskan oil without spilling, seemed to confirm they were safe until the *Challenger* and Deepwater Horizon blew up and the *Exxon Valdez* ran aground, with disastrous consequences. There were nevertheless danger signs that should have prompted measures to prevent disaster if organizations and regulators had been vigilant. For example, the Deepwater Horizon had experienced powerful spurts of natural gas that provided ominous forewarnings from the high pressure deep underground that a blowout was imminent. These gushes led BP's drilling engineer to call it a 'nightmare well' before it blew out, yet key safety systems had been disabled or placed in bypass mode (Freudenburg and Gramling 2011).

The Deepwater Horizon disaster disproved the hypothesis that economic self-interest and market incentives prevent disasters by pushing companies to avoid excessive risk and costly losses. Limited liability laws set liability so low ($75 million in the USA) compared to profits that they encourage taking the risk of low probability, high impact dangers. Only public pressure, potential criminal charges, and the likelihood of being excluded from drilling in the Gulf of Mexico forced BP to pay more.

Old rail lines pass through all cities and towns in North America. Many had fallen into disuse since automobiles and trucks emerged, but others carried non-hazardous goods like lumber, grain, corn syrup, and canola oil. This changed dramatically with the development of fracking shale, which resulted in abundant crude oil, but the additional supply exceeds pipeline capacity to transport it to refineries. Risk-taking railway entrepreneurs contracted to transport it using tankers designed for inert canola oil or corn syrup. Indications that shale tight oil from North Dakota was more flammable and corrosive than other crude oils were ignored. Costs were reduced by decreasing inspectors from 1 per 14 tankers to 1 per 4,000 and by allowing railways to regulate themselves, following the ideology of deregulation. Productivity and profits were increased by lengthening the train to 100 tankers and reducing the number of crewmen to one. On 6 July 2013, a 72-tanker train filled with crude oil was parked on a siding on a hill. Its brakes were set according to accepted railway procedures by that one crewman, which proved inadequate, so it became a runaway train that overturned on a curve in the centretown of Lac Megantic, Canada, exploded, killed 47 people, demolished the centretown, and polluted the lake with 6.5 million litres of oil (Robertson and McNish 2013). Legal liability is yet to be determined because the refinery and oil extraction companies contracted out transportation to a large railway that subcontracted this part of the journey to a small railway which is now bankrupt. This disaster was explained away as a once-in-a-lifetime event, a hypothesis that was subsequently refuted by similar explosions of a 90-tanker crude oil train in Alabama four months later and a 100-oil tanker train in North Dakota a month after that. It was mere luck that neither of these explosions occurred in highly populated cities such trains travelled through. A crude oil tanker train derailed and nearly toppled off a bridge in Philadelphia in January 2014, fortunately without exploding.

Transportation of hazardous materials has increased exponentially, but safety enforcement has not kept pace. The justification that 99.9 per cent of oil shipments arrive safely at their destination is not reassuring when the remainder cause a disaster, when new types of crude oil are more hazardous than before, and when the number of oil tankers in North America has increased from 8,000 in 2009 to 400,000 in 2013 (McNish and Robertson 2013). The more oil and natural gas are extracted, the more they are transported by pipelines and rail, and the more spills and accidents occur. Hazardous materials are being extracted, recombined, and transported as never before to promote economic growth, so safety and sustainability require that adequate monitoring, regulation, and enforcement be done, but often they are not. Tomorrow's disasters are being incubated today. Risk is being mismanaged to maximize economic growth and profit. Freudenburg and Gramling (2011: 158) conclude from their study of the Deepwater Horizon blowout that there 'needs to be prevention, not a mistaken belief that we can actually "clean up" such a mess', a conclusion very instructive for fostering sustainable development.

The incubation of slow-onset disastrous unsustainability

The above studies documented that the pursuit of economic benefits led to the dismissal of danger signs and the failure of foresight needed to prevent disasters in particular locations. Could this be occurring on a global scale for a growing population? Indifference to warning signs of long-run unsustainability suggests this is the case, with examples being apathy toward conclusions of the IPCC (2013) concerning the carbonization of the atmosphere through fossil fuels and land use, toward scientific evidence about biodiversity loss and ocean degradation, etc. International conferences to implement binding commitments to mitigate anthropogenic climate change have failed, and local initiatives have not had the scale or resources to tackle such a global problem. In North America peak oil has been lost from view and replaced by the appearance of an abundant supply, but this threatens to be a temporary cornucopia followed by scarcity of economically extractable oil and gas, depletion of these non-renewable resources, and carbon removed from safe storage in the ground and placed menacingly in the atmosphere. The likelihood is high that oil extraction in deep water, in Far North tar sands, in the Arctic, and in Amazon jungles will become error-inducing and accident-producing systems because everything is hidden from view in these remote locations. Freudenburg and Gramling's (2011: xiii) study of the BP oil spill disaster led them to conclude that 'literally and figuratively, and both in the Gulf of Mexico and elsewhere, we have been getting into increasingly dangerous waters, doing so without being sufficiently vigilant about the implications of our actions'. From an ecological perspective, Hughes et al. (2013) refer to this as living dangerously on borrowed time during slow, unrecognized regime shifts.

Threats to the long-term sustainability of development, such as climate change, biodiversity decline, deforestation, freshwater scarcity, ocean acidification, accumulation of nuclear waste, etc., have rarely produced present-day disasters and hence are relegated to back-of-mind issues that do not incite remedial action. This has resulted in talk but little corrective action (Milne et al. 2009), so threats grow under these incubation conditions. Without immediate focusing events like disasters, leaders and populations typically discount the future even when there are scientific predictions of harm such as those of the IPCC:

> Since the dangers posed by global warming aren't tangible, immediate or visible in the course of day-to-day life, however awesome they appear, many will sit on their hands and do nothing of a concrete nature about them. Yet waiting until they become visible and acute before being stirred to serious action will, by definition, be too late.
>
> *(Giddens 2009: 2)*

Busenberg (1999) documented in a case study of the *Exxon Valdez* disaster that vigilance is maintained in hazardous systems only if a disaster leads to institutionalized improvements in regulatory procedures and to sentinel organizations that promote improvements. He argued that complacency creeps in when: (1) disasters are rare; (2) disasters do not act as focusing events that promote learning from errors; and (3) organizations pursue goals that compete with safety. These three conditions fostering atrophy of vigilance are precisely those applicable to slow-onset environmental problems caused by economic development that threatens its own long-term sustainability by producing global climate change, acidification of oceans, biodiversity loss, deforestation, freshwater scarcity, nuclear waste accumulation, etc. A century from now, disasters resulting from such development may be frequent and close to home, but presently they are rare or geographically distant. Hence they are out-of-focus possibilities that only lead to circumscribed mitigation and adaptation, and rarely to regulatory prevention and sentinel organizations promoting sustainability and safety appropriate for these global threats. Corporations and governments pursue near-term economic benefits that compete with long-term safety and sustainability, hence are prone to downplay inconveniently foreseeable dangers, overestimate safety, and reassure the population. Most ominous is the possibility that irreversible tipping points will be reached before improvements are made, much like smokers by the time they cough up blood may already have terminal lung cancer. Societies will then be locked into a degraded environment that provides inferior services to humans. For slow-onset threats where there are significant time lags and geographical distance between causes and effects, latent irreversibility can set in before a disastrous event provokes a focus on the problem.

Conclusion

Research on disasters has documented that needs are not always met, and that lessons which should be learned are sometimes not learned or are forgotten as time passes. This social construction of vulnerability and the failure of foresight to take preventive action lead to the incubation of disaster, to man-made disasters, and to repeat disasters. Sustainable development becomes an oxymoron if there is inadequate learning from disasters, but disasters and unsustainability do not have to be incubated by development. Warning signs can be heeded and can incite action to prevent such incubation. Sustainable development is a variable, not a universal constant, and can be either an oxymoron or an achievable goal.

Some long-term risks are unforeseeable, which is the ultimate challenge for sustainability. But most are foreseeable, however inconvenient that may be, even if their precise impact, location, and timing are unpredictable. Some hazards are naturogenic, like earthquakes. For these, sustainability and safety require adaptation: monitoring, enhanced robustness through building codes, disaster preparation to diminish harm, and efficient organization to promote resilience. Others, like modern global warming, are anthropogenic. To promote sustainability and safety, prevention must be added to the above strategies.

Long-term sustainability is being trumped by short-term economic development because adverse consequences are time-delayed and/or distant on a huge planet. Time lags and geographical distance between anthropogenic causes and harmful consequences are conditions that push unsustainability and danger out of focus and make them very different from the experience of disaster that becomes a focusing event. These conditions foster complacency which impedes action to avoid incubating disasters. Hence this chapter argues that, though sudden disasters temporarily hamper development, slow-onset dangers constitute longer-lasting and greater threats to sustainability.

Complacency is not nevertheless inevitable. The chapter also argues that learning how past disasters have been incubated is crucial for countering complacency, for avoiding the incubation of unsustainability, and for making the prophecy of unsustainability self-denying. This involves learning to avoid the failure of foresight, the atrophy of vigilance, indifference to danger signs, error-inducing systems, normalization of deviance, tightly coupled systems that magnify normal human errors, fantasy risk analyses, laxity of regulations and enforcement, capture of regulatory institutions by industries being regulated, limited liability laws incentivizing recklessness, uselessness of potential market losses in preventing calamities, etc.

The most dangerous threat is hubris and excessive faith in technology, the market, and organizations to create eternal sustainable development. The attractiveness of technological fixes is that they enable society to avoid inconvenient social innovation, but such fixes often fail or bring adverse consequences. In 1954, the chairman of the U.S. Atomic Energy Commission asserted that nuclear energy would result in electricity 'too cheap to meter' (Strauss 1954), but subsequent requirements to make it safe instead made it expensive. The U.S. Surgeon-General declared in 1969 that modern medicine had vanquished infectious diseases, which became an embarrassment because it was stated on the eve of the AIDS outbreak. Technological breakthroughs do occur, but not always, and often not in a timely fashion. It is imprudent to pin all of society's hopes for sustainability on technological fixes. Lung cancer has yet to be cured by science despite almost a century of research, but has been greatly diminished by anti-smoking campaigns and cigarette taxes. Just as there was resistance to taxes on cigarettes and anti-smoking bylaws, there is resistance to carbon taxes, polluter-pays regulations, up-front costs to innovate efficiencies and renewable energy, etc. Maximizing sustainability and minimizing long-term danger require socio-cultural innovations taking into account the long term and steering societies away from only short-term economic benefits. Sustainable development and safety are fostered if and only if societies learn from the incubation of previous disasters and accept the chronic burden of being vigilant and paying up-front costs necessary to maintain the services that nature provides.

Note

1 The chapter avoids expressions like 'collapse' and 'unnatural sixth extinction' to prevent accusations of overkill, but such threats cannot be ruled out over the long run. Societies that over-exploit their environment have collapsed (Diamond 2005) and there are compelling reasons and evidence that render imprudent the dismissal of the possibility that the present type of development is incubating a sixth mass extinction (Kolbert 2014).

References

Adam, B. (1995) *Timewatch*. Cambridge: Polity Press.

Adam, B. (1998) *Timescapes of Modernity*. London: Routledge.

Birkland, T. (1997) *After Disaster: Agenda Setting, Public Policy, and Focusing Events*. Washington, DC: Georgetown University Press.

Busenberg, G. (1999) The evolution of vigilance: disasters, sentinels and policy change. *Environmental Politics*, 8(4): 90–109.

Clarke, L. (1999) *Mission Improbable: Using Fantasy Documents to Tame Disaster*. Chicago: University of Chicago Press.

Davidson, D. and Andrews, J. (2013) Not all about consumption. *Science*, 339(6125): 1286–1287.

Davis, L. (1998) *Environmental Disasters*. New York: Facts on File, Inc.

Del Moral, R. and Walker, L. (2007) *Environmental Disasters, Natural Recovery, and Human Responses*. Cambridge: Cambridge University Press.

Diamond, J. (2005) *Collapse: How Societies Choose to Fail or Succeed*. New York: Viking.

Foster, J. B., Clark, B. and York, R. (2010) *The Ecological Rift: Capitalism's War on the Earth*. New York: Monthly Review Press.

Freudenburg, W. (1992) Nothing recedes like success? Risk analysis and the organizational amplification of risks. *Risk: Issues in Health & Safety*, 3(1): 1–35.

Freudenburg, W. and Gramling, R. (2011) *Blowout in the Gulf: The BP Oil Spill Disaster and the Future of Energy in America*. Cambridge, MA: MIT Press.

Freudenburg, W., Gramling, R., Laska, S. and Erikson, K. (2009) *Catastrophe in the Making: The Engineering of Katrina and the Disasters of Tomorrow*. Washington, DC: Island Press.

Giddens, A. (2009) *The Politics of Climate Change*. Cambridge: Polity Press.

Hannigan, J. (2012) *Disasters Without Borders*. Cambridge: Polity.

Hernan, R. (2010) *This Borrowed Earth: Lessons from the 15 Worst Environmental Disasters Around the World*. New York: Palgrave Macmillan.
Hughes, J. D. (2009) The energy issue. In T. Homer-Dixon (ed.) *Carbon Shift*. Toronto: Random House, pp. 59–95.
Hughes, T., Linares, C., Dakos, V., van de Leemput, I. and van Nes, E. (2013) Living dangerously on borrowed time during slow, unrecognized regime shifts. *Trends in Ecology & Evolution*, 28(3): 149–155.
IEA International Energy Agency (2012) *World Energy Outlook 2012: Executive Summary*. Paris: OECD/IEA. Available at: www.iea.org/publications/freepublications/publication/English.pdf (accessed 22 November 2012).
IPCC Intergovernmental Panel on Climate Change (2013) *Working Group I Contribution to the IPCC Fifth Assessment Report Climate Change 2013: The Physical Science Basis Summary for Policymakers*. Available at: www.climatechange2013.org/images/uploads/WGIAR5-SPM_Approved27Sep2013.pdf (accessed 28 September 2013).
Jaccard, M. (2009) Peak oil and market feedbacks. In T. Homer-Dixon (ed.) *Carbon Shift*. Toronto: Random House, pp. 96–131.
Jasanoff, S. (2010) A new climate for society. *Theory, Culture & Society*, 27(2–3): 233–253.
Kingdom, J. (1995) *Agendas, Alternatives, and Public Policy*, 2nd edn. New York: HarperCollins.
Kolbert, E. (2014) *The Sixth Extinction: An Unnatural History*. New York: Henry Holt & Co.
Kondratyev, K., Grigoryev, A. and Varotsos, C. (2002) *Environmental Disasters: Anthropogenic and Natural*. London: Springer.
Laffont, J. J. and Tirole, J. (1991) The politics of government decision making: a theory of regulatory capture. *Quarterly Journal of Economics*, 106(4): 1089–1127.
LaPorte, T. (1996) Highly reliable organizations. *Journal of Crisis and Contingency Management*, 4(2): 60–71.
Latin, H. (2012) *Climate Change Policy Failures*. Singapore: World Scientific Publishing.
Levine, M. E. and Forrence, J. L. (1990) Regulatory capture, public interest, and the public agenda. *Journal of Law Economics & Organization*, 6: 167–198.
McNish, J. and Robertson, G. (2013) The dangerous secret of Lac-Megantic's oil. *Globe and Mail*, 3 December: A1, A10–11.
Milne, M. J., Tregidga, H. M. and Walton, S. (2009) Words not actions! The ideological role of sustainable development reporting. *Accounting, Auditing & Accountability Journal*, 22(8): 1211–1257.
Mol, A. P. J.. Sonnenfeld, D. and Spaargaren, G. (2009) *The Ecological Modernisation Reader*. London: Routledge.
Mulvihill, P. and Ali, S. H. (2007) Disaster incubation, cumulative impacts and the urban/ex-urban dynamic. *Environmental Impact Assessment Review*, 27: 343–358.
Murphy, R. (2006) The challenge of disaster reduction'. In A. McCright and T. Clark (eds) *Community and Ecology*. Oxford: Elsevier.
Murphy, R. (2009) *Leadership in Disaster: Learning for a Future with Global Climate Change*. Montreal: McGill-Queen's University Press.
Murphy, R. (2010) Environmental hazards and human disasters. In M. Redclift and G. Woodgate (eds) *The International Handbook of Environmental Sociology*, 2nd edn. Cheltenham: Edgar Elgar.
Murphy, R. (2011) The challenge of anthropogenic climate change for the social sciences. *International Review of Social Research*, 1(3): 167–181.
Murphy, R. and Murphy, M. (2012) The tragedy of the atmospheric commons. *Canadian Review of Sociology*, 49(3): 247–270.
Ottawa Citizen (2005) Anarchy: relief effort called a 'national disgrace'. 2 September.
Patt, A., Schroeter, D., Klein, R. and de la Vega-Leinert, C. (eds) (2009) *Assessing Vulnerability to Global Environmental Change*. London: Earthscan.
Perrow, C. (1984) *Normal Accidents*. Princeton, NJ: Princeton University Press.
Pielke, R. Jr. (2010) *The Climate Fix*. New York: Basic Books.
Prins, G. et al. (2010) *The Hartwell Paper*. LSE/Oxford. Available at http://eprints.lse.ac.uk/27939/1/HartwellPaper_English_version.pdf (accessed 29 October 2013).
Quarantelli, E. (1998) *What Is a Disaster?* London: Routledge.
Rayner, S. (2010) How to eat an elephant: a bottom-up approach to climate policy. *Climate Policy*, 10: 615–621.
Redclift, M. (2005) Sustainable development (1987–2005): an oxymoron comes of age. *Sustainable Development*, 13: 212–227.

Robertson, G. and McNish, J. (2013) A pipeline on wheels. *Globe and Mail*, 2 December: A8, 10.
Rudel, T. K. (2013) *Defensive Environmentalists and the Dynamics of Global Reform*. New York: Cambridge University Press.
Schnaiberg, A. (1980) *The Environment: From Surplus to Scarcity*. New York: Oxford University Press.
Stigler, G. (1971) The theory of economic regulation. *Bell Journal of Economic Management Science*, 2: 3–21.
Strauss, L. (1954) Speech to the National Association of Science Writers, New York, 16 September, *New York Times*, 17 September.
Tenner, E. (1997) *Why Things Bite Back*. New York: Vintage.
Turner, B. and Pidgeon, N. (1978) *Man-Made Disasters*. London: Wykeham.
Vaughan, D. (1996) *The Challenger Launch Decision*. Chicago: University of Chicago Press.
Weick, K., Sutcliffe, K. and Obstfeld, D. (1999) Organizing for high reliability. *Research in Organizational Behavior*, 21.
York, R. (2012) Do alternative energy sources displace fossil fuels? *Nature Climate Change*, 2: 441–443.
York, R., Rosa, E. and Dietz, T. (2003) A rift in modernity. *International Journal of Sociology and Social Policy*, 23: 31–51.

27

WOMEN'S 'RIGHT TO SUSTAINABLE DEVELOPMENT'

Integrating religion and a rights-based approach

Yamini Narayanan

Introduction

The combined importance of the advances in three distinct discourses inform the way this chapter argues for a reconceptualization of women's inclusion and role in sustainable development practice and policy-making. First, it specifically focuses on 'women' rather than 'gender' as a way of thinking about women's roles, inclusion and participation in sustainable development. Critics of the GAD (gender and development) theory, particularly the post-development feminists, have argued for some time that the focus on 'gender' can obscure the specific inequities and inequalities that women continue to suffer, especially in developing nations. The emphasis on 'gender' in the sustainable development discourse can actually perpetuate the exclusion that women of the South continue to face. In 'Dismantling the master's house with the master's tools', Kathleen Staudt (2004: 61–62) notes:

> In the hierarchy among English-speaking critics, most of them excluded from national and international institutions, gender discourse was privileged and pure; the word women was passé. Never mind that gender was obscure terminology from sociology and linguistics, disciplinary narrative and by definition elitist in activist terms. Never mind also that gender did not translate well into many languages . . . Not surprisingly, some of the most virulent bureaucracies, hostile to women and to budgetary redistribution more inclusive of women, adopted the gender terminology.

Second, the human rights approach has been a strong theme in the sustainable development discourse in the past two decades, and particularly since the UN Conference on Environment and Development (the Earth Summit) in 1992. Principally, this has been articulated in terms of the 'right to a healthy environment' (UN-NGLS 2002). This chapter seeks to expand this discussion and frame it specifically in terms of 'women's right to sustainable development'. This includes not only an analysis of women's right to the environment, but also other areas integral to their leadership and expanded agency in sustainable development, such as rights to safety, health and education and right to mobility.

Third, religion has played a definitive role in the international human rights and liberties discourse from the very inception of the Universal Declaration of Human Rights in 1948, and the UN Commission on Human Rights included comprehensive regional representation from all the major world religions. Witte and Green (2013: 15) argue that religion as a category of analysis in human rights has since become ever more increasingly relevant for three reasons: (1) religion continues to play a significant role as a social, cultural political force (in spite of the dark predictions about the demise of religion from the public spaces from the combined effects of modernization and urbanization); (2) the discussion of human rights without religion becomes questionable as religions in fact endorse human rights as a way of discharging religious duties; and (3) religion is important to ensure that the analytical framework remains relevant for non-Western cultures. Witte and Green write (ibid.: 15), 'without religion, human rights become too captive to Western libertarian ideals', thus rendering themselves significantly irrelevant to the realities of non-Western societies.

The chapter brings a religion and human rights perspective to the discussions on women and their participation in sustainable development, and demonstrates that it is a crucial way of understanding the particular ways in which these connections actively restrict – or alternatively provide the opportunity to enable – women's active leadership and role in sustainable development. The discourses on religion and human rights, as well as those on women and religion, have been concerned about the fact that women's liberties, freedom of self-expression, capabilities and access to resources have been particularly compromised by patriarchal and restrictive religious practices. Sharon Bong (2004: 241), the Malaysian activist, argues that while it is far from uncomplicated, religion-based analyses *must* inform the theory, practice and debates on women's rights as it is 'a moral and political imperative to negotiate women's human rights with cultures and religions, in order to complement other strategies for their empowerment'.

The chapter is structured as follows: the next section discusses feminist perspectives on sustainable development. It then provides an overview of the discourse on religion as an obstacle or opportunity to women's fundamental human rights. In the second half of the chapter, it discusses the intersections between religion, women's rights and sustainable development by specifically focusing on issues that starkly illustrate the need for a religion-based human rights approach to women's participation in sustainable development: (1) the right to a clean environment and environmental resources; (2) the right to safety and security; and (3) the right to health and education.

Women and sustainable development

Ideas about women and development are among the weakest links in the sustainable development discourse. This is despite the extensive feminist scholarship that has critically interrogated the concept of 'development'. In the early twentieth century, Charlotte Perkins Gilman pioneered the concept of 'eco-communities' in her ([1915] 2007) book *Herland*, which envisioned a utopian community in a geographical space blessed with few natural resources, but which lived by principles and practices such as equity, recycling, clean technology, cooperation, citizen participation and community lifestyles. Ester Boserup's path-breaking work on *Women's Role in Economic Development* ([1970] 2007) noted that development based on the Western model was exploitative of women, and that capitalism was inherently patriarchal. This led to demands that development be planned in a gender-sensitive manner, such that women's productive as well as reproductive roles were recognized.[1] Subsequent research has repeatedly urged the crucial need to consider women's rights at the centre of development, in both defining the problem, as well as in articulating solutions (Anand 1992; Shiva 1993).[2]

Despite this long-standing complaint from feminist development planners that the gender perspective be centrally incorporated into development, the sustainability model continues, in general, to ignore this concern. The Brundtland Report's definition of sustainable development has been criticized because it does not give specific attention to the gender perspective (Shiva 1993). Braidotti et al. (1994) point out for instance, that the two issues of environmental degradation and population explosion, identified by the Brandt Report (ICIDI 1980) as the greatest sustainability challenges in the coming decades, both involve women centrally.[3] This is of particular concern for the developing world because as Shiva (1993) notes, agriculture is possibly the single most critical means of ensuring a livelihood for the majority of the women from these countries, where most of the farmers are women. However, even mainstream sustainability arguments persist in viewing women as an 'add-on' to the overall sustainability problem (Braidotti et al. 1994). In 1994, Cairo hosted the International Conference on Population and Development. Health issues, particularly reproduction, were connected to development, as part of the continued focus on demography. In more recent times, the Millennium Development Goals 2000 included an agenda to 'promote gender equality and empower women' (World Bank 2004). The specific aims of this goal include a commitment to 'eliminate gender disparity in primary and secondary education, preferably by 2005, and to all levels of education no later than 2015' (World Bank 2004).

Mainstreaming women in sustainable development continues to be a massive political challenge. The Rio+20 UN Conference on Environment and Development in June 2012 was criticized for missing a 'historic opportunity to affirm the critical link between investing in women and achieving sustainability goals' (Worldwatch Institute 2012). The events of 9/11 and the subsequent 'War on Terror' have brought back religion into public policy debate and foregrounded religion as a 'development' as well as a 'foreign policy' issue. The nexus between women, (mal-) development and religion is a particularly strong narrative in the discussions on development. The UN Economic Commission for Europe (UNECE 2012) states that the notion of gender justice must underpin gender-sensitive sustainable development concepts and approaches. A number of issues challenge gender equity and justice, such as unequal access to income, natural resources, good health and education.

There is increasing interest in providing funding to faith-based NGOs (FBOs), even leading to concerns that such FBOs may be receiving preferential treatment (Tomalin 2012). Worryingly, it is also assumed that FBOs that engage with feminist critiques are well equipped to mitigate any of the sexist approaches of development and religion, and enable the most equitable outcomes for women from both concepts and practices. Tadros (2011: 9) expresses concern about the unquestioned notion that 'a feminist re-engagement with religious texts within a religious framework is a panacea for altering gender bias in laws, policies and practices'. These abilities may in fact be overestimated when the reactions of many Muslim women are considered, who regard such feminist interpretations of their faith with suspicion and voluntarily choose to continue with their traditional practices (Tomalin 2013).

In analysing the nexus between women and development, religion is typically viewed in three ways (Balchin 2003): first, as an 'obstacle' to gender justice and thus good development. Viewing religion as a development evil allows international development and political policy to pretend that 'local men' and 'local culture' are responsible for local women's subjugated status, thus negating the substantial role that unfair global restructuring policies may have on the low status of local men *and* women (Balchin 2003). The second approach is to treat religion as an 'issue', which while subtly different from being regarded as a 'problem' is itself a problem for its tendency to essentialize or homogenize an understanding of women's lives based on universal understanding of their shared religion. Third, religion may be viewed in an instrumentalist manner as a 'solution' to identified development issues. This latter dimension has led to the emergence of notions like 'Islamic feminism', for instance, a sanitized view of Islam as rich in its potential for women's empowerment which has been viewed with some alarm by critics like Mojab (2001) for its potential to divide the global feminist movement on the basis of religion, and for ignoring the diversity of realities within the lives of Islamic women.

At the heart of the debate on the nexus between religion, women and development is the concern over religiously-sanctioned violation of human rights, and specifically women's rights. In the next section, I discuss the need for sustainable development's critical engagement with religion that rejects polarized views of religion purely as evil or an opportunity for development.

Women's human rights and religion

In 1993, 45 years after the Universal Declaration of Human Rights, the United Nations World Conference on Human Rights in Vienna found it necessary to explicitly explain that women's rights indeed were also human rights. Incredibly, it appeared that the ambit of human rights and equality was understood to automatically refer only to men. African feminist theologian Oduyoye observed (1995: 4–5):

> The concept of women's rights has been generated by the contemporary articulation of women's experience that suggests that human rights have tended to mean men's rights . . . women in the past decade or so have had to insist that human rights are women's as well.

Religion is generally treated as one of the significant reasons for women's inequality for its perceived sanction of the compromise or even violation of their fundamental human rights (King and Beattie 2005). Religious institutions and structures are thought to be fundamentally patriarchal in privileging male interests and status; King (2005: 3298) writes, 'Religious beliefs, thoughts, and practices are not only profoundly patriarchal but often also thoroughly *androcentric*, that is to say predominantly, if not exclusively, shaped by male perspectives and experiences.' Seclusion of women and their physical, psychological and social repression continue to be common in many orthodox Hindu, Muslim and Christian communities (Ahmed 2002). The various fundamentalist movements, most recently, the Taliban regime, the spread of Islamic terrorism or the rise of Hindu nationalism, have arguably marginalized women in several important ways, and ignored the vibrant and composite relationship that women and religion share. Robinson (1999: 197) puts forth some pertinent questions:

> Does this imply that religion is inevitably and irredeemably associated with the oppression of women and hence that it is imperative to raise women's consciousness about the evils of religion? Or does this imply that religion has been abused by being implicated in the oppression of women and hence that it is imperative to draw to women's attention the true meaning of religion?

Ahmed (2002: 8) writes that to be convinced of the validity of religion in circumstances of extreme subjugation is 'an act of courage'. However, she clarifies, 'it is courage gained through a creative engagement with religion in which faith and different types of sacred and secular knowledge reinforce each other' (ibid.: 8). Ahmed (ibid.: 81) calls extremist interpretations of both religious and secular principles a 'hypermasculine approach to the construction of both knowledge and meaning regarding self and the other'. She explains that secularism places humans at the forefront, trusting that through good will and reason, people will find a way to live ethically. However, she points out, as demonstrated by the Holocaust, communism, and Bosnia, men have proved that they are 'as ready to kill in God's *absence* as they are in His name' (ibid.: 81). Extremism is not an offspring of religion, she concludes, but is a deeper psychological problem. Balchin notes (2003: 40) that adopting a rigid and essentialist view of the relationship between women and religion may also ironically compromise modernity, and result in 'the narrowing of spaces for secular alternatives (preferred even by many believers)'.

Development theory and policy have only recently begun to engage in some measure with religion, but even so, have generally avoided considering religion in articulating gender-sensitive development planning. I suggest, however, that the question of religion's relevance or irrelevance itself is not a valid one – development's approach to religion is more accurately pitched around critical *engagement* with religion. Where religion is clearly complicit in women's subordination, active consideration of the role of religion is vital to its solution. Religion can also have a major role in expanding women's capabilities and agency (Nussbaum 2000), providing a space for drawing out women's voices (Bradley 2010) and thus their access to their fundamental rights. Women may also seek out religion because of its strategic potential for greater personal empowerment. For instance, the majority of the converts to Pentecostalism sweeping through Africa are women, who are attracted by the promise of economic power and wealth accumulation that Pentecostalism endorses (Spinks 2003). Inter-generational and intra-generational equity, one of the main tenets of sustainable development, which should also include gender equity, can be more easily achieved through a considered engagement with religion, for as Carroll (1983: 3) noted as early as three decades ago:

> [P]olicy makers have been reluctant to confront the religious powerful and their supporters for fear of a backlash against their developmental efforts or to disturb the religious beliefs of the masses for fear of causing a revolt. Yet the failure to recognize, research, and discuss the prevalence of religion and its impact on people's lives very often leads to the precise problems that development experts seek to avoid.

Ahmed believes (2002: 70–71) that the problem is *not* that religions in general are prejudiced against women. The issue is the conceptual perspective about gender and religion, which she says, 'is that of the Western intellectual tradition's "dead white male", the legacy of Freud and Marx', who argued that those who believe don't think, and that those who think don't believe. She believes that their ideas have caused some of people's most elemental assumptions about women and religion to be distorted, thus thwarting a realistic understanding of both religion and women's spirituality. No matter where one is located geographically, the problem has become a global phenomenon, of 'psychological *monotheism*, which makes a monolith of any religion . . . and this is an overwhelmingly literal and masculine way of looking at issues' (Ahmed 2002: 81).

Such an 'overwhelmingly literal and masculine' approach was exemplified in France's controversial legislation in 2004 to ban all personal symbols of religious affiliation in the public space. This was particularly seen as a move to specifically target Muslim women and their headscarf and was decried for its violation of religious freedom and freedom to practise religion without oppression. French public debate implicitly assumed that Muslim girls and women wearing the headscarf had no choice in the matter, negating the possibility that while some degree of compulsion may be assumed to exist, it was also indeed very likely that many Islamic women wore the scarf out of their own choice. Sunder (2013: 282) writes, '[i]ncreasingly, women in the modern world reject this binary – *religious liberty versus gender equality* – as a false and unacceptable choice in the twenty-first century'. These reformers – New Enlightenment reformers, as Sunder calls them – are pursuing the novel right to *enjoy* religious freedom as a fundamental liberty on its own and significantly, from *within* the religious communities to which they belong (ibid.). Maloutas (2006) had argued in her feminist critique of democracies that women's *unobvious* inequalities in democratic societies stem from cultural and religious roots which cannot be addressed by secularist legislation alone; they must be considered at a deeper level of societal reform from within the religio-cultural context of those communities. Thus, in order to enjoy freedom of religion, women need to 'be guaranteed freedom from discrimination within these communities' (Sunder 2013: 283). This will also enable women's leadership and capabilities to flourish in a moral and ethical framework that meets their needs from 'private' religion and its fulfilments, as well as allow them a meaningful role through religion as 'agents' in development and public policy.

Religion: informing women's 'right to sustainable development'

The religious dimensions of women's right to sustainable development is further elaborated in discussions specifically on a range of indicators integral to sustainable development such as women's rights to a healthy environment, safety and security, health and education (UN-Habitat 2013).

Right to environment

The Worldwatch Institute (2012) identified certain areas of relevance to the links between women and environmental sustainability, and the achievement of global sustainable development. Each of these issues is also intimately interconnected with religion. The first of these is women's reproductive health and women's reproductive rights, which may ostensibly decrease carbon emissions by up to 14 per cent. Orthodox religious values have been held as particularly responsible for withholding women's right to contraception and agency as well as fostering a strong culture of son preference. The second is environmental conservation, for nearly 80 per cent of African women and 50 per cent of Asian women depend directly upon the natural ecology for their livelihood. Though it would be misleading to assume that all women are interested in ecological protection or utilize religious resources to do so, the role of poor women's capacity for environmental stewardship through religious environmentalism has been well established (Shiva 1993), highlighted in illustrative movements in India, for instance, such as the Chipko Movement in Uttar Pradesh and the Narmada Bachao Andolan. The underlying and unstated concern behind both these issues is one of patriarchy's dominion over women's lives, typically seen to be privileged by religion.

Seen through the eyes of ecofeminists, the analysis of religion should be at the centre of any approach seeking to fully expand women's right to the environment and by extension and association, their rights to their own bodies. Feminist inquiry, especially ecofeminism, has been prominent among those seeking to explore philosophical, cultural and religious frameworks to link environmental issues to problems of justice, particularly social justice (Jenkins and Chapple 2011). Ecofeminism and ecophilosophy have sought to place women at the centre of these discourses in explaining their vulnerability to environmental and socio-political problems. Ecofeminists have been particularly instrumental in illustrating how the patriarchal ideology and 'logic of domination' (Warren 1994: 2) and control are responsible for both strands of problems, thus requiring a unified response. Reuther (2005) criticizes science for its innate violent, even patriarchal, ideology in treating nature as a malleable object. She notes that religions have a unified world-view which is not splintered by multiple and distinct responses to different problems; this thus offers the scope for a critical evaluation of responses to social, environmental and gendered developmental problems in an integrated way.

Right to safety

One of religion's worst offences against women has been its perceived sanction to inflict a range of violence against women (VAW) from physical battering and rape, to emotional and psychological abuse. The Women's International Network (WIN News 1998) argues that organized religions are guilty of explicitly sanctioning abuse of women; they quote from the *Rules of Marriage*, a fifteenth-century Catholic text that says: 'Scold your wife sharply, bully and terrify her', and further describes wife beating as a noble act that will bring spiritual merit to husband and wife. Surah 4.34, in the Islamic context, likewise describes the will of Allah approving wife-beating, which the Taliban offered as a rationale for their gross mistreatment of women and human rights abuse (WIN News 1998). Statistics forewarn of an escalating trend of VAW; the UN-Habitat (2009: 1) made the grim observation that:

> women aged between 15–44 are more at risk from rape and domestic violence than from cancer, motor accidents, and war and malaria. It is estimated that one in five women globally will become a victim of rape or attempted rape in her lifetime.

I have argued that violence against women (VAW) and thus *any* violations of women's right to safety and good health, must be explicitly framed and treated as a problem of sustainable development because of its capacity to compromise intra-generational and inter-generational equity, one of the fundamental tenets of sustainable development (Narayanan 2012). The Convention to Eliminate All Forms of Discrimination against Women (CEDW) recognized that 'violence against women is an obstacle to equality, development and peace and that the opportunities for women to attain legal, social economic and political equality are constantly being limited by violence' (UMP 2000). VAW can compromise sustainability in all areas of development; in the context of cities, for instance, the UN-HABITAT (2007) noted that if women consider the space safe, then it is safe for everyone, since women have the highest fear of violence in urban areas as the most vulnerable group. According to the Beijing Platform for Action, adopted at the Fourth United Nations World Conference on Women in 1995:

> Violence against women is an obstacle to the achievement of the objectives of equality, development and peace. Violence against women both violates and impairs or nullifies the enjoyment by women of their human rights and fundamental freedoms. The long-standing failure to protect and promote those rights and freedoms in the case of violence against women is a matter of concern to all States and should be addressed.
>
> *(paragraph 112)*

Cultural analyses of VAW often tend to view VAW as 'cultural' rather than simply as a violent act, and those seeking a religious explanation may tend to focus on essentialist interpretations of religion (Rew 2011). Yet others tend to seek solutions within religion; for instance, Bradley (2010) suggests that religious rituals and women-only spaces of religiosity can afford women the space and emotional and intellectual praxis that they need to respond to the violence that they may be subjected to within a patriarchal family system. She argues that religious organizations, places of worship such as temples and other sacred spaces that are regulated by an institution can offer women the private space for revitalization, or to 'formulate her response to violence', away from the scrutiny and judgement of her male relatives (ibid.: 362). However, it is not the case 'that religious institutions as currently structured provide a pathway for the amelioration of women's unequal status' (Seguino 2011: 1317); indeed, it is likely that the drawbacks to gender equity and equality are greater through the interventions of religious organizations than any benefits to women these interventions offer. While sustainable development policy must engage with religion, it needs to tread carefully while engaging with any of these views for they can, ironically, also result in more restricted and terrorized spaces for women (Rew 2011) and a greater violation of their fundamental rights to safety, and lack of fear and vulnerability.

Right to health and education

Access to good health and education is among the key indicators of a high quality of life for women (UN-Habitat 2013) and overall sustainable development, and constitutes their fundamental human rights. Investing in women's education is also one of the most important tasks for national development and economic growth. The Worldwatch Institute (2012) observes that the links between women and sustainable development are particularly strong in the areas of education and economic empowerment, in which NGOs and microfinance organizations are greatly involved. Religion has also been involved extensively in a range of women's health-related issues, especially the lack of contraception which compromises their reproductive rights and heightens their exposure to HIV/AIDS (Lewis 2006). In Mexico, for instance, gender equality rests crucially on the interface between religion and politics, and further, 'religion and gender equality intersect precisely on the issue of women's sexuality and reproductive rights' (Amuchastegui et al. 2010: 990). Studies have explored for some time women's education, in particular sectarian and religious institutions and the corresponding size of their families and number of pregnancies (Westoff and Potvin 1966). Of particular interest has been the differential impact on women's health and education that different religions may have. Do specific religions empower women more? Are certain religions more guilty of abusing women's rights?

Njoh and Akiwumi (2012: 1) note that Christianity, for instance, can be seen to have a positive correlation with each of the four targets of the Millennium Development Goals (MDGs), under the third MDG related to women's empowerment, namely, raising the percentage of school-aged girls in school; female adult literacy rates; female share of non-agricultural employment; and female representation in government. They note that higher levels of affiliation to the Christian faith can correspond to higher levels of success in their achievement while Islam, on the other hand, can be argued to have an 'inverse relationship' with all four of the targets under Goal 3. They suggest (2012: 6) that the policy of gender-based social exclusion practised by Islam (even under the guise of 'benevolent sexism' in preventing women from joining the military, for example) may produce 'gender-based power differentials' that can consequently have implications for development. Kuran (1997) likewise has noted that Muslims in poor countries constitute the largest proportion of the demography, and have one of the highest rates of illiteracy. Norton and Tomal (2009) also found a strongly negative co-relation between women's education and adherents of the Islamic and Hindu faith, particularly of the Orthodox denominations.

However, while this does not fully explain Islam's (or any other religion's) correlation with women's retrogressive status in society, the complexity of trying to delineate the impact of one religion in isolation on women's development is a somewhat fraught task. In the perception of

Islam's role in seemingly diminishing women, Christianity had some part to play. Africans were accepted into mission schools only if they had converted to Christianity (Njoh and Akiwumi 2012). Consequently, the rates of educated Christians, whose instruction corresponded with education as understood by colonialism and thereafter by development indicators appeared higher than rates of educated Muslims. Njoh and Akiwumi conclude that, overall, any attempts to implement the MDGs in Africa must consider the influence of the three dominant religious forces – indigenous African religion, Christianity and Islam – in determining the role and status of women in Africa. Essentially, this points to the need to enable women's agency and complete access to their rights to health and education in order to be participants in as well as recipients of the benefits of sustainable development.

Conclusion

The nexus between religion and development is no longer neglected. However, there is urgent need for the sustainable development meta-narrative which arguably has considerable political force to take religion seriously as an analytical category, particularly in strategizing women-inclusive development. Obstacles to women's full participation in development in effect constitute and are also a result of their compromised human rights. Women's complete 'right to sustainable development' cannot be achieved without engaging with religion in rethinking a range of women's rights, including the right to a healthy ecology and environmental resources, safety and security, health and education, and mobility and space.

Such an approach places sustainable development practice and policy in a very precarious position of engaging with religion without 'taking over' or 'managing' religion. These approaches are bound to have reactionary or fundamentalist outcomes from religion, which may ironically intensify the very retrogressive characteristics of religion for women that sustainable development seeks to redress. The challenge for gender-sensitive sustainable development is to retain a flexibility, commitment to research and genuine understanding of religion wherein the productive partnerships between women, religion and sustainable development can be constantly maintained by planning being aware of the rituals/practices/values and political context that may enable a mutually autonomous and yet working partnership. Carroll (1983: 4) suggests, 'Policy makers need to distinguish between mere religious sanctions (termed here religiosity) and the fundamental visionary tenets or philosophy of religion.'

In this way, she argues, the fundamental principles of religion are retained and in fact actively mainstreamed into society *via* sustainable development policy, but at the same time, the outdated interpretations that keep women and other minority groups in submissive positions are deconstructed and invalidated. In partnership with sustainable development policy, the reform capacity of each religion would be foregrounded, rather than their chauvinistic aspects. This would be a significant step in achieving the 'right to sustainable development' for women.

Acknowledgements

This chapter uses some material previously pubished in my doctoral thesis, and I gratefully acknowledge Professor Bev Thiele and Doctor lan Barns for their intellectual mentoring.

Notes

1 However, the global women's movement was neither united nor necessarily just in representing the cause of women worldwide. Feminists differed sharply in their views on the modernization theory, which depicted traditional societies as authoritarian, conservative and male-dominated, and modern communities as democratic and egalitarian (Kishwar 1999). Third World feminists have since pointed out that this distorts and negates the reality of the lives and achievements of their women (ibid.).

2 However, in the 1960s, international development continued to view women as beneficiaries of development and was focused mostly on issues like population policies, family planning and literacy programmes, particularly in developing countries (Anand 1992). Over the next couple of decades, Anand notes, women increasingly came to the realization that they needed to organize, but separately – their issues merited acknowledgement and attention in their own right – and the women's movement started to address development from their own perspectives. Boserup's work was important in this area.

3 Bitter debates have arisen between the feminists of the South and the North, because the Northern feminists tend to squarely place the responsibility of population containment on the women of the South and see 'sufficient justification for stringent population control measures directed mainly at women in the South' (Braidotti et al. 1994: 89).

References

Ahmed, D. (2002) The last frontier. In D. Ahmed (ed.) *Gendering the Spirit: Women, Religion and the Postcolonial Response*. London: Zed Books.

Amuchastegui, A., Guadalupe Cruz, E. A. and Consuelo, M. M. (2010) Politics, religion and gender equality in contemporary Mexico: women's sexuality and reproductive rights in a contested secular state. *Third World Quarterly*, 31(6): 989–1005.

Anand, A. (ed.) (1992) *The Power to Change: Women in the Third World Redefine Their Development*. New Delhi: Women's Feature Service, Kali for Women.

Balchin, C. (2003) With her feet on the ground: women, religion and development in Muslim communities. *Development*, 46(4): 39–49.

Bong, S. A. (2004) An Asian postcolonial and feminist methodology: ethics as a recognition of limits. In U. King and T. Beattie (eds) *Religion, Gender and Diversity: Cross-Cultural Perspectives*. London: Routledge, pp. 238–249.

Boserup, E. ([1970] 2007) *Women's Role in Economic Development*. London: Earthscan.

Bradley, T. (2010) Religion as a bridge between theory and practice in work on violence against women in Rajasthan. *Journal of Gender Studies*, 19(4): 361–375.

Braidotti, R., Charkiewicz, E., Hausler S. and Wieringa, S. (1994) *Women, the Environment and Sustainable Development: Towards a Theoretical Synthesis*. London, New Jersey and Santa Domingo: Zed Books in association with INSTRAW.

Carroll, Foster, T. (1983) *Women, Religion, and Development in the Third World*. New York: Praeger Publishers.

Gilman, C. P. ([1915] 2007) *Herland*. Bibliobazaar.

ICIDI (The Independent Commission on International Development Issues) (1980) *North-South: A Programme for Survival* (The Brandt Report).

Jenkins, W. and Key Chapple, C. (2011) Religion and environment. *Annual Review of Environment and Resources*, 36: 441–463.

King, U. (2005) Gender and religion: an overview. In L. Jones (ed.) *Encyclopedia of Religion*, vol. 5, 2nd edn. Detroit: Macmillan, pp. 3296–3310.

King, U. and Beattie, T. (eds) (2005) *Gender, Religion, and Diversity: Cross-Cultural Perspectives*. London: Continuum.

Kishwar, M. P. (1999) *Off the Beaten Track: Rethinking Gender Justice for Indian Women*. New Delhi: Oxford University Press.

Kuran, T. (1997) Islam and underdevelopment: an old puzzle revisited. *Journal of Institutional and Theoretical Economics*, 153: 41–71.

Lewis, S. (2006) *Race Against Time: Searching for Hope in AIDS-Ravaged Africa*. Melbourne: Text Publishing.

Maloutas, M. P. (2006) *The Gender of Democracy: Citizenship and Gendered Subjectivity*. New York: Routledge.

Mojab, S. (2001) The politics of theorizing Islamic feminism: implications for international feminist movements. *Dossier*, 23/24.

Narayanan, Y. (2012) Violence against women in Delhi: a sustainability problematic. *Journal of South Asian Development*, 7(1): 1–22.

Narayanan, Y. (forthcoming) *Hinduism, Heritage and the Sustainable City: Religion and Urbanisation in Jaipur*. London: Routledge.

Njoh, A. J. and Fenda Akiwumi, A. (2012) The impact of religion on women empowerment as a millennium development goal in Africa. *Social Indicators Research*, 107(1): 1–18.

Norton, S. W. and Tomal, A. (2009) Religion and female educational attainment. *Journal of Money, Credit and Banking*, 41(5): 961–988.

Nussbaum, M. C. (2000) *Women and Human Development: The Capabilities Approach*. Cambridge: Cambridge University Press.

Oduyoye, M. A. (1995) *Daughters of Anowa: African Women and Patriarchy*. Maryknoll, NY: Orbis Books.

Reuther, R. R. (2005) *Integrating Ecofeminism, Globalization, and World Religions*. Lanham, MD: Rowman and Littlefield.

Rew, M. (2011) Religion and development I: Anthropology, Islam, transnationalism and emerging analyses of violence against women. *Progress in Development Studies*, 11(1): 69–76.

Robinson, C. (1999) *Tradition and Liberation: The Hindu Tradition in the Indian Women's Movement*. Surrey: Curzon Press.

Seguino, S. (2011) Help or hindrance? Religion's impact on gender inequality in attitudes and outcomes. *World Development*, 39(8): 1308–1321.

Shiva, V. (1993) The impoverishment of the environment: women and children last. In M. Mies and V. Shiva (eds) *Ecofeminism*. Halifax, NS: Fernwood Publications.

Spinks, C. (2003) Panacea or painkiller?: The impact of Pentacostal Christianity on women in Africa. *Critical Half: Annual Journal of Women for Women International*, 1(1): 20–25.

Staudt, K. (2004) Dismantling the master's house with the master's tools. In K. Saunders (ed.) *Feminist Post-Development Thought: Rethinking Modernity, Post-Colonialism and Representation*. London: Zed Books, pp. 57–68.

Sunder, M. (2013) Keeping faith: reconciling women's human rights and religion. In J. Witte, Jr and C. Green (eds) *Religion and Human Rights: An Introduction*. Oxford: Oxford University Press.

Tadros, M. (2011) Introduction: gender, rights and religion at the crossroads. *IDS Bulletin*, 42(1): 1–9.

Tomalin, E. (2012) Thinking about faith-based organisations in development: where have we got to and what next? *Development in Practice*, 22(5–6): 689–703.

Tomalin, E. (2013) Gender, religion and development. In M. Clarke (ed.) *Handbook of Research on Development and Religion*. Cheltenham: Edward Elgar, pp. 183–200.

UMP, Urban Management Program (2000) Violence against women in urban areas. Working Series Paper 17. Available at: www.unhabitat.org/downloads/docs/1900_46700_ViolAgWomUrbnpm_pt2EN.pdf (accessed 15 April 2013).

UNECE (2012) Empowering women for sustainable development. Available at: www.unece.org/fileadmin/DAM/Gender/publication/UNECE_Discussion_Paper_2012.1.pdf (accessed 4 December 2013).

UN-Habitat (2007) Women's safety audits for a safer urban design. Available at: www.unhabitat.org/downloads/docs/5544_32059_WSA%20Centrum%20report.pdf (accessed 15 April 2013).

UN-Habitat (2009) *The Global Assessment on Women's Safety*. Available at: www.unhabitat.org/downloads/docs/7380_832_AssesmentFinal.pdf (accessed 15 April 2013).

UN-Habitat (2013) *State of Women in Cities 2012–2013: Gender and the Prosperity of Cities*. Available at: www.unhabitat.org/pmss/listItemDetails.aspx?publicationID=3457 (accessed 26 November 2013).

UN-NGLS (2002) Human rights approaches to sustainable development. Available at: www.un-ngls.org/orf/pdf/ru90hrsd.pdf (accessed 1 December 2013).

Warren, K. (1994) *Ecological Ecofeminism*. New York: Routledge.

Westoff, C. F. and Raymond Potvin, H. (1966) Higher education, religion and women's family-size orientations. *American Sociological Review*, 32(4): 489–496.

WIN News (1998) Women and violence: how organized religions support violence against women. *WIN News*, 24(1): 45.

Witte, J, Jr. and Green, C. (2013) Introduction. In J. Witte Jr and C. Green (eds) *Religion and Human Rights: An Introduction*. Oxford: Oxford University Press, pp. 3–26.

World Bank (2004) *Millennium Development Goals*. Available at: www.worldbank.org/mdgs/ (accessed 17 December 2013).

Worldwatch Institute (2012) The critical role of women in sustainable development. Available at: www.worldwatch.org/critical-role-women-sustainable-development (accessed 4 December 2013).

28

FROM SUSTAINABLE DEVELOPMENT TO GOVERNANCE FOR SUSTAINABILITY

Ashwina Mahanti and David Manuel-Navarrete

Introduction

Sustainability in its myriad forms is being increasingly framed as a governance challenge (Adger and Jordan 2009; Mason 2011). However, the concrete relationship between governing processes and sustainability outcomes remains obscure despite more than three decades of debate and academic exploration. This might partly be due to the fact that both governance and sustainability are 'moving targets' in the sense that globalization is constantly reshaping the contexts within which both new sustainability challenges, and novel governance configurations emerge. Nevertheless, there is little doubt that novel governance arrangements, and the theories formulated to explain them, have contributed to framing sustainability agendas and actions in the last decades. At the same time, the notion of sustainability has strongly influenced international efforts towards building governance systems that can tackle emerging global challenges such as climate change or financial instability. A recent example is the United Nations Environment Program's (UNEP) Finance Initiative, which is guided by principles of sustainable insurance, sustainable finance, and banking sustainability.

Academia is rising to the challenge of formulating explicit theories and approaches for effective 'governance for sustainability' in the context of an increasingly globalized planet (Kemp et al. 2005; Jordan 2008). In this chapter we propose to reconcile two distinctive perspectives, social-political and social-ecological, which have traditionally framed, in contrasting but complementary ways, the debates about the governance challenges of sustainable development and sustainability. This chapter is not a compendium of governance approaches, but rather is a synthesis of two overarching perspectives on the link between sustainability and governance.

Governance and sustainable development both emerged as popular terms in the late 1980s. Sustainable development has been since its inception a normative concept aimed at achieving principles of inter- and intra-generational equity, making it fundamentally an ethical and political question of distribution. The recognition of mutually reinforcing dynamics between loss of ecological integrity, rising inequalities, and a world paradoxically characterized by increasing wealth and consumption consolidated the idea that the world was on an unsustainable trajectory. Thus, sustainable development emerged as an attempt to address ecological degradation, justice, and human development in a context of sustained economic prosperity (Kemp et al. 2005).

Sustainable development was rapidly adopted by international organizations and governments and emerged as a term with broad public appeal, but little public or private action. Its condition as an all-encompassing concept, though it might have contributed to render the concept largely inconsequential in terms of actual applications, enabled energetic and constructive discussions about future visions, desirable societal goals, and inter-generational justice (Jordan 2008). Nevertheless, while the universal appeal of the normative ideals central to sustainable development encourages verbal agreements, declarations and charters; it is the translation of these concepts into action that is fraught with controversy. In any case, governance is playing a central role in discussions about making sustainable development an actionable concept (Loorbach 2007).

After decades of sluggish implementation, pundits are concluding that in practice sustainable development might have just been a means of subordinating nature and society to economic growth (Redclift and Woodgate 2013). Furthermore, global financial crises are increasingly seen as systemic threats to even purely economic sustainability and new labels such as green economy or green growth are emerging as alternatives that provide less ambitious but more coherent goals (Urhammer and Røpke 2013). As a result, the very notion of sustainable development appears to be in crisis, a situation worsened by the meager performance of the Rio+20 'landmark' conference. In fact, practitioners have started to re-think what the concept really means in a post-Rio+20 world and to craft new, more engaging narratives to calls for more radical reforms in global environmental governance (Halle et al. 2013).

While the idea of sustainable development and the associated governance institutions might be at a crossroads, the notion of 'sustainability' is growing in popularity as a principle that can guide transitions in the ways in which corporations, educational institutions, and other organizations currently operate (Nidumolu et al. 2009). In this context, 'sustainability governance' becomes a 'metagovernance for sustainable development' associated with the steering of companies and other organizations towards transitions that might tip the system over into larger societal transformations (In't Veld 2011: 282).

An important question associated with the emergence of 'sustainability', which could arguably be seen as an alternative to failed sustainable development global governance institutions, is to what extent non-governmental institutions will be interested, have the capacity, and might end up proving to be more effective in addressing equity, social justice, and human–environment relations. These are legitimate concerns considering the common critique that much of the sustainable development debate since the 1990s has been influenced (even hijacked) by neo-liberal forces, evident, for instance, in the attempts to translate environmental choices into market preferences (Redclift 2005). Accordingly, if 'sustainable development' evolved from being an environmental and social movement addressing fundamental needs and rights of people and the environment to becoming a conversation on how to increase the role of markets and private sector, then should not we see current 'sustainability' agendas as the culmination of this process of cooption?

A fundamental difference between sustainable development and sustainability is that each has emerged in a different global governance context. 'Sustainability' emerged more recently in a context characterized by climate change consensus, the concatenation of systemic financial and economic crises affecting almost every single nation on Earth, accelerating socio-economic changes, and the global hegemony of neo-liberal discourse (Swyngedouw 2010). The acknowledgment of this particular contextual situation should inform the inquiry on whether sustainability might be better poised to deliver on social and environmental objectives, and whether sustainability governance, as defined above, is likely to deliver better outcomes.

This chapter explores these questions and argues that the main advantage brought about by sustainability governance is its emphasis on deliberate social transitions and transformations, and that this positively transcends the old paradigm of sustainable development focused on balancing out environmental, economic and social spheres. This transformational focus does not guarantee the formulation and effective implementation of radically new alternatives (Redclift 2005). However, we argue that it provides an opportunity to integrate the two dominant perspectives on governance that have informed the sustainability debate. The chapter provides insights on how the 'balancing out' and better combination of these two perspectives can enable more effective and functional governance systems for sustainability.

Sustainability and governance

The notion of governance was a natural fit to the sustainable development debate because both concepts are founded on the balancing out of their constituent dimensions: private sector, government and civil society, in the case of governance, and environmental, social and economic spheres, in the case of sustainable development. Thus, incorporating governance into sustainable development research, and vice versa, was eased by the fact that they are homologous conceptual constructs. The combination gave rise to the concept of 'governance for sustainable development', which was originally framed as a goal-oriented activity involving the deliberate adjustment of governance practices in order to promote sustainable outcomes (Meadowcroft 1997). However, the recognition that sustainable development is not an end state, but a social process (Redclift 2002), has influenced the progressive re-signification of this conceptual combination as the dynamic process of transforming the structures that regulate socio-ecological interactions (Meadowcroft et al. 2005). The emphasis on process is central in emerging understandings of sustainability as a design principle for socio-ecological transformation, versus just a new approach to 'development' (Leach et al. 2010). The terms sustainability governance, pathways for sustainability or transgovernance and sustainability transitions are now commonly used to stress socio-ecological transformation while emphasizing the anticipatory, reflexive and political dimensions of sustainability. According to In't Veld (2011: 288), sustainability governance brings about a new approach to governance that goes:

> beyond disciplinary scientific research, towards more transdisciplinarity; beyond borders formed by states and other institutions, towards trans-border approaches; beyond conventional means to measuring progress, towards new and more interactive measuring methods; beyond linear forms of innovation, towards open innovation; beyond cultural integration or assimilation, towards looking for compatibility.

This chapter explores the genesis and conceptual foundations of sustainability governance and the new discipline of sustainability science, which we broadly conceive as an emerging design principle for governing socio-ecological transitions in the context of our increasingly globalized world. We identify two broad perspectives to governance in the literature that converge into the notion of 'governance for sustainability'. These two perspectives have respectively evolved from social sciences, and socio-ecological research applications of governance.

Governance perspectives

Meadowcroft summarizes that, in order to govern effectively, one needs: clear goals, a good understanding of relevant causal relationships, and the power to influence outcomes. In the context of sustainability, each of these three requirements appears challenging. Goals are vague and contested, we are plagued by uncertainties and power is distributed among many actors and across many subsystems. We do not fully understand complex, evolving, and interlinked natural and social systems, and power is so broadly dispersed that policy-makers lack the ability to make things happen (Meadowcroft 2007). In light of this assessment, the question of how sustainable development and sustainability science scholars have addressed these governance challenges is vital to answer. While some authors believe that these challenges have plagued governance in any realm and are not new to sustainability, only more politically contested; others posit that the globalized world we live in is a complex inter-linked system and governing a complex system requires a governance revolution. Different disciplines have both framed these challenges differently and built on different perspectives to address governance for sustainability.

The first perspective, which we call social-political, addresses primarily the third challenge of distributed power and authority. Globalization is described as the process of the reconfiguration of power structures that have challenged the authority of governments and introduced new actors into novel governance architectures. This body of literature starts with a discussion on governance and power and evolves to address the question of what this redistribution of power means for sustainability governance. Sustainability in this conversation is regarded as both a new agenda and a novel set of ideals for inclusive governance (ibid.).

The second perspective, which we call socio-ecological, is often adopted by complex systems thinking and resilience scholars, and has evolved considerably in these three decades. As we grow dangerously close to depleting natural resources and crossing tipping points and planetary boundaries, the need for a complex systems approach to governance grows more and more imperative. This social-ecological perspective has evolved from trying to understand system dynamics and mapping causal interactions to proposing governance solutions for local social-ecological systems (SESs) characterized by uncertainty. Scholars also seek to understand the characteristics that are desirable in a governance structure, or the functions that governance must perform in order to govern for sustainability in bounded systems characterized by uncertainty, incomplete information and inevitable surprises (Young et al. 2006; Underdal 2010; Young 2010). The role of globalization is limited in this perspective to its impacts on local system dynamics while the social, political and economic ramifications of globalization are conspicuously absent.

These two perspectives are discussed in further detail in the next sections. Their synthesis is proposed as a platform to advance sustainability governance ideas and practices.

The socio-political perspective: determining power and authority to govern while pursuing sustainable trajectories

Globalization is the defining feature of our era and has undoubtedly shaped the sustainability and governance challenges of our generation (Young 2010). In the wake of globalization, the main question that emerged was to what extent the transfer of power from state to non-state actors means that the state is no longer the primary vehicle for governance (Rosenau 2003). Oran Young contends that globalization has brought about a bi-directional flow of power: upwards towards new global centers and downwards to specialized nodes of global governance (Young 2010). Globalization has simultaneously caused fragmentation and integration, globalism and localism and a disintegration of authority (Rosenau 2005). Others state that while new actors have appeared on the governance stage, governments have always been and will remain the primary vehicle for governance (Pierre and Peters 2004; Meadowcroft 2007). Scholars further posit that the rising power of non-state actors and civil society is the new 'rationality' through which the government orchestrates governance. Governments, as viewed from this governmentality lens, would acquire the capacity to orchestrate the actions of non-state actors in order to achieve their ends (Sending and Neumann 2006).

In terms of sustainability governance, the concerns of the socio-political perspective regarding the role of the government, including its eventual weakening position and the power vacuum this would create, have been discussed as both a threat, and an opportunity. On the one hand, when governance is conceived as the exercising of authority, the absence of a central authoritative figure paints a bleak future for sustainability governance (Rosenau 2007). On the other hand, the weakening of a central authority is paralleled with growing optimism on the ability of governance networks and hybrid forms of collaboration to advance sustainability goals (Lemos and Agrawal 2006). Thus, the social-political perspective includes two contrasting views on the ramifications of power distribution for sustainability governance, where de-centralization and polycentricity are seen as either a threat, or an opportunity.

Some authors state that the challenges of fragmented power and disintegrated authority eclipse any chance of consensus, collaboration or emergence of coordinated institutional steering mechanisms. This disintegration of authority is usually associated with the weakening of the state. Rosenau introduces a new unit of analysis called 'Spheres of Authority' to explore this fragmentation. The basic idea is that every rule system acquires and exercises authority differently. Compliance is the evidence of ascertaining the presence of a Sphere of Authority. Governance is thus the ability to exercise authority and engender compliance. While governments generate compliance through constitutional legitimacy, other actors and rule systems may derive legitimacy from traditional norms, informal agreements, negotiations, and other governance mechanisms (Rosenau 2005).

For other authors, fragmented power brings about opportunities for alternative forms of ordered rule and collective action (Stoker 1998). In this view, the political and economic hollowing out of the state can be seen as a chance to advance sustainability governance. This possibility has been explored from multiple disciplinary perspectives: political science, political ecology, geography, and even ecology in the context of resilience thinking and complex systems theory. Indeed, the changing configuration of power dynamics has spawned new disciplines and approaches to grapple with the meaningful integration of governance and sustainability.

The social-ecological perspective: governing complex systems

The second broad perspective on sustainability governance focuses on the social ecological system (SES) as the basic unit of analysis to explore mechanisms governing interconnectedness of human and environmental components (Walker et al. 2004). The conceptualizations of the SES by Gallopin et al. (1989) and Berkes and Folke (1998) led to wide recognition that the social and ecological dimensions of a problem are inextricably linked and require holistic forms of problem-solving. Adaptation, vulnerability and resilience started being described as properties of the dynamics of the SES and as amenable to governance analysis (Lebel et al. 2006). Resilience scholars became interested in the evolution of institutional systems and the factors that enable them to maintain stability. It became increasingly evident that the resilience of natural systems cannot be studied in isolation, and that social and natural systems are inextricably linked (Brown and Westaway 2011). Summing up, resilience thinking evolved from regarding social pressures as exogenous threats to natural systems to encompassing social elements as integral components of human–environment systems that co-evolve (Manuel-Navarrete 2013).

SES governance was initially conceptualized as a novel means of managing ecosystems (Manuel-Navarrete et al. 2004). Uncertainty, incomplete information and poor understanding of complex system interactions characterize the governance–sustainability dilemma in complex systems. Tipping points and non-linear changes further add to the dilemma and it was soon recognized that the management of these systems would have to move away from trying to control change to learning to deal with changes in these systems (Walker et al. 2004).

Adaptive governance was born with an emphasis on managing for complexity within the SES. This led a definition of the social components of SESs as complex systems in themselves. The role of learning by experimentation, social capital, networks and leadership became key elements in the shaping of adaptive governance (Folke et al. 2005). Young et al. (2006) contend that in seeking to understand complex and uncertain coupled systems, we need to move beyond conventional notions of risk, stability and control, and instead shift our attention to the dynamics of resilience, vulnerability and adaptability. These authors view sustainability governance as a natural vehicle for the shift from governing SESs as static entities for maximum benefits, to governing them as dynamically evolving systems requiring adaptive responses to problems, shocks and surprises. The act of governing these systems has also been recognized as being complex and dynamic in itself (Young 2010). Thus, the challenges of sustainability governance do not merely lie in a lack of understanding of the complex systems within which sustainability problems originate and manifest. They also include challenges related to the dynamics of governing systems themselves.

Resilience scholars have been criticized for using analogies from ecological dynamics to analyze social (and governance) systems without due consideration of factors such as politics, power, justice and ethics (Davidson 2010). There are fundamental differences between natural systems and governance systems, which appear to have been initially overlooked. However, it is being increasingly acknowledged that social and governance system consists of: 'Individuals who are capable of reflecting over their situation and actions, and who are endowed with intrinsic moral rights and who hold normative convictions' (Duit et al. 2010: 365).

Further, societies have the capacity to collectively work towards translating such normative convictions into collective action and to produce and distribute collective goods as well as to steer society towards attaining desired goals. The strong normative facet of social systems, inherent in governance and sustainability is naturally absent in resilience thinking and its incorporation is highly problematic (Folke 2006; Rockström et al. 2009).

Adaptive management supported the redefinition of governance in the field of natural resource management through promoting the idea that socio-ecological systems are best governed in the light of uncertain events and surprises (Folke et al. 2005; Folke 2006; Armitage et al. 2009). This sought a form of governance that is itself dynamic and that allows the system to transform. Adaptive management assumes policy failures will occur and that they provide a valuable contribution for learning, while other approaches seek to avoid policy failure. Avoiding failures may reinforce the status quo and precludes opportunities for learning while doing (Olsson et al. 2006). The emphasis is on desirable attributes in a governance system rather than current structures of governance as described by the social-political approach.

Integrating the socio-political and socio-ecological perspectives

Discussions within both socio-political and socio-ecological perspectives describe different structural configurations of how governance should be organized. However, the complexity and dynamism of the governance system itself are often framed by both perspectives as a multi-level and multi-scale challenge (Gibson et al. 2000). Bach and Flinders (2004) define multi-level governance as 'the dispersion of central governmental authority both vertically to actors located at other territorial levels, and horizontally to non-state actors'. The multi-level character of governance might become a hinge between the socio-political and socio-ecological perspectives. In the previous section we discussed Rosenau's (2005) use of Spheres of Authority, which in his view constitute the Möbius strip or web of global governance. From a socio-political perspective, too much fragmentation of authority may lead to a governance stage overwhelmed by an 'organizational explosion' that may become a barrier to effective governance (Rosenau 2007: 209). As the state loses control over increasing flows of goods, wealth, raw materials, people, pollution, or ideologies, new spheres of authority spawn across borders to govern social and ecological functions. These spheres of authority assume different forms as described by multi-level governance, polycentric governance, network governance, hybrid collaborations, and also sustainability governance.

The socio-ecological approach provides an analytic perspective on multi-scale and multi-level governance, which can complement equivalent socio-political framings. For instance, Marks and Hooghe (2004) distinguish between Type I and Type II multi-level governance. Type I multi-level governance comprises general-purpose jurisdictions at a limited number of levels with non-overlapping membership and is a descendant of federalism. The European Union is an oft-cited example of Type I multi-level governance. Type II multi-level governance is characterized by task-specific jurisdictions and intersecting memberships (ibid.). The prevalence of multiple jurisdictions that overlap bears close resemblance to the polity or 'collective consumption units' described by Vincent Ostrom in the context of metropolitan cities in the United States (Ostrom et al. 1961). Flexibility in jurisdictional units is also illustrated by the conception of Functional, Overlapping and Competing Jurisdictions (FOCJ). An FOCJ is flexible since it can be established or discontinued when required, and is the 'institutional way to vary the size of public jurisdiction in order to minimize spillovers' (Frey and Eichenberger 1999). Each of these building blocks, jurisdictions, polity or FOCJs is a lineage of different disciplines trying to construct a structure for the 'new' governance that the world is witnessing. The concept of 'multi-level governance for sustainability' can be seen as providing an umbrella or arena to articulate these building blocks and provide coherent understandings of governance across disciplines and approaches. NGOs, transnational environmental networks, and epistemic communities; defined as networks of knowledge-based expertise, all have a role to play in this new arena of global sustainability governance (Lemos and Agrawal 2006). Indeed, the past two decades have seen the rise of inter-governmental panels debating governance of the global commons, multi-lateral organizations collaborating with the private sector to enable the adoption of sustainability solutions, public–private partnerships and hybrid governance arrangements of all kinds steering development at different scales on alternative development trajectories (IPCC, IFC, CGIAR). These innovative collaborations, boundary organizations bridging the traditional science–policy divide and emerging polycentric structures have all been indispensable to weave emerging structures for sustainability governance.

Sustainability governance: insights from the socio-political and socio-ecological approaches

Avoiding past failures and the disappointments of the sustainable development agenda might require a fundamental change in the way we approach governance. Novel hybrid conceptualizations of governance are proliferating and empirical evidence will be needed to test their effectiveness (Lemos and Agrawal 2006). In this section we discuss the concept of sustainability governance as one possible form of hybridization that combines socio-political and socio-ecological perspectives in order to foster a sustainability agenda based on governance transformations (Table 28.1).

Table 28.1 A synopsis of two perspectives on governance for sustainability

Criteria	*Social-political perspective*	*Social-ecological perspective*
Definition of sustainability governance	The steering of society towards a more sustainable trajectory.	Decision-making process to maintain the functional integrity of SES.
Fundamental question	Who is doing the steering? This approach focuses on agency, the actors and their ability to steer society towards sustainability. It is concerned with power distribution and authority.	What structures (e.g. polycentric) or modes (adaptive) of governance are required to govern (maintain) socio-ecological functions?
Main frameworks	• Multi-level governance as characterized by Marks and Hooghe (2010). • Governmentality: States govern by delegating pre-established tasks that are required to their government. • Möbius strip of governance: fragmented authority characterizes global governance in a globalized world. • Hybrid governance: drawing synergistic collaborations to address multi-faceted problems.	SES as the unit of analysis for governance. Resilience of SES. Adaptive governance: enables better preparation for crisis by means of experimentation and learning rather than an attempt to avoid crises. Polycentric governance: the focus is on cross-scale linkages. Telecoupled systems: framework to understand the influence that two or more SESs exert on each other.
Role of globalization	Globalization as a process: flow of power to non-state actors. New actors multiply and create an 'organizational explosion' that results in fragmentation and integration, globalism and localism, thus creating dualities that make coordinated governance challenging.	A systemic approach to globalization is adopted. Role of globalization is discussed as altering local systems' dynamics: increasing connectedness, reducing diversity and redundancy.
Unit of analysis	Jurisdictional units (multi-level) Spheres of Authority (SOA).	Socio-ecological systems.

The emergence in the 2000s of sustainability science as a solution-driven research agenda was supported by the World Congress 'Challenges of a Changing Earth 2001' in Amsterdam, organized by the International Council for Science, The International Geosphere-Biosphere program and the International Human Dimensions program on Global Environmental Change and the World Climate Research Program. Sustainability science emerged as a field 'defined by the problems it addresses rather than by the disciplines it employs'; it serves the need for advancing both knowledge and action by creating a dynamic bridge between the two (Clark and Dickson 2003). Since its inception, sustainability science has drawn heavily on both socio-political and socio-ecological perspectives to governance. Integral to sustainability science are systems thinking, anticipating future scenarios and problem-solving for the present and the future (Wiek et al. 2011). Problem-solving involves a governance process and thus sustainability science emphasizes the exploration of structures for governance that promote sustainable trajectories (Kates et al. 2001; Komiyama and Takeuchi 2006). Among the core questions put forward in a seminal article on sustainability science is: 'What systems of incentive structures including markets, rules, norms and scientific information can most effectively improve scientific capacity to guide interactions between nature and society to a more sustainable trajectory?'(Kates et al. 2001).

These systems of incentives, rules and norms have long been discussed by authors from socio-political perspectives, while the focus on nature–society interactions is a result of socio-ecological perspectives. The normative goal of guiding interactions along a more sustainable trajectory is another way to describe the process of governance and governing that have been employed by both perspectives.

The emphasis on using problems and solutions to structure research agendas is the lynchpin of both sustainability science and governance for sustainability. It is perhaps these unique elements that have allowed sustainability governance to transcend the older sustainable development paradigm of first segregating the environmental, social and economic dimensions of a problem and then seeking to balance them out, as problems and solutions were often at the interface of these spheres (Robinson 2004). In this section, we cite two examples of recent attempts at combining both governance perspectives in order to address sustainability problems.

The first example is the use of hybrid forms of governance by the Dutch government to steer energy transitions in the 2000s. This process involved both bottom-up participation with top-down support. The resulting knowledge network for system innovations and transitions is a knowledge community to better understand, identify and influence transitions. With a mandate of promoting deliberate shift to a sustainable society by creating both fundamental knowledge as well as practical knowledge that enables transitions, they have undertaken a number of projects and research initiatives (Knowledge Network for System Innovations and Transitions: www.ksinetwork.nl/research/projects).

Another relevant example is the Earth System Governance project. The Earth System Governance project is a research network on governance and global environmental change. The network explores 'political solutions and novel, more effective governance systems to cope with the current transitions in the biogeochemical systems of our planet'. Scholars using this approach view earth system governance not only as a question of governance effectiveness, but also as a challenge for political legitimacy and social justice. The discussion on social justice was largely absent from the socio-ecological approach and the Earth System Governance project seeks to address that shortcoming. With an emphasis on power, knowledge, norms and scale as cross-cutting themes across research over earth systems such as food, water climate and economic systems, they thus account for architecture, agency, adaptiveness, accountability, allocation and access (Biermann 2007). Arguably, the selection of these criteria and dimensions are reflective of their efforts to integrate socio-political and socio-ecological perspectives.

These two examples demonstrate the potential of governance for sustainability research that integrates socio-political and socio-ecological perspectives. Their approach towards fragmented authority, however, is quite different. While the transition management policy of the Dutch government leverages bottom-up participation with top-down support by involving different actors to constitute a transition arena; the issue of fragmented authority is viewed as a problem by scholars of the Earth System Governance project. This is perhaps due to the scale at which both approaches have been adopted. While earth system governance seeks to inform intergovernmental panels in an era of declining government power, transition management has largely been adopted at regional scales. Thus while questions of legitimacy and accountability are emphasized more in the Earth Systems Governance project, transition management emphasizes multi-stakeholder dynamics.

Within the last decade, the application of telecoupling as a heuristic to define the sustainability challenges of our generation has offered some interesting insights on how to combine socio-political and socio-ecological perspectives. As an extension of research on coupled SESs, telecoupling has been used to understand the influence that two or more SES exert on each other (Liu et al. 2013). It brings about new opportunities to think about bridging socio-political and socio-ecological perspectives in order to jointly explore the sustainability-governance-globalization *trilemma*. Telecoupled systems illustrate that concomitant with the overwhelming multiplicity of organizations involved in governance is a 'governance vacuum' which comes to the fore when distant interactions unfold, causing 'unanticipated consequences', 'shocks' and surprises in systems which were considered unconnected. These sustainability challenges are thus viewed as manifestations of a governance deficit (Eakin et al. 2014).

The shift in focus from a single socio-ecological system to interactions among SESs is a response to increased global connectedness and interactions. The term teleconnections has been used in climate and atmospheric science for a long time and was originally used to refer to atmospheric circulation and processes in one location having climatic consequences in geographically distant places (Trenberth and Hurrell 1994). This notion of 'acting at a distance' when applied to SES illustrates the role of distant interactions affecting issues of global importance. These distant interactions are shaping the contemporary problems of this generation. Climate change, food security, changes in land use, biodiversity loss, and public health and water scarcity are a few examples (Liu et al. 2013). Further, this heuristic challenges the way we conceptualize our world, bounded in discrete geographic units and urges us to draw on integrated socio-political and socio-ecological perspectives that provide new units of analysis to re-think governance.

Conclusion

In this chapter we have posited that sustainable development did not live up to the expectations of the international community since technocratic attempts at balancing out the social, economic and environmental aspects of a problem necessitate governance structures that we are still lacking. The concept of sustainability governance has been presented here as the means to transition to a future in which such structures thrive. We have shown how sustainability governance needs to draw on and integrate two academic perspectives to governance: the socio-political and the socio-ecological.

While the socio-political perspective focuses on agency, power, authority, legitimacy and accountability, which are key concepts for transformational social change, the socio-ecological perspective conceptualizes governance as a dynamic process. It also contributes to a new language to talk about change that is rooted in complexity and system dynamics related to tipping points, abrupt changes, surprises and uncertainty. Recognizing the fact that the systems we govern for sustainability are fundamentally unpredictable, and thus governance would have to be adaptable, is a valuable insight from this perspective. The need for a complex systems approach and the utility of resilience thinking in governance systems are no longer moot points. It has been widely acknowledged that resilience thinking holds potential for broadening the wider governance research agenda (Young 2010). In particular, it urges us to consider fundamental issues of change and stability, adaptation and design, hierarchy and self-organization in the study of multi-level governance systems. In addition to traditional benchmarks such as efficacy, accountability, and equity used when assessing public governance, a resilience perspective on governance would also consider issues of human–environmental interactions, vulnerability resulting from mal-adaptations, and innovation capacity as integral parts of evaluating a given governance system; facets that are indispensable when governing for sustainability (Nelson et al. 2007). However, the challenge remains of better integrating resilience and complexity insights with cultural and political aspects of governance. The role of culture, local and traditional knowledge, is often ignored in governance for sustainability frameworks (Armitage et al. 2009). While the need to study power is increasingly mentioned, few studies have discussed how power can be studied in social ecological systems and few have taken on this challenge (Manuel-Navarrete 2010). Discussions on power and authority thus remain a subject mostly discussed within the social-political approach.

As global environmental change gains momentum and we grow aware of our limited 'safe operating space', a long-term agenda for sustainable development appears to be increasingly insufficient. Problems requiring urgent solutions are now at the fore and the 'concerns for future generations' are gaining immediacy and being rapidly replaced with a focus on solution-driven approaches under the banner of sustainability. The sustainable development agenda is being re-framed as the term sustainability gains currency among corporations, academic institutions and NGOs. Within academia a new sustainability science is proposed as a response to urgent problems that characterize our globalized world as well as the inability of conventional science to address the normative dilemmas of sustainability.

References

Adger, W. N. and Jordan, A. (eds) (2009) *Governing Sustainability*. Cambridge: Cambridge University Press.

Armitage, D. R., Plummer, R., Berkes, F., Arthur, R. I., Charles, A. T., Davidson-Hunt, I. J., Diduck, A. P., Doubleday, N. C., Johnson, D. S., Marschke, M., McConney, P., Pinkerton, E. W. and Wollenberg, E. K. (2009) Adaptive co-management for social-ecological complexity. *Frontiers in Ecology and the Environment*, 7(2): 95–102.

Bach, I. and Flinders, M. (2004) *Multi-Level Governance*. Oxford: Oxford University Press.

Berkes, F. and Folke, C. (eds) (1998) *Linking Social and Ecological Systems: Management Practices and Social Mechanisms for Building Resilience*. Cambridge: Cambridge University Press.

Biermann, F. (2007) Earth system governance as a crosscutting theme of global change research. *Global Environmental Change*, 17(3): 326–337.

Brown, K. and Westaway, E. (2011) Agency, capacity, and resilience to environmental change: lessons from human development, well-being, and disasters. *Annual Review of Environment and Resources*, 36(1).

Clark, W. C. and Dickson, N. M. (2003) Sustainability science: the emerging research program. *Proceedings of the National Academy of Sciences USA*, 100(14): 8086–8091.

Davidson, D. J. (2010) The applicability of the concept of resilience to social systems: some sources of optimism and nagging doubts. *Society and Natural Resources*, 23(12): 1135–1149.

Duit, A., Galaz, V., Eckerberg, K. and Ebbesson, J. (2010) Governance, complexity, and resilience. *Global Environmental Change*, 20(3): 363–368.

Eakin, H., DeFries, R., Kerr, S., Lambin, E. F., Liu, J., Marcotullio, P. J., Messerli, P., Reenberg, A., Rueda, X., Swaffield, S. R., Wicke, B. and Zimmerer, K. (2014) Significance of telecoupling for exploration of (sustainable) land use change. In K. C. Seto and A. Reenberg (eds) *Rethinking Global Land Use in an Urban Era*. Cambridge, MA: MIT Press.

Folke, C. (2006) Social-ecological systems and adaptive governance of the commons. *Ecological Research*, 22(1): 14–15.

Folke, C., Hahn, T., Olsson, P. and Norberg, J. (2005) Adaptive governance of social-ecological systems. *Annual Review of Environment and Resources*, 30(1): 441–473.

Frey, B. and Eichenberger, R. (1999) *The New Democratic Federalism for Europe: Functional, Overlapping and Competing Jurisdictions*. Cheltenham: Edward Elgar.

Gallopin, G. C., Gutman, P. and Maletta, H. (1989) Global impoverishment, sustainable development and the environment: a conceptual approach. *International Social Science Journal*, 121: 375–397.

Gibson, C. C., Ostrom, E. and Ahn, T. K. (2000) The concept of scale and the human dimensions of global change: a survey. *Ecological Economics*, 32(2): 217–239.

Halle, M., Najam, A. and Beaton, C. (2013) *The Future of Sustainable Development: Rethinking Sustainable Development after Rio+20 and Implications for UNEP*. Winnipeg, Canada: The International Institute for Sustainable Development.

In't Veld, R. J. (2011) *Transgovernance: The Quest for Governance of Sustainable Development*. Potsdam: IASS Institute for Advanced Sustainability Studies.

Jordan, A. (2008) The governance of sustainable development: taking stock and looking forwards. *Environment and Planning C: Government and Policy*, 26(1): 17–33.

Kates, R. W., Clark, W. C., Corell, R., Hall, J. M., Jaeger, C. C., Lowe, I., McCarthy, J. J., Schellnhuber, H. J., Bolin, B., Dickson, N. M., Faucheux, S., Gallopin, G. C., Grübler, A., Huntley, B., Jäger, J., Jodha, N. S., Kasperson, R. E., Mabogunje, A., Matson, P., Mooney, H., Moore III, B., O'Riordan, T. and Svedin, U. (2001) Sustainability science. *Science*, 292: 641–642.

Kemp, R., Parto, S. and Gibson, R. B. (2005) Governance for sustainable development: moving from theory to practice. *International Journal of Sustainable Development*, 8(1): 12–30.

Komiyama, H. and Takeuchi, K. (2006) Sustainability science: building a new discipline. *Sustainability Science*, 1(1): 1–6.

Leach, M., Scoones, I. and Stirling, A. (2010) *Dynamic Sustainabilities: Technology, Environment, Social Justice*. London: Earthscan.

Lebel, L., Anderies, J. M., Campbell, B., Folke, C., Hatfield-Dodds, S., Hughes, T. P. and Wilson, J. (2006) Governance and the capacity to manage resilience in regional social-ecological systems. *Ecology and Society*, 11(1).

Lemos, M. C. and Agrawal, A. (2006). Environmental governance. *Annual Review of Environment and Resources*, 31(1): 297–325.

Liu, J., Hull, V., Batistella, M., Defries, R., Dietz, T., Fu, F., Hertel, T. W., Izaurralde, R. C., Lambin, E. F., Li, S., Martinelli, L. A., McConnell, W. J., Moran, E. F., Naylor, R., Ouyang, Z., Polenske, K. R., Reenberg, A., deMiranda Rocha, G., Simmons, C. S., Verburg, P. H., Viousek, P. M., Zhang, F. and Zhu, C. (2013) Framing sustainability in a telecoupled world. *Ecology and Society*, 18(2).

Loorbach, D. A. (2007) *Transition Management: New Mode of Governance for Sustainable Development*. Rotterdam: Erasmus University Rotterdam.

Manuel-Navarrete, D. (2010) Power, realism, and the ideal of human emancipation in a climate of change. *Wiley Interdisciplinary Reviews: Climate Change*, 1(6): 781–785.

Manuel-Navarrete, D. (2013) Human-environmental integration and social power in global environmental change research. In L. Sygna, K. O'Brien and J. Wolf (eds) *A Changing Environment for Human Security: Transformative Approaches to Research, Policy and Action*. London: Routledge, pp. 305–315.

Manuel-Navarrete, D., Kay, J. J. and Dolderman, D. (2004) Ecological integrity discourses: linking ecology with cultural transformation. *Human Ecology Review*, 11(3): 215–229.

Marks, G. and Hooghe, L. (2004) Contrasting visions of multi-level governance. In L. Hooghe and G. Marks (eds) *Multi-Level Governance*. Lanham, MD: Rowman and Littlefield, pp. 15–30.

Mason, M. (2011) The sustainability challenge. In J. Brady, A. Ebbage and R. Lunn (eds) *Environmental Management in Organizations*, 2nd edn. London: Earthscan, pp. 525–532.

Meadowcroft, J. (1997) Planning for sustainable development: insights from the literatures of political science. *European Journal of Political Research*, 31: 427–454.

Meadowcroft, J. (2007) Who is in charge here? Governance for sustainable development in a complex world. *Journal of Environmental Policy & Planning*, 9(3–4):. 299–314. doi:10.1080/15239080701631544

Meadowcroft, J., Farrell, K. N. and Spangenberg, J. (2005) Developing a framework for sustainability governance in the European Union. *International Journal of Sustainable Development*, 8(1): 3–11.

Nelson, D. R., Adger, W. N. and Brown, K. (2007) Adaptation to environmental change: contributions of a resilience framework. *Annual Review of Environment and Resources*, 32(1).

Nidumolu, R., Prahalad, C. K. and Rangaswami, M. R. (2009) Why sustainability is now the key driver of innovation. *Harvard Business Review*, 87(9): 56–64.

Olsson, P., Gunderson, L. H., Carpenter, S. R., Ryan, P., Lebel, L., Folke, C. and Holling, C. S. (2006). Shooting the rapids: navigating transitions to adaptive governance of social-ecological systems. *Ecology & Society*, 11(1).

Ostrom, V., Tiebout, C. M. and Warren, R., (1961) The organization of government in metropolitan areas: a theoretical inquiry. *American Political Science Review*, 55: 831–842.

Pierre, J. and Peters, B. G.(2004) Multi-level governance and democracy: a Faustian bargain? In L. Hooghe and G. Marks (eds) *Multi-Level Governance*. Lanham, MD: Rowman and Littlefield, pp. 75–89.

Redclift, M. (2002) *Sustainable Development: Exploring the Contradictions*. London: Routledge.

Redclift, M. (2005) Sustainable development (1987–2005): an oxymoron comes of age. *Sustainable Development*, 13(4):. 212–227.

Redclift, M. and Woodgate, G. (2013) Sustainable development and Nature: the substitution of capitals. Environment, Politics and Development Working Paper Series, WP#46. Department of Geography, King's College London.

Robinson, J. (2004) Squaring the circle? Some thoughts on the idea of sustainable development. *Ecological Economics*, 48: 369–384.

Rockström, J., Steffen, W., Noone, K., Persson, Å., Chapin, F. S., Lambin, E. F., Lenton, T. M., Schefoer, M., Folke, C., Schellnhuber, H. J., Nykvist, B., deWit, C.A., Huges, T., van der Leeuw, S., Rodhe, H., Sorlin, S., Snyder, P. K., Costanza, R., Svedin, U., Falkenmark, M., Karlberg, L., Corell, R. W., Fabry, V. J., Hansen, J., Walker, B., Liverman, D., Richardson, K., Crutzen, P. and Foley, J. A. (2009) A safe operating space for humanity. *Nature*, 461(7263): 472–475.

Rosenau, J. N. (2003) *Distant Proximities: Dynamics beyond Globalization*. Princeton, NJ: Princeton University Press.

Rosenau, J. N. (2005) Globalization and governance: sustainability between fragmentation and integration. *Governance and Sustainability: New Challenges for States, Companies and Civil Society*, 1, 31: 19–38.

Rosenau, J. N. (2007). Globalization and governance: bleak prospects for sustainability. In A. Pfaller and M. Lerch (eds) *Challenges of Globalization: New Trends in International Politics and Society*. New Brunswick, NJ: Transaction Publishers, pp. 201–217.

Sending, O. J. and Neumann, I. B. (2006) Governance to governmentality: analyzing NGOs, states, and power. *International Studies Quarterly*, 50(3): 651–672.

Stoker, G. (1998) Governance as theory: five propositions. *International Social Science Journal*, 50(155): 17–28.

Swyngedouw, E. (2010) Apocalypse forever? Post-political populism and the specter of climate change. *Theory, Culture & Society*, 27(3): 213–232.

Trenberth, K. E. and Hurrell, J. W. (1994) Decadal atmospheric-ocean variations in the Pacific. *Climate Dynamics*, 9: 303–319.

Underdal, A. (2010) Complexity and challenges of long-term environmental governance. *Global Environmental Change*, 20(3): 386–393.

Urhammer, E. and Røpke, I. (2013) Macroeconomic narratives in a world of crises: an analysis of stories about solving the system crisis. *Ecological Economics*, 96: 62–70.

Walker, B., Holling, C. S., Carpenter, S. R. and Kinzig, A. (2004) Resilience, adaptability and transformability in social-ecological systems. *Ecology and Society*, 9(2).

Wiek, A., Withycombe, L. and Redman, C. L. (2011) Key competencies in sustainability: a reference framework for academic program development. *Sustainability Science*, 6: 203–218.

Young, O. R. (2010) Institutional dynamics: resilience, vulnerability and adaptation in environmental and resource regimes. *Global Environmental Change*, 20(3): 378–385.

Young, O. R., Berkhout, F., Gallopin, G. C., Janssen, M. A., Ostrom, E. and van der Leeuw, S. (2006) The globalization of socio-ecological systems: an agenda for scientific research. *Global Environmental Change*, 16(3): 304–316.

INDEX

NOTES

(1) The word order is letter by letter.
(2) Locators to figures and tables are in *italics*.
(3) The letter 'n' refers to a chapter end note.